A Companion to
Genethics

Blackwell Companions to Philosophy

This outstanding student reference series offers a comprehensive and authoritative survey of philosophy as a whole. Written by today's leading philosophers, each volume provides lucid and engaging coverage of the key figures, terms, topics, and problems of the field. Taken together, the volumes provide the ideal basis for course use, representing an unparalleled work of reference for students and specialists alike.

A Companion to Genethics

Edited by Justine Burley and
John Harris

Copyright © Blackwell Publishers Ltd 2002

First published 2002

2 4 6 8 10 9 7 5 3 1

Blackwell Publishers Inc.
350 Main Street
Malden, Massachusetts 02148
USA

Blackwell Publishers Ltd
108 Cowley Road
Oxford OX4 1JF
UK

Library of Congress Cataloging-in-Publication Data has been applied for.

ISBN 0-631-20698-1 (hardback)

British Library Cataloguing in Publication Data
A CIP catalogue record for this book is available from the British Library.

Typeset in 10 on 12.5 pt Photina
by Kolam Information Services Pvt. Ltd., Pondicherry, India
Printed in Great Britain by T.J. International Padstow, Cornwall

This book is printed on acid-free paper.

Contents

Contributors

George J. Annas is the Edward Utley Professor and Chair of the Health Law Department of Boston University School of Public Health and Professor at the Boston University School of Medicine and the Boston University School of Law. He is the author or editor of a dozen books on health law and human rights, including *The Rights of Patients* (1975), *Reproductive Genetics and the Law* (1987), *Judging Medicine* (1988), *Standard of Care* (1993), and *Some Choice* (1998). He also co-authored "The Genetic Privacy Act" prepared for the ELSI program of the US Human Genome.

Inez de Beaufort is Professor in Healthcare Ethics in the Medical Faculty of Erasmus University in Rotterdam. Her original background is theology. She is a member of the National Council for Health and Healthcare, a member of the Dutch Health Council, and a member of the Central Committee for Ethics and Medical Research. She has a wide experience in the field of bioethics, both nationally and internationally. She has participated in many Dutch public debates. Over the past years she has participated in six BIOMED projects. She is presently coordinating a research project for the European Commission on Ethics and Appearance (1998–2001). She has published on human experimentation, reproductive technologies, personal responsibility, beauty and ethics, and ethics and genetics.

Diemut Bubeck is Senior Lecturer in Political Theory in the Department of Government, London School of Economics. She has done research on Marx and justice, theories of women's work, the ethics or care debate, and citizenship. Her current research focuses on gender issues in political theory, feminist ethics, and Nietzsche. She is the author of *Care, Gender and Justice* (1995).

Justine Burley is currently Simon Fellow in the Department of Government, University of Manchester and Lecturer in Politics at Exeter College, Oxford. In addition to *A Companion to Genethics*, she is editor of *The Genetic Revolution and Human Rights* (1998), and *Ronald Dworkin and His Critics* (in preparation). Her monograph, entitled *Genetic Justice*, is in preparation.

Scott Burris is Professor of Law at the James E. Beasley School of Law, Temple University. He is a graduate of the Yale Law School and writes extensively on public health law. One of his main research interests has been HIV/AIDS. In this area he has published, amongst other things, *AIDS Law Today: A New Guide for the Public* (1993). His research has been supported by the leading health philanthropies in the United States, including the Robert Wood Johnson Foundation, the Milbank Memorial Fund, and the Kaiser Family Foundation.

Ruth Chadwick is Professor of Bioethics in the Institute for Environment, Philosophy and Public Policy, Lancaster University. She is Vice-Chair of the Ethics Committee of the Human Genome Organization and a member of the Medical Research Council's Advisory Committee on Scientific Advances in Genetics.

Matthew Clayton is Lecturer in Government at Brunel University. He has edited (with Andrew Williams) *The Ideal of Equality* (2000).

Richard Dawkins is Charles Simonyi Professor of the Public Understanding of Science, University of Oxford, where he is also a Fellow of New College. Professor Dawkins is the author of *The Selfish Gene* (1989, 2nd edition), *The Extended Phenotype* (1982), *The Blind Watchmaker* (1986), *River out of Eden* (1995), *Climbing Mount Improbable* (1996), and *Unweaving the Rainbow* (1998). His awards include the Zoological Society of London Silver Medal for 1989, the Royal Society Michael Faraday Award for 1990, the Nakayama Prize for 1994, and the International Cosmos Prize for 1997. He holds honorary degrees in literature as well as in science.

Lawrence Gostin is Professor of Law, Georgetown University Law Center, Washington, DC and Professor of Public Health, the John Hopkins School of Hygiene and Public Health, Baltimore, Maryland. Professor Gostin is also Co-director of the Georgetown/ John Hopkins Program on Law and Public Health. He sits on advisory committees for various organizations including the US Centers for Disease Control and Prevention (CDC), the National Academy of Sciences, and the World Health Organization. Professor Gostin has published extensively. His most recent books are *American Public Health Law* (2000) and *Human Rights and Public Health in the AIDS Pandemic* (1997).

John Harris is Sir David Alliance Professor of Bioethics at the University of Manchester where he is also Director of the Centre for Social Ethics and Policy and of the Institute of Medicine, Law and Bioethics. He is a member of the United Kingdom Human Genetics Commission, and was a member of the UK government Advisory Committee on Genetic Testing from its inception in 1966 to its closure in 1969. He is the author of *Violence and Responsibility* (1980), *The Value of Life* (1985), *Wonderwoman and Superman* (1992), and *Clones, Genes and Immortality* (1998). He has also co-edited *Experiments on Embryos* (1990), *Ethics and Biotechnology* (1994), and *The Future of Human Reproduction* (1998). He is the editor of the Oxford Readings in Philosophy volume on *Bioethics* published in 2001.

Adam Hedgecoe is Research Fellow in the Department of Science and Technology Studies at University College London. He has a Wellcome Trust postdoctoral fellowship to look at "Pharmacogenetics and the genetic reclassification of common disease." Interested in ethical issues in science and medicine (particularly genetics), public communication of science, and policy issues in the life sciences, Adam has worked for both the European and British parliaments' technology assessment units. He has also carried out research on a European Union funded project into the ethics of genetic screening, as well as consultancy for a number of organizations including the OECD.

Søren Holm is Professor of Clinical Bioethics at the University of Manchester and Professor of Medical Ethics at the University of Oslo. He holds degrees in medicine, philosophy, and healthcare ethics. He has written extensively about the problems in transferring American bioethics to a European context.

Hussein Kassim is Lecturer in Politics at Birkbeck College, University of London. His interests span European Politics, Public Policy, and Social Theory. Formerly in charge of the M.Sc. in Race and Ethnic Relations, he is currently Director of the M.Sc. in European Politics and has published several books and articles in that field.

Tom Kirkwood is a Professor at the Institute of the Elderly, Wolfson Research Centre, University of Newcastle. He is Chairman of the British Society for Research on Aging as well as a member of the Gerontological Society of America, the British Geriatrics Society, the Royal Statistical Society, and the Biometric Society. He has written many scientific publications and won the F. E. Williams Lecture Prize from the Royal College of Physicians and the Fritz-Verzar Medal in gerontology.

Philip Kitcher is Professor of Philosophy at Columbia University. He has written books and articles on many issues in the philosophy of science. Most recently, he is the author of *The Lives to Come: The Genetic Revolution and Human Possibilities* and *Science, Truth, and Democracy*.

Bartha Maria Knoppers is Canadian Research Chair in Law and Medicine and is Professor of Law at the Faculté de droit, Université de Montréal, where she directs the "Genetics and Society Project." She is also Chair of the International Ethics Committee of HUGO (Human Genome Organization).

P. R. Lowenstein is Director of the Gene Therapeutics Research Institute in Cedars-Sinai Medical Center, California. He has more than 85 publications, including papers, reviews, and book chapters, and he has edited (with Lynn Enquist) *Protocols for Gene Transfer in Neuroscience: Towards Gene Therapy of Neurological Disorders* (1996). He is on the editorial board of *Gene Therapy*, adviser to the Gene Therapy Advisory Committee of the United Kingdom, and a Research Fellow of the Lister Institute of Preventive Medicine.

Ruth Macklin's Ph.D. is in philosophy. She is Professor of Bioethics at Albert Einstein College of Medicine in the Bronx, New York, and President of the International Association of Bioethics. Her latest book, *Against Relativism*, was published in 1999.

Gerald P. McKenny is Associate Professor and Chair of the Department of Religious Studies at Rice University. He is the author of *To Relieve the Human Condition: Bioethics, Technology and the Body* (1997) and co-editor of *Theological Analyses of the Clinical Encounter* (1994). His other publications include articles on Christian ethics, bioethical theory and the ethics of gene therapy, and physician-assisted suicide. He holds adjunct appointments at the University of Texas Health Science Center and the Institute of Religion, Houston, Texas, and a visiting appointment at Mahidol University in Thailand.

Stephen R. Munzer is Professor at the UCLA School of Law in Los Angeles, California. His most recent work is an edited collection entitled *New Essays in the Legal and Political Theory of Property* (2001).

Pilar N. Ossorio is the Section Director of the Genetics Division of the Ethics Institute of the American Medical Association. She is currently on the editorial review board of *Microbial & Comparative Genomics*. In 1996 she won the Prosser Award for both Legal Ethics and Patent Law and Policy. She is the author of many bioethics and scientific publications.

Madison Powers is Senior Research Scholar at the Kennedy Institute of Ethics and Associate Professor of Philosophy at Georgetown University. He has written widely on issues of privacy related to law, medicine, and genetics, as well as healthcare allocation and distributive justice. Together with Ruth Faden he is the recipient of a Robert Wood Johnson Health Policy Investigator Award and is working on a book on healthcare inequalities.

Janet Radcliffe Richards is currently Reader in Bioethics and Director of the Centre for Bioethics at the Royal Free and University College Medical School, University College London. Prior to this appointment she was Lecturer in Philosophy, Open University, and has held visiting appointments at UCLA, NYU, the University of Pennsylvania Law School, and the University of San Diego Law School. She is author of *Human Nature after Darwin* (2000) and *The Sceptical Feminist* (1980), as well as many articles in a number of areas of philosophy, including biomedical ethics. She has served on the ethics committees of several of the Royal Colleges of Medicine and various other bodies.

Bernard E. Rollin is Professor of Philosophy, Professor of Physiology, and University Bioethicist at Colorado State University. He is the author of numerous books and articles on many topics in bioethics, including veterinary ethics, animal ethics, animal experimentation, animal consciousness, animal agriculture, genetic engineering, animal pain, and other areas.

Lainie Friedman Ross MD, Ph.D. is an Assistant Professor in the Departments of Pediatrics and Medicine at the University of Chicago. She is an Assistant Director of the MacLean Center for Clinical Medical Ethics at the University of Chicago where she directs the Ethics Case Consultation Service. Her first book, *Children, Families, and Healthcare Decision Making*, was published in 1998.

Carol Rovane is Associate Professor of Philosophy at Columbia University. Her publications include *The Bounds of Agency: An Essay in Revisionary Metaphysics* (1997) as well as numerous articles in the areas of metaphysics, philosophy of language, philosophy of mind, action theory, and history of philosophy.

Mark Sagoff is a Senior Research Scholar at the Institute for Philosophy and Public Policy at the School of Public Affairs, University of Maryland, College Park.

Tom Sorell is Professor of Philosophy at the University of Essex. He is author of *Moral Theory and Capital Punishment* (1987); (with John Hendry) *Business Ethics* (1994); and *Moral Theory and Anomaly* (2000). He edited *Healthcare, Ethics, and Insurance* (1998).

Bonnie Steinbock is Professor and Chair of the Department of Philosophy at the State University of New York at Albany. She is the author of *Life Before Birth: The Moral and Legal Status of Embryos and Fetuses* (1992), and the editor or co-editor of several anthologies in bioethics. She is currently writing a book, *Rethinking Reproduction*.

Hillel Steiner is Professor of Political Philosophy at the University of Manchester and a Fellow of the British Academy. He has published papers on liberty, rights, and moral reasoning, and is the author of *An Essay on Rights* (1994) and *A Debate Over Rights* (1998, with Matthew Kramer and Nigel Simmonds).

Clive Svendsen is Wellcome Career Development Research Fellow, Principle Investigator, and Director of Training at the MRC Centre for Brain Repair, University of Cambridge. Dr. Svendsen is currently working with animal models of Parkinson's, Huntington's, Multiple Sclerosis, and stroke to assess the possible use of human neural stem cells to restore function in patients suffering these diseases. He has also had a long-standing interest in the mechanisms of neuronal cell death and growth factors. In addition to publishing extensively in accredited science journals, Clive Svendsen promotes public understanding in a variety of forums.

Mary Anne Warren is Professor of Philosophy at San Francisco State University. She writes on a range of issues in biomedical and applied ethics, including abortion, affirmative action, medical means of preselecting the sex of children, in vitro fertilization and embryo research, animal rights, and environmental ethics. She has published three books, *The Nature of Woman: An Encyclopedia and Guide to the Literature* (1980); *Gendercide: The Implications of Sex Selection* (1985); and *Moral Status: Obligations to Persons and Other Living Things* (1997).

David Wasserman is a Research Scholar at the Institute for Philosophy and Public Policy at the University of Maryland. He is the author of a book on the appellate representation of indigent defendants, *A Sword for the Convicted*. His other publications include *Let Them Eat Chances: Probability and Discretion* (1996), *Some Moral Issues in the Correction of Impairments* (1996), *Disability and Discrimination and Fairness* (1993), and *Can a Sense of Place be Preserved?* (1997).

Professor Sir David Weatherall FRS, is Emeritus Regius Professor of Medicine in the University of Oxford and formerly Director of the Institute of Molecular Medicine, University of Oxford.

Paul Weindling is Wellcome Trust Research Professor in the History of Medicine, School of Humanities, Oxford Brookes University. His publications include *Health, Race and German Politics between National Unification and Nazism, 1870–1945* (1989), *Epidemics and Genocide in Eastern Europe 1890–1945* (1999), and the edited volume *International Health Organisations and Movements 1918–1939* (1995). His current research is on the Nuremberg Medical Trial and on medical refugees in the UK, 1930–45.

Dorothy C. Wertz is Research Professor and Senior Scientist in Social Science and Ethics at University of Massachusetts Medical School, Shriver Division. She has conducted surveys of ethical issues in genetics for 20 years and is author of *Ethics and Human Genetics: A Crosscultural Perspective* (1989) and a forthcoming book on *Ethics and Genetics in Global Perspective*.

Ian Wilmut is currently Principal Investigator in the Division of Development and Reproduction at the Roslin Institute, Edinburgh. At the Institute he is contributor/joint leader of the team that produced transgenic sheep which secrete large quantities of human proteins in their milk, work that is now being commercialized. The focus of his research over the past three years has been on the factors regulating embryo development in sheep after nuclear transfer. This research led to the birth of live lambs from embryo derived cells and then to the live birth of lambs derived from fetal and adult cells, including "Dolly" the sheep.

Michael S. Yesley is an attorney at Los Alamos National Laboratory, Los Alamos, New Mexico. Yesley coordinated the US Department of Energy's Program on the Ethical, Legal, and Social Implications of the Human Genome Project and was the Staff Director of the National Commission for the Protection of Human Subjects of Biomedical and Behavioral Research (US Department of Health, Education, and Welfare).

Acknowledgments

Naturally a first, but wholehearted, word of thanks must go to all our contributors. They have not only produced a superb collection of papers but have been very patient with the editors over the very long production process which a volume like this entails. Beth Remmes of Blackwell has been the very picture of patience and of efficiency and without her help and encouragement this book would certainly not exist. Cameron Laux, our desk editor, has been simply outstanding; we are all in his debt. Finally we must acknowledge the generous support of the Institute of Medicine, Law and Bioethics of the Universities of Manchester and Liverpool. A Research Fellowship of the Institute supported Justine Burley's work on this volume.

Introduction

JUSTINE BURLEY AND JOHN HARRIS

No branch of science has created more acute or more subtle and interesting ethical dilemmas than genetics. There have been and still are branches of science that create problems of greater moral importance. Nuclear physics, for example, which gave us atomic weapons and hence the capability, literally, to destroy the world, has presented us with perhaps the ultimate moral dilemma. But it is genetics that makes us recall, not simply our responsibilities to the world and to one another, but our responsibilities for how people will be in the future. For the first time we can begin to determine not simply who will live and who will die, but what all those who live in the future will be like.

Identifying the 45,000 or so genes that make up the human genome affords great diagnostic benefits. Developing techniques for modifying genes gives us the capacity to change people in all sorts of ways. The impetus for this research has largely been therapeutic. The more we know about disease the more we understand the influence of genes. In single-gene disorders, such as sickle cell disease, the presence or absence of a particular gene will determine whether or not the individual will be affected. In other cases, for example, the BRCA 1 and 2 genes, which influence the onset of breast cancer, the presence or absence of the gene is not decisive but will act as a predisposing factor. Clearly, the ability to influence these genes and their operation is of immense potential benefit. However, genes also determine or influence a whole spectrum of other things. These range from factors with therapeutic importance like the ability to fight disease or the ability of tissue to repair itself, to traits like height, weight, build, and stature; hair, eye, and skin color.

The rate at which we age, and our life expectancy, are also matters which are genetically influenced and highly likely to be manipulable by human beings in the future. Here we begin to see more clearly why therapeutic concerns and ethical ones are inextricably linked. The business of medical science may be described as a combination of life-saving and life-enhancing techniques. The alleviation of distressing symptoms is important because it is life-enhancing, it makes lives go better, but so does improving the capacities that influence how our lives go; capacities such as intelligence, or stamina, or other traits like those connected with physical appearance. Life-saving, a practice universally admired and applauded, whether carried out by doctors, firemen, or those who watch bays, is really only the term we use for acts

1

that further postpone death. Once we realize that life-saving is just death-postponing we are left with a series of dilemmas when we imagine postponing death indefinitely. Would such a thing, if it became possible, be more therapeutic than cosmetic or vice versa? Would it be desirable? Some people have regarded the idea of immortality with dread and loathing, others have aspired to it with tenacity and passion. Here, the ethical challenge posed by scientific advances is formidable. What might be good for us as individuals might not be good for society as a whole? What age distribution in society would be best; would it make everyone happier or more at ease with one another? Which age distribution would be economically or politically most advantageous? Are we entitled to attempt to influence such things; would we be right not to?

Genetic science has had great influence in sensitizing us to our capacity to make changes to human beings, and the necessity of attempting to evaluate the desirability of these changes for individuals, for society, and for the future of the species. Over and above this, however, genetic science has had two other major effects of ethical interest which we should note.

The first concerns increasing awareness of the fact of how closely we are genetically related not only to one another but also to other species. Any child, for example will be 99.95 percent the same as its genetic mother in terms of genetic information, but it will also share 99.90 percent of its genetic information with any randomly chosen person. Such facts may begin to profoundly influence how we understand such concepts as "relatedness" and "kinship." Moreover, just as it is true that we share the vast majority of our genes with everyone else, we also share the vast majority of our genetic information with animals. Chimpanzees, for example, share with us some 95 percent of their genetic information. How should this fact guide our ethical relations with each other and with other species? On the one hand, such knowledge seems to bring all of creation closer together; on the other, it seems to highlight the crucial importance of quite minute differences at the level of genetic information.

Finally, we should note a new and radically important consequence of the new genetics. This involves a change in attitude to one of the most basic and traditional of distinctions, that between what is given and what is done. There is the realm of things and events that come to us as given, that seem to us to be governed by "fate." There is also the realm of things which, because they are susceptible to our influence, are in some sense down to us, are our responsibility. Genetics has radically enlarged this latter category by showing us that something as basic as "human nature," so far from being a stable, unchanging inheritance, is in fact changing both in ways that are out of our control *and* in ways that, increasingly, we can influence. The first of these new understandings we owe to Darwin. The second comes both from more recent advances in genetics and from philosophy. Progress in genetics has shown us just how much we can actually and potentially do to influence and alter the genetic constitution of individuals, and all that flows from that. And it is philosophy that has reminded us that once we have the capacity to make things different, and of course the knowledge that we have that capacity, then we are responsible for the consequences of our choices as to whether or not to exercise it.

In this book, we have attempted to bring together some of the best and most influential of contemporary writing about genetics which affects our ethical understanding of this explosive science, both at the level of individual decision-making and at the level of policy. To this end we have had to adopt a truly multidisciplinary approach. To understand the ethical importance and the implications of genetics you have, of course, to know something of the science, both what it is and what it might be able to achieve. But to think through the ethical and policy implications, one also needs to consider legal, philosophical, and to some extent social, cultural, and religious issues as well. This book has brought together new and important work in all these fields from 37 of the most prominent contributors to contemporary debate, to provide wide-ranging, scholarly analysis of, and sometimes provocative insights into, all the major issues of moral, political, and social significance which arise from what has understandably come to be called "the genetic revolution."

We have divided the book into five broad sections. In Part I, "Genetics: The Basics," the scientific stage for the remaining sections is set. We attempt here to give both a realistic picture of what can be done now and what the foreseeable future may hold in store for us and our descendants. Part II is focused on research issues and begins to explore the specific ethical issues raised by developments in genetics. Although these are in a sense the subject matter of the whole book, we attempt here to introduce major themes and major concerns. Genetics has grown up with the legacy of the eugenics movement of the last century and with the specter of Nazi atrocities. This history has colored many people's thinking about genetics, and we explore this legacy and its lessons for the future. Following the Second World War, many international conventions and protocols attempted to prevent future abuses by setting out guidelines for the ethical conduct of future research. The cornerstone of these and indeed of much contemporary thinking about the ethics of scientific research is the notion of informed consent. People are generally presumed to be the best guardians of their own interests and hence their fully informed consent to involvement in research is an obvious first safeguard. This of course raises problems about research on and for the benefit of those who cannot give an autonomous informed consent, namely children, those with impairments that diminish autonomy, and animals.

Part III looks specifically at gene manipulation and gene selection. The ability to alter or influence the genetic constitution of individuals raises profound issues both of personal identity and of our responsibilities to future generations. Because so much about us is determined or influenced by genes, they have come to have a special role in our understanding of, and indeed our feelings about, ourselves and our sense of our own uniqueness. In this role genes have replaced the previous contenders for this special place, the heart, and more recently, the brain. Because most manipulations would have to be done on embryos, or even perhaps on gametes, and because embryos are a source for human stem cells which may come to have enormous therapeutic benefit, our rights and responsibilities concerning human reproduction and the moral status of the human embryo have become a central focus and have been fiercely debated.

These themes continue into Part IV, which takes the debates further into the domain of public policy concerning science. The commercial importance and potential of all scientific advances is of crucial importance. Research is expensive and benefits that flow from research have huge commercial value. The ownership of the products of research then obviously comes to be of the first importance. When the research involves elements that are also part or may become part of the human body,

3

issues of ownership and patenting are complicated by concerns about privacy and autonomy. Genetic information is of commercial importance in another sense also: it has powerful predictive force about the future health and life expectancy of the individual. Since in many societies life and health insurance play a key role not only in the lives of individuals but in the provision of healthcare on a society-wide basis, the interests of insurance companies, including the state, have assumed immense importance in these debates. Not only because of the inheritance from the eugenics movement but also because some genetic conditions are associated with particular "races" or ethnic groups, genetics also triggers racial awareness in both desirable and less desirable manifestations. The unfairness of a genetic inheritance which makes for so many hugely important differences between people has also increasingly set the moral and political agenda of genetics. Issues of so-called "genetic justice" will continue to shape our thinking about the future of genetics and our sense of the legitimacy or illegitimacy of the genetic manipulation of human beings.

In the final part, we turn to the role of law and regulation in science. Information about individuals and their genetic constitution obviously has immense importance for public health. It also gives opportunities for selection and discrimination in many fields: employment, healthcare provision, insurance, reproduction, parenting, to mention only the most obvious. Except for monozygotic twins or clones, genetic information is also a unique personal identifier. A person's identity can be established from and traced to any sample of DNA, however small. Sufficient DNA for these purposes can be obtained even from a smear of saliva or a flake of skin. From paternity and maternity testing to the investigation of crime, the forensic uses and possible abuses of genetics are clearly immense. And because genetic samples can now be obtained non-invasively, the opportunities for illicitly obtaining genetic information are greatly increased, raising acutely different issues of genetic privacy and personal liberty.

Following someone's death, stored genetic material can be of enormous benefit scientifically. What has come to be called "the human tissue archive," that is, the sum total of all stored human tissue, products of surgical operations, *post mortem* examinations, samples of blood, and other tissue taken during the course of a life for a myriad of purposes, can all generate important information of personal significance and general utility. Who owns this material? Who has the right to use it? Who should reap the financial and other benefits of its use? Whose consent is required before it may be used?

We do not here profess to have answered definitively all of the above questions raised by genetics in the ensuing pages. Rather we have provided a forum in which some of the leading contemporary contributors to this field and analysts of the issues it generates can present their current thinking, and to which any reader of this book can respond and find some basis for making their own contribution.

Part I

GENETICS: SETTING THE SCENE

1

Stem Cells

C. N. SVENDSEN

Introduction

The world of genetics has taken biology by storm over recent years. A four-letter code, strung together in different patterns within our genes, appears to determine everything from eye color, through various diseases to, perhaps, even intelligence. Through this blueprint, all the components of the living cell are encrypted. But it requires consistent repair and replacement – and, inevitably, flaws do occur leading to malformations of cell architecture and, in turn, disease. Thus, correcting genetic deficits through "gene therapy" is one of the goals of modern medicine and has attracted enormous investment both from international governments and industry. This research is spearheaded by a massive collaborative effort to sequence the entire human genome (the Human Genome Project). However, it is clear that in using these modern gene methods the doctor becomes the architect, correcting flaws in the human design, even enhancing the original plans with new ideas. Clearly this raises enormous philosophical and ethical issues, a core feature of this volume. But quietly, alongside this wild exuberance among all genetically inclined, a revolution of another sort is gaining momentum. A revolution that may soon compete alongside the four letters. Stem cell biology is developing at such a rapid pace it is almost impossible to keep up with the latest developments – and each new experiment raises tantalizing possibilities for novel types of therapy for a wide range of disorders. At the same time, stem cell research raises complex moral and philosophical questions with regard to who we are and the limits of medicine. This chapter is an attempt to explain the science behind the hype, and discuss the possible implications of stem cell biology for our modern and rapidly changing society.

The Mother of All Cells

If the genes are thought of as a blueprint for life, cells could be considered the building materials. Some are even shaped like bricks, such as the short-lived epithelial cells with their simple rectangular structures. Others are more complex, like rows of elegant ornaments placed in strategic locations within the building. The neuron of the brain, for example, which can have a lifespan of over 100 years, has a small cell body, enormous dentritic tentacles, and a single thin cable of communication with other cells which can reach over a meter long. Together, these and many other cell types bind together to form multicellular life. But how do these different type of cells arise in the body? For many years scientists have known one simple fact – we all develop from a single cell. A sperm penetrates the thick wall of a receptive egg and generates a charged cell, or oocyte, with a full complement of 46 chromosomes – half from the mother and half from the father. This is the miracle of life, and the combining of the two sets of chromosomes, each carrying their own genetic history, underlies the wonderful and unique characteristics of each new being. The oocyte is truly totipotent, capable of producing total organism. It first splits into 2 cells, then 4, 8, 16 – the rate of growth is exponential and astounding, for it only takes 30 divisions to produce 1 billion individual cells from the single oocyte. At each division, both daughter cells are thought to inherit an identical copy of genes. However, different parts of various genes are switched on in different cell types by crucial molecules known as transcription factors (molecules capable of switching on specific sets of genes), leading to the cellular differences we see throughout the body. Some become brain cells, others heart, muscle, blood, or kidney. But how do cells from the mother egg know what to turn into and where? These are the fundamental issues of developmental biology and have been pondered over for many years. It is now becoming clear that cellular development involves the sequential expression of specific genes and transcription factors and is based around common founder cells, or *stem cells*.

Embryonic Stem (ES) Cells

The oocyte rapidly develops into a small, hollow ball of cells termed a blastocyst. The blastocyst is a remarkable structure which floats along the fallopian tubes until it reaches the uterus, dividing as it goes. It becomes polarized with primitive "head" and "tail" regions, crucial for subsequent development into a developing fetus once implantation to the womb has taken place. From it, a primitive form of stem cell, the embryonic stem cell, or ES cell, can be derived in the test tube (Svendsen and Smith 1999). This requires that the blastocyst is torn apart into single cells which are then no longer able to make a whole organism – a crucial procedure which is often misunderstood and deserves highlighting futher. Unlike the totipotent fertilized egg, ES cells are an artificial type of cell generated in the test tube and *cannot form a whole organism alone*, and as such could not be used to clone either animals or people. For this reason they are termed pluripotent, to emphasize the point that they cannot form a total organism. However, ES cells do retain the capacity to turn into any tissue type either within the culture dish or following transplantation. This has led to the term "therapeutic cloning" where single cells are replicated in the culture dish, as opposed to "reproductive cloning" where whole organisms are cloned. In mice, ES cells can be injected back into fresh blastocysts, which are then allowed to implant and develop. The resulting animals are chimeric, containing some tissues from the ES cells and some from the original blastocyst; they have been used widely to generate genetically modified animals. ES cells are also capable of extensive self-renewal (where a cell makes an identical copy of itself) in the culture dish. So here is a cell that can essentially recapitulate most of the developmental steps leading to the generation of specific tissues in the body, without being capable of making a whole organism.

Specialized Stem Cells

There are also other types of stem cells that are more restricted in their potential. These are termed multipotent stem cells. These cells form founder colonies in specific regions of the developing embryo, which lay down the progenitor cell colonies required to build specific tissue types. Progenitor cells are rapidly dividing with a limited self-renewal potential – programmed to make one type of tissue fast and then stop. They are the workhorses of development, while the true stem cells remain quietly in the background, dividing just enough to maintain the progenitor cell pool. Once an organ is complete, a pool of stem cells will often reside in its deeper layers. These divide slowly under normal circumstances, but can be induced to divide faster by tissue damage, and have a remarkable capacity for self-renewal. The stem cells of the blood system are perhaps the most studied, and were discovered over 50 years ago. The blood is one body tissue that needs continual replacement. Blood stem cells lie deep within the bone marrow, producing enough progeny to replace cells lost through wear and tear. Other tissues such as skin, gut, and liver have their own multipotent stem cell pools. Thus, the body is in fact a mosaic of different tissue types, each with their own founder colonies of cells which in many cases can be recruited to repair damage or replace lost cells.

If this system is so efficient, why do tissues wear out at all? Why can't the cells simply replace each other continually? Herein lies one of the mysteries of the body – the process of aging. Clearly, if every tissue in the body could replace itself continually throughout life, aging would not take place. However, as discussed extensively in another chapter (see Kirkwood), there appears to be either a genetic preponderance or a preset program which leads to errors in both dividing and nondividing cells as they age. It is this accumulation of damage that leads to loss of skin tone, wrinkles, organ malfunction, and possibly brain diseases of old age. The adult stem cell pools appear to have a finite period in which they can continue to divide efficiently and replace their offspring in most organs. This process of regulating cell division is one of the major challenges our bodies face, and one can imagine a powerful struggle between cells which want to divide and cells which don't in the aging and tiring body. Get it wrong and the result is massive cellular division and the formation of a tumor. As cancer remains one of the most common killers in modern medicine, and the risk increases with age, it is clear that the body often loses this struggle, a rogue cell reverting to lost youth and immortality, with deadly consequences. Thus, once in place through the miracle of development, many of our cells live in a fine balance between division and death. Stem cells, buried deep within our organs, are perhaps the closest link with the past, and a potential target for increasing health in later life or following disease.

9

Therapeutic Implications of Stem Cell Biology

A major part of medicine has traditionally been linked with preventing diseases of advancing age, using either drugs or surgery. Novel chemical compounds, capable of changing or supplementing our existing biology, have been churned out in their millions in the never-ending quest for health. Surgeons have performed miracles by removing growths or repairing old or broken joints. But until recently the thought of replacing diseased parts of the body was pure science fiction.

Blood donation has been a feature of modern medicine and is one of the most basic types of cell transplantation from one patient to another. In some cases this is in the form of infusion following injury and massive loss of blood. In many forms of cancer, treatment using high-dose chemotherapy often destroys both the cancer and the patient's blood and the cells of the immune system. However, blood stem cells can be removed prior to chemotherapy, and then replaced to repopulate the bone marrow afterwards. In fact, there are now companies who specialize in storing blood stem cells from young, fit people just in case they need them later following chemotherapy (e.g. Stem Cell Science Inc.: www.stem-cell.com). Whole-organ transfer from "brain dead" patients on life support to patients with kidney, liver, or heart failure has also become part of everyday medicine. The final hurdles in organ transplants were not in fact surgical at all, but to do with the power of the body's immune system to repel all invaders. Any tissue not recognized as "self" was immediately destroyed by the immune system, and it took the development of powerful antirejection drugs to allow the first kidney transplants to take place. The success of these operations is tempered by the rather tragic waiting list which now faces all patients with serious heart or kidney disease, and the side-effects of the various types of antirejection drugs which have to be taken for extended periods of time. Less well known are brain transplant studies. Parkinson's disease involves the loss of specific neurons within the brain that produce the chemical dopamine. A number of reports have now shown that these neurons can be replaced by new dopamine neurons transplanted into the affected patient. Here, brain tissue harvested from terminal patients on life support cannot be used, as the neurons within the adult brain do not survive the trauma of being removed. However, postmortem fetal tissue survives with the brain of Parkinson's disease patients, and can develop into mature neurons, which in turn reverse some symptoms of the disease. The idea of using cells rather than whole organs to alleviate disease has led to the term "cell therapy." Keyhole heart surgery is already being considered, where fresh heart muscle cells are injected into the ailing organ and may possibly integrate and revitalize without total replacement. In diabetes, pancreatic transplants are already available and new cell therapy approaches are already in clinical trials. These consist of using specialized cells, called "Islets of Langerhans" which produce insulin, as a source of tissue for grafting into the pancreas, thus obviating the need for a whole organ transplant.

In all of these transplant scenarios, a major problem continues to re-emerge. Where will the tissue come from? Clearly, there are not enough donations to provide for the numbers of patients who could benefit from transplantation. This is related to shortages in the blood supply, the small number of organ donor card holders, and the specific requirements of harvesting organs. One approach is the use of animal organs. Pigs share many characteristics with humans with regard to organ size and function. In addition, they have large litters and can be bred with relative ease. Recently, a genetically modified pig has been produced which has "humanized" cells which are less likely to produce an acute immune response. However, there remains the problem of long-term chronic rejection with pig organs, and following the BSE scare there is always the worry of transmitting an innocuous pig virus to man, where its effects would be unpredictable.

In November 1998 the world woke up to the discovery that human embryonic stem cells could be grown in culture. A research group, funded by a biotech company called Geron, reported in the journal *Science* that they had successfully grown human ES cells and that these cells could give rise to all the major tissue types of the body (Thomson et al. 1998). Although not all of the tests had been carried out to prove that these cells were bonafide ES cells, they had many characteristics that suggested they were at least very similar. Suddenly, it was possible to generate human tissues at will in the culture dish. The worlds of ES cell biology and medicine were now on a collision course, at least theoretically. In general, the idea of generating whole organs from single stem cells is simple to grasp. Yet, in practice this has been difficult to achieve. Although skin can now be artificially generated in the culture dish, complex three-dimensional organs again are proving more difficult. However, the field of complex polymers, combined with novel stem cell culture techniques, is pushing the field forward, with the first artificial bladder grown in a test tube currently awaiting clinical trials. Huge amounts of money are being invested in this field of research, and large companies such as Advanced Tissue Sciences (ATS) already provide bioengineered skin and cartilage substitutes and are working hard to develop the first artificial kidney or heart outside the body. The impact of these techniques on organ transplantation is obvious, and the idea of combining human ES cell technology with organ factories comes closer to reality with each passing day.

Although exciting, there are certain drawbacks to all of the above therapeutic possibilities of using human stem cells to treat various diseases. Of these the most serious might be the immune response to foreign cells. Although not as serious as xenografts (where cells from another species such as a pig are used), there is still rejection of transplanted cells derived from another human. Antirejection drugs are of course available, but they can have serious side-effects in certain patients. How might this be circumvented? There are two major possibilities.

The first approach is to take adult stem cells from the patient under treatment, expand these in the culture dish, genetically modify them, and then transplant them back. If organ construction in the culture dish becomes a reality, similar adult stem cells might be used to "seed" polymer matrixes with the patient's own cells to generate a new organ. A second approach has more ethical considerations. Nuclear transfer involves the removal of a nucleus from one cell into another. Early studies using amphibian embryos showed that it was possible to transfer the nucleus of one oocyte to another, and then generate a new organism. Years of speculation and controversy were ended with the production of Dolly, the world's first cloned mammal. Although this method was very inefficient, it proved that the DNA from

11

adult cells retains all the potential to generate a whole new organism, or clone (see Ian Wilmut's chapter 3) providing it was put into a quiescent state and transferred to a receptive egg. Using these methods, the nucleus from a patient's skin cell could be transferred to a donor egg, which could then be induced to grow to the blastula stage. ES cells isolated from this blastula and induced to turn into the appropriate tissue type could subsequently be transplanted back into the patient. The benefit here of course is that the cells would appear to belong to the patient (as they had copies of the patient's own DNA) and thus not be rejected. However, these methods involve generating and destroying a human blastocyst for medical reasons. This has prompted enormous debate in most countries and led to the formation of a new government advisory body, the Human Genetics Commission, to tackle this issue in the UK.

It is perhaps becoming clear that stem cells may come close to providing a panacea for certain areas of medicine. New cells, new organs: when its worn out, replace it. Are there philosophical issues here? Certainly, the borders between a person and their individual parts become blurred when thinking in terms of cells and man. Continual replacement of tissues and organs also raises the idea of immortality – for those who can afford it. Because these new technologies will not come cheap, state-run hospitals will be hard pressed to keep up with demand. But another major issue remains: it may be possible to have forever-young bodies, but what of the mind?

Cellular Philosophy and the Mind Problem

Although the presence of stem cells in tissues requiring many new cells during life, such as the skin and blood, may seem obvious, it was more of a surprise to find similar stem cells also existed within the adult brain. Why? Because the brain is classically thought of as a static structure. The old dogma reads, "we are born with so many brain cells and then they die gradually as we get older – our memory often dying with them." Recent developments in neuroscience have put this idea to rest. Certain regions of the adult brain have cells which divide all through life, generating new neurons which may even contribute to new memories. Early remarkable studies in songbirds showed that new nerve cells replace old ones each year and contributed to novel songs. Although this was long thought to be an isolated avian example, more recent studies in rats have shown conclusively that stem cells lining the ventricular caverns of the brain continue to proliferate in two regions. The first is in the front of the brain. Here, dividing cells migrate along established pathways down to the olfactory bulbs, the region of the rodent brain devoted to smell. Once they arrive in the olfactory bulb, these cells turn into neurons that integrate and begin to function as a new component of this brain region. A remarkable number of newly generated cells migrate along this pathway throughout the rodent's life, although the exact function of this process remains a mystery. Another region of the brain where new neurons are produced is the hippocampus (the region of the brain responsible for short-term memory). When rats are exposed to an enriched environment (i.e. their cages have toys and bigger areas of space), more new neurons are produced in the hippocampus, suggesting that the process of cell division in this brain region is linked to the environment. Some of these new cells may also play a role in new memory formation, although this is a hotly debated topic at present. Remarkably, similar cells have also been found in the human brain, and thus represent a fascinating feature of the adult nervous system (Kempermann and Gage 1999). These dividing cells can be removed from the adult brain and grown in the culture dish. There they continue to divide if given the right nutrient broth, and have been intensely studied. In most cases, a percentage of the dividing cells are multipotent neural stem cells, capable of making new neurons and glia, the major cell types of the brain. New ways of growing these neural stem cells have shown that large numbers can be generated in the culture dish over relatively short periods of time.

Human neural stem cells can more readily be isolated from postmortem fetal tissue and subsequently grown for long periods of time in the culture dish. These cells retain the ability to survive and integrate into the damaged rodent brain (Svendsen et al. 1999). Other groups have shown that using a cocktail of genetic manipulation and certain chemicals in the culture, similar cells from the rodent can be turned into dopamine neurons. These types of cells may bring partial relief in diseases such as Parkinson's, through simply releasing chemicals within a defined brain region. However, restoring full neural circuitry may be far more of a challenge, requiring that the cells not only survive and release specific chemicals, but also that they link up in the correct fashion. Only then will full brain repair be possible.

For most body parts it may appear that we are simply taking the next logical step in medicine. Instead of treating the diseased tissues of the body, we are replacing them with new ones. But how long can this go on? How many cells do we have to replace before the "self" is lost? If one thinks of the body as a machine, controlled by the brain, then perhaps it is allowable to exchange all of our body parts on a regular basis in order to stay at maximum health, rather like a conscientious owner changes the parts of a car as they wear out. The car continues to age, but its parts are kept in premium condition. At the end of its life it is still an MGB or E-type Jaguar, even though its original parts have been replaced many times. But change the shape of the car and suddenly it's not the same anymore. It has been modified, adapted to a form that is no longer recognizable. With the human body it is obviously possible to change looks through plastic surgery or reconstruction of the face. But a friend or family member would soon realize it was the person they knew once a conversation had begun, memories were rerun, likes and dislikes discussed. But changing the mind is a different concept.

For diseases such as Parkinson's, where the idea of transplants at present is to simply replace a missing chemical responsible for the flow of movement, there appears to be no philosophical problem. But if diseases such as Alzheimer's are considered for cell therapy, an interesting conundrum arises. In its early stages, Alzheimer's consist of episodic short-term memory loss and changes in personality. As it progresses the memory impairments become worse and there is a dramatic transition in character, back to an almost childlike state. In its final stages, the sufferer is practically uncon-scious to the surrounding world, living in a body with no free mind, no past or present, no sense of being, and no recognition of family or friends. As brain studies have shown an enormous loss of cells in many regions of the brains of patients with Alzheimer's, it is clear that one possible therapeutic approach would be to replace these with new ones. But even if this were possible in the future (at present restoring these types of connections is very difficult), what would be the outcome of such a transplant? "Who" would the resulting person be? Would the new cells link the patient's past world with the current one? Or would they simply feel as if they had been born into an old body? This same argument could be applied when considering using neural cell therapy to restore memory loss and cognitive decline seen in normal aging.

In a way this problem touches on the complex issue of what "self" is, or perhaps, depending on definitions, consciousness (see Carol Rovane's chapter 18). Are we simply a collection of neurons organized in a specific way, or is there a grander plan to things, which only arises during the mystery of development, among the millions of dividing cells in the brain. Of course we are not born with a feeling of self. At birth we are only able to communicate in a very basic way, perhaps less than a dog or cat, and we have no concept of good and evil, no social skills, no ability to predict the future or even rationalize about the past. Yet the entire brain is there. What is missing is experience. Experience is known to shape the brain from the moment we are born. If cats are prevented from seeing the outside world throughout development it might be predicted that once able to see again these animals would regain normal sight. However, experiments designed to test this revealed a different outcome. The adult cats showed visual deficits not only just after regaining vision, but also for an indefinite period of time afterwards. It is now clear that during development, it is not enough to have the cells in place, they must have input in order to organize. The example for vision is almost certainly true for other senses, and is probably true for our overall character, which is forged during our formative developmental years and difficult to change in later life. Thus, the destruction of the basic character of a person through disease will not readily be reversed by simply transplanting cells. One could take this argument further. Assuming stem cells can be transplanted into the brain of Alzheimer's patients and encouraged to restore circuits, would the recipient "come back" to the world as a young child? Would the transplanted cells then require new experiences to mature and develop? There is some evidence from animal studies that transplanted cells will respond to new environmental stimuli – in particular with regard to memory tasks. In other words, the animal needs to learn how to use the new transplant, which without this new training does nothing. Therefore, to restore the lost personality of a patient (or elderly person with many replacement organs) may be difficult, but it may well be possible to give the patient an opportunity to develop a new personality. Perhaps we really will be able to teach an old dog new tricks in the future!

There is a genuine concern that stem cell transplants, or other types of transplant, will drastically change the personality of a patient. This led to the suggestion that brain transplants be limited to a certain percentage of the whole brain to avoid drastic changes in personality. But with the current trend of continual improvement in health, intelligence, and life expectancy it may not be long before healthy people begin to ask for transplants to improve their basic learning abilities. Surely more cells will mean more intelligence? Mind improving drugs may be supplemented with mind improving cells, carefully topping up regions of the brain which undergo the greatest reduction in cell number during normal aging. It is perhaps this idea of continually replacing damaged or worn out cells during *normal aging*, or improving our natural brain capacity, which highlights one of the potential discussion points of this type of research.

Of course in some cases the actual memories may remain in undamaged parts of the brain, but the conduit to these is destroyed. One may think here of more focal brain damage, such as that which occurs in stroke patients. Specific key parts of the brain can be destroyed with apparently global effects, as those parts serve as the platform upon which thoughts are translated into actions. In these cases, stem cell or other cell transplants may have better effects and "bring back" lost personalities through providing a new interface between intact brain regions and the outside world.

The New Alchemists

The pace of research in stem cell biology is such that every month one has to reassess the field in light of new papers. And the really exciting experiments are just beginning. If a single adult cell, from the skin for example, has the capacity to generate a whole organism, surely it could be made to produce different tissue types in a test tube. In fact, this type of research is now becoming the focus of a number of companies and academic labs. As discussed previously, the reason a skin cell is a skin cell is not that it has lost all the other genes required to make different tissues, but that only a subset of genes ("skin cell genes") are expressed within that cell, while the others are silenced. By waking up dormant genes using specific transcription factors, it may be possible to generate a wide variety of cells from such a humble skin cell. A recent report has shown that stem cells derived from mouse brain tissue can convert into blood cells under certain circumstances (Bjornson et al. 1999). This lends support to the idea that cells from the skin or brain may be switched into other cell types providing the correct genes are turned on or off, or the cells are exposed to an appropriate environment.

In relation to this chapter, the idea of manipulating any cell to change its "personality" suddenly frees this area of research from the ethical and moral dilemmas it currently finds itself in when dealing with human embryos. Surely there can be no opposition to removing a skin cell from a Parkinson's patient, growing it in culture and changing it into a nerve cell, and then transplanting it back into the patient's brain to alleviate some aspects of the disease? The added beauty of this approach is that the patient's own cells are the source for transplantation, so there are no rejection issues. If the skin cell can be modified to produce kidney or liver cells, and the combined technologies applied to produce whole organs, this type of method may prove enormously powerful in all aspects of cell therapy. The bottom line with these studies, once again, is understanding the genes which direct our cells to be what they are.

Stem Cell Biology: God in a Test Tube?

We stand on the threshold of a new era of cell biology. We evolved over millions of years from a single cell in the primordial soup of the cooling earth, a process which is

15

replayed millions of times as the human fetus develops. As we struggle to understand this remarkable event where a few billion cells come together to form human beings, the reductionists are beginning to win. We are starting to control the very process of life – cellular division and differentiation. In controlling this we get closer to playing God. Cloning animals from single oocytes may become routine. Replacing worn out organs, even worn out brain cells, could become normal practice – in effect providing a form of immortality. Therefore, the combination of genetics and cell biology will throw up some of the most important philosophical, moral, ethical, and theological questions faced by modern man. Inevitably this will lead to enormous amounts of scare-mongering, exaggeration of the facts, and in some cases vindictive and ill-informed attacks on the scientists doing this work. It is the cutting edge of science that leads this process. It is equivalent to the space race of the 1960s and every bit as competitive. Everyone wants to be first, to take the next step – and the top journals encourage these steps. Publish or perish. Under these pressures are the scientists able to make moral decisions about their research? Caught up in the race, is it possible to look rationally at where the work is going and the possible implications?

In some cases the issues are taken out of the hands of the scientists and into the hands of politicians. The transplantation of fetal tissue to treat Parkinson's disease was not funded by the National Institutes of Health in America (the largest government biological science funding body) for a number of years because the Reagan administration banned any funding of studies using human aborted fetuses. Clinton recently overturned this law, and new clinical trials involving transplantation for Parkinson's are currently underway in the USA. A similar ruling banning the use of fertilized eggs for research and the generation of ES cells has been in place in the USA for some time. Ironically, it was an American lab which published the first data showing that human ES cells could be grown in culture which highlights one of the major problems when government attempts to restrict science. Industry simply stepped in and provided the funding required to do the research. There is a danger here that companies will end up in the role of God, rather than society, which is surely less acceptable. There is certainly money in both reproduction and immortality, not to mention restoring function following disease, which will drive companies to pursue this type of research.

What is needed is debate and decisions such that effective laws can be passed and extended, where possible, to a worldwide set of guidelines. It also needs timely and extensive investment from government research councils throughout the world. This type of biology is going to keep going in some form, and by avoiding solid funding, governments run the risk of losing regulatory control. Research using human embryonic tissues is highly emotive and ethically complicated. Who is to determine when life really begins and how the early fertilized egg should be treated? Should there be commercial gain from using cells derived from human embryos? If there is commercial gain, the woman donating the eggs or terminating her pregnancy must be made aware of this as part of the informed consent process. This has the danger of encouraging egg and fetal donations simply for financial gain, and should clearly not be encouraged. One possible way to avoid this scenario is for government to take a more active role in embryo-based stem cell technologies, to regulate this field of research and invest in developing cell therapy methods, from the basic science to the establishment of "cell factories" for the production of tissues for transplantation. In this way, although it would be expensive at the start, governments would be able to utilize these technologies within nonprofit systems, thus overcoming commercial complications connected with selling human tissues. Because of these issues, many cell-based companies are focusing on modifying normal adult human cells grown in culture – either using gene transfer techniques or environmental switches. Here the ethical issues are less involved, although the impact on medicine and society will be no less dramatic if they are successful.

Clearly, as outlined in this chapter, stem cell biology could deliver real therapy for diseases affecting millions of people, and may lead to many exciting discoveries with regard to how humans develop. As such it must be worth pursuing. But in the process of generating human embryos or continually renewing body tissues with "spare parts" we will open a Pandora's box of ethical and moral issues. Just what we should take out will be the focus of the next millennium, and the center of many interesting discussions. Let's hope that these are based on reasoned thought, rather than radical and extremist science phobias. This will only come about if the scientists, public, government, industry, and religious bodies work together in a transparent fashion. We all derive from a single cell, but its clear that the miracle of life has produced a plethora of different views on these issues – in itself a testament to the majesty and power of biology.

References and Further Reading

Bjornson, R. L. et al. (1999), "Turning Brain into Blood: A Hematopoietic Fate Adopted by Adult Neural Stem Cells In Vivo," *Science* 283, pp. 534–7.

Kempermann, G. and Gage, F. H. (1999), "New Nerve Cells for the Adult Brain," *Scientific American* 280, pp. 48–53.

Svendsen, C. N. and Smith, A. G. (1999), "New Prospects for Human Stem-cell Therapy in the Nervous System," *Trends in Neuroscience* 8, pp. 357–64.

Svendsen, C. N. et al. (1999), "Human Neural Stem Cells: Isolation, Expansion and Transplantation," *Brain Pathology* 9, pp. 499–513.

Thomson, J. et al. (1998), "Embryonic Stem Cell Lines Derived from Human Blastocyts," *Science* 282, pp. 1145–7.

2

Gene Therapy for Neurological Disorders: New Therapies or Human Experimentation?

P. R. LOWENSTEIN

Marry, and you will regret it. Do not marry, and you will also regret it. . . . Marry or do not marry, you will regret it either way. . . . Whether you laugh at the stupidities of the world or you weep over them, you will regret it either way . . . Whether you trust a girl or do not trust her, you will regret it either way . . . Whether you hang yourself or do not hang yourself, you will regret it either way. This, gentlemen, is the quintessence of all the wisdom of life.

Søren Kirkegaard, Either/Or

Introduction

In the prolific debate over gene therapy, gene therapy for *neurological diseases* has not figured prominently (Anderson and Fletcher 1980; Anderson 1984, 1989; Nichols 1988; Walters 1986; Wivel and Walters 1993; Ledley 1996; Dyer 1997; Heyd 1992; Harris 1993; Harris 1998; Walters and Palmer 1997). Gene therapy is potentially a novel clinical tool for the treatment of human disease. Most work in gene therapy is thus geared towards the development of useful strategies that *could be* implemented clinically for the treatment of disease in human patients. My ensuing exploration of the issues surrounding the implementation of novel molecular therapies for the treatment of neurological disease is a search for answers to practical dilemmas. I believe that clarifying the pros and cons of gene therapy, and establishing more accurately what gene therapy can and cannot deliver, will help to provide a basis for moving scientific- ally sound ideas and technical proposals more rapidly into human clinical trials, avoiding the delays usually imposed on new therapeutic approaches. I also believe that although current gene therapy trials are carefully evaluated and monitored, and have proceeded to the considerable benefit of science and affected patients, gene therapy continues to pose ethical challenges. Further explorations into the ethics limits of human gene therapy are needed. Also, the historical, cultural, social, and bioethical context of gene therapy will need to be carefully considered in the future (Cooter 1995). Below, I aim first to make clear the premises and aims of clinical gene therapy. I shall then indicate which ethical aspects of gene therapy trials require further attention, and why.

A (re)Definition of what Human Gene Therapy is About

Gene therapy is the use of nucleic acids as drugs (Kay et al. 2001). Thus, as for any drug, its application will be mainly restricted to therapeutic uses. Four categories or types of gene therapy have been defined: (i) somatic gene therapy, (ii) somatic genetic enhancement, (iii) germline gene therapy, and (iv) germline genetic enhancement (Anderson 1985 and 1989; Wivel and Walters 1993; reviewed in Walters and Palmer 1997). Therapeutic applications refer to treatment of disease in a strict sense, while enhancement applications are used to define all nontherapeutic uses of gene therapy. Somatic gene therapy refers to the treatment of any organ, tissue, or cells, excluding the germ cells (i.e. the spermatozoids of males, and the oocytes of females). An ethical boundary has been drawn beyond somatic gene therapy. All other uses in humans have been deemed unethical at the present time. Purposeful modification of germline cells is specifically forbidden by law in the USA, UK, and most other countries with relevant legislation (Clothier et al. 1992). Although the dividing line between somatic gene therapy and enhancement will not always be clear-cut, e.g. when considering certain human attributes like height, and while experimentation on possible germline modifications through gene therapy continues to be developed (Brinster and Avarbock 1994), all current clinical gene therapy trials are clearly true *somatic* gene therapy applications. Nevertheless, several misconceptions still remain regarding gene therapy and clinical trials of gene therapy which I shall now address in turn.

Misconception one: gene therapy is something completely new

Gene therapy is *not* (strictly speaking) new. It has been discussed under the same name for at least the last 30 years, if not longer. Recently, though, Professor Theodore Friedmann of the University of San Diego in California has convincingly argued that the whole field has left the "conceptual phase" to enter the "implementation phase" (Friedmann 1996). Prior to this, the conceptual basis of gene therapy was still being questioned (i.e. "will it ever work?"). Now, with successful clinical trials (Cavazzana-Calvo et al. 2000; Fischer et al. 2001), dedicated gene therapy professional societies (e.g. the American Society of Gene Therapy and the European Society of Gene Therapy) and specialized journals (*Gene Therapy, Human Gene Therapy, Molecular Therapy, Current Gene Therapy, Journal of Molecular Medicine*), and gene therapy commercial enterprises, in summary, the professionalization of gene therapy and its differentiation and recognition from other scientific subdisciplines, the implementation phase (i.e. how to get it to work clinically throughout different medical specialties) is proceeding ahead at full steam.

Misconception two: gene therapy is to be applied only to the treatment of inherited disease

Gene therapy is *not* restricted to the treatment of inherited diseases even if it did arise as a novel approach to treat hitherto incurable inherited diseases (Lowenstein 1997).

19

Even if in its origins gene therapy was closely associated with inherited disease, nowadays most gene therapy is for the treatment of many nonprimarily-inherited diseases, e.g. cancer. This is indicated by the fact that, since 1989, more than 70 percent of gene therapy clinical trials have been for cancer – something not predicted by the main leaders in the field, even five years prior to the commencement of the trials (Roth and Cristiano 1997). This change in the selection of target diseases is more a reflection of the power and limitations of gene therapy as a therapeutic tool, than it is of the irresistible influence of the big pharmaceutical houses on research directions and/or of the high incidence of cancer as a major contributor to morbidity and mortality in advanced societies (see detailed arguments for this in Lowenstein 1997). In principle, it is more straightforward to devise a successful scientifically sound strategy for the treatment of cancer, than to do the same in an inherited disorder (Lowenstein 1997); although gene therapy for inherited disorders has now achieved true cures (Cavazzana-Calvo et al. 2000).

Misconception three: gene therapy is "different" from other current therapeutic approaches, i.e. it will provide magic bullets to cure disease overnight

Gene therapy is the therapeutic use of genetic material and/or nucleic acids, instead of the small, simple chemical molecules used by classical pharmacology. It is best characterized as a *kind of pharmacology*, though a new kind. Where "classical" pharmacology has been (and will always remain) limited to *modifying* existing cellular functions, gene therapy can direct cells to perform *new functions*. Since biological information is encoded by nucleic acids, cells can now be *engineered* effectively to function in ways that biology has not programmed them to do; classical pharmacology cannot force cells to perform functions for which they are not genetically programmed. Thus, gene therapy is a new *branch* of therapeutics, which, through the use of nucleic acids can reprogram cells to perform almost any chosen function, even if such a function is not normally performed by the target cells. As with classical pharmacology, gene therapy could, in principle, be used to treat a wide variety of both inherited and sporadic disease. Moreover, neither requires detailed understanding of underlying disease pathophysiology for the implementation of a putative therapeutic strategy.

How long will it take for gene therapy to become a widespread clinical tool? The short answer to this question is that we just do not know. Should this necessarily worry us? It should not. Acute lymphoblastic leukemia of childhood now has a 5-year survival rate of 80 percent, while in 1948 this value was 0 percent. It took classical cancer chemotherapy almost 50 years to arrive at such a remarkable result.

Neurological Gene Therapy

How gene therapy works

Having reviewed briefly what gene therapy is, and what it is not, I will now examine in detail how gene therapy actually works. Nucleic acids, the "drugs" of gene therapy, do not have any magical powers in themselves. However, given that life on earth is nucleic acid-based, essentially all products forming part of any living organism are encoded by particular nucleic acids, i.e. "stretches" of DNA. DNA is said to encode proteins. This refers to the fact that DNA, which is formed by nucleotides, will be translated to give rise to a protein, which is built from amino acids. Proteins are synthesized by DNA being transcribed into RNA first. There is a direct correspondence in which each three nucleotides are interpreted by the cellular protein synthetic machinery as an individual amino acid. This then allows translation of the nucleic acid sequence into an individual protein sequence. Thus, if I know the sequence of amino acids in a protein, I can deduce a corresponding sequence of DNA, which will be decoded into the predetermined protein structure. Further, given that protein function depends on its three-dimensional structure, and such structure depends on the particular sequence of amino acids, even nonnatural structures and functional capacities could be created and synthesized by cells expressing the designed DNA sequences. In short, given a protein, a nucleic acid can be made that encodes this protein.

A nucleic acid encoding a protein structure, *even a theoretical one*, can be devised following simple construction rules. Thus, although a "natural" nucleic acid sequence encodes a "natural" protein, alternative sequences can be artificially synthesized that give rise to the same sequence. Nucleic acid structures can also be constructed that encode for chimeric or even naturally non-existent protein structures. This can be used to combine useful parts of different proteins into one. For example, an antibody (a molecule produced by specific cells of the immune system and designed to recognize just a single antigen) can be linked to a receptor ligand (a molecule that fits a particular receptor; e.g. insulin is the ligand for the insulin receptor) on one side, and a cytotoxic protein on the other, thus allowing the specific delivery of the cytotoxic protein (a protein which causes a cell to die), to cells able to bind the complex. In cancer treatments in which antibodies are used to specifically direct a cytotoxic protein to cancer cells, the antibody recognizes the cancer cells, and when it is fused to a cytotoxic protein, the cytotoxic protein is delivered to the cancer cells, which are killed as a result.

What the techniques known as gene therapy now allow, is the re-engineering of *single adult members* of any species. Therefore, at least at the moment, it differs from "transgenic technologies" i.e. a technique which produces animals that are genetically engineered to express a particular protein not normally expressed by such animals through germline engineering. In this case a particular lineage is engineered, rather than an individual adult. Gene therapy also differs at the present from "knock-out animals," that is, the technique that produces an animal lineage (rather than an individual adult) which is genetically engineered not to express a particular protein (to study the effects of its absence on the animal's physiology). Gene therapy is further unrelated to cloning (see Ian Wilmut's chapter 3 in this volume).

In theory, gene therapy strategies could be devised to be applied to any conditions suffered by individuals which are currently treated (or not) by classical pharmacology. While any disease that can be treated by drugs might be treated by gene therapy, this does not necessarily imply that gene therapy will be more efficient than classical pharmacological tools. What gene therapy allows is the re-engineering of single adult members of any species.

Re-engineering cell function through gene therapy

Gene therapy targeted at neurological disorders ought to be potentially effective in the treatment of any neurological disease through the re-engineering of brain cells, whether such disease can be currently treated by classical pharmacology or not. What is meant by the "re-engineering of cells"? What a cell does or does not do depends exclusively on which regions of the cell's DNA are active and which are not. Thus, a liver cell expresses liver proteins, while a neuron expresses neuronal proteins. To date, for the treatment of liver disease, drugs can interfere with the function of liver proteins to achieve a desired therapeutic result. They cannot, however, change the kind of proteins expressed by a liver cell. This means that a liver cell cannot be made to express a nonliver protein, even if the gene encoding such a protein will be present (but not expressed) in the liver cell's genome. Thus, it is conceivable that drugs could be developed that would turn on the expression of nonliver proteins in the liver. However, pharmacology could not make a human liver cell express a plant, bacterial, or viral protein, since the liver cell's DNA certainly does not encode for any such proteins.

Gene therapy, because it consists of efficient ways of inserting foreign and biologically active nucleic acids into target cells, in such a way that they are then expressed by the engineered cells, has the capacity to achieve the expression of any protein in any cell type. This is the case independent of whether the target cell contains any DNA encoding for such a protein. Using the techniques of gene therapy, several proteins could be expressed in novel locations, sites where they are normally absent. Hence, cells could be endowed with new properties which they never had before, nor would otherwise have displayed in the absence of such genetic modification. This is what is meant by cell engineering through the techniques of gene therapy.

While this can be achieved through other means in cells grown in vitro, gene therapy provides the tools and "know-how" to do this in single, intact adult organisms, including humans. Of course the pharmaceutical industry is trying to develop simple (i.e. chemical) drugs which will be able to turn genes on and off in predetermined cell types. Although much effort is being put into this kind of research, only a handful of drugs already exist which can directly modify the expression of specific genes. What classical pharmacology aims to achieve with simple chemicals, gene therapy aims to achieve by targeting specific genes directly to target organs. The main advantage of gene therapy over classical approaches will be the capacity to achieve expression of proteins not encoded by the cells' genome.

The re-engineering of the brain

Having explained the concept of re-engineering through gene therapy, it becomes easier to apply this concept to the brain and its disorders. Neurological disorders being targeted by gene therapy involve metabolic disorders, neurodegenerative disorders, and brain tumors. Inherited metabolic disorders are caused by the lack of individual enzymes' activity due to inherited mutations in the genes encoding such enzymes (i.e., hypoxanthine-guanine phosphoribosyl-transferase in the Lesch-Nyhan syndrome, or α-L-iduronidase in Hurler's disease). Loss of enzymatic activity leads to disarrangement of neuronal or brain intermediary metabolism in a way that ultimately leads to brain cell death, widespread neurodegeneration, and global neurological dysfunction.

Neurodegenerative diseases are those in which specific areas of the brain progressively die. They can be inherited (e.g. Huntington's disease), or sporadic (e.g. Parkinson's disease). As our understanding of the genetic predisposition to some neurological diseases improves, it is becoming very clear that at least certain neurodegenerative diseases have both inherited and non-inherited components (e.g. Alzheimer's disease). The genetic basis of the risk to develop particular diseases is actively being pursued, thus defining the molecular components underlying the predisposition to develop certain diseases. Each of these molecular genetic lesions will thus become a reasonable target for reengineering by gene therapy or modification by classical pharmacology. (This explains why the big pharmaceutical houses have such vested interests in the Human Genome Project.)

It is not a coincidence that most current developments for gene therapy in neurological diseases are for the treatment of the kind of diseases mentioned above, i.e. metabolic diseases, neurodegenerative disorders, or cancer. These constitute important targets; patients suffering from these diseases are only helped partially by available drugs, and improved treatments would be of great help to them. However, if one takes for granted the statement that "gene therapy can be effective in any disease, amenable or not to classical pharmacology," the logical conclusion becomes that gene therapy will eventually also be used to develop new treatments for depression, schizophrenia, autism, as well as other so-called neuropsychiatric disorders. It would be technically easy to devise a logical and sound practical strategy to implement gene therapy for the treatment of mental disorders like depression.

While treatment of Parkinson's or Huntington's disease will initially focus on achieving therapeutic changes in motor behavior, Huntington's disease and Alzheimer's disease disrupt higher brain functions, i.e. memory and cognition. Engineering the brain to combat some of the most dire consequences of Alzheimer's disease will involve attempting to re-engineer the cognitive capacities of the brain. Whether such strategies will be of value for other patients suffering from cognitive disorders, or even whether they would eventually become "cognitive enhancers," cannot be predicted today with any accuracy.

It is likely that those mechanisms that lead to neurodegeneration in Alzheimer's disease occur more frequently in this disease than in the brains of normal aging people. It may be that an inhibition of such processes could preserve or maybe even enhance cognitive abilities. Whether powerful *cognitive enhancers* derived from gene therapy will become available may be difficult to predict, but not impossible to design. Much has already been learned on how to enhance cognitive abilities from early intensive stimulation of Down's Syndrome children and of children subjected to high doses of radiotherapy (which also leads to impaired intellectual abilities), as well as from the generalized cognitive enhancing effects claimed for Ritalin, Prozac, and other currently used antidepressants.

We should also learn from the interesting cases of mental pathologies in which patients excel at a particular cognitive function, to the exclusion of all others.

23

Currently, there is much work being done on the identification of the genetic basis of these diseases. It is still not known how the brain achieves such remarkable capacities – for example, calendrical calculation, or musical or drawing abilities, sometimes displayed by the so-called "idiot-savants" (Treffert 1988). Were it possible to understand how such capacities came about, it may become possible to use this knowledge to engineer a normal brain to outperform in a given predetermined mental capacity. In theory, if the genetic and cellular basis for this behavior is understood, the tools developed by gene therapy could be used to engineer such changes.

It is important to note here that for many centuries, human mental capacity has been under the influence of drugs, used either for therapeutic, recreational, or religious purposes. These various drugs have had the capacity to manipulate human behavior in crude but not unpredictable ways. The study of the responses of humans to psychoactive drugs has led to the development of behavioral and psychopharmacology, which has developed sophisticated ways to treat, reasonably successfully, diseases like depression, manic-depression, or schizophrenia. Currently, the main pathway to the discovery of new drugs has been the serendipitous finding of molecules which display the sought-after effects, usually developed using brute-force trial and error methods, or more modern rational chemical engineering protocols. Gene therapy thus enhances the rational power to improve on human brain engineering. Currently, true discovery and innovation remain in the hands of serendipity.

In summary, gene therapy re-engineering techniques could be used in the future to change cognitive function, mood, pain perception, motor behavior, the regulation of the neuroendocrine system, or consciousness levels. Vectors could be developed to deliver individual proteins to particular groups of brain cells in order to modify their activity in predetermined ways to achieve such aims. These vectors would be engineered to express individual proteins at the right level, and under the control of appropriate regulatory functions, such that only sufficient amounts of the required proteins would be expressed. Furthermore, control functions could be engineered such that the activity of the vectors could be made to be regulated in accordance with the overall activity of the brain, thus tailoring its operation to the demands imposed by the whole system. Control functions could be further engineered to permit the regulation of gene therapy vectors (i.e. through the ingestion of a small chemical compound). Safety controls can also be easily engineered to be used in conditions in which a vector needs to be eliminated from the patient's body.

Ethics and Gene Therapy

Clinical trials and human experimentation

experiment:
1a. The action of trying anything, or putting it to proof; a test, trial.
 b. An expedient or remedy to be tried.
 2. A tentative procedure; a method, system of things, or course of action, adopted in uncertainty whether it will answer the purpose.

3. An action or operation undertaken in order to discover something unknown, to test a hypothesis, or establish or illustrate some known truth, as in science.

4a. The process or practice of conducting such operations; experimentation.

trial:

2a. The action of testing or putting to the proof the fitness, truth, strength, or other quality of anything; test, probation.

3. Inquiry or investigation in order to ascertain something; examination, elucidation.

4a. Action, method, or treatment adopted in order to ascertain the result; investigation by means of experience, experiment.

b. The result ascertained by testing; effect; efficacy.

13. Of or pertaining to trial; made, done, used, or taken for or as a trial: as *trial animal*, etc. (*The Oxford English Dictionary*, 2nd ed., 1992)

Rule 3 of the Nuremberg Code:

"The experiment should be so designed and based on the results of animal experimentation and a knowledge of the natural history of the disease or other problem under study that the anticipated results will justify the performance of the experiment." (From the final judgment of the tribunal at the Doctors' War Crimes Trial, Nuremberg, 1946; cited in Kennedy and Grubb 1994.)

There is a difference in our perception of what constitutes a human "experiment," and what constitutes a clinical "trial." But the reality is that, notwithstanding our emotional reactions to the term "experiment," trials and experiments are the same thing! The future of gene therapy will involve more and more trials to test what works and what does not, just as with any other new medical technology. It is important that all new trials are based on thorough in vitro and in vivo experimental data, rather than "desperate treatments for desperate patients." However, one important fact about clinical trials should be noted. Clinical trials are, in the early stages, human experiments. Our society already makes decisions about whether to proceed with human clinical experimentation, in the absence of an absolute certainty about the trials' outcomes. Clinical trials are subdivided into phase I, II, III, and IV trials. Clinical trials start as phase I trials, which are essentially toxicity trials. The aim is to see whether, in moving a new experimental treatment from animals to humans, unforeseen toxicity will occur. As a matter of fact, phase I clinical trials of anticancer agents are dose escalation studies in which the new drugs' dose is increased until any specific toxicity appears. These trials are not designed as tests to measure efficacy, even if certain journalists and researchers would like to convert them into such trials. Efficacy trials only occur later, as phase III/IV clinical trials which are performed on sufficient numbers of patients to allow for valid statistical analysis. Thus it is my view that the differential emotional response to "trial" and to "experiment" is not wholly warranted.

Consent

"A study is ethical or not at its inception; it does not become ethical because it succeeds in producing valuable data...The fundamental principle is that it should be determined in advance that the probable benefits outweigh the probable risks." (Beecher 1966)

What are the implications for the requirement of informed consent of the new therapeutic genetic technologies? Do the technological intricacies of gene therapy have an effect on the capacity of human patients to provide informed consent? Informed consent was introduced into the planning and ethics of human clinical trials in the aftermath of the Second World War, and the cruel and unethical human experiments carried out by medical doctors in German concentration camps. The judges sitting at the Nuremberg Doctors' Criminal Trial tried to engrave the requirement for informed consent in stone, as point 3 of their final judgment. What is not widely known is that, although what has become known as "the Nuremberg Code" was written under the advice of the medical experts present in Nuremberg, it really was the closing statement of the presiding judges at the Doctors' trial. This statement was written by judges, not by doctors, researchers, or ethical experts. Its aim was to ensure that patients participating in clinical trials would decide whether or not to undergo treatment on the basis of full information.

Much has been written on informed consent, and arguments presented elsewhere (see Holm, Chapter 7, in this volume) will not be rediscussed here. The main difficulty with consent to gene therapy concerns the high degree of technological sophistication of the technique. Even if the patient is told in detail about the gene therapy trial, its potential benefits and potential harms, it is virtually impossible (unless the patient is already well versed in the field of genetics and allied disciplines) that the patient will have a thorough understanding of the procedures to be performed. Even if the patient is put through a basic "course" to improve her knowledge of the field, it is unlikely that she will gain an indepth understanding of the scientific problems involved. The strong claim that the patient has all the necessary information available to make a knowledge-based decision on his own treatment in the face of a life-threatening neurological disorder, becomes difficult to fully support. What patients really consent to is placing their faith (and life) in the hands of the physician/scientist. This, I believe, cannot be easily changed in the near future by thorough informed consent procedures, or even a "crash course" on human molecular genetics and gene therapy. True knowledge-grounded informed consent is, in the case of gene therapy, very hard to achieve. We should be open about this and not hide behind the words "informed consent" as if they can be applied unproblematically in all cases. Thus societies, rather than individual patients, need to decide on whether they want to proceed with human clinical experimentation in the absence of foolproof assurance of effectiveness. The only way to progress and improve medical treatments is through continued human experimentation.

When is it ethical not to start a clinical trial?

"Three general requirements . . . are that it should be shown in animal studies that (i) the new gene can be put into the correct target cells and will remain there long enough to be effective; (ii) the new gene will be expressed in the cells at an appropriate level; and (iii) the new gene will not harm the cell or, by extension, the animal." (Anderson 1985)

Most of the time when we deliberate over a proposed clinical trial it is asked: "When is it ethical to start?" This question is misleading. I suggest that the question, especially in the context of gene therapy trials, is: "When is it ethical *not* to start?" Societies have to take the ethical risk of deciding whether novel clinical experiments and technologies should be implemented. Implementation will carry a risk. Non-implementation will carry a grave risk too.

In 1980, at the time of the now infamous "Cline" gene therapy trial,[1] ethically-minded critics rightly argued that no gene therapy should proceed before it could be shown beyond reasonable doubt that the gene could be expressed long enough, that gene expression could be regulated, and that long-term transgene expression would not lead to untoward effects (Anderson and Fletcher 1980). Nevertheless, when the first Recombinant DNA Advisory Committee (RAC) approved gene therapy trials[2] began in 1989, not all of these basic scientific issues had been completely resolved. Nor could they be by animal experimentation alone.

The central need for animal experiments preceding human clinical trials was sanctified by "The Nuremberg Code." This Code asks the researcher to provide as much evidence as possible in support of the new treatments proposed. This requirement has been implemented in the normal process of scientific and medical discoveries and all potential new treatments are tested first in animals.

However, results from animal experiments are indicative, but they are not absolutely predictive. Moreover, animal models of human disease, while very important, are not perfect. Much is learned from such animal models, but differences in metabolism, physiology, life span, and even size, make it difficult to test out new therapeutics in accurately predictive animal trials. Although necessary, they are not fail-safe, nor do they protect fully against side-effects in human patients. In view of the advances of our understanding and practical implementation of medical ethics safeguards over the last two decades, it is time to reanalyze the criteria set out by the Nuremberg judges, and ask if they still apply and, if so, to what degree, or whether they should be re-evaluated.

A critical discussion of the above-quoted statement by W. F. Anderson relates to the extent of requirement for animal studies, and what exactly is to be expected of them in preparation of clinical gene therapy trials. A focus on animal experimentation, while crucial in providing very important avenues to understand the efficacy and potential side-effects of gene therapy (Dewey et al. 1999), cannot answer all questions relating to *human* gene therapy. The concepts laid down in the above-quoted foundation of clinical gene therapy while very useful, will require further refinement. They are justified because they are similar to those criteria used in the testing of drugs, and thus are solid enough to be generalized to gene therapy. However, are they sufficient? As W. French Anderson himself discusses: "The exact definitions of what is 'long enough to be effective,' what level is 'an appropriate level,' and how much harm is meant by 'harm,' are questions for ongoing discussion as more is learned about gene therapy" (Anderson 1985). Even if these criteria are mostly uncritically repeated, they continue to be challenged and discussed in various forums. It is thus very likely that in the future, revised criteria, more accurately representing the reality of challenges imposed by clinical gene therapy trials, will be developed.

27

Slippery slopes and the possibilities of abuse: gene therapy and eugenics

Gene therapy could certainly be used for eugenic purposes. We need, however, to be circumspect about the use of the term "eugenics." Eugenics is usually understood to mean the study of ways to improve the quality of the human race. Note that currently available medical technologies like the pharmacological treatment of infectious disease, organ transplantation, selective abortion of fetuses suffering from inherited disorders, or the pre-implantation selection of normal fertilized eggs in parents suffering from inherited disease, are all "eugenic" practices. Gene therapy is potentially no more a facilitator of eugenic aims than these.

While gene therapy and allied genetic engineering strategies do have the potential for achieving permanent and irreversible changes in the workings of the human brain, this is not a new phenomenon. Even current pharmacological agents used in the treatment of Parkinson's and schizophrenia many times lead to irreversible changes in brain function (i.e. dystonias and dyskinesias). The point is this: not all eugenic practices are bad ones, eugenics can be positive: such practices can be aimed at helping people who suffer pain and face early death or a life not worth living.

Scientific and regulatory authorities worldwide have agreed that gene therapy ought to remain limited to somatic cell gene therapy. The same techniques used in the context of a diseased person as "therapy," could nevertheless be judged to constitute "enhancement" in a different human being. Many believe any "enhancement" use of gene therapy to be unacceptable, and fear it will produce a two-tier society – the "gene-abled" and the "gene-disabled." This is a slippery-slope argument and, as such, it is an empirical argument.

One of the most notorious examples of a slippery slope in the practice of medicine occurred in Germany in the first half of this century. Work in progress on medicine in the Third Reich indicates that it may be possible to follow the development from normal to murderous medicine, that the boundaries may be very thin indeed, and that much of our "post-hoc" assessments of the boundaries of "ethical human experimentation" are indeed contingent on changing historical contexts (Lowenstein, in preparation). Consider that in the first decades of the twentieth century it was normal practice among German and Japanese anatomists to utilize the bodies of executed criminals for scientific research. Much German anatomical research of the time was being done with those bodies, and a complex network of scientific interactions and collaborations existed which allowed the exchange of "human scientific material" among interested researchers.

As Germany moved into the thirties, anatomists continued performing the same kind of research, even if the justice system that was executing prisoners and providing the scientific material became that of a totalitarian state. Furthermore, suddenly the euthanasia program provided an enormous amount of material, and there was no shortage of physician-scientists who accepted the large inflow of anatomical "specimens." Whether these were then being used in the teaching of anatomy, the provision of anatomical museums, or scientific research, has yet to be traced in detail. In a similar way to the "euthanasia program" which proceeded in Germany before 1939,

German prisons, concentration, and extermination camps started to provide an even larger number of bodies during the mid-thirties. Just as in the twenties no one was protesting against the use of bodies of executed prisoners, no one protested against the use of bodies from so called "legal" executions following the changes imposed in the German legal system after 1933, the "euthanasia program" (the killing of mentally disabled people), or later, the experiments and medical teaching performed on concentration and extermination camp inmates. The bottom of the slope was effectively reached when prisoners were experimented on, and killed, to provide the research material for scientific experimentation, which was directly financed by the German medical research council (Deutsche Forschungsgemeinschaft), and presented throughout contemporary German medical conferences (cited in Weindling 1989).

The implementation of radical eugenic measures in pre-Second World War Germany and the United States occurred before even the structure of DNA was solved. Technologists and professionals did play a role in the mass genocide of the Jews and other *persona non grata*, but they did not need the use of extremely sophisticated tools. This fact is worth stressing, because some people think that *because* gene therapy is technologically complex it will lead to abuses. But the most important point here is that we must not lose sight of the fact that the blame for any abuses in medicine resides squarely with its human users, and not with the technology itself. The best we can do to prevent gene therapy from being misused is to implement workable safeguards and ensure that they are respected. Of course, safeguards are never a guarantee that individuals' interests will be respected. Abuses have occurred before and following the introduction of "The Nuremberg Code" (e.g. the Tuskegee Syphilis study) (Lederer 1992, 1995; Pappworth 1967). Moreover, regulations cannot always be designed to foresee future developments, or even to control them effectively. We cannot disallow gene therapy trials just because they could be used to violate individuals' rights. After all, we would not wish to disinvent fire just because we know that next year arsonists will kill and maim people and cause costly damage.

Changing historical context

Humanity has gained much from the advances of clinical medicine. But we should be aware that what we accept now may not be judged ethical in the future, just as we now regard certain historical medical practices to be unethical. The fact that currently adults, who as children were saved from certain death (i.e. acute leukemias), take their old "saviors" to court for having rendered them sterile while saving their lives, emphasizes how quickly attitudes can change. That historical context is important is also shown by our unquestioning attitude to universal vaccination for a great number of infectious diseases. These vaccinations are not judged against the ethical status of the clinical experiments which first demonstrated their validity. Few in our society refrain from vaccinating their children. Yet part of the true story behind the "safe" introduction of universal vaccination is that many trials were performed using orphans, mentally retarded children, or were done in Third World countries where ethical standards were easier to abuse (Lederer 1992; Pappworth 1967). Indeed, many human clinical trials and experiments could be subjected to criticism, even some performed during the first half of the twentieth century (Lederer 1995). One future day, it may be the case that our current caution regarding gene therapy trials will be deemed to have been immoral. People might even be surprised that genetic enhancement was considered frightening and a focus of debate. These remarks are not to say that anything endorsed by a given society is necessarily right, only that we should be aware that phrases like "respect for the patient" may take on different *legitimate* meanings.

Acknowledgments

I wish to thank Justine Burley and John Harris for editorial comments, which have greatly improved the manuscript.

Notes

1   A list of ongoing and authorized human clinical gene therapy trials is published regularly by the journal *Human Gene Therapy*.
2   In the early 1970s, Martin Cline from UCLA in the US wished to perform a clinical gene therapy trial for thalassemia, an inherited disease in which particular globin proteins are not produced. The affair, described in *Correcting the Code*, by Larry Thompson (1994, chs. 6 and 7), was a very complex one. Cline wished to deliver the gene encoding the missing protein into blood cells of affected patients. Because of difficulties in obtaining permission for performing such a trial in the USA, he decided to carry out trials in Italy and Israel, where he sought and obtained local ethical approval. He performed the gene transfer as planned. It was then found out that he had never obtained permission from his local hospital Institutional Review Board, or the US National Institutes of Health, to use the particular DNA constructs available to him in humans, and was thus found guilty of scientific and ethical misconduct: the DNA plasmids he used were classified as recombinant DNA, and because they had been produced with federal funds from the NIH, even if he planned to use them abroad he needed NIH approval. Although most people have regarded Cline's attitude as unethical, the whole affair was complicated by a mixture of scientific, ethical, and political issues. Cline has claimed that he could detect the activity of one of the genes administered to patients six months posttreatment. These data were never published. If Cline's claim was indeed proven to be correct, it would have represented a major breakthrough. The definitive history of the "Cline" affair remains to be written.

References

Anderson, W. F.: "Prospects for human gene therapy." *Science* 226 (1984), 401–9.
Anderson, W. F.: "Human gene therapy: scientific and ethical considerations." *Journal of Medicine and Philosophy* 10 (1985), 275–91.
Anderson, W. F.: "Human gene therapy: why draw a line?" *Journal of Medicine and Philosophy* 14 (1989), 681–93.
Anderson, W. F. and Fletcher, J. C.: "Gene therapy in human beings: when is it ethical to begin?" *The New England Journal of Medicine* 303 (1980), 1293–7.

Beecher, H. K.: "Ethics and clinical research." *New England Journal of Medicine* 274 (1966), 1354–60.

Brinster, R. L. and Avarbock, M. R.: "Germline transmission of donor haplotype following spermatogonial transplantation." *Proceedings of the National Academy of Sciences*, USA 91 (1994), 11303–7.

Cavazzana-Calvo, M., Hacein-Bey, S., de Saint Basile, G., et al.: "Gene therapy of human severe combined immunodeficiency (SCID)-XI disease." *Science* 288 (2000), 627–9.

Clothier, C. et al.: *Report of the Committee on the Ethics of Gene Therapy.* London: HMSO, 1992.

Cooter, R.: "The resistible rise of medical ethics." *Social History of Medicine* 8 (1995), 257–70.

Dewey, R. A., Morrissey, G., Cowsill, C. M., Stone, D., Bolognani, F., Dodd, N. J. F., Southgate, T. D., Klatzmann, D., Lassmann, H., Castro, M. G., and Lowenstein, P. R.: "Chronic brain inflammation and persistent herpes simplex virus 1 thymidine kinase expression in survivors of syngeneic glioma treated by adenovirus-mediated gene therapy: Implications for clinical trials." *Nature Medicine* 5 (1999), 1256–63.

Dyer, A. R.: "The ethics of human genetic intervention: a postmodern perspective." *Experimental Neurology* 144 (1997), 168–72.

Fischer, A., Hacein-Bey, S., Le Deist, F., et al: "Gene therapy for human severe combined immunodeficiencies." *Immunity* 15(1) (2001), 1–4.

Friedmann, T.: *Gene Therapy: Fact and Fiction.* Cold Spring Harbor Laboratory, Cold Spring Harbor, New York, 1983.

Friedmann, T.: "Progress toward human gene therapy." *Science* 244 (1989), 1275–81.

Friedmann, T.: "Human gene therapy – an immature genie, but certainly out of the bottle." *Nature Medicine* 2 (1996), 144–7.

Friedmann, T. and Roblin, R.: "Gene therapy for human genetic disease?" *Science* 175 (1972), 949–55.

Harris, J.: "Is gene therapy a form of eugenics?" *Bioethics* 7 (1993), 178–87.

Harris, J.: *Clones, Genes, and Immortality: Ethics and the Genetic Revolution.* Oxford: Oxford University Press, 1998.

Heyd, D.: *Genethics: Moral Issues in the Creation of People.* Berkeley: University of California Press, 1992.

Kay, M. A., Glorioso, J. C., and Naldini, L.: "Viral vectors for gene therapy: the art of turning infectious agents into vehicles of therapeutics." *Nature Medicine* 7 (2001), 33–40.

Kennedy, I. and Grubb, A.: *Medical Law: Text with Materials*, 2nd ed. London: Butterworths, 1994.

Kersey, J. H.: "Fifty years of studies of the biology and therapy of childhood leukemia." *Blood* 90 (1997), 4243–51.

Lederer, S. E.: "Orphans as guinea pigs: American children and medical experimenters, 1890–1930." In Cooter, R, ed.: *In the Name of the Child, Health and Welfare, 1880–1940.* London: Routledge, 1992.

Lederer, S. E.: *Subjected to Science: Human Experimentation in America before the Second World War.* Baltimore: Johns Hopkins University Press, 1995.

Ledley, F. D.: "Our study is man (and woman)." *Human Gene Therapy* 7 (1996), 1193–5.

Lowenstein, P. R.: "Degenerative and inherited neurological disorders." In Dickson, G., ed.: *Molecular and Cell Biology of Human Gene Therapeutics.* London: Chapman and Hall, 1995, 301–49.

Lowenstein, P. R.: "Why are we doing so much cancer gene therapy? Disentangling the scientific basis from the origins of gene therapy." *Gene Therapy* 4 (1997), 755–6.

McGleenan, T.: "Human gene therapy and slippery slope arguments." *Journal of Medical Ethics* 21 (1995), 350–5.

Mercola, K. E. and Cline, M. J.: "The potentials of inserting new genetic information." *The New England Journal of Medicine* 303 (1980), 1297–1300.

Nichols, E. K.: *Human Gene Therapy.* Cambridge, MA: Institute of Medicine, National Academy of Sciences; Harvard University Press, 1988.

Pappworth, M. H.: *Human Guinea Pigs.* London: Routledge, 1967.

Roth, J. A. and Cristiano, R. J.: "Gene therapy for cancer: what have we done and where are we going?" *Journal of the National Cancer Institute* 89 (1997), 21–39.

Thompson, L.: *Correcting the Code.* New York: Simon and Schuster, 1994.

Treffert, D. A.: "The idiot savant: a review of the syndrome." *American Journal of Psychiatry* 145 (1988), 563–72.

Walters, L. R.: "The ethics of human gene therapy." *Nature* 320 (1986), 225–7.

Walters, L. R. and Palmer, J. G.: *The Ethics of Human Gene Therapy.* New York: Oxford University Press, 1997.

Weindling, P.: *Health, Race and German Politics between National Unification and Nazism, 1870–1945.* Cambridge: Cambridge University Press, 1989.

Wivel, N. A. and Walters, L. R.: "Germ-line gene modification and disease prevention: some medical and ethical perspectives." *Science* 262 (1993), 533–8.

3

Cloning in Biology and Medicine: Clinical Opportunities and Ethical Concerns

IAN WILMUT

The birth in July 1996 of Dolly the sheep, the first mammal to be cloned from an adult animal by nuclear transfer, attracted international interest because of both the new medical, biological, and agricultural opportunities and the ethical concerns raised by her birth (Wilmut et al. 1997). Of all potential uses of cloning, the possibility of making copies of people received most attention, perhaps because it generates anxiety and excitement. As I will discuss, there are no proposed reasons for copying a person that I find ethically acceptable. By contrast, research stimulated by the birth of Dolly will lead to many new therapies in human medicine. It is a superficial paradox that the technique that could be used to make identical copies could, in principle, provide a means of introducing precise genetic change. This ability will generate the means to provide organs, such as kidneys or hearts, from animals for transplantation to human patients. In addition, cell therapy will provide more effective treatment of diseases associated with damage to cells that are not repaired or replaced: diseases such as Parkinson's disease, heart attack, blindness caused by macula degeneration or diabetes type 1. This could be achieved with cells from animals, or by taking cells from the patient, growing them in the laboratory, treating them so as to obtain cells of the damaged type, and returning these to the patient. In the first half of this chapter I will describe the cloning procedures as they are at present, including the clear limitations, before discussing some ways in which they may develop and other avenues of research. In the second section, the possible applications and their ethical implications will be considered.

Nuclear Transfer at Present

Two cells are involved in nuclear transfer: a recipient and a donor cell to control development (for a detailed description see Campbell et al. 1996). In most cases the recipient cell is an egg, an oocyte, recovered from a donor female shortly after it is shed by the ovary at the time when mating would normally occur. At this time the chromosomes are assembled in a group at the periphery of the egg. Although they are not visible by light microscopy, an indication of their situation may be gained from localized differences in the cytoplasm. A fine needle is placed against the outside of the cell, before suction is applied to remove cytoplasm which it is hoped contains the chromosomes. To provide confirmation that the chromosomes have been removed the cells are preincubated with a dye that binds to chromosomal DNA and fluoresces in UV light. The oocyte is removed from the field of illumination to prevent damage to the cytoplasm, before UV light is used to confirm that the chromosomes are in the needle.

The donor cell that is to provide the nucleus to control development may be a cell from an animal at any stage of development. Early research concentrated upon the use of cells from very early embryos, as the nuclei are still expected to resemble those of the fertilized egg and so are likely to support normal development after nuclear transfer. However, in more recent experiments, donor cells were obtained by culture of cells taken from fetal and adult tissues. In this way, large numbers of cells, and so potentially of offspring, may be obtained. The nucleus is introduced into the recipient cell either by cell fusion or by direct injection of the nucleus. It is then necessary to induce the egg to begin development, either by administration of electric pulses or exposure to stimulating chemicals. The reconstructed egg then begins development and in some cases is able to develop to term.

The present procedures have proved to be repeatable, and essentially the same method has led to the birth of offspring from mice and cattle (Wakayama et al. 1998, Wells et al. 1999). Furthermore, a variety of different cell types have proved to be suitable as nuclear donor cells. However, there are several significant limitations, regardless of the species, the type of donor cell, or variation in procedures. Firstly, the proportion of embryos that develop to become offspring is very small. In the great majority of cases between 1 and 5 percent of cloned embryos develop to term. Rarely do more than half develop for a week, when they reach the stage known as a blastocyst, at which time they are transferred to a recipient female. Different methods are used to follow subsequent development. In our sheep at Roslin, ultrasound scanning is used; in just the same way that it is used in women. Of the fetuses at day 50 of pregnancy, approximately half failed to survive to term, a loss that was 10 times greater than in commercial mated sheep. The pattern of loss was also very different, as an unusual proportion of cloned lambs are lost late in pregnancy, some within days, even hours, of expected birth. Among those lambs born live, around 20 percent died within a few days of birth, three times more than in commercial flocks. These deaths were sometimes associated with abnormal development of major organs such as the heart or kidney. Similar patterns of loss are described in other reports, including in experiments with cattle and mice. Indeed, in one experiment a normal calf became ill 7 weeks after birth and died apparently because of acute lymphoid hypoplasia (Renard et al. 1999)

The inadequacies of the current procedures for cloning from differentiated cells taken from fetal or adult tissues probably reflect the failure to reverse changes in the functioning of the genetic information that had brought about the development of those tissues in the first place. During development of an animal from the single-cell embryo there are many cell divisions and progressive changes into all of the different tissue. This "differentiation" is thought to result from changes in the function of the genes brought about by interactions between the DNA of the genes and proteins binding to the DNA. Until the birth of Dolly these changes were believed to be irreversible. With present techniques it seems that they can be reversed, but not efficiently. Although there are very few direct observations, it is assumed that as the transferred nucleus enters the oocyte, and during the first few cell cycles, factors in the cytoplasm interact with the chromosomes and influence gene expression, making it more like that of a newly fertilized egg. However, there are profound differences between the situation during fertilization and that after nuclear transfer. During fertilization half the chromosomes arrive in the sperm head, packed in unique proteins, the protamines. They join those assembled during growth of the egg before ovulation. By contrast, the proteins appropriate for the specific donor cell type assembled the transferred nucleus. In these circumstances, it would not be surprising if regulation of gene function in the developing embryos was not exactly like that after fertilization. There are many human genetic diseases resulting from abnormal function of just one gene. The patients with Huntingdon's chorea, for example, loose control of their limbs because of such an error. In this case the disease only becomes apparent in early middle age. Similar situations may occur after nuclear transfer. Gene function is presumably almost normal in those cloned conceptuses that begin development, but die late in gestation. Death follows malfunction of one or more genes at a stage when normal function is essential for further survival.

Cloning technology is in its infancy, and it would be naive to pretend that future approaches can all be envisaged already or that it is possible to predict when more effective procedures will become established. Novel approaches that will lead to improvements may include treatment of donor cells before nuclear transfer, isolation of nuclei and their "reprogramming" in the laboratory before transfer, and treatment of recipient cells before or after transfer. All that is certain is that the nature of future developments is uncertain. As the technical challenge is enormous, it is possible that development of embryos reconstructed by nuclear transfer will never be as efficient as that after fertilization.

Potential Applications

The practical opportunities from cloning arise from three different aspects. The most obvious use is to produce genetically identical copies, but nuclear transfer will also have the potential to introduce precise genetic changes in mammals. While the donor cells are in culture, molecular biology techniques may be used to make precise genetic changes (gene targeting). Although methods have been used to add genes to mammals, nuclear transfer will make it possible for the first time to change any function of existing genes. Animals produced in this way would be genetically identical to one another and, except for the one precise modification, to the source of the cells. The third opportunity is in the production of undifferentiated (embryonic) cells that will be used to treat cell-based diseases. The greatest ethical concerns are raised by the suggestions of making a human embryo that would have the potential to develop into a copy of another person. This is considered either as a means of obtaining cells for human therapy or of producing the copy. These applications will be considered first.

Copying people

The use of cloning to produce copies of people has been suggested for several reasons, but any suggestion that a person be copied raises the concern that these circumstances treat the child as less than a full individual and impose unacceptable limitations and expectations. In some cases, the proposals also raise false expectations, because human personality is only partly determined by our genes. Copying is suggested for four reasons: as a means for an infertile couple to have a child, to bring back a lost relative, to have a child as a copy of a person held in high esteem, or fourthly as a source of tissues for a sick person.

In considering these choices it is important to recognize first the probable outcome of human reproductive cloning. A clone would be genetically identical to the original and so very similar. However, clones would be less alike than genetically identical twins, because in most cases they would be derived from a different recipient egg, develop in a different womb, be fed by a different mother, brought up in a different era, and subject to a different chapter of accidents and illnesses. Although identical twins have similar personalities, more similar for example than non-identical twins of the same sex, they do have some differences. People are not machines whose fate is determined absolutely by their genes, as our personalities are only partly determined by our genes. Whatever the exact degree of similarity, the relationships between copy and original would also be unusual and might be expected to influence the development of the child.

The wish to have a child is clearly one of the strongest human emotions. Although there is no form of infertility for which cloning is the only possible means of having a child, it is important to recognize that many couples are childless, despite recent advances in assisted reproduction. What is suggested is that such couples might choose to have a copy of one of them. My concern would be that the relationships within the family would be inappropriate for the child. Would the parent that had been copied treat the copy like a child conceived by fusion of sperm and egg? To a far greater extent than with a sexually produced child, I believe that there would be a tendency to think that you knew better than the young copy: to say, "I can tell you from my experience that what you are doing now is not going to work out for you (us)." In general this would set even greater expectations and limitations than usual. How would the other parent react to the younger copy, particularly as it approached maturity? Out with the old and in with the new? Finally we should ask if it is helpful for a child to see their physical future alongside them? Sometimes this might be encouraging, but in other cases a child will learn that they are vulnerable to a cancer or mental illness. The impact of this type of information can be seen now in young women, who learn that they have the genes associated with breast cancer that killed their mothers.

In considering this possible use of reproductive cloning, it is important to try to imagine yourself in such a situation, rather than to treat potential cloned children as abstract entities. How do you think that you would react to a copy of yourself? Or of your partner? Those of us who have children have probably already reflected upon the way in which chance has mixed the characteristics of ourselves and our partners in the children, producing physiques and personalities that have flashes of similarity to ourselves, but very distinct differences. While I understand the wish of people to have children, I do not believe that it would be appropriate to make a copy of a partner as a way of fulfilling that wish. I do not believe that the parents would be able to treat the child in an appropriate manner.

Everyone must understand the wish of parents who lose a child to "have that child back." Unfortunately, that is not what cloning would offer. As has been discussed already, the child produced would be a different individual. The original might have developed interests in music and played in a band, partly because of a relationship with a fellow student or a particular teacher, while the copy would sometimes develop quite different interests because of different chance circumstances. In the minds of the parents, how long would the recollection of the lost child form the expectations of the copy? Could the parents, having started with the wish to copy the original, accept the new child for itself? If the baby were to be treated as a new individual, then why not have a baby by sexual reproduction and cherish the memory of the lost child?

As sperm banks are used, it may be that people would use cloning to make copies of people who they admired greatly, including film stars or sportsmen and women. While the copy would be likely to develop the same physique as the original, their personality would be expected to differ because of the effect of their upbringing. Would it be fair to have a child with the expectation that they become a specific type of person, even a copy of the original, rather than accepting each child as an individual? I accept that most parents impose limitations and expectations upon their children, but suggest that in such selected breeding the pressures would be of an altogether greater order of magnitude.

In a number of well-known cases, parents have conceived another child in the hope, sometimes granted, that the new baby would have a similar tissue type to that of a sick child. Cells taken from the new child and transferred to the invalid have provided a cure for lethal illnesses such as leukemia. How much more tempting it would be to make a copy of the child and so be confident of a successful tissue match. Emphasis is placed on the pride, pleasure, and esteem that the child enjoys because they helped their elder sibling, but surely the child will also feel from time to time that they were only wanted because of the older child? It was really the other child that the parents were concerned about. This would surely have a depressing effect upon the copy?

The detailed causes for concern are different in each case, but center around a common fear that it would not be possible to treat children who were a copy in an appropriate manner. Emphasis is often placed upon the right of an adult to reproduce in the way that they wish. More important is the right of the child to be wanted and treated as an individual.

Cell therapy

Several of the more unpleasant human diseases are associated with damage to cells that are not repaired or replaced. These diseases include Parkinson's disease, diabetes (type 1), muscular dystrophy, heart attack, and those caused by autoimmune attack on nerve or cartilage tissues, including MS and arthritis. There is no fully effective treatment for any of these diseases. Indeed some have scarcely any treatment. Research is now considering the possibility of providing cells to replace those that are damaged. This might be either from animals, from another person, or from the same patient. This is a comparatively young area of research and there is much still to learn. Let us first consider the different cell types, before contrasting their possible value in therapy.

There are many different cell types in a person. Their "differentiation" is thought to occur in stages. Initially, the cells of an early embryo have the potential to form any of the adult cell types. They then develop along one of three different lines, or lineages, from which the different tissues arise. At specific stages along the path of differentiation stable populations of cells form, from which only cells of certain specific types arise as required. Such source populations are known as "stem cells." When stem cells divide they may form either more stem cells or differentiate into one of the cell types obtained from that source. Thus they act as a reservoir for cells required during a life span that may be many times longer than the life of one of the differentiated cells. While stem cells have been characterized for many different types of tissues, it is not known if they are present in all tissues.

Unique populations of cells that are able to form all of the different tissue types of an adult have been isolated from embryos. Detailed studies of such "embryo stem cells" have only been carried out in the mouse (see Hooper 1992), but cells that appear to be similar have been isolated recently from human embryos and cultured for a prolonged period in the laboratory. These embryo stem cells provide a unique resource for cell therapy. In time it will be possible to control their differentiation into all of the different cell types.

Therapy depends upon isolating (stem) cells of the appropriate type and being able to grow a sufficient number in culture. These cells would then be placed in an appropriate location in the patient. New understanding of developmental biology has created three new approaches to cell therapy. Cells might be obtained from the patient, be derived from a previously established embryo stem cell population, or be cultured from an embryo produced by nuclear transfer from a patient's own donor cell. Different practical and ethical issues arise in each of these three cases.

Terminally differentiated cells taken from the patient are expected to have only a very short life span, leaving an inadequate opportunity for them to grow in culture before transfer to the patient. Recent observations suggest that cell life may be artificially prolonged by introducing into the cells an enzyme, telomerase, which is usually only active in eggs and some stem cells (Bodnar et al. 1998). Each time that other cells divide, a small portion is lost from the specialized structure at the end of the chromosome, the telomere. Cells are believed to be unstable if the telomeres become very short. Telomerase is active in eggs and some stem cells and acts during normal reproduction to restore the length of the telomeres. Further studies are required to discover if somatic cells in which telomerase is active are healthy and able to function in an appropriate tissue-specific manner. Research is also required to discover which of the many different types of cell may be obtained from adults and respond to treatment with telomerase. As the cells would be returned to their source, no immune rejection is expected.

Alternatively, stem cells may be isolated from the patient's tissue, as these would be expected to have a greater potential for multiplication. Furthermore, exciting recent research has shown that stem cells derived from some tissues have a greater potential for differentiation than had been expected. Stem cells from the brain of mice were able to give rise to blood cells (Bjornson et al. 1999), while stem cells derived from rat bone marrow gave rise to oval cells in the liver (Petersen et al. 1999). The studies add to the evidence that some adult cells have a greater degree of plasticity than previously recognized. It is not clear to what extent these observations reflect dedifferentiation of a cell back along an earlier path of differentiation, or alternatively a wider developmental potential than previously recognized. Is our thinking being limited by the naming of the cells after the first tissue from which they were derived? In use for cell therapy, no immune rejection is expected, as the cells would be returned to their source.

Human pluripotential stem cells offer many potential advantages for cell therapy. Their isolation stimulated research into methods to control stem cell differentiation and protocols will soon be described for the derivation of some specific cell types. Experience with the mouse embryo stem cell populations suggests that they will have essentially limitless life in culture and that some populations will prove to be far more robust and reliable than others. In principle, methods could be established for isolation of any cell type in a predictable manner. However, use of donated human stem cells in therapy would depend upon immune suppression to overcome the rejection that would be expected, except in the very rare cases of matched tissue type occurring by chance. While immunosuppression is effective, it is not without significant side-effects. In considering the comparative value of this approach to cell therapy it will be necessary to balance the disadvantage from immunosuppression against the comparatively ready availability of the pluripotent cells. The balance of advantage may vary with cell types, as some sites, including the brain, are protected from immune response, at least to some extent. The third strategy would employ nuclear transfer to produce an embryo from which cells of the appropriate type would be derived. In principle this would provide the ideal cell population, being immunologically identical to the patient, available in limitless number, and with a full life span ahead. However, it is also the most demanding strategy as it depends upon three technologies, each of which is at present in its infancy and very inefficient. These are nuclear transfer to produce an embryo, isolation of pluripotential stem cells, and the control of their differentiation to the required cell type.

Ethical concerns are raised by the use of human embryos, either for the isolation of a small number of stem cell lines or to derive stem cells for each patient. Some people grant an embryo the same status as an adult. It is human. For them it is unacceptable to consider using an embryo, even in the cause of providing therapy for a patient. However, it is inappropriate to judge such an early embryo as being equivalent to a newborn baby. The embryo from which stem cells are derived, 6 or 7 days after fertilization, is a small ball of some 250 cells, only just visible to the naked eye. The cells are embryonic in nature, with no evidence of the formation of a nervous system. Indeed the nervous system will not begin to form for several weeks. As the embryo is not yet aware, it is a potential person, but not yet a person in that critical sense. In these circumstances, I would use the cells of the embryo. After successful IVF treatment, we accept that embryos at similar stages are destroyed because the patient does not require them. There is no fundamental difference between the use of a small number of embryos donated after IVF treatment or the deliberate production of embryos for each patient.

In the longer term there is another possible route to cell therapy, as one day it may be possible to derive some cell types without the production of an embryo. The birth of Dolly showed that differentiation is reversible, at least in some cases. After transfer of the nucleus into the cytoplasm of the occyte, factors in the cytoplasm act to regulate gene expression to be appropriate for embryonic development to term. "Dedifferentiation" of this kind was previously judged to be impossible. This observation raised the revolutionary thought that if the oocyte factors could be identified it might be possible to take a cell from a human patient and cause it to dedifferentiate directly, either to a lineage-specific stem cell or perhaps something equivalent to a pluripotential cell. There are likely to be differences between cell types in the extent to which they can be dedifferentiated, and the ideal donor cells must be identified. This approach is speculative at present. False expectations are raised if it is used as an argument against the production of embryos as a source of pluripotential cells.

Ambitious research should begin to assess the practicality of each of these strategies for cell therapy. As the outcome of research is always unknown we cannot know how successful it will be. It may well be that each approach will provide effective treatment for some conditions.

Cloning livestock

Genetic modification of livestock will provide new opportunities in medicine and research, and two examples will be considered. Genetic modification of pigs is suggested as a means to provide organs for transplantation to human patients: xenotransplantation. Thousands of people die each year at present before organs become available from suitable human donors, and research is dedicated to the provision of organs from an animal, probably a pig. Organs transplanted between species are usually destroyed within minutes by an acute immune response, because of differences in the sugars on the surface of the cells. Several strategies are being developed to modify pigs so that this acute immune rejection does not occur. Concern is also raised by the possibility of infection being introduced to the human population from the pigs. In particular, most pigs carry, in their DNA, sequences derived from viruses, and it is not known if these might ever infect the patient. Studies are in progress to monitor patients who have already received pig tissues, with no evidence of infection in the first report. In future, viral sequences could be removed either by precise genetic selection or the use of techniques for genetic modification. Xenotransplantation has the potential to restore to fully active lives many patients who suffer terminal failure of one organ, so extending their health span.

There are a very large number of genetic diseases of humans, of which cystic fibrosis is the most common in the Caucasian population. It is caused by errors in a single gene. The most obvious symptom is an accumulation of mucus in the lungs, leading to infection and a shorter than normal life span, but there are effects in other tissues and organs. There is no effective treatment for the disease, and patients expect a shorter than average life span. At present new treatments are assessed by administration to human patients and to mice bred with the disease, and both approaches have serious limitations. There is a limit to risks that may be taken with human patients. There are significant differences between the respiratory systems of mice and humans, and the small size of mice prevents detailed physiological studies. Furthermore, there are differences between mice and humans in the structure of the gene. By contrast, both the gene and physiology of sheep are more similar to those of humans. Methods for genetic change through cloning could be used to study the disease in sheep.

There are a variety of ethical responses to these proposals. To some it is intrinsically wrong to change a species, but those advancing this view must acknowledge that conventional genetic selection has brought about profound changes in livestock and pet species. Others welcome the availability of organs from animals provided that there is no suffering for the animals, as this will extend the life of otherwise healthy people. Many people are disturbed at the suggestion of deliberately making animals ill, and some would prohibit such use whatever the benefit. Such experimental animals must be given exactly the same treatment as human patients. Provided that the advance in knowledge from the experiment is likely to lead to improvements in treatment, most societies accept that the benefit from such studies in animals justifies the distress caused to the animal. In most countries, legislation only allows such research under strict supervision.

Implications of the Present Inadequacies

Apart from the ethical judgment as to whether a specific application is acceptable or not, the safety of the procedures must also be considered. Clearly any suggestion that people should be produced with the present procedures is distressing. It is distressing enough when deaths occur with experimental animals, but it is surely unthinkable that women should be subjected to the greatly increased risk of fetal death late in pregnancy or to death of their newborn child. In considering any of the other potential uses, the question must be asked, what would we need to know about the outcome of the proposed treatment before novel treatments can be justified? If an organ is to be transplanted into a patient from an animal, what information should we have on life span or cause of death of such animals? When human cells are to be transferred into patients, what tests are possible to ensure that they do not form tumors? While there is a clear need for caution, most of the patients who might benefit from the proposed treatments would die or have a very unpleasant life without the treatment. To what extent is it acceptable to allow a person to take greater risks when the alternative is death anyway? Comparatively little attention has been paid to these important issues.

General Conclusions

There is a great potential benefit for regulation of the use of these new techniques by an independent body equivalent to the FDA in the USA or the HFEA in the UK in their

41

respective fields. There should also be extensive public discussion, because those involved may not be the most appropriate people to make recommendations. Patients, doctors, scientists, and companies developing new methods are all perhaps too closely involved, with the best of intentions, to make the decision. Time should be allowed for the social decisions as to whether these procedures should be permitted or not. This is because the underlying biological mechanisms and implications are not fully understood by anybody, and the choices should be made cautiously.

Experience shows that predictions as to the value and uses of new techniques are often wrong and that society changes its assessment of a new procedure. Fifty years ago, the church was scandalized at the introduction of methods for the artificial insemination of cattle, a procedure which helped to eliminate sexually transmitted diseases and provided the single biggest advance in livestock breeding. Great concern was raised at the time of the birth of Louise Brown, the first baby to be produced after *in vitro* fertilization. Since then, thousands of babies have been born to previously infertile couples and the technique is widely, although not universally, accepted. It remains to be seen how methods of cloning will be used and how they will be accepted.

References

Bjornson, C. R. R., et al., 1999. "Turning Brain into Blood: A Hematopoietic Fate Adopted by Adult Neural Stem Cells in Vivo." *Science* 283, 534–7.

Bodnar, A. G., et al., 1998. "Extension of Life-span by Introduction of Telomerase into Normal Human Cells." *Science* 279, 349–52.

Campbell, K. H. S., McWhir, J., Ritchie, W. A., and Wilmut, I., 1996. "Sheep Cloned by Nuclear Transfer from a Cultured Cell Line." *Nature* 380, 64–6.

Hooper, M. L., 1992. In: Evans, H. J., ed., *Embryonal Stem Cells: Introducing Planned Changes into the Germline*. Chur, Switzerland: Harwood Academic Publishers.

Petersen, B. E., et al., 1999. "Bone Marrow as a Potential Source of Hepatic Oval Cells." *Science* 284, 1168–1170.

Renard, J.-P., et al., 1999. "Lymphoid Hypoplasia and Somatic Cloning." *Lancet* 353, 1489–91.

Thomson, J. A., et al., 1998. "Embryonic Stem Cell Lines Derived from Human Blastocysts." *Science* 282, 1145–7.

Wakayama, T., et al., 1998. "Full-term Development of Mice from Enucleated Oocytes Injected with Cumulus Cell Nuclei (see comments)." *Nature* 394, 369–74.

Wells, D. N., et al. 1999. "Production of Cloned Calves Following Nuclear Transfer with Cultured Adult Mural Granulosa Cells." *Biology of Reproduction* 60, 996–1005.

Wilmut, I., et al., 1997. "Viable Offspring Derived from Fetal and Adult Mammalian Cells." *Nature* 385, 810–13.

4

The Genetics of Old Age

THOMAS B. L. KIRKWOOD

Introduction

When Jeanne Calment died in 1997 aged 122 years many commentators speculated that she must have been endowed with an exceptionally robust genetic constitution. While it is certainly true that Mme. Calment cannot have suffered from any important heritable frailty, her relatives and particularly her descendants were not conspicuous for their longevity. Her ancestors had unremarkable life spans, two of her siblings died before she was born, her only daughter died at age 36, and her only grandchild (male) died also at age 36. However, her brother lived to age 97. What these data reveal, small as this sample is, are some of the difficulties that arise in clearly identifying the genetic component in aging.

Life span is, of course, a trait that is strongly influenced by chance. The immediate cause of death is often some extrinsic hazard, such as an accident or disease. Even among genetically homogeneous populations of laboratory animals, maintained in protected conditions, there is a considerable variance in the length of individual life spans. Nevertheless, there are patterns in the statistics of animal and human mortality which indicate clearly that genetic factors are important. Most obviously, there are large differences in species-specific life spans, which among mammals vary by more than forty-fold. These differences must derive from differences between species' genomes. There is also a growing body of evidence that human longevity is partly heritable. Danish records for monozygotic and dizygotic twins born last century provide some of the strongest data (McGue et al. 1993), from which an estimate of the coefficient of heritability of life span has been calculated at around 25 percent.

An important and as yet unresolved question touching on the genetics, as well as the general biology, of human aging concerns the relationship between so-called "normal" aging and the spectrum of diseases whose incidence rises progressively with advancing years. Are age-associated conditions such as Alzheimer's disease and osteoarthritis distinct from normal aging, or are they part of a continuum of degenerative processes that are intrinsic to senescence? Most of us, if we live long enough, will develop the neuritic plaques and neurofibrillary tangles which are hallmarks of Alzheimer's disease. Most of us will also develop wear and inflammation of our joints. However, whether we will reach the point of being clinically diagnosed as having either Alzheimer's disease or osteoarthritis is much less certain. In the case of both these diseases, genes have been identified in which certain mutations are risk factors for the familial, early-onset forms. In the case of Alzheimer's disease, it also appears that particular alleles at certain polymorphic genetic loci confer increased risk of the commoner, late-onset form of the disease. Thus, the genetic assessment of risk for age-associated diseases is becoming ever more possible, even though we do not yet know how these genetic factors exert their effects within the context of the aging body.

These data all contribute to the emerging science of the genetics of old age which will be reviewed within this chapter. The prime motivation of most research within the field is directed at understanding the complex genetic basis of aging in order to enable intervention (not necessarily genetic intervention) to improve quality of later life, rather than life extension *per se*.

Genetic Architecture of the Life Span

We need first to consider how genes might affect the aging process, before we can meaningfully discuss the implications of genetic research in this field. Valuable insight into the genetic architecture of the life span comes from considering the evolutionary basis of the aging process (Kirkwood and Rose 1991; Partridge and Barton 1993). For the present purpose we define aging as a process which leads to progressive, generalized impairment of function and results in an increasing age-specific death rate. There exist some animals (e.g. hydra) which appear not to age, and therefore the challenge is to understand why our own species, along with many others, is not in this state. From a Darwinian perspective, aging is a puzzle because of its clearly deleterious impact on fitness.

Because aging is so obviously deleterious for the individual, a number of early attempts were made to explain its evolution in terms of an advantage to the population as a whole (Kirkwood and Cremer 1982). Typically, it was suggested that senescence functions as a form of population control to prevent overcrowding. Although this idea continues to resurface periodically, it commands little or no evolutionary support. Firstly, there is scant evidence that animal numbers in the wild are regulated to any important extent by senescence, mortality from extrinsic causes such as predation, starvation, cold, and disease being so great that few individuals live long enough to grow old. Secondly, the idea is intrinsically unsound because it relies upon "group selection" rather than selection on the individual genotype. We have just argued that aging does not appear to have an important effect upon survival in the wild, but if exceptionally such were the case, the weakness of the group selection argument would become readily apparent. In such circumstances, selection would favor any mutation that inactivated or postponed the aging process. This would render any adaptive mechanism of aging evolutionarily unstable. In conclusion, therefore, the adaptive theory is both damned if aging is not important in the wild, and damned if it is.

The flaws in the adaptive argument are of major account because they remove any basis for supposing that aging is an actively programmed process like development. In other words, we should not expect to discover genes *for* aging.

44

If aging is not an evolutionary adaptation in its own right, its widespread phylo-genic distribution must be explained through the indirect action of natural selection. Two factors are thought to be important: (i) the force of natural selection weakens with age; and (ii) longevity is only obtained at some metabolic cost, through the action of mechanisms for somatic maintenance and repair.

The first of these observations arises from a point made earlier, namely, that extrinsic mortality is the predominant cause of death in the wild. Because of this, any genetic factor that causes the organism harm, but does so only at an age when the chances of still being alive are negligible, escapes the force of natural selection. Medawar (1952) pointed out that this observation on its own is sufficient to account for the evolution of aging. It is the basis of the so-called mutation accumulation theory of aging. Natural selection is relatively powerless to act against novel muta-tions which express their effects late in the life span at ages when, because of extrinsic mortality, survivorship has already fallen to a very low level. It is envisaged that over many generations late-acting deleterious mutations might therefore accumulate within the genome. The practical consequence of such an accumulation will be negligible in the wild environment but will have a serious effect if a population is moved to a protected environment. In the protected environment, the reduction in extrinsic mortality permits survival to ages when the intrinsic effects of the accumu-lated mutations are felt.

The second observation invokes the idea that trade-offs may be important in the evolution of aging. Williams (1957) first introduced the idea of trade-offs when he postulated that pleiotropic genes might be important in aging, specifically, genes which are beneficial in the early stages of life but produce harmful effects later on. The trade-off principle has found more concrete expression in the form of the dispos-able soma theory of aging (Kirkwood 1977), which first recognized the evolutionary importance of the physiological costs of "longevity assurance" mechanisms, i.e. the mechanisms for somatic maintenance and repair.

Somatic maintenance promotes the survival and longevity of the organism but only at the expense of metabolic investments that must detract from the resources avail-able for growth and reproduction. All that is required of somatic maintenance is that the organism remains in reasonably sound condition through its natural expectation of life in the wild environment. Because of this, the optimum strategy for allocation of metabolic resources between maintenance, growth, and reproduction results inevit-ably in a smaller investment in maintenance of the soma than would be required for indefinite life span. (N.B. Investments in the maintenance of the reproductive cell lineage, or "germ-line", are subject to a different consideration.) The germ-line must, in a fundamental sense, be immortal. This is presumably the reason why animals like hydra, which reproduce by budding and therefore do not have a distinct soma, do not age.

The theories just considered help us to understand the likely genetic architecture of the life span. The disposable soma theory is the most specific in its predictions; it suggests that the primary determinants of life expectancy are genes that regulate the processes of somatic maintenance and repair. These include genes that code for DNA repair enzymes, genes that provide resistance to the array of intrinsic and extrinsic stressors that may give rise to damage (e.g. genes coding for antioxidant enzymes), and genes that code for elements of the complex intracellular mechanisms that secure accurate synthesis of macromolecules and accurate control of gene expression. Additional to longevity assurance genes may be genetic factors that are involved in other kinds of trade-off that benefit young organisms at the expense of their later survival, as well as purely deleterious, late-acting mutations that have escaped the force of selection.

A number of implications follow from this analysis of the genetic architecture of the life span. Firstly, it is predicted that multiple kinds of genes contribute to senescence and that the total number of such genes may be large. This suggests that uncovering the genetic basis of senescence will be a complex task requiring a combination of approaches, such as quantitative trait locus (QTL) mapping, adaptation of methodologies for analysis of polygenic diseases, transgenic animal models, and so on.

Secondly, the theories readily explain differences in the rate of aging between different species, which are likely to be the result of different levels of extrinsic mortality. This is because extrinsic mortality determines the rate of decline in the force of natural selection. Extrinsic mortality also has a major effect on the optimal allocation of energy between maintenance, growth, and reproduction. The disposable soma theory predicts higher levels of maintenance in somatic cells of long-lived species, for which there is growing evidence.

Thirdly, in the case of the disposable soma theory, there is a clear prediction that the actual mechanisms of senescence will be stochastic, involving processes like the random accumulation of somatic mutations or oxidative damage to macromolecules. Biological gerontology has long been divided between the "program" and "stochastic" views. The idea that aging might be due to the accumulation of random damage, but that the rates of damage are programmed in a statistical sense through the evolved settings of the maintenance systems, offers some accommodation of these apparently opposite views.

Genetics of Longevity

Studies in model organisms, notably the nematode worm *Caenorhabditis elegans* and the fruit fly *Drosophila melanogaster*, have shown how genes can affect longevity (Tower 1996). In these organisms, the assessment of the aging phenotype is based mainly on the measurement of mean and maximum life span, as there is little opportunity to study pathology. Mutations in several nematode genes have been found which increase life span, whereas in flies artificial selection for increased longevity has produced genetic strains which live significantly longer than the wild-type populations.

Two strategies have been delineated to identify genetic polymorphisms associated with human longevity (Schächter et al. 1993). The major interest is in alleles that confer above-average or extreme longevity, since there is potentially a large number of alleles that shorten life span through mechanisms that are unconnected or only indirectly connected with aging. One strategy involves the candidate gene approach using the methodology of epidemiological case-control studies. The aim with this method is to identify extremely long-lived individuals (the cases) and compare their allele frequencies at the candidate gene locus to the allele frequencies of a control population, who will be young individuals from the same genetic background. This assumes that the controls are unlikely themselves to reach the extreme old age of the cases, which is not unreasonable if the age criteria are appropriately defined. Candidate gene studies have identified significant differences in allele frequencies between centenarians and controls at the HLA, apolipoprotein E, and angiotensin converting enzyme (ACE) loci (Proust et al. 1982; Schächter et al. 1994). The second approach is the sibling-pair method designed to detect loci that segregate within kin groups with traits of interest, such as inherited diseases. In the case of aging, the trait of interest is extreme longevity. This method requires the recruitment of a sufficiently large sample of extremely long-lived sibling pairs, and its application has not yet been reported.

Genetic studies of human longevity may identify alleles that are associated with low risk of late-life diseases, and they may also identify alleles that confer reduced rates of aging. The alleles identified to date all belong to the former category and there is as yet no direct evidence in humans for genes affecting the overall rate of aging. However, certain rare genetic conditions, in particular Hutchinson-Gilford and Werner syndromes, cause acceleration of many (but not all) aspects of the normal aging phenotype.

Recently, the gene responsible for Werner syndrome was identified by positional cloning and shown to code for a DNA helicase (Yu et al. 1996). Helicases are important in preparing the DNA for replication and repair. This finding is therefore highly significant in that it supports the idea that accumulation of DNA damage may be a contributing factor to aging, especially in dividing cells. In patients with Werner syndrome, postmitotic tissue is relatively spared, which is consistent with the discovery that the gene defect is one that will principally affect DNA replication. However, the fact that a defective helicase may accelerate some aspects of aging does not mean that the normal helicase plays a primary role in determining the rate of aging in individuals in whom the helicase gene is intact.

Indirect evidence that human aging may vary in rate within the population comes from data showing that average age-specific mortality slows its rate of increase among centenarians (Smith 1994). A plausible explanation of this observation is that it reflects genetic heterogeneity within the population. If there is genetic variation in aging rate, individuals with the fastest aging rates will tend to die first, so that by the time most of the population has died, as is the case by age 100, those who survive may be a distinct subset with intrinsically lower rates of aging than the average. However, an alternative explanation for the slowing of the mortality rate increase at very old ages may simply be that the oldest old receive more assiduous care.

Genetics and the Future of Old Age

Our present understanding of the genetics of human aging permits some consideration of how human life spans might conceivably change in the future, although a great deal more research is needed. Human longevity may be altered as a result of (i) genetic engineering, (ii) genetic risk assessment coupled with prophylactic measures,

(iii) drug interventions, (iv) behavioral and lifestyle modifications, (v) natural selection, (vi) artificial selection.

In the popular mind, advances in genetic research are often linked to the idea of genetic engineering. Genetic engineering is a conceivable route to modification of human longevity, although this presupposes major advances in the technology of gene therapy and in the detailed dissection of the genetic factors influencing life span. At present, effective gene therapy is still unavailable even for monogenic inherited diseases like cystic fibrosis which are, rightly, the most urgent targets of research. Whether genetic modification of a general process like aging will ever become practically feasible is far from clear, and meaningful discussion must await the further identification of possible genetic targets. Nevertheless, the broad ethical issues can and should be addressed as part of the wider debate on application of the "new genetics."

One of the major successes of genome research to date has been the identification of risk alleles for conditions such as Alzheimer's disease and breast cancer. The discovery of alleles linked to late life diseases is likely to continue at an accelerating pace. If such discoveries are coupled with the development of effective drug treatments or prophylaxis, they are likely to result in further extension of average life expectancy through reducing the negative impact of risk alleles on survivorship. It will be surprising if this approach has much effect on *maximum* life span, however, since the longest lived at present are probably those who are at lowest genetic risk.

Drug interventions based on understanding of genetic mechanisms involved in late life diseases like Alzheimer's disease are the most likely immediate benefits to emerge from genetic advances in aging research. Whether these will in time have the cumulative effect of altering underlying life spans remains to be seen, but in any case the more immediate and attainable goal is to improve the quality of the later years of life.

Advances in genetic understanding of aging will not necessarily require genetic or drug-based interventions to produce enhancement in the quality of later life, or even life extension. Knowledge of genetic mechanisms is also likely to help to identify nongenetic factors (nutrition, exercise, etc.) which may be beneficial. It is already clear that genes are only a part of what influences duration of life. The identification and exploitation of gene–environment and gene–lifestyle interactions will be of great importance too.

Even though human populations now live under circumstances that many regard as unnatural, natural selection has not ceased. The fact that so many humans now live to experience old age will, in principle, expose the genetic factors involved in aging to new selection forces tending to increase life span. On the other hand, selection against inherited weaknesses has diminished, through medical interventions and the generally more comfortable circumstances of life, and this may lead to the accumulation of minor gene defects that will eventually have deleterious effects on long-term survival. Patterns of reproduction have also altered profoundly through the development of reliable contraception, resulting in extensive family planning governed mostly by social and economic circumstances. The net effect of these changes on the genetics of the future human life history are hard to predict, but merit consideration.

Artificial selection has produced significant effects on the life histories of fruit flies, but such procedures are neither ethical nor feasible in human populations. Nevertheless, the fruit fly experiments are interesting for the information that they provide on genetic variance in populations and on the rate and extent of the response to selection. The genetic variance within a population reflects the evolutionary history of that population, however, and there are likely to be major differences between fruit flies and humans with regard to the genetic variance in factors affecting life span.

Conclusion

To judge from some public reactions to recent advances in the genetic understanding of aging, research in this field is seen differently from other areas of biomedical research, such as heart disease, cancer, and stroke. Fundraising by charities for basic research on aging is more difficult (Elizabeth Mills, Director, Research into Aging, personal communication), even though such research may provide the underpinning knowledge to enable more effective treatment of a broad range of age-related diseases. Whereas it is taken for granted that it is a good thing to prevent or cure a degenerative disease, research on the general cause of most degenerative diseases, i.e. aging itself, is not so straightforward. The question is often asked, is research on the genetics of old age seeking to prevent or cure aging, and if not, then what is it for?

Advances in the genetics of old age will undoubtedly inform research on many of the specific age-associated diseases. Such research thereby stands to gain readier ethical approval when its objectives are couched in these terms. Demographic trends make research on aging an increasingly urgent priority, as has been recognized by governments and agencies around the world. It is worth emphasizing that the goals and objectives of biomedical aging research should take particular account of the overall quality of life. For example, a breakthrough in the cure or prevention of an age-related cause of sudden death might seem less of a benefit if the survivors are spared only to suffer slow and distressing declines from other degenerative conditions.

It is revealing that media accounts of advances in genetic research on aging tend towards sensationalism, and that public reaction to these reports is ambivalent. On the one hand there is excitement that a great "secret," the elixir of youth, may be revealed. On the other hand, there exist widespread misgivings about the desirability of extending the life span. Genetic research is as yet a long way from extending the human life span. However, the fact that public opinion varies so markedly on the desirability of this outcome suggests that debate on the goals and objectives of research on the genetics of old age is timely.

References

Kirkwood, T. B. L.: "Evolution of aging." *Nature* 270 (1977), pp. 301–4.
Kirkwood, T. B. L. and Cremer, T.: "Cytogerontology since 1881: a reappraisal of August Weismann and a review of modern progress." *Human Genetics* 60 (1982), pp. 101–21.

Kirkwood, T. B. L. and Franceschi, C.: "Is aging as complex as it would appear? New perspectives in aging research." *Annals of the New York Academy of Sciences* 663 (1992), pp. 412–17.

Kirkwood, T. B. L. and Holliday, R.: *Proceedings of the Royal Society* (London, Series B, 205, 1977), pp. 531–46.

Kirkwood, T. B. L. and Rose M. R.: "Evolution of senescence: late survival sacrificed for reproduction." *Philosophical Transactions of the Royal Society* (London, Series B, 332, 1991), pp. 15–24.

Lithgow, G. J.:. "Invertebrate gerontology: the age mutations of *Caenorhabditis elegans*." *Bio-Essays* 18 (1996), pp. 809–15.

McGue, M. et al.: "Longevity is moderately heritable in a sample of Danish twins born 1870–1880." *Journal of Gerontology* 48, B (1993), pp. 237–44.

Medawar, P. B.: *An Unsolved Problem of Biology* (London: H. K. Lewis, 1952).

Partridge, L. and Barton N. H.: "Optimality, mutation and the evolution of aging." *Nature* 362 (1993), pp. 305–11.

Proust, J. et al.: "HLA antigens and longevity." *Tissue Antigens* 19 (1982), pp. 168–73.

Schächter, F., Cohen, D., and Kirkwood, T. B. L.: "Prospects for the genetics of human longevity." *Human Genetics* 91 (1993), pp. 519–26.

Schächter, F. et al.: "Genetic associations with human longevity at the *APOE* and *ACE* loci." *Nature Genetics* 6 (1994), 29–32.

Smith, D. W. E.: "The tails of survival curves." *BioEssays* 16 (1994), pp. 907–11.

Takata, H. et al.: "Influence of major histocompatibility complex region genes on human longevity among Okinawan-Japanese centenarians and nonagenarians." *The Lancet* ii, (1987), pp. 824–6.

Tower, J.: "Aging mechanisms in fruit flies." *BioEssays* 18 (1996), pp. 799–807.

Williams, G. C.: "Pleiotropy, natural selection and the evolution of senescence." *Evolution* 11 (1957), pp. 398–411.

Yu, C. E.: "Positional cloning of the Werner's syndrome gene." *Science* 272 (1996), pp. 258–62.

Further reading

Finch, C. E. and Kirkwood, T. B. L.: *Chance, Development and Ageing.* (Oxford: Oxford University Press, 1999).

Kirkwood, T.: *Time of Our Lives: The Science of Human Ageing.* (London: Weidenfeld & Nicolson, 1999; New York: Oxford University Press, 1999).

Kirkwood, T. B. L. and Franceschi, C.: "Is aging as complex as it would appear? New perspectives in aging research." *Annals of the New York Academy of Sciences* 663 (1992), pp. 412–17.

Kirkwood, T. B. L. and Rose M. R.: "Evolution of senescence: late survival sacrificed for reproduction." *Philosophical Transactions of the Royal Society*, London, Series B, 332, (1991), pp. 15–24;

Partridge, L. and Barton N. H.: "Optimality, mutation and the evolution of aging." *Nature* 362 (1993), pp. 305–11.

Schächter, F., Cohen, D., and Kirkwood, T. B. L.: "Prospects for the genetics of human longevity." *Human Genetics* 91 (1993), pp. 519–26.

Part II

GENETIC RESEARCH

5

The Ethical Legacy of Nazi Medical War Crimes: Origins, Human Experiments, and International Justice

PAUL WEINDLING

Genetics under National Socialism

The case of Mengele and the KWI for Anthropology

In 1984 the Cologne professor of genetics, Benno Müller-Hill, documented how the Auschwitz camp doctor, Josef Mengele, continued academic collaboration with the human geneticist, Otmar von Verschuer. Müller-Hill's work represented a turning point in demonstrating how genetic precepts underlay what had hitherto been perceived as racial fanaticism. The "Angel of Death," notorious for selections for the gas chambers, and for gruesome experimental butchery, took part in collaborative research on hereditary pathology, supported by Germany's main scientific funding body, the Deutsche Forschungsgemeinschaft (Müller-Hill 1984).

Did Mengele have the credentials of a geneticist? He gained doctorates both in medicine and anthropology in 1935 with work on the physical anthropology of the jaw, demonstrating that variations in the alveolar region of the jaw were racially specific. As Verschuer's assistant in Frankfurt, he focused on the inheritance of cleft lip, jaw, and cleft palate as caused by a dominant gene (Mengele 1939; Weindling 561). Mengele kept abreast of advances in genetics in the United States, using crossover patterns to demonstrate inherited frequencies. The Mengele–Verschuer axis raised intriguing issues as regards the interpretation of German biology under National Socialism. The research project on "hereditary pathology," of which Mengele formed part, involved a range of distinguished scientists: notably the geneticist Hans Nachtsheim, the biochemist (and later President of the Max Planck Gesellschaft) Adolf von Butenandt, and the psychologist (and later East German professor) Kurt Gottschaldt. It indicated that the Nazi state was pumping massive funds into both basic and applied biology (Weindling 1989: 558–61).

Verschuer's senior position at the Kaiser Wilhelm Institute (KWI) for Anthropology, Human Heredity, and Eugenics indicates the high prestige of genetics in Nazi Germany. The Institute offered courses to physicians to train them in basic genetics. Physicians were to determine fitness for marriage. The SS had had an elaborate

53

hereditary screening for prospective marital partners since 1931. Geneticists lobbied for compulsory sterilization for a range of hereditary defects in 1933, and endorsed the reporting of newly born babies with congenital abnormalities from circa 1936. Here was the scheme of a genetically based medicine, suited for the racial state. Mengele was at the fore of the movement to geneticize medical practice with a chilling ruthlessness. Race in Nazi Germany was no mere vapid rhetoric of Nordic warriors and rustic maidens – genetic practice was to be ruthlessly applied to realize the racial state.

Müller-Hill shattered the complacency that human genetics was a post-1945 academic sphere, untainted by Nazism. He achieved his breakthrough by applying a historical research technique of examining the records of a major funding organization, revealing the Verschuer–Mengele axis, and broadening his findings to the research community of human geneticists under Nazism. Most chillingly, he showed how the recollections of surviving academics often covered up serious scientific crimes. His work coincided with a rise of studies on Nazi medicine, dating from the late 1970s, on such topics as the exclusion of Jewish doctors from the sickness insurance system and the Nazis' racial purge of the sciences. Historians reinterpreted German eugenics as embedded in public health, and the biomedical sciences. The new wave of historical research meant that Nazi racial policies were seen as tied closely to professional power, and to the ruthless realization of research programs, as political and ethical safeguards were swept away by the tide of academic enthusiasm for Nazism.

The situation suggested that biologists were not just Nazi fanatics. Nazi leaders often made wild claims about National Socialism as applied biology. There was a movement for "German biology" paralleling that of the "German physics" attack on Einstein. The attack on mechanistic rationalism in favor of holistic notions of organic integration made more sense in biology than physics. The leader of the German biology movement, the botanical geneticist Ernst Lehmann, had in the early 1920s fought the Marxist view of theoretical biology advanced by Julius Schaxel; moreover, this movement was circumscribed. In the Third Reich debates on holism and reductionism, selection and cytoplasmic inheritance continued. The Nazis did not endorse a single position: within the SS there were holists and genetic reductionists. The Ahnenerbe of the SS supported a range of projects in biology, including applied entomology at Dachau. It showed how biological funding had links to human experiments and anthropological and ethnological research.

The movement to racialize medicine drew on biological sciences, which accorded with international standards. The statistical methods of Ernst Rüdin and Fritz Lenz were developed by J. B. S. Haldane and the social biologist Hogben (Mazumdar 1992). Similarly, the Rockefeller Foundation did not withdraw from scientific funding in Nazi Germany, funding anthropological, serological, and neuroanatomical research. Racial purity was often a motive, but the basic scientific components were internationally acceptable. There was a small army of biologists drawing funds from the Nazi state to research on a range of problems relating to plant sciences, human biology, and disease control.

Although there was a situation of reckless pursuit of research goals, the achievements of medicine in the Nazi state require critical evaluation and due reference to context. Advances in cancer epidemiology and on the hazards of tobacco occurred in the context of a highly racialized public health administration. Certainly massive scientific resources were lavished by the Nazi state on the life sciences. Yet it is artificial to focus on the research of a scientific elite without reference to why the authorities made funds available for strategic priorities. The enhanced funding for and status of virology well exemplifies this. It is important not just to focus on elite areas of the KWI institutes and prestige university departments, and overlook the field of applied biology, which fitted the Nazi action-oriented mentality (cf. Deichmann 1996). A crucial question is why did the Nazi state inject large funds into the life sciences? It was in the interest of the Nazi state to support a functioning scientific community, in order to win the war in the east, and impose German racial hegemony on the wider world.

The eugenic legacy

There was a broad rethinking of German science. The interpretation holding sway until the 1980s was that the scientific lead taken by Germany in the second half of the nineteenth century was lost if not by 1914, then certainly in 1918 with the ensuing financial crash and political disarray. In genetics the crucial work was in such locations as Morgan's fly room; the Rockefeller Foundation (RF) in the US, and innovative biologists such as J. B. S. Haldane and J. D. Bernal in the UK showed an Anglo-American supremacy in the life sciences. Yet in terms of organization, the Germans did much to establish a new infrastructure for the sciences during the 1920s. The chemist Fritz Haber founded the Notgemeinschaft der Deutschen Wissenschaft as the precursor organization for the Deutsche Forschungsgemeinschaft. German biology retained a stunning experimental capacity in areas like radiation biology. Here was an organization which could draw funds from the RF. Harwood has shown that the 1920s were a glittering period of innovation and diversity in areas like cytoplasmic inheritance.

But what of eugenics? Germany saw pioneering ideas of racial hygiene as chromosomal engineering as proposed by Alfred Ploetz in 1895. The German racial hygiene tried to steer clear from racist mysticism in order to establish its credentials as a branch of anthropology and medicine. Ploetz, who coined the term "Rassenhygiene," in 1895, was influenced by Galton and the utopian schemes of Edward Bellamy's *Looking Backward from the Year 2000*. An even clearer eugenic paradigm for German medicine was developed by the psychiatrist Wilhelm Schallmayer, who outlined a scheme for socialized medical services. He outlined how the physician's duty to the individual patient meant that therapeutic medicine prolonged the lives of the eugenically undesirable: the physician as state official should oversee a scheme of annual genetic checks registered in health passports. There was a new concern to regulate access to marriage to prevent the spread of sexually transmitted diseases and chronic diseases. Turn of the century studies pointed to the inheritance of a range of physical, medical, and psychological traits, such as myopia, alcoholism, schizophrenia, and homosexuality. Prior to 1914, eugenic notions pervaded schemes to eliminate chronic degenerate diseases, such as sexually transmitted diseases, tuberculosis, and alcoholism. While only very few conditions were proven as inherited on a genetic basis, contracting an infection was attributed to an inherited

55

susceptibility. Holistic notions of genetic susceptibility created the expectation that a range of psychological and physical conditions, as well as many diseases, were the result of the inheritance of a basic genetic core.

These ideas of predisposing genetic factors gained increasing acceptance in Weimar Germany. During the First World War the German state recognized a duty to promote the well-being of future generations, and geneticists lobbied for a national institute and clinics for hereditary health. In the trauma of the loss of the war and the unstable economic conditions, biologists warned of the need to protect the "genetic treasury" of the nation. State-sponsored eugenic committees promoted a range of positive eugenic measures. These received some influential (although far from unanimous) support from Catholic and socialist circles. The Prussian Welfare Ministry generally had a Catholic Center Party minister. The former Jesuit biologist Hermann Muckermann drummed up funds for the KWI for Anthropology, Human Heredity, and Eugenics, which was established at the time of the international genetics conference of 1926/7. Positive eugenic measures included school health services, dietary supplements, schemes to promote exercise and fresh air, additional welfare for the "child rich." Negative measures were targeted at youth psychopaths. There were proposals, deemed unacceptable, for sterilization and preventive detention. A distinctive form of eugenics lay at the core of the Weimar welfare state.

What of Weimar genetics? Jonathan Harwood (1985) discerned a different style between encyclopedic biologists who saw genetics as a component of general biology, and those concentrating on genetics as applied science. This view has many merits, although it artificially drew a line between genetics and eugenics. Is this sustainable? The dichotomy has to confront the situation that key geneticists such as Erwin Baur and general biologists were leading eugenicists. The demarcation between genetics and eugenics appears to be somewhat contrived. Of greater interest is to specify the different forms of eugenics.

There are good reasons for distinguishing between the Weimar and Nazi periods in the life sciences. The overall context changed fundamentally. Thus Eugen Fischer came to the KWI for Anthropology as a supporter of the Catholic Center Party. He remained in office as someone prepared to work alongside the Nazis. Verschuer had deeply held religious views. Initially in 1933 the Nazi authorities looked at him quizzically with the verdict that they liked his science, but he was naive about the ultimate aims of Nazism. Yet he too made a headlong leap into the Nazi fold. He could be characterized as serving the God of Christianity and Hitler. He was thus a fitting successor to Fischer in 1941, when the Nazi state stood on the brink of ruthless genocide.

The 12 years of the Nazi era were less a unified era when the state regimented biologists than a rapidly changing sequence of biologists opportunistically reorienting their priorities and forging new alliances with factions in the Nazi power system. The rapidity with which the compulsory sterilization legislation was introduced and operationalized provides a good example. Already on the statute books in July 1933, it proved a powerful force in the wholesale reform of public health, in that it accelerated the shift to a unified state and municipal public health system with an office for race and heredity at its core. Sterilization also achieved the widespread interest of geneticists, who backed its implementation. The schizophrenia researcher Ernst Rüdin took a leading role in drawing up the law. This was targeted at a range of clinical conditions, notably schizophrenia, muscular dystrophy, and Huntington's chorea.

There was widespread international interest in German sterilization measures, as other countries enacted sterilization laws: Denmark and the Swiss canton of Vaud led the way in 1931; the German legislation coincided with new laws in Ontario and British Columbia in 1933, followed by Sweden and Norway in 1934 and Finland in 1935. The centrality of incurable mental illness in all these laws makes comparison reasonable, although paths were soon to diverge. It is necessary to distinguish between the medical framework of the laws and the Nazi context of their enactment. No one – according to the law – could be sterilized for belonging to a supposedly pathogenic racial group such as the Jews or gypsies. Moreover, a heavy drinker who happened to be a Nazi might be sterilized. That was the theory. But the practice was different. The black German half-castes (offspring of the French colonial troops who occupied the Rhineland) were sterilized: although this was technically illegal, the Nazi state was permissive when it came to racial brutalities. There were variations in sterilization, such as in Hamburg and Erlangen, which were both Protestant areas, but Hamburg saw a higher incidence of sterilization. It was mainly (but not exclusively) the working class who were sterilized.

Nazi eugenics can be seen not so much as unethical, but as deploying ethics in keeping with the Nazi values. The stress was on the priorities of the nation and race; the sick individual was seen as a burden on the fit (a category defined in physical and racial terms). The state had coercive powers of intervention not only in terms of power to detain and segregate, but also to intervene in the body.

Nazi Germany became notorious for coercive euthanasia. After many years of virtual neglect this area too has become a focus of major historical reinterpretation (Burleigh 1995; Friedlander 1995). The origins of euthanasia remain obscure: the standard story that a family petitioned the Führer derived from Karl Brandt's testimony at the Nuremberg Medical Trial. Benzenhöfer has shown that the child indeed existed, but was not called Knaur, and that the dates of birth and death mean that any petition to Hitler occurred later in 1939 after the decision to unleash euthanasia had been reached. Brandt (who at the time was Hitler's escort surgeon) was one of a circle of medical advisers around Hitler who convinced the Führer of the need to go for the more radical solution of euthanasia. Hitler, who in any case favored radical solutions, particularly when they showed ruthless disregard for liberal and humane values, was readily convinced at a time when he foresaw that the war economy could do without the "burdens" of the incurably mentally ill and physically incapacitated. To what extent did euthanasia have a genetic rationale? As with sterilization, there was a panel of expert adjudicators but now, instead of a legal procedure of notification and appeal, a single doctor made decisions on the basis of cursory scrutiny of clinical records.

Factors precipitating the Nazi euthanasia measures included strategic concerns with clearing hospitals for war casualties, and economic concerns with the burden of the incurably mentally ill. Malformed and disabled children were targeted in separate programs. The killing occurred in special pediatric units by means of long-term starvation and lethal medication: the norms of clinical medicine were readily perverted once the concept of lives no longer worth living was accepted.

Geneticists rallied to the attempt to solve mental health problems. In the context of Verschuer's "Hereditary Pathology" program, Kurt Gottschaldt studied German twins, sent to a special observation camp, and Hans Nachtsheim studied epilepsy as genetically inherited in rabbits, developing a cardiazol test for inherited epilepsy. Nachtsheim induced seizures in children from one of the euthanasia centers in low-pressure chambers (Deichmann 1996: 236–7).

In terms of the concept and organization, euthanasia shows how Nazi medicine was on the road to genocide. Anatomists exploited victims' body parts. Researchers interested in hereditary biology showed intense interest in exploiting euthanasia for scientific ends. For example, Julius Hallervorden of the KWI for Brain Research obtained brain specimens from patients whose clinical records were "of interest." Patients were killed to order by researchers, who followed clinical studies with autopsies. The euthanasia program was expanded to concentration camps and the killing of inmates of psychiatric hospitals from occupied territories. The staff operating the carbon monoxide gas chambers in the special killing centers were transferred to extermination camps in occupied Poland. While euthanasia did not provide a direct pattern for the gas chambers of Auschwitz, it did for the smaller carbon monoxide gas chambers.

Were there biological motives for the brutal butchery of the Holocaust? The SS continued to screen for ethnic identity – for instance, Wolfgang Abel of the KWI for Anthropology sought to locate racially valuable elements in occupied Russia. Consideration was given to Germanization programs. The Nazis sought to determine who among the populations under occupation were ethnically German, and the extent that the Germanic qualities were corrupted. Gypsy children were held for scientific observation in a German children's home to study their capacities for Germanization. The negative verdict by the researcher Eva Justin meant transfer to Auschwitz for these children. Eugenics thus supported the killing of a range of ethnic and supposedly asocial groups.

The overall context of the Holocaust was a vast scheme of "clearance" of the east for resettlement. Extermination of the Jewish "race" was considered a means of regenerating what were variously referred to as the German, Aryan, or Nordic races. For example, the Nazis attempted to transfer the politically inconvenient South Tyrol "Germans" to the east. There was also interest in a takeover of Soviet plant breeding and biological institutions to support the resettlement program.

A mass of biological and genetic activity was pervaded by a distinctively Nazi ethics. The Nazi medical anthropologists hunted for body parts to illustrate their grotesque views on racial history. Brains, eyes, skeletons, and internal organs were assiduously collected. Yet it is tendentious to refer to a "Genetik-Labor Auschwitz" (Klee 1997: 473): the camp arose from the intersection of multiple historical factors, including economic and policing factors. Even within medicine, there were several strands operating. Mengele as camp doctor applied sanitary precepts of bacteriological hygiene ruthlessly in the control of typhus and other infections. Yet at the same time the racial killing and experimentation had the rationale of isolating and eradicating the carriers of pathogenic genes. Genetics flourished in Nazi Germany in often gruesome research programs, and as an incentive to racial policy.

From "Medical War Crimes" to the Nuremberg Code

Allied concern with the medical war crimes resulted in the promulgation of the Nuremberg Code in August 1947. The principle of informed consent and the obligations of research workers to ensure the safety and health of their subjects had – in the long term – profound implications for clinical practice and research. The Code has offered guidelines for genetic counseling, genetic screening, the use of body parts, and therapeutic trials. But the Code did not arise from Allied recognition of the genetic abuses of Nazi Germany. As this formative period is poorly documented and less well understood, I will examine the origins of the Nuremberg Code, and Allied views on genetics.

A key feature of the postwar situation was the Western Allies' strategic aims. Faced in 1945 with the continuing war in the Far East, the Allies initially were concerned with how German medical research in fields such as aviation physiology or poison gas could be exploited. Considerable effort was devoted to sifting through German research of the Nazi period for strategic rather than ethical or judicial ends. The Allies were reluctant to condemn sterilization. The laws were suspended and victims were not regarded as victims of Nazism, unless the law was shown to have been flouted. The Allied medical investigators were unwilling to risk a wholesale condemnation of science.

Only one associate of the KWG for Anthropology was a defendant at the Nuremberg Medical Trial: Helmut Poppendick of the race and settlement office of the SS. He had been seconded for a year's course in genetics. No other human geneticist was prosecuted at Nuremberg, and senior researchers were de-Nazified with just a small financial penalty or wholly acquitted. Mengele came to the attention of the US War Crimes investigators for the killing of gypsies to obtain heterochromic pairs of eyes. But the Nuremberg prosecutor, Telford Taylor, passed on information to a former prisoner, Gisela Perl, who was keen to testify against Mengele, that Mengele had died. The researchers into the psychology of gypsies, Robert Ritter and his assistant Eva Justin, found a postwar niche in public health work.

The Kaiser Wilhelm Institute for Anthropology was continued after the war. How can the virtual immunity of Nazi genetics be explained? There was a smooth continuity of racial hygiene to human genetics: Fritz Lenz was professor of racial hygiene in Berlin under the Nazis; in 1946 he became professor of human genetics in Göttingen. Verschuer initially tried to convince the Americans that his expertise was fundamental for solving problems of postwar health. Once he detected their animosity, he made headway in the British zone. Significantly, Verschuer eventually obtained a chair at the University of Münster. Other human geneticists who saw themselves rehabilitated included (to name but a few) W. Lehmann at Kiel in 1948, Hans Grebe (Verschuer's former assistant) at Marburg, with a teaching post in human genetics in 1948, and Lothar Loeffler at Hanover in human genetics in 1953. The eugenicist Hans Harmsen was appointed to a chair of public health in Hamburg (Weindling 1989: 567). Significantly, Göttingen, Hamburg, Hanover, and Münster were in the British zone. The

British adopted a policy of restarting the motors of German science, and basic biological research was favored. Later the family policy of the Federal Republic held to eugenic values during the 1950s, with restrictions on abortion and birth control, and nationality laws requiring a German pedigree. These nationality laws subsequently encountered much criticism, as persons deemed ethnic Germans retained the right to nationality, whereas those for many generations residents in Germany retained no such right. West Germany of the postwar era remained deeply stained by authoritarian values.

Several factors explain the transitions, and the question arises whether geneticists elsewhere were willing to confront the Nazi atrocities. Verschuer was befriended by the geneticist R. A. Fisher, who assisted in his international rehabilitation. Eugenics was not regarded as inherently Nazi. C. P. Blacker of the Eugenics Society argued that the Nazis corrupted sound eugenic science. Nor was sterilization categorized as a Nazi measure. Radiation genetics increased in importance, initially with the dropping of the atomic bombs on Japan, and then in the context of the Cold War. Ideological factors joined strategic calculations. Geneticists could exploit the Lysenko issue to gain Allied support. Hans Nachtsheim, who became professor at the largely US-sponsored Free University Berlin, considered that genetics fared worse under the Soviets than under the Nazis. Soviet support for Lysenko meant that the Western Allies were reluctant to scrutinize the record of geneticists under Nazism.

The onset of the Cold War increased the Western Allies' focus on medicine, which at first sight appeared to be a clearer case of Nazi criminality. Whereas the International Military Tribunal at Nuremberg was a Four Power Trial, the Nuremberg Medical Trial (NMT) was conducted solely by the US as the first of a series of trials focusing on key groups within the Nazi state. The British were opposed to a second Four Power Trial because of a commitment to try industrialists like Friedrich Flick and Krupp, and financiers, and because of the prospect of the trial being held in Berlin under Soviet authority. The British encouraged the US to proceed unilaterally. For political reasons the US prosecution team did not wish to tackle the controversial industrialists in the first trial of the series. So the British obligingly transferred several German doctors to US custody once the US decided in late August 1946 to hold a medical trial. The US prosecutors considered that medicine was not so much a sphere with a distinctive set of ethical norms, but that Nazi medicine amounted to hands-on murder, which was orchestrated by the SS. The NMT approached German racial medicine selectively: it looked at X-ray sterilization experiments in Auschwitz (but not the general sterilization program), and the links between the concentration camps and euthanasia rather than the general euthanasia program. One of the observers, Alice Platen-Hallermund (now Ricciardi-Platen), published in 1948 a succinct and eloquent account of Nazi euthanasia. Otherwise the prosecution showed little interest in the place of genetics in Nazi medical atrocities. Race was important, but as a link to the genocidal SS. The scientific components of Nazi medical racism were ignored.

Despite this restricted approach to Nazi medical atrocities, the Nuremberg Trial saw the formulation of the principle of informed consent in the shape of the Nuremberg Code. A turning point came when one investigator, John West Thompson, coined the concept of a medical war crime in November 1945. He concluded from investigating experiments at German universities, clinics, and hospitals that human experiments involved either death or permanent wounding. In December 1945 he alerted the (British) War Office that, "similar researches at other institutions throughout Germany would show that something like 90 per cent of the members of the medical profession at the highest level were involved in one way or another in work of this nature" (PRO FO 937/165 BWCE Nurnberg to War Office Dec. 12, 1945). Thompson organized a legal medical conference with the Americans and French, as he was convinced that inaction would condone the experiments, and that "there is equally a danger that these practices may continue in Germany or spread to other countries" (ibid.). This led to an inter-Allied meeting of war crimes investigators on May 15, 1946, with British, French, and US representatives "to consider evidence bearing on the commission of war crimes by German scientists believed to be guilty of inhuman experimentation on living men and women." The key issue was "unethical experiments on living human beings." "Professor LEPINE [a bacteriologist from the Pasteur Institute] expressed the opinion that a pronouncement of moral condemnation of the unethical practice of German scientists should be made and that this should be done by the representatives of the scientific bodies of the four Powers" (PRO WO 307/ 471; Weindling 2001). The Allies had two options: a tribunal of scientists evaluating the Nazi research record, or full-scale judical proceedings.

Between March and August 1946 there were intensive forensic investigations, interviews with victims, interrogations of captured doctors – and ethical discussions. The British lawyer in charge, Somerhough, explained on June 17, 1946, that: "a case involving gross breaches of medical ethics should be given all the publicity available so as to engender the interest of other powers in cases of a similar nature" (UK PRO WO 309/471).

It was in response to these discussions that on May 17, 1946, the American Medical Association nominated Andrew Ivy to the Commission. The Secretary of State for War endorsed the recommendation and assigned to Ivy additional tasks of evaluating Nazi scientific research. Ivy was a physiologist and professor of physiology at the University of Illinois College of Medicine and head of the Department of Clinical Science, a founder of the Naval Medical Research Institute during the war, when he experimented on making sea water drinkable, and later executive director of the National Advisory Cancer Council from 1947 to 1951 (US NAW RG 153 86– 1 Box 10 Book 1, 16 May 1946 to SG). Ivy saw matters from the point of view of a scientist, seeking a legitimate ethical framework for research, as a patriot engaged in strategic research (as he had been for the Naval Research Institute), as a medical educator concerned with inculcating sound morals in medical students and physicians, and as a physician seeking scientifically based therapies to alleviate human suffering. This distinctive combination of values made Ivy a fitting choice as AMA representative, despite his lack of acquaintance with German science; his later support for a cancer therapy brought these elements into conflict, leaving Ivy marginalized, discredited, and ultimately condemned by the AMA.

Ivy's ethical guidelines stressed that animal experimentation was to safeguard humans from harm. At a meeting at the Pasteur Institute on July 31, 1946, Ivy pursued the issue of experimentation without consent: "It was agreed that there is already considerable indication that the experimental use of human beings without the subjects' consent and with complete disregard of their human rights was carried out on nationals of various nations, under the Nazi regime." "Doctor Ivy warned that unless appropriate care is taken the publicity associated with the trial of the experimenters in question, and also the publicity which is bound to be attached to the official report of this meeting, may so stir public opinion against the use of humans in any experimental manner whatsoever that a hindrance will therefore result to the progress of science." Ivy's attempt to demarcate between legitimate clinical research and criminal abuses drew on the defense of science against antivivisectionists; he stressed that animal research was a fundamental prerequisite for clinical research.

"Therefore, Dr Ivy felt that some broad principles should be formulated by this meeting enunciating the criteria for the use of humans as subjects in experimental work." Ivy's draft code contained the germ of the principle of providing experimental subjects with information on hazards. His "Outline of Principles and Rules of Experimentation on Human Subjects" contained the following terms:

I. Consent of the subject is required; i.e. only volunteers should be used.
(a) The volunteers before giving their consent, should be told of the hazards, if any.
(b) Insurance against an accident should be provided, if it is possible to secure it.
II. The experiment to be performed should be so designed and based on the results of animal experimentation, that the anticipated results will justify the performance of the experiment; that is, the experiment must be useful and be as such to yield results for the good of society.
III. The experiment should be conducted
(a) So as to avoid unnecessary physical and mental suffering and injury, and
(b) by scientifically qualified persons.
(c) The experiment should not be conducted if there is a prior reason to believe that death or disabling injury will occur.

The requirement that volunteers should be told of hazards before giving their consent represented an important step towards the principle of informed consent. Thus an embryonic formulation of the Nuremberg Code was tabled before a panel of research scientists at the Pasteur Institute, before a decision to hold a dedicated medical trial. Given the abuses of German bacteriology, the contrast could be drawn with German experimentation in Buchenwald, which involved the Robert Koch Institute of bacteriology in Berlin.

At a meeting on August 6, 1946, with General Telford Taylor, the Chief Prosecutor at Nuremberg, Ivy again cautioned that "caution should be exercised in the release of publicity on the medical trials so that it would not jeopardise ethical experimentation." "Mr Anspacher (in charge of pubic relations) agreed that the publicity on the medical trials should be pointed so as to emphasize the difference between ethical and unethical experimentation. He suggested that it would be advisable for the A.M.A. and perhaps the B.M.A. to publish an article providing the rules for ethical experimentation as conducted by us during the war and condemning the Nazi practices. We then discussed with Messrs. McHaney and Hardy [Taylor's assistant prosecutors] various aspects of the medical crimes, including specific cases, the ethics of human experimentation, the legal aspects of euthanasia, and the probable arguments of the defense." Ivy supplied them "with written statements regarding the ethics and also a list of questions which should be used in questioning witnesses and potential defendants." Ivy's ethical strategy was agreed between US legal and medical experts just when a decision to mount a medical trial was made (NAW RG 153/86-3-1/box 11/ folder 4/book 3 Andrew Ivy, Outline of Itinerary).

The German defendants counterattacked that their research did not differ from wartime research in the US on infectious diseases and the human metabolism. Ivy sought additional support for his experimental rules. In his report to the Judicial Council of the AMA in December 1946, Ivy required that: "Before volunteering the subjects have been informed of the hazards, if any." He elaborated criteria allowing the pursuit of experiments as "a method for doing good," and argued that the Hippocratic precepts of benefiting the sick, not giving any deadly medicine, and of a duty of confidentiality to the patient "cannot be maintained if experimentation on human subjects without their consent is condoned" (Ivy, Report on War Crimes of a Medical Nature, AMA Archives, pp. 10, 13, 14). The references to Hippocratic duty to the individual patient, and the need to provide information, appear not to have found favor with the AMA.

The AMA responded by promulgating its own Principles of Medical Ethics, which demanded far less than Ivy's original formulation of consent provided after information on potential hazards. The AMA required:

1 The voluntary consent of the individual on whom the experiment must be performed must be obtained.
2 The danger of each experiment must be previously investigated by animal experimentation.
3 The experiment must be performed under proper medical protection and management. (JAMA, 133 (1946) 35)

Appearing discreetly in small print and without comment in JAMA, gone were Ivy's postulates of informing the subject of the hazards, and the notion of the good of society; the avoiding of suffering, injury, and disability were attenuated (cf. Katz 1964).

The US prosecutors at Nuremberg hoped that if they proved the authorization of human experiments by the SS – and they had Himmler's papers to hand – they would show that these were a clear-cut case of Nazi-inspired murder. The lawyers regarded medical experiments as hands-on murder (cf. Shuster 1997: 1437). The murderers' motive was political. In fact, despite US publicity, most were not SS members.

The War Department commissioned Ivy to spearhead an ethical strategy: "Ivy will serve as observer expert witness at Med[ical] Trial. Can come from opening of the Trial for at least two weeks. Will bring History of Medical Experimentation on Humans. Fishbein editorial to appear 23 Nov. Code of ethics being prepared for adoption 9 Dec. Will forward by TT if possible. Affidavits as to practice being prepared from leading centers of Med Research. Pub Health Office collecting material as to state standards" (NAW RG 153 86-3-1, book 1, box 10, War Dept to USCC Nuremberg 16 Nov 46). The AMA nominated Ivy as medical adviser to the Nuremberg prosecution. The plan was for Ivy to come to Nuremberg for just two weeks armed with a

History of Medical Experimentation on Humans, the AMA editorial, and code of ethics prepared.

When congratulating Irving Ladimer, Roger Newman, and W. J. Curran, professors of legal medicine at Boston University, on their volume on "Clinical Investigation in Medicine," Ivy reminisced: "I accepted the invitation to serve at the Nuernberg trials only because I had in mind the objective of the place human beings may serve as subjects in a medical experiment, so that these conditions would become the international common law on the subject. Otherwise I would have had nothing to do with the nasty and obnoxious business. I believe in prevention, not a 'punitive cure'" (Ivy to Irving Ladimer, Roger W. Newman, W. J. Curran, March 23, 1964, Ivy Papers box 89, folder 5).

Ivy reiterated his aim of a Code on human experimentation at a meeting of April 9 at the War Department to discuss possible US participation at the International Scientific Commission on Medical War Crimes:

> Dr Ivy explained his reasons for believing that a report on Nazi legal and unethical experimentation should be made by an international group of scientists under government sponsorship. He feels that the attitude of scientists towards the evidence collected for the medical trial of Nuremberg is somewhat different from that of the prosecutors. He is interested in an international code of ethics on experimentation on humans which would condemn Nazi practices and be a guide for the future. (NAW RG 153/ 86-3-1/ box 11, folder 4, book 3, International Scientific Commission; Belton O. Bryan to Ivy, March 25, 1947)

In line with Ivy's suggestion of August 6, 1946, that the prosecutors be reinforced by a physician-scientist, the neurologist Leo Alexander was appointed Chief Medical Expert for the Prosecution in November 1946. Alexander had compiled various intelligence reports on German aviation experiments, sterilization, and euthanasia in 1945. He moved the agenda towards the ethically relevant spheres of sterilization and euthanasia. Countering the defense that Germans were experimenting on "prisoners condemned to death," Alexander concluded that experimental wards were a death mill from which few emerged alive. He showed that Himmler's concession of April 1942, that certain prisoners should be pardoned after undergoing a potentially lethal experiment, was never acted on. "Our evidence is that they were picked at random, that none of them was asked whether he was willing, that none of them signed any written agreement . . . That should explode the German claim that these experiments were voluntary, quite apart from the fact that a concentration camp was certainly no setting for anything voluntary."

The British entomologist, Kenneth Mellanby, acting as correspondent for the *British Medical Journal*, defended the German research work as scientifically valid. The prosecution's medical experts realized that the Trial could turn into a trial of American medicine unless a more sophisticated strategy was pursued. Alexander promptly contacted the genocide theorist Raphael Lemkin, and tried to rescue the case by collecting evidence that human experiments on US prisoners and the mentally ill were voluntary. Alexander realized that the legal basis of the trial – the prosecution of war crimes as crimes against humanity – was too narrow. The NMT was not in origins a genocide trial, but more a trial concerned with medical research. Indeed, the lawyer who coined the term genocide in 1944, Raphael Lemkin, pointed out that annihilation of whole peoples involved such measures as the medical uses of poison gas. Lemkin's ideas had been rejected by the US military lawyers. However, Alexander reworked the genocide concept, arguing that the experiments were designed not to sustain life but to destroy it. He drew up a memo to General Taylor on December 5, 1946, on "Thanatology as a Scientific Technique of Genocide." He argued that "The German research therefore definitely constitutes an advance in destructive methodology – as killing methods for a criminal state," and as "an aggressive weapon of war" (Memorandum to Taylor McHaney and Hardy, "The Fundamental Purpose and Meaning of the Experiments in Human Beings of which the Accused in Military Tribunal No. 1, Case No. 1, have been Indicted: Thanatology as a Scientific Technique of Genocide"). The experiments were designed to develop the science of killing – termed by Alexander "ktenology." Alexander redrafted the memo, substituting the term ktenology for thanatology so that its title became "Ktenology as a Scientific Technique of Genocide." Alexander concluded: "The frightful body of new methods of killing ... constitute a formidable body of new and dangerous knowledge, useful to criminals everywhere, and to a criminal state if another one is permitted to establish itself again, so as to constitute a new branch, a destructive perversion of medicine worthy of a new name, for which the term ktenology is herewith suggested. This ktenological medicine supplied the technical methods for genocide, a policy of the German Third Reich which would not have been carried out without the active participation of its medical scientists" (Alexander, "One Aim of the German Vivisectionists: Ktenology as a Scientific Technique of Genocide," released Dec. 31, 1946, and read before the International Scientific Commission (War Crimes) in Paris, France, on Jan. 15, 1947).

The NMT prosecution and the ISC were parallel enterprises. At the meeting of January 15, 1947, Lord Moran signaled the Commission's ethical objectives: "a. To strengthen the stand against disregard for human life and for human rights. b. To aid in maintaining the public's confidence in ethical research and to this end lay down criteria for the justifiable use of human beings as experimental subjects."

"Doctor Alexander was called on by the President to present his report, which he did by presenting his thesis that the medical and associated scientific world in Germany was enticed by the Hitler regime to utilize its knowledge in developing methods for exterminating human beings. He pointed out that whatever scientific advance had been the result of the experimental work in question, it was primarily of a destructive nature and that running throughout all the experimental work, one could see a 'fine red thread' of measures designed either to kill or sterilize." The negative paradigm of Nazi medicine as criminal destruction was to become pervasive, ironically obscuring the linkages between mainstream medical research and the Nazi system.

Alexander as a neurologist defined what constituted consent. His criterion was "legally valid voluntary consent of the experimental subject" requiring "a. The absence of duress. b. Sufficient disclosure on the part of the experimenter and sufficient understanding of the exact nature and consequences of the experiment for which he volunteers, to permit an enlightened consent on the part of the experimental subject ... The nature and purpose of the experiment must be humanitarian,

65

with the ultimate aim to cure, treat, or prevent illness and not concerned with the methods of killing or sterilization (ktenology)."

Ivy and Alexander both claimed authorship of the Code. Grodin reasonably suggests that Alexander and Ivy consulted together to pull together their testimony (Grodin 1992: 121–44). As Ivy's contribution became confused with the subsequent saga of his defense of the cancer therapy Krebiozen, his significant contribution has been obscured (see Shuster 1998). Historians have restricted their evaluation of Ivy's contribution to the rudimentary AMA code; however, the evidence suggests that he initiated the scheme of a code and provided a more ambitious (albeit highly permissive) formulation. As Ivy later reflected: "The Judges and I were determined that something of preventative nature had to come out of the 'Trial of the Medical Atrocities'" (Ivy to Ladimar March 23, 1964). Alexander's engaging with the evidence of the atrocities contributed to the substance of the Code.

Alexander's paper, "Ethical and Non-ethical Experiments on Human Beings," developed Ivy's criteria, and was submitted to Taylor on April 15, 1947:

1 Alexander now defined voluntary consent more fully – as a. the absence of duress, and b. "Sufficient disclosure on the part of the experimenter and sufficient understanding on the part of the experimental subject of the exact nature and consequences of the experiment for which he volunteers to permit an enlightened consent. A mentally ill patient should have the consent of next of kin or their legal guardian, and where possible should give his own consent."

2 Experiments should be humanitarian, "with the ultimate aim to cure, treat or prevent illness, and not concerned with killing or sterilization."

3 No experiment is permissable when there is the probability that death or disabling injury of the experimental subject will occur.

4 A high degree of skill and care of the experimenting physician is required.

5 The degree of risk taken should never exceed that determined by the humanitarian importance of the problem. It is ethically permissable to perform experiments involving significant risks only if not accessible by other means and if he is willing to risk his own life.

6 ...the experiment must be such as to yield results for the good of society and not be random and unnecessary in nature.

Finally, there was a move to protect the research subject. Taylor attributed the Code to one of the judges, Harold Sebring, and it may well be that Sebring recognized the value of a Code, both as regards the Trial and as a broader ethical outcome ("Biomedical Ethics" 1976). Shuster argues that the judges shifted the focus away from the physician to the research subject. She suggests that the requirement for informed consent was "new, comprehensive, and absolute." Certainly, what was novel was the right to withdraw from the experiment, while Ivy had initiated the requirement of informing the subject of just hazards. Shuster's view (1997: 1437) that the Code "grew out of the Trial itself" omits the formative preliminary period, and the crucial inter-Allied discussions.

The key issues, what contact the judges had with the medical experts at the Trial, and the discussions between the judges, have to date not been resolved. Again, Ivy provided crucial information to Ladimar: "I did not reveal my objective to anyone except Messers Haney and Hardy until January, 1947. And, at that time I was invited by a member of the Tribunal (late in January, 1947) to have lunch with them. At luncheon the Judges indicated that the prosecution had not made a case since the defense was arguing that medical scientists had done to prisoners and 'Conscientious objectors' in the U.S.A. the same thing and under the same conditions that the Nazi physicians had done to their prisoners. This opening was the first opportunity that I had to inform the Tribunal of my objective and the reasons for it. I also told them that I had outlined the rules for the use of prisoners at Stateville, Illinois, and that I had used and was using conscientious objectors. I was then asked by the Presiding Judge if I would return in June, 1947, as a rebuttal witness, since it was not proper at that stage of the Trial to give direct testimony" (Ivy to Irving Ladimar, March 23, 1964). While one might doubt whether it was foreseen that the trial would last as long as June, Ivy does provide a plausible explanation of how he nurtured the judicial interest in the Code. He concluded his letter, "The foregoing is a brief review of the origin and development of the Nuernberg Code. The Judges and I were determined that something of a preventative nature had to come out of the 'Trial of the Medical Atrocities.' Handling patients as though they had no sacred or inalienable rights, as individual[s], is a bad means which will negate the good end or reason for the existence of the medical profession in Society, namely to prolong life and alleviate suffering in so far as possible."

Alexander and Ivy frequently cited the Hippocratic notion of the doctor's duty of care for a patient. Indeed, Hippocratic ideas became a political ideology. Medical opposition to interference in the doctor–patient relationship meant that – in Ivy's words – "We must oppose any political theory which would regiment the profession under a totalitarian authority or insidiously strangle its independence" (Ivy, "Nazi War Crimes of a Medical Nature"). An editorial in the *British Medical Journal* (1947: 143) diagnosed the problem as political: "the surrender, in fact, of the individual conscience to the mass mind of the totalitarian state." References were increasingly made to the abuses of Nazi medicine as a rallying cry by physicians against the socialization of medical services. The autonomy of science reflected a situation of doctors opposing central state planning and the welfare state. The scales of justice were heavily tilted by the weight of Cold War requirements for clinical research into radiation and professional defense of the status of the individual practitioner.

It can be concluded that the Nuremberg Code arose from the concerns of Allied medical war crimes investigators as they encountered the survivors of the human experiments and the records of extensive human experiments in concentration camps. Thompson took a crucial initiative in bringing together an international committee of forensic pathologists and other medical and legal investigators. Joint Franco-British investigations during the summer of 1946 provided the crucial impetus. The International Commission offered an alternative model to a public trial, that of expert evaluation conducted in secret. The debates on research were crucial in providing the initial stimulus for the formulation of a code of experimental ethics.

The scheme for a Code should be credited to Ivy, who insisted on the voluntary status of the experimental subject, and who convinced the prosecution and the judges of the necessity of a Code. Alexander amplified the obligations of the medical experimenter, defined what constitutes consent, and insisted on humane aims. Finally, the judges recognized the rights of the experimental subject.

The legacy of Nuremberg was the principle of informed consent, which has been an important factor in genetic counseling and research. The Allies did not scrutinize German genetic atrocities in any meaningful way. Because of the concern to protect the legitimacy of clinical research in general, as well as eugenics, the Allies were reluctant to make the connection between a high-prestige scientific institute like the KWI for Anthropology and an SS camp doctor, particularly when, as in Mengele's case, the research was of no strategic significance. The legitimacy of eugenics as a science of racial improvement, designed to curb the reproduction of the biologically "unfit," went unquestioned. The conflation between eugenics and human genetics remained problematic until geneticists at last began to apply informed consent to their work.

The Nazi era is therefore salutary both as an example of an ethically unbridled medical research program, and an object lesson in how limited subsequent scrutiny can be. The high prestige and funding enjoyed by geneticists contrasts with the refusal to accept that victims of sterilization were entitled at least to compensation. Not only were the sums derisory, but the position that the law was in general validly applied has not been conceded. Despite the wave of historical research on Nazi biomedical sciences, James Watson, who was awarded the Nobel Prize as a co-discoverer of the structure of DNA, has issued the call for geneticists to put Hitler behind them, and look forward rather than ruminate on the abuses of Nazi science. Should they? This chapter contends that scrutiny not only of genetics under Nazism but also the broader international responses casts light on some very fundamental issues concerning clinical practices and the place of science in society. It should be kept in mind that it was in scrutinizing the medical atrocities of Nazi Germany that the fundamental concept of informed consent was first used as a safeguard against any abuses in the future.

It might be objected that human genetics marked a fundamental break with racial hygiene. Yet the research paradigm in which Mengele was to be found – hereditary pathology – marked a problematic bridge between racial biology and human genetics. It was with good reason that the physiologist and Nobel laureate A. V. Hill raised the issue of whether a new biologists' Hippocratic oath was required, in parallel with medicine. The call remains unheeded.

References

Benzenhöfer, Udo (1998), "Der Fall 'Kind Knauer,'" *Deutsches Ärzteblatt* 95: B- 954–5.

"Biomedical Ethics and the Shadow of Nazism: A Conference on the Proper Use of the Nazi Analogy in Ethical Debate," *Hastings Center Reports*, vol. 6, no. 4 (1976), Supplement, pp. 1–20.

British Medical Journal (1947), "Doctors on Trial," *BMJ* 25 (Jan.).

Burleigh, M. (1995), *Death and Deliverance: "Euthanasia" in Germany c. 1900–1945*. Cambridge: Cambridge University Press.

Davey Smith, G., Sabine, A., and Ströbbele, M. E. (1994), "Smoking and Health Promotion in Nazi Germany," *Journal of Epidemiology and Community Health* 48: 220–3.

Deichmann, U. (1996), *Biologists Under Hitler*. Cambridge, Mass.: Harvard University Press; original German ed. 1992.

Friedlander, H. (1995), *The Origins of Nazi Genocide: From Euthanasia to the Final Solution*. Chapel Hill: University of North Carolina Press.

Grodin, M. A. (1992), "Historical Origins of the Nuremberg Code," in G. Annas and Grodin (eds.), *The Nazi Doctors and the Nuremberg Code*. Oxford: Oxford University Press.

Harwood, J. (1985), *Styles of Scientific Thought: The German Genetics Community, 1900–1933*. Chicago: University of Chicago Press.

Hill, A. V. (1962), "The Ethical Dilemma of Science," in *The Ethical Dilemma of Science and Other Writings*. London: Scientific Book Guild.

Katz, J. (1966), "Human Experimentation," *New England Journal of Medicine*, 790.

Katz, J. (1972), *Experimentation with Human Beings*. New York: Russell Sage Foundation.

Klee, E. (1997), *Auschwitz, die NS-Mediizin und ihre Opfer*. Frankfurt: S. Fischer.

Mazumdar, P. (1992), *Eugenics, Human Genetics and Human Failings: The Eugenics Society, its Sources and its Critics in Britain*. London: Routledge.

Müller-Hill, B. (1984), *Tödliche Wissenschaft. Die Aussonderung von Juden, Zigeunern und Geisteskranken 1933–1945*. Cologne: Reinbek, 1984.

Platen-Hallermund, A. (1948), *Die Tötung Geisteskranker in Deutschland: Aus der deutschen Ärzte-Kommission beim amerikanischen Militärgericht*. Frankfurt: Verlag der Frankfurter Hefte.

Proctor, R. (1999), *The Nazi War on Cancer*. Princeton: Princeton University Press.

Shuster, E. (1997), "Fifty Years Later: The Significance of the Nuremberg Code," *New England Journal of Medicine*, 1436–40.

Shuster, E. (1998), "The Nuremberg Code: Hippocratic Ethics and Human Rights," *Lancet* 351 (1998): 974–7.

Weindling, P. J. (1989), *Health, Race and German Politics between National Unification and Nazism*. Cambridge: Cambridge University Press.

Weindling, P. J. (1996a), "A Biological Sonderweg," *Nature* 380: 399400.

Weindling, P. J. (1996b), "Human Guinea Pigs and the Ethics of Experimentation: The BMJ's Correspondent at the Nuremberg Medical Trial," *British Medical Journal* 313: 1467–70.

Weindling, P. J. (2001), "The Origins of Informed Consent: The International Scientific Commission on Medical War Crimes and the Nuremburg Code," *Bulletin of the History of Medicine* 75, no. 1.

6

Biotechnology and Animals: Ethical Issues in Genetic Engineering and Cloning

BERNARD E. ROLLIN

Introduction

Despite the scientific community's unfortunate tendency to declare that science is "value free" and to relegate ethics to "subjective opinion," it is manifest that any society must have a socially objective consensus ethic in order to avoid chaos and anarchy. Given that any major technological innovations, especially ones as profound as genetic engineering and cloning, are bound to have significant effects on how we live, we can articulate two related axioms directly relevant to social ethics and biotechnology:

1 Any major technological innovation will create a vacuum in social ethics, wherein people recognize that new issues are occasioned by the technology, but where they are unsure what these issues are.
2 "Bad ethics drives good ethics out of circulation;" what I have called in my book on genetic engineering of animals a "Gresham's Law for Ethics." (Rollin 1995b)

Recall that Gresham's Law states that bad money drives good money out of circulation. Thus, in post-First World War Germany, wherein it took millions of marks to buy a loaf of bread, people obviously paid off debts with marks, not with gold. Given the ethical void we mentioned, we see something like Gresham's Law operative: The failure of the biotechnology community to articulate the real ethical issues emerging from biotechnology leads to the proliferation of bad ethical issues seizing center stage. In short, the vacuum demands filling, so the universe of discourse becomes defined by opportunists with vested interests such as Jeremy Rifkin and church leaders, who assert slogans with little meaning that seize the social imagination, viz.: Genetic engineering "desacralizes nature," "violates species boundaries," shows "no respect for the gift of life," has man "playing God," etc. (In fact, a politically odd coalition opposed to genetic engineering has recently sprung up between fundamentalist Christians and biotechnology opponent Rifkin, with leaders promising to dwarf the antiabortion movement!) In the absence of good ethical discussion, slogan-mongering dominates the social mind, and the resulting dogmas are extremely difficult to refute since they, in essence, have no clear meaning.

The "Frankenstein" Myth

I have argued at length that various aspects of the Frankenstein myth capture and encapsulate both the real and spurious social issues associated with genetic engineering and cloning of animals. For example, in ABC-TV's documentary, *The Real Frankenstein*, genetic engineering is depicted as the latest manifestation of the Frankenstein archetype. The three aspects of the Frankenstein story that are utilized in the social mind to symbolize its unanalyzed concerns about biotechnology can be quickly characterized as follows.

Aspect one of the myth

"There are certain things humans were not meant to do," best uttered in a comic opera Mittel-Europaeische accent. Concerns of this sort are an example of bad ethics driving good ethics out of circulation – I have argued at length that there are no real rationally-based ethical issues here (Rollin 1995b). Nonetheless, such concerns are politically powerful, since they often enjoy considerable religious and public support. It was largely in the face of such emotional responses to the cloning of the sheep Dolly by Scottish scientists that the British government decided to withhold funds from research into cloning. Similarly, in the US, 75 percent of the public asserted that cloning is "against God's will," and 56 percent affirmed that they would not eat cloned animals (CNN/Time Poll 1997).

Aspect two of the myth

"Rampaging monsters" – the image of the human creation run amok. This concern is more prudential than ethical – *no one* benefits from biotechnology run amok – and can be cashed out as the demand for public education as to the dangers of genetic engineering, and as to the safeguards for managing them. I have argued that the public will never accept genetic engineering until it has been so educated and until it feels it has been party to deciding the *ethical question* of what risks are justified by what benefits. These risks are far from negligible (Rollin 1995b). In the area of genetic engineering of animals they include environmental despoliation or catastrophe occasioned by release of transgenic animals; risk of new disease growing out of changing animals in both immunological and non-immunological ways and unwittingly selecting for new pathogens dangerous to humans and/or other animals; risk of genetically engineered animals such as the SCID mouse, designed to be susceptible to infection by the AIDS virus, either infecting humans or having the endogenous mouse viruses interact with the AIDS virus to produce pathogens with unpredictable characteristics (Lusso et al. 1990); risk of developing weaponry by way of genetic engineering; risk of increasing our unfortunate tendency in agriculture towards monoculture; risks of sociocultural disruptions, for example further elimination of small farms in favor of large corporate industralized agribusiness. While, for example, scientists may deploy one set of values in weighing heavily for example the benefits of the SCID mouse, and correlatively minimize the importance of the risks associated with creating such a mouse and emphasize their ability to control these risks, ordinary citizens may well be unwilling either to suffer any risks in order to create a mouse model for AIDS, or to place their own security in the hands of scientists' assurances about the certainty of containment. Fairly weighing these competing values and interests represents the key ethical issue in aspect two of the myth.

What are the risks of cloning animals? The most significant risk seems to me to arise from the potential use of cloning to narrow the gene pool of animals, particularly in agriculture. With the advent in the mid-twentieth century of an agriculture based in a business model, and emphasizing efficiency and productivity rather than hus-bandry and way of life as supreme values for agriculture, it is now evident that sustainability has suffered at the hands of productivity – we have sacrificed water quality to pesticides, herbicides, and animal wastes; soil quality to sod-busting and high tillage; energy resources to production; air quality to efficiency (as in swine barns and chicken houses), rural ways of life and small farms to large, industrialized production techniques. What is less recognized but equally significant is that we have also sacrificed genetic diversity on the same altar.

A lecture I once attended by one of the founders of battery cage systems for laying hens provides an excellent example of how this works. He explained that, with the rise of highly mechanized egg factories, the trait most valued in chickens was high production, i.e. numbers of sellable eggs laid. Laying-hen genetics focused with great skill and success on productivity. Inevitably, the production horse race was won by a few strains of chicken, with other traits deemed of lesser significance. Given the efficiency of artificial selection and rapid generational turnover in chickens, the laying chicken genome grew significantly narrower. Thus today's laying hens are far more genetically uniform than those extant in the 1930s. In fact, said the speaker, such selection has so significantly narrowed the gene pool that, had he known this consequence, he would never have developed these systems!

Why not? Because the narrowing of the gene pool in essence involves, pardon the execrable pun, putting all our eggs in one basket, and reduces the potential of the species to respond to challenges from the environment. Given the advent of a new pathogen or other dramatic changes, the laying hens could be decimated or even permanently destroyed because of our inability to manage the pathogen. The pres-ence of genetically diverse chickens, on the other hand, increases the likelihood of finding some strains of animals able to weather the challenge.

Cloning will almost inevitably augment modern agriculture's tendency towards *monoculture*, i.e. cultivation and propagation only of genomes that promise, or deliver, maximal productivity at the expense of genetic diversity. Thus, for example, given a highly productive dairy cow, there will be a strong and inevitable tendency for dairy farmers to clone her, and stock their herds with such clones. And such cloning could surely accelerate monoculture in all branches of animal agriculture. Cloning could also accelerate our faddish tendency to proliferate what we think are exemplary animals, rather than what we might really need. For example, very high production milk cows for which we have selected have very short productive lives; very lean pigs are highly responsive to stress, etc.

At the moment, agriculture's only safety net against ravaged monocultures are hobby fanciers and breeders. Although commercial egg production disdains all but productive strains, chicken fanciers, hobby breeders, and showmen perpetuate many exotic strains of chickens. Given a catastrophe, it would surely be difficult to diversify commercial flocks beginning with hobby animals as seed stock, but at least some genetic diversity has been preserved.

Aspect three of the myth

"The plight of the creature," eloquently captured in Mary Shelley's novel and in the recent Kenneth Branagh film. This is the aspect of the myth most directly relevant to a pure moral issue, namely, the well-being of animals. Unlike controlling the dangers of genetic engineering, dealing with this issue is not patently a matter of self-interest, for concern for the animals can limit, constrain, and even nullify some of the economic and human benefit emerging from genetic engineering and cloning. What makes this third concern about biotechnology especially dramatic is that the technology is emerging at precisely the same historical moment that the traditional social ethic for animal treatment is undergoing rapid and dramatic change.

What is the nature of this new ethic for animals and how does it differ from the traditional ethic?

Although society has paid formal attention to limiting human behavior regarding animals for over 2000 years, such attention was restricted to the prohibition of overt, intentional, willful, extraordinary, malicious, or unnecessary cruelty or deviant or outrageous neglect – for example, not providing food or water. This ethic can be found even in the Bible – for example in the injunction not to yoke the ox and the ass to a plow together, or in the restriction against muzzling the ox when he is being used to mill grain.

This minimalistic, lowest common denominator ethic was formally encapsulated in the anticruelty laws during the nineteenth century. These laws were as much designed to ferret out sadists and psychopaths who might begin with animals and, if left unchecked, move to venting their twisted urges upon human beings, as to protect the animals in themselves. The same view of prohibiting animal cruelty can be found in Catholic theology where, although animals do not in themselves count morally, animal cruelty is forbidden for its potential consequences for people, since people who are cruel to animals will "graduate" to abusing people. Interestingly enough, contemporary research has buttressed this insight.

Within the purview of this traditional ethic, any suffering inflicted on animals for "acceptable," "normal," "necessary" reasons, such as economic benefit, food production, pursuit of scientific knowledge, cures for disease, or, as one law puts it, otherwise "ministering to the necessities of man," was morally and legally invisible, shrouded by the all-encompassing cloak of "necessity." By and large, therefore, the "normal" use of animals for human benefit in research, agriculture, hunting, trapping, rodeo, and the like was not the concern of social moral thought about animals.

During the past two decades society has begun to move beyond the overly simplistic ethic of cruelty and kindness and to reach for a more adequate set of moral categories for guiding, assessing, and constraining our treatment of other animals. Perhaps the key insight behind this change is the realization that the overwhelming majority of animal suffering at human hands is not the result of cruelty, but rather, the animals suffer because of normal animal use and socially acceptable motives. To prove this, I ask the reader to perform a thought experiment. Imagine a pie chart representing the total amount of suffering that animals experience at human hands. Then ask yourself, what percentage of that suffering is the result of intentional, sadistic, useless, deliberate infliction of pain or suffering on the animals for no purpose? Interestingly enough, all of my lecture audiences, be they Montana rodeo people or San Francisco animal rights activists, say the same thing – well under 1 percent. Most animal suffering comes from reasonable human motives and goals. Scientists may be motivated by benevolence, high ideals, and noble goals, yet far more animal suffering is occasioned by people acting in pursuit of these motives than by the actions of overt sadists. Confinement agriculturalists may be motivated by the quest for efficiency, profit, productivity, low-cost food, and other putatively acceptable goals, yet again, their activities occasion animal suffering in orders of magnitude traditionally unimaginable.

As mentioned, the old ethic opposing cruelty doesn't apply to these normal, non-deviant uses of animals. This is true not only conceptually, but practically. The limitations of the ethic and the laws based in it were dramatically illustrated when the Animal Legal Defense Fund, a group of attorneys whose *raison d'être* is raising the moral status of animals in society by use of the legal system, attempted to extend the scope of the anticruelty laws by a test case. As animal advocates, they generate many fascinating lawsuits which test, press, and expose the limits of the legal system's control over the treatment of animals. In 1985, they brought suit against the New York State Department of Environmental Conservation, that branch of New York State government charged with administering the use of public lands. Specifically, they charged the department with violating the anticruelty laws by permitting trapping on public lands utilizing the steel-jawed trap. Since there are no laws regulating how often a trapper must check his trap line, an injured animal could be trapped without food, water, medical care, or euthanasia for long periods of time which, according to the plaintiffs, constituted unnecessary cruelty. They were thus seeking an end to such trapping. (*Animal Legal Defense Fund v. The Department of Environmental Conservation of the State of New York*, 1985.)

Given the laws, the judge made a very wise decision. He opined that the steel-jawed trap was, in his view, an unacceptable device. But given the way the anticruelty laws have been written and interpreted, the actions of the agency in question did not constitute cruelty. After all, steel-jawed trapping is widely done as a means to achieving pest control, supplying fur, and providing a recreational pastime. Thus the activity of trapping is a legitimate one from a legal point of view, and does not fit either the intent, judicial history, or statutory language of the anticruelty laws. If one wishes to change the status of the steel-jawed trap, he asserted, one should therefore go not to the judiciary, but to the legislature. In other words, one must change the laws, i.e., the social ethic.

This case neatly illustrates some important features of what is happening in social thought: First of all, social thought is moving "beyond cruelty." Second, society is attempting to create new social rules and laws to protect animals. The best illustration of this point is the passage in the US in 1985 and in Britain in 1986 of new laws to protect laboratory animals after society realized that the research community was not regulating itself. Third, society is moving beyond concern about traditional cute and cuddly animals to concern about all animals who can suffer.

Why is society suddenly concerned about the 99 percent of animal suffering that is not the result of deliberate cruelty? One can speculate as to why the demand for such an ethic has emerged only recently. First, society has just lately focused its concern on disenfranchised human individuals and groups, such as women, Blacks, the handicapped, and the Third World. This same emphasis on moral obligation rather than patronizing benevolence toward the powerless has led to a new look at animal treatment. Second, the urbanization of society makes the companion animal, not the food animal, the paradigm for animals in the social mind. Third, graphic media portrayal of animal exploitation fuels social concern. As one reporter said to me, "animals sell papers."

Fourth, numerous rational voices have been raised to spearhead the articulation of a new ethic for animals. Although concern for animals was traditionally seen (with much justice) as largely a matter of inchoate emotion, such a charge cannot be leveled against the numerous scientists, philosophers, and other intellectuals of today who eloquently and forcefully nudge the social mind in the direction of increasing moral awareness of our obligations to animals.

Fifth and by far the most important, the nature of animal use has changed significantly. The major use of animals in society was and is, of course, agricultural. Before the mid-twentieth century, the essence of agriculture was husbandry. People who used animals put those animals into environments for which they were evolved and adapted and then augmented their natural ability to cope with additional food, shelter, protection from predators, etc. The biblical shepherd who leads the animals to green pastures is the lovely paradigm case of this approach. Producers did well if and only if animals did well. This is what has been aptly called "the ancient contract" – "we take care of the animals and they take care of us," as US Western ranchers say. No producer could, for example, have attempted to raise 100,000 egg-laying chickens in one building – he would have had all his animals succumb to disease in weeks.

In contrast, when "animal husbandry" departments in the US symbolically became "animal science" departments in the 1940s and 1950s, industry replaced husbandry, and the values of efficiency and productivity above all else entered agricultural thinking and practice. Whereas traditional agriculture was about putting square pegs in square holes, round pegs in round holes, and creating as little friction as possible while doing so, "technological sanders" such as antibiotics and vaccines allowed us to produce animals in environments which didn't suit their natures but were convenient for us. For example, we could now raise 100,000 chickens in one building.

Similarly, the rise of significant amounts of research and toxicity testing on animals in the mid-twentieth century also differed from the ancient contract – we inflict disease on animals, wound, burn, and poison them for our benefit, with no benefit to them.

These, then, are the reasons society seeks a new ethic for animals. We have no time here to explain the form the new ethic is taking – I have done this in detail elsewhere (Rollin 1995a, 1995b, 1993) – but the conclusion is clear. While society wants to continue to use animals, it wants to make sure they live happy lives, or at least that they don't live miserable lives. US society felt so strongly about this that, despite years of laissez faire and dire threats from the research community about endangering human health, it passed two major federal laws regulating the use of animals in biomedicine and aimed at limiting pain and suffering.

The Responsibility of Researchers for Animal Welfare

Thus there is a significant onus on those who genetically engineer or clone animals to attend to the suffering of these animals.

a) In *research* on creating these animals, this is relatively easy to deal with. Indeed, in the US and Britain laws militate in this direction by specifying proper use of anesthesia, analgesia, and early euthanasia. For example, one of my colleagues was attempting to genetically engineer cattle for double muscling, and in fact succeeded in producing what I believe was the first transgenic calf. Though the calf was born showing no apparent problems, within a month it could not stand up on its own, for reasons which are not yet clear. To the researcher's credit, the calf was immediately euthanized at the first sign of problems.

b) In *agriculture*, attempts to engineer animals have been largely based on increasing animal efficiency and productivity. Based on the history and the development of confinement systems in industrialized agriculture, it is clear that if the pain, suffering, and disease of the animal does not interfere with economic productivity, the condition is ignored. (Hence the existence of the so-called "production diseases" endemic to confinement agriculture.) Most important, there are in the US no legal or regulatory constraints on what can be done to animals in pursuit of increasing agricultrual productivity, either in agricultural research or in industry. Given the absence of such constraints and the historical willingness of industrialized agricultrue to sacrifice animal welfare for productivity, the moral problem inherent in genetically engineering animals for production agriculture is obvious.

Many of the attempts which have thus far been made to genetically engineer farm animals have generated serious welfare problems. For example, attempts to increase the size of pigs, chickens, and sheep by insertion of modified genes to control growth, while achieving that result, have engendered significant suffering (Pursel 1989). The desired results were to increase growth rates and weight gain in farm animals, reduce carcass fat, and increase feed efficiency. While certain of these goals were achieved – in pigs, rate of gain increased by 15 percent, feed efficiency by 18 percent, and carcass fat was reduced by 80 percent – unanticipated effects, with significantly negative impact on animals' well-being, also occurred. Life-shortening pathogenic changes in pigs including kidney and liver problems were noted in many of the animals. The animals also exhibited a wide variety of diseases and symptoms, including lethargy, lameness, uncoordinated gait, bulging eyes, thickened skin, gastric ulcers, severe synovitis, degenerative joint disease, heart disease of various kinds, nephritis, and pneumonia.

Sexual behavior was anomalous – females were anestrous and boars lacked libido. Other problems included tendencies toward diabetes and compromised immune function. The sheep fared better for the first six months, but then became unhealthy.

There are certain lessons to be learned from these experiments. In the first place, although similar experiments had been done earlier in mice, mice did not show many of the undesirable side effects. Thus it is difficult to extrapolate in a linear way from species to species when it comes to genetic engineering even when, on the surface, the same sort of genetic manipulation is being attempted.

Second, as we mentioned, it is impossible to effect simple one-to-one correspondence between gene transfer and the appearance of desired phenotypic traits. Genes may have multiple effects, traits may be under the control of multiple genes. The relevance of this point to welfare is obvious; one should be extremely circumspect in one's engineering until one has a good grasp of the physiological mechanisms affected by a gene or set of genes. A good example of the welfare pitfalls is provided by recent attempts to genetically engineer mice to produce greater amounts of interleukin 4, in order to study certain aspects of the immune system (Lewis et al. 1993). This, in fact, surprisingly resulted in these animals experiencing osteoporosis, a disease resulting in bone fragility, clearly a welfare problem.

Yet another bizarre instance of totally unanticipated welfare problems can be found in the situation where leglessness and cranio-facial malformations resulted from the insertion of an apparently totally unrelated gene into mice.

Thus welfare issues arise both in research on genetically engineered agricultural animals and, more drastically, in potential commercial production. As we said, the research animal issues can best be handled with judicious use of anesthesia, analgesia, and, above all, early end points for euthanasia if there is any suffering. The issues associated with mass production of suffering genetically engineered animals must be dealt with in a different way. For this reason, I have proposed "the Principle of Conservation of Welfare" to guide the agricultural industry (Rollin 1995b). This principle states that *genetically engineered animals should be no worse off than the parent stock would be if they were not so engineered, and ideally should be better off.* Genetically engineering disease resistance, e.g., for Marek's disease in chickens, is a good example of the latter case.

What of cloning animals? The first such possible negative welfare consequence arises out of the possibility that cloning *per se* can have unexpected and deleterious effects on the animals. Although one is putatively creating an organism that ought to end up indistinguishable from a naturally derived animal, it is conceivable that the process of cloning could itself have deleterious effects that emerge at some stage in the life of the organism. This phenomenon has already been manifested in cattle clones created by splitting embryos by nuclear transfer. According to veterinarians working with these animals, they have been oversized and thus difficult to birth, had difficulty surviving, and have also been behaviorally retarded, requiring a good deal more care at birth than normal calves (Garry et al. 1996). (Indeed there seem to be problems in noncloned animals created by *in vitro* fertilization.) The cause of this is not known, and it is quite possible that clones could "crash" later in life in virtue of some unknown mechanism. At this point, there is no evidence for this concern – it is an empirically testable possibility that will be verified or falsified as our experience with cloned animals develops. If it turns out that there are in fact unanticipated welfare problems for animals that are cloned, this should and likely will abort the technology until the problems are solved.

There is a more subtle sense in which cloning can conceivably create problems for animal welfare and thus give rise to genuine social moral concerns. Many people believe that cloning will contribute to the mind-set of "commodification" of animals that underlies industrialized agriculture. In such an agriculture, animals are products, pounds of pork, eggs per cage, commodities. The ability to clone them, one might argue, augments and reinforces this view. After all, cloned animals are manufactured, and, like cars or soup cans coming off an assembly line, are "identical."

I have some sympathy with this concern, the same concern that informs animal advocates' vigorous opposition to patenting animals. But the issue here is far more basic than cloning – it is the industrialization of animal agriculture and the correlative loss of the ethic of husbandry. On traditional hog farms, for example, sows had *names* and received individual attention. In today's huge production units, they do not. Cloning *per se* is perhaps a reflection of this industrialization, but there is no necessary connection between the two. After all, one can imagine a strongly husbandry-based agriculturalist caring a great deal for his herd of cloned pigs. Just because cloning has emerged from a questionable mind-set, does not mean that it could not thrive in a highly morally acceptable agriculture. Admittedly cloning is far likelier to be developed and employed in an industrial mind-set, but it does not follow that there could not be a use for it in a softer, more morally concerned agriculture. Just because cloning is a spin-off from industrialized agriculture does not mean that it is conceptually incongrous with sustainable husbandry. Western ranchers – the last husbandry agriculturalists – will continue to provide husbandry for their animals whether they are produced by AI, cloning, or natural breeding; after all, they are still animals under our care.

It could perhaps be claimed that cloning will accelerate public apathy about farm animal treatment, based on the psychological fact that the more of something we encounter, the more we see the units as interchangeable, the less we care about each unit. I doubt that cloning will worsen the situation we already have – though it won't improve it either. Phenotypically all noncloned laying hens, all broilers, all black cattle, all white sheep or pink pigs or white laboratory rodents look alike to the average urban citizen. But this has not served to diminish social concern about their treatment – concern for the treatment of these uniform animals in the laboratory or on the farm has continued to grow, not diminish, as evidenced by legislation in the US, the UK, Sweden, and the EU.

Animal models for human disease

The most vexatious issue regarding the welfare of genetically engineered animals arises out of the potential for creating transgenic models for human disease that were historically unresearchable in animals. (Cloning is relevant here as a potentially rapid modality for proliferating such animals.) A recent chapter in a book devoted to transgenic animals helps to focus the concern:

There are over 3,000 known genetic diseases. The medical costs as well as the social and emotional costs of genetic disease are enormous. Monogenic diseases account for 10% of all admissions to pediatric hospitals in North America...and 8.5% of all pediatric deaths...They affect 1% of all liveborn infants...and they cause 7% of stillbirths and neonatal deaths...Those survivors with genetic diseases frequently have significant physical, developmental, or social impairment...At present, medical intervention provides complete relief in only about 12% of Mendelian single-gene diseases; in nearly half of all cases, attempts at therapy provide no help at all. (Karson 1991)

This is the context in which one needs to think about the animal welfare issues growing out of a dilemma associated with transgenic animals in biomedical research. On the one hand, it is clear that researchers will embrace the creation of animal models of human genetic disease as soon as it is technically feasible to do so. Such models, which introduce the defective human genetic machinery into the animal genome, appear to researchers to provide convenient, inexpensive, and most importantly, high-fidelity models for the study of the gruesome panoply of human genetic diseases outlined in the over 3,000 pages of text comprising the sixth edition of the standard work on genetic disease, *The Metabolic Basis of Inherited Disease* (Scriver et al. 1989). On the other hand, such animals will live lives of considerable suffering, since they would be used for long-term studies, and we cannot control such suffering occasioned by these diseases in the humans these animals model.

The very first attempt to produce an animal "model" for human genetic disease by transgenic means was the development, by embryonic stem cell technology, of a mouse which was designed to replicate Lesch-Nyhan's disease, or hypoxanthine-guanine phosphororibosyltransferase (HRPT) deficiency. Lesch-Nyhan's disease is a particularly horrible genetic disease, leading to a "devastating and untreatable neurologic and behavioral disorder" (Kelley and Wyngaarden 1983). Patients rarely live beyond their third decade, and suffer from spasticity, mental retardation, and choreoathetosis. The most unforgettable and striking aspect of the disease, however, is an irresistible compulsion to self-mutilate, usually manifested as biting fingers and lips. This disease is so dramatic that I predicted in 1985 that it would probably be the first disease for which genetic researchers would attempt to create a model by genetic engineering.

Though the asymptomatic mouse is still a useful research animal, clearly a symptomatic animal would, as a matter of logic, represent a higher-fidelity model of human disease, assuming the relevant metabolic pathways have been replicated. This case provides us with an interesting context for our animal welfare discussion. Although the animals were in fact asymptomatic, presumably at some point in the future researchers will be able to generate a symptomatic model transgenically. Let us at least assume that this can occur – if it cannot, there is no animal welfare issue to concern us! Cloning is relevant here since it can be used to rapidly proliferate such animals once they are produced, assuming the technology were perfected.

The creation of such animals can generate inestimable amounts of pain and suffering for these animals, since genetic diseases, as mentioned above, often involve symptoms of great severity. The obvious question then becomes the following: Given that such animals will surely be developed wherever possible for the full range of human genetic disease, how can one ensure that vast numbers of these animals do not live lives of constant pain and distress? Such a concern is directly in keeping with the emerging social ethic for the treatment of animals; one can plausibly argue that minimizing pain and distress is the core of recent US and British legislation concerning animal use in research.

To my knowledge, no one in the research community is addressing this issue.

Conclusion

People in the biotechnology industry cannot ignore the pressing socio-ethical concerns about genetic engineering and cloning of animals. By meeting the issues head on, they can first of all separate good ethical coin from bad and avoid the pernicious consequences of our "Gresham's Law for ethics." Second, they can listen to and dialogue with the public, engage their concerns about risk, and thereby bridge the gulf of fear and ignorance distancing ordinary people from this new technology. Finally, they can help ensure that the unfortunate tendencies in modern agriculture to place emphasis on productivity and efficiency above genetic diversity and animal well-being can be checked in this new technology, and that biomedical advances do not come at the expense of inestimable animal suffering.

References

Animal Legal Defense Fund v. The Department of Environmental Conservation of the State of New York. Index no. 6670/85.

CNN/Time Poll: "Most Americans say cloning is wrong." March 1, 1997.

Garry, F., Adams, R., McCann, J. P., and Odde, K. G.: "Post-natal characteristics of calves produced by nuclear transfer cloning." *Theriogenology* 45 (1996), pp. 141–52.

Karson, E. M.: "Principles of gene transfer and the treatment of disease." In First, N. and Haseltine, F. P., eds.: *Transgenic Animals* (Boston: Butterworth-Heinemann, 1991), ch. 16.

Kelley, W. N. and Wyngaarden, J. B.: "Clinical syndromes associated with hypoxanthine-guanine phosphororibosyltransferase deficiency." In Stanbury, J. B. et al., eds.: *The Metabolic Basis of Inherited Disease*, 5th ed. (New York: McGraw-Hill, 1983), ch. 51.

Lewis, D. B., et al.: "Osteoporosis induced in mice by overproduction of interleukin-4." *Proceedings of the National Academy of Sciences* 90 (1993), pp. 1618–22.

Lusso, P. et al.: "Expanded HIV-1 cellular tropism by phenotypic mixing with murine endogenars retroviruses." *Science* 247 (1990), pp. 848–51.

Pursel, V. et al.: "Genetic engineering of livestock." *Science* 244 (1989), pp. 1281–8.

Rollin, B. E.: *The Unheeded Cry: Animal Consciousness, Animal Pain and Science* (Oxford: Oxford University Press, 1989).

Rollin, B. E.: *Animal Rights and Human Morality*, 2nd ed. (Buffalo, NY: Prometheus Books, 1993).

Rollin, B. E.: *Farm Animal Welfare* (Ames, Iowa: Iowa State University Press, 1995a).

Rollin, B. E.: *The Frankenstein Syndrome: Ethical and Social Issues in the Genetic Engineering of Animals* (New York: Cambridge University Press, 1995b).

Rollin, B. E.: "Send in the clones...Don't bother they're here." *Journal of Agricultural and Environmental Ethics*, 10 (1997), pp. 25–40.

Scriver, C. R. et al., eds.: *The Metabolic Basis of Inherited Disease*, vols. 1 and 2, 6th ed. (New York: McGraw-Hill, 1989).

Further reading

Holland, A. and Johnson, A., eds.: *Animal Biotechnology and Ethics* (London: Chapman and Hall, 1998).

Rollin, B. E.: *The Unheeded Cry: Animal Consciousness, Animal Pain and Science* (Oxford: Oxford University Press, 1989).

Rollin, B. E.: *Animal Rights and Human Morality*, 2nd ed. (Buffalo, NY: Prometheus Books, 1993).

Rollin, B. E.: *Farm Animal Welfare* (Ames, Iowa: Iowa State University Press, 1995).

Rollin, B. E.: *The Frankenstein Syndrome: Ethical and Social Issues in the Genetic Engineering of Animals* (New York: Cambridge University Press, 1995).

Rollin, B. E.: " 'Keeping up with the clones': issues in human cloning." *Journal of Ethics* 3 (1999), pp. 51–71.

7

The Role of Informed Consent in Genetic Experimentation

SØREN HOLM

Introduction

At some point in the development of any diagnostic, therapeutic, or preventive intervention intended for use in humans, it becomes necessary to test its efficacy in research involving humans. Theoretical arguments and animal experimentation cannot tell us exactly how a given method will work in humans. The history of medicine is replete with horrific examples of dangerous, in some cases lethal therapies which were introduced because they had a good theoretical rationale and promising results in animal studies.

When we begin human experiments we are therefore in a situation where we have reason to believe, but do not know for certain, that the intervention which is tried out will be effective in humans. The person asked to participate in a trial of a new method has to make this decision in a context of larger uncertainty than in the normal therapeutic context. The experimental and the therapeutic contexts also differ with regard to the interests of the doctor/researcher. In the idealized therapeutic context the doctor's only interest is the benefit of the patient, while in the research context the doctor is also interested in generating knowledge which may benefit future patients (even if the project shows that the method is dangerous this is a benefit to *future* patients who will then not run the risk of being subjected to it). In the experimental context the patient is thus partly being used as a means to further the project of somebody else.

The special features of the experimental context raise the specific ethical issues that are at the core of biomedical research ethics. Traditionally many of these issues have been dealt with through requiring informed consent from the research subjects (see below).

There are, however, certain characteristics of genetic experimentation which place the concept of informed consent under strain. Some have even claimed that informed consent to certain kinds of genetic experimentation is either impossible or invalid, and that these kinds of experimentation are thus always unethical. It is this claim, and other less radical claims, which will be examined in this chapter.

In the present chapter genetic experimentation will be understood in a fairly broad sense including all experimental uses of genetic testing, gene therapy, and other forms of gene manipulation in humans. The chapter also includes a discussion of the ethical problems connected to informed consent which occur in genetic investigations on previously stored tissue or cell samples.

The Doctrine of Informed Consent

The concept of "informed consent" has almost reached the status of an infallible dogma in biomedical research ethics. Today, informed consent is seen as a necessary and, in some cases, perhaps even sufficient condition for the ethical acceptability of the enrollment in a biomedical research project of a person as a "research subject" (Faden and Beauchamp 1986; ICH 1996). But this has not always been so, and it is still not the case in many other areas of research involving humans (e.g. in the social sciences) (Kimmel 1988). For this second reason I shall employ the term "research subject" and not "research participant" throughout this chapter; it is the former that most accurately describes the position of the majority of persons enrolled in biomedical research. (I have sympathy with the recommended move to adopt "participant," but only because it expresses a hope for the future.)

The doctrine of informed consent to research has gradually been developed since the Second World War. The doctrine was first clearly enunciated in the Nuremberg declaration which was a result of the trial of the Nazi doctors, but it has ancient roots in the prohibition found in most legal systems against touching another person without his or her permission. Since 1947 the doctrine of informed consent has been incorporated as a basic principle in the Helsinki I and II declarations of the World Medical Association and in many national legal regulations of biomedical research (ICH 1996).

In its present form the doctrine of informed consent as applied to research projects states that consent is necessary if a person is to be used as a research subject, and that this consent is only valid if (a) the person is competent to consent, (b) the consent is uncoerced, and (c) the consent is informed, that is, the research subject has been given the relevant information about the project, and this information has been understood and has figured in an appropriate way in the reasoning leading to consent.

There has been a protracted debate on how the sufficient "amount" of information should be specified. The discussion has mainly centered on whether the appropriate standard for sufficient information should be an objective standard or a subjective standard. An objective standard defines and describes the amount of information independent of the characteristics of any individual research subject, whereas a subjective standard takes into account the information needs and wants of each specific research subject. This debate has both legal aspects and ethical aspects, and it is important to keep the two aspects separate. The standard supported by the best ethical arguments may not be the same as the standard which is most suitable for legislative purposes or in the court room. In the legal context, additional factors like standards of evidence play a considerable role in selecting the best legal standard of information. The debate has not found any final resolution, but there seems to be general agreement in the research ethics literature that the information given always

83

has to fulfill some minimal objective criteria. It must, for instance, contain information about the objective of the research, the role of the research subject, and the risk and inconvenience caused by being part of the project. The information ideally has to be objective, and the researcher must not try to persuade the potential research subject. This standard information must then be further expanded to suit the informational needs of each individual research subject.

With regard to genetic experimentation there may be problems with informed consent both concerning the voluntariness of the consent and concerning the information component.

Genetic experiments can in some cases be very complicated and this can make it doubtful whether it is possible to inform the average person to such an extent, that he or she is able to give informed consent. This problem is a problem which genetic experimentation shares with a whole range of other biomedical research projects. It is usually not acknowledged as a serious problem by biomedical researchers, but when one takes into account that a significant proportion of the population of the industrialized countries are functionally illiterate, it should probably receive more consideration. In the genetics context we have further reason to believe that many people who are not illiterate in the usual sense of the word, are actually genetically illiterate (i.e. have no knowledge of modern genetics).

In an early paper on research ethics Hans Jonas suggested that research subjects should be chosen according to their ability to understand the research project (Jonas 1972). The researcher should first ask colleagues, then other academics in nearby fields, then other college graduates, and only as a last resort the general public. There are good ethical arguments for choosing this order of priority in recruiting research subjects in contexts where there is no need to use patients with a specific disease, since it will undoubtedly improve the validity of the consent. The priority has never caught on, and it seems to be a stable feature of biomedical research that it often "exploits" socioeconomically disadvantaged groups. By adopting this priority in recruiting research subjects to genetic research the researchers could, however, circumvent the objection that genetic research is so complicated that it is impossible for ordinary people to give valid consent.

I will make you an offer you cannot refuse!

In some kinds of research on gene therapy the potential research subject is placed in a situation where he or she has to choose between the following options:

1 No participation = certain death in the not too distant future.
2 Participation = an unknown chance of getting some extra months of life or perhaps being cured, together with an unknown risk of side-effects.

None of these options is especially appealing, but option 2 is the only one which offers the slightest glimmer of hope. It is in a sense an offer the patient cannot refuse if he or she wants to live. Does this constitute coercion in a way which vitiates the consent of the patient?

It is obvious that the patient is actually coerced, but he or she is coerced by nature, and not by the researcher. It is not the researcher who has brought the patient into the situation where the offer becomes potentially coercive.

The offer is put forward by a researcher who, as mentioned above, probably has an interest in getting the consent of the patient. The research project can only progress if a sufficient number of patients consent. This is, however, still not sufficient to support a claim of unethical coercion.

But what about exploitation? Is it the case that the researcher exploits the research subject in an ethically problematic way?

Normally we do not regard offers as exploitative, even though they may change people's actions. If I offer you a job with twice your present salary, I have not exploited you if you accept the offer, although I have changed the way in which you would have acted had I not presented the offer.

Our intuitions may, however, be different if we look at offers presented to persons in more difficult situations. What would we for instance say if I offered an Indian day laborer 5,000 pounds for one of his kidneys or, perhaps even more problematic, 50,000 pounds for his heart? In both situations it might be rational for him to accept, because he could secure the future well-being of his family with the money gained in the transaction; but would this not be a case of an exploitative offer?

I think such an offer is exploitative, and that its exploitative nature stems from the combination of the offer and the condition of severe material deprivation in which the Indian day laborer finds himself. What makes the offer exploitative is, paradoxically, that it is an offer he ought to accept, at least as far as the kidney is concerned – I ignore here the question of whether giving your life for others can ever be an obligatory and not a supererogatory act, but only because he is in a situation where no human being ought to be. Or to put it more formally, an offer is an exploitative offer if (a) the recipient of the offer is in a severely materially or socially deprived situation, (b) this situation is not a situation in which the recipient ought to be on the account of his own wrongdoing, and (c) the giver of the offer is aware of (a) and intends to use the situation to his own advantage.

This would mean that an offer does not become exploitative just because it has abnormal potency in a situation. If I offer a job to somebody, knowing that this is the job he has dreamt of all his life, I have not exploited him, although the offer has an abnormal potency in this situation.

An alternative explanation of our different intuitions about the two offers could be that whereas accepting the job offer does not harm me, the Indian day laborer is harmed in some sense by accepting the offer because it involves physical harm to his body. That would imply that the offer is wrong, not by being exploitative but by being harmful. But consider the following example. I offer the job, knowing (a) that your wife has a good job which she won't leave, and (b) that you will have to move if you accept the job. If you accept the job, as you probably will because it is the job you have always dreamt about, then you have been harmed, because you and your wife will have to live apart from each other. (You may not have been harmed on balance, if all factors are taken into account, but the same is true of the Indian day laborer.)

Does that make the offer wrong in some sense? Perhaps, but even if the psychological harm is of the same magnitude as the physical harm in the transplant case,

85

few would think that the two offers are equally bad. This residue seems to be explainable only by the exploitative element of the transplant case.

A somewhat similar view on coercive/exploitative offers is presented by Robert Nozick in his seminal article "Coercion" (Nozick 1969), and has recently been defended in a modified form by Alan Wertheimer (1987). Nozick's basic idea is that the feature which makes certain offers coercive is, that the situation in which the person giving the offer finds himself departs from what could normally be expected. The problem which Nozick realizes is that what could normally be expected can be understood in two quite different ways, either as an empirical statement about the normal development of a state of affairs in a given society, or as a normative statement describing what the person in question is morally justified in expecting. Nozick himself prefers the moral interpretation, but delivers a counterexample which he thinks shows that the empirical interpretation must be used from time to time. In Wertheimer's version this example runs as follows:

> The Drug Case. A is B's normal supplier of illegal drugs for $20 per day. One day, A proposes to B that he will supply B's drugs if and only if B beats up C. (Wertheimer 1987: 209)

Nozick believes that his idea of a moral baseline cannot show coercion to be present in this case, but since he believes that the situation is coercive he proposes to use the baseline which the person in question (B) would like to see used.

Wertheimer rejects Nozick's claim that the choice of baseline is to be decided by the person receiving the offer and expands the number of possible baselines to 3:

The statistical (what is normal in a given society);
The moral (what morality requires);
The phenomenological (what the person in question expects).

He further claims that there is no right answer to which baseline one ought to choose, and that each baseline gives rise to a coercion claim with a particular moral force. And he maintains that offers are only coercive if they involve a threat to make somebody worse off than he presently is in respect to one of these baselines.

I think that this is a mistake. In the Indian day-laborer case discussed above, there is little doubt that actually he is not worse of with respect to any of these baselines after having received the offer. The offer is normal in his society, he has no moral right to expect that this particular person is going to help him (the person may have a general obligation to help the poor, but he would have no specific obligation to help *this* day laborer), and before the offer was given he could not expect any help, since he did not know the person giving the offer. Nevertheless the offer must be considered as coercive. This can only be achieved by a theory which accepts that some cases of severe material or social deprivation may make any offer coercive, if the intention of the offer is to exploit the deprived condition of the person.

The implication for genetic experimentation of this analysis of coercive offers seems initially to be that genetic experimentation using research subjects who have lethal diseases/conditions falls within the category of morally problematic coercive offers.

On further analysis it can, however, be shown that the implications are not as far-reaching. First, the genetic researchers have no part in creating the unfortunate situation of the potential research subject and they cannot alleviate or change this situation. The same is in most cases true of the society of which the researchers are a part.

Second, the carrying out of genetic research is in many cases directly aimed at the long-term benefit of all sufferers from the disease/condition in question, and is often a necessary component in an attempt to change the unfortunate situation of these persons.

These considerations show that although the offer of participation in genetic research can be coercive in the sense that it is an offer it would be irrational to refuse, the offer is not in all cases ethically problematic. This does not mean that no offers of this kind are ethically problematic. Offers to participate in genetic research that offers personal benefits to the research subjects, but which is mainly carried out because of its basic scientific value, may still be coercive in a problematic sense.

Consenting to an Unknown Future

In all cases of clinical research there is an element of uncertainty. If we knew the result of the research project before it was conducted it would be unethical to perform it and to involve research subjects. In many cases of standard clinical research the degree of uncertainty is, however, fairly small. It is customary to divide clinical research into four phases:

Phase I: Research on safe and effective dosage in humans.
Phase II: Small-scale clinical research aimed at substantiating efficiency.
Phase III: Large-scale clinical research aimed at establishing proof of efficiency and detecting rare side-effects.
Phase IV: Postmarketing research aimed at widening the recognized indications for use.

Any pharmaceutical product has to go through phase I–III before it can be marketed, whereas phase IV is optional.

This scheme is most directly applicable to clinical research involving pharmaceutical products, but it is also useful outside this specific area.

In the present context it is important to note that the uncertainty decreases as a product goes through successive phases, whereas the numbers of research subjects increase. In phase I the number of research subjects may be fairly small (<100) whereas phase III trials often involve several thousand subjects.

In research on gene therapy these phases are often compressed, so that phase I and II occur simultaneously, and phase III is omitted. As soon as some evidence of efficacy is produced, the therapy often enters routine clinical use immediately. This is problematic because many patients will be offered "therapies" where there is still a large element of uncertainty about efficacy and side-effects. These patients are therefore in essence research subjects, but they are not offered the same protections and extended information as true research subjects. The problem here is therefore a problem about informed consent in the sense that patients are told that they are being offered "therapy" when they are really being offered "experimental treatment."

Consenting for Future Generations

Some genetic experiments change the genes in the germ cells. If a person who has participated in such an experiment procreates at some later point, the change will be transmitted to his or her children and possibly to many future persons that are genetically related to him or her.

It has been suggested that this specific feature precludes valid informed consent to some kinds of genetic experimentation, because nobody is in a position to consent on behalf of any of these future persons.

There are three problems with this argument. First, it is quite usual to make decisions which have far-reaching implications for ones' descendants without thinking explicitly about these implications. My choice of education, place of residence, timing of procreation, etc. influence the life of my children in profound ways. These differences are not just differences in the material conditions and environment, but may also be very profound differences in culture and language. Just think of the difference between growing up having Danish or Finnish as a first language. Second, it is unclear why I should concern myself with future generations if I cannot foresee some definite future harm coming from my present actions. Everything I do influences future generations in some way, most often unpredictably. Third, the most popular variant of the argument implicitly assumes that some harm will befall the future persons. It is seldom mentioned that the lack of consent from the future persons must be an equally serious problem, if my present actions will unequivocally benefit these future persons.

A version of this argument which is perhaps more interesting could be built on the ideas put forward by Hans Jonas in *The Imperative of Responsibility* (Jonas 1984). Jonas argues that there is a certain class of acts which it is ethically forbidden to perform, even if they seem to promise great benefits. These are acts which may potentially lead to the extinction of the human species. According to Jonas we have no right to endanger the future of the species, even if the risk of extinction is minute and the benefits immense.

If this is applied to genetic experimentation it would entail, that any kind of genetic experimentation which could potentially lead to the extinction of the human species should be prohibited. This argument could speak against certain forms of gene therapy.

The problem with the argument lies in exactly specifying what kinds of acts fall within the scope of the prohibition. It is logically possible that any human act can turn out to be one of the necessary acts in the chain of acts leading to the extinction of the human species. It is, for instance, not logically impossible that the act of writing the present sentence could be such an act. It is, nevertheless, highly unlikely. If the argument prohibits all actions which could possibly endanger the human species, it will therefore prohibit all actions. A more plausible version could build on a distinction between a class of acts that are risk-free in practice, a class of acts that may contain risk, and a class of acts that are definitely risky. Such a distinction could, for instance, be based on the perceived likelihood of the scenarios in which a certain act really caused the extinction of the human species. The limits between the three classes will necessarily be arbitrary, but the distinction may be useful in practice anyway.

Research without Consent?

Every hospital, research laboratory, and major museum of natural history has stored human tissues which can be used for genetic research. This may be in the form of samples specifically collected for research, or it may be samples originally collected for other purposes (diagnostic, therapeutic, etc.). In many cases the persons from whom the tissue originates have not given explicit consent to the collection and storage of the material, and in some cases there is not even implicit consent (e.g. in the case of Egyptian mummies or other sources of ancient DNA). A lot of interesting and worthwhile genetic research can be conducted on such tissue samples. This does, however, raise the question whether such research is only ethically acceptable if the researcher gets consent from the persons from whom the tissue was acquired. It is fairly obvious that there are cases where it is impossible to get consent from the actual person, for instance because he or she is dead. In those cases it could be proposed that consent should be sought from the descendants of the person, but even this may be impossible in many cases. There may be no descendants, the descendants may not be known, or there may be so many descendants that it becomes unclear which of these should be asked.

Is research unethical in all those cases where consent cannot be obtained? To answer this question it is important to remember why informed consent is seen as an important principle in research ethics. As it was outlined above, informed consent in research is important because it protects the research subjects' right to self-determination and prevents the researchers from "using" persons as pure means to further their own ends. In the context of stored tissue samples we could on this basis argue (a) that people in the future ought to be told that their tissues could be stored and later used for research, and (b) that if persons are traceable, and we have reason to believe that they have an interest in whether or not the stored sample of their tissue is used in a specific research project, then we ought to ask their consent.

Some of the interests of a person may conceivably persist after his or her death, for instance the interest in maintaining a good reputation, but most interests become void when the person dies. If we accept surviving interests in reputation this could have implications for those kinds of genetic experimentation that can posthumously tarnish a person's reputation. Such experimentation would be *prima facie* wrong.

There are, however, problems with this initially promising argument. We have to decide which code of honor and reputation to apply in deciding whether somebody's reputation has been tarnished. For a modern monarch or politician it would be problematic if it was shown that they were the result of an incestuous relationship, and themselves engaged in incest with their siblings. For an Egyptian pharaoh of certain dynasties it would be equally problematic if he was not the result of an

89

incestuous relationship, or if he did not marry one of his sisters, since this would show him not to be a true Son of the Sun. Initially it would seem that the right code of reputation to choose was the present, since it is at the time of the experiment and the revealing of the results that the reputation may be tarnished, but this just raises the problem in a new form. If codes of reputation change, then results obtained today may achieve a negative valuation in the future when the code has changed. If we look at the development of our ideas of proper behavior over time, there are very few kinds of behavior which have not been considered disreputable in some society at some point in history, and even if we limit our scope to presently existing societies we will see a wide divergence in ideas about proper behavior. We can therefore argue that there is really no way in which we can protect the reputation of the deceased for more than a few generations, and perhaps not even for so long. Taking account of the reputation of the long deceased in considerations of the ethics of genetic experimentation may be an honorable idea, but it may well be practically absurd, and it should not stand in the way of important research projects.

Conclusion

This chapter has shown that there are a number of problems concerning informed consent to genetic experimentation. None of these problems do, however, provide us with a knock-down argument showing that informed consent to genetic experimentation is impossible and that all genetic experimentation is therefore ethically problematic. The reasons why this radical conclusion does not follow are primarily the following: (a) there is a whole range of genetic experimentation from the simple and trivial to the complicated and contentious, (b) some of the problems concerning informed consent can be circumvented by proper choice of research subject and by attention to the context and process of getting informed consent, and (c) it may not be all genetic experimentation which, seen from an ethical point of view, requires informed consent (but this is obviously not a determination which should be made by the individual researcher).

References

Faden, R. R. and Beauchamp, T. L.: *A History and Theory of Informed Consent* (New York: Oxford University Press, 1986).

ICH Harmonised Tripartite Guideline for Good Clinical Practice (Brookwood: Brookwood Medical Publications, 1996).

Jonas, H.: "Philosophical reflections on experimenting with human subjects." In Freund, P. A., ed.: *Experimentation with Human Subjects* (London: Allen and Unwin, 1972).

Jonas, H.: *The Imperative of Responsibility – In Search of an Ethics for the Technological Age* (Chicago: University of Chicago Press, 1984).

Kimmel, A. J.: *Ethics and Values in Applied Social Research* (Newbury Park, CA: Sage Publications, 1988).

Nozick, R.: "Coercion." In Morgenbesser, S., Suppes, P., and White, M., eds.: *Philosophy, Science, and Method – Essays in Honor of Ernest Nagel* (New York: St. Martin's Press, 1969).
Wertheimer, A.: *Coercion* (Princeton: Princeton University Press, 1987).

Further reading

Harris, J.: *Wonderwoman and Superman: The Ethics of Human Biotechnology* (Oxford: Oxford University Press, 1992).
Harris, J. and Dyson, A., eds.: *Ethics and Biotechnology* (London: Routledge and Kegan Paul, 1993).
Kevles, D. J. and Hood, L., eds.: *The Code of Codes: Scientific and Social Issues in the Human Genome Project* (Cambridge, MA: Harvard University Press, 1992).
Marteau, T. and Martin, R., eds.: *The Troubled Helix: Social and Psychological Implications of the New Human Genetics* (New York: Cambridge University Press, 1996).
Suzuki, D. and Knudtson, P.: *Genethics: The Clash Between the New Genetics and Human Values* (Cambridge, MA: Harvard University Press, 1989).
Walter, L. and Palmer, J. G.: *The Ethics of Human Gene Therapy* (New York: Oxford University Press, 1997).

8

Testing Children and Adolescents

DOROTHY WERTZ

Introduction

Many geneticists around the world (38 percent) have had requests from parents to test children or adolescents for adult-onset genetic disorders, including Huntington's chorea, that are neither treatable nor preventable (Wertz 1998). Most of us assume that knowledge is a "good," but is this really so? Sophocles, in *Oedipus Rex*, cautioned that "It is not wisdom to be wise, when wisdom profits not." How much do we really want to know about our own future, or at least our medical future? Most of us would probably like to know about diseases we could prevent, but would we really like to know that we will develop Alzheimer disease? If we do (and there may be a sound reasons for wanting to know), at least we are making the decision as (presumably) competent adults. But what about the child whose medical future in adulthood, middle and old age becomes predictable as a result of genetic testing? What about the image-conscious adolescent? What is it like to live with a predictable but unchangeable future? Once provided, the knowledge cannot be returned to Pandora's box. Did others have the right to let it out?

There are several types of genetic testing. Perhaps the most common is diagnostic testing for a symptomatic child or adolescent. This is part of medical practice generally and does not pose an ethical problem. The potential problems arise from testing apparently healthy children or adolescents. Testing of healthy children may be of three types. The first is carrier testing for recessive or X-linked genes that will not affect the child but may affect the child's own children. Examples are genes for cystic fibrosis (recessive) or hemophilia (X-linked). (In a few X-linked conditions, such as fragile X, girls who are carriers may also be mildly affected, in which case testing becomes part of ordinary diagnostic procedures.) A second type of testing is for susceptibility to common diseases such as breast cancer. Susceptibility testing provides a risk, but not a certainty, that one will develop the disease over the course of a lifetime, for example, an 80 percent risk of breast cancer by age 80. It does not provide information about the age at which the disease will appear or about the course of the disease or responsiveness to treatment in a particular individual.

A third type of testing is presymptomatic testing, which identifies the presence of a gene that definitely will cause a genetic disorder if the person lives long enough. The most frequently mentioned example is Huntington's chorea, an untreatable degenerative neurological disease that usually begins around age 40 and leads to death over a course of 10 to 20 years.

Testing below the age of legal majority falls into several different categories of age, each of which may have different purposes. Starting backwards, these are: adolescence, childhood, newborn, and prenatal. In adolescence, testing may be done to provide information relevant to reproduction, perhaps at the adolescent's own request. An example might be a girl whose brother has cystic fibrosis and who is dating a boy whose cousin has cystic fibrosis; she wants carrier testing to find out if their children might have cystic fibrosis. Childhood testing is usually requested by parents who are anxious about their child's future and wish to resolve the anxiety. Newborn screening, which is usually mandated by governments to identify and treat diseases of infancy, has been limited, for ethical reasons, to disorders where early diagnosis and treatment would benefit the newborn, but with multiplex tests the focus of testing may be expanding to include some nontreatable disorders. Kitcher (1996) foresees the day when parents will receive an entire "genetic report card" at the child's birth predicting lifetime health. By extension, prenatal diagnosis for an adult-onset disorder such as Huntington's chorea becomes testing of a child, if the fetus is carried to term. That child, tested before birth, will grow up with parents who know that it will inevitably develop a severe, incurable disease.

Why is Testing Children a Moral Problem?

If early diagnosis increases possibilities for treatment, as is the case for disorders typically covered under state-mandated newborn screening, offers avenues for prevention, as is the case for genetic disorders that cause high levels of cholesterol, or avoids years of uncomfortable monitoring procedures, as may be the case with familial adenomatous polyposis, which requires frequent colonoscopies, ethics would appear to require testing as early in postnatal life as is medically beneficial. The problems occur in situations where there is no clear benefit in the near future (Harper and Clarke 1990; Clarke and Flinter 1996; Bloch and Hayden 1990). These situations include carrier testing, presymptomatic testing for disorders that occur later in life, and susceptibility testing (e.g., for certain cancers, heart disease, or mental illness). Potential benefits of testing – to both child and family – must be weighed against potential harms. At this point there are few data on which to make judgments; there is a virtual absence of research on psychosocial outcomes among children who have been tested.

Parents (and also children or adolescents) tend to see mostly the benefits. They want relief from anxiety, which will enable them to plan for the future. What they really want to find out, like most people facing possible "bad" results from medical tests, is that their child does not have the gene in question. It seems that most of the benefits of testing may accrue to those who do not have the gene (50 percent in the case of Mendelian dominant disorders such as Huntington's chorea). Testing may actually prevent stigmatization. In the absence of definitive information, some families have already picked out a particular child as the one who has the "bad" gene. Testing can remove the label from this child (but may place it on another child).

Favorable test results may be a mixed blessing, however. Children who are free of the gene in question may feel "survivor guilt" if they have an ill sibling or parent (Fanos and Johnson 1992; Kessler 1987), just as some survivors of Hiroshima felt guilty for being alive when family and friends were dead. There is a real possibility of disrupting sibling relations (Fanos 1997). Some parents may not fully believe the test results and may continue to dwell on the possibility that the test was inaccurate and that their child really has the gene after all. This phenomenon, called the "vulnerable child syndrome" (Green and Solnit 1964), is common among parents whose children have had a serious illness and who can never quite believe afterward that the child is wholly well. They may go through life anticipating that the illness, or one like it, will recur. So a favorable outcome from testing may not be a panacea for all families.

For those with unfavorable test results, there will at least be closure. This may be a psychological benefit to all. However, the benefits may not be proportional to the potential harms, which have been described in detail elsewhere (Wertz, Fanos, and Reilly 1994). The child may later be subjected to discrimination by health insurers (in countries with private insurance), life insurers, employers, schools, and other institutions. Although discrimination on the basis of carrier status or genetic susceptibility is rare (Wertz 1997), it does exist (Wertz 1997; Lapham 1996; Geller et al. 1996). Discrimination and stigmatization within the family itself may be a more likely possibility. In a recent survey, several US genetics professionals reported parental requests to test children for genes for Huntington's chorea because the parents wanted to know whether or not they should set aside money for college tuition (Wertz 1995). If a child had the Huntington gene, they would shift family resources away from that child and toward the other children. Damage to the child's own self-image is another possibility, even for those who are carriers of recessive genes, especially if the parents regard them as somehow damaged, less healthy, or less reproductively fit than other children.

In view of the real, though as yet undocumented, possibilities for harm, professional societies in the United Kingdom (CGS 1994) and the United States (AMA 1995; ASHG 1995; NSGC 1995) have recommended that testing be postponed until adulthood unless there is a proven medical benefit in the near future.

The clinching argument against testing children, however, is that most adults, when offered testing for themselves, have decided that they don't want to know. About 16 percent of adults at risk have chosen to be tested for the Huntington gene (Tyler et al. 1992; Bloch and Hayden 1990). Except for pregnant women (concerned about the baby's health), the US public has evinced little interest in cystic fibrosis carrier tests (Miller 1993; Flinter et al. 1992). Between 1 percent and 77 percent (mostly pregnant) have accepted free offers of carrier testing for cystic fibrosis in the US pilot studies (*Science* 1996). The uptake for breast cancer genetic testing has also been well below expectations (*Science* 1997). If adults do not want to know, why should parents or professionals be able to impose tests on children or adolescents, who might not have wanted to know when they became adults? Are there "questions that parents should resist" (Ruddick 1989)?

A 37-Nation Survey of Ethical Views

The following essay refers from time to time to a major international survey of geneticists' ethical views, which included questions on testing children and on adolescents' rights. We surveyed 4,609 genetics services providers in 37 nations, including 1,538 in the US, 846 primary-care physicians (pediatricians, obstetricians, family practitioners) in the United States, 718 first-time visitors to 12 genetics clinics in the United States and Canada, and 1,000 members of the US public. The 37 nations included all those known to have at least 10 practicing geneticists. A geneticist colleague in each country identified geneticists and distributed and collected the anonymous questionnaires. In the United States, Canada, and United Kingdom, master's-level genetic counselors and genetic nurses were included. The primary-care physicians, all certified by their specialty board (Pediatrics, Obstetrics, or Family Practice), were randomly selected from the American Medical Association's (AMA) *Physician Masterfile*, which lists all US physicians regardless of whether they are members of the AMA.

The questionnaires included questions about both professional and personal socio-demographic data and 50 questions about ethical situations related to clinical genetics, mostly presented in the form of case vignettes. Respondents were asked what they would do (or, for patients, what they thought the doctor should do), from a checklist of possible actions, and also to explain, in their own words, why they had chosen this course of action.

Geneticist, primary-care physician, and patient and public questionnaires covered the same issues, but primary-care physician questionnaires used common medical parlance instead of genetic terminology (e.g., Turner syndrome instead of 45,X). Patient and public questionnaires used simpler statements. The geneticist questionnaire was translated into 12 languages. Geneticists and primary-care physicians received three waves of mailings with telephone follow-up. Parents received the questionnaires by mail before their first clinic visit, in order to ensure that their views were not influenced by genetic counseling. Members of the public were surveyed by printed questionnaires delivered in person, using a quota sample developed by Roper-Starch Worldwide, a professional survey firm.

In all, 2,903 (63 percent) geneticists around the world returned questionnaires, including 1,084 (70 percent) of those who received questionnaires in the United States and 102 (47 percent) in the United Kingdom (table 8.1). Egypt was removed from the analysis because of the small number (2) responding. 499 (59 percent) primary-care physicians, 473 (66 percent) patients, and 988 (99 percent) members of the public responded. Most patients lived in the United States (93 percent), were women (91 percent) and white (89 percent). They had a median of 13 years of education; 13 percent had not finished high school, and 28 percent were college graduates (including 11 percent with some postgraduate training). Most were in working-class occupations (clerical or sales, 29 percent service, 19 percent, or production factory work, 8 percent, with a minority in professional or managerial work, 30 percent). The majority of their spouses were also working class, with 31 percent in factory production work, 23 percent in clerical or sales, and 15 percent in service occupations. Median income

95

was US $25,000–45,000. This group appeared closer to "middle America" than the college-educated or consumer support groups sometimes surveyed about "genetic discrimination" (Lapham et al. 1996). The following tables report responses of the 409 who were parents of minor children. The median age of child patients was 5 years, and the most frequently mentioned conditions were neurofibromatosis, Marfan syndrome, Down syndrome, cleft/lip palate, and cancer syndromes.

Table 8.1 Survey response rates

Country	Invited to participate	Responded	% Responding
Argentina	57	19	33
Australia	26	15	58
Belgium	40	15	38
Brazil	131	74	56
Canada	212	136	64
Chile	25	16	64
China	392	252	64
Colombia	27	15	56
Cuba	96	18	19
Czech Republic	137	81	59
Denmark	54	28	52
Finland	53	22	42
France	102	75	74
Germany	418	255	61
Greece	12	12	100
Hungary	78	38	46
India	70	23	33
Israel	27	23	85
Italy	23	21	91
Japan	174	113	65
Mexico	89	64	72
Netherlands	41	27	66
Norway	18	9	50
Peru	16	14	88
Poland	250	151	60
Portugal	22	11	50
Russia	66	46	69
South Africa	21	16	76
Spain	82	51	62
Sweden	15	12	80
Switzerland	10	6	60
Thailand	38	25	66
Turkey	30	22	73
United Kingdom	217	101	47
United States	1538	1084	70
Venezuela	22	16	73
Total	**4629**	**2906**	**63**

A Clash of Autonomies: Parent and Child

Respect for individual autonomy appears to be increasing among genetics profession-als, and presumably among the cultures from which they come. A comparison between the 1993–6 survey and a similar survey in 1984–5 (Wertz et al. 1990; Wertz and Fletcher 1989) shows greater willingness to disclose full information to individuals and families and greater willingness to accede to patient requests, includ-ing sex selection, in all but three (India, France, and Sweden) of the 19 nations previously surveyed (Wertz and Fletcher 1998). There was also greater willingness to disclose fully a psychologically sensitive diagnosis (XY genotype) to a woman patient than in the earlier survey. Many professionals think that withholding any service is paternalistic and a denial of patients' rights (46 percent), that providers should support all patient decisions, including those with which they disagree (71 percent), that patients should be offered a referral if the provider finds a request morally objectionable (84 percent), that patients have a right to whatever service they can pay for out-of-pocket (33 percent), and that people have a right, even *after* being tested, to decide *not* to know the results (73 percent) (table 8.2).

Patients in the United States were even more in favor of autonomy than were professionals (table 8.2, row 7); 59 percent thought patients were entitled to any service they asked for and could pay out-of-pocket. (Patients rejected the "right not to know" because they said they could not understand why someone would change their mind after taking a test.) Their views could well represent the wave of the future, at least in societies like the US, where medicine is a commercial enterprise and patients prefer to be called "consumers." Parents think they have a right to have their children tested. Having been taught that knowing more about oneself will improve health, most probably think that in requesting tests they are doing "the best" for their children.

It appears that autonomy has triumphed, or is about to do so, in most of the world. Many providers seem to have forgotten that it is ethically acceptable to refuse requests for medicines or procedures that serve no medical purpose (Brett and McCullough 1986, Beauchamp and McCullough 1984). The classic example in bioethics is a request for antibiotics to cure the common cold.

This trend toward greater respect for autonomy accords with classical principles of medical ethics (Beauchamp and Childress 1994) and with recommendations of national and international groups (US National Commission 1977; US President's Commission 1982; WHO 1995, 1997). The question is, *whose* autonomy? The parents' or the child's? In both the US (Ambuel and Rappoport 1992; Holder 1977, 1988, 1989) and the UK (Nicholson 1986), courts have awarded increasing auton-omy to adolescents and children. In many states in the US, adolescents may request testing for sexually transmitted diseases (including HIV), may receive birth control information and devices, and may have abortions on their own initiative, without their parent's knowing (Gans 1993). An adolescent who is living independently, is a parent caring for a child, or is pregnant may be legally regarded as a "mature minor" and legally entitled to manage her/his own healthcare regardless of age. However,

Table 8.2 Views on patient autonomy: rights to services, % agreeing

Country	Withholding any requested service is paternalistic	Patients are entitled to any service they request and can pay for out-of-pocket	PND should be provided regardless of intended use	Women should have unqualified right to abortion before viability
English-speaking nations				
Australia	50	27	40	67
Canada	38	11	28	71
South Africa	56	38	38	50
United Kingdom	51	4	20	46
United States	56	36	47	85
US Primary care physicians	57	26	44	63
US Patients (n = 476)	69	59	80	n/a
Northern/Western Europe				
Belgium	53	0	21	39
Denmark	67	19	44	70
Finland	29	0	41	38
France	45	8	86	14
French Patients	48	54	68	n/a
Germany	28	13	23	29
German patients (n = 593)	66	48	94	n/a
Netherlands	37	7	37	46
Norway	56	22	22	56
Sweden	58	8	17	75
Switzerland	67	33	50	50
Southern Europe				
Greece	50	33	31	58
Italy	55	35	52	30
Portugal	36	27	18	46
Spain	41	20	18	32

Eastern Europe				
Czech Republic	48	41	42	51
Hungary	15	29	6	74
Poland	67	68	61	35
Russia	55	67	65	88
Near East				
Israel	59	57	50	55
Turkey	63	23	5	91
Latin America				
Argentina	50	43	39	43
Brazil	30	48	30	58
Chile	47	33	27	7
Colombia	54	31	23	79
Cuba	36	46	7	93
Mexico	54	36	8	74
Peru	31	43	14	43
Venezuela	40	38	13	50
Asia				
China	23	28	13	61
India	43	26	27	30
Japan	32	64	6	12
Thailand	32	36	29	18
Total (geneticists)	**46**	**33**	**35**	**59**
Total, excluding US	**40**	**30**	**29**	**46**

parents may learn of procedures that will be billed to their health insurance and may be able to exert control by refusing permission for payment.) Federal law governing federally-funded research recognizes the child's autonomy by requiring "assent" from children old enough to understand that they are being asked to participate in a research project (45 CFR 46, 408). Although no set age is given in the regulations, usually children age 7 and over are assumed to be capable of assent. Children's assent parallels the elements of adult informed consent, but in simplified form (Fletcher et al. 1989). It is not legally binding, is not a substitute for parental informed consent, and may be overridden if the research has therapeutic benefits.

This growing respect for the autonomy of children may sometimes clash with the growing respect for autonomy of adults. Testing a child, even with the child's assent, robs that child of the right to make a later decision about whether to be tested in the light of the greater self-understanding that should accompany adulthood (Brock 1989; Buchanan and Brock 1989). The "future autonomy" of the child is sacrificed to the present autonomy of the parents.

In many parts of the world, autonomy of the child is a new idea. The traditional ethic, that parents should be able to exert rights over the child, or even that the child is a form of chattel (property), still holds in many cultures, as it did until the mid-nineteenth century in the United States (Platt 1969; Kett 1977).

Survey Results

Table 8.3 shows the national differences in willingness to test children and adolescents among respondents to our survey.

In English-speaking nations other than the US, the percents of geneticists who would test for Huntington's chorea, Alzheimer's disease, or susceptibility to alcoholism (assuming that such a test were possible) were lower than in the United States (table 8.3). The low percents who would test in the United Kingdom (2 percent, 2 percent, and 4 percent) are especially striking. This reluctance to test may stem in part from greater experience with requests for testing in the UK than anywhere else in the world except Switzerland and the Netherlands. In the UK, 76 percent had had requests to test children for adult-onset disorders, as compared with 38 percent in the US and 49 percent in western Europe. Percents in northern/western Europe who would test were also lower than in the US (table 8.3). In southern Europe, eastern Europe, the Near East, Asia, and Latin America, however, majorities would test children for all conditions listed (table 8.3). Willingness to test in these regions appears to stem from cultural beliefs about the rights of parents and their authority over their children.

Respondents were asked to explain, in their own words, their responses regarding testing. We recorded two reasons behind each write-in comment, using categories developed in an earlier survey. In giving reasons for their responses, 66 percent of geneticists in the United States said they wished to avoid harm, through early treatment or prevention, from familial hypercholesterolemia (a condition predisposing to heart disease), cancer, or possible alcoholism, or to avoid harm from premature knowledge of Huntington's chorea or Alzheimer's disease. 43 percent said the

Table 8.3 Testing children: % who thought parents should be able to have minor children tested for...

Country	Huntington's disease	Alzheimer's disease	Alcoholism (predisposition)	Cancer mutations	Familial hypercholesterolemia	Had requests to test children for adult-onset disorders	Would tell a minor results of Alzheimer test
English-speaking nations (totals)	**9**	**9**	**19**	**62**	**69**	**65**	**16**
Australia	13	13	7	64	73	93	0
Canada	12	11	26	63	71	56	22
South Africa	25	25	67	81	81	50	0
United Kingdom	2	2	4	58	67	76	12
United States	27	25	48	70	81	38	18
US Primary Care Physicians	66	58	76	81	89	20	44
US Patients	n/a	61	n/a	93	92	n/a	32
US Public	**n/a**	**54**	**n/a**	**85**	**82**	**n/a**	**n/a**
Northern/Western Europe (totals)	**16**	**14**	**27**	**51**	**63**	**49**	**12**
Belgium	15	15	50	62	92	57	17
Denmark	33	33	33	56	67	37	14
Finland	18	18	23	41	64	41	13
France	21	19	37	72	85	51	9
French patients	45	n/a	n/a	97	97	n/a	n/a
Germany	14	10	24	45	56	44	12

Table 8.3 *(contd)*

Country	Huntington's disease	Alzheimer's disease	Alcoholism (predisposition)	Cancer mutations	Familial hypercholesterolemia	Had requests to test children for adult-onset disorders	Would tell a minor results of Alzheimer test
German patients (n = 593)	37	n/a	n/a	86	87	n/a	n/a
Netherlands	11	11	18	36	57	84	13
Norway	11	11	11	56	78	67	0
Sweden	8	8	25	50	42	58	0
Switzerland	40	20	33	80	67	83	20
Southern Europe (total)	**66**	**62**	**66**	**80**	**89**	**34**	**1**
Greece	90	70	70	80	90	40	0
Italy	48	48	57	76	91	38	0
Portugal	64	64	64	82	91	27	0
Spain	70	66	70	82	88	33	2
Eastern Europe (total)	**73**	**70**	**78**	**88**	**93**	**16**	**5**
Czech Republic	73	70	78	86	95	30	5
Hungary	58	56	58	75	81	17	0
Russia	86	80	93	91	93	12	7
Near East							
Israel	41	38	59	82	91	77	15
Turkey	68	68	91	86	91	18	20

Latin America						
Argentina	69	85	85	85	23	0
Brazil	69	80	89	90	8	15
Chile	73	81	93	94	19	6
Colombia	64	79	71	79	21	8
Cuba	100	100	100	100	0	15
Mexico	82	77	84	85	32	4
Peru	100	93	100	100	7	0
Venezuela	73	73	100	93	25	15
Asia						
China	85	69	85	84	18	6
India	74	54	82	87	14	9
Japan	58	59	74	73	13	25
Thailand	84	92	96	96	4	16
Total geneticists	**40**	**50**	**71**	**79**	**35**	**14**
Total, excluding US	**48**	**51**	**72**	**77**	**34**	**11**

information was necessary to make decisions about medical management. Fewer mentioned parental autonomy (13 percent) or preparing for the future (9 percent) as reasons for testing. More (25 percent) mentioned protecting the child's autonomy as a reason not to test, and 13 percent said there was no need to know at this time. Few (3 percent) mentioned the possibility of stigmatization.

In contrast to geneticists, the majority of both primary-care physicians and parents thought parents should be able to have their minor children tested for both Huntington and Alzheimer. In a separate survey of 988 members of the US public, most thought parents should be able to have their children tested for conditions that were "treatable if found early" (84 percent), or "preventable" (81 percent). A slight majority (53 percent) approved testing for conditions that were "neither preventable nor treatable." These results point to a dichotomy between geneticists and the rest of the US medical community, whose views closely paralleled those of their patients.

In a separate question, asked only in the United States, Germany, Japan, and Hungary, 20 percent of US geneticists would urge a woman with a dominant breast cancer gene to have her 13-year-old daughter tested now; 71 percent of parents said it was moderately (22 percent), very (17 percent), or extremely (32 percent) likely that if they themselves had a breast cancer gene they would encourage their own 13-year-old daughters to be tested now. Some parents wrote in that they would impose radical lifestyle changes on a daughter who had a breast cancer gene.

The results suggest (1) a need for international discussion about potential effects of testing on minors and about minors' autonomy; and (2) discussion with parents' groups about their different rationales for testing. It may be that some kinds of tests – especially the carrier testing that parents seem most to want – pose less likelihood of harm than do presymptomatic or susceptibility tests for adult-onset disorders such as Huntington's chorea or breast cancer. Carrier testing may also provide a real benefit for those adolescents who wish to exert some control over reproduction.

In the United Kingdom, the Genetic Interest Group (GIG) has argued in favor of carrier testing but against presymptomatic testing (Genetic Interest Group 1995). As knowledge about genetics increases, the possibility of carrier stigmatization may decrease, and self-acceptance after learning one is a carrier should increase. Follow-up studies of adolescents tested for Tay-Sachs carrier status in Canada have shown no measurable psychosocial harms from testing (Clow and Scriver 1977), but several years later, 19 percent of carriers were still worried about the information (Zeesman et al. 1984).

When is a Child or Adolescent Ready to Know?

Even very young children may understand the basic mechanisms of disease and the reasons for procedures such as immunizations (Lewis 1983; Lewis et al. 1978). Given enough education, they should also be able to understand the basis of inheritance and the characteristics of the disorder for which they are tested, though this has not yet been documented. Being able to list the symptoms of a disorder or to answer questions about Mendelian inheritance, however, is not the same as understanding how this may affect one's own life and one's self-image. For example, young children who appear to understand the germ theory of disease may have no understanding of the finality of death (Perrin and Garrity 1981, Millstein et al. 1981; Susman et al. 1987). The classic components of legal "competence to consent" – voluntariness, awareness of oneself as a being with a past and future, ability to assess the effects of an action on one's present and future (even if the factual assessment may be incorrect, the logical process leading to it should be reasonable), consistency of one's decisions with one's own future well-being – presume greater maturity than mere learning of facts (Brock 1989). Some children start to project their lives into the future quite early on. Girls of 9 and 10 may start thinking of themselves as mothers and may wonder if they will pass on a sibling's genetic condition to their children. Some of the world's great religions have set the "age of discretion" at 11 or 12, when the child formally becomes an adult, religiously speaking, by making certain statements of belief at a special ceremony. If one can make decisions about one's future in eternity, why not about learning one's future here on earth, through genetic testing?

On the other hand, many adults never became ready to know, as evidenced by the majorities who have rejected presymptomatic testing. Psychologists, legal scholars, and bioethics commissions have agreed that no fixed age can be set for minors' competence (Grisso 1981; Grisso and Vierling 1983; US President's Commission 1982; Wertz et al. 1994). Usually, competence is not presumed below the age of 14 (US President's Commission 1982) or 15 (Nicholson 1986), though it may exist earlier in some individuals. Fifteen is also the age at which adolescents are considered ready to ask for some medical procedures on their own. There was no agreement among our respondents, however, about the rights of even a 16-year-old to refuse testing for a treatable condition (table 8.3).

Taking a test is not necessarily equivalent to learning the results, because parental disclosure to the child may be delayed or may never occur. Table 8.3 (righthand column) shows the percents of geneticists who thought parents should tell the child about results of a test for Alzheimer's disease before the age of legal majority. Although most thought parents should *not* tell the child, some disagreed. (Percents were similar for Huntington's chorea; there was no consensus in regard to suscepti- bility to alcoholism, which some respondents thought was preventable and others thought was stigmatizing.) In actuality, it may be very difficult to conceal test results from a child of any age, especially if parents' behavior toward that child changes after the test. Openness may be preferable to attempts at concealment, once a test has been performed, because of the erosion of trust that results from keeping secrets (Bok 1984). This would be an argument against testing, unless parents are prepared to disclose soon afterward. On the other hand, disclosure denies the child the "right not to know," a right that most professionals support (table 8.2). The problem with testing is that one cannot simply say, "You had a test and your mother and father know the results. Would you like to know, too, or would you rather wait?" Whoever tells the child that the information exists and that people close to her/him have it, has already let half the cat out of the bag. It becomes very difficult for the child to refuse the information.

Parents in the survey were ambivalent about even wanting to know information about themselves. Although most patients (85 percent) and members of the public (77 percent) said they would want to know about a risk of serious incurable disease in

105

their own future, fewer patients (47 percent) thought that the doctor should tell them even if they didn't want to know. Testing and telling a child is analogous to the latter situation, because it may be difficult to tell whether the child really wants to know or would want to know if the decision about knowing were postponed until adulthood. The percent of parents who would actually choose to know, given the opportunity, is probably far lower than 85 percent, in view of the low uptake of presymptomatic testing.

The psychosocial effects of knowing may vary according to age. Pre-adolescents may accept genetic information the way they accept other medical information such as being allergic to peanut butter, without feeling a blow to their self-image, especially if the parents present the information in a matter-of-fact manner that indicates that it does not affect their love for the child. Young children may accept the news of even very serious cancers without becoming emotionally upset (Susman et al. 1987; Koocher 1986; Spinetta 1981). If testing is going to be done, it may be preferable to test before the emotional stress of adolescence, as some parent groups have suggested (GIG 1995). All this is speculative, however, in the absence of research, and suggests that ordinarily testing is best postponed, unless the child or adolescent has some compelling reason for requesting a test.

One extreme is telling a child too soon; the other is not telling the child at all. Few survey respondents believed in concealing test results forever. Unfortunately, there is no way of making certain that the child will have the opportunity to learn the results, if desired, upon reaching adulthood (Fanos and Johnson 1995). Sometimes genetic test results are kept separately from medical records in order to avoid possible discrimination by insurers or employers. Even if the information is retained in the child's medical record, there is no certainty that anyone will read the entire medical record and pass the information on to the child as a young adult. This argues for postponing testing until the child can make an informed decision about testing and about learning results.

Newborn Screening: The "Genetic Report Card"

Philip Kitcher (1996; and see chapter 17 in this volume) believes that the day is coming when all children will be tested at birth for genetically-influenced disorders that may appear throughout their lifetimes. Parents and child will presumably benefit from knowing what to expect. Kitcher's proposed "genetic report card" is a departure from classical newborn screening, which tested only for disorders where early diagnosis and treatment benefitted the newborn (Knoppers and Laberge 1990; US President's Commission 1983; Institute of Medicine 1994). Newborn screening is already moving away from this model, with the advent of multiplex tests that identify some nontreatable disorders along with those that are treatable. This has some benefits for the parents, because they will not have to go from doctor to doctor seeking a diagnosis when the child falls ill, and will not blame themselves for the illness. They will also be counseled about their own carrier status and the chances of conceiving another child with the same disorder. Parental counseling of this sort is already done in some sickle-cell screening programs, when a newborn is identified as a carrier. In the survey, 74 percent of geneticists (including 86 percent in the UK) thought this counseling was an important goal of newborn screening. The majority of parents (71 percent) said they would want their newborns tested, even if the condition were not treatable, so that they find out if their next child might have the same condition. They shied away from government-mandated newborn screening for this purpose, however; only 27 percent thought governments should require screening for nontreatable conditions. In other words, they wanted to know, but they did not want the government to require them to know.

Preserving patient autonomy presents both ethical and logistical problems, because most newborn screening is state-mandated. Even if a special informed consent were required for any screens on a multiplex that did not offer early medical benefits to the newborn, as suggested by several commissions (Institute of Medicine 1994; Holtzman and Watson 1997), the pressure of the hospital setting, the parents' physical and emotional condition immediately after birth, and the cultural belief that "medical testing is good for you" will lead most parents to consent. It may be possible to draw lines against tests for adult-onset, nontreatable disorders such as Huntington's chorea, but these single-gene disorders are fairly rare. It may be difficult to draw lines against testing for "risk genes," such as BRCA1 and 2 for breast cancer, especially since many people believe that early lifestyle changes (diet) may reduce risk.

In the future, today's arguments about testing children may shift to the newborn period. This will be a gradual shift, starting with the "accidental" findings of some multiplexes that also identify nontreatable childhood diseases as part of the process of searching for treatable diseases. As acceptance grows, future generations may wonder why ethicists questioned the testing of children. There is still a real possibility of harm, however. Kitcher's (1996) "genetic report card" of the twenty-first century assumes that the public is well educated about genetics and is also conditioned, through a process of ethical training, not to stigmatize people who look or act differently. According to Kitcher, antidiscrimination laws will have effectively prevented refusals of insurance, employment, schooling, or adoption. We have to ask ourselves whether this utopia is really likely and also whether the benefits of education will be distributed among all social groups.

What may be more likely than the Kitcher scenario is that the "democratization" of newborn testing for a wide variety of disorders and susceptibilities will serve to place genetics within the realm of general medicine. Genetic testing would become a routine on the order of childhood immunizations and would frighten fewer and fewer people, as most of us came to realize that we all carry genetic susceptibilities to one or more common and ultimately deadly diseases such as diabetes, heart disease, cancer, or respiratory infections. This could reduce the possibility of stigmatization, though it would not necessarily help people with uncommon conditions, especially those with disfiguring conditions or mental or behavioral disorders.

What Kitcher has overlooked, however, is the possibility that some people will simply ignore the test results. Many people, especially minority groups or those who have received part of their care through the welfare system, distrust all tests and prognoses, whether genetic or not. Too often medicine has been wrong. One result of having newborn genetic report cards may be that "nothing happens;" people will go on with their lives as if the tests had never existed.

Prenatal Tests for Adult-onset Disorders

Testing a fetus for a later-onset disorder becomes the psychosocial equivalent of testing a newborn or a child, if the fetus is carried to term. The child will be labeled for life, even if not told, and will be deprived of the right to decide about whether to be tested. In the United States, this situation will become more frequent, as prenatal diagnosis spreads into the general population and includes women who do not accept abortion under most conditions, but who feel that they should accept the offer of a test that will tell them the baby is healthy. A minority of parents (25 percent) or members of the general public (21 percent) would abort for "severe incurable mental illness at age 40"; parents of children with cystic fibrosis in an earlier survey had similar responses (Wertz et al. 1991). At present, most disorders of this kind are not identified by routine amniocentesis for advanced maternal age. With a multiplex, however, it could be possible to test for Huntington's chorea, BRCA, and susceptibility to Alzheimer's disease inexpensively on the same prenatal test. Given that most people will not abort for conditions where the child may have 40 or more years of useful life, this could lead to a generation of children who have been tested prenatally.

The classic case in medical ethics of testing children before birth was the "nondisclosing" or "exclusionary" test for Huntington's chorea, where a parent at 50 percent risk wanted to learn about the fetus but not about her/himself. It was generally assumed that if parents knew the fetus had the gene, they would always abort, though this has turned out not to be the case. For ethical discussion, the exclusionary test made a better case than direct testing, because it gave the fetus only a risk – either 50 percent or 4 percent – rather than a certainty, and it was assumed that some parents would decide not to abort a fetus at 50 percent risk. The question is, should professionals draw a line against testing a child prenatally for a later-onset disorder, assuming that the child will be born? In the survey, the majority (57 percent around the world, 75 percent in the United Kingdom) would perform the test if requested, honoring prenatal autonomy; 18 percent would do the test only if the couple committed in advance to abortion, and 25 percent would refuse the test altogether unless the at-risk parent agreed to learn his/her own status. Changes in technology and in the pool of parents being screened will lead, in the future, to births of more children who will be labeled in advance as inevitably developing a genetic disorder at midlife. The alternative – restricting prenatal diagnosis to parents who would abort – is ethically unacceptable in societies that respect autonomy. Besides, it may be impossible to draw lines between people who would and wouldn't abort, because few people are absolutely certain, in advance, about what they would do in each and every situation.

Commercialization

The trend toward autonomy, combined with increasing commercialization in many countries, will inevitably lead to more home test kits and direct approaches by parents to testing laboratories. In the United States, parents may approach testing laboratories directly (depending on the state). In a recent survey of testing children among 105 laboratories in the Helix research network (an informational network of laboratories, mostly university-based) that also provided clinical services, 45 percent reported that they had provided tests directly to consumers, without a physician intermediary (Wertz and Reilly 1997). Of the 46 percent that had policies on testing asymptomatic children, most had only fragmentary or single-disease policies, such as refusal to test for Huntington's chorea. Yet 22 percent of those who performed Huntington tests had tested asymptomatic children under the age of 12. The laboratories surveyed were not commercial laboratories. There are no published studies of the private sector.

It may be possible to limit direct testing by regulations, or at least to require that laboratories and makers of home test kits provide pretest counseling that would inform parents of the pros and cons (and limits) of testing. A confounding difficulty in trying to limit testing is the ignorance of primary-care physicians, who may order most of the tests and who tend to favor testing, both in the US and the UK (CGS 1994), but who may be woefully ignorant about the clinical manifestations of some disorders and also about the person's ability to function over the life course.

Conclusion

Cautionary statements by professional bodies (CGS 1994; AMA 1995; ASHG 1995; NSGC 1995) have pointed to the major ethical issues of weighing harms and benefits and of preserving the future autonomy of the child. They have recommended postponing tests until adulthood unless there is a medical benefit in the near future. Some parent groups, on the other hand, believe that carrier testing may provide real psychological benefits, provided that families understand the meaning of the results and that the child is actively involved in the decision (GIG 1995). Professional groups will need to work with parent groups to update their statements as social, educational, and technological conditions change. In the future, the issue may shift from isolated parental requests on behalf of older children or adolescents to inclusion of nontreatable later-onset disorders in newborn or prenatal multiplex screens. This could mean that an ever-larger proportion of children could grow up having been tested. Before this happens, we need to know how testing affects children of different ages and their families, so that policy-makers and counselors can act in the child's best interests. In other words, we need research soon in this underresearched area, before the reality of widespread testing is upon us.

Acknowledgments

The survey was supported by grant R01-HG00540-02 from the Ethical, Legal, and Social Implications Branch of the National Human Genome Research Institute (National Institutes of Health) and by contract N01-HD-1-3136 from the Mental Retardation and Developmental Disorders Branch of the National Institute of Child Health and Human Development (NIH).

References

Ambuel, B. and Rappoport, J.: "Developmental trends in adolescents' psychological and legal competence to consent to abortion." *Law and Human Behavior* 16 (1992), pp. 129–54.

American Medical Association (AMA) Council on Ethical and Judicial Affairs: "Testing children for genetic status." *Code of Medical Ethics, Report 66* (Chicago: American Medical Association, 1995).

American Society of Human Genetics (AMHG) Board of Directors and American College of Medical Genetics Board of Directors: "Points to consider: ethical, legal, and psychosocial implications of genetic testing in children and adolescents." *American Journal of Human Genetics* 57 (1995), p. 1233.

Beauchamp, T. L. and Childress, J. F.: *Principles of Biomedical Ethics* (New York: Oxford University Press, 1994).

Beauchamp, T. L. and McCullough, L. B.: *Medical Ethics: The Moral Responsibilities of Physicians* (Englewood Cliffs, NJ: Prentice-Hall International, 1984).

Bloch, M., Adam, S., Wiggins, S., Huggins, M., and Hayden, M. R: "Predictive testing for Huntington disease in Canada: the experience of those receiving an increased risk." *American Journal of Medical Genetics* 42 (1992), pp. 499–507.

Bloch, M. and Hayden, M. R.: "Predictive testing for Huntington disease in childhood: challenges and implications." *American Journal of Human Genetics* 46 (1990), pp. 1–4.

Bok, S.: *Secrets: On the Ethics of Concealment and Revelation* (New York: Vintage Books, 1984).

Brett, A. S. and McCullough, L. B.: "When patients request specific interventions: defining the limits of the physician's obligation." *New England Journal of Medicine* 315 (1986), pp. 1347–51.

Brock, D. W.: "Children's competence for healthcare decision-making." In Kopelman, L. M. and Moskop, J. C., eds.: *Children and Healthcare: Moral and Social Issues* (Dordrecht, Netherlands: Kluwer Academic Publishers, 1989), pp. 181–212.

Buchanan, A. E. and Brock, D. W.: *Deciding for Others: The Ethics of Surrogate Decision Making* (Cambridge: Cambridge University Press, 1989), pp. 215–66.

Clarke, A. and Flinter, F.: "The genetic testing of children: a clinical perspective." In Marteau, T. and Richards, M., eds.: *The Troubled Helix: Social and Psychological Implications of the New Human Genetics* (Cambridge: Cambridge University Press, 1996), pp. 164–76.

Clinical Genetics Society (CGS): "The genetic testing of children: report of a working party of the Clinical Genetics Society." (Angus Clarke, Chair.) *Journal of Medical Genetics* 31 (1994), pp. 785–97.

Clow, C. L. and Scriver, C. R.: "Knowledge about and attitudes toward genetic screening among high school students: the Tay-Sachs experience." *Pediatrics* 59 (1977), pp. 86–96.

Fanos, J. H.: *Sibling Loss* (Mahwah, NJ: Lawrence Erlbaum, 1997).

Fanos, J. H. and Johnson, J. P.: "Still living with cystic fibrosis: the well sibling revisited." *Pediatric Pulmonology* suppl. 8 (1992), pp. 228–9.

Fanos, J. H. and Johnson, J. P.: "Barriers to carrier testing for adult cystic fibrosis sibs: the importance of not knowing." *American Journal of Genetics* 59 (1995), pp. 85–91.

Fletcher, J. C., Van Eys, J., and Dorn, L. D.: "Ethical considerations in pediatric oncology." In Pizzo, P. A. and Poplack, D. C., eds.: *Principles and Practice of Pediatric Oncology* (Philadelphia: J. B. Lippincott, 1989).

Flinter, F. A. et al.: "Population screening for cystic fibrosis." *Lancet* 339 (1992), pp. 1539–40.

45 CFR 46, 408, US Dept. of Health and Human Services: 45 Code of Federal Regulations 46, Support D – Additional Protection for Children Involved as Subjects in Research. 48 *Federal Register* 9818.

Gans, J. ed.: *A Policy Compendium on Confidential Health Services for Adolescents* (Chicago: American Medical Association, 1993).

Geller, L. N., Alper, J. S., Billings, P. R., Barash, C. I., Beckwith, J., and Natowicz, M. R.: "Individual, family, and societal dimensions of genetic discrimination: a case study analysis." *Science and Engineering Ethics* 2 (1996), pp. 71–88.

Genetic Interest Group (GIG): *"GIG Response to the Clinical Genetics Society Report" The Genetic Testing of Children* (London: GIG, Farringdon Point, 1995).

Green, M. and Solnit, A. J.: "Reactions to the threatened loss of a child: a vulnerable child syndrome." *Pediatrics* 34 (1964), pp. 58–77.

Grisso, T.: *Juveniles' Waiver of Rights: Legal and Psychological Competence* (New York: Plenum Press, 1981).

Grisso, T. and Vierling, L.: "Minors' consent to treatment: a developmental perspective." *Professional Psychology* 9 (1983), pp. 412–27.

Harper, P. S. and Clarke, A.: "Should we test children for 'adult' genetic diseases?" *Lancet* 335 (1990), pp. 1205–6.

Holder, A. R.: *Legal Issues in Pediatrics and Adolescent Medicine* (New York: John Wiley & Sons, 1977).

Holder, A. R.: "Disclosure and consent problems in pediatrics." *Law Medicine and Healthcare* 16 (1988), pp. 219–28.

Holder, A. R.: "Children and adolescents: their right to decide about their own healthcare." In Kopelman, L. M. and Moskop, J. C., eds.: *Children and Healthcare: Moral and Social Issues* (Dordrecht, Netherlands: Kluwer Academic Publishers, 1989), pp. 161–72.

Holtzman, N. A. and Watson, M. S., eds.: *Promoting Safe and Effective Genetic Testing in the United States: Final Report of the Task Force on Genetic Testing* (Washington, DC: National Institutes of Health, 1997).

Institute of Medicine: "Committee on Assessing Genetic Risks." *Assessing Genetic Risks* (Washington, DC: National Academy Press, 1994), p. 276.

Kessler, S.: "Attitudes of persons at risk for Huntington disease toward predictive testing." *American Journal of Medical Genetics* 16 (1987), pp. 257–66.

Kett, J. F.: *Rites of Passage: Adolescence in America 1790 to the Present* (New York: Basic Books, 1977).

Kitcher, P.: *The Lives to Come: The Genetic Revolution and Human Possibilities* (New York: Simon & Schuster, 1996).

Knoppers, B. M. and Laberge, C. M.: *Genetic Screening: From Newborns to DNA Typing* (Amsterdam: Elsevier, 1990), pp. 243–56.

Koocher, G. P.: "Psychosocial issues during the acute treatment of pediatric Cancer." *Cancer* 58 (1986), pp. 468–72.

Lapham, E. V. et al.: "Genetic discrimination: perspectives of consumers." *Science* 274 (1996), p. 621.

Lewis, C. E.: "Decision making related to health: when could/should children act responsibly?" In Melton, G. B., Koocher G. P., and Saks, M. J., eds.: *Children's Competence to Consent* (New York: Plenum Press, 1983), pp. 75–91.

Lewis, C. E., Lewis, M. A., and Ifekwanigue, M.: "Informed consent by children and participation in an influenza trial." *American Journal of Public Health* 68 (1978), pp. 1979–2082.

Miller, S. K.: "Few take up offer of genetic screening." *New Scientist* (Sept. 18, 1993), p. 139.

Millstein, S. G., Adler, N. E., and Irwin, C. E.: "Conceptions of illness in young adolescents." *Pediatrics* 68 (1981), pp. 834–9.

National Society of Genetic Counselors (NSGC): "Prenatal and childhood testing for adult-onset disorders." *Perspectives in Genetic Counseling* 17 (1995).

Nicholson, R. H.: *Medical Research with Children: Ethics, Law, and Practice* (Oxford: Oxford University Press, 1986).

Perrin, E. C. and Gerrity, J. S.: "There's a demon in your belly: children's understanding of illness." *Pediatrics* 67 (1981), pp. 841–9.

Platt, A. M.: *The Child Savers: The Invention of Delinquency* (Chicago: University of Chicago Press, 1969).

Ruddick, W.: "Questions parents should resist." In Kopelman, L. M. and Moskop, J. C., eds.: *Children and Healthcare: Moral and Social Issues* (Dordrecht, Netherlands: Kluwer Academic Publishers, 1989), pp. 221–30.

Science: "ELSI's cystic fibrosis experiment" (editorial). *Science* 274, (1996), p. 489.

Science: "Gene tests get tested" (editorial). *Science* 275 (1997), p. 781.

Spinetta, J. J.: "Adjustment and adaptation in children with cancer." In Spinetta, J. J. and Deasy-Spinetta, P., eds.: *Living with Childhood Cancer*, (St. Louis: Mosby-Yearbook, 1981), pp. 5–17.

Susman, E. J., Dorn, L. D., and Fletcher, J. C.: "Reasoning about health and illness in ill and healthy children and adolescents: cognitive and emotional developmental aspects." *Developmental and Behavioral Pediatrics* 8 (1987), pp. 266–73.

Tyler, A., Morris, M., Lazarou, L., Meredith, L., Myring, J., and Harper, P.: "Presymptomatic testing for Huntington's disease in Wales 1987–1990." *British Journal of Psychiatry* 161 (1992), pp. 481–8.

United States, National Commission for the Protection of Human Subjects of Biomedical and Behavioral Research: *Report and Recommendations: Research Involving Children. US Dept. of Health, Education, and Welfare* (Washington, DC: DHEW publication OS 77–0004, 1 (1977)), p. 1213.

United States, President's Commission for the Study of Ethical Problems in Medicine and Biomedical and Behavioral Research: *Making Healthcare Decisions.* (Washington, DC: US Government Printing Office, 1982), pp. 175–91.

United States, President's Commission for the Study of Ethical Problems in Medicine and Biomedical and Behavioral Research: *Screening and Counseling for Genetic Conditions.* (Washington, DC: US Government Printing Office, 1983).

Wertz, D. C.: "Geneticists' ethical views: a survey in 37 nations." Paper presented at the European Society of Human Genetics, Berlin (May, 1995).

Wertz, D. C.: "Society and the not-so-new genetics: what are we afraid of? Some future predictions from a social scientist." *Journal of Contemporary Health Law and Policy* 13 (1997), pp. 299–346.

Wertz, D. C.: "International perspectives." In Clarke, A., ed.: *Genetic Testing of Children* (Oxford: Bios Scientific Publishers, 1998).

Wertz, D. C., Fanos, J. H., and Reilly, P. R.: "Genetic testing for children and adolescents: who decides?" *Journal of the American Medical Association* 272 (1994), pp. 875–81.

Wertz, D. C. and Fletcher, J. C. eds.: *Ethics and Human Genetics: A Cross-cultural Perspective* (Heidelberg; Springer-Verlag, 1989).

Wertz, D. C. and Fletcher, J. C.: "Ethical and social issues in prenatal sex selection: a survey of geneticists in 37 nations." *Social Science and Medicine* 46 (1998), pp. 255–73.

Wertz, D. C., Fletcher, J. C., and Mulvihill, J. J.: "Medical geneticists confront ethical dilemmas: Cross-cultural comparisons among 18 nations." *American Journal of Human Genetics* 46 (1990), pp. 1210–13.

Wertz, D. C. and Reilly, P. R.: "Laboratory policies and practices for the genetic testing of children: a survey of the Helix network." *American Journal of Human Genetics* 61 (1997), pp. 1163–8.

Wertz, D. C., Rosenfield, J. M., Janes, S. R., and Erbe, R. W.: "Attitudes toward abortion among parents of children with cystic fibrosis." *American Journal of Public Health* 81 (1991), pp. 992–4.

World Health Organization (WHO): *Guidelines on Ethical Issues in Medical Genetics and the Provision of Genetics Services*, prepared by Wertz, D. C., Fletcher, J. C., and Berg, K. (Unofficial publication, 1995, Hereditary Diseases Program, WHO, Geneva).

World Health Organization (WHO): *Proposed International Guidelines on Ethical Issues in Medical Genetics and Genetics Services* (draft document, 1998), http://www.who.int/ncd/hgn/hgnethic.htm, World Health Organization, Human Genetics Program, Division of Noncommunicable Diseases.

Zeesman, S., Clow, C. L., Cartier, L., and Scriver, P. R.: "A private view of heterozygosity: eight-year follow-up study on carriers of the Tay-Sachs gene detected by high school screening in Montreal." *American Journal of Human Genetics* 18 (1984), pp. 769–78.

Further reading

American Medical Association Council on Ethical and Judicial Affairs: "Testing children for genetic status." *Code of Medical Ethics, Report 66* (Chicago: American Medical Association, 1995).

Clarke, A.: *The Genetic Testing of Children* (Oxford: Bios Scientific Publishers, 1998).

Clinical Genetics Society: "The genetic testing of children: report of a working party of the Clinical Genetics Society." (Angus Clarke, Chair.) *Journal of Medical Genetics* 31 (1994), pp. 785–97.

Kopelman, L. M. and Moskop, J. C., eds.: *Children and Healthcare: Moral and Social Issues* (Dordrecht, Netherlands: Kluwer Academic Publishers, 1989).

Melton, G. B., Koocher, G. P., and Saks, M. J., eds.: *Children's Competence to Consent* (New York: Plenum Press, 1983).

Nicholson, R. H.: *Medical Research with Children: Ethics, Law, and Practice* (Oxford: Oxford University Press, 1986).

Wertz, D. C., Fanos, J. H., and Reilly, P. R.: "Genetic testing for children and adolescents: who decides?" *Journal of the American Medical Association* 272 (1994), pp. 875–81.

World Health Organization (WHO): *Proposed International Guidelines on Ethical Issues in Medical Genetics and Genetic Services* (draft document, 1998), http://www.who.int/ncd/hgn/hgnethic.htm, World Health Organization, Human Genetics Program, Division of Noncommunicable Diseases.

9

Genetic Testing of Children: Who Should Consent?

LAINIE FRIEDMAN ROSS

Introduction: Informed Consent and the Doctor–Patient Relationship

Informed consent is at the foundation of clinical ethics and the doctor–patient relationship. Informed consent is meant to be a process in which physicians provide medical information and discuss its significance with an individual patient so that the patient can make decisions that best reflect his or her own values. Informed consent is important both at the diagnostic stage as well as at the therapeutic stage. It includes discussing the risks and benefits of the proposed procedures or therapies, the possible alternatives, and the decision to forgo testing or treatment. Ideally, the consent process is a dialogue that proceeds through time, but the final decision belongs to the patient.

Informed consent and the doctor–patient relationship are more complicated in genetics. The traditional confidential nature of the doctor–patient relationship is challenged by genetics because an individual's diagnosis is not an isolated diagnosis but reflects disease probability or risk factors in siblings, parents, children, and other blood relatives. This raises consent issues because information about one individual may inadvertently give information about other family members, including those who may not wish to know. Informed consent for genetic services is further complicated by the fact that results often signify disease predilection, not definitive diagnoses. Even when testing provides a definitive diagnosis, treatments are only in the experimental stages. Add to this the fact that studies reveal that both physicians and patients have a difficult time grasping probabilities, and that many physicians and patients do not understand genetics.[1]

Informed consent and the doctor–patient relationship are even more complicated in pediatrics where the doctor–patient dyad is a triad that includes the physician, the child, and his or her parents. Traditionally, parents made decisions for their children, although currently there are movements around the world to increase the child's own voice,[2] particularly the older child. And in fact, some argue that mature children (specifically adolescents) should be allowed to make their own decisions without their parents' permission, even without their parents' awareness (Holt 1974; Cohen 1980; Alderson and Montgomery 1996). Whether this autonomy should be expanded to genetic services depends on what role one believes that children should have in healthcare decisions generally and whether one believes that decision-making in genetics is comparable to other healthcare decisions. In this chapter, I examine the process of informed consent for genetic testing of children.

The Role of Children in the Informed Consent Process

With rare exception, parental consent is sought for all pediatric healthcare decisions in the United States.[3] There is, however, a movement in the United States as well as in many other countries to allow older children to consent to their own medical treatment. For the consent to be informed means that the consent is informed (made knowingly), is competent (made intelligently), and is voluntary (Grisso and Vierling 1978: 415). The literature shows that most healthcare decisions do not fulfill the three components of informed consent, and this is true for adults (Appelbaum et al. 1987: 57–62) and children (Grisso and Vierling 1978: 415).

Intuitively one would postulate that the biggest difference between children and adults is their ability to understand diagnostic or treatment alternatives and the consequences of each possible decision. But the empirical data are insufficient to show whether consent given by adults is significantly different (presumably better) than consent given by competent children. The few studies that do compare adolescent and adult decision-making have not shown marked differences in process or content (Grisso and Vierling 1978; Weithorn and Campbell 1982; Gardner et al. 1989). If competency is all that is necessary for healthcare autonomy, then adolescents should be given healthcare autonomy, and this also would hold true for genetic services, unless there are particular facts about genetic services that make adolescents particularly vulnerable.

The moral argument against giving adolescents independent autonomy to consent to healthcare is based on the general claim that competency is necessary but not sufficient for autonomy (Ross 1997). Two arguments to support the continued participation of parents in their children's healthcare decisions are (1) to provide children with a protected period in which to develop "enabling virtues" – habits, including the habit of self-control, which advance their lifetime autonomy and opportunities (Purdy 1992: 45) rather than rely on a mere threshold level of competency; and (2) to provide children with the opportunities to gain world experience, the lack of which "distorts [one's] capacity for sound judgement" (Gaylin 1982: 35). Parental participation is also supported by the pragmatic argument that parents are responsible for the moral, physical, and emotional well-being of their children, and this requires them to ensure for their child's medical well-being as well. The parents' role may even be stronger in the context of genetics because treatment may not be available, the results may be ambiguous, and the value of testing may depend upon how one interprets and integrates the psychosocial implications of the results. Data are scant (Michie 1996), although theoretically it would seem that even mature adolescents are at a disadvantage due to their lack of world experience, and focus on short-term considerations rather than long-term or overall impact. This does not argue against a role for children in the decision-making process for genetic testing, but it may argue against giving them independent autonomy.

In this chapter I examine four clinical contexts in which genetic testing of children occurs. I discuss what roles the parents and children should play. The issues regarding consent for genetic research, particularly experimental gene therapies and the storage of blood by researchers for future uses, are even more complex and are deferred for another time.

Newborn Screening: Mandatory Screening versus Informed Consent

The whole issue of consent for genetic testing of children has been overridden in the US in newborn screening programs which are universally state-mandated in 49 of the 50 states.[4] Although each state has a different panel of tests, the most common tests are phenylketonuria (PKU), hypothyroidism, hemoglobinopathies (including sickle-cell disease), congenital adrenal hyperplasia (CAH), and galactosemia (AAP 1996: 474). All of the conditions listed above are autosomal recessive conditions (except hypothyroidism, which is sporadic), meaning that an affected child has two asymptomatic parents who carry this recessive allele, and the affected child is homozygous recessive (received a recessive gene from each parent).

Each of the conditions listed above meets the criteria for universal screening: each represents an important health problem for which there is an accepted cost-effective treatment which, if begun early, can prevent many if not all of the negative sequella of the condition. The screening test is simple and cheap and the follow-up testing is highly accurate (Wilson and Jungner 1968: 8).

The major benefit of mandatory screening is to ensure that all children are screened in order to treat quickly and accurately those who are affected (true positives) and to reassure those who do not have the disease (true negatives).

The major danger of mandatory screening is that tests may become institutionalized prior to an adequate understanding of what the test can and cannot do. Consider, for example, the history of PKU screening. In 1963, Massachusetts adopted a mandatory screening program despite the fact that a collaborative project to study the effects of dietary restriction on the physical, cognitive, and psychosocial development of PKU testing did not begin until 1967. Many other states implemented mandatory PKU statutes before it was known that there were children with elevated levels of phenylalanine who would not respond to a phenylalanine-free diet, or that there were some benign causes of elevated levels of phenylalanine which did not require treatment (Acuff and Faden 1991: 64–7). The result was that some healthy children were placed on these diets, which led to malnourishment if not iatrogenic retardation (Holtzman 1970).

The major arguments against requiring parental consent for newborn screening are that the process is time-consuming and that even when consent is sought, the consent is perfunctory and not informed (Statham et al. 1993). But these arguments do not support the conclusion that consent is unnecessary The time required does not need to be excessive (Holtzman et al. 1983), and is justified by its value in educating women about medical tests that can promote their child's well-being. If the consent is perfunctory, that does not argue against the need for consent, but is a criticism of the physicians who are not fulfilling their role in the consent process. Universal testing in the newborn period is desirable and achievable because virtually all parents want to do what is best for their children, and for most parents this means diagnosing and treating medical conditions safely and effectively.

In contrast, the arguments in favor of parental consent are persuasive. Parental consent serves several important functions. First, parental consent is sought for all medical care of children to promote their well-being and to protect them from harm. Consent serves as a symbol of respect for the family, respect which is well-placed given that families are the primary source of child rearing, and given that families, and not the state, will bear the greatest costs if an affected child is not screened and diagnosis is delayed. Second, procuring parental consent serves a valuable educative role. By requiring consent, parents must be educated about the purpose and limitations of screening, which may give them an incentive to follow up on abnormal screening results. Knowledge of negative test results also may be reassuring to parents, particularly those with personal knowledge of any of the conditions being tested. I support the repeal of the mandatory statutes in favor of laws that mandate physicians to recommend newborn screening yet still require parental consent.

Testing Young Children for Early-onset Genetic Conditions

Testing young children (children who do not have decision-making capacity) for early-onset conditions includes two very different categories of conditions: those, like retinoblastoma and familial adenomatosis polyposis, for which early diagnosis and treatment save lives; and those, like Duchenne's muscular dystrophy and cystic fibrosis, for which early diagnosis and treatment does not affect the course of the disease. The value of presymptomatic testing in the first category is to prevent serious morbidity and mortality. Children in at-risk families should be tested or undergo frequent surveillance exams. Failure to do either is neglectful as it places children at unnecessary and imminent risk. Physicians morally can respect parental refusal for genetic testing provided that the parents arrange for frequent surveillance. If parents refuse diagnostic work-ups (in a child who has a positive genetic test or in a child whose genetic status is unknown or inconclusive), physicians should feel compelled to seek state permission to override their refusal.

In the second category, the value of presymptomatic diagnosis are (1) to help avoid delay in diagnosis when early symptoms are nonspecific, (2) to target surveillance screening more accurately, (3) to allow parents to prepare for a child who will have special needs, and (4) to be useful for parents in their own reproductive planning. There are also potential psychological benefits of reducing family uncertainty about the future and allowing for more practical planning (ASHG/ACMG 1995). Particularly for families in which there is another affected child, a negative result may serve to reassure parents that nonspecific symptoms are not signs of impending disease. On the other hand, early diagnosis may create a vulnerable child, have adverse impact on parent–child bonding, adversely impact on the child's self-image and self-esteem, may cause difficulties for the parents to obtain appropriate health insurance for the child and even healthy siblings, and parental expectations for the future also may be unnecessarily limited (ASHG/ACMG 1995).

117

The risk–benefit balance of presymptomatic testing for conditions like cystic fibrosis will depend on the values and needs of each family. Physicians need to be aware of the possibility for presymptomatic diagnosis and must be prepared to counsel families about the risks and benefits of testing. Some parents may value such information, particularly if they know an affected biological relative; other parents may choose to remain uninformed unless (until) the child develops symptoms, so as to avoid treating the child as vulnerable before the child becomes ill. Given that early testing has not been shown to improve morbidity or mortality, such presymptomatic testing clearly goes beyond the definition of what states can morally mandate.[5] Physicians should be nondirective in their dialogue and respect a decision to test as well as a decision not to test.[6] If testing is deferred, the physician should keep in mind the patient's risk factors and be vigilant in clinical practice in case the child develops related symptoms.

Testing Children for Late-onset Genetic Conditions

Testing children for late-onset genetic conditions is highly controversial and has been the focus of much of the debate on consent for genetic testing in pediatrics (Working Party of the Clinical Genetics Society 1994; Wertz et al. 1994; Hoffman and Wulfsberg 1995; Clayton 1997; AAP 2001). These conditions can be divided into two categories. In the first category are conditions like Huntington's disease in which presymptomatic testing virtually guarantees the development or freedom from the disease, but for which there are no known treatments to modify or prevent the course of illness. In the second category are the majority of conditions for which genetic testing only reveals an increased or decreased probability for a particular condition. For example, women who carry the BRCA1 gene have as high as an 85 percent lifetime risk of developing breast cancer (Ford et al. 1994; Struewin et al. 1997), with variability depending on particular genetic mutations as well as other genetic, dietary, hormonal, and environmental factors. This compares with an 11 percent lifetime risk of developing breast cancer in the general population (Feuer et al. 1993).

Studies have been done to understand the knowledge, attitudes, and practices of individuals in families at risk for late-onset genetic conditions. One of the most studied conditions is Huntington's disease (HD), an autosomal dominant condition of early-onset dementia. Before genetic testing became available, studies found that most individuals in at-risk families claimed that they would want to know their HD risk status (Schoenfeld et al. 1984; Meissen and Berchek 1987), even if nothing could be offered to change the course of their illness. But as testing became available, the number of at-risk individuals who sought testing was much lower than predicted. Currently, less than 15 percent of individuals at risk for HD have been tested despite the availability of genetic testing for over five years (Craufurd et al. 1989; Bloch et al. 1992; Benjamin et al. 1994).

When predictive testing is done in asymptomatic adults, testing is done in a setting in which recipients receive pre- and post-test counseling. For some, knowledge is important for making career decisions, family reproductive decisions, and for reducing the anxiety of the unknown. For many, however, uncertainty allows them to remain hopeful that they are unaffected. Recipients of both positive and negative results may have surprising psychological reactions to their test results. While one might expect those who test positive to suffer depression, distress, or increased anxiety, some find the result liberating as they can now make realistic plans about the future. For many who test negative, there is great relief, but some suffer what is known as survivor's guilt. These reactions cannot be predicted *a priori* (Marteau and Croyle 1998).

In the early years of predictive testing, particularly when testing for Huntington's disease required linkage analysis, the desire not to know was deemed to trump the desire to know, and individuals whose family members refused to participate in linkage analysis were not able to be tested. Now that the specific gene has been located, direct genetic testing is available. Individuals are counseled about the possible negative impact on family members, but an informed request is usually honored.

What about children? Should they be tested for late-onset diseases, particularly for those conditions for which no treatment exists? If parents can choose to have their children tested, the children lose the right not to know as adults, and it is well-known that many patients choose not to know. On the other hand, an outright ban prohibits adults from having the right to have known since childhood, and this may interfere with their ability to incorporate this information into their personal identity.

The empirical data about the psychological impact of testing children for late-onset conditions are lacking. Despite the lack of evidence, virtually all geneticists and specialists argue against providing such services.[7] General pediatricians, on the other hand, are more divided about whether parents should have the right to have their children tested for these conditions.[8] In some cases, there may be reasons why families will benefit (or at least believe they will benefit) from such knowledge. The potential benefits of testing children for late-onset diseases are that it may foster openness within the family, allow the child to adjust to his genetic destiny, reduce the anxiety associated with not knowing, and identify children who will need genetic counseling before child-bearing. A positive result, however, may adversely affect the parent–child relationship, distort the family's perception of the child, lead to unnecessarily limited expectations of the child, adversely affect the child's self-esteem, and lead to discrimination in education, employment, or insurance. Of course, data show that many families often label or scapegoat one or more children as positive, and treat the child differently than siblings, even without testing (Kessler 1988). If the child tests negative, in contrast, it may bring great relief, although that too may distort family relationships if some children test negative and others positive.

The issue then becomes whether families have the right to decide what is best for them (Sharpe 1993), or whether this should be imposed by professionals. Generally, when the balance between benefits and harms of a medical option are unknown, decision-making is left to the family. There is an expectation that parents will act to promote their child's best interest, although many ethicists realize that parents often need to balance an individual child's interest with the needs and interests of the family (Ross 1997; Clayton 1997: 234–7). This is morally acceptable as long as the child's interests are promoted, even if they are not maximized.

For those who believe that the decision belongs to the family and not the professional, there is still the question of what role the child should play in the decision-making process. Some argue that testing should be deferred until the child can at least assent, which is often defined as school age (6 or 7 years); others would argue to defer testing until adolescence when the child can give an informed consent. Most ethicists would hold the child's dissent as binding when such testing does not offer clear and direct medical benefits (Wertz et al. 1994). I support a policy of discouraging parental requests for children of all ages because it allows the child to decide whether to know or not to know as an adult. However, I would not prohibit testing of the young child, as there may be children and families in which the benefits of testing outweigh the risks. Still, even in these cases, I would try to convince parents to defer testing until their child can participate in the decision-making process, at which time the child's dissent should be binding.

Should adolescents have the right to make these decisions independently? Even if one supports confidential healthcare for older children, one must ask whether genetic services are different. Several arguments against granting adolescents autonomy for genetic services are: (1) they potentially provide a great deal of information about one's parents (including nonbiological parentage); (2) they have significant short-term and long-term psychosocial implications which children are neither emotionally nor cognitively fully able to grasp (Fanos 1997; Clayton 1997: 246); and (3) the pragmatic arguments that support adolescent autonomy for sexually transmitted diseases, for example, do not apply, as there are no advantages, only potential disadvantages, to expediency. Given the serious psychosocial risks of genetic testing for late-onset diseases, particularly those for which no current treatment can modify the course, I do not support a policy which allows adolescents to seek genetic testing for late-onset conditions without parental involvement. There may be reasons that parents refuse to allow their adolescents to be tested, including (1) concerns for their child's future health insurability and employability; (2) concerns of misattributed paternity; and (3) concerns regarding the parents' ability to cope with their sense of guilt about their child's genetic risk factors.

Testing Children for Carrier Status

All individuals carry recessive genes that can result in significant health conditions if their children are born with two such genes. Usually carriers are asymptomatic and unaware. Although carrier status may be integral for reproductive decision-making, it is rarely relevant to an individual's medical well-being. In general, then, it is unnecessary to test children for carrier status.

Do parents have the right to know the carrier status of their children? The issue comes in two forms. First, in some newborn screening programs such as testing for sickle-cell anemia, screening identifies carriers as well as those affected with the disease. The follow-up test distinguishes children with disease from children with trait. The Institute of Medicine (IOM) of the National Academy of Science has argued against informing parents of their child's carrier status (Andrews et al. 1994: 174–5), although most screening programs currently do inform parents. In part, the rationale for disclosure is pragmatic: how do you ask a parent to bring her or his child for follow-up testing and not disclose the reason why follow-up is necessary? There is also a moral argument in favor of informing parents: to withhold trait status from parents implies that the state, and not the parents, are the guardians or the owner of such information on behalf of the child.

Another argument in favor of disclosing trait status is that carrier status may have important implications for the child's parents. If parents do not know that they carry such alleles, learning that a child is a carrier can serve as a warning that future children may be at risk. It may lead each of them to be tested for carrier status. The Institute of Medicine specifically rejected using the child's test result as a means for providing reproductive information to parents. Their argument is based on a flawed understanding of Kant's categorical imperative: "Act in such a way that you treat humanity, whether in your own person or in the person of another, always at the same time as an end and never simply as a means" (Kant 1981, para. 429). The IOM misunderstood the categorical imperative to prohibit the use of persons as means; when, in fact, the categorical imperative prohibits the use of persons *solely* as a means. Testing a child for sickle-cell anemia is done because early prophylaxis with penicillin is known to decrease morbidity and mortality (AAP 1996: 491–3). In the process of determining disease status, the child may be found to be a carrier, which has reproductive implications for the child's parents and for him- or herself in years to come. As such, the primary goal is to promote the child's well-being, and only secondarily does the child serve as a means by which his or her parents learn of their potential reproductive genetic risks.

The second type of case in which carrier status information is sought comes in the form of parents who request carrier testing for their child on a "want-to-know" basis. Often the interest is prompted by the diagnosis of a relative with the disease. Other parents may seek such information in response to an educational outreach program. The main arguments for refusing parental requests for carrier testing of children are: (1) it frustrates the child's right not to know as an adult; (2) it fails to respect the child's right to confidential reproductive knowledge; and (3) it may adversely impact on the child's self-concept. There is also concern that parental misunderstanding of test results will lead to treating the child with trait as an ill or potentially ill child (Fanos 1997: 25). The arguments in favor of honoring the parents' requests are that being informed of carrier status in childhood may be easier to accept and incorporate into one's personal identity (Fanos 1997: 23), that it may be useful for other family members, and that parents, not the state, are in a better position to decide if the benefits of knowledge outweigh the risks for a particular child.

I disagree with the IOM's recommendation to withhold from parents carrier status information that is determined as an incidental finding, and I support the current practice of disclosure. The more interesting question is whether to respect parental requests to test their children for carrier status without clinical indications, or to defer testing until the child is able to participate in his or her own medical decisions and can be counseled directly about testing. Here, I support a policy of discouraging carrier testing of children because it serves no immediate medical benefit. At minimum, I would try to convince parents to defer testing until their child can participate in the decision-making process. But I would not prohibit testing of the young child, as there may be cases in which parents do decide that the benefits outweigh the risks.[9]

121

Should the adolescent be able to learn of his or her trait status without parental involvement? Given the potential for serious psychological stress and misunderstanding of genetics (Ponder et al. 1996), and the public's poor understanding of genetics,[10] I believe that such testing is best done with parental involvement. As such, I do not advocate state- supported programs which encourage mass screening of adolescents in high schools without parental consent (Clow and Scriver 1977).

Conclusion

Genetics is a rapidly evolving field. It has great potential for changing how we see ourselves, how health is understood, and how medicine is practiced. It also has great potential for being misused or abused, particularly while our knowledge is incomplete. As such, informed consent for genetic testing is critical. This is particularly true in pediatrics, where errors may lead to long-term morbidity or lifelong social stigmatization.

In this chapter, I have argued that parents should play a major role in deciding whether their children should undergo genetic testing. I encourage policies which require parental consent for all genetic testing of children, even in the newborn nursery. I believe that there are some genetic tests which are best deferred until adulthood, but I am willing to respect the request of well-counseled parents to test their children, as they are in the best position to determine what is best for their child and their family.

I have also argued for the inclusion of children in the consent process, even when their consent is not binding. I believe that the child's dissent should be binding for genetic testing of late-onset conditions for which there are no known therapies or preventive measures that can be introduced in childhood. However, I have also argued that I do not believe that adolescents should have independent autonomy in deciding whether or not to undergo genetic testing for any of the clinical cases discussed.

Acknowledgments

I would like to thank Angela Scheuerle, MD, for her comments on this manuscript. This paper was supported in part by DOE grant, Geneticization of Primary Care, DE-FG02-95ER611990PI, and by an Irving Harris Grant; Ethical Analysis and Public Policy Recommendations Regarding the Genetic Testing of Children.

Notes

1   With respect to physicians, see, for example, Geller, G. and Holtzman, N. A.: "Implications of the human genome initiative for the primary care physician," *Bioethics* 5 (1991), pp. 318–25; Hofman, K. J et al.: "Physicians' knowledge of genetics and genetic tests," *Academic Medicine* 68 (1993), pp. 625–32; and Giardiello, F. M. et al.: "The use and

interpretation of commercial APC gene testing for familial adenomatous polyposis," *New England Journal of Medicine* 336 (1997), pp. 823–7.

With respect to patients, see, for example, Andrews, L. B.: "Compromised consent: deficiencies in the consent process for genetic testing," *Journal of the American Medical Women's Association* 52 (1997), pp. 39–42, 44; Durant, J. et al.: "Public understanding of the new genetics," in Marteau, T. and Richards, M., eds.: *The Troubled Helix: Social and Psychological Implications of the New Human Genetics* (Cambridge: Cambridge University Press, 1996), pp. 235–48.

2   In Great Britain, the legal age of healthcare decisions is 16 (Family Law Reform Act, 1969), in contrast with 18 in the US. The *Gillick* decision encouraged physicians to respect the consent of minors younger than 16 on a case-by-case judgment of competency (*Gillick v. W Norfolk & Wisbech* HA [1985] 3 All ER 402). However, several more recent cases substantially limit this ruling. See, *Re R* [1991] 4 All ER 177; *Re W* [1992] 4 All ER 627; *Re E* [1993] 1 FLR 386; and *Re S* (1994) 2 FLR 1065.

In the US, the recent policy statement by the Committee on Bioethics of the American Academy of Pediatrics recommends that competent children be given sole decision-making autonomy and that the dissent of the child with developing competency should be determinative when the therapy can be deferred without substantial risk. If the child dissents to life-saving care, the child can be overruled; nevertheless, attempts should be made to persuade the child to assent for "coercion in diagnosis or treatment is a last resort." Committee on Bioethics, American Academy of Pediatrics, "Informed consent, parental permission, and assent in pediatric practice," *Pediatrics* 95 (1995), pp. 314–17.

3   Exceptions include (1) healthcare for mature minors or emancipated minors, (2) medical emergencies for any child, (3) treatment for conditions which fall under the specialized consent statutes (statutes which grant adolescents the right to seek confidential care for contraception, for the diagnosis and treatment of sexually transmitted diseases, and for mental health), and (4) mandatory newborn screening (which is discussed later in the chapter).

4   Maryland had state-mandated screening but repealed it in 1976 for a statute and regulations requiring informed parental consent.

5   In reality, some states do mandate testing for cystic fibrosis. Internationally, some countries test newborns for Duchenne's muscular dystrophy.

6   This is the position taken by The American Society of Human Genetics Board of Directors/ American College of Medical Genetics, Board of Directors (ASHG/ACMG), "Points to consider: ethical, legal and psychological implications of genetic testing in children and adolescents," *American Journal of Human Genetics* 57 (1995), pp. 1233–41, and the Working Party of the Clinical Genetics Society (UK), "The genetic testing of children," *Journal of Medical Genetics* 31 (1994), pp. 785–97.

7   See the position taken by the ASHG/ACMG, p. 1233, the Working Party of the Clinical Genetics Society, p. 785, and the report of the Institute of Medicine of the National Academy of Science (US): Andrews, L. B. et al., eds.: *Assessing Genetic Risks: Implications for Health and Social Policy* (Washington DC: National Academy Press, 1994). Two position statements by subspecialty organizations are: "Guidelines for the molecular genetics predictive test in Huntington's disease," *Neurology* 44 (1994), pp. 1533–6; and "Gene testing in autosomal dominant polycystic kidney disease: results of National Kidney Foundation workshop," Scientific Advisory Board of the National Kidney Foundation, *American Journal of Kidney Diseases* 13 (1989), pp. 85–7.

8   The Working Party of the Clinical Genetics Society sent out a survey to several thousand healthcare professionals and then published their findings as an appendix to their article (pp. 795–7). Whereas only 2 of 49 geneticists would test a 5-year-old for Huntington's disease at the parents' request, 100 out of 189 pediatricians would (p. 796).

9   Again, this issue was raised in the questionnaire sent out by the Working Party. The issue came up over the question of testing healthy siblings of affected patients. Pediatricians were more likely to test than were geneticists.

10 Durant et al. cite many of the international studies which show poor understanding of genetics in many developed countries. Durant et al.: "Public understanding of the new genetics," in Marteau, T. and Richards, M., eds.: *The Troubled Helix: Social and Psychological Implications of the New Human Genetics* (Cambridge: Cambridge University Press, 1996), pp. 235–48.

References

(AAP) American Academy of Pediatrics, Committee on Genetics: "Newborn screening fact sheets." *Pediatrics* 98 (1996), pp. 473–501.

(AAP) American Academy of Pediatrics, Committee on Bioethics: "Ethical issues with genetic testing in pediatrics." *Pediatrics* 107 (2001), pp. 451–5.

Acuff, K. L. and Faden, R. R.: "A history of prenatal and newborn screening programs: lessons for the future." In Faden, R., Geller, G., and Powers, M., eds.: *AIDS, Women and the Next Generation* (New York: Oxford University Press, 1991), pp. 59–93.

Alderson, P. and Montgomery, J.: *Healthcare Choices: Making Decisions with Children* (London, UK: Institute for Public Policy Research, 1996).

Andrews, L. B. et al., eds.: *Assessing Genetic Risks: Implications for Health and Social Policy* (Washington, DC: National Academy Press, 1994).

Appelbaum, P. S., Lidz, C. W., and Meisel, A.: *Informed Consent: Legal Theory and Clinical Practice* (New York: Oxford University Press, 1987).

(ASHG/ACMG) The American Society of Human Genetics Board of Directors/American College of Medical Genetics, Board of Directors: "Points to consider: ethical, legal and psychological implications of genetic testing in children and adolescents." *American Journal of Human Genetics* 57 (1995), pp. 1233–41.

Benjamin, C. M. et al.: "Proceed with care: direct predictive testing for Huntington disease." *American Journal of Human Genetics* 55 (1994), pp. 606–17.

Bloch, M. et al.: "Predictive testing for Huntington disease in Canada: the experience of those receiving an increased risk." *American Journal of Medical Genetics* 42 (1992), pp. 499–507.

Clayton, E. W.: "Genetic testing in children." *The Journal of Medicine and Philosophy* 22 (1997), pp. 233–51.

Clow, C. L. and Scriver, C. R.: "The adolescent copes with genetic screening: a study of Tay-Sachs screening among high-school students." In Kaback, M., ed.: *Tay-Sachs Disease: Screening and Prevention. Progress in Clinical and Biological Research* 18 (1977), pp. 381–93.

Cohen, H.: *Equal Rights for Children* (Totowa, NJ: Rowman and Littlefield, 1980).

Craufurd, D., Dodge, A., Kerzin-Storrar, L., and Harris, R. "Uptake of presymptomatic predictive testing for Huntington's disease." *Lancet* 2, 8663 (Sept. 9, 1989), pp. 603–5.

Fanos, J. H.: "Developmental tasks of childhood and adolescence: implications for genetic testing." *American Journal of Medical Genetics* 71 (1997), pp. 22–8.

Feuer, E. J. et al.: "The lifetime risk of developing breast cancer." *Journal of the National Cancer Institute* 85 (1993), pp. 892–7.

Ford, D. et al.: "Risks of cancer in BRCA1-mutation carriers." *Lancet* 343 (1994), pp. 692–5.

Gardner, W., Scherer, D., and Tester, M.: "Asserting scientific authority: cognitive development and adolescent legal rights." *American Psychologist* 44 (1989), pp. 897–9.

Gaylin, W.: "Competence: no longer all or none." In Gaylin, W. and Macklin, R., eds.: *Who Speaks for the Child: The Problems of Proxy Consent* (New York: Plenum Press, 1982), pp. 27–54.

Grisso, T. and Vierling, L.: Minor's consent to treatment: a developmental perspective." *Professional Psychology* 9 (1978), pp. 412–27.

Hoffmann, D. E. and Wulfsberg, E. A.: "Testing children for genetic predispositions: is it in their best interest?" *Journal of Law, Medicine, and Ethics* 23 (1995), pp. 331–44.

Holt, J.: *Escape from Childhood* (New York: E. P. Dutton and Co., 1974).

Holtzman, N.: "Dietary treatment of inborn errors of metabolism." *Annual Review of Medicine* 21 (1970), pp. 335–56.

Holtzman, N. A. et al.: "Effect of informed parental consent on mothers' knowledge of newborn screening." 72 *Pediatrics* (1983), pp. 807–12.

Kant, I.: *Grounding for the Metaphysics of Morals* (1785). Trans. J. W. Ellington (Indianapolis, IN: Hackett Publishing Co., 1981).

Kessler, S.: "Preselection: a family coping strategy in Huntington disease." *American Journal of Medical Genetics* 31 (1988), pp. 617–21.

Marteau, T. M. and Croyle, R. T.: "The new genetics: psychological responses to genetic testing." *British Medical Journal* 316 (1998), pp. 693–6.

Meissen, G. J. and Berchek, R. L.: "Intended use of predictive testing by those at risk for Huntington disease." *American Journal of Medical Genetics* 26 (1987), pp. 283–93.

Michie, S.: "Predictive genetic testing in children." In Marteau, T. and Richards, M., eds.: *The Troubled Helix: Social and Psychological Implications of the New Human Genetics* (Cambridge: Cambridge University Press, 1996), pp. 177–83.

Ponder, M. et al.: "Family history and perceived vulnerability to some common diseases: a study of young people and their parents." *Journal of Medical Genetics* 33 (1996), pp. 485–92.

Purdy, L. M.: *In Their Best Interest? The Case Against Equal Rights for Children* (New York: Cornell University Press, 1992).

Ross, L. F. "Healthcare decision making by children: is it in their best interest?" *Hastings Center Report* 27 (1997), pp. 41–5.

Schoenfeld, M. et al.: "Potential impact of a predictive test on the gene frequency of Huntington disease." *American Journal of Medical Genetics* 18 (1984), pp. 423–9.

Sharpe, N. F.: "Presymptomatic testing for Huntington disease: is there a duty to test those under the age of eighteen years?" *American Journal of Medical Genetics* 46 (1993), pp. 250–3,

Statham H., Green, J., and Snowdon, C.: "Mothers' consent to screening newborn babies for disease." *British Medical Journal* 306 (1993), pp. 858–9.

Struewin, J. P. et al.: "The risk of cancer associated with specific mutations of BRCA1 and BRCA2 among Ashkenazi Jews." *New England Journal of Medicine* 336 (1997), pp. 1401–8.

Weithorn, L. and Campbell, S.: "The competency of children and adolescents to make informed treatment decisions." *Child Development* 53 (1982), pp. 89–98.

Wertz, D. C., Fanos, J. H., and Reilly, P. R.: "Genetic testing for children and adolescents: who decides?" *Journal of the American Medical Association* 272 (1994), pp. 875–81.

Wilson, J. M. G. and Jungner, F.: "Principles and practice of screening for disease." *Public Health Papers* 34. Geneva: WHO, 1968.

Working Party of the Clinical Genetics Society (UK): "The genetic testing of children." *Journal of Medical Genetics* 31 (1994), pp. 785–97.

Further reading

(ASHG/ACMG) The American Society of Human Genetics Board of Directors/American College of Medical Genetics, Board of Directors: "Points to consider: ethical, legal and psychological implications of genetic testing in children and adolescents." *American Journal of Human Genetics* 57 (1995), pp. 1233–41.

Clayton, E. W.: "Genetic testing in children." *The Journal of Medicine and Philosophy* 22 (1997), pp. 233–51.

Hoffmann, D. E. and Wulfsberg, E. A.: "Testing children for genetic predispositions: is it in their best interest?" *Journal of Law, Medicine, and Ethics* 23 (1995), pp. 331–44.

Wertz, D. C., Fanos, J. H., and Reilly, P. R.: "Genetic testing for children and adolescents: who decides?" *Journal of the American Medical Association* 272 (1994), pp. 875–81.

Working Party of the Clinical Genetics Society (UK): "The genetic testing of children." *Journal of Medical Genetics* 31 (1994), pp. 785–97.

10

Mapping the Human Genome and the Meaning of "Monster Mythology"

GEORGE J. ANNAS

Introduction

Pre-Columbian cartographers drew their maps to the extent of their knowledge, and then wrote in the margins, "Beyond this point there are dragons." With the voyage of Columbus, we lost both our fear of the geographic frontier and our innocence. We accept that knowledge can generally overpower fear; but we have also learned that the application of new knowledge often has a dark side that can lead to brutality and disaster. The discovery of America, for example, led to unforeseen value conflicts of justice and fairness involving native Americans that were "resolved" only by their merciless subjugation and genocidal destruction. The Columbus metaphor is a powerful one, one that emphasizes both the need to confront mythical dragons with knowledge, and the need to anticipate and plan for the real monsters, the value conflicts that new knowledge produces. Perhaps nowhere is the promise of benefit and the risk of harm so great as in genetic research. The plan to map and sequence the 3 billion base pairs that make up the genetic blueprint of a human being – the "Human Genome Project" – provides an opportunity to examine the relationship between science and society (Annas 1990). How can scientists and social policy-makers work together to maximize the benefits of this project while minimizing its dangers?

Monster Mythology

Since at least Elizabethan times, English literature has reflected a fascination with stories of scientists and physicians who have attempted to change the attributes of humankind, and the monsters their attempts have created. Shakespeare set the tone and provided the language and the setting for much of this cautionary literature. *The Tempest*, which is set on an island, forces us to confront the meaning of the natural. The lowly and grotesque Caliban is often seen as a monster, as when Trinculo says of him: "That a monster should be such a natural!" If we see nature as orderly, then the disorderly and deformed Caliban must be a monster (Langbaum 1964).

When Prospero's daughter Miranda, who has grown up with Caliban and the spirits but has seen no other humans, sees the shipwrecked party from Italy, she exclaims of them:

> O, wonder!
> How many goodly creatures are there here!
> How beauteous mankind is! O brave new world
> That has such people in't! (V.i.181–4)

At the end of the play, as Prospero prepares to return to the real world and reclaim his place as Duke of Milan, he breaks his magic wand. This gesture is properly been seen as the author's commentary on the relationship between art and life: art, or at least an enchanted island, is no place for man to live life longer, "but rather a place through which we pass in order to renew and strengthen our sense of reality" (Langbaum 1964: 9).

Huxley, of course, took the title of his most famous work on the social implications of the new genetics, *Brave New World*, from Miranda's description. Between Shakespeare and Huxley are two other writers that have altered our collective consciousness with the creatures they created: Mary Shelley and H. G. Wells.

Mary Shelley's masterpiece, *Frankenstein*, has become the metaphor for all scientific attempts to create life (Gaylin 1977). In her gothic novel, Victor Frankenstein is obsessed with creating life from a construction of dead body parts. Shelley does not explain how Victor was able to "infuse a spark of being into the lifeless thing," but she does describe Victor's emotions upon seeing "the dull yellow eye of the creature open":

> His limbs were in proportion, and I had selected his features as beautiful. Beautiful! Great God! His yellow skin scarcely covered the work of muscles and arteries beneath; his hair was of a lustrous black, and flowing; his teeth of a pearly whiteness . . . (Shelley 1817: 56)

But Victor's burst of emotion at achieving his goal quickly changes to horror as he gazes at the creature's "watery eyes . . . his shriveled complexion and straight black lips": "now that I had finished, the beauty of the dream vanished, and breathless horror and disgust filled my heart." Victor leaves his laboratory, sleeps, and the creature escapes. The remainder of the novel deals with the creature, which is never given a name but simply referred to as "the monster," and its relationship to Victor. Indeed, it seems most reasonable to consider the monster either as Victor's alter ego, or as a projection of his inner thoughts made flesh. Perhaps this is why we often think of the monster, instead of its creator, as Frankenstein. Victor's creation eventually kills his young nephew William, his friend Clerval, his wife Elizabeth, and, indirectly, Victor himself.

At one point in the story, the monster convinces Victor to create a wife for him. In this scene Victor is seen as God the creator, and the monster as his Adam, or alternatively, as Lucifer, the fallen angel. But having constructed the monster's would-be mate on a remote island, Victor decides he cannot give her life for fear that she and the monster might propagate a "race of devils" that would "make the very existence of the species of man a condition precarious and full of terror." Victor consequently tears the female's body apart while the monster looks on, letting out a "howl of devilish despair and revenge." This scene, as much as any other, focuses the theme of the novel: the scientist's simultaneous capacity for creation and destruction.

In *The Tempest*, Shakespeare sees the chaos of nature as a constructive force that helps renew social order. Mary Shelley's vision seems different: the orderliness of scientific research produces chaos and ultimately death. As one critic has put it, a "fitting epigraph" for *Frankenstein* may be the taunt of a Fury to Mary's husband, Percy Shelley's, Prometheus: "And all best things are thus confused to ill" (Bloom 1987).

Written 10 years before the word "gene" was coined in 1909 (according to the *OED*), H. G. Wells's *The Island of Dr. Moreau* brings us into the twentieth century. Like Prospero before him, Dr. Moreau is depicted as a god, if not as God himself, and rules over his island. And like Victor Frankenstein, the story involves the making of human beings by nonnatural means. Moreau has discovered how to combine transplant surgery and drugs to transform animals into creatures with a human-like shape and a human-like brain. His animal-men talk, and reject their animal (natural) ways. But they are grotesque in appearance, and their transformation is not permanent. When the shipwrecked Charles Prendick, the narrator of the tale, accuses Moreau of creating "an abomination," Moreau replies simply: "To this day I have never troubled about the ethics of the matter. The study of Nature makes a man at least as remorseless as Nature. I have gone on, not heeding anything but the question I was pursuing."

Eventually the creatures turn on Moreau and kill him; and the remainder of the tale relates the "slow and inevitable" reversion of the creatures from human to animal:

> Of course these creatures did not decline into such beasts as the reader has seen in zoological gardens – into ordinary bears, wolves, tigers, oxen, swine, and apes. There was something strange about each; in each Moreau had blended this animal with that; one perhaps was ursine chiefly, another feline chiefly, another bovine chiefly, but each was tainted with other creatures – a kind of generalized animalism appeared through the specific dispositions. And the dwindling shreds of the humanity still startled me every now and then, a momentary recrudescence of speech perhaps, an unexpected dexterity of the forefeet, a pitiful attempt to walk erect. (Wells 1896)

This brings us to Aldous Huxley's *Brave New World*, and his vision of how the state could use newfound techniques, including those of genetics, to keep its citizens controlled and contented. The novel is not about scientific research and discovery, but about the application of knowledge to specific governmental goals. Huxley's work presaged the Nazi eugenics program, with its rigid biologically-based class system. In his *Brave New World*, natural human reproduction has been abolished; all reproduction is done artificially in state hatcheries and conditioning centers. The key to social control is the "Bokanovsky Process" in which a single embryo is stimulated to divide into 96 identical copies. These 96 embryos (or all the survivors; 72 was the average) are artificially gestated together under identical conditions designed to produce four basic classes of workers: gammas, deltas, epsilons, and alphas. Specific "batches" are conditioned to perform specific tasks and to love performing them. As the Director of the Hatcheries put it, conditioning "is the secret of happiness and virtue – liking what you've *got* to do. All conditioning aims at that: making people like their unescapable social destiny."

The resulting society is compactly described by Mustapha Mond, the Resident World Controller for Western Europe, to a man who had been brought back to "civilization" from the reservation, and who is known as "the Savage." He explains to the Savage why it would be impossible to write *Romeo and Juliet* or *Othello* now:

> Because our world is not the same as Othello's world: you can't make flivvers [inexpensive autos] without steel – and you can't make tragedies without social instability. The world's stable now. People are happy; they get what they want, and they never want what they can't get. They're well off; they're safe; they're never ill; they're not afraid of death; they're blissfully ignorant of passion and old age; they're plagued with no mothers or fathers; they've got no wives, or children, or lovers to feel strongly about; they're so conditioned that they practically can't help behaving as they ought to behave. And if anything should go wrong, there's *soma*. (Huxley 1969: 10)

Huxley thus seems to reject Shakespeare's view of art and order being in harmony, and suggests that at least some disorder is necessary to produce real art – order itself produces only sterile contentment.

These four works of art from three different centuries help frame the emotional and intellectual debate about the ends of genetic research today. They keep us centered on the critical issues: What does it mean to be human? and, How can human "happiness" be enhanced? Some scientists continue to insist that these questions are none of science's concern. They insist that their job is simply to explore the world in search of new knowledge; society's job is to use, misuse, apply, and misapply that knowledge. The Human Genome Project is the effort to map and sequence the approximately 3 billion base pairs of nucleotides that make up the 23 different human chromosomes that compose the human "genome." It provides us with a contemporary megaproject that can be used as a vehicle to explore the proper relationship between science and society as science seeks to understand the genetic basis of human characteristics.

The Legal and Ethical Issues Raised by the Human Genome Project

To oversimplify somewhat, there are three levels of issues that the Human Genome Project raises: individual/family, society, and species. Almost all of our work on genetics to date has involved the individual/family level, where questions of genetic screening and counseling have center stage. Negligence in failing to offer or to properly perform these tests has resulted in lawsuits for wrongful birth and wrongful life; and standards for genetic screening and counseling have been set by professional organizations.

The level 2 issues implicate society more directly: population-based genetic screening, resource allocation and commercialization, and eugenics. More specifically, to what uses should its fruits be put in screening groups of people, such as applicants for the military, government workers, immigrants, etc.; what priority should the genome project have for federal funding and what role should patenting laws play; and finally, should we attempt to use the new genetics to improve our citizens, either by trying to eliminate specific genetic diseases or by enhancing desirable traits?

The level 3 issues are somewhat more speculative, and involve how a genetic view of ourselves could change the way we think about ourselves. This level raises recurrent philosophical questions involving determinism, reductionism, normalcy, and the meaning of health and disease.

This brief cataloging of the major issues raised on each level suggests that there probably are no *unique* issues raised by the Human Genome Project. On the other hand, this project raises all of the issues in a much more focused manner (certainly a difference in degree if not in kind), and the fact that *all* of these issues are implicated in the genome project may itself make the project societally unique.

Level 1. (individual/family) issues

Genetic screening and counseling are techniques that have been in widespread use in the United States for almost three decades. Stated concisely, "Genetic counseling is the process whereby an individual or family obtains information about a real or possible genetic problem" (NAS 1975: 9). Counseling is usually primarily directed toward couples deciding whether or not to have children based on their risk of having a child with a genetic handicap; counseling pregnant women about the existence of genetic tests to determine the status of the fetus; and counseling parents of newborns about the genetic condition of their child. Genetic screening bridges level 1 and level 2 issues because it is primarily a public health endeavor that actively seeks out asymptomatic people, many of whom would not otherwise seek medical care or discover their condition.

Although we have not solved any of the major issues raised by past genetic screening and counseling cases, we have been able to identify the major factors to be considered before initiating a screening program: (1) the frequency and severity of the condition; (2) the availability of treatment of documented efficacy; (3) the extent to which detection by screening improves the outcome; (4) the validity and safety of the screening tests; (5) the adequacy of resources to assure effective screening and counseling follow-up; (6) the costs of the program; and (7) the acceptance of the screening program by the community, including both physicians and the public (Elias and Annas 1987: 54; Holtzman 1977). This list primarily relates to the scientific validity and a cost/benefit analysis of the testing procedure. In addition, two major legal issues are implicit in all genetic screening programs: autonomy and confidentiality. Autonomy requires that all screening programs be voluntary, and that consent to them is sought only after full information concerning the implications of a positive finding is disclosed and understood. Confidentiality requires that the finding not be disclosed to anyone else without the individual's consent.

131

Provided that testing remains voluntary, and that the results are only disclosed with the individual's permission, genetic testing based on one's genome raises questions only of degree rather than kind. The degree is that instead of one or even hundreds of conditions that can be screened for, there may be thousands. Perhaps even more important, we may find that certain genes predispose a person to specific illnesses, such as breast cancer or Alzheimer's disease. This information may be very troubling to individuals, but will be of great interest to health insurance companies and employers.

We have so far managed to develop genetic screening and counseling as tools that we have permitted individuals and families to use or not use as they see fit. This has followed the "medical model" of the beneficent doctor–patient relationship: a model of mutual consent in which decisions are made for benefit of the patient. This model has served us well to date in expanding the reproductive options of individuals. Level 2 concerns move us away from concern with the individual, to concern with society itself.

Level 2 (societal) issues

Societal issues involved in the genome cluster around three areas: population-based screening, resource allocation and commercialism, and eugenics. Of these, the first overlaps level 1 concerns (since population screening can be used to identify individuals to help them), and the last is the most unique and troubling. All merit discussion.

Population-based screening has already been discussed in level 1, and can be aimed at the attempted elimination of a genetic condition, or simply at identifying the incidence of a genetic condition in a population, or the presence of a genetic condition in an applicant for a particular benefit (employment, insurance, immigration, etc.). As previously discussed, autonomy and confidentiality are the major legal issues involved, and this type of screening becomes problematic primarily when it is mandatory and the results are made known to others without consent. The other two areas are more uniquely "societal."

The issue of resource allocation itself has its own three levels. The first is the obvious one: what percentage of the nation's research budget should be devoted to the Human Genome Project? Answering this question requires us to consider how research priorities are set in science, and who should set them. The second level involves making the fruits of the genome project available to all those who want them. This involves at least two questions. The first is the issue of commercialism, and who "owns" and can patent the products that are produced by the genome initiative. Should the fact that much of this research is nationally funded mean that its fruits should be in the public domain? Or should individual companies and scientists be able to patent or copyright maps and sequences of specific areas of human genome in order to encourage them to become involved in mapping research? The other issue can be summed up in three words: national health insurance, i.e., should the genetic tests and their follow-up procedures be made part of a "minimum benefit package" under national health insurance (or some other scheme for universal access), or should they only be available to those who can pay for them privately? This, of course, is an issue that society must confront with every new medical technology.

132

The third level of the resource allocation issue is probably the most intrinsically interesting. It involves determining the balance of resource priorities between how much we should spend on identifying and treating genetic diseases, as opposed to how much we should spend directly on *other* conditions that cause disease, such as poverty, drug and alcohol addiction, lack of housing, poor education, and lack of access to decent medical care. In a country like the United States, is it ethical or rational to develop medical technologies that large segments of the population would not have access to today if they were available, or to develop technologies that even if universally available, would only be useful to a few individuals? What is the social impact of putting the spotlight on a project like the Human Genome Project? Could the fact that we are vigorously pursuing this project lead us to downplay environmental pollution, work-site hazards, and other major social problems that cause disease, based on the hope that we will someday find a "genetic fix" to permit humans to "cope" with these unhealthy conditions?

The third level 2 issue, and the most important one, is the issue of eugenics. This issues is perhaps the most difficult to address because of the highly emotional reaction many individuals have to even mentioning the racist genocide of the Nazis, which was based on a eugenic program founded on a theory of "racial hygiene" (Proctor 1988). Although repugnant, the Nazi experience and legacy demands careful study to determine what led to it, why scientists and physicians supported and collaborated in developing its theory and making possible its execution, and how it was implemented by a totalitarian state. In this regard other national experiences with racism, sterilization, and immigration quotas will have to be reexamined. In so doing, we are likely to rediscover the powerful role of economics in driving our own views of evolution (in the form of social Darwinism) and who should propagate. In 1927, the US Supreme Court wrote with clear reference to the First World War, that eugenics by involuntary sterilization of the mentally retarded was constitutionally acceptable based on utilitarianism:

> We have seen more than once that the public welfare may call upon the best citizens for their lives. It would be strange if it could not call upon those who already sap the strength of the State for these lesser sacrifices often not felt to be such by those concerned, in order to prevent our being swamped with incompetence. It is better for all the world, if instead of waiting to execute degenerate offspring for crime, or to let them starve for their imbecility, society can prevent those who are manifestly unfit from continuing their kind. (*Buck* v. *Bell*, 274 U.S. 200, 207 (1927))

That may seem ancient history, but in 1998 the US Congress's Office of Technology Assessment, in discussing the "Social and Ethical Considerations" raised by the Human Genome Initiative, developed a similar theme:

> Human mating that proceeds without the use of genetic data about the risks of transmitting diseases will produce greater mortality and medical costs than if carriers of potentially deleterious genes are alerted to their status and encouraged to mate with noncarriers or to use artificial insemination or other reproductive strategies. (1988: 21–4)

133

The likely primary reproductive strategy, mentioned only in passing in the report, will be genetic screening of human embryos, already technically feasible, but not nearly to the extent possible once the genome is understood. Such screening need not be required; people will want it, even insist on it as their right. As OTA notes, "New technologies for identifying traits and altering genes make it *possible for eugenic goals to be achieved through technological as opposed to social control*" (ibid., italics added).

So far most writers have insisted that it is at least premature to follow the example of Dr. Moreau and try to *improve* upon the species, either by enhancing certain genetic characteristics, such as height, or by altering sex cells so that characteristics modified in an individual can be passed down to future generations. (Anderson 1985; Andrews and Mariner 1989). Just as population-based screening provided a bridge between levels 1 and 2, enhancing genetic traits provides a bridge between levels 2 and 3.

Level 3 (species) issues

Level 3 issues relate to the fact that powerful new technologies do not just change what human beings can do, they change the way we think, especially about ourselves. In this respect, maps may become particularly powerful thought transformers. Maps model reality to help us understand it. Columbus changed the shape of the world's map forever: from a flat chart to a spherical globe. Monsters could no longer either prowl or guard the edge of the world: there was no edge of the world. Copernicus and Vesalius published their great works in the same year, 1543. *On the Motions of Heavenly Bodies* made it clear that the earth rotated around the sun, not the other way around. The earth could no longer be seen as the "center" of the universe.

Vesalius's "maps" of the human anatomy may have been even more important metaphors for us, for in dissecting the human body, Vesalius insisted that human beings could nonetheless only be understood as whole beings: *human* beings rather than as parts that can be fitted together to manufacture life forms. For Vesalius, who shows 21 of 73 drawings in his *Fabrica* as full-figured humans, and 10 of 12 drawings in his *Epitome* as full-figured humans, the emphasis is firmly on the person, even though the treatise is concerned with the person's body parts (Saunders and O'Malley 1950). This is in stark contrast to the bar-graph illustrations used by contemporary geneticists in "mapping" the genome which are totally devoid of human reference, almost life without life. A similar lifeless, reductionist phenomena can be seen in the "maps" of areas of the human brain, which are said to correspond to various human emotions and the ability to think and conceptualize (Eccles 1989). Does this reconceptualization of the human to a new "map" encourage us to travel into areas that could lead us to simultaneously misunderstand and demean what it is to be human?

What new human perspectives, or what new perspectives on humans, will a sequential map of the 3 billion base pairs of the human genome bring? The most obvious is that breaking "human beings" down into 6 billion "parts" is the ultimate in reductionism. James Watson himself has used such reductionist language in promoting the Human Genome Project. In his words, the project will provide "the ultimate tool for understanding ourselves at the molecular level" (Jaroff 1989). Just what this means is unclear, but Watson continues: "How can we not do it? We used to think our fate is in our stars. Now we know, in large measure, our fate is in our genes" (ibid.). Seeing our fate in our genes, of course, resonates with level 2 concerns: if genes determine our fate, then we can alter our fate by altering our genes. Maybe we really can look forward to the day that mental illness, and therefore at least some homelessness, can be prevented by genetic manipulation. Such a view suggests most of the level 3 concerns.

The first is the consequence of viewing humans as an assemblage of molecules, arranged in a certain way. The almost inevitable tendency in such a view is that expressed in *Brave New World*. People could view themselves and each other as products which can be "manufactured," and subject to quality-control measures. People could be "made to measure," both literally and figuratively. If people are so seen, we might not only try to manipulate them as embryos and fetuses, but we might also see the resulting children as products themselves. This raises the current stakes in the debates about frozen embryos and surrogate mothers to a new height: if children are seen as products, the purchase and sale of the resulting children themselves, not only embryos, may be seen as reasonable. Secondly, to the extent that genes are seen as more important than environment, our actions may be viewed as genetically determined, rather than as a result of free will. We have already witnessed an early example with this type of reasoning in the use of the "XYY defense." Those possessing the XYY karyotype were thought to be more prone to commit crime. Accordingly, individuals accused of crime who also had an extra Y chromosome consequently argued that their genetic composition predisposed them to crime and therefore they should not be held criminally responsible for their actions. This defense was generally rejected, and in the few cases where it was accepted, the defendant was confined to a mental institution until "cured." Of course, since it is impossible to remove the extra Y chromosome from any cell, let alone every cell, in one's body, a cure is not possible (Dershowitz 1976).

Finally, we know that most diseases and abnormalities are social constructs, not facts of nature. Myopia, for example, is well accepted; whereas obesity is not. We won't discover a "normal" or "standard" human genome, but we may invent one. If we do, what variation will society view as permissible before an individual's genome is labeled "substandard" or "abnormal"? And what impact will such a construct of genetic normalcy have on society and on "substandard" individuals? For example, what variation in a fetus should prompt a couple to opt for abortion, or a genetic counselor to suggest abortion? What variation should prompt a counselor to suggest sterilization? What interventions will society deem acceptable in an individual's life based on his or her genetic composition? Should health plans, for example, be able to disclaim financial responsibility for the medical needs of a child whose parents knew prior to conception or birth that the child would be born with a seriously "abnormal" genome? Should employers be able to screen out workers on the basis of their genomes? These and many other similar issues exist today based on screening for single-site genes. But the magnitude of the screening possibilities that may result from analysis of the map of the human genome will raise these issues to new heights, and will almost inevitably change the way we think about ourselves and what it means to be human.

What options exist for policy-makers who would like to have the benefits of the human genome initiative and minimize or control the potential harms?

Strategies to Regulate Genetic Technology

English literature provides us with a rich backdrop from which to begin our consideration, but actual examples of successful regulatory intervention into either scientific research or technological application are much less plentiful. Nor have scientists and policy-makers worked together well in the past. As C. P. Snow has noted, "Non-scientists tend to think of scientists as brash and boastful" (Snow 1964). This attitude it certainly exemplified in the literature herein summarized, as is the view that scientists underestimate the danger in their work, and vastly overestimate its importance. Scientists, on the other hand, tend to think of social policy and ethics as fields that "lag behind" science and cannot "keep up with" scientific progress and advance. It is almost as if they believe that morality is a field of knowledge "in the charge of unidentified, but presumably rather incompetent experts" (*Science* 1978). Experts in both fields have little experience with each other, and generally only meet in the courtroom or in the government hearing room. Scientists then often revert to the old slogan, "What is good for General Motors is good for the country"; or more precisely, as James Watson has put it, "Science is good for society."

The challenge is to get beyond the literary archetypes, the stereotypes, and the clichés, and to work together to develop a coherent set of goals to judge scientific priorities and actions against. Once these goals are agreed upon in an open and public forum, it will be reasonably easy to devise methods to attempt to accomplish them. A few such methods merit further discussion because they are the ones most likely to be used: moratoriums and bans, regulatory agencies, advisory groups, and private lawsuits.

Moratoriums and bans

At a Workshop on International Cooperation for the Human Genome Project held in Valencia in October, 1988, French researcher Jean Dausset suggested that the genome project posed great potential hazards that could open the door to Nazi-like atrocities. To attempt to avoid such results, he suggested that the conferees agree on a moratorium on genetic manipulation of germ line cells, and a ban on gene transfer experiments in early embryos (Swazy et al. 1978; Berg et al. 1975). Reportedly, the proposal won wide agreement among the participants, and was watered down to a resolution calling for "international cooperation" only after American participant Norton Zinder successfully argued that the group had no authority to make such a resolution stick.

Zinder was correct. A moratorium and ban on research that no one wants to do at this point would have only symbolic value – and negative symbolic value at that. It would signal that the scientists could handle the ethical issues alone, and could monitor their own work. It would tend to quiet the discussion of both germ line research and gene transfers in early embryos – both subjects that deserve wide public debate. But Dausset also had a point. The Nazi atrocities grew out of the combination of a public health ethic that saw the abnormal as disposable, and a tyrannical dictatorship that was able to give the physicians and public health authorities unlimited authority to put their bestial program into practice.

Regulations

The US federal government has specific guidelines governing the conduct of rDNA research by facilities receiving federal funds. These guidelines primarily relied upon a series of biological and physical containment measures that increased as the risk of the rDNA experiment increased (Roberts 1989). Compliance was to be supervised locally by an Institutional Biosafety Committee (IBC), which was requested, but not required, to open its meetings "to the public whenever possible, consistent with protection of privacy and proprietary interests" (DHHS 1983).

A few cities and states were not content to rely upon the federal guidelines, and developed their own. In Cambridge, Massachusetts, the home of Harvard and MIT, as well as many private biotechnology firms, Mayor Al Vellucci said in 1976, "They may come up with a disease that can't be cured – even a monster. Is this the answer to Frankenstein's dream?" (Areen et al. 1984). Recombinant DNA research is not, of course, the answer to Frankenstein's dream of animating dead tissue; it is more the answer to Dr. Moreau's dream of combining various species into a new creature, a unique creature. Nonetheless, as Lewis Thomas observed, having man don the mantle of creator of life raises the fundamental questions that the Frankenstein myth exemplifies:

> The recombinant DNA line of research is upsetting...because it is disturbing in a fundamental way, to face the fact that the genetic machinery in control of the planet's life can be fooled around with so easily. We do not like the idea that anything so fixed and stable as a species line can be changed. The notion that genes can be taken out of one genome and inserted in another is unnerving. (President's Commission 1982: 23)

The Frankenstein myth resonated because of rDNA's ability to create new life forms that the creator could not control, and also because of the public's concern that scientists were doing this work for their own enjoyment rather than society's betterment. As Mayor Vellucci put it: "I don't think these scientists are thinking about mankind at all. I think that they're getting the thrills and excitement and the passion to dig in and keep digging to see what the hell they can do" (ibid., 24). The Mayor here encompasses not only the driving force behind Dr. Frankenstein, but that behind Dr. Jekyll and Dr. Moreau as well. The President's Commission on Bioethics summarized the "Frankenstein factor" in rDNA research as follows: "The fear was that for researchers creating a new life form – even a monster – would be a matter of curiosity; for the public, it would be an assault on traditional values" (ibid., 16–17). As a result of their concern, the City of Cambridge developed regulations that called for laboratory inspections by a publicly-appointed committee.

137

Oversight committees

Closely related to regulation is the establishment of oversight committees. The most prominent of these in the US genetics research field has been the Recombinant DNA Advisory Committee (the "RAC") and its subcommittee on genetic engineering. The RAC is a National Institutes of Health Committee advising the Secretary of HHS on all matters relating to rDNA research, and reviewing certain genetic experiments and approving them before they can be carried out. The three specific areas over which the RAC has retained oversight even in private facilities are: (a) cloning toxin-producing genes; (b) introducing drug resistance into an organism; and (c) deliberately releasing genetically engineered organisms into the environment (ibid).

Self-regulation and private tort suits

In most areas, even those heavily regulated, the professionals themselves will have much, if not everything, to say about the standards applied to their work. Under almost any standards, Victor Frankenstein and Dr. Moreau would be guilty of gross negligence and cruelty in abandoning their creations, and in inflicting suffering upon them. Dr. Jekyll might properly argue that he was experimenting on himself, but would still, of course, be criminally responsible for the murders committed by Mr. Hyde. The murderous experiments of the Nazi physicians during the Second World War led to the Doctors' Trial at Nuremberg, and to the articulation of the Nuremberg Code (Nuremberg Military Tribunals, 1950). It is now clear, although it should have been prior to 1947 as well, that experimentation on individual human beings without their consent (in exceptional circumstances proxy consent may suffice) is criminal activity, as well as being a civil wrong against the person (Annas and Grodin 1992).

Future lawsuits are likely to be of three kinds. The first will involve the accidental or purposeful release of a dangerous organism into the environment. This is the type of harm Mayor Velluci worried about, and could give rise to traditional tort suits alleging nuisance, trespass, battery, and/or negligent failure to contain the organism. The second kind of suit will involve those who apply the new knowledge gained by the genome initiative to the clinical setting: cases involving wrongful birth (for failure to counsel about existing technology that results in a couple having a child they would not otherwise have had, and who is genetically handicapped); and cases involving wrongful life (suits by a child alleging that the child would have been better off not having been born, and would not have been born if the physician had properly counseled its parents or properly performed agreed-to screening tests). The third type of lawsuit will be one for breach of confidentiality leading to a loss on the basis of discrimination. For example, a physician may be sued for improperly disclosing a genetic diagnosis to an employer, who then fires the employee on the basis of the genetic information. As can be seen from this listing, tort suits will be most useful *after* genetic screening tests have been developed, and will likely have little impact on their ultimate development itself. In this regard it is at least of some interest that many physicians already consider the legal profession to be Victor Frankenstein's monster incarnate, and consider the actions of malpractice attorneys every bit as destructive as the creatures on Dr. Moreau's island.

Where do we go from here?

It seems reasonable to conclude from the various methods that have been employed to review genetic research and the clinical applications of that research that level 1 concerns will be dealt with by a combination of oversight committees, regulation, self-regulation, and private law suits. Level 2 concerns are not readily approached by private lawsuit, and so will likely require a combination of governmentally-mandated regulation, most likely based on suggestions by one or more advisory committees with broad public input. Level 3 concerns are not subject to legal regulation at all, except insofar as specific practices, such as the purchase and sale of "high-grade embryos" can be outlawed altogether. But this may be the area that has the most long-term impact on us as a species, and the one about which we therefore need the most careful and creative thinking.

It is on "level 3" that the cautionary tales with which this chapter opened focus. Mary Shelley's tale, for example, teaches us a lesson that we find hard to deal with seriously: as difficult as it is to create a monster, it is even more difficult to control it or to restore order after the creation has spawned chaos. In seeking to control our world, we may in fact lessen our control over it. Dr. Robert Oppenheimer unwittingly made this point in reference to the Manhattan Project to a Congressional Committee in 1945. He was testifying on the role of science in the development of the atomic bomb:

> When you come right down to it, the reason that we did this job is because it was an organic necessity. If you are a scientist, you cannot stop such a thing. If you are a scientist, you believe that it is good to find out how the world works; that it is good to find what the realities are; that it is good to turn over to mankind at large the greatest possible power to control the world. (Rhodes 1986: 761)

The striking thing in Oppenheimer's testimony is his emphasis on the notion that science is unstoppable with the simultaneous insistence that its goal is *control* over nature, irreconcilable concepts that seem equally at the heart of the human genome project. Of course, with the atomic bomb, control quickly became illusory. The bomb, which carries with it the promise of the total annihilation of mankind, has made the nation-state ultimately unstable and put it at the mercy of every other nation with the bomb. Necessity has forced all nuclear powers to move, however slowly, toward a transnational community.

Scientists working on the Human Genome Project say they are working on an interesting scientific question to gain new knowledge and insight into what genes do, and what we can learn about man's origins and relationship to other species. If we take the scientists at face value, they have given no more thought to the potential social applications of genome mapping and sequencing than Victor Frankenstein had given to the consequences of creating his monster, or than Dr. Moreau had given to the consequences of his experiments in modifying life forms.

139

Our own "brave new world" will not be ruled by scientists, any more than scientists decided whether or not to use the atomic bomb, or whether to send a man to the moon. Social policy will ultimately be set by elected politicians and their advisers. It is already past time to begin to involve the electorate in a national debate about the appropriate uses (and the misuses) of the products of the Human Genome Project.

In this discussion, the focus should be on two central questions: What does it mean to be human? And how can human "happiness" be enhanced? One leading commentator, psychiatrist Willard Gaylin, has thoughtfully suggested that we should develop guidelines by which to judge which changes to encourage and which to discourage. His suggested set of human characteristics to encourage is instructive, and provides a useful basis on which to begin such a national discussion:

> a life of imagination, esthetics, and hope; autonomy and freedom; a range of feeling that includes joy and pride, but *also* guilt and shame; a romantic sexuality; a joy in work (as distinguished from labor); a developed conscience; and a line of traits that leads from identification to friendship and love. (Gaylin 1990)

Gaylin's plea is that we focus on our goals, rather than on the "Frankenstein Factor," which he defines as being overly intimidated by high technology that has the capacity to alter the nature of the human species. In this he is surely correct. He could have added that we now focus on neither; and it is past time to begin the national discussion on both. He could also have added that fear that produces constructive action is valuable, and a lack of fear that proceeds from ignorance or denial of potential disaster itself produces disaster, and not just in fiction. The public and policy-makers need to understand the Human Genome Project, and the cartographers of the human genome need to be able to recognize and deal with the real monsters lurking outside their laboratories.

With both real and psychological walls crumbling around the world, the time may be at hand for meaningful international dialogue and cooperation on the Human Genome Project. It may also be possible, although perhaps this is wishful thinking, to engage the world in a responsible debate about all of our futures, and to do so in a manner that strives to enhance the dignity of all human beings. Playwright, former political prisoner, and current president of Czechoslovakia, Vaclav Havel, expressed it well in a 1984 speech on "Politics and Conscience":

> To me the smokestack soiling the heavens is...the symbol of an age which seeks to transcend the boundaries of the natural world and its norms and to make the matter merely a private concern, a matter of subjective preference and private feeling. The process of anonymisation and depersonalization of power, and its reduction to a mere technology of rule and manipulation, has a thousand masks...
>
> The question about socialism and capitalism...is beside the point. The question is wholly other, deeper and equally relevant to all: whether we shall, by whatever means, succeed in rehabitating the personal experience of human beings as the measure of things, placing morality above politics and responsibility above our desires, in making human community meaningful, in returning content to human speaking, in reconstituting, as the focus of all social activity, the autonomous, integral and dignified human "I," responsible for himself because he is bound to something higher...If we can defend our

humanity, then, perhaps, there is a hope of sorts that we shall also find some more meaningful ways of balancing our natural claims to shared economic control, to digni-fied social status... As long, however, as our humanity remains defenseless, we will not be saved by any better economic functioning, just as no filter on a factory smokestack will prevent the general dehumanization. To what purpose a system functions is, after all, more important than how it does so; might it not function quite smoothly, after all, in the service of total destruction? (Havel 1989: 136).

Havel then adds, "I speak of this because I cannot avoid the impression that many people in the West still understand little of what is actually at stake in our time... that Western culture is threatened far more by itself than by SS-20 rockets" (ibid., 150). He then goes on to elaborate that the task of all of us is to resist "at every step and everywhere, the irrational momentum of anonymous, impersonal and inhuman power – the power of ideologies, systems, *apparat*, bureaucracy, artificial languages and slogans... whether it takes the form of consumption, advertising, repression, technology, or cliché... We must not be ashamed that we are capable of love, friendship, solidarity, sympathy and tolerance, but just the opposite: we must set these fundamental dimensions of our humanity free from their 'private' exile and accept them as the only genuine starting point of meaningful human community" (ibid., 153).

Havel's image of the smokestack is striking: the inanimate destroyer has replaced the animate monster in industrial society. Governments grow more machine-like, and in consequence treat their citizens as interchangeable parts of that machine. The machine-men become alienated even from themselves; and technology cannot save them from artificiality; only their "natural" humanness and their ability to distin-guish good from evil.

Havel obviously did not have the Human Genome Project in mind when he delivered his 1984 speech, nor when he delivered a speech to a joint session of the US Congress in February, 1990. Nonetheless, his 1984 words aptly summarize the challenge we face, and his 1990 words to the Congress properly insist that we all take personal responsibility for our own actions and the future of our world:

Without a global revolution in the sphere of human consciousness, nothing will change for the better in the sphere of our being... We still don't know how to put morality ahead of politics, science and economy. We are still incapable of understanding that the only genuine backbone of all our actions, if they are to be moral, is responsibility – responsibility to something higher than my family, my country, my company, my success. (Havel 1992)

Can the "new world" United States learn from the old; and can new science learn to take its social responsibilities seriously? It will not happen easily in a country where new is still seen as better, and where the future is still seen as limitless. It is, after all, not Mary Shelley's but Gatsby's view of the US's future that still prevails:

Gatsby believed in the green light, the orgiastic future that year by year recedes before us. It eluded us then, but that's no matter – tomorrow we will run faster, stretch our arms further... And one fine morning –
  So we beat on, boats against the current, borne back ceaselessly into the past. (Fitzgerald 1925: 182)

141

Acknowledgments

This chapter is based on Annas 1990.

References

Anderson, W. E.: "Human gene therapy: scientific and ethical considerations." *Journal of Medicine and Philosophy* 10 (1985), pp. 275–91.

Andrews, L. and Mariner, W. K.: "National Conference on Birth, Death and Law." *Jurimetrics* 29 (1989), pp. 403, 434.

Annas, G. J.: "Mapping the human genome and the meaning of monster mythology." *Emory Law Journal* 39 (1990), pp. 629–64.

Annas, G. J. and Grodin, M., eds.: *The Nazi Doctors and the Nuremberg Code: Human Rights in Human Experimentation* (New York: Oxford University Press, 1992).

Areen, J. et al.: *Law, Science, and Medicine* (Mineola, NY: Foundation Press, 1984).

Berg, P., Baltimore, D., Brenner, S., et al.: "Asilomar Conference on Recombinant DNA Molecules." *Science* 188 (1975), pp. 991–4.

Bloom, H.: Afterword to *Frankenstein*, by Mary Shelley (New York: New American Library ed., 1963).

Department of Health and Human Services (DHHS): "National Institutes of Health: Guidelines for Research Involving Recombinant DNA Molecules." 48 *Fed. Reg.* 24556; sec. IV- B-2-f (1983).

Dershowitz, A.: "Karyotype predictability and culpability." In Milunsky, A. and Annas, G. J., eds.: *Genetics and the Law* (New York: Plenum, 1976).

Eccles, J.: *Evolution of the Brain: Creation of the Self* (New York: Routledge, 1989).

Elias, S. and Annas, G. J.: *Reproductive Genetics and the Law* (St. Louis: Yearbook-Mosby, 1987).

Fitzgerald, F. S.: *The Great Gatsby* (New York: Charles Scribner's Sons, 1925).

Gaylin, W.: "The Frankenstein factor." *New England Journal of Medicine* 179 (1977), p. 665.

Gaylin, W.: "Fooling with mother nature." *Hastings Center Report* 17 (1990), p. 21.

Havel, V.: "The end of the modern era." *New York Times* (March 1, 1992), p. E17.

Havel, V.: *Living in Truth* (London: Faber & Faber, 1989).

Holtzman, N. A.: "Newborn screening for genetic-metabolic diseases: progress." *Principles and Recommendations* (1977).

Huxley, A.: *Brave New World* (New York: Perennial Library, 1969).

Jaroff, L.: "The gene hunt." *Time* (March 20, 1989), p. 62.

Langbaum, R.: Introduction to Shakespeare's *The Tempest* (New York: New American Library edition, 1964).

Law no. 10, vols. 1 & 2, *US Gov. Print. Office*, Washington, DC, 1950.

National Academy of Sciences (NAS): *Genetic Screening: Programs, Principles and Research* (Washington, DC: National Academy of Sciences, 1975).

President's Bioethics Commission for the Study of Ethical Problems in Medicine and Biomedical and Behavioral Research: *Splicing Life: The Social and Ethical Issues of Genetic Engineering with Human Beings* (Washington, DC: US Gov. Print. Office, 1982).

Proctor, R.: *Racial Hygiene* (Cambridge, MA.: Harvard University Press, 1988).

Rhodes, R.: *The Making of the Atomic Bomb* (New York: Simon & Shuster, 1986).

Roberts, L.: "Who owns the human genome?" *Science* 237 (1987), pp. 358–61.

Roberts, L.: "Watson versus Japan." *Science* 246 (1989), pp. 576, 578.

Roszak, T.: *The Making of a Counter Culture: Reflections on the Technocratic Society and its Youthful Opposition* (London: Faber, 1970).

Saunders, J. and O'Malley, C.: *The Illustrations from the Works of Andreas Vesalius* (Cleveland: World Publishing, 1950).

Shelley, M.: *Frankenstein* (New York: New American Library, 1817).

Snow, C. P.: *The Two Cultures* (New York: Cambridge University Press, 1964).

Swazey, J., Sorenson, J., and Wong, C. B.: "Risks and benefits, rights and responsibilities: a history of the recombitanant DNA research controversy." *Southern California Law Review* 51 (1978).

US Congress, Office of Technology Assessment: *Mapping Our Genes: Genome Projects, How Big, How Fast?* (Washington, DC: US Gov. Print. Office, 1988).

US Supreme Court: *Buck v. Bell*, 274 US (1927).

Wells, H. G.: *The Island of Dr. Moreau* (New York: New American Library, 1988). First published 1896.

Further reading

Annas, G. J.: *Standard of Care: The Law of American Bioethics* (New York: Oxford University Press, 1993).

Annas, G. J.: *Some Choice: Law, Medicine and the Market* (Oxford: Oxford University Press, 1998).

Annas, G. J. and Elias, S., eds.: *Gene Mapping: Using Law and Ethics as Guides* (New York: Oxford University Press, 1992).

Annas, G. J., Glantz, L. H., and Roche, P. A. "Drafting the Genetic Privacy Act: science, policy and practical considerations." *Journal of Law, Medicine and Ethics* 23 (1995), pp. 360–6.

Elias, S. and Annas, G. J.: *Reproductive Genetics and the Law* (St. Louis, IL: Mosby-Yearbook, 1987).

Mann, J., Gruskin, S., Grodin, M., and Annas, G. J., eds.: *Health and Human Rights: A Reader* (New York: Routledge and Kegan Paul, 1999).

US National Research Council (NRC): *Evaluating Human Genetic Diversity* (Washington, DC: National Academy Press, 1997).

Part III

GENE MANIPULATION AND GENE SELECTION

11

The Moral Status of the Gene

MARY ANNE WARREN

Introduction

Do genes have moral status? Can we, in other words, have moral obligations towards the DNA of human beings or other organisms? My question is not whether we can have obligations regarding genes. We obviously have moral obligations towards other human beings regarding what may and may not be done to (parts of) their bodies, including their DNA. The question is, rather, whether we can have moral obligations towards genes, independent of any obligations we may have towards the organisms of which they are, were, or will be part.

I shall argue that genes do not have independent moral status. There are powerful objections to some current or potential uses of recombinant DNA techniques. For instance, it would probably be irresponsible deliberately to produce hereditary alterations in human germline DNA, so long as the risks to future persons are not well understood. However, it is implausible to construe obligations to avoid irresponsible uses of genetic technologies as obligations to DNA. A better approach is to focus upon the likely benefits, risks, and harms to present and future human and nonhuman organisms, and ecosystems, of each application of genetic technology. According DNA a special moral status, unlike that of other bodily parts, organs, or systems, can only distort the ethical issues.

I will begin with an overview of some major theories of moral status, each of which provides a basis for the recognition of moral obligations towards living organisms of specific types. None of the theories provides a basis for the recognition of obligations towards parts of organisms. There are, however, medical, ecological, social, and other long-term risks associated with the development and marketing of recombinant DNA techniques. If these risks are sufficiently severe, then perhaps they may be used to argue for a special moral status for DNA. This would mean that we could have moral obligations towards genes, separate from our obligations to the organisms from which they are derived, or of which they are or will be part.

The suggestion might seem plausible, especially in the light of the symbolic and religious meanings that genes have accrued in some cultural contexts. However, these special symbolic meanings are not well grounded in empirical evidence about the biological functions of DNA. Moreover, according moral status to genes will not facilitate the moral, social, economic, and ecological analyses that are essential to the development of enforceable national legislation and international agreements regarding acceptable and unacceptable uses of genetic technologies.

Why Parts of Organisms Do Not Have Moral Status

To have moral status is to be an entity towards which moral agents can have moral obligations. We usually assume that human beings have moral status, but that their blood, bones, and other body parts, systems, or tissues do not. Of course, it is generally wrong deliberately to injure a person's body; but the wrong is assumed to be a wrong against the person, and not against the injured part. We also assume that any nonvital body part, such as a tonsil, may – with the person's consent – be removed, if it has become incurably diseased, and a serious liability to the person's health. And when a person's survival is at stake, even so vital an organ as a heart may – with the prior consent of donor and recipient – be removed and replaced with another one, with no independent moral concern for the organ that is removed.

These common-sense assumptions are consistent with the major philosophical theories of moral status. Each of these theories promulgates a single criterion of moral status, based upon some property possessed by some or all living organisms. One of the most inclusive criteria is that of Albert Schweitzer, who defends a principle of equal moral status for all living organisms, from human beings to the simplest microorganisms (Schweitzer 1929: 247). In contrast, Immanuel Kant's theory is one of the more exclusive: he argues that only rational moral agents are ends in themselves (Kant 1948: 90); and that all other organisms are mere things, towards which we can have no moral obligations (Kant 1963: 151). Between these extremes lie theories of intermediate inclusiveness, such as the sentience-based criterion defended by Peter Singer, and the subject-of-a-life criterion defended by Tom Regan.

Singer's criterion of moral status is the capacity for sentience, i.e., the ability to experience pleasure and pain. His utilitarian principle of equal consideration requires that, in our moral calculations, equal consideration be given to the comparable interests of all sentient beings (Singer 1975: 8–9). All sufficiently developed vertebrate animals are probably sentient, and many complex invertebrates, such as insects, arachnids, and crustaceans, are also likely to have a degree of sentience. Thus, the sentience standard grants an equal moral status to all these animals, though (probably) not to plants, simple invertebrate animals, or microorganisms.

Tom Regan's theory is more exclusive than Singer's; he accords equal basic moral rights to only those sentient beings that are subjects-of-lives. Subjects-of-lives are beings that are capable of such relatively sophisticated mental activities as memory, anticipation of the future, and intentional action in the pursuit of conscious goals (Regan 1983: 243). Regan suggests that all mammals over a year of age are subjects, and that some other animals may also be subjects (p. 78).

Each of these theories focuses upon an intrinsic property of some organisms, which is relevant to the moral consideration that we owe to them. However, none of these theories is plausible as a complete account of moral status. To more accurately represent common-sense convictions about moral status that we are unlikely to surrender, we need to combine the insights of these and other theories. We need to take into account not only whether an organism is alive, and its sentience and mental sophistication, but also its importance to the ecosystem in which it exists, and its social or other relationships to human beings. Respect for all living organisms is a worthy ideal; but it is necessary to permit the destruction of some organisms – e.g., pathogenic microbes – on the basis of reasons that would not justify the destruction of equal numbers of human beings.

Similarly, it is reasonable to hold that not even spiders should be made to suffer needlessly; but it is unreasonable to demand that human beings be as deeply concerned with the suffering of spiders as with the suffering of other human beings. Regan rightly argues that we have stronger moral obligations towards more mentally sophisticated beings, such as humans and other mammals, who probably can suffer more intensely than spiders, and who also probably have lives that are of greater value to them.

Yet, however smart some nonhuman mammals may be, we cannot always treat the protection of their lives as a moral imperative on a par with the protection of human lives. For instance, it is sometimes necessary to kill mice and rats that invade our homes and food storage areas, or to introduce cats or other predators. Kant is probably right to hold that moral agents are entitled to a higher level of respect for their lives and liberty than are most sentient nonhuman animals. The possibility of reciprocity and cooperation between moral agents makes this higher level of respect possible; and because it is possible, it may be held to be morally obligatory. Kant's mistake is to suppose that we can never have moral obligations towards living things that are not moral agents.

My purpose, however, is not so much to compare the relative merits of these four theories, as to note their agreement on the point at issue. On none of these theories is there a plausible basis for asserting that we can have moral obligations towards part of a human being that are not entirely derivative from our obligations towards the human being. The same criteria that help to explain why organisms have moral status, and why some of them have a stronger moral status than others, also help to explain why the parts of organisms do not have independent moral status.

One reason for regarding living organisms as worthy of moral consideration is that they are teleological systems, with a good of their own. They are organized to maintain and reproduce themselves; and to interact with their environments in ways that have evolved because they tended to serve these ends (Taylor 1983: 124, 153). The teleological organization exhibited by organisms is only derivatively exhibited by their parts. Tissues and organs take on specific forms and functions in particular plant or animal species, because these traits have promoted (or at least been compatible with) the transgenerational reproductive success of ancestral organisms. Thus, the "goals" of a liver, or any other bodily organ, are other-directed in ways that the goals of the organism generally are not (Agar 1997: 164). That is one reason why it is generally inappropriate to demand that parts of organisms be accorded independent moral status.

In the case of organisms that are sentient, there is an even stronger reason for according moral status to them rather than to their parts. Sentience – the experience of pleasure, pain, and other felt mental states – occurs at the level of the organism. I may feel pain in my foot, but it is unlikely that my foot has private pains that I cannot feel. To feel such private pains, it would need a central nervous system of its own, and it does not appear to have one. Pain, emotions, and other felt experiences, are states of organisms, not of their isolated parts. Thus, it is reasonable to argue that we have special obligations to sentient organisms, such as not to needlessly cause them pain or suffering. But if parts of organisms cannot experience pleasure and pain, then we do not have that reason for recognizing moral obligations towards them.[1]

Similarly, memory, conscious anticipation of the future, and intentional action in pursuit of conscious goals, are capacities possessed by certain organisms, i.e., those that have sufficiently sophisticated brains. The moral respect that an organism may deserve by virtue of these mental capacities does not transfer to the creature's constituent parts, which are not endowed with the same capacities. And moral agency, while it may exist only amongst beings who have social as well as intellectual capacities, is nevertheless a capacity exercised by individual organisms. The biological parts of organisms are not moral agents, and cannot plausibly be held to have the rights that follow from moral agency.

These points may help to explain why it is odd to suggest that genes enjoy a moral status independent of the organisms of which they are part. If blood and bones do not have such status, then why should DNA? Present and future human and nonhuman organisms can be harmed by damage done to their DNA; but they can be harmed by damage to virtually any organ, system, or subsystem within their bodies. We do not need to accord moral status to parts of organisms in order to explain why it is morally wrong avoidably to harm the bodies of living persons, or to cause needless suffering to sentient nonhuman animals.

A Pragmatic Case for the Moral Status of Genes?

But perhaps there are reasons for treating DNA differently from other body parts. There are strong arguments for regarding human germline DNA as an inappropriate target for alteration, at least at the present time. There are also legal, social, and ecological arguments against the patenting and monopolistic commercial exploitation of either human or nonhuman genes. If people throughout the world agreed to grant a special moral status to genes, perhaps some of the gravest risks posed by the new genetic technologies could be avoided.

In *The Biotech Century*, Jeremy Rifkin explores the medical, ecological, and social risks of the unfettered commerical development of technologies of genetic manipulation. For instance, the release of genetically altered plants, animals, and microbes over large parts of the earth may damage natural ecosystems. Just as the introduction of nonnative species of plants and animals has often led to the decimation of native species, so genetically altered plants and other organisms may compete, or hybridize, with wild species and subspecies, thereby decreasing valuable natural biological diversity. If only a small percentage of the new bioengineered organisms have ecosystemic consequences comparable to (for instance) the introduction to Australia of rabbits, domestic cats, foxes, cane toads, and other nonnative animals, major trouble can be expected in ecosystems throughout the world.

Genetically engineered plants and animals also threaten to reduce the genetic diversity of human cultigens, by replacing older and more diverse domesticated varieties of plants and animals. This diversity is important to the avoidance of large- scale catastrophes caused by excessive reliance on genetically homogenous stock and crops, which have uniform vulnerabilities to parasites, diseases, and other threats. The use of transgenic animals for research and as a source of transplant organs and pharmaceuticals introduces another set of potential dangers, including the risk of infecting human beings with new animal viruses, for which no treatments exist. Transgenic animals themselves may be caused considerable suffering by the biological effects of the insertion of foreign genes, which may disrupt their growth and development in unpredictable ways.

The risks attendant upon the emerging ability to alter the genes of living human beings are also great. Even the alteration of somatic cell DNA, for legitimate thera-peutic purposes, carries some risk of inadvertently damaging germline DNA, thereby causing new hereditary illnesses or disabilities (Boyce 1998). If the current *de facto* moratorium on alterations of germline DNA is eventually ended, human beings in the distant future may face hereditary health problems caused by the side-effects of well-intended alterations carried out in earlier generations.

They may also inherit a social world more deeply divided by socioeconomic class and ethnicity. Lee Silver envisions a time when those who can afford it, routinely use genetic therapy to "improve" upon their germline DNA. In his scenario, the class distinction between the wealthy "GenRich" and the impoverished "Naturals" be-comes so deeply institutionalized that there is no movement from one class to the other, and no intermarriage between them; and in time humanity divides into mutually infertile species (Silver 1997: 4–7).

This unappealing scenario has a degree of plausibility, not because the genetic engineering of more capable human beings is likely to be easy, but because of the widespread belief in the almost exclusively genetic determination of human abilities. In a world of genetically enhanced children, this belief is likely to lead to systematic discrimination against the genetically "imperfect," or "unimproved." As Ruth Hub-bard points out, the idea that traits like intelligence are determined primarily by the genes is eagerly embraced by supporters of the status quo; for it seems to show that the wealthy classes and nations owe their wealth to inherent genetic superiority (Hubbard and Elijah 1993: 9).

Another legitimate concern is the rush by corporations, many of them large transnationals, to gain patent rights to the use of genetic material from plant and animal species from around the world, and even to portions of the human genome. The granting of ethically inappropriate and overly-broad patents, e.g., to the genomes of plants or animals that have been known and used by indigenous people for generations, is a form of what some call "biopiracy." The potentially enormous profits to be made in this genetic goldrush make it reasonable to question whether the corporations will spontaneously share the proceeds with the nations and ethnic groups from which genetic material is taken, or undertake sufficiently careful evalu-ations of the medical, agricultural, and ecosystemic risks.

If the potential biological and sociological consequences of the marketing of new genetic technologies are this dire, then perhaps a long-term ban on at least some of

151

the riskier applications is called for. Perhaps some DNA, such as human germline DNA, should be accorded a sacred status that precludes altering it.

The Sacred Gene

Some extraordinary religious and symbolic meanings have already become associated with the human genome. As Dorothy Nelkin and M. Susan Lindee point out, human DNA has been used as a symbol of individual human identity, and of the human spirit, soul, or essence. Many people are horrified by the prospect of cloning human beings from the DNA of adults or children, in part because they fear that humans whose genetic constitution is not unique would not be real human beings, with individual minds, wills, and souls. Many are inclined to view the human genome as "a sacred territory, a taboo area, that by virtue of its spiritual importance should never be manipulated" (Nelkin and Lindee 1995: 54).

The tendency to attribute a special moral or spiritual significance to DNA can be found in both religious and scientific writing. For instance, opponents of abortion have often pointed to the presence of the full complement of chromosomes in the nucleus of a human zygote, as evidence that the zygote is already a human being, possessed of the right to life.

John Noonan maintains that conception is "the decisive moment of humanization," because,

> at conception the new being receives the genetic code. It is this genetic information which determines his characteristics, which is the biological carrier of the possibility of human wisdom... A being with the human genetic code is a man. (Noonan 1993: 59)

Scientists, too, have been willing to view the gene "not only as a powerful biological entity but also as a sacred text that can explain the natural and moral order" (Nelkin and Lindee, p. 39). For instance, Richard Dawkins speaks of genes as, in effect, the true locus of human agency. He is aware that "Genes have no foresight. They do not plan ahead" (Dawkins 1976: 24). Yet he describes their activities as though they were conscious agents, with a sense of self, and their own self-centered interests:

> Individuals are not stable things, they are fleeting... the genes... change partners and march on... they are the replicators and we are their survival machines. When we have served our purpose we are cast aside. But genes are denizens of geological time; genes are forever. (Dawkins, p. 35)

Both Noonan and Dawkins impute to genes properties that might once have been attributed to the soul. For Noonan, genes constitute the human essence, that which makes us uniquely valuable beings. Thus, a single cell may be regarded as the moral equal of an adult human being, if it contains a complete set of human chromosomes. For Dawkins, genes are powerful – even godly – beings, which call us into existence, and which enjoy a form of immortality that human and other organisms do not.

Empirical Arguments Against Sanctification

Both these authors ascribe to DNA a more impressive form of causal agency than the empirical evidence warrants. It takes more than a package of DNA to constitute an organism. The DNA within a human zygote does not make the zygote already a human being, or even necessarily a potential human being. Without the soon-to-be-pregnant woman, and her personal, social, and biological support systems, the zygote has no potential to become a new human being. The invention of ectogenesis machines would not fundamentally change the absolute dependence of the DNA upon the rest of the embryonic organism, and its nurturing environment.

Even in favorable circumstances, the form and behavior of an organism is only partially determined by its nuclear DNA. In Stuart Newman's words, DNA provides "a list of ingredients, not a recipe for their interactions" (cited in Rifkin 1998a: 157). Genes function as parts of organisms, responding to complex influences from elsewhere in the organism and the larger environment. That is why even monozygotic twins are often different in appearance and personality, and why cloned humans, originating from different ova and gestated in different wombs and/ or at different times, would be even more different from one another. Newman says that:

> The "environment" of the genome includes not only externally controllable factors like temperature and nutrition, but also numerous maternally-provided proteins present in the egg cell at the time of fertilization. These proteins influence gene activity, and by virtue of variations in their amounts and spatial distribution in the egg can cause embryos even of genetically identical twins to develop in uniquely different ways. (Rifkin, p. 157)

DNA is not the sole source and shaper of organisms, and neither is it an immortal being. It is not an immaterial entity that is eternally reincarnated in new physical bodies. It is a physical part of living and mortal organisms, one that has a central but not omnipotent role in the organism's development, functioning, and reproduction. Like other parts of an organism, it usually dies (i.e., stops functioning and begins to degenerate) more or less at the same time that the organism does. Like any other part of the organism, it is replicated, more or less accurately, in the organism's progeny. To speak of genes as immortal is, at best, a misleading way to indicate that their replication is sufficiently consistent that plant and animal species often retain fairly stable hereditary traits over long periods of time.

In short, we can look to genes to explain much about biology, but we should not expect to find in them the essence of humanity, the locus of human agency, or the fulfillment of the dream of personal immortality. Like other elements of living organisms, genes are replicated in new organisms because they have served the reproductive success of ancestral organisms. That we need DNA in order to develop, live, and reproduce, does not make our genes the sum of our humanity, or our omnipotent masters, any more than our need for kidneys makes us into passive vehicles for the production of more kidneys.

Pragmatic Arguments Against Sanctification

I have argued that genes are unsuitable candidates for independent moral status. It is possible, nevertheless, that many cultures will come to treat them as sacred, for pragmatic and perhaps spiritual reasons. But, despite the dangers of the new genetic technologies, there are at least two good reasons to resist the sanctification of the gene.

In the first place, the moral objections to particular applications of genetic technology are contingent upon current estimates of their dangers, as weighed against the realistic hope of benefit. The possibility of harm to future generations and planetary ecosystems must be taken seriously, even though the magnitude of the risks is still uncertain. The risks of altering the human germline DNA, at the present time, almost certainly outweigh any likely benefits, or any that could not be achieved in other ways. But this may not always be the case. Suppose it were possible to modify the human immune systems to resist HIV, or some other lethal and pandemic pathogen, through carefully targeted modifications of the DNA of human gametes or zygotes. Might there not be a point at which the expected saving of life would ethically outweigh the risk of harmful side-effects? It would be premature to suppose that modification of the human genome will always be more dangerous than the alternatives. Yet the ascription of either sacredness or moral status tends towards permanence, and towards strong resistance to reevaluation in the light of changing conditions.

The second reason to resist the ascription of sacred status to the gene is that it will tend to suggest, wrongly, that applications of genetic technology that do not involve the direct alteration of genes are always less morally problematic than those that do. But many of the possible harms to present and future human beings resulting from these technologies are not genetic harms, i.e., harms to their DNA. For instance, testing to detect genetic markers for a particular illness, such as Huntington's Disease, does not in itself alter the DNA within living human beings. However, it can lead to serious problems for individuals, such as the denial of medical insurance or employment discrimination. No putative moral obligations to DNA can have been violated; but the information has been used to the unfair disadvantage of the individual. The denial of employment based upon genetic liabilities that do not preclude doing the job well is unjust, for much the same reason that racist or sexist discrimination is unjust. Denying medical insurance, on the grounds that the applicant has genes that are likely to cause illness, is also unjust, especially in the absence of alternative means of access to adequate medical services. The genes of persons who are discriminated against in these ways will not feel wronged; but the persons will.

Similarly, many of the important objections to the patenting of plants, animals, and parts of the human genome cannot be expressed in terms of obligations to genes. When John Moore's spleen tissue was used without his knowledge to develop a patented cell line now thought to be worth billions of dollars (Rifkin 1998a: 60), the offense was not to Moore's cells, but to his legitimate expectation that they would not be commercially exploited without his consent. Although he may have suffered no medical harm from the appropriation of his cells, he was wronged by the secret taking of potentially valuable parts of his body, to which he provided access only to facilitate his own medical treatment. He was entitled – morally, if not legally – to the opportunity to give or withhold consent to this use of his cells; and perhaps also to make his consent contingent upon receiving a modest share of any profits.

Similarly, when plant and animal resources of a region are found to be valuable for genetic research or commercialization, simple justice would suggest that profits be shared with the people of the region. Quite often, they have known of the species for generations, and made use of its medicinal, nutritional, or other properties. Patenting the species may reasonably be regarded a theft of their moral property. The patenting of biological resources that are derived from the bodies of human beings is also arguably a form of wrongful taking. When patents were sought in 1993 on a virus derived from the cell line of a Guaymi Indian woman from Panama, Isidro Acosta, President of the Guaymi General Congress, protested in the following terms:

> I never imagined people would patent plants and animals. It's fundamentally immoral, contrary to the Guaymi view of nature, and our place in it. To patent human material...to take human DNA and patents its products...that violates the integrity of life itself, and our deepest sense of morality. (Rifkin 1998a: 14)

The offense here is perceived by Mr. Acosta as an offense against life itself; and perhaps he is right. But there is also an offense against the woman, who presumably did not donate biological material in order that it could be commercially exploited, with no benefits accuring either to her or to her community. This offense is more readily explained in terms of established moral and legal concepts than in terms of the sacredness of DNA. The disrespect to the Guaymi woman is clear enough; but disrespect to life, or to DNA, is a more subjective charge, difficult to prove or disprove. After all, who can say whether DNA is harmed by being patented, or recombined into new patterns?

The ascription of moral status to the gene does not help us to understand either the impact of genetic technologies upon individual persons and groups, or its potential contribution to economic inequality, globally and within nations. There is no necessary connection between the alteration of plant or animal genes, and the granting of patents on the use of particular species or genes. National and international law could promulgate the principle that knowledge about human and nonhuman genes is an international "commons," free to be accessed and utilized by anyone, for any ethically defensible purpose. Altering DNA, or marketing products of recombinant DNA techniques, is neither good nor evil except insofar as it produces harms or benefits to human and other organisms; and it is on these that our moral analysis needs to be focused.

Regulation without Sanctification

In an episode of the television series *Deep Space Nine*, a young physician is revealed to have been subjected to illegal genetic enhancement therapy as a child, because his ambitious parents were unsatisfied with the speed of his intellectual development. These treatments make him legally ineligible for his job on the space station, or any other post in Star Fleet. While it is harsh to visit the sins of the parents on the child, a long-term ban on the alteration of either human somatic DNA or human germline DNA, solely for the purpose of enhancing socially valued traits, might be called for. Even therapeutic alterations of germline DNA could be very dangerous in the present state of the art; but attempts to improve upon genetic traits that are clearly within the normal range are even more dubious. The risks of harmful side-effects for future persons who have not consented to be genetically altered mitigates against trying to "fix" parts of the genome that are not broken.

The establishment of effective international conventions for the regulation of genetic technologies will require the cooperation of people of all nations. The hope of success rests upon keeping the focus of analysis and advocacy on the likely impacts of the development and marketing of genetic technologies upon present and future human beings, nonhuman organisms, and ecosystems. International agreements are needed to establish nonmonopolistic ways of marketing the products of these technologies, and just ways of defining intellectual property rights. These are concerns that people of all spiritual persuasions may share.

Arguments for a special moral status for genes are more religious than secular in nature, depending as they do upon empirically unsupported beliefs about the moral and spiritual significance of DNA. These religious or quasi-religious views are entitled to respect, so long as they do not issue in demands that are seriously harmful to persons who do not share those beliefs. Except in special circumstances (e.g., certain sorts of criminal investigation), nothing should ever be done to any part of the body of a competent person, or to biological materials derived from it, that is contrary to that person's will. When the parts or products of a person's body are used in ways that violate their deeply held moral or religious convictions, the insult is deep. Such insult should be avoided, regardless of whether the person's convictions are widely shared. Yet, because personal or cultural convictions about the sacredness of genes are neither generally shared, nor well based in empirical science, they are inadequate as a guideline for the development of law and public policy.

Conclusion

I have argued that genes have no moral status, and no special sacredness, separate from that of the organisms of which they are part. Like other body parts, our chromosomes can malfunction in ways that endanger our health and survival. When they do, altering them becomes a morally legitimate option – provided that the knowledge exists to do this safely, and without risking the health of present or future persons. Similarly, genetically altered crops may significantly benefit growers and consumers. There is no *a priori* reason not to permit such alterations – provided that we know enough to avoid the associated risks, such as the risk of genetically contaminating wild species, or fostering a dangerous level of human dependence on genetically uniform crops.

Unfortunately, we are far from having this knowledge. What we need now is not a new moral status for genes, but an enhanced appreciation of the vulnerability of future human and nonhuman organisms, and natural ecosystems, to the unwise development and use of genetic technologies.

Note

1   Some people make an exception to this rule when the injured part is a fetus; but that is usually either because they regard the fetus as already a separate human being; or because they are concerned for the well-being of the future human being who may develop from the injured fetus.

References

Agar, N.: "Biocentrism and the concept of life." *Ethics* 108 (1997), pp. 147–68.

Boyce, N.: "Suffer the children: the great taboo of gene therapy may have been broken." *The New Scientist*, 2125 (March 1998), p. 7.

Dawkins, R.: *The Selfish Gene* (Oxford and New York: Oxford University Press, 1976).

Dworkin, R.: *Taking Rights Seriously* (Cambridge, MA: Harvard University Press, 1978).

Hubbard, R. and Elijah, W.: *Exploding the Gene Myth: How Genetic Information is Produced and Manipulated by Scientists, Physicians, Insurance Companies, Educators, and Law Enforcers* (Boston: Beacon Press, 1993).

Kant, I.: *The Moral Law: Kant's Groundwork of the Metaphysics of Morals*, Paton, H. J., trans. (London: Hutchinson, 1948).

Kant, I.: *Lectures on Ethics*, L. Infield, trans. (New York: Harper and Row, 1963).

Nelkin, D. and Lindee, S.: *The DNA Mystique: The Gene as a Cultural Icon* (New York: W. H. Freeman, 1995).

Noonan, J.: "An almost absolute value in history." In Dwartz, D. M.: *Arguing About Abortion* (Belmont, CA: Wadsworth, 1993).

Paton, H. J.: *Lectures on Ethics*, trans. Louis Infield (New York: Harper & Row, 1963).

Regan, T.: *The Case for Animal Rights* (Berkeley and Los Angeles: University of California Press, 1983).

Rifkin, J.: *The Biotech Century: Harnessing the Gene and Remaking the World* (New York; Jeremy T. Farcher/Putnam, 1998a).

Rifkin, J.: "The biotech century; human life as intellectual property." *The Nation* April 13, 1998b, pp. 11–19.

Schweitzer, A.: *Civilization and Ethics: The Philosophy of Civilization* (London: A. & C. Block, 1929).

Silver, L. M.: *Remaking Eden: Cloning and Beyond in a Brave New World* (New York: Avon Books, 1997).

Singer, P.: *Animal Liberation: A New Ethic for Our Treatment of Animals* (New York: Avon Books, 1975).

Singer, P.: *Practical Ethics* (Cambridge: Cambridge University Press, 1979).

Taylor, P.: *Respect for Nature: A Theory of Environmental Ethics* (Princeton: Princeton University Press, 1983).

12

The Ethical Use of Human Embryonic Stem Cells in Research and Therapy

JOHN HARRIS

The use of human embryonic stem cells (ES cells) raises a number of important issues. Some of these issues have to do with the moral status of the embryo, some with the consents required to us ES cells, some with the intentions behind (a) the production of the embryos/fetuses and (b) the use of the embryonic material, and finally there are issues of symbolic as opposed to utilitarian accounts of the meaning of what is done.

Before considering the ethics of such use in detail we need to understand the possible therapeutic and research uses of stem cells and, equally, the imperatives for research and therapy.

Why Embryonic Stem Cells?

Embryonic stem cells were first grown in culture as recently as February 1998 by James A. Thomson of the University of Wisconsin. In November of that year Thomson announced in *Science* that such human ES cells formed a wide variety of recognizable tissues when transplanted into mice (Thomson et al. 1998). As Roger A. Pedersen noted recently (Pedersen 1999):

> Research on embryonic stem cells will ultimately lead to techniques for generating cells that can be employed in therapies, not just for heart attacks, but for many conditions in which tissue is damaged . . . If it were possible to control the differentiation of human embryonic stem cells in culture the resulting cells could potentially help repair damage caused by congestive heart failure, Parkinson's Disease, diabetes and other afflictions. They could prove especially valuable for treating conditions affecting the heart and the islets of the pancreas, which retain few or no stem cells in an adult and so cannot renew themselves naturally.

This might eventually enable us not only to grow tailor-made human organs which, using cloning technology of the type that produced Dolly the sheep, could be made individually compatible with their designated recipients. In addition to tailor-made organs or parts of organs, such as heart-valves, for example, it may be possible to use ES cells to colonize damaged parts of the body including the brain, and to promote the repair and regrowth of damaged tissue. These possibilities have long been theoretically understood, but it is only now with the isolation of human ES cells that the reality is reasonably close (Harris 1992).

Talking of these possibilities recently, Mooney and Mikos (1999) noted:

> An exciting new strategy, however, is poised to revolutionize the treatment of patients who need new vital structures: the creation of man-made tissues or organs, known as neo-organs. In one scenario, a tissue engineer injects or places a given molecule, such as a growth factor, into a wound or an organ that requires regeneration. These molecules cause the patient's own cells to migrate into the wound site, turn into the right type of cell and regenerate the tissue. In the second and more ambitious, procedure, the patient receives cells – either his or her own or those of a donor – that have been harvested previously and incorporated into three-dimensional scaffolds of biodegradable polymers, such as those used to make dissolvable structures. The entire structure of cells and scaffolding is transplanted into the wound site where the cells replicate, reorganize and form new tissue. At the same time the artificial polymers break down, leaving only a completely natural final product in the body – a neo-organ. The creation of neo-organs applies the basic knowledge gained in biology over the past few decades to the problems of tissue and organ reconstruction just as advances in material science make possible entirely new types of architectural design.

In addition to these new therapies which will include organ and tissue replacement and cures for many diseases including diabetes, neurodegenerative disorders, and heart disease, human ES cells could have major research applications including the discovery of rare proteins.

One therapeutic use of stem cells that should be highlighted is the case of skin grafts, as Mooney and Mikos have emphasized:

> The need for skin is acute: every year six hundred thousand Americans suffer from diabetic ulcers, which are particularly difficult to heal; another six hundred thousand have skin removed to treat skin cancer; and between ten thousand and fifteen thousand undergo skin grafts to treat severe burns . . . The next tissue to be widely used in humans will most likely be cartilage for orthopedic, craniofacial, and urological applications. Currently available cartilage is insufficient for the half a million operations annually in the US that repair damaged joints and for the additional twenty-eight thousand face and head reconstructive surgeries.

Having noted some of the research and therapeutic possibilities, it is important to remind ourselves of the moral reasons we have to pursue them. "Research" always sounds such an abstract and even vainglorious objective when set against passionate feelings of fear or distaste. We need to remind ourselves of the human benefits that stem from research and the human costs of not pursuing research.

Stem Cells for Organ and Tissue Transplant

It is difficult to estimate how many people might benefit from the products of stem cell research should it be permitted and prove fruitful. Perhaps the remotest of the likely products of such research would be tailor-made human organs, but at least in this field we have some reliable data on the numbers of human lives that wait on the development of better ways of coping with their need to replace or repair damaged organs.

"In the world as a whole there are an estimated 700,000 patients on dialysis . . . In India alone . . . 100,000 new patients present with kidney failure each year" (few if any of whom are on dialysis and only 3,000 of whom will receive transplants) . . . "Almost 3 million Americans suffer from congestive heart failure . . . deaths related to this condition are estimated at 250,000 each year . . . 27,000 patients die annually from liver disease . . . In Western Europe as a whole 40,000 patients await a kidney but only . . . 10,000 kidneys" become available (Cooper and Lanza 2000). Nobody knows how many people fail to make it onto the waiting lists and so disappear from the statistics.

While the days of genetically modified tailor-made organs are still very far off, compatible organs may one day supply many of the needs for tissue repair and replacement, releasing more donor organs to meet transplant needs which cannot be met in other ways.

Immortality

Finally, we should note the possibility of therapies that would extend life, perhaps even to the point at which humans might become in some sense "immortal." We are all 'designed' to age and die, but this looks increasingly like a design fault. If cells weren't programmed to age, if the telomeres, which govern the number of times a cell may divide, didn't shorten with each division, if our bodies could repair damage due to disease and aging "from within," we would certainly live much longer and healthier lives. Cloned ES cells appropriately reprogrammed might be made to colonize particular tissue and organs, triggering constant regeneration. Precise combinations of growth factors injected directly into muscle or tissue might put the body into a state of constant renewal. If we could discover all the genes that trigger the aging process and switch them off in the early embryo, and also programme the capacity for regeneration into cells, we could then "write immortality into the genes of the human race." We should note, of course, that immortality is not the same as invulnerability, and even these "immortals" could die or be killed. Steven Austed has calculated that, based on the death rate of 11-year-olds (who have ceased to die of childhood illnesses and haven't yet begun to die of the diseases of old age), life expectancy might eventually average 1,200 years (Harris 2000; Kirkwood 1999).

A Guarded Welcome for Stem Cell Research

On January 22, 2001, the United Kingdom became the first country, certainly in Europe, to approve human embryonic stem cell research, albeit with what the government described as "adequate safeguards." The UK government had set up an "expert group" under the Chief Medical Officer (CMO's Expert Group) and this group finally reported in June 2000 (*Stem Cell Research: Medical Progress with Responsibility*). In August 2000, the government published its response, broadly welcoming the report and accepting all of its major recommendations (Government Response 2000). These recommendations were the subject of a free vote in both houses of the UK parliament, and this vote was overwhelmingly for approval of stem cell research and so-called "therapeutic cloning." Given the isolation of this approach in Europe, it is important to be clear about the arguments that might sustain the ethical respectability of such research. The CMO's Expert Group relied for such argument mainly on the consistency of the research, with embryo research already permitted and well established in the United Kingdom under the Human Fertilization and Embryology Act 1990, and the regulation of research under that Act by the Human Fertilization and Embryology Authority (the HFEA). Basically under that act research on embryos is permitted to investigate problems of infertility and for other limited purposes. Now the list of permitted purposes is extended to include human embryonic stem cell research. The government also gratuitously (but perhaps expediently) has repeated the unsupported claim that human reproductive cloning was "ethically unacceptable" and should continue to be outlawed,[1] and has promised firm legislation to outlaw human reproductive cloning.

The Precautionary Principle

People often believe that there is some moral imperative to be ultracautious in permitting new research, particularly in the general field of genetics. This has now been elevated into a principle, commonly called "the precautionary principle." It is not unusual to find this so-called "precautionary principle" being invoked in circumstances in which it is far from clear in which direction (if any) caution lies. A similar problem is familiar from discussions about germline gene therapy (British Medical Association 1992, Harris 1994). Precaution was urged to prevent the introduction of germline gene therapy on the principal ground that germline changes would affect future generations indefinitely and are probably irreversible. Any damage done if germline therapy were to go wrong would therefore (a) be magnified and (b) continue as long as procreation continued. However, given that the germline therapy would likely be introduced to correct genetic defects, to fail to carry out the therapy would also adversely affect future generations indefinitely, and thus the harm caused by the genetic defect would (a) be magnified and (b) continue as long as procreation continued. We would only know which way lay caution, if we could compare the number of times the germline therapy would go wrong and the magnitude of the damage thereby caused, with the number of times a defective gene would be disastrously expressed and the magnitude of the harm that would cause.

Similarly in the present case. We cannot know which way lies caution without having some rational basis for establishing the scale of likely dangers from pursuing stem cell research and comparing those with the ongoing costs of failing to pursue the research to a successful conclusion. These costs may include the vast numbers of people dying for want of donor tissue and organs or from other diseases for which ES cells might prove therapeutic.

161

What is clear is that, as has been indicated above, with hundreds of thousands, perhaps millions of people dying annually worldwide from damaged organs and tissue and from the other diseases we have reviewed, any possible dangers accruing from ES cell research would have to be "real and present" before any moratorium or delay could be defended on ethical or even precautionary grounds. It is unclear how ES cell research presents any real and present dangers (with the possible exception of loss of popularity by politicians), but it is to the possible moral dangers that we must now turn.

The Ethics of ES Cell Research

Since stem cells, which might be used for research and therapeutic purposes, can, at present, only be obtained either from aborted fetuses or from preimplantation embryos, their recovery and use for current practical purposes turns crucially on the moral status of the embryo and the fetus.

This may not remain the case for long. It has recently been reported that the Geron Corporation, following it's collaboration with the Roslin Institute (Dolly's birthplace), is working on more efficient and less controversial ways of producing ES cells. Dr. Thomas Okarma, Geron's vice-president for Research, reports that the new company, Roslin Bio-Med, will pursue research to understand how eggs "reprogram" the nucleus of an adult cell to make it function like embryonic pluripotent cells. If this process can be understood and replicated, then 'cloned' stem cells might be produced by using the reprogramming factors found in an egg to alter the properties of cells taken from adults and produce ES cells for use in the adult donor. It might even be possible to use animal rather than human eggs for this purpose. In neither case would the resulting ES cells have to be derived from embryos or fetuses (New York Times website).

If and when such techniques become possible and safe, or when we are able to collect and use the stem cells that remain in humans throughout their lives, or successfully reprogram adult cells, most of the current 'ethical' objections to the creation and use of ES cells would disappear. However, many believe that embryonic stem cells will always be the best type of stem cells to use, because they have proven and well-researched characteristics compared to other sources of stem cells. It is therefore likely to be and remain important to see whether the use of human embryos and fetuses as sources of cells is morally objectionable.

There are three possible solutions to the ethical problems of using human embryonic stem cells. The first is the use of cells from the early embryo, which survives the removal of such cells. The second is the deployment of arguments about the moral status of the embryo. This is the line taken, for example, by the CMO's Expert Group in the United Kingdom, which relies on a moral distinction, used in previous legislation and regulation, between the early embryo prior to the development of the primitive streak at around 14 days' development, and later stages of embryonic development. The third solution is a reminder about the role of embryo loss in reproduction.

Stem Cells from Early Embryos

It is possible to remove cells from early preimplantation embryos without damage to the original embryo. This may be one solution to the problem of obtaining embryonic stem cells. However, if the cells removed are totipotent (capable of becoming literally any part of the creature including the whole creature), then they are in effect separate zygotes, they are themselves "embryos," and so must be protected to whatever extent embryos are protected. If, however, such cells are merely pluripotent (capable of development in many ways but not in all, and not capable of becoming a new separate creature), then they could not be regarded as embryos and the use of them would presumably not offend those who regard the embryo as sacrosanct. Unfortunately it is not at present possible to tell in advance whether a particular cell is totipotent or simply pluripotent. This can only be discovered retrospectively by observing the cell's capabilities.

The Moral Status of the Embryo

While everyone has views about the moral status of the embryo and some of those who have views even have arguments to support their views, attempts to solve problems about issues which depend on the use of embryonic or fetal material by recourse to establishing the moral status of the embryo have proved intractable. Arguments about the moral status of the embryo are convincing and in some cases conclusive; however, they notoriously fail to persuade the groups crucial to achieving consensus on vexed policy issues. Most people are neither puzzled as to the moral status of the embryo or fetus, nor do they welcome arguments which challenge their views. What they seek from philosophical reflection on these issues is not enlightenment but confirmation of prejudice.

While this may appear a depressing conclusion, I believe that progress in the field of social policy may still be made. This is because many members of these same groups, and if not them, then certainly established principles and practices in the societies in which they live and to which they owe allegiance, are committed to policies which indicate the permissibility and acceptability of a number of crucial practices.

Lessons from Sexual Reproduction

I will try now to indicate what follows about the ethics of the use of ES cells from practices or principles that are well established in many of the relevant societies, and these will of course include societies with the capacity to pursue such research. This involves exploration of the third way. We will start with the ethics and law of human reproduction.

While there are of course better or worse reasons for creating an embryo or establishing a pregnancy, people who can do so without medical assistance are not

163

usually required either to provide reasons or to qualify for the right or liberty to do so. I will assume that the practice of refraining from interfering with unassisted reproduction is both morally defensible and legally acceptable, and that public policy on reproductive liberty for the consenting fertile is unlikely to change. Even the use of assisted reproductive technologies (ART) is now commonplace, and although in some circumstances parents have to demonstrate their fitness (for example, in the UK, under the Human Fertilisation and Embryology Act 1990, doctors must take account of the welfare of the child to be born as a result of using the technologies), the creation of embryos using ART is very common and subject to relatively few restrictions.

Establishing a Pregnancy by Sexual Reproduction

Let us start with the free and completely unfettered liberty to establish a pregnancy by sexual reproduction without any "medical" assistance.

What are people and societies who accept this free and unfettered liberty committing themselves to? What has a God who has ordained natural procreation committed herself to?

We now know that for every successful pregnancy which results in a live birth, many, perhaps as many as five, early embryos will be lost or "miscarry" (although these are not perhaps "miscarriages" as the term is normally used, because this sort of very early embryo loss is almost always entirely unnoticed). Many of these embryos will be lost because of genetic abnormalities, but some would have been viable. How are we to think of the decision to attempt to have a child in the light of these facts? One obvious and inescapable conclusion is that God and/or nature has ordained that "spare" embryos be produced for almost every pregnancy, and that most of these will have to die in order that a sibling embryo can come to birth. Thus the sacrifice of embryos seems to be an inescapable and inevitable part of the process of procreation. It may not be intentional sacrifice, and it may not attend every pregnancy, but the loss of many embryos is the inevitable consequence of the vast majority of (and perhaps all) pregnancies. For everyone who knows the facts, it is conscious, knowing, and therefore deliberate sacrifice; and for everyone, regardless of 'guilty' knowledge, it is part of the true description of what they do in having or attempting to have children.

We may conclude that the production of spare embryos, some of which will be sacrificed, is not unique to ART; it is an inevitable (and presumably acceptable, or at least tolerable?) part of all reproduction.

Is it a blessing that in the present state of technology, all of these spare embryos, byproducts of natural sexual procreation, are lost, for the most part unnoticed and their stem cells irretrievable and unusable? If, perhaps *per impossibile*, we found a way of monitoring and collecting stem cells and perhaps other usable material from these early miscarriages, would there be any ethical objection to our so doing? I shall assume for the moment that this is a rhetorical question, because the answer is clearly that it is not a moral advantage that no stem cells are recoverable from this process, it is merely an unfortunate fact.

It might be responded that mothers do not usually wish or intend the death of their embryos when they become pregnant (although many who conceive will not have wished to become pregnant), and that this process cannot therefore reasonably be compared to the deliberate creation of spare embryos for research or therapy, or the deliberate use of embryos which might otherwise be implanted. There are important differences of course, but it is not clear that these differences are material.

Both natural procreation and ART involve a process in which embryos, additional to those which will actually become children, are created only to die. I will continue to call these "spare" embryos in each case. If either of these processes are justified it is because the objective of producing a live, healthy child is judged worth this particular cost. So far we will assume that the purpose in each case is the securing of a successful pregnancy and a new, live human child.

The intentions of the actors, appealed to in the frequently deployed but fallacious doctrine of double effect,[2] are not here relevant. What matters is what the agents knowingly and voluntarily bring about. That this is true can be seen by considering the following example.

Suppose we discovered that the use of mobile phones within 50 meters of a pregnant woman resulted in a high probability, near certainty, of early miscarriage. No one would suggest that once this is known, it would be legitimate to continue use of mobile phones in such circumstances on the grounds that phone owners did not intend to cause miscarriages. Any claim by phone users that they were merely intent on causing a public nuisance, or, less probably, that they were making telephonic communication with another person and therefore not responsible for the miscarriages, would be rightly dismissed. It might of course be the case that we would decide that mobile communications were so important that the price of early miscarriage and the consequent sacrifice of embryos, was one well worth paying for the freedom to use mobile phones. And this is, presumably, what we feel about the importance of establishing pregnancies and having children. Mobile phone users of course usually have an alternative method of communication available, but we'll suppose they do not.

To be sure, using a mobile phone is trivial by comparison with the moral significance of creating a new human life, and it might be argued that the comparison is misleading; however, the point of the analogy lies elsewhere. This example shows the incoherence of the so-called doctrine of double effect. The motives or primary purposes of the phone user are clearly irrelevant to the issue of their responsibility for the consequences of their actions. They are responsible for what they knowingly bring about. The only remaining question is as to whether, given the moral importance of what they are trying to achieve (phoning their friends), the consequent miscarriages are a price it is morally justifiable to exact to achieve that end. Here the answer is clearly "no." However, when we pose the same question about the moral acceptability of sacrificing embryos in pursuance of establishing a successful pregnancy, the answer seems different. My point is that the same issues arise when considering the use of embryos to obtain ES cells. Given the possible therapeutic uses we have reviewed, it would be difficult, I suggest, to regard such uses as other than morally highly significant.

We may conclude that there can be no absolute prohibition on the conscious, voluntary destruction of human embryos in pursuit of a particular morally important goal: that of producing a live, healthy child.

The Incoherence of Current US Federal Law

In the United States, current federal law prohibits the use of federal funds for "the creation of a human embryo" explicitly for research purposes or, more crucially, for "research in which a human embryo or embryos are destroyed, discarded or knowingly subjected to the risk of injury or death" (Pub.L. 1998). Such law is presumably animated by concern about the morally problematic nature of such actions. As we have noted, normal sexual reproduction inevitably involves a process in which "a human embryo or embryos are destroyed or discarded." It is also incontrovertibly an activity in which "a human embryo or embryos" are "knowingly subjected to the risk of injury or death"; at least for anyone who knows the facts of life. It is interesting that the framers of this federal legislation chose to concentrate on the "knowing," rather than say the "intended," risk of injury or death to embryos. It seems natural to regard this as some evidence that the framers of this legislation implicitly accept a premise of this chapter: that it is the knowledge of consequences that carries with it responsibility, and not the more narrow idea of intending or willing those consequences as a primary objective of decisions or conduct.

The conscious, voluntary production of embryos for research, not as the byproduct of attempts (assisted or not) at reproduction is a marginally different case, although some will think the differences important. However, if the analysis so far is correct, then this case is analogous in that it involves the production and destruction of embryos for an important moral purpose. All that remains is to decide what sorts of moral objectives are comparable in importance to that of producing a child. Although some would defend such a position, some preference utilitarians for example, it would seem more than a little perverse to imagine that saving an existing life could rank lower in moral importance to creating a new life. Assisted reproduction is, for example, given relatively low priority in the provision of healthcare services. Equally, saving a life that will exist in the future seems morally comparable to creating a future life. In either case the moral quality and importance of the actions and decisions involved and of their consequences seem comparable.

The Symbolic Value of Life

At this point it is important to consider whether appeals to the symbolic, intrinsic, or deontological value of life and its link with procreation offers support for any distinctions that would enable us to separate the creation of embryos for procreation and for other life-saving moral purposes.

Although it mixes arguments of many different sorts, the following quotation from a paper by George Annas, Art Caplan, and Sherman Elias (1996) is typical of appeals to the symbolic value of life.

> The moral problem with making embryos for research is that as a society we do not want to see embryos treated as products or as mere objects, for fear that we will cheapen the value of parenting, risk commercializing procreation and trivialize the act of procreation.

166

It is society's attitude toward procreation and the interests of those whose gametes are involved in making the embryos that provide the moral force behind the restriction or prohibition of the manufacture of embryos for nonprocreative uses.

Of course it could not be "society's attitude toward procreation" that provides the "moral force" behind the nonprocreative production of embryos, rather it must be some values or moral features of procreation that animates and justifies society's attitude. There are two ways of understanding the moral value of procreation. One is in terms of the moral importance of future generations and the continuation of the human species. The other is in terms of the value of the individual lives that result from particular procreative acts. We can, I believe, ignore the former dimension since it would be implausible to suppose that the manufacture of embryos for nonprocreative uses impacts upon the viability of, or probability of there being, future generations in any significant way. To be sure, creating embryos that will never become persons has a certain symbolic meaning; but this meaning needs to be understood, interpreted if you like, in the light of two relevant facts. The first is that, as we have noted, natural sexual reproduction produces nonviable embryos in not dissimilar circumstances. The second is that there are life-saving and life-enhancing purposes behind the creation of such embryos, again comparable to those of normal sexual reproduction. If, on the other hand, procreation is a sacred and symbolic act because it results in an entity that will grow into a new human being and such a person is morally important; then it is indeed possible to see the point of attaching symbolic importance to such an act. However, as we have noted, it is a necessary, or at least inevitable, part of natural procreation that embryos miscarry and die without ever becoming such a morally important new human being. Moreover, insofar as procreation symbolizes or is expressive of the value of life, it is difficult to see why the creation of embryos for therapy, and research well calculated to cure or prevent life-threatening conditions of future human beings, is not equally expressive of the sacred and symbolic importance of human life.

As John Robertson has persuasively suggested:

> Although embryos do not themselves have rights, they are an occasion for expressing or symbolising one's views about the importance or value of human life, thereby constituting one's moral or national character in the process. People differ, however, over the degree and intensity of the symbolic associations that attach to non-rights-bearing entities such as embryos. The importance of signifying or constituting a highly protective attitude towards human life by objecting to certain kinds of embryo research is thus more determined by personal or public preferences than it is by the obligations of moral duty. (Robertson 1999)

Now let's consider the ethics of production and use of ES cells against the background of the production of spare embryos as a result of ART.

ART and Spare Embryos

In IVF and some other ARTs, spare embryos are often created. These are either frozen for the future use of the woman or may be donated by her for implantation in other women or for research; they may be destroyed at her direction. Many such stored embryos are never claimed, and in the United Kingdom around 5,000 such embryos had to be destroyed. This so-called "orphaned embryos opera"[3] was performed in the summer of 1996. It came about because under the provisions of the Human Fertilisation and Embryology Act 1990 a maximum storage period of 5 years had been permitted for frozen embryos. Shortly after (and certainly because of) this tragic waste of embryonic tissue, the law was changed to permit storage for 10 years.

It is difficult to see how a society that could allow so many spare embryos to be destroyed for no good purpose could object to such embryos, or others like them, being used as sources for ES cells or for other therapeutic purposes.

We must now ask what sorts of reasons would justify using embryos for experimentation or for therapeutic purposes? Let's pose this question broadly for all fetal and embryonic material.

Tissue from Fetuses

In the United Kingdom, thinking on this issue began to crystallize with the publication of the report of the Polkinghorne Committee, which advised the UK government on these matters (*Review* 1989).

One of the key recommendations of the so-called Polkinghorne code of practice was that a woman's decision to have an abortion should not be influenced by consideration of the possible uses which might be made of the fetus, and that the initiation or termination of a pregnancy, in order to provide suitable fetal material, is unethical.[4] The Polkinghorne Committee's main preoccupation was with the ethics of using fetal ovarian tissue for reproduction. However, their conclusions were general and I will, for the sake of completeness, look at both reproductive and possible research and therapeutic uses including ES cell retrieval together.

Many people, including the Chairman of the Committee which produced the code of practice referred to, believe that people have a special interest in controlling the destiny of their own genetic material. They further believe that because the gametes contain genetic material which will be passed on indefinitely to future generations, any consent to the use of one's own genetic material in this way must be specific and must encompass the knowledge of its ultimate destiny.

For this reason, Polkinghorne suggested that consent to the use of fetal ovarian tissue by the mother must be specific. However, the Polkinghorne code of practice insists that consent to the use of fetal tissue must in general, be general; in order to avoid the possibility that women might be induced to have abortions in order to secure some specific outcome. If this is sound, the ethics of fetal ovarian donation are incompatible with the ethics of general fetal donation, and it would consequently be unethical to use fetal ovarian tissue for transplant purposes. One cannot easily resist the conclusion that the insistence on specific consent for ovarian tissue transfer in the face of a previous report demanding general consent for fetal tissue more generally, is designed to achieve a particular outcome – namely the impossibility of approving ovarian tissue transfer from fetuses.

The report thus contains a sort of Catch-22 which neatly preempts fetal ovarian donation. Even if we grant (which surely we should not) that women donors of fetal material should not be influenced by the possible uses of such material, it is completely unclear as to why a *specific* consent would be more influential than a general consent. Of course, if separation is to be maintained then one would have to ensure that the women who are asked to consent to the use of their fetal material after abortion, are so asked only *after* they have finally determined to have an abortion, and have satisfied whatever the legal requirements are which entitle them to an abortion. If this is done and, if and only if, only then are they asked specifically whether they will consent to the fetal ovaries being used, there can surely be minimal danger that they could be induced to have an abortion for that reason alone. An added security would be to deny such women any right to *direct* the particular destination of fetal ovarian tissue, but merely give specific consent as to the nature of its potential use.

Polkinghorne and others have further claimed that it would be unethical for the woman to delay the timing of her abortion until the fetus had developed to a point where certain tissue, including ovarian tissue, was usable for transplant purposes. Why this would be unethical has never been adequately explained. It is true that by delaying the abortion the woman puts herself under increased physical risk and mental strain, but if she does this freely, having been fully informed, it is surely her own decision to make. We must remember that giving birth is almost always more risky than abortion, and yet women are seldom criticized on the grounds of the increased risks involved for deciding to continue a pregnancy.

Moreover, having decided on an abortion it might be a great comfort to the woman to know that although the fetus will die, its organs, tissue, and cells will be used for beneficial purposes to save life, restore health, and perhaps to allow another woman to have the child that she so desperately wants.

Doing Something Good is Better than Doing Nothing!

Surely no one could believe that it could be better (more ethical) to allow the fetal material to go to waste than to use it for some good purpose? It must, logically, be better to do something good than to do nothing good; it must be better to make good use of something than to allow it to be wasted. It is doubtful as to whether it could be *more* ethical to help no one than to help someone. This principle, that other things being equal it is better to do some good than no good, provides the woman with a good reason to delay an abortion so that these good outcomes may be achieved (given that she has already fully determined to have an abortion for reasons independent of the good outcome for others). Those who disapprove of abortion would surely also welcome the possibility that, in postponing abortion, the woman has further time to reflect as to whether it is what she truly wants, and therefore has time to change her mind.

Of course among the other things that must be equal is the general acceptability of the practices that give rise to the fetal material. It would not follow (although it might nonetheless be the case) that there was a moral imperative not to waste valuable resources that had been generated by wicked practices.

We should note that the Polkinghorne report considers some of these points, but concludes that the arguments for not permitting a woman to vary the method and timing of her abortion so that fetal material will be available are "of such ethical importance that they outweigh those for allowing the mother to make any direction regarding the use of her fetus or fetal tissue." However, the report does not identify these ethically important arguments, and so it is difficult to know what weight, if any, to give them.

In a subsequent paper John Polkinghorne (1992) stated specifically, in the context of fetal ovarian tissue transfer, that since in such a case "the fetus would be the genetic mother of the resulting child, and the mother providing the tissue[5] would be its genetic grandmother. It seems clear to this writer that it would be ethically wrong to allow the creation of a human person linked in this way with a family without the *explicit* consent of the mother involved." It is difficult not to agree that specific consents should be required if consent is to be required at all. No consent which is not specific could be fully informed if the woman is not made aware of all the possible uses to which her fetus's tissue might be put. However, it cannot be for this reason that the creation of a genetically linked human person might be unethical, since this would give the mother, any mother, an effective veto on the production of grandchildren, whether those grandchildren were produced from the eggs of her dead fetus or from her live, 25–year-old daughter. This is not of course the circumstance envisaged by Polkinghorne, but since he specifically makes the genetic nature of the link the central feature that requires consent, it is difficult to know why other genetic parenting would not equally require specific consents.

To enable parents to veto the production of their grandchildren because their explicit consent for their children to have such grandchildren had not been given, seems somewhat excessive. Moreover this insistence on the importance of *specific* consent to the transmission of genetic material sits oddly with Polkinghorne's insistence on denying donors of fetal ovarian tissue the right to direct where such material should go. Why not permit women to do this so long as they meet the qualification for abortion first, and of course so long as their directions are not unethical for some independent reason? Obvious examples of such unethical independent reasons are where donors direct that only people of a particular race or religion should be beneficiaries.

Interim Conclusions

The use of embryonic and fetal organs and tissue including ES cells is permissible if it is for a serious beneficial purpose, either therapeutic or research. An interesting question arises as to what consents if any are required for the use of such material?

Is the consent of both "parents" of the embryo or fetus required? There seems to be a difference when we consider the case of tissue from aborted fetuses or embryos on the one hand and preimplantation embryos on the other.

Products of abortion

Let's take the case of material from aborted fetuses and embryos first. In many cases the identity of the father may not be known to the mother, even if she believes she knows it; or if his identity is known, it may not be possible to trace him at the time consent is being considered. Indeed the mother may wish to have no further contact with him. Should the genetic father have the right to veto the donation of his genetic material present in the fetus he has engendered? The question is complicated, but I think the father's preferences must ultimately be ignored. To cut through complexities which are beyond the purview of this discussion, we can note that to give the father such a right would, as discussed above, give him an effective veto on the production of any grandchildren. Either he is entitled to control the destiny of his genes or he is not; if he is, then the intervening preferences of his daughter are irrelevant, or if they are not, their special and overriding importance must be demonstrated. The reason the mother's specific consent is required, if it is, is not because she has a special interest in the destiny of her genes, but rather because of the special emotional ties of a mother to the embryo or fetus she has nurtured.

Preimplantation embryos

Here the case is rather different, because although, as in most issues of human reproduction, the woman's role is the greater and more important, the issue seems more clearly one of the rights to control the destiny of genetic material. In cases where the embryos will never become human individuals but will be the sources of organs, tissue, or cells, it seems unclear that there are any important rights to control the destiny of these. However, since people are usually confused about their connection with organic material which contains their genes it seems prudent, although not, I believe, morally required, to insist on consents from all those who have made a genetic contribution to the embryo.

Genetic Identity

Invocations of notions of genetic identity and genetic rights are often confused. As Lee Silver has noted: "The psychological power of the gene lies far out of proportion to its actual contribution to the relationships established between individuals. We should keep in mind that while a child is 99.95% the same as its genetic mother at the level of genetic information, it is also 99.90% the same as any randomly chosen person on the planet earth" (Silver 1999). Moreover we share approximately 98.5 percent of our genetic information with chimpanzees and 40 to 50 percent with bananas and cabbages. In view of these facts it is difficult to see clearly what rights to control the destiny of one's genes or genetic privacy might amount to, or indeed, on what they might be based. Do I have rights over genetic information of which I am the immediate source but which might be shared with millions of other people, or do I only have rights or interests in genes or alleles that are unique to myself if there are any such unique genes

171

or alleles? It is in fact the *combinations* of such genes and alleles that are unique. Again, as Lee Silver has noted: "If you are not a member of an identical twin pair, the chances that someone else in the world has the same combination of alleles at all 70–100,000 genes is essentially zero, even though none of your alleles is unique."

Moral Complicity

Many writers have suggested that because ES cells are not embryos and "lack the awesome potential of an intact embryo" their use in research or therapy is unproblematic (Pedersen 1999). Whether or not this is true depends on whether the destruction of the organism to obtain the cells was wrongful and the extent to which the subsequent use of material from embryos of fetuses wrongfully killed share the moral taint of that initial wrongdoing. John Robertson has produced a useful analysis of these issues distinguishing between a causative theory of moral complicity in wrongdoing and a "no benefit from another's wrongdoing" theory. As Robertson observes: "under a causative theory of complicity, neither derivation nor later use of ES cells from abortions that would otherwise have occurred would make one morally complicit in the abortion itself because there is no reasonable basis for thinking that donation of tissue for research after the decision to abort has been made would have caused or brought about the abortion." Robertson points out that while the "no benefit" view would prohibit use of embryo or fetal material if people thought the fetus death was wrongful, such a position is difficult to maintain with any consistency, "because many common activities, practices and social arrangements may be traceable to some past wrongdoing, e.g., wresting land from Native Americans. Persons holding that view, if they are consistent, would have a difficult time living in the contemporary world" (Robertson 1999). Of course the fact that all wrongdoing of this sort might be unavoidable could not show that attempts to minimize such wrongdoing were irrational or morally incoherent.

Ultimately the issue of the moral respectability of ES cell research and use can only be resolved either by resort to a discussion of the moral status of the embryo,[6] or by showing, as this paper has attempted to do, that those who object to ES cell research are morally inconsistent. They are inconsistent not, as Robertson eloquently suggests, because they do not or cannot renounce all complicity in wrongdoing, but because they do not in fact believe that the creation and use of embryos or fetuses for morally important objectives is in fact morally wrongful. Since, so far as I am aware, none of those who object to the use of fetal and embryonic material have objected to attempts at normal sexual reproduction, a reasonable inference is that they accept the creation and death of embryos as a price it is reasonable to pay for the creation of a new human life. Since the death of human embryos to achieve such an objective is not wrongful, it would be difficult to imagine why the use of cells or tissue from such dead embryos might become wrongful.

Those who would nonetheless object to the harvesting and use of embryonic tissue and cells, must show how the death and use of those particular embryos is different in morally relevant ways from those which die in pursuit of normal sexual reproduction. They must also show that the price, in the same coin, that is paid for obtaining embryonic material and cells is somehow distinct from the case of normal sexual reproduction, or that it is too high a price to pay for the prospect of saving millions of future lives and alleviating untold human misery.

Acknowledgments

I am grateful to my colleague Søren Holm for incisive criticism and comments on an earlier draft of this paper. The paper was presented to the Smithkline Beecham Ethics and Public Policy Board, July 11–12, 1999, and I am grateful to all the participants in that board meeting for helpful comments.

Notes

1   See my "Genes, Clones and Human Rights," in Justine C. Burley, ed., *The Genetic Revolution and Human Rights: The Amnesty Lectures 1998* (Oxford: Oxford University Press, 1999), pp. 61–95.
2   For a conclusive refutation of that doctrine see Harris 1980. For a more recent discussion of these broad issues see F. H. Kamm, "The doctrine of triple effect and why a rational agent need not intend the means to his end," and John Harris, "The moral difference between throwing a trolley at a person and throwing a person at a trolley: A reply to Francis Kamm," in *The Proceedings of the Aristotelian Society*, 2000.
3   Here the arguments follow that developed in my "Rights and reproductive choice," in Harris and Holm, eds., *The Future of Human Reproduction* (1998).
4   I have argued elsewhere that neither of these courses of action is necessarily unethical. See *Clones, Genes and Immortality* (Oxford: Oxford University Press, 1998), ch. 5.
5   This should surely read: "the mother *consenting to the provision of* the tissue would be its genetic grandmother."
6   Something I have attempted in a book-length study some time ago. See John Harris, *The Value of Life* (London: Routledge & Kegan Paul, 1985).

References

Annas, George, Caplan, Art, and Elias, Sherman: "The politics of human embryo research – avoiding ethical gridlock". *New England Journal of Medicine*, 334 (1996), pp. 1329–32.
BBC (British Broadcasting Corporation): http://news.bbc.co.uk/hi/english/health/newsid_281000/281404.stm
British Medical Association: *Our Genetic Future*. Oxford: Oxford University Press, 1992.
Committee on the Ethics of Gene Therapy. London: HMSO, 1992.
Cooper, David K. C. and Lanza, Robert P.: *Xeno: The Promise of Transplanting Animal Organs into Humans*. Oxford: Oxford University Press, 2000.
Government Response to the Recommendations made in the Chief Medical Officer's Expert Group Report, "Stem Cell Research: Medical Progress with Responsibility." Presented to Parliament by the UK Secretary of State for Health By Command of Her Majesty, Aug. 2000. London: HMSO, Cm4833.
Harris, John: *Violence and Responsibility*. London: Routledge and Kegan Paul, 1980.
Harris, John: *The Value of Life*. London: Routledge & Kegan Paul, 1985.

Harris, John: *Wonderwoman and Superman: The Ethics of Human Biotechnology*. Oxford: Oxford University Press, 1992), esp. ch. 1.

Harris, John: "Biotechnology: friend or foe." In Dyson, A. and Harris, J., eds.: *Ethics and Biotechnology*. London: Routledge, 1994.

Harris, John: "Intimations of immortality." *Science* 288, no. 5463 (April 2000).

Harris, John and Holm, Soren, eds.: *The Future of Human Reproduction: Choice and Regulation*. Oxford: Oxford University Press, 1998), pp. 5–37.

Kirkwood, Tom: *Time of Our Lives*. London: Weidenfeld and Nicolson, 1999.

Mooney, David J. and Mikos, Antonios G.: "Growing new organs." *Scientific American*, April 1999, pp. 38–43.

New York Times: www.nytimes.com/library/national/science/061599sci-stem-embryos.html

Pedersen, Roger: "Embryonic stem cells for medicine." *Scientific American*, April 1999.

Polkinghorne, J. C.: "Law and ethics of transplanting foetal tissue." In Edwards, Robert G., ed.: *Foetal Tissue Transplants in Medicine*. Cambridge: Cambridge University Press, 1992.

Pub.L.105–277. Section 511, Oct. 21, 1998, Slip Copy. 1998 H.R. 4328.

Review of the Guidance on the Research Use of Fetuses and Fetal Material. London: HMSO, 1989; Cm762.

Robertson, John: Presentation to Smithkline Beecham Ethics and Public Policy Board, Chewton Glen, July 11 and 12, 1999.

Silver, Lee: "The meaning of genes and 'genetic rights.'" *Jurimetrics: The Journal of Law, Science, and Policy* 40, no. 1 (Fall 1999), pp. 77–93.

Stem Cell Research: Medical Progress with Responsibility. UK Dept. of Health, June 2000.

Thomson, J. A. et al.: "Embryonic stem cell lines derived from human blastocysts." *Science* 282 (1998), pp. 1145–6.

UK Dept. of Trade and Industry: www.dti.gov.uk/hgac/papers/papers-d.htm

Further Reading

1 Harris, John: *Clones Genes and Immortality*. Oxford: Oxford University Press, 1998.

2 Harris, John and Holm, Søren, eds.: *The Future of Human Reproduction*. Oxford: Clarendon Press, 1998.

3 Harris, John, ed.: *Bioethics*. Oxford Readings in Philosophy Series, Oxford University Press, 2001.

4 Harris, John: "Goodbye Dolly: the ethics of human cloning." *The Journal of Medical Ethics* 23, no. 6 (Dec. 1997), pp. 353–60.

5 Harris, John: "Ethical genetic research." *Jurimetrics: The Journal of Law, Science, and Policy* 40, no. 1 (Fall 1999), pp. 77–9.

6 Harris, John: "Genes, clones and human rights." In Burley, Justine C., ed.: *The Genetic Revolution and Human Rights: The Amnesty Lectures 1998*. Oxford: Oxford University Press, 1999. 61–95.

7 "Opinion of the European Group on Ethics in Science and the New Technologies to the European Commission." No. 15, Nov. 14, 2000.

8 "Stem cell research: medical progress with responsibility." UK Dept. of Health, London: HMSO, June 2000.

9 US National Bioethics Advisory Commission, *Ethical Issues in Human Stem Cell Research*, vols. I–III. Rockville, Maryland, Sept. 1999.

10 "Stem cell research and ethics." *Science* 287, Feb. 2000.

11 The Wellcome Trust: *Public Perspectives on Human Cloning: A Social Research Study*. London: Wellcome Trust, 1998.

13

Preimplantation Genetic Diagnosis and Embryo Selection

BONNIE STEINBOCK

Introduction

Preimplantation genetic diagnosis (PGD) is a recently developed technique to determine genetic defects in embryos created by *in vitro* fertilization prior to implantation in a uterus for gestation. The diagnosis occurs at the 6 to 10 cell stage of embryonic development, when one or two cells can be removed without harm to the embryo or affecting its potential to implant. The cellular DNA is then tested for chromosomal abnormalities or genetic mutations, using polymerase chain reaction (PCR) for mono-genic diseases and fluorescent in-situ hybridization (FISH) for chromosomal aberrations (Lissens and Sermon 1997). Embryos carrying serious genetic diseases are discarded (or frozen indefinitely); embryos free of disease can be implanted for gestation. The proced-ure is still experimental, but there is little doubt that rapid developments in molecular biology will permit detailed genetic analysis of single embryonic cells in the foreseeable future, enabling PGD to be offered for wide range of conditions (Botkin 1998).

PGD can be used as an alternative to traditional prenatal diagnosis (such as chori-onic villus sampling – CVS – and amniocentesis) and selective abortion for couples at risk of transmitting inherited disorders. Because the affected embryos are discarded prior to implantation, PGD avoids the need for abortion, and many people find it preferable to traditional prenatal diagnosis for that very reason. For example, Lord Winston was cited in an article in *The Times* as saying, "Ethically it [PGD] is better than termination of pregnancy" (Murray 1998). However, this is an oversimplification.

Better Alternative Than Abortion?

The moral status of the embryo

Whether one views discard of a preimplantation embryo as ethically superior to abortion depends on one's view of the moral status of embryos and fetuses. A few writers on abortion (Warren 1973; Tooley 1983) view even well-developed fetuses as having little or no moral status, and abortion at any stage as morally unproblematic. On this view, presumably PGD would not be *ethically* preferable to abortion, though it might be preferable for psychological reasons. At the other end of the spectrum are those conservatives on abortion who claim that even a fertilized egg is a human person with all the rights of any other human person (John Paul II 1993). For them as well, PGD is not ethically preferable to abortion, as both are forms of homicide, indeed, murder. In fact, from the perspective of loss of prenatal life, PGD is worse than traditional prenatal diagnosis and abortion, because PGD requires the creation of numerous embryos for each live birth produced. According to one research group, 137 embryos were created to get 5 births (Ao et al. 1996). Botkin comments, "Clearly the loss of prenatal life is substantially greater through PGD than would have resulted from the 12 at-risk couples pursuing traditional prenatal diagnosis and selective termination. PGD will not be an ethically appropriate alternative to selective abortion for those individuals who adhere to the conservative position" (1998: 21).

Avoiding the termination of a wanted pregnancy

Most people are in neither of these extreme camps. Most people regard fetuses, even fairly early-gestation fetuses, as having a different moral status than preimplantation embryos, and this view has been reinforced by various commissions, including the Warnock Report (1984) and the Glover Report (1989), as well as by bioethicists such as John Robertson (1990). Not only is the very early embryo nonsentient (a characteristic it probably shares with first-trimester fetuses), but it does not even have the neural substrate necessary for the development of consciousness and sentience. Even at the 100-cell blastocyst stage, the early embryo consists of undifferentiated cells, some of which will go on to become the placenta and some the fetus. Indeed, until implantation and the formation of the embryonic axis occurs, at about 14 days after fertilization, it is not yet certain that a biological individual exists, as twinning could still occur, producing two individuals (Robertson 1990: 445). All of these biological facts about early embryos suggest a different and lesser moral status for preimplantation embryos than for fetuses. In addition, many people regard the fact of pregnancy as itself morally as well as psychologically significant. Even people who are generally pro-choice are likely to find the termination of a pregnancy, especially a wanted pregnancy, as a serious, often difficult, decision, and one that is more problematic than the discarding of embryos prior to implantation. For people at risk of passing on serious genetic disorders, PGD may be a preferable choice. Consider, for example, the story of Paula and Noah Huffman (Rowland 1996). They had two sons, both born with a rare, deadly genetic disease which affects only male offspring. One son lived two months, the other a week. Rather than take another risk of bearing another affected male child, the Huffmans decided to go with PGD in order to select and implant a female embryo. Paula Huffman says, "There was no other option at that point, other than having an abortion if you found out it was a boy, which we don't believe in."

Disadvantages of PGD to traditional prenatal diagnosis

It does not follow, however, that PGD is always preferable to ordinary prenatal diagnosis. While PGD can detect the sex of an embryo, making it useful for sex-linked disorders, as well as single-gene diseases, it cannot detect other conditions, such as spina bifida, anencephaly, encephalocele, omphphalocele, hypoplastic left heart syndrome, bladder extropy, renal aenesis, and many others (Botkin 1998). For such conditions to be detected, traditional prenatal diagnosis is required.

Another factor complicating the use of PGD is that it requires IVF, which is physically burdensome, risky, and often costly. The woman must be subjected to drugs which cause superovulation and have significant side-effects, including bloating, weight gain, fatigue, hot flashes, depression and mood swings, and possibly an increased risk of ovarian cancer (Rossing et al. 1994). The invasive procedures used to retrieve the eggs also pose risks to the woman, including bleeding, adverse reaction to anesthesia, and infection. The replacement of the fertilized ovum in the uterus may cause infection, physical damage, or ectopic pregnancy.

In addition to the physical risks and burdens imposed by IVF, there are the complexities of genetic analysis and the subsequent instantiation of pregnancy. As Botkin notes, this entire procedure requires dedication by the couple and collaboration of a small army of physicians, scientists, and technicians. Nor does it completely obviate the need for prenatal diagnosis. Botkin (1998: 17–18) cites Lissens et al. as saying:

> Preimplantation diagnosis is . . . a procedure requiring the multidisciplinary collaboration of a clinical IVF unit, a laboratory IVF unit with micromanipulation facilities, a molecular biology and cytogenetics laboratory, and a clinical genetics unit. Most centers still consider [PGD] an experimental method and request and advise follow-up prenatal diagnosis in cases of pregnancy.

In addition, IVF is usually not a one-shot deal. Typically, two or more cycles of egg retrieval, genetic testing, and implantation are required to establish a successful pregnancy. It requires months of time, multiple drugs, and withstanding repeated failures of implantation or loss of early pregnancy.

These realities mean that PGD is unlikely to be attractive to most couples, including those who prefer discard of preimplantation embryos to early abortion. In any event, the need for a confirmatory prenatal diagnosis means that PGD does not completely avoid the need for abortion. Thus, speculation that "Even couples with no reason to think they are at risk might try to buy the treatment if it were more widely available" (Murray 1998) seems implausible.

Another issue is cost, which depends on the country in which it is done. Cost does not seem to be a major concern in the UK, where the few programs doing PGD charge about £2,000–2,500. In the United States, however, the cost of PGD would be substantial. While there is no data yet available on the cost specifically of PGD, there is data on the cost of IVF. Each cycle costs between $5,000 and $7,000, which is often not covered by insurance. Currently 85 percent of the costs of IVF are not covered by insurance in the US (Collins et al. 1995). Since two or more cycles may be required, the cost is likely to be between $10,000 and $30,000. However, indirect costs make the total much higher, estimated by one researcher to be $43,000 per delivery of an infant (Van Voorhis et al. 1997). It seems unlikely that insurance carriers or governmental funding agencies will want to cover these costs when there are cheaper and more reliable alternatives. Most experimental PGD cycles at the present time are being done for maternal age-related chromosomal aneuploidy (trisomy 21, trisomy 18, etc.). The risk of having a child with a chromosomal aneuploidy for a 40-year-old woman is about 2.5 percent, while the chance of a woman over 40 getting pregnant on a cycle of IVF is about 5 percent.

Botkin asks:

> Assuming future costs will not be covered by experimental programs or insurance, we have to wonder how many older mothers will be willing to undergo multiple interventions at high cost to address a modest risk that can otherwise be addressed through CVS or amniocentesis (or, perhaps, through adoption). To be more specific, how many women would spend $40,000 for a procedure with a 5% success rate to ensure an outcome that would occur 97.5% of the time anyhow? (1998: 17)

Targeted uses of PGD

However, even if PGD is unsuitable as a general means of preventing birth defects, a targeted use of PGD may be appropriate. For example, it may be appropriate for individuals who would avoid procreation unless they could be sure of not passing on serious genetic diseases to their offspring, and who want to avoid abortion. It may also be useful for patients undergoing fertility treatment who have had repeated IVF failures. There is evidence that these failures may be due to chromosomal abnormalities in the embryos. Embryos with chromosomal abnormalities are less likely to implant, and more likely to spontaneously abort. Moreover, the abnormalities in the embryos are not always morphological. The possibility of identifying normal embryos using fluorescent in-situ hybridization (FISH) could improve the chance of pregnancy in this category of patients (Gianaroli et al. 1997).

The Morality of Prenatal Diagnosis

Aside from the issue of whether PGD is ethically preferable to traditional prenatal diagnosis, there is the deeper issue of the morality of prenatal diagnosis altogether. For prenatal diagnosis has, as a primary aim, the avoidance of having a child with a disability. Admittedly, some users of traditional prenatal diagnosis may not use the information to terminate the pregnancy, but rather to prepare themselves for a child who is likely to have a serious disability. Information about certain conditions, such as spina bifida, may also be relevant to the method of delivery or care of the newborn. But in most cases, the reason for prenatal diagnosis is to prevent the birth of a child with a disability. In the case of PGD, this is the only point. There would be no point in going through the IVF procedures and then implanting affected embryos. As Botkin says, "The purpose of PGD is not to simply inform couples about the genetic nature of their embryos. The explicit purpose is to implant healthy embryos and discard those destined to be affected" (1998: 19). The question, then, is whether wishing to avoid having a child with a disability is morally problematic.

This question may strike some readers as odd. Surely there is nothing wrong with desire to avoid having a child with a disability. After all, the goal of obstetrics is usually expressed as "a healthy mother and a healthy baby." Pregnant women are expected to do whatever they can to have healthy babies: to avoid tobacco, alcohol, and other drugs, to get a nutritious diet, to engage in enough (but not too much) exercise, to avoid environmental hazards, and so on (Steinbock 1997). Why, then, is prenatal diagnosis to prevent disability morally problematic?

An obvious reason is that traditional prenatal diagnosis "prevents" disability by preventing the child; that is, by abortion. Those who regard fetuses as having the moral status of born human beings can no more regard abortion for fetal indications as acceptable than they can regard infanticide for disability as acceptable. Most people regard fetuses as having some moral status, but not full moral status, and regard abortion as needing a justification, even if they also think that the decision belongs to the pregnant woman. Within this group, fetal indications are considered among the strongest of reasons for terminating a pregnancy, right behind serious threats to the woman's life or health and certainly above the need to postpone her education or the loss of career opportunities. In general, there seems to be considerable social support for prenatal diagnosis and termination for so-called "serious" conditions, such as Tay-Sachs disease, spina bifida, cystic fibrosis, sickle-cell disease, hemophilia, and muscular dystrophy. At the same time, there is also a generally held conviction that prenatal diagnosis and abortion for "trivial" conditions is ethically troubling. The usual example of a "trivial" condition is sex, or as we say these days, gender. George Annas argues that physicians should not engage in prenatal testing for gender. It is unacceptable medical practice because "[g]ender is not a disease. Moreover, identifying female fetuses for abortion is viciously and destructively discriminatory and undermines our fundamental belief in equality. Not only is prenatal sex selection nonmedical, it's destructive of core values" (1994: 263).

The disability perspective

Precisely the same argument has been made against prenatal diagnosis and selection for disability. Those in the disability community argue that identifying fetuses or embryos as candidates for termination or discard because they will, once born, have a disability, is equally viciously and destructively discriminatory. They maintain that the view that "fetal indications" justify termination or discard stems from the ignorant and prejudiced belief that having a disability makes life unbearable, and that those who are disabled are "better off unborn." Disability rights advocates maintain that disabilities are largely socially constructed. The appropriate response is to change society's attitude toward disability, not to try to get rid of disabled individuals. Moreover, prenatal screening cannot prevent all disability. It is useless to prevent disabilities caused during the birth process, e.g., some cerebral palsies, or those caused postnatally. As long as there are going to be people with disabilities, it is argued, an attitude of inclusion is better than an attitude of removal. Moreover, according to this view, prenatal screening increases intolerance of imperfection. It leads parents to expect a "perfect baby."

179

Disability rights activists have performed a much-needed service in making the larger community aware that most people with disabilities find their lives rewarding and worthwhile. They do not wish they were dead, or that they had never been born. A disability rights perspective also forces us to recognize the extent to which socially constructed barriers, rather than natural conditions, prevent equal opportunity. At the same time, the claim that disability is totally a social construction is surely an exaggeration. Society can do a great deal to offer opportunities to people with disabilities, but not all disabilities can be overcome. Someone who is severely mentally retarded may have a life worth living, but cannot hold a job, marry, or raise children. This is not a matter of social prejudice but of reality. This is acknowledged even by disability rights advocates like Adrienne Asch, who writes:

> Not all problems of disability are socially created and, thus, theoretically remediable... The inability to move without mechanical aid, to see, to hear, or to learn is not inherently neutral. Disability itself limits some options. Listening to the radio for someone who is deaf, looking at paintings for someone who is blind, walking upstairs for someone who is quadriplegic, or reading abstract articles for someone who is intellectually disabled are precluded by impairment alone... It is not irrational to hope that children and adults will live as long as possible without health problems or diminished human capacities. (Asch 1988)

However, while Asch supports preventive measures to avoid disability, she finds abortion for "fetal indications" profoundly troubling. This is not because she regards fetuses as persons and abortion as seriously morally wrong. Her view is that abortion is morally acceptable if the woman does not want to become a mother. However, she distinguishes between abortion to prevent having a child (any child) and abortion to prevent having *this* child. Why, Asch asks, would someone who wants to be a mother reject this pregnancy and this (future) child because of one thing about that child, that is, that he or she will have, or is likely to have, a disability? Such rejection can only stem from inaccurate and prejudiced ideas about what it is like to have a disability or to parent a child with a disability. Asch considers aborting to avoid having a child with a disability morally on a par with abortion to avoid having a child of the "wrong" sex. It embodies the view that there is something undesirable about being a person with a disability; so undesirable that it is better that such people do not get born. Others in the disability community argue that prenatal testing "sends a message" that "we don't want any more of your kind."

The disability rights critique of prenatal diagnosis is not limited to traditional prenatal testing and selective abortion; it applies also to PGD. Indeed, it might be said to apply even more to PGD, since PGD is never used to prepare prospective parents for the birth of a child with a disability, as prenatal testing might be, but only to prevent such births. From a disability rights perspective, this is unacceptable. Instead of trying to rid the world of people who have disabilities, we should attempt to change the world so that it provides all people, those who are (temporarily) abled and those who are disabled, with opportunities to live good lives. PGD and embryo selection, just as much as prenatal diagnosis and abortion, imply that it is better that children who have disabilities are not born.

180

Defending prenatal testing from the disability critique

Any defense of prenatal diagnosis must confront this critique. Does prenatal testing reflect prejudice toward or an inability to accept fully people with disabilities? George Annas finds this implausible because he thinks that prenatal testing is used only to prevent the births of individuals whose lives would be so awful that they are better off not being born. He writes:

> Historically, prenatal screening has been used to find life-threatening or severely debilitating disease where a reasonable argument can be made that actually the fetus is better off dead than living a, usually, short life. (Annas 1994: 265)

But this is simply false. Prenatal testing has not been, and is not today, used only or even primarily to detect life-threatening, extremely severe fetal anomalies. One of the most common reasons for screening women over 35 in the US (40 in the UK) is to detect trisomy 21 (Down Syndrome (DS)). DS is not a fatal disease; many people with Down's live into their fifties and sixties. Moreover, it is compatible with a good quality of life, with appropriate medical treatment and educational opportunities. It is simply not true that someone who has DS would be better off dead or unborn.

What, then, should we say about most prenatal testing, which is used to screen for conditions that are compatible with a life worth living? Should we say that such screening is wrong, comparable to screening for sex? I do not think we need to concede this. There is another way to defend prenatal screening, one that does not require the fiction that it is used only to prevent the births of children whose lives will be so awful that they are better off unborn.

Prenatal Genetic Testing as Prevention

This defense turns on the idea that prenatal screening, along with abortion and embryo selection, is a form of prevention. As a form of prevention, it is comparable to recommending folic acid supplements to pregnant women to prevent the births of children with neural tube defects. Both kinds of measures are intended to, and can be expected to, reduce the number of individuals with disabilities. Yet no one, not even the most radical disability rights advocates, suggests that giving pregnant women folic acid supplements betrays a prejudiced attitude toward individuals with spina bifida. The issue, then, is whether PGD can be seen as a form of prevention. Obviously, anyone who considers embryos to be human persons cannot regard embryo discard as a form of "prevention"; there is a difference between preventing a person from acquiring a disabling condition and killing that person. But how should those who reject the claim that embryos are people (see, for example, Dworkin 1993; Steinbock 1997; Sumner 1981), regard the matter? If embryos are not people at all, they are not people with disabilities. Hence, destroying embryos found to have genetic or chromosomal disorders is not "getting rid of disabled people." It is choosing for implantation those embryos that are more likely to develop into people without health problems or diminished human capacities. If it is desirable that people live their lives without health problems or diminished human capacities, it is hard to see what is wrong with a technique that selects healthy and normal embryos for implantation, or why it is ethically different from taking a folic acid supplement when pregnant to avoid the birth of a child with a neural tube defect. Both measures express the attitude: I prefer not to have a child with a neural tube defect. That is an outcome to be avoided. It is to be avoided partly because of reasonable expectations about what life will be like for the parents, if their child has a serious health problem. But it is to be avoided also because of expectations of what their child's life will be like. Repeated hospitalizations and operations, paralysis, mental retardation – all of these are outcomes that prospective parents reasonably wish to avoid. Nor does the wish to avoid these outcomes imply that if a child with disabilities is born, that child will be rejected or unloved. There is no inconsistency in thinking, "If I have a child who has a disability, or becomes ill, or has special needs, I will love and care for that child; but this is an outcome I would much prefer to avoid." Allen Buchanan illustrates this point with a thought experiment:

> Suppose God tells a couple: "I'll make a child for you. You can have a child that has limited opportunities due to a physical or cognitive defect or one who does not. Which do you choose?" Surely, if the couple says they wish to have a child without defects, this need not mean that they devalue persons with disabilities, or that they would not love and cherish their child if it were disabled. Choosing to have God make a child who does not have defects does not in itself in any way betray negative judgments or attitudes about the value of individuals with defects. (Buchanan 1996: 33–4)

Disability activists have a laudable goal: to change society so that it is welcoming and accepting of people with disabilities. However, there is no reason why society cannot both attempt to prevent disability and to provide for the needs of those who are disabled. As a matter of fact, the rise of prenatal screening has coincided with more progressive attitudes toward the inclusion of people with disabilities, as evidenced in the United States by the passage of the Americans with Disabilities Act.

To summarize, those who reject embryo selection for disability, but are generally pro-choice, seem to take inconsistent positions. They accept measures that are intended to reduce the number of people with disabilities (like giving pregnant women folic acid supplements), so long as these measures do not involve killing embryos. But they have no objection to killing embryos in general. They support the right to abortion and presumably embryo research. They object to the destruction of embryos only when the intention is to prevent the birth of someone who will have a disability. It is difficult to see why this is objectionable when other measures to accomplish the same goal are viewed as neutral or even desirable, and when killing embryos is not regarded as intrinsically wrong.

Disability rights advocates are right to insist that the larger community have a better understanding about the lives of people with disabilities and to advocate that couples get complete, unprejudiced, factual information before undergoing prenatal testing or making a decision about the result of such testing. This falls under the uncontroversial principle of informed consent to medical procedures. Nevertheless, the decision (to test or not to test, to terminate or not to terminate) has to be made by the people who will live with its consequences, namely, the expectant couple. Their decision will be based on their own moral, religious, and spiritual values, and a sense of what is best for themselves and their family. They have a right to make their own decision about such a personal, intimate choice, without recriminations from others who might choose differently.

The Line-drawing Question

I have been arguing that prenatal testing for serious genetic or chromosomal disorders is morally permissible and a matter of individual choice. In part, my argument is based on the impact of raising a child likely to have serious health problems or diminished capacities. However, there are hundreds of syndromes associated with chromosomal abnormalities, of varying degrees of seriousness. Should pregnant women be offered genetic tests for all these conditions? If not, on what basis should we decide which conditions it is reasonable to test for prenatally? This is sometimes called "the line drawing question." It will become more complicated as more genetic tests are developed. According to Botkin:

> This fundamental problem with traditional prenatal diagnosis will be exacerbated by the rapid increase in genetic tests for a wide range of conditions, including late onset conditions, conditions with a limited impact on health and, possibly, behavior or physical characteristics that fall within the normal range. (1998: 21)

The line-drawing question will be even more important for PGD. As we learn more about the role genetics plays in predisposition to various diseases, we may be able to give couples a chance to select against embryos carrying these defects. Couples who would be reluctant to terminate an established and otherwise normal pregnancy in the case of a late-onset disorder are already starting to show an interest in preimplantation diagnosis as a means of reducing the risk of passing on the disease (Delhanty et al. 1997). At some point, genetic testing may be able to identify embryos with increased risk of homosexuality, mental illness, increased intelligence, musical or artistic talent, etc. Ought prospective parents to be able to select for or against traits of these kinds?

The fallacy of genetic determinism

First, a cautionary note. Genetic testing of embryos *may* indicate increased risk of a trait, but it would be an enormous oversimplification to suggest that genetic analysis of an embryo can tell us what traits the person will have. The reason is that genes are only part of the story. Many genetic diseases are caused, not by a single gene or defect on a single gene, but rather by the interaction of many genes. Such disorders are called "polygenic." In addition, environmental factors often play a crucial role in whether a particular trait or condition is expressed. When this is the case, the inheritance is deemed "multifactorial." Some common abnormalities considered to be inherited in polygenic/multifactorial fashion include neural tube defects, congenital hip dislocation, peptic ulcer disease, most forms of congenital heart defects, hypertension, clubfoot, scoliosis, most forms of epilepsy, hydrocephalus, and asthma (Elias and Annas 1987). The more complex the interaction of genes and environment, the less likely it is that the disorder can be predicted.

Behavioral traits are even more complicated than disease traits. While genetic inheritance undoubtedly plays some role in traits such as intellectual ability and musical talent, it is impossible to predict from the genetic make-up of an embryo whether or to what extent the resulting child will be brilliant or musical. There are simply too many factors and too much that is unknown.

Jeffrey Botkin suggests that perhaps much of contemporary interest in genetic testing will collapse as our overly deterministic genetic paradigm progressively fails. "Nevertheless," he goes on, "we only may need a popular *perception* of genetic determinism, fueled by creative marketing and weak regulation, to move poorly predictive tests from the lab into the clinic" (1998). If this is right, the response of professionals, whether ethicists or scientists, should be to resist this perception and to correct the tendency toward genetic determinism. This was nicely done in the report of the National Bioethics Advisory Commission, *Cloning Human Beings* (1997), which said:

> This belief, that genes alone determine all aspects of an individual, is called "genetic determinism." Although genes play an essential role in the formation of physical and behavioral characteristics, each individual is, in fact, the result of a complex interaction between his or her genes and the environment within which they develop, beginning at the time of fertilization and continuing throughout life. As social and biological beings we are creatures of our biological, physical, social, political, historical, and psychological environments. Indeed, the great lesson of modern molecular genetics is the profound complexity of both gene–gene interactions and gene–environment interactions in the determination of whether a specific trait or characteristic is expressed. (NBAC 1997: 32)

Appropriate public education should help to reduce demand for genetic testing. The public needs to understand that embryo selection or manipulation is unlikely to be an effective means of producing healthier, smarter, or more talented children. More traditional means, from better diets and better schools to less time spent in front of the television, are better bets. Nevertheless, even after education and understanding, some people will be interested in embryo selection, not to avoid the birth of a child with a serious congenital disorder, but rather to avoid an increased risk of a late-onset disease, such as Alzheimer's disease, or behavioral traits, such as alcoholism or homosexuality. Should people be able to request such testing for the purpose of embryo selection, or should there be restrictions on the kinds of genetic tests that will be offered? There are basically three responses to the line-drawing question.

Total prenatal autonomy

Some commentators (e.g., Robertson 1992, 1993) argue that no lines should be drawn. Prospective parents should be able to use prenatal screening and embryo selection for any offspring characteristics they want. Robertson argues that selection of offspring traits is part of procreative liberty, and thus presumptively protected, unless some tangible harm to specific individuals can be demonstrated. The strongest case for embryo selection is to ensure healthy offspring, but ultimately Robertson thinks that individuals should not be denied access to embryo biopsy and selection, for any condition or trait.

George Annas characterizes the total parental autonomy view as "the market or consumer product model." He writes:

> It basically holds that prenatal testing is not just a medical decision, but is really more a lifestyle decision, an intimate and personal decision, so individuals should make their own decisions based on their own belief systems...Prenatal tests become a consumer product, and as with other consumer products it should be up to the individual whether or not to buy the product, and physicians and companies should be free to advertise and sell the product in any nonmisleading way. (1994: 264)

Annas worries that this model inclines us toward treating children themselves as products. The more we try to engineer children to have desirable traits, the less we will be able to love them for themselves. Moreover, as we "create" these children, "we will simultaneously create a genetic underclass – to which the vast majority of us will belong" (1994: 265).

Others (e.g., Murray 1997) have expressed similar concerns about commodification and objectification of children. But why, it may be asked, should prenatal testing and selection be regarded as specially likely to result in regarding children as products, any more than existing and accepted methods of improving children? Robertson writes:

> parents now have wide discretion to enhance offspring traits after birth with actions that range from the purely social and educative, such as special tutors and training camps, to the physio-medico as occurs with orthodontia, rhinoplasty, and exogenous growth hormone. Such actions may give the child advantages over other children, exacerbate class and socioeconomic differences, and risk treating the child like a product or object to serve the parent's interests. Yet they fall within a parent's discretion in rearing offspring, and could not constitutionally be banned. (1993: 164)

Although Robertson's argument is couched in terms of what may not be banned as a matter of law, it seems clear that he is unimpressed by moral arguments against PGD or traditional prenatal testing based on commodification or objectification of children. For Robertson, then, prospective parents are morally and legally entitled to use PGD for nondisease or benign traits, so long as they can find willing professionals to do the testing. At the same time, physicians have discretion not to make PGD or other prenatal testing available for reasons they regard as "trivial or less important than the prenatal life that will be sacrificed to achieve that goal" (1993: 172), so long as they make their disagreement known in advance, enabling consumers to seek services elsewhere.

The medical model

The medical model advocates drawing the line at serious disability or disease. This model is exemplified by the following statement from The Council on Ethical and Judicial Affairs of the American Medical Association:

> In general, it would be ethically permissible to participate in genetic selection (abortion or embryo discard) or genetic manipulation to prevent, cure, or treat genetic disease. It would not be ethical to engage in selection on the basis of benign characteristics. (Council on Ethical And Judicial Affairs, AMA, 1994: 633)

The medical model rules out prenatal testing for sex selection, for example, since being male or being female is not a genetic disease. It also forbids selection on the basis of disease conditions viewed as "benign" though the criteria for benign traits is not spelled out. Is a cleft palate which can be surgically corrected benign? At a conference on the Human Genome held in 1998, Professor George Annas suggested that prenatal testing for cystic fibrosis, usually considered a serious genetic disease, might not be warranted, since the life expectancies of people with CF are being extended, and a cure may be on the horizon. Clearly, there is disagreement on what counts as a "benign characteristic," and thus for what conditions it is permissible to do prenatal testing.

Line-drawing on the medical model is not determined solely by the seriousness of the genetic disease or defect. Other relevant factors include the probability of disease and the age at onset (Post et al., 1992), as well as the possibility of remedial treatment.[1] To understand how these factors relate to the justification of prenatal testing, consider Tay-Sachs disease, one of the clearest examples of a genetic disease for which prenatal testing is appropriate. First, Tay-Sachs has a dire impact on health. The disease causes severe and progressive psychomotor degeneration, ending in a vegetative state and death typically by the age of 3 to 5. Second, the age of onset is infancy. This differentiates Tay-Sachs from Huntington's Disease (HD), which is equally severe, but does not occur typically until the late forties. Thus, the person with HD can have a healthy, normal life for 40 or more years before the disease manifests itself. Third, Tay-Sachs can be diagnosed prenatally with a high degree of certainty, given homozygous status in the fetus. This contrasts with many genetic defects which merely put the child at risk of developing a particular disease. Fourth, there is no cure or even ameliorative therapy for Tay-Sachs. This contrasts with a disease like cystic fibrosis, with several new genetically engineered drugs and gene therapy on the horizon. These four factors – impact on health, age of onset, probability of disease, and potential for therapy – provide a useful framework for discussing the appropriateness of prenatal testing. The case for morally permissible prenatal testing is strongest where there is serious impact on health, a high probability of disease, non-existent or ineffective therapy, and early age of onset. Where the impact on health is less serious, the probability that disease will occur becomes less certain, there exist useful therapeutic interventions, or the age of onset is relatively late in life, the case for prenatal testing becomes weaker. For example, it is unlikely that prenatal testing for, say, Alzheimer's disease (AD) could be justified. While AD is a very serious disorder, for which there is no cure and little effective therapy, it typically develops at the very end of life, in the seventies, eighties, or even nineties. Prenatal testing and embryo selection would not avoid extra burdens in child-rearing, since the parents will probably be dead long before onset of the disease. Nor do considerations of the interests of offspring seem persuasive in this case, since the disease typically does not affect the person until after a life of normal length and health. It is unfortunate to undergo dementia at the end of life, and something to be avoided if possible. However, we all have to die of something, sometime. The prospect of eventual illness and deterioration is not a reason against getting born.

Most important, there is, at this time, no prenatal test for Alzheimer's disease. This differentiates AD from other late-onset diseases such as Huntington's disease. The APOE genotype has been discovered to be the single most important genetic determinant of susceptibility to AD, but some individuals with that genotype do not develop AD and some who have a different genotype do. The consensus is that while genetic testing may prove useful in diagnosing individuals with cognitive impairment, it is not appropriate to use as a predictive test in asymptomatic patients at this time (Roses 1995). Furthermore, AD is a multifactorial disease. It is affected by environmental as well as genetic factors, making it unlikely that there will ever be a reliable genetic test to determine who will and who will not develop the disease. On the medical model, then, there is no justification for developing or offering APOE prenatal testing, even if there might be some people who would "want to know" and who would terminate a pregnancy simply because of increased risk of a serious, though late-onset, genetic disease.

What about PGD? As noted above, discard of preimplantation embryos seems morally less problematic to most people than abortion. Given the inability to predict AD from the presence of the APOE gene, it would not make sense for anyone to undergo IVF and PGD in order to avoid the birth of a child at higher risk of getting AD. At the same time, if a couple were already undergoing IVF for infertility, and were particularly concerned about AD, perhaps because of a family history on both sides, they might want to use PGD to reduce the risk. As Robertson says, "If one has to choose three out of seven embryos to place in the uterus, it is not irrational to exclude those which have genetic markers for susceptibility to major disease" (Robertson 1993: 156).

The disability rights view

As noted above, many disability rights activists are morally opposed to prenatal testing, except for the narrow purpose of preparing for the birth of a child with a disability, because of what they believe such testing expresses about the worth and lives of people with disabilities. In its rejection of prenatal testing, the disability rights model contrasts with both the total parental autonomy model and the medical model. However, some disability rights advocates, such as Adrienne Asch, regard line-drawing as even more detrimental to the disability community than prenatal testing itself, because line-drawing suggests that there are some conditions so terrible that they make life not worth living. By contrast, if parents can select for or against *any* trait, based on personal preference, there is no suggestion that selecting against these traits is "medically indicated." Thus, for very different reasons, Robertson and Asch end up on the same side of the line-drawing question: Let parents decide for themselves what conditions or traits they wish to test and select for.

However, this approach poses serious practical difficulties, especially if viewed from the perspective of social policy. Prospective parents cannot be informed, much less counseled, about the thousands of genetic conditions which might be detected. Nor is it economically feasible to perform all possible genetic tests on pregnant women. There has to be some way of identifying conditions likely to be of interest to most people. The parameters identified by the medical model perform that function. Moreover, if, as I have argued, line drawing in prenatal testing does not imply discriminatory attitudes toward people with disabilities, there is no reason to insist on total parental autonomy, which is impractical. It should be emphasized that the decision to test or not to test belongs with the prospective parents. Physicians and genetic counselors should give parents the relevant information and support them in their decision, whatever it is.

Conclusion

While PGD is not a panacea, and is unlikely to replace traditional prenatal testing, it can be useful for targeted groups of individuals. In particular, it may be indicated for some couples whose infertility problems are due to chromosomal abnormalities, as well as for couples at high risk of passing on serious genetic diseases. As with most technologies, there exists a risk of inappropriate or over-use. This risk is best opposed, not by legal restrictions, which are likely to be hard to enforce, but rather by statements by various professional organizations about the appropriate use of PGD. If, as I have argued, it is reasonable to wish to avoid genetic disease and disability, PGD is an acceptable means of achieving that goal.

Note

1   The following section borrows from my paper "Prenatal genetic testing for alzheimer disease," in Post, S. G. and Whitehouse, P. J., eds.: *Genetic Testing for Alzheimer Disease: Ethical and Clinical Issues* (Baltimore: Johns Hopkins University Press, 1998).

References

Annas, G. J.: "Noninvasive prenatal diagnostic technology: medical, market, or regulatory model?" *Annals of the New York Academy of Sciences* 731 (1994), pp. 262–8.
Ao, A., Ray, P., Harper, J. et al.: "Clinical experience with preimplantation genetic diagnosis of cystic fibrosis." *Prenatal Diagnosis* 16 (1996), pp. 137–42.
Asch, A.: "Reproductive technology and disability." In Cohen, S. and Taub, N., eds.: *Reproductive Laws for the 1990s* (Clifton, NJ: Humana Press, 1988), pp. 69–124.

Botkin, J. R.: "Ethical issues and practical problems in preimplantation genetic diagnosis." *Journal of Law, Medicine & Ethics* 26 (1998), pp. 17–28.

Buchanan, A.: "Choosing who will be disabled: genetic intervention and the morality of inclusion." *Social Philosophy & Policy* (1996), pp. 18–46.

Collins, J. A., Bustillo, M., Visscher, R. D., and Lawrence, L. D.: "An estimate of the cost of in vitro fertilization services in the United States in 1995." *Fertility and Sterility* 64 (1995), pp. 538–45.

Council on Ethical and Judicial Affairs, American Medical Association: "Ethical issues related to prenatal genetic testing." *Archives of Family Medicine* 3 (1994), pp. 633–42.

Davis, D. S.: "Genetic dilemmas and the child's right to an open future." *Hastings Center Report* 27:2 (1997), pp. 7–15.

Delhanty, J. D. A., Wells, D., and Harper, J. C.: "Genetic diagnosis before implantation: applications of the technique are growing." *British Medical Journal* 315 (1997), p. 828.

Dworkin, R.: *Life's Dominion: An Argument About Abortion, Euthanasia, and Individual Freedom* (New York: Knopf, 1993).

Elias, S. and Annas, G. J.: *Reproductive Genetics and the Law* (Chicago: Year Book Medical Publishers, Inc., 1987).

Gianaroli, L., Magli, M. C., Munne, S., Fiorentino, A., Montanaro, N., and Ferraretti, A. P.: "Will preimplantation genetic diagnosis assist patients with a poor prognosis to achieve pregnancy?" *Human Reproduction* 12:8 (1997), pp. 1762–7.

Glover, J. et al.: *Ethics of New Reproductive Technologies: The Glover Report to the European Commission* (DeKalb, IL: Northern Illinois University Press, 1989).

John Paul II: *Evangelium Vitae*, Encyclical Letter, Aug. 16. Libreria Editrice Vaticana. Reprinted in Dwyer, S. and Feinberg, J., eds.: *The Problem of Abortion*, 3rd ed. (Belmont, CA: Wadsworth Publishing Company, 1993), pp. 21–3.

Lissens, W. and Sermon, K.: "Preimplantation genetic diagnosis: current status and new developments." *Human Reproduction* 12 (1997), pp. 1756–61.

Lissens, W., Sermon, K., and Staessen, C. et al.: "Review: Preimplantation Diagnosis of Inherited Disease." *Journal of Inherited Metabolic Disease* 19 (1996), pp. 709–23.

Murray, I.: " 'Designer baby' inquiry ordered." *The Times* (Jan. 17, 1998), p. 36.

Murray, T.: *The Worth of a Child* (Berkeley: University of California Press, 1997).

National Bioethics Advisory Commission (NBAC): *Cloning Human Beings* (1997).

National Human Genome Research Institute: "Should preimplantation genetic diagnosis be used to select for traits?" GenEthics Consortium Case Literature. Http://www.nhgri.nih.gov/About_NHGRI/Dir/Ehics/pre.html.

Post, S. G., Botkin, J. R., and Whitehouse, P.: "Selective abortion for familial Alzheimer disease?" *Obstetrics and Gynecology* 79 (1992), pp. 794–8.

Purdy, L. M. "Genetic diseases: can having children be immoral?" In Munson, R., ed.: *Intervention and Reflection: Basic Issues in Medical Ethics* third edition (Belmont, CA.: Wadsworth Publishing Company, 1998), pp. 364–71.

Robertson, J. A.: "In the beginning: the legal status of early embryos." *Virginia Law Review* 76 (1990), pp. 437–517.

Robertson, J. A.: "Ethical and legal issues in preimplantation genetic screening." *Fertility and Sterility* 57:1 (1992).

Robertson, J. A.: *Children of Choice: Freedom and the New Reproductive Technologies* (Princeton: Princeton University Press, 1993).

Roses, A. D.: "Point of view: APOE genotyping in the differential diagnosis, not prediction, of Alzheimer's disease." *Annals of Neurology* 38:1 (1995), pp. 6–14.

Rossing, M. A., Daling, J. R., Wiess, N. S., Moore, D. E., and Self, S. G.: "Ovarian tumors in a cohort of infertile women." *New England Journal of Medicine* 331:12 (1994), pp. 771–6.

Rowland, R.: "Embryo screening helps cut chance of birth defects." News show, Cable News Network, Inc., Transcript # 1295–6, March 9, 1996.

Steinbock, B.: *Life Before Birth: The Moral and Legal Status of Embryos and Newborns* (New York: Oxford University Press, 1997).

Sumner, L. W.: *Abortion and Moral Theory* (Princeton: Princeton University Press, 1981).

Tooley, M.: *Abortion and Infanticide* (New York: Oxford University Press, 1983).

Van Voorhis, B. J., Sparks, A. E., Allen, B. D. et al.: "Cost-effectiveness of infertility treatments: a cohort study." *Fertility and Sterility* 67 (1997), pp. 830–6.

Warnock, Mary: *A Question of Life: The Warnock Report on Human Fertilization and Embryology* (Oxford: Blackwell, 1984).

Warren, M. A.: "On the moral and legal status of abortion." *The Monist* 57 (1973), pp. 43–61.

Further reading

Beauchamp, D. and Steinbock, B, eds: *New Ethics for the Public's Health* (New York: Oxford University Press, 1999).

Dworkin, R.: *Life's Dominion: An Argument About Abortion, Euthanasia, and Individual Freedom* (New York: Knopf, 1993).

Glover, J. et al.: *Ethics of New Reproductive Technologies: The Glover Report to the European Commission* (DeKalb, IL: Northern Illinois University Press, 1989).

Robertson, J.: "Ethical and legal issues in preimplantation genetic screening." *Fertility and Sterility* 57 (1992).

Steinbock, B.: *Life Before Birth: The Moral and Legal Status of Embryos and Newborns* (New York: Oxford University Press, 1997).

14

Individual Autonomy and Genetic Choice

MATTHEW CLAYTON

Introduction

Modern liberal society holds respect for personal autonomy as one of its core moral norms. Its vision is that of individuals having control over their own lives, pursuing the lifestyle which they have freely chosen without coercion or manipulation by others. This vision is, for many, the heart of the case for a tolerant legal attitude to abortion, contraception, and the genetic screening of one's would-be offspring. To inhibit or prohibit a person's choice with respect to these services would be a serious violation of her autonomy and, as such, unjustified in a liberal society.

Some who value autonomy maintain that abortion, for example, is morally wrong but it is a kind of moral wrong which should not be prohibited by law. For them, autonomy is essentially a matter of not having one's informed choices coercively interfered with by others: it generates a legal right to do moral wrong. Similarly, parental design of their children's genetic make-up might be deemed morally wrong but, in cases in which the wrongness does not involve harm to the offspring, it may be regarded as a moral wrong which people should be legally free to perform, just as the expression of particular views may be blasphemous but legally permitted in a liberal society.

Others argue that abortion should be legally prohibited in many cases even though we have reason to respect personal autonomy. They might argue that, since respect for autonomy has value, it would be *in one way* wrong for government to restrict women's access to abortion. However, they might also believe that respect for the sanctity of human life or a concern for the welfare of the fetus are also weighty moral considerations and, they might argue, our reasons to allow abortion out of a concern for women's autonomy are defeated by these other values: although a prohibition on abortion is *in one way* wrong for reasons deriving from the right to autonomy, a prohibition is, *all things considered*, justified. Similar claims could be made about the relationship between personal autonomy and gene selection. Even though a person might value autonomy, she might attach different weights to its importance and, consequently, arrive at different policy conclusions.

To avoid disputes of this kind it is clearer to start with the following type of question: "to the extent that respect for autonomy matters what policy must we advocate with respect to abortion, contraception, and so on?" More specifically, we focus here on what a concern for autonomy requires of public policy regarding gene selection. Once we have an answer to this question we can go on to discuss what weight should be given to considerations of autonomy compared to other moral values and norms. However, answering the question about what personal autonomy, considered alone, requires of genetic policy is not as simple as it might first appear, for there are different groups of people whose autonomy might be affected by gene selection. First, we must be attentive to the autonomy of procreators. Access to abortion and contraception are often defended on grounds of autonomy, because control of one's procreative decisions has been thought to be central to personal autonomy: frustration of one's desire not to found a family, for example, is a serious infringement of one's autonomy. Similar thoughts often inform discussions of gene selection. It is sometimes claimed that, since the character and ability of one's children greatly matters to some people, we should respect the genetic choices people make for their children as an aspect of their right to personal autonomy, just as many educational decisions parents make on behalf of their children should be respected.

However, it may also be the case that other people's autonomy should figure prominently in the debate about gene selection. A second potential constituency is comprised of the offspring of people's procreative choices. Can one's procreative decisions violate the right to autonomy of one's child? Some answer "no," on the grounds that, since autonomy is centrally concerned with not interfering with people's choices, the right to autonomy cannot be employed to condemn or justify any particular conduct towards individuals before they are born. However, if we decide that a person's autonomy can be violated by actions taken before her birth or even, perhaps, prior to conception, we must establish which types of gene selection, if any, are questionable on grounds of autonomy.

Finally, a third set of people whose autonomy might be thought to count includes third parties who find that the degree of control they have over their lives is inhibited by society's attitude or policy towards the creation of persons with similar genetic characteristics. For example, it is sometimes claimed that prenatal screening followed by selective abortion for the purposes of eradicating certain genetically determined conditions (e.g. cystic fibrosis) from the germline would show disrespect for existing people with those conditions, or make it harder for them to take control of their lives. Such fears, if well-founded, would have considerable force since, other things equal, people with these conditions are worse off than others and, therefore, their complaints have greater moral force.

Types of Gene Selection

Gene selection operates in current medical practice in a number of different ways. It is common to distinguish between various means by which genes can be selected. In addition, different moral problems attend the various types of gene selection. We can distinguish between two types of genetic screening, as follows.

Carrier testing

Carrier testing with genetic counseling prior to conception might be done through an assessment of the risks of passing on a particular disease by reconstructing a family tree of medical problems. Another method of carrier screening is to identify the genetic constitution of would-be parents to establish the probability of their offspring having a particular condition. Both techniques may be followed by prenatal diagnosis of the fetus and, possibly, abortion if the fetus suffers from particular conditions. Alternatively, the results of carrier testing may be taken by potential parents as a reason to refrain from procreating or to procreate by artificial insemination with a donor egg or sperm which has a different genetic make-up. Screening of these kinds might, for example, be performed for hemophilia, Huntington's disease, Tay-Sachs disease, cystic fibrosis, and sickle-cell anemia.

Prenatal screening

Prenatal screening can be effected through a number of techniques, including ultrasound, amniocentesis, measuring levels of alpha-fetoprotein in the pregnant woman's blood, and chorionic villus sampling in which part of the placenta is removed and tested. Such tests are used in the diagnosis of a number of conditions including Down's syndrome, spina bifida, sickle-cell disease, and Tay-Sachs disease. If the presence of an abnormal condition is established an abortion may be offered. In the case of in vitro fertilization, genetic tests may be performed on the cells of embryos prior to implantation and a decision then made whether to implant some, all or none of them.

Issues Relating to Gene Selection and Personal Autonomy

Different moral issues attend the various methods of gene selection. In the case of selection by the termination of a pregnancy, for example, issues relating to the sanctity or otherwise of human life and the moral status of the fetus, as well as concerns about the procreator's personal autonomy, are central. Similar issues are relevant to the emerging practice of testing in vitro fertilized embryos with selective implantation. However, in cases of carrier screening with genetic counseling or artificial insemination by donor (AID) these moral issues may to some extent be avoided, since the selection is made at the pre-conception stage. Instead, other issues arise relating to the ethics of donating eggs and sperm and the possible effects of AID on the offspring who are created using such techniques.

In debates about the implications of respect for autonomy for the morality of gene selection two issues are central. First, would it be morally permissible for political institutions through the law or medical codes to encourage the production or selection of people with particular characteristics: those with high rather than low intelligence; people who are free of certain diseases or conditions; females rather than males; homosexuals rather than heterosexuals? Second, if it is not the appropriate business of the state to take a stand on these matters, can would-be parents legitimately do so? Is it ever morally permissible, for example, for a couple to choose the sex of their child?

These debates about personal autonomy and the creation of different types of people are, in a way, somewhat unreal. Current practice with respect to genetic counseling and prenatal screening is limited to the identification of only a limited number of medical conditions. Hence discussions of whether, for example, the state may legitimately use genetic screening to increase the number of homosexuals in society are insensitive to the fact that the causes of homosexuality are unknown and, therefore, the technical feasibility of such a policy in the short or long term is uncertain. Moreover, it might be claimed that the more urgent moral problems concern the permissibility of gene selection in the case of those conditions for which it is currently practiced. Nevertheless, the lack of reality in these debates should not be a reason to ignore them. Such discussions may help us to assess the desirability of selecting particular characteristics for those we beget. It might be that society should adopt a generally tolerant attitude to parents choosing the genotype of their children, in which case further mapping of the human genome and effecting techniques for the manipulation of genes would have a stronger rationale. Alternatively, it might be that there are moral limits to parental design. If so, defining these limits could enhance our understanding of how we should employ a technical advance in genetic screening or engineering. In addition, if it is established that genetic engineering to eradicate certain characteristics is morally wrong, it becomes less pressing to perfect techniques for their identification and manipulation. Thus, the debate about personal autonomy and gene selection has value *even when* the genetic status of the characteristics under consideration is disputed or unknown.

Individual Autonomy in a Liberal Society

An individual's interest in leading an autonomous life is at the core of the debate about whether the state can legitimately enforce particular conceptions of the good life – through the law or in other ways, such as subsidizing or advertising the benefits of particular conceptions. Conceptions of the good life embody a set of claims about personal virtue, the aims and projects which people should pursue and, perhaps, the meaning of life. The ideal of personal autonomy is often employed in justification of an anti-perfectionist political morality, that is, a morality which asserts that the state should not endorse as intrinsically valuable particular conceptions of the good life and promote them though the use of its powers. This view is associated with a number of thinkers (Rawls 1993; Dworkin 1985, 1990, 2000; Ackerman 1980; Larmore 1990). In Rawls's view, for example, there are good reasons for the state to uphold certain views of the right or social justice: it should, for instance, maintain various liberal rights – the freedoms of conscience, expression, association, and other familiar democratic rights – as well as pursue a policy which seeks to maintain fair equality of opportunity and reduce the inequalities of wealth that are characteristic of contemporary industrial societies. Nevertheless, people may agree on the desirability of such measures but affirm very different views about religion, sexuality, art, work and sport. Antiperfectionists argue that the state and its justification should ideally be premised on arguments which rise above the controversies relating to these matters, such as whether or not there is a God, or the value of art as against science. These disputes are ones which should be conducted within the constraints and opportunities that liberal society provides, but the state should not take a stand on such disputes or endorse the view of any particular party to the controversy.

Personal autonomy is the ideal of individuals being, to a large extent, in control of their own lives. Included within the ideal is the claim that they should be able rationally to form, revise and pursue a particular conception of the good life. This power requires a number of developmental conditions, such as an appropriate education which enables individuals to reflect critically on the various choices available to them and assess, for instance, which of these best accords with their fundamental goals in life. It also supports the maintenance of the social, economic, and political conditions which enable people to bring about what they have reflectively chosen. Respect for autonomy, then, provides a basis for a range of liberal policies, from upholding the freedoms of expression, conscience, and association – which protect the individual's interests in leading an autonomous life from the interference of others – to the provision of education, healthcare and economic assistance to ensure that each has sufficient internal and external resources rationally to reflect on and pursue her chosen life plan.

The ideal of autonomy is invoked in a second way in some liberal conceptions: in defense of antiperfectionism. One striking feature of a society marked by free institutions of the kind outlined above is that there exists a diversity of allegiance with respect to conceptions of the good life. Whereas some are devout, others regard religious belief as unhealthy superstition. Some liberal thinkers argue that the content and justification of the principles which regulate the liberal political order should be, so far as is possible, independent of particular claims about conceptions of the good life. They claim that the public's endorsement of the state is an attractive ideal and, given the diversity of conceptions in a free society, if the state were to affirm any particular conception of the good and promote it through its powers, some section of the citizenry would fail to affirm the prevailing political arrangements (Rawls 1993: 3–40, 47–72).

The ideal of public acceptability in politics follows from a concern for autonomy as self-government. Personal autonomy, as we have seen, is the ideal that individuals should have the power to make uncoerced choices and bring about what they have chosen. In the case of political institutions, however, this is not fully possible: we cannot choose to be born into society and since, realistically, we exit from it only at death, we are subject to society's coercive laws throughout our lives. How can the involuntary nature of political association be rendered consistent with autonomy? This is a central problem of political philosophy. One solution is to insist that the constraints necessary for social cooperation must be capable of being regarded as legitimate by citizens in light of their own reason. Being constrained by the law is not autonomy-inhibiting for an individual provided she identifies freely with or embraces the constraints she is under. When there exists a diversity of conceptions of the good life, the state can hope to deliver autonomy in this sense only if it takes an antiperfectionist stance. This is because any perfectionism is bound to be deemed unacceptable to some section of the citizenry (Rawls 1993: 68, 77–8, 137; Cohen 1994).

This, in outline, is the position taken by certain prominent liberal thinkers who treat autonomy as a significant part of their view. What are the implications of this ideal for gene selection? If the argument for antiperfectionism in politics is sound, then a *political* policy of gene selection for the purposes of creating people with a tendency to align themselves to some controversial conception of the good would be morally impermissible. Consider, for example, the issue of sexuality. The issue here concerns the moral status of using the law, tax and subsidy arrangements, or educational/advertising techniques, to encourage through gene selection (if that were feasible) the creation of people who favor what is taken to be a superior conception of sexuality. Suppose the state proposed to offer tax incentives to encourage would-be parents to create straight rather than gay offspring in the belief that heterosexuality is superior. The appeal to autonomy as self-government would rule such a policy to be morally impermissible on the grounds that it would violate the autonomy of the many people in society who regard homosexuality as either better or no worse than heterosexuality. They would be forced to live under a political regime animated by ethical values they reject. (Note, however, that there may be nonperfectionist reasons to increase the number of people who exhibit a particular conception of sexuality. Suppose, for example, that increasing the number of gay people in society would make it easier for gays to find a suitable partner. Such a policy may have a nonperfectionist justification which rests on a principle of *equality of opportunity to find a sexual partner*, which does not presume that homosexuality is better than, or even as good as, heterosexuality.)

In the liberal view, then, any state-sanctioned policy must be publicly endorsed by free and equal persons, that is, persons who have a sense of justice and the powers necessary to lead an autonomous life. The upshot of this view with respect to genetic policy involves the *ideal of undominated diversity*: the state is morally permitted to enforce a policy of selection of genotype A over genotype B only if it is universally accepted that having genotype B places a person at a disadvantage compared to A. However, if there exists disagreement over the comparative benefits of A and B, a policy of gene selection in favor of either would be morally impermissible (Ackerman 1980: ch. 4).[1] For example, if some in society align themselves to the view that homosexual practices are better than heterosexual ones, it would be a violation of autonomy as self-government if the state's genetic policy sought to eradicate homosexuality. Nevertheless, undominated diversity may allow gene selection with respect to a different range of conditions. It is likely that everyone will agree that having Tay-Sachs disease or sickle-cell anemia is worse than not having these conditions. That agreement would justify a policy of encouraging carrier testing and, perhaps the use of AID to avoid begetting children who suffer from these conditions. This kind of policy would not violate anyone's autonomy, because everyone would agree that the policy is legitimate. Other policies with respect to the elimination of these genes, however, may prove to be more questionable. If the policy were to encourage selective abortion after genetic testing, this may be rejected by some citizens who regard fetal life to be sacred. This kind of objection would constitute a reason to refrain from a policy of encouraging abortion even when everyone agrees that Tay-Sachs disease is a condition which it is always better to be without. This reiterates the point that the morality of gene selection is rendered complex in virtue of the variety of techniques available for its implementation.

The ideal of undominated diversity has been criticized for having implications for genetic policy that are too restrictive. Ackerman himself cites as a potential problem for the view the case of a person who regards the possession of some serious disabling condition as "a mark of divine approbation upon him" (Ackerman 1980: 118), and, consequently, denies that the condition is universally dispreferred to another. The existence of idiosyncratic characters of this kind seems to render a genetic policy which sought to screen out these disabilities impermissible. Yet, it could be responded that this possibility merely implies that the ideal of undominated diversity is implausible: it erects unjustifiable restrictions on the goal of preventing the creation of people who suffer from serious disabilities (Glover 1984: 162).

One response to this problem, defended by Ackerman, distinguishes between those with conscientious but idiosyncratic beliefs about disabilities and those who wish to create disabled persons who can be dominated and exploited by others. The existence of the first might ideally render the policy of selecting against the particular disability impermissible, but the voice of the second may legitimately be disregarded, because they disrespect the ideal of equal citizenship which forms the basis of the liberal view. However, Ackerman also claims that it is quite easy for the would-be dominator to conceal his view and pass himself off as conscientiously idiosyncratic. Thus he proposes a second-best policy, namely one which ignores the existence of conscientious idiosyncratics. Only in this way can we circumvent the problems associated with identifying the real reasons an individual values a disability (Ackerman 1980).

An alternative response to this problem is to highlight the first respect in which personal autonomy is valued within the liberal view. The power critically to reflect, revise, and pursue one's conception of the good is required if one is to be in control of one's life in the relevant way. In addition, it is important for individuals to have an adequate range of significant options from which to choose their goals and projects. Now both kinds of goods can be enhanced by gene selection. The power to conceive, revise and follow rationally a set of goals requires a set of physical and mental abilities which are denied to people who suffer disabilities of the kind for which routine screening is already offered. Thus, to the extent that autonomy is an ideal, a large number of disabilities might be legitimately screened for, even though some might take them to be ennobling or a mark of God's blessing. Such idiosyncratic objections can be seen to involve a rejection of the value of autonomy.

However, these autonomy-supporting considerations do not justify the state encouraging gene selection when the aim is to change people's motivations and desires, as in the case of sexuality, or change their abilities in a way that does not enhance their powers of autonomy or the range of options available to them: for example, if changing a genotype to increase the offspring's scientific abilities could be delivered only at the expense of a decline in the offspring's aesthetic powers. These kinds of genetic policy regard particular conceptions of the good as more valuable than others and are bound to be rejected by some citizens who agree about the value of freedom and equality.

197

Parental Choice

We have been discussing the relationship between the ideal of autonomy and state-directed genetic policy. According to many liberals, that policy must be antiperfectionist to the extent that respect for autonomy figures within one's political view. Nevertheless, even though *government* cannot legitimately take a stand on the intrinsic merits of, say, homosexual and heterosexual lifestyles, the permissibility of would-be *parents* doing so remains open. In addition, this may meet with the approval of existing citizens and show a concern for the autonomy of procreators. Potential parents often do care about how many children they have and they sometimes prefer to have certain sorts of children rather than other sorts. Now, since procreation and the upbringing of children are projects of considerable significance, to deny people freedom of choice with respect to matters of quantity and quality may seem a serious violation of their autonomy (Harris 1989, 1997). Bearing this in mind, it might be argued that although the government should resist engaging in perfectionist genetic policy itself, it should allow parents to beget offspring of the genotype of their choice. Because a decentralized policy of this nature would not be premised on any controversial view of the good life, it may also meet with the approval of the whole citizenry.

Jonathan Glover discusses and, in a qualified form, defends Nozick's idea of a genetic supermarket which embodies such a scheme of decentralized gene selection (Glover 1984: 45–56; Nozick 1974: 315). The ideal of parental design which is accommodated by the genetic supermarket is attractive, in part, because it overcomes certain worries about a particular group of people controlling genetic policy. These worries relate to the abuse of power which might attend such centralized control and the loss of variety in human characteristics that might result from it. Since the parental design model gives each set of parents control over the characteristics of their own offspring, human diversity may not be threatened and there should be little fear of abuse of the system, since no one would enjoy the right to determine the characteristics of more than a few children.

Nevertheless, the supermarket model may need to be regulated in certain respects. Glover cites two powerful reasons in support of regulation. First, even though an unrestricted choice may not be problematic when each choice is considered in isolation of other people's choices, the collective consequences of unrestricted choice may be disastrous or repugnant. For example, allowing parents to choose the sex of their child may lead to a marked imbalance between males and females in society which might, in turn, cause social problems in the future. Thus, the genetic supermarket might need to be regulated by, for instance, a licensing scheme which rationed the supply of particular genetic make-ups. Second, the supermarket would have to be constrained by the concern that the child should be capable of developing a sense of justice and the powers necessary for leading an autonomous life. Hence, the supermarket must not offer genotypes which restrict the offspring's opportunities in these respects or harm them in serious ways.

Subject to constraints of this kind a genetic supermarket would show respect for procreative autonomy. It seems to be a natural extension of the argument that autonomy requires access to contraception and abortion. However, a number of objections must be considered before the notion of a genetic supermarket is accepted.

The first objection is that the supermarket model would exacerbate the already large inequalities which exist in society. It is often noted that the children of wealthy parents are advantaged by the larger share of monetary resources that are devoted to their upbringing compared to the share enjoyed by less privileged children. A supermarket in which desirable genes are priced more highly than those in less demand might merely accentuate this inequality of opportunity. Whereas the rich would be able to afford to purchase the genes of their choice, the poor may not have the means to take advantage of the goods offered in the market. People who care about justice in the distribution of opportunity and resources might raise this potential inequality-generating feature of the genetic supermarket as an objection to its legitimacy.

The complaint raised above constitutes a strong case against the parental design of offspring. To accommodate the objection, the model would need to prevent rich parents from seeking an advantage for their children through the purchase of expensive beneficial genes. One means of effecting this might be to regulate the selection of genes through vouchers which are priced in a means-tested manner, so that the poor are not disadvantaged in the choice of genes available to them. However, given the abysmal record of democratic societies when it comes to securing equality of opportunity in the political and educational domains, it may well be that social justice would be better served by preventing the existence of, rather than by trying in vain to regulate, genetic supermarkets.

A second objection to the model has wider significance. If gene selection is practiced it is likely that parents would seek to avoid having children who suffer from various disabilities, such as spina bifida and cystic fibrosis. It is sometimes objected that this policy is harmful to people who already live with these disabilities. The harm might be spelled out in various ways. The disabled might regard the policy as denying them respect as an equal; the policy might cause the disabled to lose self-esteem because it would be seen as validating the attitude that these disabilities should be avoided; and it might deflect attention away from providing adequate aids or compensation for people who suffer from disabilities. In these ways gene selection, whether it is practiced by the state or parents, can have harmful side-effects for third parties and, especially, people who suffer from the disabilities which the policy allows to be screened out.

If personal autonomy is valuable, we must ensure that a policy of gene selection does not frustrate the disabled in their desire to be in control of their lives by making it harder for them to pursue their goals or through a diminution of their self-confidence. Nevertheless, these worries might be mollified without abandoning gene selection (Glover 1992: 133–4). The case for respecting the rights of the disabled to social, economic, and political goods and to compensation for their disadvantage does not vary with the presence or absence of a policy which seeks to avoid the creation of people with disabilities. The elimination of genetic disabilities from the germline, for instance, is perfectly compatible with the acknowledgement that people with disabilities have equal moral status, are entitled to the means to pursue their life plans and, more generally, should be shown concern and respect: just as, mutatis mutandis, offering a cure for certain causes of blindness is compatible with respecting the rights of the blind whose sight cannot be restored.

Procreative Autonomy versus Children's Autonomy

A final set of issues for discussion concerns whether the offspring's right to autonomy generates any moral limits to parental selection of genes. One limit has been identified above: parental genetic choice must not restrict the child's future opportunity to lead an autonomous life. Since gene selection which sought to deprive a person of various mental and physical capabilities would have that effect, it is morally forbidden on grounds of respect for autonomy.

This illustrates a general claim about the nature of autonomy, namely, that it is not merely threatened by others interfering in the pursuit of one's informed desires. The ideal of personal autonomy also asserts the desirability of people having and exercising the capacity to form, revise, and pursue their lifestyles in an informed and rational manner. This ideal can be frustrated in childhood by depriving individuals from developing the mental resources necessary for this capacity (Feinberg 1992). In addition, it can be denied to individuals in the choice of the genes which are chosen to constitute them. If my parents created me through a genetic choice which deprived me of the capabilities necessary to lead an autonomous life, it would be perfectly intelligible for me or my representative to claim that they have violated my right to autonomy. They would have done so because they would have created a person unable to lead an autonomous life and, thereby, violated their duty to promote and respect personal autonomy in persons. (Note that if this is the case then, arguably, the duty to respect people's autonomy cannot always be construed as a person-affecting moral principle. In some cases involving gene selection (e.g., ones which involve selective implantation of eggs or sperm) the moral wrongness involved in not promoting personal autonomy in the creation of a person does not rest on the fact the person who is created is, all things considered, worse off than he otherwise would be. That person-affecting account is implausible, because were an autonomous person created he would be a different person and, therefore, the nonautonomous person would never have existed. And, although personal autonomy is of considerable value to a person, it is not true to say that all nonautonomous persons would have been, all things considered, better off had they never existed (Parfit 1984: ch. 16; 1986; cf. Woodward 1986, 1987).)

Does this feature of autonomy pose a problem for the (regulated) parental design model of gene selection outlined by Glover? On one view of the duty to respect autonomy the answer is "no." On this view autonomy is an *end-state* to be achieved. Whatever else parents do to and with their children, they must not prevent them from eventually leading an autonomous life. In their choice of education, for example, parents must not restrict below adequacy their children's mental or physical development or prevent them from being exposed to a range of lifestyles from which they may eventually choose goals and projects. Similarly, they cannot legitimately choose to have children who, for easily avoidable genetic reasons, are incapable of becoming autonomous. Nevertheless, on the end-state view, provided these opportunities are preserved for their offspring, parents are permitted to steer their children towards certain conceptions of the good rather than others. One can legitimately engage in the religious instruction of a child, for example, on condition that this instruction is consistent with the child's development of the mental resources necessary for autonomy (Feinberg 1992). Similarly, the end-state view is compatible with parental gene selection. The desire to have a *female* who has *scientific* rather than aesthetic abilities and is *straight* rather than gay, is consistent with the imperative that the child should be able appropriately to form and revise her life plan with an understanding of the options available and pursue it rationally. If these abilities and motivations have a genetic basis, the end-state view of autonomy would find nothing problematic about this kind of gene selection.

On a different view, autonomy is not merely an end-state to be achieved. Instead, its possession is a *precondition* of being treated in certain ways. The central claim of this view is that there are certain things that cannot legitimately be done to people without their free consent. This account highlights the fact that autonomy has an *interpersonal* dimension which cannot be reduced to the ideal of ensuring that individuals have the capacities necessary to deliberate and choose between an adequate range of options. This dimension has been termed a condition of *independence* (Raz 1986: 377–8). The condition requires one's choices not to be coerced or manipulated by others.

An example of this concern is expressed in the principle of informed consent in medicine. Requiring an individual to consent to medical interventions in a free and informed manner ensures that her independence is respected. Another instance of our affirmation of the independence condition relates to the common objection to genetic engineering on the basis that we do not have the right to "play God." The thrust of the objection, on its more plausible interpretation, is not that it is never appropriate to interfere in nature; rather it is that humankind should not treat other people in the way that God is thought entitled to treat humanity, namely, as beings whose abilities and interests can legitimately be molded to his values. Playing God is wrong because it subjects people in their creation and education to the will of others. Thus Raz states: "[L]oss of options through coercion is deemed to be a greater loss of autonomy than a similar loss brought about by other means. That is why slaves are thought to lack autonomy even if they enjoy a range of options which, were they free, would have been deemed sufficient. Manipulation, unlike coercion, does not interfere with a person's options. Instead it perverts the way that a person reaches decisions, forms preferences or adopts goals. It too is an invasion of autonomy whose severity exceeds the importance of the distortion it causes" (Raz 1986: 377–8).

The precondition account of autonomy asserts, then, that it is an affront to an individual's autonomy if others coerce her into doing certain things or having particular attributes without her consent. It can plainly be seen that this requirement is violated when others coerce or manipulate an individual *against* her will. It is less commonly recognized that an individual's independence is violated when others manipulate or force her to participate in activities the value of which can reasonably be rejected *before* she has a well-developed will of her own.

Consider the moral wrongness of practices such as the genital mutilation of young children or the use of young children in pornographic pictures. Liberals standardly condemn these practices because of the mental and physical harm they inflict on children. However, even when these practices are not particularly harmful in these respects the objection remains that they violate the autonomy of the children concerned. Respect for individual autonomy provides us with a reason to allow bodily mutilation and the production of pornography between consenting adults. However, an individual's autonomy is violated if others involve her in these activities without her consent. For others would then be deciding the particular conception of the good that governs her life: her life would be marked by unjust manipulation and coercion.

The precondition account can plausibly be extended to the case of genetic choice. On that account an individual's autonomy is reduced if the genes which constitute her and shape her motivations and abilities are manipulated or chosen on the basis of her parents conception of the good. Even if she possesses the other conditions of autonomy her life will always have a particular history marked by her interests and abilities having been to some extent chosen by her parents. Viewed from the perspective of the parents, they can be seen to violate their duty to respect autonomy in their procreative choices. Their choice of, say, a girl rather than a boy, or a gene for heterosexuality (if such a gene exists) would involve manipulation of a future child's characteristics such that they conform to their own particular conception of the good, a conception which can reasonably be rejected. The precondition account insists that one has a permission to encourage an individual to adopt a particular conception of the good when, but only when, she has realized the mental capacities to deliberate rationally about that encouragement. This insistence respects the independence of the individual by ensuring that no one is coerced or manipulated by others. Moreover, it might be that this aspect of autonomy explains the view that while no injustice has been done if a straight child is born through natural reproductive methods, it would be wrong to use genetic screening to create such a child. Whereas in the first case the child's sexuality is not chosen by others, in the second case her characteristics are the manipulated product of her parents pursuing their particular conception of the good.

Conclusion

The precondition account of autonomy offers a liberal objection to procreative freedom. Liberals typically defend that freedom in terms of respect for the value of individual autonomy. However, if the importance of independence for autonomy is accepted, respect for autonomy can be seen to place significant moral limits on choice in procreation. These limits are motivated by respect for the autonomy of the child that is begotten.

To be sure, the precondition account must be elaborated in greater detail if it is to be a plausible guide to genetic policy. That elaboration must attend to a number of issues. First, the account asserts that it violates the child's autonomy if her particular talents and interests are chosen for her by others. Yet it might be objected that this condemns too much genetic screening. For example, the attempt to eliminate genes that produce blindness, deafness, low life expectancy, and various mental disabilities, seem to be instances of genetic selection which affect the child's talents and interests. But these kinds of interference seem morally unobjectionable.

So, the precondition account must explain why particular choices, such as the choice of sex or sexuality for example, are illegitimate while the ones itemized above are acceptable.

Second, there is a question about the *weight* that should be attached to the independence dimension of autonomy. An advocate of parental choice might accept that the future child has a legitimate claim to lead a life the particular character of which has not been shaped in advance by others. Moreover, they may note that this establishes a potential conflict between acknowledging the autonomy of the offspring and parents respectively. However, she may argue that the conflict should be resolved in favor of the procreator since her claim has greater weight. Thus, the critic of procreative freedom must explain why the independence of the offspring should operate as a moral constraint on procreative decisions, or why it has sufficient importance to override the procreative freedom of adults.

Finally, and relatedly, we may return to the issue with which we began. Let us grant that the precondition account of autonomy justifies significant moral limits on procreative choice. The question remains whether it is legitimate coercively to enforce this moral result through a legal prohibition on genetic screening that exceeds these limits. Here we encounter the problem of designing a public policy which is enforceable without having "special and grave" effects on particular groups in society (Dworkin 1993: 157). If the enforcement of these moral limits is unrealizable, or realizable only at the cost of significant harm to procreators, the best policy might remain one which offers a legal right to procreative choice. But consideration of these issues must await another occasion.

Acknowledgments

For their helpful suggestions I am grateful to Bob Blank, Justine Burley, Andrew Mason, Mark Philp, Katherine Watson, and, especially, Andrew Williams.

Note

1   The notion of undominated diversity has been applied in a rather different context by Van Parijs as a standard for establishing whether there exists an inequality in different individuals' enjoyment of personal resources (such as their mental or physical capabilities). See Van Parijs 1995: ch. 3. For a critique of Van Parijs's position see Williams 1999: 97–106. It should be noted that Ackerman's use of undominated diversity as a constraint of justice on any policy of genetic choice is compatible with the rejection of Van Parijs's use of the idea as an indicator of inequalities in personal resources.

References

Ackerman, B.: *Social Justice in the Liberal State* (New Haven: Yale University Press, 1980).
Cohen, J.: "A more democratic liberalism." *Michigan Law Review* 92 (1994), pp. 1503–46.

Dworkin, R.: *A Matter of Principle* (Cambridge, MA: Harvard University Press, 1985).

Dworkin, R.: "Foundations of liberal equality." In Peterson, G., ed.: *The Tanner Lectures on Human Values* 11 (Salt Lake City: University of Utah Press, 1990), pp. 3–119.

Dworkin, R.: *Life's Dominion: An Argument about Abortion and Euthanasia* (London: HarperCollins, 1993).

Dworkin, R.: *Sovereign Virtue: The Theory and Practice of Equality* (Cambridge, MA: Harvard University Press, 2000).

Feinberg, J.: "The child's right to an open future." In his *Freedom and Fulfillment* (Princeton: Princeton University Press, 1992).

Glover, J.: *What Sort of People Should There Be?* (Harmondsworth: Pelican Books, 1984).

Glover, J.: "Future people, disability, and screening." In Laslett, P. and Fishkin, J., eds.: *Justice Between Age Groups and Generations* (New Haven: Yale University Press, 1992).

Harris, J.: "The right to found a family." In Scarre, G., ed.: *Children, Politics, and Parents* (Cambridge: Cambridge University Press, 1989), pp. 133–53.

Harris, J.: " 'Goodbye Dolly?' The Ethics of Human Cloning." *Journal of Medical Ethics* 23 (1997).

Larmore, C.: "Political liberalism." *Political Theory* 18 (1990), pp. 339–60.

Nozick, R.: *Anarchy, State, and Utopia* (Oxford: Blackwell, 1974).

Parfit, D.: *Reasons and Persons* (Oxford: Oxford University Press, 1984).

Parfit, D.: "Comments." *Ethics*, 96 (1986).

Rawls, J.: *Political Liberalism* (New York: Columbia University Press, 1993).

Raz, J.: *The Morality of Freedom* (Oxford: Clarendon Press, 1986).

Van Parijs, P.: *Real Freedom for All: What (if Anything) can Justify Capitalism?* (Oxford: Clarendon Press, 1995).

Williams, A.: "Resource egalitarianism and the limits to basic income." *Economics and Philosophy* 15 (1999).

Woodward, J.: "The non-identity problem." *Ethics* 96 (1986), 804–31.

Woodward, J.: "Reply to Parfit." *Ethics* 97 (1987), pp. 800–16.

Further reading

On liberalism and individual autonomy:

Dworkin, G.: *The Theory and Practice of Autonomy* (Cambridge: Cambridge University Press, 1988).

Dworkin, R.: "Foundations of liberal equality." In Peterson, G., ed.: *The Tanner Lectures on Human Values* 11 (Salt Lake City: University of Utah Press, 1990).

Rawls, J.: *Political Liberalism* (New York: Columbia University Press, 1993).

Raz, J.: *The Morality of Freedom* (Oxford: Clarendon Press, 1986), chs. 12, 14, 15.

On autonomy and genetic choice:

Ackerman, B.: *Social Justice in the Liberal State* (New Haven: Yale University Press, 1980), ch. 4.

British Medical Association, *Human Genetics: Choice and Responsibility* (Oxford: Oxford University Press, 1998).

Burley, J., ed.: *The Genetic Revolution and Human Rights* (Oxford: Oxford University Press, 1999), esp. chs. 1, 2, 4, and 5.

Dworkin, R.: *Sovereign Virtue: The Theory and Practice of Equality* (Cambridge, MA: Harvard University Press, 2000), ch. 13.

Glover, J.: *What Sort of People Should There Be?* (Harmondsworth: Pelican Books, 1984).

Harris, J.: *Clones, Genes, and Immortality: Ethics and the Genetic Revolution* (Oxford: Oxford University Press, 1998).

Harris, J. and Holm, S., eds.: *The Future of Human Reproduction* (Oxford: Clarendon Press, 1998).

Heyd, D.: *Genethics: Moral Issues in the Creation of People* (Berkeley: University of California Press, 1992).

Holm, S.: "A life in the shadow: one reason why we should not clone humans." *Cambridge Quarterly of Healthcare Ethics* 7 (1998), pp. 160–2.

Karin-Frank, S.: "Genetic engineering and the autonomous individual." In Evans, J., ed.: *Moral Philosophy and Contemporary Problems* (Cambridge: Cambridge University Press, 1987), pp. 213–29.

McGee, G.: *The Perfect Baby: A Pragmatic Approach to Genetics* (Lanham, MD: Rowman and Littlefield, 1997).

Robertson, J.: *Children of Choice: Freedom and the New Reproductive Technologies* (Princeton: Princeton University Press, 1993).

15

Cloning and Public Policy

RUTH MACKLIN

Introduction

It seemed like only minutes after a team of Scottish scientists announced, in late February 1997, that they had successfully cloned a sheep, that governmental officials and private citizens throughout the world called for a ban on cloning human beings. The rush to legislate or issue executive orders was so swift, it is reasonable to wonder why the news that a mammal had been cloned ignited such a stampede to prohibit, even criminalize, attempts to clone humans. These events raise a series of separate, yet related questions. Why does the prospect of cloning human beings incite such strong reactions? What reasons have been proposed for enacting national laws or international conventions to prohibit cloning? Can these prohibitions be justified by sound ethical arguments? Before attempting to answer these questions, let us look first at the responses that called for public policy measures to ban human cloning.

Public Policy Actions

On March 4, 1997, the US president, Bill Clinton, issued an immediate moratorium on the use of federal funds for human cloning and requested scientists in the private sector to voluntarily comply with this temporary ban. President Clinton asked the National Bioethics Advisory Commission (NBAC) to thoroughly review the legal and ethical issues associated with the use of this technology and report back in 90 days. (ASBMB Public Affairs News, Friday, March 7, 1997). In the US Congress, the Technology Subcommittee of the House of Representatives Science Committee held public hearings, as did the Subcommittee on Public Health and Safety of the Committee on Labor and Human Resources of the US Senate. Officials from governmental agencies, scientists from the private sector, bioethicists, and others testified at these hearings. At the same time, members of both houses of Congress and of state legislatures introduced bills into their chambers to prohibit human cloning.

In June 1997, the NBAC issued a 110-page Report and Recommendations. The chief recommendations of the commission were to continue the current moratorium on the use of federal funding in support of any attempt to create a child by somatic cell nuclear transfer, and to request all parties in the private sector to comply voluntarily with the intent of the federal moratorium (NBAC 1997: 109). The Commission based its recommendation on its judgment that current scientific information indicates that this technique is not safe to use in humans at this time. The Commission further recommended that federal legislation should be enacted to prohibit anyone from attempting to create a child through somatic cell nuclear transfer cloning.

In the United Kingdom, the House of Commons Select Committee on Science and Technology quickly issued a report on March 18 (Shapiro 1997). Earlier legislation, the 1990 Human Fertilisation and Embryology Act, had intended to ban human cloning by prohibiting "replacing a nucleus of an embryo with a nucleus taken from a cell of any person, embryo or subsequent development of an embryo." However, there was some uncertainty whether that prohibition covers the specific technique employed in cloning Dolly, the sheep, since Dolly was created by the transfer of a cell nucleus to an ovum. The House of Commons Scientific and Technology Committee urged that the existing law be tightened to ensure that human cloning does not occur in the UK (Nicholson 1997: 5). The issue was turned over to the Human Fertilization and Embryology Authority for further study.

On the European continent, President Jacques Chirac of France called on the French national committee for advice and subsequently ordered a ban on cloning in his country. In Italy the Minister of Health issued a decree forbidding cloning for one year, during which legislation was to be developed and presented to parliament. The parliament in Norway voted 153 to 2 to ban cloning and prepared to take the next step, drafting a law. A law in Germany dating back to 1990 was designed to prevent cloning but, like the UK law, did not envision the technique used to produce Dolly (Nicholson 1997: 5).

European commissions, which have no legislative authority in individual countries, also weighed in on the issue. The European Parliament issued a resolution confirming its opposition to the cloning of human embryos and calling for an explicit worldwide ban on the cloning of human beings. The Group of Advisers on the Ethical Implications of Biotechnology to the European Commission issued an opinion that included the following items regarding the human implications of cloning:

2.6 ... any attempt to produce a genetically identical human individual by nuclear substitution from a human adult or child cell ("reproductive cloning") should be prohibited.
2.8 Multiple cloning is a fortiori unacceptable ...
2.10 The European Community should clearly express its condemnation of human reproductive cloning ... (Group of Advisers on the Ethical Implications of Biotechnology, p. 6)

The Steering Committee on Bioethics of the Council of Europe drafted an additional protocol to the already existing Convention for the Protection of Human Rights and Dignity with Regards to the Application of Biology and Medicine. This additional protocol asserted in Article 1 that "Any intervention seeking to create a human being genetically identical to another human being, whether living or dead, is prohibited" (Steering Committee on Bioethics of the Council of Europe 1997). The International Bioethics Committee of the United Nations Educational, Scientific, and Cultural Organization (UNESCO) issued a consensus statement, which declared that reproductive cloning of human beings should not be permitted. The following three reasons were given:

- it undermines genetic indeterminability (by intervening on the "genetic lottery");
- it overrates the biological link;
- it could reduce human beings to the level of a tool, and as such would be contrary to human dignity. (Bioethics Unit of UNESCO, undated)

The fiftieth World Health Assembly met in Geneva on May 14, 1997, and issued a statement entitled "Cloning in Human Reproduction." The statement affirmed that "the use of cloning for the replication of human individuals is ethically unacceptable and contrary to human integrity and morality." The statement further requested the Director-General of the World Health Organization (WHO) to take the lead in clarifying and assessing the ethical, scientific, and social implications of cloning, to consult with other international organizations and national governmental and nongovernmental bodies, and to report to the results of these assessments to the fifty-first World Health Assembly (World Health Assembly 1997).

One commentator on this flurry of activity noted the speed with which most of these various reports were issued and questioned whether the bodies that prepared them took the time to reflect. Writing in the *New Scientist*, David Shapiro commended the British select committee for its speed and sobriety of judgment, adding that the French and German reports "bear some marks of intense political pressure for speed" (Shapiro 1997: 47). According to Shapiro, both of these reports suffer from dogmatism and "overuse the rhetoric of cloning being 'an attack on human dignity.'" Shapiro is most critical of the French report because of its apparent inconsistency. That report begins by stating that genetic identity must not be confused with a person's identity, but then goes on to stress the "unique character of human beings."

It was all but inevitable that the rush to propose legislation to ban cloning would run into problems. A bill to prohibit human cloning was introduced in the US House of Representatives containing language that might have had a limiting impact on medical research, a restriction probably not intended by the bill's sponsor. The original bill called simply for a prohibition on the use of federal funds to conduct or support research on the cloning of humans. A representative who sought to amend bill argued that it "was drafted imprecisely and could harm continued genetic research and biomedical innovation" (*Life Science* 1997). The amended bill changes the original wording from "the cloning of human beings" to "any project of research that involves the use of a human somatic cell to produce an embryo." The need to amend these legislative proposals underscores the haste with which they were introduced and the lack of careful preparation that might have enabled their proponents to foresee the unwanted implications.

Strong Reactions to Human Cloning

It is not clear why the prospect of human cloning prompts such strong reactions in many people, be they scientists, bioethicists, governmental officials, or ordinary citizens. Scientists voiced passionate opposition as strong as that of the Pope. The first reports of the sheep cloning quoted the lead scientist in that effort, Dr. Ian Wilmut, as saying that it would be ethically unacceptable to clone humans (Kolata 1997a: 22). Dr. Wilmut was further quoted as saying: "There is no reason in principle why you couldn't do it; but all of us would find that offensive" (Kolata 1997b: B8).

Dr. Harold Varmus, the Director of the National Institutes of Health, the agency responsible for most of the funding of biomedical research in the United States, said in his testimony before a Congressional subcommittee that he personally considered the idea of cloning humans to be "offensive" and not scientifically necessary. However, Dr. Varmus did not support an immediate legislative ban and said that any future legislation should be drawn very carefully so as not to prohibit important scientific research.

A medical epidemiologist from Rome, Giovanni Berlinguer, was interviewed in Buenos Aires and told the journalist that "the first argument against human cloning is based on the liberty and the autonomy of each individual." Professor Berlinguer added that he had no doubts that cloning is a violation of individual human rights, together with the human rights of the species (Halperin 1997: 20, original in Spanish). However, the Italian professor did not specify just which "individual human rights" would be violated or why, nor did he elucidate the rather odd notion of "the human rights of the species."

Two prominent bioethicists in the United States based their opposition to human cloning on an individual's "right to genetic identity." Daniel Callahan stated that cloning would compromise a person's "right to a unique identity" (Callahan 1997: A23), and George Annas argued that "replication of a human being by cloning would radically alter the very definition of a human being" because the cloned individual would have only a single genetic parent. That, according to Annas, would constitute "the potential loss of individuality" (Annas 1997: p. D1). Callahan contended that the impulse to clone humans should be resisted, "if not by law, at least by a countervailing social pressure." Annas went further, saying that "only government has the authority to restrain science and technology, and we must use it" (Annas 1997: D2).

Initial reactions among the general public and in the media in the United States stemmed in large part from images taken from science fiction. Most of the great harms envisaged are the ones depicted in literature and films. Scenarios of armies of Hitlers, clones used as organ farms for already existing individuals, and the imaginative portrayal in a Woody Allen movie of cloning the nose of a dictator, are only some of the images television news broadcasts presented to viewers. Science fiction is a poor basis for making public policy. Science fiction stories that involve cloning have not portrayed the evils of producing human beings by this method but rather, the abuses of one application in the production of multiple clones or clones of consummately evil people. Many options exist besides outright prohibition of an activity even when great harms can be conceived. We regulate research involving human subjects with a variety of mechanisms in order to prevent unbridled and unethical human experimentation from going forward. But we do not ban research on human beings altogether just because we can imagine some madman designing and implementing atrocities in the name of science.

When scientists and scholars use strong emotional language to condemn an activity, it is evident that deeply rooted sentiments are at play. One of the most vigorous opponents of cloning in the United States has been Leon R. Kass, a professor at the University of Chicago. Kass testified on March 14, 1997, before the National Bioethics Advisory Commission, and later expanded his testimony into a magazine article (Kass 1997). Kass based his opposition to human cloning on three rather different considerations: first, what he perceived to be virtually inevitable, horrible consequences; second, on the familiar but still obscure consideration of human dignity, and third, on the deep-seated emotions he attributed to almost everyone who considers cloning. But what he claimed are the "easily foreseeable consequences" are by no means evident, the concern about human dignity is only vaguely articulated, and the "revulsion," "repugnance," "repulsion," and other visceral reactions he attributed to most people (Kass 1997: 19) are far from universal.

Kass argued that the stakes are very high, as he put it in his testimony before the NBAC, "whether human procreation is going to remain human, whether children are going to be made rather than begotten." When a scientist, rather than a theologian, casts the problem in these terms it is truly puzzling. Since the clone of a human being would still be a human being, it is certainly the case that human procreation will remain *human* if cloning is permitted. The conceptual question is whether we should still call it "reproduction." But even if the answer to that conceptual question is "no," replication is not reproduction, nothing automatically follows with regard to the ethical implications for public policy. Furthermore, contrary to Kass's contention, use of the technique of cloning would not result in the "manufacture" of children. An embryo that results from cloning would still be implanted in a woman's uterus, and gestation and birth would occur in the usual manner. Whether this means that children who come about in this way are "begotten," to use this rather archaic biblical term, is irrelevant. The task is to determine what governmental policies should permit modern medical science and technology to seek to accomplish, when it is justifiable to restrict such attempts, and on what grounds.

Like other commentators, Kass worries about the "serious issues of identity and individuality." A cloned person would be identical to another human being in genotype, the same as identical twins. But cloned individuals would almost certainly not be exactly identical in appearance to their sources. Most identical twins lack precise physical identity. A person cloned from an adult would surely not appear identical to the other person because the two would be chronologically separated and therefore, not identical in appearance at the same time. Cloned individuals would have a different intrauterine environment from the persons of their origin, they would have different life experiences and different memories. They would be distinct individuals, respected and cherished for themselves. A child brought into existence by this method would not be a commodity nor would its worth be any less than that of other children.

Again like other commentators, Dr. Kass uses the terminology of "manufacture," "artifice," and "technological production," concluding that this mode of bringing into existence human beings is "profoundly dehumanizing." But why? There is no obvious basis for his assertion that "the violation of human equality, freedom, and dignity are present even in a single planned clone." Whose equality or freedom is violated? And whose dignity? Of course we should all be morally opposed to violations of equality, freedom, and dignity of human beings. But it requires an argument to show how such "violations" occur simply by the act of bringing a human being into existence in some ways rather than in other ways. A child who came into the world through cloning would no more be the "property" or the "possession" of its creator than are children who are "begotten" or who result from *in vitro* fertilization.

Kass and others take as axiomatic the proposition that to be cloned is to be harmed, or at least to be wronged. Axioms are underived postulates, so they must be known by means of divine revelation, by a method of intuition, or in the way that the axioms of logic are known. I leave to theologians the question whether propositions about cloning are knowable by divine revelation. Intuition has never been a reliable epistemological method, especially since people notoriously disagree in their moral intuitions. The other drawback of reliance on intuition is that it admits of no argument or justification. It is absurd to maintain that the proposition "cloning is morally wrong" is self-evident in the way that axioms of logic like Leibniz's law are knowable. The mere assertion that cloning is the replication of humans – a process radically different from reproduction – and therefore it should be outlawed, fails to identify the moral wrong involved. In a moral argument it is necessary to specify the precise nature of the wrong done either to the individual from whom a clone is derived or to the resulting cloned person. The question remains: *Who* would be harmed in instances where individual humans – not herds of humans – might be cloned? Whose rights would be violated, if cloning were legally permitted only in cases where people initiated a voluntary request?

Kass concludes that human cloning is "deeply unethical in itself and dangerous in its likely consequences." That statement embodies two different types of ethical judgments. The first is a judgment about the intrinsic worth (good or evil) of something; the second evaluates an action or activity by its consequences. Judgments about intrinsic worth still require a justification, and judgments about consequences should rest on empirical evidence or at least, extrapolations from analogous circumstances. Kass has neither provided a justification for his claim that human cloning is "deeply unethical in itself," nor has he provided evidence that masses of dehumanized beings will be a likely consequence of failing to enact a ban on cloning. He is certainly right to urge that we not be slaves of unregulated progress. But he is mistaken in thinking that the only way to regulate progress is with a sweeping legal prohibition.

In testimony presented to the NBAC, Dorothy Wertz, a sociologist, correctly observes that "the level of public discourse...has not advanced much since the early 1970s, when Mayor Al Velucci of Cambridge, Massachusetts said that if the Massachusetts Institute of Technology (MIT) made genetically engineered bacteria, 'little green monsters would come out of the sewers'" (Wertz 1997: 1). Unfortunately, bioethicists opposed to cloning have done little to introduce sanity or clarity into the discourse. Surely we need to educate the public better than the media have done in the recent aftermath of the cloning of a single sheep. The usual polls following a breaking news story revealed that a considerable majority of those questioned were opposed to human cloning. Did they base their opposition on scenarios of a hundred Hitlers? Or on the hastily mustered worry: "I don't want *them* to clone me!"

A Rational Approach to Public Policy

Leon Kass and others fearful of cloning employ an array of adjectives – revolting, repugnant, repulsive – that represent one set of emotional reactions some people have expressed at the prospect of human cloning. Unfortunately, however, Kass makes the move of so many commentators on cloning when he cites the main source of that repugnance: the "mass production of human beings, with large clones of look-alikes..." Is this a realistic worry? Even if it might be, in the hands of some hypothetical dictator or totalitarian government, public policy could include a perfectly sensible restriction as suggested by Dorothy Wertz: prohibition of the use of cloning to produce more live births than would ordinarily occur in nature, say five (Wertz 1997).

What is left unexamined is whether widespread revulsion (if it exists) is good grounds for instituting legal prohibitions. Kass acknowledges that "revlsion is not an argument" (p. 20). Yet he adds that "repugnance is the emotional expression of deep wisdom, beyond reason's power fully to articulate it" (p. 20). The history of philosophy includes examples of thinkers who have embraced a moral epistemology of intuitionism or the view that ethical judgments are merely expressions of the speaker's feelings or attempts to get other people to have similar feelings. To base public policy on "what we intuit and feel," as Kass would have us do, is questionable at best, and irrational at worst.

There is no evidence that human dignity (whatever might be meant by this concept) has been compromised by the introduction of other forms of assisted reproduction, nor is it threatened by the prospect of cloning. Rhetorical flourishes, even eloquent appeals, and vague references to human dignity are no substitute for reason and argument. The many commentators who contend that it is important to respect and preserve human dignity need to provide a more precise account of just what constitutes a violation of human dignity if no individuals are harmed and no one's rights are violated. Dignity is a fuzzy concept, and appeals to dignity are often used to substitute for empirical evidence that is lacking or sound arguments that cannot be mustered. If objectors to cloning can identify no greater harm than a supposed affront to the dignity of the human species, that is a flimsy basis on which to erect barriers to scientific research and its applications, and to enact prohibitionist legislation.

One incontestable ethical requirement is that no adult person should be cloned without his or her consent. Even the term "consent" is misplaced here. It is more accurate to say that cloning an adult person should be ethically permitted only if that person initiates a request. But if adult persons sought to have themselves cloned, would the resulting individuals be harmed by being brought into existence in this way? One harm that some envisage is psychological or emotional distress to a person who is an exact replica of another. As already noted, some opponents have elevated this imagined harm to the level of a right: "the right to our own individual genetic identity." But it is not at all clear why the deliberate creation of an individual who is genetically identical to another living being (but separated in time) would violate anyone's rights. The person from whom the clone is derived must initiate the process voluntarily, and thus waives any alleged right to genetic identity. The cloned individual would not otherwise have come into existence. He or she would have the presumed benefit to enjoy life and would, of course, deserve all the legal protections of any human being brought into the world by any means, natural or with the aid of assisted reproductive technology. Evidence, not mere surmise, is required to conclude that the psychological burdens of knowing that one was cloned would be of such magnitude that they would outweigh the benefit of life itself.

Some commentators have expressed concerns about the potential negative consequences and violations of rights that may result if human cloning is legally *prohibited*. John Robertson, a bioethicist and professor of law argued that "an optimal public policy on human cloning would respect human rights and individual freedom and dignity, including scientific freedom" (Robertson 1997). Robertson also points out that cloning is much less radical than gene alteration technologies on the horizon, so it is important to place this technique in the context of others that may need to be regulated in some way but will probably not face an absolute ban. Robertson's view is echoed by Susan Wolf, another lawyer-ethicist, who claimed that a "ban of all public and private cloning may well violate [US] constitutional guarantees of academic freedom for researchers and procreative liberty for infertile couples" (Wolf 1997).

It is certainly possible that there may be no substantial benefits to society that would result if human cloning were to become a reality. Yet this would constitute a good argument for banning cloning only if considerable harms are a likely consequence. The question is whether public policy prohibitions should be based on a relative absence of prospective benefits or on a demonstration of probable harms. The problem is further complicated in that what some people construe as benefits, other think of as harms. This is the case regarding some of the potential benefits envisaged for individuals or couples who might want to use the opportunity afforded by human cloning.

A number of possible situations have been envisioned. In one, a couple suffers a tragic loss when their child is fatally injured. Let us assume further that the woman is past child-bearing. Before the child dies, the parents seek to have her cloned. In a second situation, a couple is infertile and unable or perhaps unwilling to use one of the existing techniques of assisted reproduction. Cloning is the only way for them to have a genetically related child.

In the first situation we may sympathize with the grieving parents yet still wonder if a child brought into existence from such motives might be psychologically damaged. But is replacing a beloved child by the technique of cloning more ethically suspect than having another baby be the usual means to serve as a replacement? In the second situation, we may question why these and other infertile couples are so desperate to have a genetically related child. But for what specific reasons would cloning be unacceptable when the couple might use the gametes of strangers, employ

213

in vitro fertilization, and implant the resulting embryo in the woman's sister who has agreed to be a gestational surrogate? No harm specific to the technique of cloning is apparent.

In the context of infertility treatment, the form of cloning that involves embryo splitting or induced twinning may save a woman from repeated exposure to drugs that cause superovulation, possibly reducing her risk of later developing ovarian cancer (Wolf 1997). Still another possibility is that couples who are seeking an embryo donation may be enabled to choose more precisely the genome of their offspring, with the result that the child will have a good genetic start in life an the couple would enjoy a happy rearing experience (Robertson 1997: 4).

The ethics of these situations must be judged by the way in which the parents nurture and rear their resulting child and whether they bestow the same love and affection on a child brought into existence by a technique of assisted reproduction as they would on a child born in the usual way. Yet commentators have termed these scenarios "grotesque," countering the supposition that these could be benefits of cloning with the response that these alleged benefits are, in reality, the harms. It is a sure sign that an ethical disagreement is deeply rooted when one side identifies as benefits precisely what their opponents construe as harms.

Human cloning should remain in a research context for an indefinitely long time, following adequate animal work. Layers of oversight more effective than the current procedures of ethical review committees would be necessary to monitor the research efforts. Both in the research phase and in any future applications, human cloning must be shielded from market forces: no payments to research subjects, no "clone banks," and no buying or selling of cloned cells or embryos in the scientific or medical community. If these sorts of restrictions go beyond what is currently in place to govern human experimentation, perhaps we need better oversight and monitoring for the entire research enterprise with human subjects.

There is probably more to fear from commercial applications of cloning than from the other evils envisioned by opponents. One has only to look at the entire area of assisted reproduction in countries where it remains unregulated to see how a profession or technology can mislead or even exploit infertile couples. Unlike the UK, which has the Human Fertilization and Embryology Authority acting as a regulatory body, the United States has no such oversight that has governmental authority to monitor or regulate a variety of clinical practices of assisted reproductive technology. Misleading advertising, deceptive use of statistics in citing "success" of *in vitro* fertilization, and other questionable practices can be traced to the economic rewards that less-than-scrupulous practitioners can reap.

Everything that is now unethical or illegal regarding the treatment of human beings would apply as well to clones. Moreover, we can enact new restrictions and regulations, if needed. The potential negative consequences of human cloning can be adequately managed by such regulation. Just as we have laws prohibiting baby selling and commerce in human organs, so can we and should we have laws prohibiting commercial transactions involving cloned human beings. Laws and regulations would be needed to protect people's rights and prevent harmful applications, and violators would have to be punished. This is a rational approach to the perfection of techniques that produced the first successful cloning of a mammal, much better than the reaction generated by panic and obscure appeals to human dignity.

References

Annas, G. J.: "Cloning: crossing nature's boundaries." *Boston Sunday Globe*, March 2, 1997, p. D1.

ASBMB Public Affairs News, Friday, March 7, 1997, transmitted via internet.

Bioethics Unit of UNESCO: undated.

Callahan, D.: "A step too far." *New York Times*, Feb. 26, 1997, A23.

Group of Advisers on the Ethical Implications of Biotechnology (GAEIB): "Opinion: ethical aspects of cloning techniques." May 28, 1997.

Halperin, J.: "Clonar personas es violar los derechos humanos." *Clarin* 25 de mayo de 1997.

Kass, L. R.: "The wisdom of repugnance." *The New Republic*, June 2, 1997.

Kolata, G.: "Scientist reports first cloning ever of adult mammal." *New York Times*, Feb. 23 (1997a).

Kolata, G.: "With cloning of a sheep, the ethical ground shifts." *New York Times*, Feb. 24 (1997b).

Life Science, July 31, 1997, subscriptions@washington-fax.com (Washington Fax: An Information Service).

National Bioethics Advisory Commission: *Cloning Human Beings* (Rockville, Maryland: 1997).

Nicholson, R.: "Two of a kind – or none?" *Hastings Center Report*, 27, no. 3, May–June 1997.

Robertson, J.A.: "A ban on cloning and cloning research is unjustified." Testimony before the National Bioethics Advisory Commission, March 14, 1997.

Shapiro, D.: "Think before you squawk." *New Scientist*, Aug. 2, 1997.

Steering Committee on Bioethics of the Council of Europe: *Draft Additional Protocol to the Convention for the Protection of Human Rights and Dignity with Regards to the Application of Biology and Medicine. Directorate of Legal Affairs* (Strasbourg, July 1997).

Wertz, D. C.: "Cloning humans: is it ethical?" Testimony before the US National Bioethics Advisory Commission, 1997.

Wolf, S.: "Why the Bioethics Commission is wrong to seek a ban on cloning." *Star Tribune*, June 19, 1997.

World Health Assembly: "Cloning in human reproduction." Document WHA 50.37, May 14, 1997 (Geneva: World Health Organization).

16

Sex Selection: The Feminist Response

DIEMUT BUBECK

Introduction

The possibility of "choosing" the sex of a baby received much discussion in the 1970s and early 1980s because of significant advances in reproductive technology or, if not advances, then at least the widely and optimistically advertised possibility of such advances in the future. There is no general consensus among feminist activists and theorists, however, over their evaluation of sex selection, with feminist responses ranging from outright rejection to at least provisional acceptance. After a brief exposition of the facts and the more general arguments, I shall present the diverse feminist responses and discuss the roots of their disagreement.

Developments in Sex-selective Technology and Practice

Sex selection can take place either before or after conception (preconceptive and postconceptive sex selection). In almost all cases,[1] postconceptive selection will involve the abortion of the fetus if her/his sex is not the desired one. Sex determination is a routine byproduct of the genetic screening of fetuses for the purposes of detecting chromosomal anomalies or other hereditary diseases, some of which are sex-linked. Such screening became first possible in the 1950s through amniocentesis in the late second trimester of pregnancy. Chorionic villus sampling, developed in the late 1970s, moved the date of genetic screening forward into the late first trimester. The sex of the fetus can also be ascertained – though not reliably in all cases – through the now widely used ultrasound method. Current research on the possibility of fetal genetic screening through blood tests of the pregnant woman, if successful, will make screening less intrusive and move it forward even further into the first weeks of pregnancy. The ever earlier availability of knowledge about the sex of a fetus means, in its turn, that the abortion of fetuses on the basis of their sex becomes a possibility at an ever earlier stage in the pregnancy.[2]

Attempts at preconceptive sex selection are age-old, but received renewed public attention in the 1970s when various methods based on differential qualities of gynogenic and androgenic sperm (female- and male-producing sperm) were discussed

216

and marketed. So far, however, none of these methods seems to work reliably, hence there is currently no certain way of selecting sex before conception (Holmes 1995). This means that sex selection, as currently practiced, involves abortion subsequent to a fetal sex diagnosis, and this in turn no doubt constrains the practice of sex selection quite considerably.

Sex selection is used at present in countries such as India, China, Korea, and Taiwan and, if used, clearly discriminates against girls. The recent rise in sex ratios at birth, indicating the birth of more male babies than normally expected, reflects this trend (Goodkind 1996; Kusum 1993; Moen 1991). This rise confirms earlier predictions based on research on sex preferences regarding children which indicates a preference for male children as well as a preference for the first-born child to be male (Williamson 1976; Steinbacher and Gilroy 1990). Various social, economic, and cultural factors seem to exacerbate son preference, among them the one-child and openly eugenic policies in China, the expense of dowries in India, patrilocal families and the ensuing need for support by sons in old age, and the need for sons for purposes of religious practice as in Confucianism or Hinduism. Misogynist gender stereotypes and gender divisions reinforce and are in their turn reinforced by these other factors.

Empirical Predictions

Many of the arguments about sex selection rely on empirical predictions about the consequences of not prohibiting it. As Powledge put it early on and very succinctly, these predictions differ not so much in their basic assessment that the sex ratio will be higher, that is, more favorable to men, but in their assessment of the size of this shift and its consequences (Powledge 1983: 205).

By how much will the sex ratio rise? Will this rise be counterbalanced over time by a subsequent fall, will it continue over time, or will it reach a certain maximum level at which it will remain? The answer to these questions depends on many further factors such as the legality, availability and cost of sex determination and abortion, the development of cheap preconceptive sex selection, and, not least, the level of son preference and misogyny in any particular culture. Furthermore, even if these predictions could be made, it is not clear what further consequences such higher sex ratios will lead to: will they have rather dire consequences for women – such as their increasing confinement (Postgate 1973) – or will they make women more valued because there are less of them, thus counteracting any existing misogyny and resulting in gender equality? (Keyfitz 1983) Will they lead to more crime, more competition, more homosexuality and less culture in societies with high sex ratios? (Etzioni 1968). Will they reduce fertility and thus reduce the population growth rate in developing countries? (Postgate 1973).

While these predictions were doubly speculative at the time they were made, supposing a rise in the sex ratio, they remain speculative to date since the consequences of the now confirmed rise cannot yet be assessed. Predictions are further complicated by possible trade-offs and knock-on effects. For example, there is some ground for assuming that prenatal discrimination through sex selection will at least to some extent replace postnatal discrimination such as female infanticide and

217

various forms of neglect of girls as expressed in their higher mortality rates (Goodkind 1996), hence the effect on the overall sex ratio in a society may not be that great if the new form of discrimination cancels out older forms.

In sum, there remains much room for speculation even though more is known now about the rise of the sex ratio at birth than was at the beginning of this discussion. More specifically, no long-term trends in sex ratios can yet be confirmed, nor, consequently, any of the other predictions hinging on them.

Consequentialist Arguments

Consequentialist considerations (as in utilitarianism, or cost–benefit analysis) attempt to evaluate the moral status of a particular practice, policy, or issue by reference to its consequences. Unlike in other forms of moral evaluation, which may refer to more abstract values such as liberty, equality, or justice, the plausibility of consequentialist argument is dependent on the reliability of its assessment of the relevant consequences.

The following main negative and positive effects of sex selection have been discussed in this literature.

Negative effects:
a) negative consequences of a higher sex ratio for societies such as higher criminality and less culture (Etzioni 1968);
b) effects on women's lives, such as their increased social confinement and policing (Postgate 1973);
c) the effect on women of being second-born, given a consistent preference for first-born boys and evidence that first-born children tend to do better in various respects (cf. Warren 1992);
d) the perpetuation or even reinforcement of misogynist gender ideology through a practice which is openly expressive of such a misogynist evaluation of women;
e) the possibility of large-scale "female feticide" or "gynicide" (discussed below).

Positive effects:
f) the increase in happiness in parents, given that they have children of a sex of their choice and that they are able to "balance" their families;
g) the increase in happiness and welfare of children, especially girls, if they are the sex their parents wanted them to be;
h) the avoidance of violence in women's lives which could have been expected had they been not been able to avoid further female children;
i) the avoidance of sex-linked diseases;
j) the possibility of population control in countries with steep rises in population.

Two specific types of consequentialist argument seem interesting enough to deserve separate mentioning. The first type is the slippery-slope argument. In the context of sex selection, three such arguments have been used:

218

k) sex selection is the first step onto the slippery slope towards the "custom-made" child, or complete "quality control" of one's offspring, an outcome which is a form of eugenics and as such repulsive (Wertz and Fletcher 1992);

l) by contrast, the prohibition of sex-selective abortion could be the beginning of the slippery slope to a complete prohibition of abortion;

m) sex selection is, if not the beginning of, then at least a significant further move onto a slippery slope ending in the mass extermination of women, or "gynicide."

Slippery-slope arguments are convincing to the extent that they convince us that we have reason to be afraid, since the only reason why we should reject a not very objectionable thing (policy, practice, state of affairs) is because it will, if accepted, lead to a much more objectionable thing (policy etc.). The most important step in slippery-slope arguments is thus the establishment of an inevitable link between the not very objectionable and the objectionable thing. Whether such a link will obtain, however, is a matter of empirical speculation.

The second type of argument focuses on the counterproductive social consequences of individual choices. Two such arguments can be found in the discussion of sex selection:

n) giving individual women the choice to abort female fetuses may indeed improve these women's lives, but the exercise of this choice has the social consequence(s) of worsening the situation of women overall and/or reinforcing misogynist gender ideology;

o) allowing women certain reproductive choices in fact undermines women's reproductive rights and freedom (Raymond 1993: xi, p. 77).

This type of argument cuts mainly against the liberal or individualist stress on rights, choice, or liberty, pointing out a particular kind of consequence which is overlooked if one's focus is too narrowly on the individual and consequences for the individual.

Ideally, each of the consequences specified in (a) to (o) could be assessed as to their magnitude and probability, and the overall balance, negative or positive, could be then computed and a verdict on sex selection be given. However, since the predictions about any of these consequences are mainly speculative, not much headway can be made except on the basis of yet further assumptions or stipulations about, e.g., magnitudes and probabilities, or further factors aiding the predictions (see my discussion above). The only exception to what seems otherwise largely guesswork is the prediction of a rise in the sex ratio at birth, but, as I have argued above, this by itself does not aid us much in the prediction of further consequences. Moreover, threshold effects may further complicate the picture: if the effects are relatively small, they might fall below the threshold which will trigger off further consequences, thus not changing the picture much at all (this might be particularly true for the counterproductive social outcome type of consequence), while if the effects are above a certain threshold, consequences may spin out of control or change qualitatively. Given the predicament of being faced largely with guesswork, two conclusions suggest themselves. First, at the more practical, policy level, the most important conclusion might be the attempt to guard against the worst possible consequences.

Second, at the theoretical level, the conclusion must be that the consequentialist approach to evaluating sex selection is simply not feasible.

Radical Feminist Argument: Patriarchy and Gynicide

In response to the initially very upbeat discussion of various new technologies in the field of reproduction (usually referred to as "new reproductive technologies," or NRTs), a number of academic and activist feminists formed FINRRAGE (Feminist International Network of Resistance to Reproductive and Genetic Engineering) to argue and campaign against NRTs, and a number of works have been published elaborating their arguments for the complete rejection of any of these technologies (Corea 1985; Corea et al. 1987; Rowland 1992; Raymond 1993). These feminists contextualize the discussion of sex selection in two ways: first, sex selection is seen as one of a number of new technologies which, especially when combined, have the potential to change women's reproductive lives enormously; second, it is seen as part of the power relations between men and women which structure women's lives. Given this patriarchal context, radical feminists argue, NRTs aggravate rather than improve women's lives.

One significant strand of the argument against sex selection is consequentialist, predicting "gynicide" or "femicide" as the outcome of its widespread use, and concluding with the necessity of its rejection if such gynicide is to be avoided. Thus Steinbacher speculates that the "conclusion" of sex selection combined with further technological developments in extrauterine development of fetuses is "femicide" and that "[u]ltimately, patriarchy can do without women – except for those few kept for the purpose of producing eggs" (Steinbacher 1984: 275), while Corea notes that

> In discussing sex predetermination, most scientists focus on foreground issues (the expansion of options; disease prevention; population control) and ignore the Background question: Gynicide. (Corea 1985: 206)

Clearly, these are suggestions more than arguments, consisting of evocative chapter headings and final paragraphs, and using terms such as "femicide" or "gynicide" to suggest the mass extermination of women in parallel to the genocide of the Jews (cf. Corea 1985; Holmes and Hoskins in Corea 1987; Hanmer and Allen 1980; Warren 1985).

It is easy to reject such argument as exaggerated or even hysterical. As Birke et al. have insightfully noted, the argument expresses mainly fear (1990: x, 22–6) and, we might add, it convinces to the extent that the reader shares these fears about the consequences of the NRTs for women. Fear, however, is a plausible response for women to have for three reasons. First, as I pointed out above, the only sound prediction about sex selection is the rising sex ratio at birth. Second, all other predictions are more or less guesswork, and such radical unpredictability leaves room for various emotional responses such as fear and despair on one hand, and hope and optimism on the other.

The third reason for fear about NRTs is a point radical feminists have emphasized throughout their writings: patriarchal social relations in which women have little power to influence outcomes to their own advantage. Women are, having been oppressed throughout most of history and oppressed in present day society, justified in fearing the worst. Fear is an adaptive response to painful experiences, warning those subjected to such experiences of the possibility of further pain, therefore, given that women have been subjected to oppressive painful conditions, it is rational for them to be afraid. Thus, as feminists have correctly pointed out, sex selection would only be a new form of killing women, but not a new phenomenon, since women have been the victims of violence, including fatal violence, in most societies: many societies had, and many continue to have, skewed sex ratios, produced, among other things, by female infanticide, neglect, starvation and mutilation of girls compared to boys, and violence against wives and other female members of the family (Corea 1985: 195–5; Warren 1985: ch. 2; Sen 1995: 260). Given this overwhelming patriarchal history as a larger context for projections into the future, fear rather than hope seems appropriate, and predictions take a much more sinister turn.

Thus by stressing the already high sex ratios in countries such as India, and then generalizing over both developing and developed countries, radical feminists suggest that femicide is indeed a possibility (Steinbacher 1984: 275; Corea 1985: 206). A more level-headed evaluation of likelihoods, however, would, first, have to distinguish between the more gender-egalitarian developed countries and the more patriarchal developing countries whose sex ratios do reflect misogyny and actual discrimination against girls and women. Given this distinction, it would then have to conclude that, (a) femicide is much less likely in the former than in the latter, and (b) that it is not very likely on a grand scale in the latter due mainly to the cost of the currently required sex determination and subsequent abortion (although this prediction might change if cheap and reliable preconceptive sex selection became possible). Second, the prediction of femicide assumes that patriarchy can only get worse, but not better: if it were to weaken, the grounds for selecting against girls would disappear, too, and the specter of femicide be banished. The very case of India, often cited as one of the worst, presents, if disaggregated, an interesting case in point: the once communist-governed and most egalitarian state of Kerala has a sex ratio of 97, while sex ratios in the northern states are far above 100, ranging from 114 in Punjab and Rajastan to 120 in Sikkim (Moen 1991: 242). The figures can be read both as an indication of the severity of patriarchy in (northern) India and thus as a ground for fear, as well as an indication of the difference a commitment to egalitarian policies, as in Kerala, makes and thus as a ground for hope.

In conclusion, fear is not necessarily an inappropriate response to sex selection, especially not regarding countries with already high sex ratios – indicating fatal violence and neglect to girls and women – to begin with. However, distinctions between countries are necessary, and the dystopic projection of ever-worsening patriarchal relations has less purchase when the achievements of feminist campaigns in the last three decades are considered (while bearing in mind their failures and the need to struggle on, however). Hence femicide is a possibility that should be taken seriously, but seems relatively unlikely a prospect at present. It may need to be reconsidered in some countries, however, should cheap and reliable preconceptive

221

sex selection become available. Last, although feminist argument seems in a position to firm up some of the predictions regarding sex selection, the problem of the guesswork on which consequentialist argument is based remains. Consequently, it might be argued that other criteria should be used, values such as liberty, equality, and justice. In the following, therefore, I shall discuss arguments attempting to evaluate sex selection on those grounds.

The Liberal Position: The Importance of Choice

The liberal position in the discussion of sex selection can be characterized as follows. The values of choice or reproductive liberty are postulated or presumed as the most important values in assessing sex selection. It follows from these values that people should have the option of choosing sex selection, regardless of whether they want to take it up or not, since not having the option reduces their choice set or reproductive liberty (Robertson 1994; cf. Warren 1985). With regard to policy, since the prohibition of sex selection (for whatever reasons) takes away such choice, prohibition is unjustifiable. Other policies short of prohibition, such as not making information about the sex of the fetus available to prospective parents (Wertz and Fletcher 1992: 248–9) or prohibiting the use of fetal screening for the purposes of sex determination (a policy endorsed in Maharashtra, India, for example), are equally unjustified to the extent to which they are indirect ways of preventing the parents from making such choices. The liberal position at least at the policy level is also endorsed by many feminists otherwise not classifiable as liberal, even if somewhat reluctantly (Birke et al. 1990; Holmes 1987; Overall 1987: ch.2).

Two main considerations lead feminists in particular towards taking a liberal position in the area of reproduction. The first and most important one refers to the fact that one of the ways in which women were, and in some places still are, oppressed is by being denied any choice regarding both their sexuality and its expression, and their ability to bear children. Hence one of the most important gains for women has been the liberty to make choices about their sexuality and reproduction, and the protection of this liberty mainly through privacy rights. Sexual and reproductive choice, liberty, and rights, therefore, remain important values to be defended (or still to be achieved). The second consideration is another slippery slope argument: whatever reproductive rights and liberty have been achieved for women are far from secure yet, indeed continue to remain under threat everywhere, hence any reduction in their reproductive rights or liberty could be the dangerous first step on the slippery slope to losing all of these rights or liberty. Now the first consideration is not likely to be objected to by any feminists as it stands. What can, however, be questioned is the interpretation of reproductive liberty or rights. A further point of possible disagreement is highlighted by the question what relation the value of reproductive liberty has to other possible values such as equality or justice. A last point relates to the slippery-slope argument: not all feminists agree that reducing some choice courts the danger of the reduction of all choice, in fact, and paradoxically, they have argued that the reduction of some choices is necessary for women to have true reproductive freedom. These points of possible disagreement go to the heart of the varied feminist response to sex selection. I shall discuss the first and last point in what follows and address the question of other values in the next section.

First, then, Raymond has objected to the conception of reproductive freedom used in defenses of sex selection and other NRTs as a "banalizing of choice" where choice is understood on the model of consumer choice and more choice, whatever it is, is better than less (Raymond 1993: 85ff). Furthermore, the choices defended by reproductive liberals, according to her, are determined by and benefit "medical-technical interests," but are not necessarily in women's interests. In fact, they raise from and are exercised in contexts in which women are oppressed. To deal with the second point first, the context of certain choices must make us no doubt suspicious about their desirability. If, on the face of it, it is desirable for any individual woman to be able to select against girls in a society where she (and her girl) would face serious negative consequences if she gave birth to a girl, the desirability of this choice clearly derives from the misogynist and oppressive context in which the woman has to survive. Choices, however, may always be desirable on other grounds, too: it is at least in principle conceivable that women may desire a certain sex in their children for other reasons (Overall 1987: 23–7). The critique, therefore, stands only if the desirability of these choices derives exclusively from their oppressive context, and this is a difficult point to establish. Furthermore, even if oppressive circumstances compromise women's choices in various ways, it would be wrong to conclude that women cannot make autonomous choices. The critique of such choices might therefore also be seen as implying a form of feminist "maternalism" which will limit women's agency even further instead of protecting it, while not allowing for the possibility of women making autonomous choices even under oppressive conditions.

Raymond's other argument against reproductive liberalism, then, is that feminists should defend a more substantive conception of reproductive freedom and self-determination for women, not just choice *tout court*. "Reproductive liberalism offers women no substantive vision of reproductive freedom or rights," according to her, because it neglects to take into account how women's sexuality and reproduction are determined and limited by women's oppression by men (Raymond 1993: 98). The solution to the problem, therefore, cannot lie in more choice or determination, and which also implies the need for a much more radical more rights for women, but only in much more fundamental changes. The refusal to discuss women's reproductive freedom in isolation from social context thus leads reproductive radicals to embrace a much more determinate vision of the future which includes the end of women's oppression and their genuine self-change in gender relations. Liberals, by embracing their "emaciated" notion of liberty, cannot address this much larger problem. Liberals might respond to this argument by pointing out that it is only through more liberty and more choice that such change will ultimately come about. While the disagreement here is based on different empirical models of social change rather than on different conceptions of freedom, there is also a more conceptual disagreement insofar as liberals and radicals disagree about how substantively freedom should be understood. Last, there is also disagreement in approach in that liberals focus on individuals and individual agency while radicals focus on social structures and context. Given these fundamental disagreements, it is not surprising that feminists have not been able to agree amongst themselves, reproducing theoretical splits that have characterized political philosophy more generally. While radicals are willing to sacrifice some liberty to bring about what they conceive of as desirable substantive liberty, liberals will decry any sacrifice of (formal) liberty as not justifiable merely in reference to a more substantive, "maternalist" conception of liberty.

The third argument against reproductive liberals, that some choices have to be restricted for freedom to be possible at all, can now be seen to be part of the more fundamental disagreement. The danger of the slippery slope towards the total restriction of women's reproductive freedom only obtains if no distinctions are made between choices. Distinctions can be argued on two grounds. First, some choices are more important than others (abortion as a choice for women is more important than different flavors of ice-cream). Second, and more strongly, some choices and some rights in fact undermine women's reproductive freedom and are therefore very different from choices and rights that are genuinely expressive of such freedom (Raymond 1993: xi). Provided these distinctions are generally recognized, the prohibition of a particular kind of choice does not necessarily lead to a more general restriction of choice. The latter point has been made in reference to sex selection, and is an interesting instance of the "unintended social consequences" type of argument: women in those countries where there is a strong preference for sons and various social, economic and cultural factors which reinforce it will not be genuinely free in making a choice about sex selection, since its very availability will increase the pressure to make use of it. Hence radicals conclude that women's *substantive* freedom is not increased by having that choice, but is in fact further compromised. Interestingly enough, most liberals agree to some restriction of choice in order to preserve liberty, such as, e.g., in their defense of the prohibition of slavery or of the necessity for laws: the defense typically is that such restrictions safeguard the liberty of everybody. It is thus perfectly possible, and indeed necessary even according to most liberals, to make distinctions between different kinds of choice. The question therefore is whether such distinctions can be made in the case of sex selection, and whether they would be recognized enough so as not to lead to further restrictions of women's reproductive freedom. While the grounds for making the distinction seem relatively strong, whether social pressure is recognized as a restriction on women's freedom unfortunately depends again on whether a more formal or a more substantive conception of liberty is endorsed. The distinction may furthermore depend on the predictability of such pressure (it may not be so bad in the more gender egalitarian countries).

In conclusion, the discussion of sex selection is riddled with conceptual divisions over liberty. While all of the arguments discussed above could be carried on at much length, similar versions of this type of argument have proved irresolvable in political philosophy. Hence an easy solution cannot be expected. An alternative way of addressing the question of reproductive liberty is by linking it to other important values.

Liberty, Equality, and Justice

Just how do we assess reproductive liberty and choice in relation to other values such as equality or justice? Is it really the most important value, "trumping" all the others, or is it one amongst a plurality of equally important values, or even subordinate to other, more important ones? It is useful to note that the above mentioned common endorsement by all or most feminists of reproductive liberty and rights as important values does not imply that they are thought to be the most important ones, and it is here that feminists have differed significantly, too.

To start with equality, then, sex selection clearly is a form of discrimination if predominantly female fetuses are selected against. Thus *prima facie* it is violating gender equality. Furthermore, if sex selection is practiced it will also likely enhance already existing gender stereotypes (Rothman 1986: ch. 5). Although it has been argued that sex selection does not necessarily discriminate against women (Warren 1985: 175–7), in societies where gender stereotypes have currency and where women's disadvantaged situation goes hand in hand with their lesser evaluation compared to men (and in fact is used to explain and justify their disadvantage), it is likely that sex selection will be influenced by such prejudice and that the expression of such prejudice through sex selection will further reinforce the prejudice, thus also reinforcing women's disadvantaged position (Keyfitz 1983a: Preface). Hence if at best, but not very probably, sex selection will have no effect on gender inequality, at worst, sex selection will aggravate it considerably in the sense that women will be valued and respected even less.

Furthermore, in addition to infringements of equality, sex selection offends gender justice in at least two respects. First, it is clearly unjust that women, simply *qua* women, have less of a chance to exist. While sex selection cannot be an injustice to any particular woman (since she will not exist, having been selected against), it is an injustice to women *as a group*, and thus to individual women *qua* members of this group: why should women's chances to exist (and live well) be less than men's, simply because they are women? Secondly, if sex selection is widely practiced and that practice is common knowledge, women have to live with the stigma of being obviously less valued and less wanted. The stigma, however, affects all women in that it will decrease their ability to develop healthy self-respect and hence their chances to succeed in life. Thus even if a particular woman was very much wanted and valued as a child, she will have to live in a society where she knows, and everybody else knows, that *her kind* is less wanted and less valued, and struggle with this stigma.

The values of equality and justice thus obviously lead to different conclusions regarding sex selection: while sex selection may enhance reproductive freedom, it also offends equality, justice, as well as a more substantive conception of freedom. Which values and thus which considerations are more important? People as well as political theorists differ in the weight they accord to any of these, and so do feminists: for liberals and libertarians, liberty is the most important value and good and thus "trumps" the others. However, it might be argued that feminist theorists can only plausibly endorse a liberal position if they make three further assumptions: first, that liberty is important even if it cannot be taken up; second, that sex selection does not fall into the class of choices that are counterproductive; and third, that increasing liberty will bring about, at least in the long run, more gender equality and gender justice (since, *qua* feminists, they have a commitment to the latter two values). The first assumption is vulnerable to criticism by those who defend more substantive conceptions of liberty, and more substantive conceptions would put more stress on gender equality and justice as necessary conditions for substantive liberty.

The last two assumptions are based on relatively optimistic further assumptions and predictions about sex selection and social change. Arguably, the comparison between the liberal, Western countries and the worst "offenders" with regard to sex selection suggests that these assumptions do not hold. Thus it is unlikely that sex selection will advance gender equality and justice in countries like India, China, or Korea – in fact it clearly aggravates the situation by discriminating against women in a new and very visible way, since unlike female infanticide or neglect it is a course of action that is officially condoned. Hence sex selection is a choice that is counter-productive at least in some circumstances: even if sex selection does not reduce women's reproductive freedom, as radical feminists have argued NRTs in general do, it does put women under new kinds of pressure and worsens their situation in other ways. Under these circumstances, the value of liberty is in outright and stark conflict with gender equality and justice, and it is arguable, as feminists in those situations have argued, that equality and justice must override liberty under those circumstances. Under the comparatively more benign and less gender discriminative conditions in Western countries, the conflict between these values is clearly less pronounced, and it may be easier for feminists in those countries to endorse if not a full liberal position then at least liberal policies regarding sex selection, while also being committed to gender equality and gender justice: if sex selection remains relatively little taken up and fails to reach a threshold of visibility, its counterproductive effects will be much reduced or even negligible, and it would thus be more neutral with respect to gender justice and equality. Given these circumstances, sex selection could be condoned, but even so it could not be positively embraced and celebrated, since its selection would continue to discriminate against girls and thus continue to threaten a more pronounced conflict between liberty, justice, and equality.

To conclude, it is important to be aware of both the more philosophical arguments about sex selection and the difference actual circumstances in various countries may make. Thus if we distinguish between the theoretical and the policy level, while arguments may be irresolvable at the theoretical level, feminists might, indeed should, come to agree that different situations may call for different solutions: while Western countries may be able to adopt a liberal wait-and-see policy without having to fear drastic consequences, the most notorious countries regarding sex selection may well need to override liberal considerations and instead affirm publicly their commitment to gender equality and justice, both because more inequality and injustice can plausibly be predicted as a result of sex selection and because women's reproductive liberty will already be compromised by social pressure to abort female children. Under such circumstances, sex selection veers too closely, if not towards the scenarios of femicide that radical feminists have wanted to urge us to take seriously, then at least towards worsening gender inequality and injustice. Surely liberty cannot be upheld as the most important value in those situations, at least as far as the issue of sex selection is concerned.

Notes

1 In *in vitro* fertilization (IVF), the sex of the embryo can be determined after conception and selected before implantation. Instances of this type are, however, relatively unlikely given the low success rate and costs involved in IVF, and the general aim of achieving a successful pregnancy. I therefore disregard this type in my discussion.

2 The issue of the morality of abortion is obviously relevant to (at least) postconceptive sex selection. However, I do not address this issue here. Instead, I concentrate on considerations regarding sex selection itself, whether pre- or postconceptive.

References

Birke, L. et al.: *Tomorrow's Child: Reproductive Technologies in the 90s* (London: Virago, 1990), x, 22–32.

Corea, G.: *The Mother Machine: Reproductive Technologies from Artifical Insemination to Artificial Wombs* (London: Women's Press, 1985).

Corea, G. et al., eds.: *Man-Made Women: How New Reproductive Technologies Affect Women* (Bloomington: Indiana University Press, 1987).

Etzioni, A.: "Sex control, science and society." *Science* 161 (1968), pp. 1107–12.

Goodkind, D.: "On substituting sex preference strategies in east Asia: does prenatal sex selection reduce postnatal discrimination?" *Population and Development Review* 22 (1996), pp. 111–25.

Hanmer, J. and Allen, S.: "Reproductive engineering: the final solution." In *Alice Through the Microscope* (London: Virago, 1980).

Holmes, H. B.: "Choosing children's sex: challenges to feminist ethics." In Callahan, C. Joan., ed.: *Reproduction, Ethics, and the Law: Feminist Perspectives* (Bloomington: Indiana University Press, 1995).

Holmes, H. B. and Hoskins, B. B.: "Prenatal and preconception sex choice technologies: a path to femicide?" In Corea, G. et al., eds.: *Man-Made Women: How New Reproductive Technologies Affect Women* (Bloomington: Indiana University Press, 1987).

Keyfitz, N.: "Preface." In Bennett, N. G., ed.: *Sex Selection of Children* (New York: Academic Press, 1983a).

Keyfitz, N.: "Foreword." In Bennett, N. G., ed.: *Sex Selection of Children* (New York: Academic Press, 1983b).

Kusum:. "The use of pre-natal diagnostic techniques for sex selection: the Indian scene." *Bioethics* 7 (1993).

Moen, E.: "Sex selective eugenic abortion: prospects in China and India." *Issues in Reproductive and Genetic Engineering* 4 (1991), pp. 231–49.

Overall, C.: *Ethics and Human Reproduction: A Feminist Analysis* (Boston: Allen & Unwin, 1987).

Postgate, J.: "Bat's chance in hell." *New Scientist* 58 (1973), 12–15.

Powledge, T.: "Toward a moral policy for sex choice." In Bennett, N. G., ed.: *Sex Selection of Children* (New York: Academic Press, 1983).

Raymond, J. G.: *Women As Wombs: Reproductive Technologies and the Battle Over Women's Freedom* (New York: Harper Collins, 1993).

Robertson, J.: *Children of Choice: Freedom and the New Reproductive Technologies* (Princeton: Princeton University Press, 1994).

Rothman, B. K.: *The Tentative Pregnancy: Prenatal Diagnosis and the Future of Motherhood* (London: Pandora, 1986), ch. 5.

Rowland, R.: *Living Laboratories: Women and Reproductive Technology* (London: Lime Tree, 1992).

Sen, A.: "Gender inequality and theories of justice." In Nussbaum, M. and Glover, J., eds.: *Women, Culture and Development* (Oxford: Clarendon Press, 1995).

Steinbacher, R.: "Sex preselection: from here to fraternity." In Gould, C. C., ed.: *Beyond Domination* (Totowa, NJ: Rowman and Littlefield, 1984).

Steinbacher, R. and Gilroy, F.: "Sex selection technology: a prediction of its use and effect." *Journal of Psychology* 124 (1990), pp. 283–8.

Warren, M. A. *Gendercide: The Implications of Sex Selection* (Totowa, NJ: Rowman and Littlefield, 1985).

Warren, M. A.: "The ethics of sex preselection." In Alpern, K. D., ed.: *The ethics of Reproductive Technology* (New York: Oxford University Press, 1992), pp. 237–8.

Wertz, D. C. and Fletcher, J. C.: "Sex selection through prenatal diagnosis: a feminist critique." In Holmes, H. B. and Purdy, L., eds.: *Feminist Perspectives in Medical Ethics* (Bloomington: Indiana University Press, 1992), 245–6.

Williamson, N.: *Sons or Daughters: A Cross-Cultural Survey of Parental Preferences* (Beverly Hills, CA: Sage, 1976).

Further reading

Birke, L. et al.: *Tomorrow's Child: Reproductive Technologies in the 90s* (London: Virago, 1990).

Corea, G.: *The Mother Machine: Reproductive Technologies from Artificial Insemination to Artificial Wombs* (London: Women's Press, 1985).

Corea, G. et al., eds.: *Man-Made Women: How New Reproductive Technologies Affect Women* (Bloomington: Indiana University Press, 1987).

Holmes, H. B.: "Choosing children's sex: challenges to feminist ethics." In Callahan, C. Joan., ed.: *Reproduction, Ethics, and the Law: Feminist Perspectives* (Bloomington: Indiana University Press, 1995).

Raymond, J. G.: *Women As Wombs: Reproductive Technologies and the Battle Over Women's Freedom* (New York: HarperCollins, 1993).

Robertson, J.: *Children of Choice: Freedom and the New Reproductive Technologies* (Princeton: Princeton University Press, 1994).

Warren, M. A. *Gendercide: The Implications of Sex Selection* (Totowa, NJ: Rowman and Littlefield, 1985).

Warren, M. A.: "The ethics of sex preselection." In Alpern, K. D., ed.: *The Ethics of Reproductive Technology* (New York: Oxford University Press, 1992).

Wertz, D. C. and Fletcher, J. C.: "Sex selection through prenatal diagnosis: a feminist critique." In Holmes, H. B. and Purdy, L., eds.: *Feminist Perspectives in Medical Ethics* (Bloomington: Indiana University Press, 1992).

17

Creating Perfect People

PHILIP KITCHER

Introduction

Within the next decade, scientists will finish constructing a fine-grained map of the human genome and will probably produce a virtually complete sequence of the 3 billion bases that constitute the nuclear DNA in a "typical" human cell. Armed with knowledge of the genomes of other organisms – particularly yeast, nematodes, fruit flies, and mice – they will be able to use computer programs to identify genetic loci and, in a significant percentage of cases, to gain some understanding of the functional role of the proteins for which various genes code. The number of loci that are involved in genetic disease, disability, or impairment of function will grow by several orders of magnitude. Because genetic variation at many of these loci may be extensive, re-searchers will probably have to be selective, focusing on those regions at which mutation is especially common and those loci where genetic modification produces the most devastating effects. It is safe to assume, I believe, that 20 years from now, people will have the ability to undergo hundreds, thousands, even tens of thousands of genetic tests.

What is far less certain is the extent to which recognition of human genes and their roles will translate into cures for diseases. One's initial thought is that knowledge of the normal and abnormal sequences of genes implicated in a disease would enable doctors to devise a treatment. Yet there are several steps that have to be negotiated. First, from the knowledge of the sequence it's often hard to discover the conformation of the protein for which the gene codes. Second, even when the three-dimensional structure of the protein is known, its function may still be obscure. Third, even when the function of the protein is recognized, the exact structure of the causal process that goes on in generating a healthy or diseased phenotype may not be fathomable. Finally, even when one has detailed causal knowledge about what goes on in normal and abnormal individuals, it may be difficult to work out a way of intervening. Despite the fact that the structure of the protein involved in Huntington's disease has been known for a decade – and, more dramatically, the molecular basis of sickle-cell anemia has been recognized for almost half a century – biomedical research has not made much advance towards any treatment. In the case of cystic fibrosis, another disease for which the underlying locus was identified relatively early, molecular knowledge has given rise to improved methods of treatment, although there is still a long way to go.

While methods of treatment trickle in, we shall be offered a number of diagnostic tools. Many of these will be refinements of the kinds of diagnoses doctors can now perform, enabling them to identify diseases more quickly in some instances and to gain insight into the form of a disease, thus distinguishing people who will benefit from a course of treatment from those who will not.

The most striking effect of a proliferation of genetic tests will not be the strengthening of the diagnostician's arsenal – important though that is – but the radical extension of preventative medicine. Even if we can't hope to intervene to correct a defect, once it has occurred, we may have the chance to head off trouble by identifying early in a person's life a propensity for disease. Indeed, there are encouraging examples: by identifying children with PKU at birth, it's possible to provide them with a special diet, free of the amino acid phenylalanine that they are unable to metabolize, that enables them to avoid the severe retardation they would otherwise suffer; those at risk for colon cancer can be monitored by sigmoidoscopy so that potential tumors are detected early and removed. Once it was thought that similar advance knowledge would prove valuable in the case of breast cancer, that identification of genes for early-onset breast cancer would give women from families at risk the chance to have frequent screenings and thus avoid a diagnosis that came too late. In the wake of the sequencing of BRCA1 and BRCA2, it has been necessary to acknowledge that the young women who are most at risk for the cancers associated with mutant alleles are typically not able to benefit from an intense course of early mammograms, since the disease is likely to strike them during their twenties and thirties, when the density of their breast tissues makes mammograms relatively poor instruments of detection.

It is not yet clear how much of the genetic knowledge we are gaining will inspire programs for avoiding or ameliorating conditions for which people are at identifiable risk. There will surely be many instances in which a genetic test, if given early, would only supply the depressing knowledge that the person tested has a high chance of future disease or disability and that there is nothing specific that can be done to lower the probabilities (beyond, perhaps, things that would have been advisable in any event). Some stoics may value early knowledge of this sort, on the grounds that it will help them better to plan their lives; others might find the knowledge completely crushing. Just as we can hope for some cures that will flow from genetic knowledge, so too we can expect that there will be cases like PKU and colon cancer in which advance knowledge really does make a difference. Yet while they will almost surely exist, they may be relatively rare.

So what is the good of genetic knowledge about ourselves, apart from improved diagnostics and some uncertain prospects of cure and preventative action? A moment's reflection produces the answer. Even if we can do nothing for the bearer of the long repeat involved in Huntington's disease, once he is born, even though we can't help the woman with the mutant BRCA1 allele, it will be possible to take action at an earlier stage. Lives that will suffer from incurable genetic disease – or even from high risks of unpreventable disease – can be foreseen in advance, and suffering can be prevented before there is a person whom we have a duty to support and help. Genetic testing already proceeds in a small way in the prenatal context. Thanks to a thorough and humane program of screening, the incidence of Tay-Sachs disease, worldwide, has been dramatically reduced. Chromosomal testing for trisomies, of which the most well-known, trisomy 21, gives rise to Down syndrome, has been available for decades and is now routinely offered to pregnant women over 35. In the short term, perhaps even in the not-so-short term, while we are awaiting preventative therapies or complete cures, genetic knowledge will readily translate into prenatal tests. Where nothing can be done for those born with genotypes that portend suffering, we can try to take advance action.

But if we begin by attempting to avoid bringing into the world human beings who would be afflicted with genetic disease, where do we stop? Doesn't the prenatal use of genetic testing start us on the road towards the creation of "perfect people"?

II

For some people, these questions have very simple answers. Life is sacred and we should not terminate a pregnancy just because it does not fit human standards. Those who adopt this approach are vulnerable to a number of counterarguments. First, we may offer the standard considerations that support the rights of women to exercise control over their bodies in general and their reproductive systems in particular. Second, we may appeal to the important neurological differences between early-stage human embryos, lacking the capacities for sentience, and subjects of pleasure and pain, who can be thought of as having rights. Third, we can insist on the continuity between efforts to avoid suffering by administering therapies that are often invasive and radical – consider neonatal surgery or the imposition of the PKU diet – and the termination of pregnancies that would give rise to extraordinary suffering: we are not obliged to take lives simply as they come. Finally, and perhaps most powerfully, one can document the consequences of the most terrible genetic diseases, syndromes like Tay-Sachs, Canavan's, Lesch-Nyhan, and San Filippo, in all of which there are disruptions of development severe enough to suggest that the quality of the bearer's life falls below any minimally acceptable standard, as well as pressures on parents and other family members that not infrequently generate ruined marriages and neglected siblings. I do not claim that these points, individually or collectively, are decisive. Some religious believers will remain unconvinced by virtu-ally any instance of human misery that a merciful abortion might have prevented. Rather than trying to articulate the four arguments in an attempt to arrive at a unanimity I think unattainable, I shall simply take for granted the idea that some uses of prenatal genetic testing, followed by termination of pregnancy, are morally legit-imate, and focus on the range of examples in which that approach ought to be allowed.

So far I have couched the discussion in terms of selection *against* undesirable traits, supposing that the prenatal use of genetic knowledge lies in rejecting genotypes that one doesn't want to issue in extrauterine phenotypes. There are two slightly different ways for this regime to proceed. One, most continuous with ordinary reproduc-tion, brings about a pregnancy in the old-fashioned way, using some technique of collecting fetal cells (at present amniocentesis or chorionic villi sampling), whose DNA can then be probed for sequences that are of concern. The other would use *in vitro* fertilization to obtain a number of zygotes, arrest each of them while genetic tests were administered, and then choose one (or more) for implantation. The second method advances slightly further in the direction of "choosing" the genetic endowment of a child, because it supplies a number of alternative genotypes from which prospective parents can select.

Two other scenarios are often discussed. One involves the deliberate engineering of a genotype, so that the parents of the future are viewed as having the ability to specify the alleles that their children will bear at the loci that interest them most. Now it is true that researchers are currently able to inject segments of DNA into cells, so that, given a zygote obtained by IVF, one could add some new DNA. But there's an important difference between getting some DNA into a cell and inserting it in a chromosome. With luck, the injected DNA will be incorporated into one of the zygote's chromosomes, rather than being broken down, but there's no way of specifying the point of insertion. This means that the new DNA may land in the middle of a functional region causing disruptions. More likely, it will figure in the intergenic wastelands, the repetitive DNA. Assuming that it has been equipped with regulatory sequences, it may be transcribed and translated to form the appropriate protein, but there are serious questions about whether the regulation of its expression will proceed properly unless it is in roughly the right place on the right chromosome and whether its expression will leave the regulation of other genes unaffected. Even more worrying is the thought that the presence of an extra chunk of DNA on one of pair of chromosomes will lead to mismatch at cell division, so that the newly inserted genetic material will simply be snipped out when the cell divides, becoming lost in the resultant cell lineages. Finally, we should recall that the genetic material at the locus of concern is still intact. The zygote is a cell with two alleles at that locus plus an allele we really like somewhere else. Perhaps the phenotypic effect of that combination will be better than if the DNA hadn't been added, but there's no reason to think that the phenotype will be that of someone who had two normal alleles at the crucial locus.

If we could do something much more delicate, then engineering cells to genetic specifications would become a real possibility, and maybe a moral threat. Imagine our having the ability to snip out genetic material we don't want, break it down or remove it from the cell, and insert just the allele we like in the resultant chromosomal gap. That's the sort of thing that seems needed if we're going to manufacture zygotes with alleles to order. But that scenario is simply fantasy. Nobody has the slightest idea how to cut and paste in such refined ways, and, I suspect, even if it were possible to do the trick in one instance, there would be no general strategy of repeating it. The preliminary results from human gene therapy show that injecting some DNA into cells in a very coarse way enables doctors to ameliorate truly terrible genetic conditions: sometimes with hypercholesterolemia or SCID it proves possible to create some approximation to normal cell function. That very rough ability will probably be improved in coming decades, but it is completely different in kind from what would be needed to do better than nature, to make zygotes with the best combinations of alleles (even supposing that that notion makes sense and that we could work out which ones they are).

However, thanks to Dr. Ian Wilmut, there may soon be a way of creating to order a zygote with a specific, antecedently existing, human genotype. Assuming that Wilmut's success in cloning sheep can be extended to our own species, prospective parents could produce a child whose nuclear genetic material was the same as that of some previously conceived person, perhaps one of themselves, perhaps someone else. The moral questions surrounding cloning easily slip out of focus because some pertinent facts aren't clearly understood. It's important to realize that the clone would be less similar to the person who supplied the nuclear DNA than identical twins are to one another. Monozygotic twins not only share their nuclear DNA but the constituents of the cytoplasm in the cells from which they develop come from a common source. Nobody yet knows how great the effect of the extranuclear character of the zygote can be (Wilmut's technique may enable that issue to be explored for nonhuman mammals), but it may be considerable. Furthermore, monozygotic twins share a common intra-uterine environment for nine months, and, typically, grow up thereafter in very similar circumstances. Especially in those cases where the source of the nuclear DNA was already an adult when the clone was formed, we can expect the changes in patterns of socialization, diet, and education to produce profound differences.

Let me sum up. I propose to set on one side blanket worries about prenatal testing, either with selective abortion or with discarding embryos formed through IVF. For the reasons I've given, we should also ignore science-fiction scenarios in which parents order the genetic qualities of their children ("We'd like the tall allele at the five principal height loci, the smart alleles at all the intelligence loci, and the straight allele at the sexual orientation locus"). This leaves us with three ways in which to exercise choice over nascent lives:

1   Deciding against continuing pregnancies;
2   Picking from a set of IVF zygotes;
3   Forming a clone of an existing person.

I aim to explore the principles that might properly guide us in these contexts.

III

Let's start with an obvious suggestion. The techniques I've been discussing are rightly viewed as *medical* techniques, directed at the correction or prevention of disease. Tay-Sachs, Down syndrome, and other conditions for which prenatal diagnosis and selective abortion are now available, are all *diseases*, and any extension of genetic testing in prenatal contexts ought to follow their precedent. So we might suggest that the sole morally legitimate use of genetic technology would be to prevent, or, at least, lower the chances of, a child's being born with a disease or disability.

There are two complementary worries about the proposal that genetic knowledge may be used in prenatal contexts when and only when it would reduce the chances of bringing into the world a new life that would suffer disease or disability. On the one hand, the criterion can be assailed because it is too permissive. Should all diseases or propensities for disease count? Would abortion be justified by the recognition that the child-to-be would be color-blind, have an allergy to hazelnuts, or have a propensity to hypertension? On the other hand, some people would protest the restriction to disease conditions. Consider the use of amniocentesis and karyotyping to identify the sex of the fetus, a process that has been used in Northern India as a prelude to selective abortion of females. Being female is not a disease and ought not to be a disability. Unfortunately, as one learns more about the women who go to the clinics and take the tests, it becomes clear that they are not moral monsters. Rather, recognizing the plight of women in their society, they try to avoid giving birth to a child who would suffer neglect, humiliation, and, often, early death. The source of the moral problem here lies in the background social environment, and it can seem callous to insist that mothers should be deprived of the chance to resist cruelty that is not of their making.

Before we attempt to judge either of these criticisms, it's important to raise a prior question: What counts as a disease? The reason this question is crucial is that, even though we might all agree on many instances, there are some cases that have either been differently classified by different people at various stages in recent history or continue to provoke different responses. It took a considerable political struggle to remove homosexuality from the official list of psychiatric disorders, and there are still disputes about whether obesity should count as a disease condition. Because there are difficulties in providing a clear definition, philosophers of medicine sometimes contend that we can manage with no explication or with an account that handles the central core of cases, but this is an illusion, so long as we are serious about limiting prenatal genetic testing to instances of disease. The examples of homosexuality and obesity make it apparent that any concept of disease adequate to ground a policy on testing must resolve the hard cases.

Two major approaches to the definition of disease have figured in recent discussions. One of these appeals directly to considerations of value: in its simplest form, it proposes that a condition would count as a disease for a community C just in case members of C would agree that the condition in question was undesirable for the bearer. I shall not argue against this definition, or weigh the merits of more refined versions of the same idea, since it seems to me that there is a simple reason for taking such approaches to be irrelevant to the problems that concern us. If the proposal to draw a line licensing just those prenatal genetic tests that test for disease has attractions, it's because we think that employing the concept of disease frees us from making judgments about the value of prospective lives. Were we to be told that diseases were linked to "undesirable conditions," then we would immediately have to face the issue of how conditions were to be judged undesirable, and, in short, we could simply short-cut the consideration of disease and tackle the valuational questions directly. Instead of discussing whether or not a valuational notion of disease can be made to work, the heart of the matter is how we are to think about the values of lives – a topic that will occupy us below.

Alternatively, we could opt for an "objectivist" notion of disease, and here the most promising view is that which links disease to breakdown in function. We can say that an organ or system of the body is diseased just in case it has a condition that impairs its function. Of course, this immediately calls for an account of the notion of function, for we shall need to be able to decide if there are systems that have broken down in people who are obese or who are attracted to members of the same sex. It's evident that functionality cannot be pinned to statistically normal behavior, since there are perfectly functional conditions that are very rare (red hair is perfectly functional) and common conditions that are dysfunctional (progressive hearing loss). Functions are best understood in terms of a connection with natural selection: to say that the function of a trait (organ, system) is F is to claim either that the trait in question has recently been maintained in the population because of its doing F or that doing F makes a causal contribution to some component of fitness (increasing survivorship, fecundity, attractiveness to mates, or something of the kind). How does the proposal to limit use of prenatal genetic testing to tests for disease fare when disease is understood in terms of breakdown of function and function explicated in these evolutionary terms?

Not well. The fact that natural selection favored organisms with some particular trait does not mean that that trait is not burdensome to us. Quite possibly women have been selected for a regime of regular child-bearing, beginning soon after menarche – and it has been suggested that the length of time between menarche and first pregnancy is positively correlated with risk of breast cancer – but that doesn't mean that women who now occupy very different environments should try to conform to that regime in the interests of health. More generally, there's no reason to claim that the deliverances of our history of evolution under natural selection are in any way sacrosanct, so that they, and they alone, should shape a proper policy with respect to genetic testing.

Nor are all breakdowns in function equally urgent. Each of us probably suffers minor modifications of a number of bodily organs or systems that reduce them below normal levels of functioning. Yet it would be absurd to insist that genetic contributions to these substandard traits are apt targets for prenatal diagnosis. An important part of any principle for employing genetic tests ought to be a differentiation of cases within those that are permissible, and this is something that the proposal in terms of disease does not supply.

In the end, I believe, we can't avoid confronting issues about values. The value-theoretic approach to disease offers us an unnecessary detour, while the "objective" notion of disease leaves us with an unrationalized policy precisely because it avoids the central issues of what matters in lives. I'm going to explore the proper use of prenatal tests by beginning with the notion of the quality of life. If we have an understanding of this concept, then we can elaborate a rationale for prenatal testing in terms of promoting the expected quality of prospective lives.

IV

Talk of the quality of life can easily inspire the protest that lives should not be evaluated "from the outside": activists regularly make the point that the value of the lives of people with disabilities is misjudged by those who do not have the experience of living and coping with handicaps. More generally, the history of western thought is full of proposals about what matters in human life, and all of us would find it oppressive to feel that our lives were to be assessed according to the standards of different epochs. This legitimate reaction does not make all talk of the quality of life otiose. In accordance with the liberal emphasis on individual choice, we

235

can understand quality of life in terms of the satisfaction of standards that are generated by the person whose life it is.

Central to the conception of quality of life that I shall develop is the thought that human lives embody decisions about what matters to them. These decisions may be taken quite explicitly, as when a person formulates definite aspirations, or they may be implicit in patterns of behavior and valuation. Self-conscious scientists who take their research as the most important facet of their lives contrast with those whose ties to family and community are expressed in their everyday actions. So I'll assume that individuals typically have a "life theme," which sets an order of priorities. In light of that theme, some hopes and desires are picked out as central, others seen as less important. So, from the perspective of the individual whose life it is, we can talk of the life as going well or going badly according to whether the desires highlighted by the theme are satisfied. To put the point in mundane terms, for a person whose life is centered on family, the flourishing of children and grandchildren is what counts in determining the happiness of the life – the triumph of the local football team or advancement at work are ultimately irrelevant (unless, of course, these are simply means to the significant ends).

I want to suggest that there are some necessary conditions for a life theme to anchor a life of high quality. One of these is that the theme reflect the agent's own choice, that it not be imposed from without. Another is that the theme should be sustainable as the agent matures, as goals are attained, and as the person gains more insight into various possible courses that life might have taken. The first condition is motivated by the importance we attach to the agent's autonomy, that the values around which his life is shaped should genuinely be his own, but there is also a link to the second condition. If a person has a theme for his life thrust upon him then, it seems, there is a distinct chance that the course of experience will lead him to regret decisions that have been guided by that theme and to see his achievements as ephemeral and unsatisfying.

When the two necessary conditions are met, the quality of a life is judged by the extent to which the aspirations given high priority by its theme are fulfilled. Lives that go well are those which freely form a sustainable theme and then achieve those things the theme identifies as important. Conversely, the expected quality of a life is adversely affected when there are low chances of autonomous choice of theme, significant probability that the theme chosen will prove unsustainable, or serious risks that the desires given priority will be unsatisfied. In this light, our fears about conditions that will afflict the lives of children are readily comprehensible. The severe genetic diseases, Tay-Sachs, San Filippo, Lesch-Nyhan, and the like, appear to preclude the possibility of the child's ever developing a theme for her life at all. In other instances, the muscular dystrophies or cystic fibrosis, for example, the range of possible themes for the life is curtailed. With this reduction, we are left wondering whether there will be any sustainable theme whose central desires have realistic chances of satisfaction. Examples of people with severe disabilities who lead rich and satisfying lives are inspiring, but they do not scotch the main worry. Surely there are sustainable themes for those who will be confined to wheelchairs throughout their lives, but they will require more good fortune than most if they are to satisfy the desires associated with these themes.

236

The account I have given so far leaves out one obvious factor in the quality of human lives, namely the balance of painful and pleasurable experience. This represents an intuitive judgment that the quality of a *human* life cannot simply be established by a plethora of hedonistic delights. There are people whose development has been so disrupted that they are permanently arrested at the normal state of a 2-year-old child, and it is imaginable, if not actual, that their lives are so arranged that they enjoy, year after year, the most unalloyed sequence of experiences that a 2-year-old would judge pleasurable. For all that, the quality of their lives is not high, and, while their caregivers are doing the best they can with a difficult situation, the lives of people who form and satisfy distinctive goals, even with struggle and pain, seem to go far better.

Even if the balance of pleasure and pain cannot be at the center of an account of the quality of human lives, it should be given some role. Other things being equal, lives that go well when evaluated by the theme-based criteria have higher quality the more pleasurable experiences they contain. When things are not equal, it does seem that the theme-based criteria exert more weight than hedonistic considerations: in assessing the quality of a life, I suggest, the central desire satisfied at some cost of pain appears more important than the painful experience. For most choices about prospective lives, avoidance of pain is not the primary criterion. There are a few known conditions which it is hard to palliate even with any administration of drugs, but, typically, pain can be controlled by medication.

My discussion so far has failed to recognize explicitly that the determinants of the quality of human lives are not intrinsic features of the individual. That point should be especially obvious when we think about the balance of pleasure and pain, for that is obviously dependent on the availability of palliative drugs. However, the resources that society is willing to place at the disposal of individuals are also highly relevant to judgments that issue from the theme-based criteria. The chances that a child born with Down syndrome, muscular dystrophy, or cystic fibrosis will be able to form a sustainable life theme autonomously and to satisfy the desires given priority by that theme depends on the support, medical, educational, and social, that the child receives. Because of this, the expected quality of a life, judged from the perspective of partial knowledge of the genotype, must be relative to the amount of social support provided for bearers of that genotype. Further, we can assess the efficiency of social support for individuals with a particular condition in terms of the increase in expected quality of life that various levels of support would produce. At this stage, it is clear that there are two major questions about the employment of prenatal testing, one of which is frequently overlooked. The first question, the relatively familiar issue, concerns how to use prenatal testing wisely *given a particular background level of social support*. The second, relatively neglected, considers how we should best combine prenatal testing and social support if we have a serious interest in enhancing the quality of human lives.

The most obvious approach to either of these questions would focus solely on the fetus who is the subject of the genetic test. So, given a fixed background of social support for people with various characteristics, it would seem appropriate to use genetic tests to identify conditions which, given the social background, would be likely to give rise to lives of low quality. But this is myopic. The envisaged new life has consequences for others, and we should not overlook the effects on the quality of those other lives. If, for example, it would only be possible to ensure for a child with a particular genetic condition a life of sufficiently high quality by neglecting an elder sibling, whose quality of life would thereby be considerably depressed, it seems permissible for the prospective parents to be able to test a fetus for the genetic condition, and to terminate the pregnancy if the test proves positive.

Siblings are not the only parties involved. The birth of a child requiring dedicated care from the parents may have an adverse effect on the parents' lives, blighting the prospects of realizing goals that had antecedently been central. While it is possible to make prenatal choices for frivolous reasons, the recognition of damaging consequences for one's own life (or the life of a partner) ought not to be ruled out of court, and a morally-informed decision to terminate a pregnancy can be based on the grounds that the efforts required to raise the quality of the prospective life to a minimally acceptable level would drastically reduce the quality of the lives of the parents. (This is not incompatible with the possibility that *in some cases* the birth of the child would reorient the parents' lives, providing them with a new theme, and that they might find fulfillment in caring for the child; but we should be very clear about the difficulties of knowing in advance that one is the sort of person whose life could be restructured in this fashion.)

Even more broadly, the birth of a child who needs special help and support affects the well-being of others. Social resources are finite, and drawing a significant amount from the available pool leaves less for others. Some parental decisions in prenatal contexts reflect the structure of the free-rider problem: parents can decide to continue a pregnancy precisely because expensive medical regimes will be available in infancy, followed by continuing medication, special social programs, schools specifically designed to cope with the disruptions of normal development, and so forth; all this exists as a result of social compassion, but it could not be sustained unless most of the pregnancies with the underlying condition are detected early and terminated. In this situation, a decision to continue a pregnancy can place in jeopardy the well-being of children born to parents who, for whatever reason, were deprived of the opportunity to identify the disability in advance.

Let me summarize. I've tried to outline an approach to the quality of human lives that will avoid judging them by standards that are not their own, and, indeed, that takes the agent's autonomy as central. According to that approach, we should use genetic testing in prenatal contexts so as to identify situations in which continuing with a pregnancy would yield lives of diminished quality, most obviously in cases in which the child who would be born would not have substantial opportunities freely to choose a sustainable theme for a life, a theme whose central aspirations have a reasonable chance of being satisfied, but also when the life in prospect could only achieve an acceptable level through serious depression of the quality of other lives, the lives of siblings, of the parents, even of other children for whom needed support might not be available. As I've noted, the envisaged decision-making takes place against the background of a set of social provisions, and it is hard to avoid the broader question of how those provisions ought themselves to be framed. I now want to examine how the three possibilities for exerting choice about prospective lives –

through prenatal genetic testing, IVF, and cloning – should be viewed within the kind of social framework currently available.

<h1 style="text-align:center">V</h1>

Let's start with the most extensive of the ways of influencing prospective lives, namely through cloning. Many popular fantasies about cloning are based on ignorance or confusion about the biological details – commentators have worried about the pro-duction of identical people (sometimes apparently produced overnight!), without recognizing that clones only agree in their nuclear genetic material and that we already know, from cases of monozygotic twins, that sharing this material is compat-ible with considerable phenotypic differences. Cloning cannot function as a device to produce a person of a very particular kind (unless one's focus is on some physiological trait under direct genetic control, the sort of trait that is not usually of concern to us). What cloning could do is raise the probability that one would bring into being a person with certain characteristics, for example, by using the nuclear genetic material from a very tall, muscular person one would raise the chances of having a child who would be athletic.

Given the perspective on quality of lives that I have recommended, it should be very clear what is wrong with this approach to reproduction. Far from respecting the autonomy of the individual, decisions to reproduce via cloning that were undertaken with these intentions would attempt to prescribe a theme to the nascent life. Of course, if parents were to use cloning to these ends, they would have a standard to which the child was supposed to conform, perhaps considering children who did not measure up to be failures, or, even if that were not so, the children might view themselves as defective if they were not to meet parental aspirations. Yet whether or not either of these harmful consequences were to ensue, the fundamental problem lies in the attempt to impose a theme.

So if there are benign uses of human cloning, it's clear how they must be generated. Cloning must be seen simply as a means to enhance the expected quality of life of offspring, to make available to them free choices that they otherwise might not have had. Perhaps there are cases in which a biological child of a couple would be at high risk for a particular form of disability, so that the chances of her finding a sustainable theme whose central desires would be satisfied are low, where cloning would circum-vent the problem. (A possible instance would involve a mutation in the maternal mitochondrial DNA, so that a healthy child could be produced by transferring the nuclear genetic material from a zygote produced by the couple to an egg supplied by another woman.) In order to defend cloning in a case like this, we must take *very* seriously the value of allowing people to produce biological children.

Turn now to the strategy of harvesting eggs, fertilizing them *in vitro*, performing genetic tests on the resultant zygotes, and deciding which one(s) to implant. Once again this strategy would be morally unjustified if it were to be driven by the search for a preferred phenotype – imagine, say, that parents wanted to ensure that they had the best possible combination of alleles at supposed "intelligence" loci – for this would be to dictate a theme to the nascent life. As in the case of cloning, permissible uses would be those in which the purpose of IVF was to guard against the high probability that a fetus conceived in the normal fashion would lack the usual opportunities for autonomously forming a sustainable theme whose central aspirations would have a reasonable chance of being satisfied. That could occur if there are risks of a disabling genetic condition and the mother would be in some danger from standard abortion procedures, or if there are several worrisome combinations of alleles, so that the probability that a fetus will carry one of them is significant.

There is a clear range of instances within which prenatal genetic testing and selective termination is morally permissible, and, equally clearly, a range of cases in which a decision to abort would be morally unjustified. For some conditions, given any amount of support we know how to provide, there is simply no way of giving their bearers any ability to formulate themes for their lives: perhaps their nervous systems degenerate soon after birth (as with Tay-Sachs) or their cognitive and emotional development is severely disrupted (Lesch-Nyhan, San Filippo). At the opposite extreme are conditions which have no obvious impact at all on the quality of life – eye color or hair texture, for example – for which any decision to end a pregnancy would be frivolous. Unfortunately, between these extremes lies a significant class of cases in which matters are by no means so clear cut.

Consider some of the possibilities: genetic testing discloses that a child will suffer from Down syndrome, or cystic fibrosis, that she will be born deaf, that she will be at high risk for early-onset breast and ovarian cancer, that she is likely to have cholesterolemia. Compatible with the test results in each case is a range of futures. Even if the parents are committed to providing support at the highest levels, they cannot be certain if the quality of the life will be close to normal or if it will be considerably depressed. In making their decision, the best the parents can do is to assess the expected quality of the child's life – not an easy task, given the absence of statistics and the fact that technological developments can sometimes improve the phenotypes associated with genotypes (as has been occurring with CF, for example). When the variance is high, as for example with Down syndrome, parents who find the risks of a low-quality life too great will be moved to abort; others will feel that they should not give up on the child. In terms of the focus on a single life, either attitude may be entirely warranted. However, if there would be serious repercussions for other family members – siblings or the parents themselves – only the decision to terminate may be morally justified.

The moral problems in this area are analogous to those parents already face in allowing their children to engage in activities that could have a profoundly adverse effect on their lives. When the chances that something terrible will occur are sufficiently low, it does seem justifiable to permit a child to participate in programs that bring benefits – learning rock-climbing or horse-riding, for instance. Increase the probabilities of trouble and the parental permission comes to seem irresponsible, and we rightly blame those parents who allow their children to hang around in dangerous neighborhoods after dark.

The cases just discussed are by no means the most disturbing. Within the next decades parents may be able to use prenatal testing in attempts to approximate perfection. Most of the traits likely to concern them are generated from a complex interaction between genotypes and environments. Nevertheless, researchers in molecular behavior genetics may discover alleles (or genetic markers) that correlate with certain forms of behavior in standard human environments, without offering any clear view about how to partition those environments more narrowly. Prenatal tests identifying those alleles or markers would give probabilistic predictions of behavioral traits, and might disclose a significant probability that the future person would have a socially unpopular trait – being obese or of below-average intelligence, for example. Should prenatal tests be used to select against characteristics that people do not like?

Here's an argument in favor of the use of genetic tests for such traits. As things now stand, people are allowed to do many things that will provide advantages for their children, and, in many middle-class enclaves, parents go to considerable lengths to ensure that their young children have broad opportunities. Their plans can be regarded as attempts to enhance the children's ability to choose, autonomously, a theme for their lives that can be sustained and that is likely to identify aspirations that can be satisfied. Use of prenatal testing is continuous with this dedicated concern, for what the parents are concerned to avoid are the characteristics that have an adverse impact on children's likely quality of life. Knowing that the children will live in a world that finds fat people unattractive and in which high intelligence is well-correlated with social success, the parents want to ensure that their offspring aren't victims of social disapproval.

I don't think that parents who reason this way are moral monsters – any more than the Indian women who reflect on the plight of their sex and decide that they cannot bring a daughter into the world. The parallel is exact, and disturbing. Because the quality of a person's life is affected by many aspects of the society in which she will grow and live, prospective parents can be moved by genuine concern for their children to recapitulate societal prejudices. From a global perspective the resultant decisions are repugnant, precisely because, when we apply more broadly the fundamental standard that the parents apply, we recognize that the society as a whole is artificially limiting the lives of some of its members.

There have been societies in which obese people haven't been objects of ridicule and condemnation and in which people who would have scored poorly on intelligence tests have lived happy and fulfilling lives. By and large, the affluent nations in which genetic testing is likely first to become prevalent are not societies of these tolerant kinds. Contemporary middle-class parents, desperate to find the right preschool programs for their children, testify to the competitive difficulties that our societies have erected and to the enormous gaps in access to resources that affect quality of life. In a world in which low intelligence likely translates into menial employment, lack of job security and uncertain health insurance, parents quite understandably want to ensure that their children avoid the lower third of the bell curve.

Notice, however, that the plausible moral principle that it is appropriate to take steps to forestall conditions that would adversely affect the quality of lives, the principle that seems to rationalize the parents' use of the prenatal tests, has a more general employment. If the factor that diminishes the quality of lives arises from social attitudes and institutions, then it's appropriate to view those attitudes and institutions as targets of reform. Instead of resting content with a permissible response to the prejudices and pressures of sick societies, we should seek to cure – or at least

241

ameliorate – the underlying social pathologies. Thus, if we want to avoid a rat-race for creating perfect people, we should be led to ask the harder, second, question I posed above – How should we combine prenatal testing and social support if we have a serious interest in enhancing the quality of human lives? – and attempt to integrate our policy on prenatal testing with broader social concerns.

Further reading

Dworkin, R.: *Life's Dominion* (London: HarperCollins, 1993).

Griffin, J.: *Well Being: Its Meaning, Measurement and Moral Importance* (Oxford: Oxford University Press, 1986).

Harris, J.: *Clones, Genes, and Immortality* (Oxford: Oxford University Press, 1998).

Kevles, D. J. and Hood, L., eds.: *The Code of Codes: Scientific and Social Issues in the Human Genome Project* (Cambridge, MA: Harvard University Press, 1992).

Kitcher, P.: *The Lives to Come: The Genetic Revolution and Human Possibilities* (New York: Simon & Schuster, 1996).

Part IV

GENOTYPE, PHENOTYPE, AND JUSTICE

18

Genetics and Personal Identity

CAROL ROVANE

Introduction: Locke's Distinction between Personal and Animal Identity

The central philosophical debate about personal identity concerns whether the condition of personal identity is the same as animal identity. This dispute was inaugurated by Locke, who asked us to imagine that the respective consciousness of a prince and a cobbler are switched into each other's body (Locke, bk. II, ch. 27). He thought that it is intuitively obvious that the prince would be the person with the prince's consciousness and the cobbler's body. And it was largely on the strength of this intuition about how a prince would remain the same person after acquiring a new body that Locke distinguished personal identity from animal identity.

It must be admitted that Locke's view conflicts with the humanist or, as it is now sometimes called, the animalist conception of ourselves that is evident in many of our commonsense attitudes and everyday practices. On the animalist conception, there is no distinction between personal and animal identity because persons just *are* animals. They are human animals whose lives are bounded by the biological events of birth and death. In contrast, Locke attached great importance to the idea that a person can stand before God on Judgment Day long after the death of its animal body and be held accountable for all of its earthly thoughts and deeds. He reasoned that this would not require the resurrection of the person's original animal body; all that would be required is that the person remain conscious of its earthly thoughts and deeds or, in other words, that the person remember them. That is why he affirmed that *consciousness alone* constitutes personal identity. According to him, there is nothing else that determines the boundaries of a person's life except its consciousness of its own personal history through memory.

Even if we do not share Locke's theological preoccupations, we might still want to embrace his distinction between personal and animal identity. Ultimately, his argument trades on an ability that we persons clearly have, namely, the ability to project imaginatively our points of view into different bodily circumstances. Thus I can easily imagine having my younger sister's body while retaining my own (as opposed to my sister's) point of view. This point of view which I regard as distinctively my own is, among other things, the point of view from which I am writing this chapter. I can imagine writing this chapter from this very point of view, but looking out from my sister's face through my sister's eyes, and seeing and using my sister's hands at the keyboard. And what makes it *my* point of view, despite its being in her body, is precisely that it includes my memories of my own personal history – that is, the very sort of personal consciousness that Locke took to constitute personal identity. We shall want to follow him in drawing a distinction between personal and animal identity, if we agree with him that: (a) what I imagine when I imaginatively project my personal point of view into my sister's body is really possible, and (b) if this were to happen, then it would be I who was living out my life in my sister's body and not she.

It is tempting to object against (a) and (b) above as follows: there is an unbreakable tie between our personal identities and our particular bodies, a tie so strong that not only is it never broken in fact, but also, it is not even broken in our imaginations when we project out personal points of view into different bodies. Consider, for example, the fact that I, a Caucasian woman of 42, can project my personal point of view into Muhammed Ali's body. When I do this, I imagine what it would be like to carry my memories in Ali's body, and to look out from his eyes and to see his hands at the keyboard instead of my own as I write this chapter. Yet although I find all of this very easy to imagine, there is also a sense in which I find it rather difficult to imagine actually living out my life in Ali's body. This is because my most cherished personal projects and relationships and commitments, such as my romantic and family in-volvements, were all undertaken with my original body in mind and not Ali's. And so it may be tempting to agree with the objection: I cannot, strictly speaking, be said to imagine being myself in Ali's body because of the way in which my personal identity is tied to my actual body. However, anyone who makes this objection has, quite simply, lost sight of the agreed terms of my thought experiment. The agreed terms are that I *can* imaginatively project my personal point of view into Ali's body. This means not only that I can imagine all the things I described above (looking out through his eyes at his hands while remembering my past and so on), but also that I can imagine what it would be like to try to adjust to this new bodily circumstance – say, by altering my personal commitments accordingly. And the crucial point is that when I imagine this, I am imagining that *I*, the *very same person*, would be doing the adjusting. These feats of imagination, then, belie the contention of the objection. This is not to say that Locke was definitely right to draw a distinction between personal and animal identity. It is only to say that we cannot reasonably reject it on this basis, by arguing that we cannot even *imagine* that our identities can come apart from our particular bodily circumstances. We surely can imagine this, as Lockean-style thought experiments clearly show. The harder question is whether what we thereby imagine is really possible.

Philosophers have raised other objections against Locke's analysis of personal identity that cannot be quite so readily dispatched. Nevertheless, neo-Lockeans have been highly resourceful in responding to them, and in doing so they have offered many important refinements of analysis. But this is not the place to review all of these objections and replies and refinements. Indeed, it would take a whole monograph to review them in a way that made them fully intelligible to those who are not

246

acquainted with the philosophical literature about personal identity.[1] And in any case, for the purposes of this chapter, all we really need to do is register the fact that, as things now stand, the philosophical dispute about personal identity that Locke inaugurated remains disturbingly far from resolution.

Having registered this fact, we can ask, *does genetics have anything to contribute toward a resolution of the dispute?* The answer is *no*. There are, however, a few points that ought to be raised in connection with this negative answer to our question. One concerns whether our newfound ability to clone sheep, and hence, presumably, human beings as well, has any relevance to the dispute about personal identity. The other is a speculation about the conditions in which future advances in genetic science might conceivably bear on the dispute – though given the present state of our understanding such a speculation is bound to be far-fetched.

The Irrelevance of Cloning

The first point about cloning, although a simple one, needs airing because it is important to be clear about the various reasons why we might or might not want to clone human beings. The point is just this: there is *no* sense in which cloning would resurrect the same person, and this is true regardless of whether Locke was wrong or right to draw a distinction between personal and animal identity.

The relation that an animal bears to its clone(s) is analogous to the relation that holds between identical twins who develop from the same zygote. They are not identical in the strict *numerical* sense; rather, they are numerically distinct animals who are *qualitatively* the same in respect of their genetic characteristics. Obviously, since cloning does not resurrect the same animal, cloning a human would not resurrect the same person even on the animalist conception of the person that Locke rejected. It would not resurrect the same person in the sense that he espoused either. For consider what cloning reproduces: only those characteristics that are genetically determined. Let us assume for the sake of argument that this includes all of a human being's distinctive psychological characteristics. Even given this assumption of radical genetic determinism of individual psychology, we still could not say that cloning resurrects the same person in Locke's sense. That would require not only that cloning reproduce all of the original human being's general psycho-logical characteristics, but also detailed memories of that original human being's particular individual history. Without such memories, there would be no continuity of consciousness between the original human being and the clone. But cloning certainly does not reproduce such memories. Just as it produces an entirely new and separate animal, so it also produces an entirely new and separate consciousness which possesses no personal memory of the original human life that preceded it. Because this is so, it does not resurrect the same person in Locke's sense any more than it resurrects the same animal.

Of course, it is easy to understand the desire to preserve and hold on to a loved one in the face of imminent biological death. And it is also easy to understand how this desire might lead us to arrange to have our loved one cloned. But we must be careful not to misdescribe what we would thereby accomplish. We would produce a human animal who shared our loved one's biological characteristics and also, depending on the degree to which individual psychologies are genetically determined, some psychological characteristics as well. But we could not coherently regard such a clone as actually living out our loved one's life in any sense – not in the biological sense of being the same animal and not in the psychological sense of having the same personal consciousness or point of view.

Personal Identity and Science

Although the sort of personal consciousness that Locke took to constitute personal identity is not reproduced by cloning, his view does presuppose that it can be reproduced *somehow* and, furthermore, that it can be reproduced in new or different bodily circumstances. Otherwise there would be no distinction between personal and animal identity.

Locke seemed to think that very little argument is required in order to establish that this is possible, over and above carrying out the relevant thought experiment – imagining that the consciousness of a prince and a cobbler are switched, or imaginatively projecting our own personal points of view into different bodies. This is a surprising attitude on Locke's part, because some of the scenarios that we find easy to imagine are not really possible. It is easy to imagine, for example, that human children can fly like Peter Pan, and yet we know that this is not really possible. In what sense are some imaginable scenarios not really possible? They are precluded by the laws of nature. So, to continue the same example, the laws of motion and human anatomy are what preclude human children from flying like Peter Pan. Clearly, we need to investigate whether the possibility that Locke asks us to imagine, the transfer of a single abiding personal consciousness from one human body to another, is consistent with the laws of nature. For if we were to discover that this is precluded by the laws of nature, then we would have to view Locke's distinction between personal and animal identity as a mere conceptual distinction that could never be realized in fact (barring miracles anyway), and its philosophical interest would be far less great than it otherwise would have been. The distinction would have no more weight or backing than the claim that human children can fly like Peter Pan. And in that case, we would be within our right to resolve the dispute about personal identity against Locke, in favor of the animalists.

It is safe to say that the task of investigating whether Locke's distinction is consistent with the laws of nature, and therefore more interesting than Peter Pan claims, lies just as much within the province of science as it does within the province of philosophy.[2] First of all, the line between philosophy and science is never sharp. And secondly, the line is especially fuzzy (and perhaps not even existent) in the domains that bear on the issue of personal identity. That issue is really just a special case of a more general issue concerning the relation between mind and body. What the theorist of personal identity needs to know is whether the same personal consciousness can continue or persist in new or different bodily circumstances, as Locke claimed it can. And it is hard to see how we could ever know this without a general understanding of how consciousness arises in human and other matter – which is to say, without a general understanding of the relation between mind and body. The special science that is most directly concerned to arrive at this understanding is cognitive science. So if we do look to science for help in resolving the philosophical dispute about personal identity, we should look first to cognitive and not to genetic science.[3]

Although various cognitive scientists and philosophers have put forward, and indeed committed themselves to, specific positions on the general issue about the relation of mind to body, the issue can hardly be pronounced as settled. This is certainly not the place to review how things presently stand in any significant detail. But a very brief and highly selective review is in order. For that will serve to put us in a position from which we can speculate about some conditions in which we might eventually want to turn to genetic science for help in solving the mind–body problem, and with it the problem of personal identity as well.

According to the functionalist theory of mind, all mental processes are computational processes. Although computational processes must always be realized in some material condition or other, they are in an important sense indifferent to their material conditions. In consequence, a single temporally extended computational process can be successively realized in different material conditions. A single mathematical calculation might, for example, begin in a particular human being's head and then expand to include scribbling on a pad of paper, the use of a pocket calculator, and finally a powerful computer. Now, if consciousness can be adequately accounted for in functionalist terms, then similar reasoning will apply. A single temporally extended consciousness, *qua* computational process, can be successively realized in different material conditions such as different human bodies. So if the functionalist theory of mind should turn out to be true, then Locke will be vindicated. The possibilities that he asked us to imagine in the course of arguing for his distinction between personal and animal identity will emerge as real possibilities, consistent with the laws of nature.

However, although the functionalist theory of mind has a significant number of staunch supporters, it also faces some severe difficulties. These concern whether certain features of conscious mental life could ever be adequately accounted for in computational terms. It has been charged, for example, that mental life has a qualitative aspect that cannot be reduced to computational terms; this qualitative residue is what it *feels* like for a person or animal to be in a mental state (Block 1978). It has also been charged that mental processes have a normative aspect which is missing in computational processes; that although the latter can be assessed from a normative point of view, as being in accord or out of accord with the normative requirements of rationality, they do not incorporate the self-conscious commitment to satisfying those requirements which characterizes genuine thinking (McDowell 1986). The most vivid way of bringing out these two alleged difficulties for functionalism is by bringing out the following implication of the doctrine: if mental processes are computational processes, then mere machines that are composed wholly of non-organic materials could in principle have mental lives, complete with feelings and normative commitments. The doctrine also implies the corollary that persons in Locke's sense could in principle survive with artificial bodies and brains as well as living ones.

249

Some philosophers hold that these implications make functionalism untenable. But committed functionalists have, on the whole, been quite happy to swallow them, and also to respond to the various difficulties that have been raised for their view, such as the two just mentioned above (Dennett 1991). One important reason why functionalists have remained committed is that they see a certain disadvantage or, at any rate, a certain weakness in the alternative. The opponents of functionalism who hold that it is in principle impossible that machines could have mental lives generally claim that machines cannot realize the very aspects of mind, such as conscious feeling and normativity, that functionalists allegedly have difficulty explaining. In claiming this, these opponents are also claiming that these aspects of mind specially require an organic basis (unless, of course, they embrace the dubious metaphysics of Cartesian dualism). Yet they have no positive account of why this should be so (Humphrey 1992; Penrose 1989). And functionalists are free to claim in turn that these aspects of mind are not any easier to explain in organic than computational terms, and that to date they have actually made more headway in giving a detailed explanation in computational terms than their opponents have in organic terms. But the truth is that we do not yet have a general solution to the mind–body problem; we do not yet know how bits of matter give rise to mental life.

With this truth in hand, we are now finally in a position from which we can speculate about how genetic science might conceivably bear on the dispute about personal identity. Recently, a philosopher has suggested that our genes must already know the solution to the mind–body problem because they know on the basis of their genetic coding how to direct the construction of organized living things that support mental life out of mere matter (McGinn 1994). Accompanying this rather extravagant suggestion came another, flamboyantly pessimistic one: we can never know what our genes know, because the constitution of our minds makes us unfit to understand the true nature of the mind–body relation. If we eschew such pessimism, then we can dare to hope to know what this philosopher says our genes know. But furthermore, even if we also eschew the suggestion that genes know anything at all, we can still dare to hope to know how genes work. And if part of their work is indeed to direct (with or without knowledge) the organization of matter into living things that support mental life, then learning how they work might well give us a general solution to the mind–body problem. And if we had this general solution in hand, we might well be in a position from which to determine whether the specific possibility that Locke raised is, after all, consistent with the laws of nature – whether, that is, the same personal consciousness really can be transferred from one animal body to another in such a way as to support a distinction between personal and animal identity.

That was a long string of *ifs*. But they spell out conditions in which future advances in genetic science might conceivably contribute to a resolution of the philosophical dispute about personal identity that Locke inaugurated. Those who find this speculation too far-fetched can rest secure in our first answer, that genetics has nothing in particular to contribute.

Notes

1   Here is a very brief statement of some of the most important and most discussed objections that have been raised against Locke's analysis of personal identity. (1) *The analysis fails to preserve the transitivity of the identity relation*. This was noticed by Thomas Reid, who asked us to consider the case of a senile general who remembers having been flogged as a young boy, and who when he was a captain remembered the flogging, but who as a general no longer remembers his actions as a captain. The analysis entails, absurdly, that the general is identical with the boy who in turn is not identical with the general. (2) *The analysis fails to preserve the one–one character of the identity relation* (this is commonly known as the duplication objection). It is conceivable that two (or more) persons could both remember, and so both be conscious of in Locke's sense, the same past thoughts and deeds. It is conceivable, for example, that my consciousness, including my memories, could be transferred to my sister's body by a process of brain-reprograming that also leaves my original consciousness intact in my original body. Both resulting persons would remember having agreed to write this chapter. So by the lights of the analysis both persons would be identical with the one person (me) who agreed to write it. But this is impossible. (3) *The analysis does not provide for the possibility that a person can be deluded about its identity*. When a person is deluded in this way, the person seems to remember having thought and done things which it did not actually think or do. But this difference, between what a person seems to remember and what the person actually did, is not visible from the point of view of its own personal consciousness. We need an independent basis from which to evaluate the person's consciousness as veridical or not, such as the life-history of a particular human being as known from a second- or third-person point of view. But no such independent basis is provided for by the analysis, since it analyzes personal identity in terms of consciousness alone. For early responses to these three objections see Perry 1975 (chapters by Shoemaker, Parfit, and Perry) and chapter 2 of my *The Bounds of Agency* (1998) for an extended discussion of why the various responses and refinements that have been offered on Locke's behalf are adequate.

2   This is not to say that philosophers have not tried to settle the dispute about personal identity on their own, without recourse to science. Typically, their strategy is to try to vindicate one side of the dispute, the Lockean or the animalist, by showing that the other side lands us in some sort of logical or metaphysical absurdity. I show in detail in my book (1998, ch. 3, pp. 40–59) why these philosophical efforts have failed. The general reason that the dispute remains unresolved is that neither side in the debate has been decisively shown to fail on purely logical or metaphysical grounds.

3   The larger claim of this paragraph, that there is a role for *some* science to play in resolving the philosophical dispute about personal identity, needs to be clarified in light of a certain ambiguity in Locke's conception of the person. Sometimes he emphasized, as this chapter does, the idea that each person has its own conscious point of view. Given this emphasis on *consciousness*, it seems perfectly appropriate to wait for the deliverances of cognitive science before pronouncing on whether he was right to distinguish personal from animal identity. But very often he emphasizes that a person is a rational agent. And given this latter emphasis on *rational agency*, it is less clear that science has an important role to play. For, as I argue in my book (1998), it is in the nature of rational agency that agents can redraw the boundaries between them so as to generate group agents composed of many human beings, and multiple agents within a single human being. Given the conception of a person as a rational agent, these group and multiple agents would qualify as persons in their own

rights, and since they clearly would not be identical with any animal they would constitute instances of Locke's distinction. But not only is it the case that persons can thus generate, through the exercise of their own agency, instances of Locke's distinction, they are also in a position to *know* that they can without waiting for the deliverances of cognitive (or any other special) science just on the basis of what they know about their own nature *qua* rational agents.

There is also another respect in which the issue of personal identity is not wholly, or exclusively, a matter for science. There are ethical reasons, I argue, for emphasizing rational agency rather than consciousness in an account of what a person is, and this emphasis is what eventually brings in train the consequence about group and multiple persons and resolution of the dispute about personal identity in favor of Locke.

However, the book's metaphysical claims about personal agency, and also its use of ethical considerations, are all part of a revisionist account of the person that takes us quite far from the usual philosophical problem of the personal identity, which shares Locke's primary emphasis on consciousness. And the important point for present purposes is that, given this emphasis, science can potentially play a role in resolving the problem.

References

Block, N.: "Troubles with Functionalism," in W. Savage, ed., *Minnesota Studies in the Philosophy of Science*, vol. 9, *Perception and Cognition* (Minneapolis: University of Minnesota Press, 1978).

Dennett, D.: *Consciousness Explained* (Boston: Little, Brown & Co., 1991).

Humphrey, N.: *A History of the Mind: Evolution and the Birth of Consciousness* (New York: Harper Collins, 1992).

Locke, J.: *Essay Concerning Human Understanding*, ed. P. Nidditch (Oxford: Oxford University Press, 1975), bk. II, ch. 27.

McDowell, J.: "Functionalism and Anomalous Monism," in E. LePore, ed., *Truth and Interpretation: Perspectives on the Philosophy of Donald Davidson* (Oxford: Blackwell, 1986).

McGinn, C.: "The Problem of Philosophy," *Philosophical Studies* 76 (1994).

Penrose, R.: *The Emperor's New Mind* (Oxford: Oxford University Press, 1989).

Further Reading

Dennett, D.: *Consciousness Explained* (Boston: Little, Brown & Co., 1991).

Nagel, T.: *The View from Nowhere* (New York: Oxford University Press, 1986).

Parfit, D.: *Reasons and Persons* (New York: Oxford University Press, 1984).

Perry, J., ed.: *Personal Identity* (Berkeley: University of California Press, 1975).

Rorty, A., ed.: *The Identities of Persons* (Berkeley: University of California Press, 1979).

Rosenthal, D., ed.: *The Nature of Mind* (New York: Oxford University Press, 1991).

Rovane, C.: *The Bounds of Agency: An Essay in Revisionary Metaphysics* (Princeton: Princeton University Press, 1998).

Shoemaker, S. and Swinburne, R.: *Personal Identity* (Oxford: Blackwell, 1984).

19

Genetic Determinism and Gene Selectionism

RICHARD DAWKINS

Long after his death, tenacious rumors persisted that Adolf Hitler had been seen alive and well in South America, or in Denmark, and for years a surprising number of people with no love for the man only reluctantly accepted that he was dead (Trevor-Roper 1972). In the First World War a story that a 100,000 Russian troops had been seen landing in Scotland "with snow on their boots" became widely current, apparently because of the memorable vividness of that snow (Taylor 1963). In our own time myths such as that of computers persistently sending householders electricity bills for a million pounds (Evans 1979), or of well-heeled welfare-scroungers with two expensive cars parked outside their government-subsidized council houses, are familiar to the point of cliché. There are some falsehoods, or half truths, that seem to engender in us an active desire to believe them and pass them on even if we find them unpleasant, maybe in part, perversely, *because* we find them unpleasant.

Computers and electronic "chips" provoke more than their fair share of such myth-making, perhaps because computer technology advances at a speed which is literally frightening. I know an old person who has it on good authority that "chips" are usurping human functions to the extent not only of "driving tractors" but even of "fertilizing women." Genes, as I shall show, are the source of what may be an even larger mythology than computers. Imagine the result of combining these two power-ful myths, the gene myth and the computer myth! I believe that I may have inadvert-ently achieved some such unfortunate synthesis in the minds of a few readers of my previous book, and the result was comic misunderstanding. Happily, such misunder-standing was not widespread, but it is worth trying to avoid a repeat of it here, and that is one purpose of the present chapter. I shall expose the myth of genetic determinism, and explain why it is necessary to use language that can be unfortu-nately misunderstood as genetic determinism.

A reviewer of Wilson's *On Human Nature* (1978), wrote: "although he does not go as far as Richard Dawkins [*The Selfish Gene*] in proposing sex linked genes for 'philander-ing,' for Wilson human males have a genetic tendency towards polygyny, females towards constancy (don't blame your mates for sleeping around, ladies, it's not their fault they are genetically programmed). Genetic determinism constantly creeps in at the back door" (Rose 1978). The reviewer's clear implication is that the authors he is criticizing believe in the existence of genes that force human males to be irremediable philanderers who cannot therefore be blamed for marital infidelity. The reader is left with the impression that those authors are protagonists in the "nature or nurture" debate, and, moreover, dyed-in-the-wool hereditarians with male chauvinist leanings.

In fact my original passage about "philanderer males" was not about humans. It was a simple mathematical model of some unspecified animal (not that it matters, I had a bird in mind). It was not explicitly (see below) a model of genes, and if it had been about genes they would have been sex-limited, not sex-linked! It was a model of "strategies" in the sense of Maynard Smith (1974). The "philanderer" strategy was postulated, not as *the* way males behave, but as one of two hypothetical alternatives, the other being the "faithful" strategy. The purpose of this very simple model was to illustrate the kinds of conditions under which philandering might be favored by natural selection, and the kinds of conditions under which faithfulness might be favored. There was no presumption that philandering was more likely in males than faithfulness. Indeed, the particular run of the simulation that I published culminated in a mixed male population in which faithfulness slightly predominated (Dawkins 1976a: 165; cf. Shuster and Sigmund 1981). There is not just one misunderstanding in Rose's remarks, but multiple compounded misunderstanding. There is a wanton eagerness to misunderstand. It bears the stamp of snow-covered Russian jackboots, of little black microchips marching to usurp the male role and steal our tractor-drivers' jobs. It is a manifestation of a powerful myth, in this case the great gene myth.

The gene myth is epitomized in Rose's parenthetic little joke about ladies not blaming their mates for sleeping around. It is the myth of "genetic determinism." Evidently, for Rose, genetic determinism is determinism in the full philosophical sense of irreversible inevitability. He assumes that the existence of a gene "for" X implies that X cannot be escaped. In the words of another critic of "genetic determinism," Gould (1978: 238), "If we are programmed to be what we are, then these traits are ineluctable. We may, at best, channel them, but we cannot change them either by will, education, or culture."

The validity of the determinist point of view and, separately, its bearing on an individual's moral responsibility for his actions, has been debated by philosophers and theologians for centuries past, and no doubt will be for centuries to come. I suspect that both Rose and Gould are determinists in that they believe in a physical, materialistic basis for all our actions. So am I. We would also probably all three agree that human nervous systems are so complex that in practice we can forget about determinism and behave as if we had free will. Neurons may be amplifiers of fundamentally indeterminate physical events. The only point I wish to make is that, whatever view one takes on the question of determinism, the insertion of the word "genetic" is not going to make any difference. If you are a full-blooded determinist you will believe that all your actions are predetermined by physical causes in the past, and you may or may not also believe that you therefore cannot be held responsible for your sexual infidelities. But, be that as it may, what difference can it possibly make whether some of those physical causes are *genetic?* Why are genetic determinants thought to be any more ineluctable, or blame-absolving, than "environmental" ones?

The belief that genes are somehow superdeterministic, in comparison with environmental causes, is a myth of extraordinary tenacity, and it can give rise to real emotional distress. I was only dimly aware of this until it was movingly brought home to me in a question session at a meeting of the American Association for the Advancement of Science in 1978. A young woman asked the lecturer, a prominent "sociobiologist," whether there was any evidence for genetic sex differences in human psychology. I hardly heard the lecturer's answer, so astonished was I by the emotion with which the question was put. The woman seemed to set great store by the answer and was almost in tears. After a moment of genuine and innocent bafflement the explanation hit me. Something or somebody, certainly not the eminent sociobiologist himself, had misled her into thinking that genetic determination is for keeps; she seriously believed that a "yes" answer to her question would, if correct, condemn her as a female individual to a life of feminine pursuits, chained to the nursery and the kitchen sink. But if, unlike most of us, she is a determinist in that strong Calvinistic sense, she should be equally upset whether the causal factors concerned are genetic or "environmental."

What does it ever mean to say that something determines something? Philosophers, possibly with justification, make heavy weather of the concept of causation, but to a working biologist causation is a rather simple statistical concept. Operationally we can never demonstrate that a particular observed event C caused a particular result R, although it will often be judged highly likely. What biologists in practice usually do is to establish *statistically* that events of class R reliably follow events of class C. They need a number of paired instances of the two classes of events in order to do so: one anecdote is not enough.

Even the observation that R events reliably tend to follow C events after a relatively fixed time interval provides only a working hypothesis that C events cause R events. The hypothesis is confirmed, within the limits of the statistical method, only if the C events are delivered by an *experimenter* rather than simply noted by an observer, and are still reliably followed by R events. It is not necessary that every C should be followed by an R, nor that every R should be preceded by a C (who has not had to contend with arguments such as "smoking cannot cause lung cancer, because I knew a nonsmoker who died of it, and a heavy smoker who is still going strong at ninety"?). Statistical methods are designed to help us assess, to any specified level of probabilistic confidence, whether the results we obtain really indicate a causal relationship.

If, then, it were true that the possession of a Y chromosome had a causal influence on, say, musical ability or fondness for knitting, what would this mean? It would mean that, in some specified population and in some specified environment, an observer in possession of information about an individual's sex would be able to make a statistically more accurate prediction as to the person's musical ability than an observer ignorant of the person's sex. The emphasis is on the word "statistically," and let us throw in an "other things being equal" for good measure. The observer might be provided with some additional information, say on the person's education or upbringing, which would lead him to revise, or even reverse, his prediction based on sex. If females are statistically more likely than males to enjoy knitting, this does not mean that all females enjoy knitting, nor even that a majority do.

It is also fully compatible with the view that the reason females enjoy knitting is that society brings them up to enjoy knitting. If society systematically trains children without penises to knit and play with dolls, and trains children with penises to play with guns and toy soldiers, any resulting differences in male and female preferences are strictly speaking genetically determined differences! They are determined, through the medium of societal custom, by the fact of possession or nonpossession of a penis, and that is determined (in a normal environment and in the absence of ingenious plastic surgery or hormone therapy) by sex chromosomes.

Obviously, on this view, if we experimentally brought up a sample of boys to play with dolls and a sample of girls to play with guns, we would expect easily to reverse the normal preferences. This might be an interesting experiment to do, for the result just might turn out to be that girls *still* prefer dolls and boys still prefer guns. If so, this might tell us something about the tenacity, in the face of a *particular* environmental manipulation, of a genetic difference. But all genetic causes have to work in the context of an environment of some kind. If a genetic sex difference makes itself felt through the medium of a sex-biased education system, it is still a genetic difference. If it makes itself felt through some other medium, such that manipulations of the education system do not perturb it, it is, in principle, no more and no less a genetic difference than in the former, education-sensitive case: no doubt some other environmental manipulation could be found which *did* perturb it.

Human psychological attributes vary along almost as many dimensions as psychologists can measure. It is difficult in practice (Kempthorne 1978), but in principle we could partition this variation among such putative causal factors as age, height, years of education, type of education classified in many different ways, number of siblings, birth order, color of mother's eyes, father's skill in shoeing horses, and, of course, sex chromosomes. We could also examine two-way and multi-way interactions between such factors. For present purposes the important point is that the variance we seek to explain will have many causes, which interact in complex ways. Undoubtedly genetic variance is a significant cause of much phenotypic variance in observed populations, but its effects may be overridden, modified, enhanced, or reversed by other causes. Genes may modify the effects of other genes, and may modify the effects of the environment. Environmental events, both internal and external, may modify the effects of genes, and may modify the effects of other environmental events.

People seem to have little difficulty in accepting the modifiability of "environmental" effects on human development. If a child has had bad teaching in mathematics, it is accepted that the resulting deficiency can be remedied by extra good teaching the following year. But any suggestion that the child's mathematical deficiency might have a genetic origin is likely to be greeted with something approaching despair: if it is in the genes "it is written," it is "determined," and nothing can be done about it; you might as well give up attempting to teach the child mathematics. This is pernicious rubbish on an almost astrological scale. Genetic causes and environmental causes are in principle no different from each other. Some influences of both types may be hard to reverse; others may be easy to reverse. Some may be usually hard to reverse but easy if the right agent is applied. The important point is that there is no general reason for expecting genetic influences to be any more irreversible than environmental ones.

What did genes do to deserve their sinister, juggernaut-like reputation? Why do we not make a similar bogey out of, say, nursery education or confirmation classes? Why are genes thought to be so much more fixed and inescapable in their effects than television, nuns, or books? Don't blame your mates for sleeping around, ladies, it's not their fault they have been inflamed by pornographic literature! The alleged Jesuit boast, "Give me the child for his first seven years, and I'll give you the man," may have some truth in it. Educational, or other cultural influences may, in some circumstances, be just as unmodifiable and irreversible as genes and "stars" are popularly thought to be.

I suppose part of the reason genes have become deterministic bogeys is a confusion resulting from the well-known fact of the non-inheritance of acquired characteristics. Before this century it was widely believed that experience and other acquisitions of an individual's lifetime were somehow imprinted on the hereditary substance and transmitted to the children. The abandoning of this belief, and its replacement by Weismann's doctrine of the continuity of the germ plasm, and its molecular counterpart the "central dogma," is one of the great achievements of modern biology. If we steep ourselves in the implications of Weismannian orthodoxy, there really does seem to be something juggernaut-like and inexorable about genes. They march through generations, influencing the form and behavior of a succession of mortal bodies, but, except for rare and nonspecific mutagenic effects, they are never influenced by the experience or environment of those bodies. The genes in me came from my four grandparents; they flowed straight through my parents to me, and nothing that my parents achieved, acquired, learned or experienced had any effect on those genes as they flowed through. Perhaps there is something a little sinister about that. But, however inexorable and undeviating the genes may be as they march down the generations, the nature of their phenotypic effects on the bodies they flow through is by no means inexorable and undeviating. If I am homozygous for a gene G, nothing save mutation can prevent my passing G on to all my children. So much is inexorable. But whether or not I, or my children, show the phenotypic effect normally associated with possession of G may depend very much on how we are brought up, what diet or education we experience, and what other genes we happen to posses. So, of the two effects that genes have on the world – manufacturing copies of themselves, and influencing phenotypes – the first is inflexible apart from the rare possibility of mutation; the second may be exceedingly flexible. I think a confusion between evolution and development is, then, partly responsible for the myth of genetic determinism.

But there is another myth complicating matters, and I have already mentioned it at the beginning of this chapter. The computer myth is almost as deep-seated in the modern mind as the gene myth. Notice that both passages I quoted contain the word "programmed." Thus Rose sarcastically absolved promiscuous men from blame because they are genetically *programmed*. Gould says that if we are *programmed* to be what we are then these traits are ineluctable. And it is true that we ordinarily use the word programmed to indicate unthinking inflexibility, the antithesis of freedom of action. Computers and "robots" are, by repute, notoriously inflexible, carrying out instructions to the letter, even if the consequences are obviously absurd. Why else would they send out those famous million pound bills that everybody's friend's friend's cousin's acquaintance keeps receiving? I had forgotten the great computer myth, as well as the great gene myth, or I would have been more careful when I myself wrote of genes swarming "inside gigantic lumbering robots..." and of ourselves as "survival machines – robot vehicles blindly programmed to preserve the selfish molecules known as genes" (Dawkins 1976a). These passages have been triumphantly quoted, and requoted apparently from secondary and even tertiary sources, as examples of rabid genetic determinism (e.g. "Nabi" 1981). I am not apologizing for using the language of robotics. I would use it again without hesitation. But I now realize that it is necessary to give more explanation.

From 13 years' experience of teaching it, I know that a main problem with the "selfish-gene survival machine" way of looking at natural selection is a particular risk of misunderstanding. The metaphor of the intelligent gene reckoning up how best to ensure its own survival (Hamilton 1972) is a powerful and illuminating one. But it is all too easy to get carried away, and allow hypothetical genes cognitive wisdom and foresight in planning their "strategy." At least 3 out of 12 misunderstandings of kin selection (Dawkins 1979a) are directly attributable to this basic error. Time and again, nonbiologists have tried to justify a form of group selection to me by, in effect, imputing foresight to genes: "The long-term interests of a gene require the continued existence of the species; therefore shouldn't you expect adaptations to prevent species extinction, even at the expense of short-term individual reproductive success?" It was in an attempt to forestall errors like this that I used the language of automation and robotics, and used the word "blindly" in referring to genetic programming. But it is, of course, the genes that are blind, not the animals they program. Nervous systems, like manmade computers, can be sufficiently complex to show intelligence and foresight.

Symons (1979) makes the computer myth explicit:

> I wish to point out that Dawkins's implication – through the use of words like "robot" and "blindly" ... that evolutionary theory favors determinism is utterly without foundation ... A robot is a mindless automaton. Perhaps some animals are robots (we have no way of knowing); however, Dawkins is not referring to *some* animals, but to all animals and in this case specifically to human beings. Now, to paraphrase Stebbing, "robot" can be opposed to "thinking being" or it can be used figuratively to indicate a person who seems to act mechanically, but there is no common usage of language that provides a meaning for the word "robot" in which it would make sense to say that all living things are robots. (p. 41)

The point of the passage from Stebbing which Symons paraphrased is the reasonable one that X is a useless word unless there are some things that are not X. If everything is a robot, then the word robot doesn't mean anything useful. But the word robot has other associations, and rigid inflexibility was not the association I was thinking of. A robot is a programmed machine, and an important thing about programming is that it is distinct from, and done in advance of, performance of the behavior itself. A computer is programmed to perform the behavior of calculating square roots, or playing chess. The relationship between a chess-playing computer and the person who programmed it is not obvious, and is open to misunderstanding. It might be thought that the programmer watches the progress of the game and gives instructions to the computer move by move. In fact, however, the programming is finished before the game begins. The programmer tries to anticipate contingencies, and builds in conditional instructions of great complexity, but once the game begins he has to keep his hands off. He is not allowed to give the computer any new hints during the course of the game. If he did he would not be programming but performing, and his entry would be disqualified from the tournament. In the work criticized by Symons, I made extensive use of the analogy of computer chess in order to explain the point that genes do not control behavior directly in the sense of interfering in its performance. They only control behavior in the sense of programming the machine in *advance* of performance. It was this association with the word robot that I wanted to invoke, not the association with mindless inflexibility.

As for the mindless inflexibility association itself, it could have been justified in the days when the acme of automation was the rod and cam control system of a marine engine, and Kipling wrote *McAndrew's Hymn*:

> From coupler-flange to spindle-guide I see Thy Hand, O God –
> Predestination in the stride o' yon connectin'-rod.
> John Calvin might ha' forged the same –

But that was 1893 and the heyday of steam. We are now well embarked on the golden age of electronics. If machines ever had associations with rigid inflexibility – and I accept that they had – it is high time they lived them down. Computer programs have now been written that play chess to International Master standard (Levy 1978), that converse and reason in correct and indefinitely complex grammatical English (Winograd 1972), that create elegant and aesthetically satisfying new proofs of mathematical theorems (Hofstadter 1979), that compose music and diagnose illness; and the pace of progress in the field shows no sign of slowing down (Evans 1979). The advanced programming field known as artificial intelligence is in a buoyant, confident state (Boden 1977). Few who have studied it would now bet against computer programs beating the strongest Grand Masters at chess within the next 10 years. From being synonymous in the popular mind with a moronically undeviating, jerky-limbed zombie, "robot" will one day become a byword for flexibility and rapid intelligence.

Unfortunately I jumped the gun a little in the passage quoted. When I wrote it I had just returned from an eye-opening and mind-boggling conference on the state of the art of artificial intelligence programming, and I genuinely and innocently in my enthusiasm forgot that robots are popularly supposed to be inflexible idiots. I also have to apologize for the fact that, without my knowledge, the cover of the German edition of *The Selfish Gene* was given a picture of a human puppet jerking on the end of strings descending from the word gene, and the French edition a picture of little bowler-hatted men with clockwork wind-up keys sticking out of their backs. I have had slides of both covers made up as illustrations of what I was *not* trying to say.

So, the answer to Symons is that of course he was right to criticize what he thought I was saying, but of course I wasn't actually saying it (Ridley 1980a). No doubt I was partly to blame for the original misunderstanding, but I can only urge now that we put aside the preconceptions derived from common usage ("most men don't understand computers to even the slightest degree" – Weizenbaum 1976: 9), and actually go and read some of the fascinating modern literature on robotics and computer intelligence (e.g. Boden 1977; Evans 1979, Hofstadter 1979).

Once again, of course, philosophers may debate the ultimate determinacy of computers programmed to behave in artificially intelligent ways, but if we are going to get into that level of philosophy many would apply the same arguments to human intelligence (Turing 1950). What is a brain, they would ask, but a computer, and what is education but a form of programming? It is very hard to give a non-supernatural account of the human brain and human emotions, feelings and apparent free will, *without* regarding the brain as, in some sense, the equivalent of a programmed, cybernetic machine. The astronomer Sir Fred Hoyle (1964) expresses very vividly what, it seems to me, any evolutionist must think about nervous systems:

> Looking back [at evolution] I am overwhelmingly impressed by the way in which chemistry has gradually given way to electronics. It is not unreasonable to describe the first living creatures as entirely chemical in character. Although electrochemical processes are important in plants, organized electronics, in the sense of data processing, does not enter or operate in the plant world. But primitive electronics begins to assume importance as soon as we have a creature that moves around...The first electronic systems possessed by primitive animals were essentially guidance systems, analogous logically to sonar or radar. As we pass to more developed animals we find electronic systems being used not merely for guidance but for directing the animal toward food... The situation is analogous to a guided missile, the job of which is to intercept and destroy another missile. Just as in our modern world attack and defense become more and more subtle in their methods, so it was the case with animals. And with increasing subtlety, better and better systems of electronics become necessary. What happened in nature has a close parallel with the development of electronics in modern military applications...I find it a sobering thought that but for the tooth-and-claw existence of the jungle we should not possess our intellectual capabilities, we should not be able to inquire into the structure of the Universe, or be able to appreciate a symphony of Beethoven... Viewed in this light, the question that is sometimes asked – can computers think? – is somewhat ironic. Here of course I mean the computers that we ourselves make out of inorganic materials. What on earth do those who ask such a question think they themselves are? Simply computers, but vastly more complicated ones than anything we have yet learned to make. Remember that our man-made computer industry is a mere two or three decades old, whereas we ourselves are the products of an evolution that has operated over hundreds of millions of years. (pp. 24–6)

Others may disagree with this conclusion, although I suspect that the only alternatives to it are religious ones. Whatever the outcome of that debate, to return to genes and the main point of this chapter, the issue of determinism versus free will is just not affected one way or the other by whether or not you happen to be considering *genes* as causal agents rather than environmental determinants.

But, it will pardonably be said, there is no smoke without fire. Functional ethologists and "sociobiologists" must have said something to deserve being tarred with the brush of genetic determinism. Or if it is all a misunderstanding there must be some good explanation, because misunderstandings that are so widespread do not come about for no reason, even if abetted by cultural myths as powerful as the gene myth and the computer myth in unholy alliance. Speaking for myself, I think I know the reason. It is an interesting one, and it will occupy the rest of this chapter. The misunderstanding arises from the way we talk about a quite different subject, namely natural selection. Gene selectionism, which is a way of talking about evolution, is mistaken for genetic determinism, which is a point of view about development. People like me are continually postulating genes "for" this and genes for that. We give the impression of being obsessed with genes and with "genetically programmed" behavior. Take this in conjunction with the popular myths of the Calvinistic determinacy of genes, and of "programmed" behavior as the hallmark of jactitating Disneyland puppets, and is it any wonder that we are accused of being genetic determinists?

Why, then, do functional ethologists talk about genes so much? Because we are interested in natural selection, and natural selection is differential survival of genes. If we are to so much as discuss the *possibility* of a behavior pattern's evolving by natural selection, we have to postulate genetic variation with respect to the tendency or capacity to perform that behavior pattern. This is not to say that there necessarily *is* such genetic variation for any particular behavior pattern, only that there must have been genetic variation in the past if we are to treat the behavior pattern as a Darwinian adaptation. Of course the behavior pattern may not be a Darwinian adaptation, in which case the argument will not apply.

Incidentally, I should defend my usage of "Darwinian adaptation" as synonymous with "adaptation produced by natural selection," for Gould and Lewontin (1979) have recently emphasized, with approval, the "pluralistic character of Darwin's own thought. It is indeed true that, especially toward the end of his life, Darwin was driven by criticisms, which we can now see to be erroneous, to make some concessions to 'pluralism': he did not regard natural selection as the only important driving force in evolution. As the historian R. M. Young (1971) has sardonically put it, "by the sixth edition the book was mistitled and should have read *On the Origin of Species by Means of Natural Selection and All Sorts of Other Things*." It is, therefore, arguably incorrect to use "Darwinian evolution" as synonymous with "evolution by natural selection." But Darwinian *adaptation is* another matter. Adaptation cannot be produced by random drift, or by any other realistic evolutionary force that we know of save natural selection. It is true that Darwin's pluralism did fleetingly allow for one other driving force that might, in principle, lead to adaptation, but that driving force is inseparably linked with the name of Lamarck, not of Darwin. "Darwinian adaptation" could not sensibly mean anything other than adaptation produced by natural selection, and I shall use it in this sense. In several other places in *The Extended Phenotype* (e.g. in chapters 3 and 6), we shall resolve apparent disputes by drawing a distinction between evolution in general, and adaptive evolution in particular. The fixation of neutral mutations, for instance, can be regarded as evolution, but it is not adaptive evolution. If a molecular geneticist interested in gene substitutions, or a paleontologist interested in major trends, argues with an ecologist interested in adaptation, they are likely to find themselves at cross-purposes simply because each of them emphasizes a different aspect of what evolution means.

"Genes for conformity, xenophobia, and aggressiveness are simply postulated for humans because they are needed for the theory, not because any evidence for them exists" (Lewontin 1979). This is a fair criticism of E. O. Wilson, but not a very damning one. Apart from possible political repercussions which might be unfortunate, there is nothing wrong with cautiously speculating about a possible Darwinian survival value of xenophobia or any other trait. And you cannot begin to speculate, however cautiously, about the survival value of anything unless you postulate a genetic basis for variation in that thing. Of course xenophobia may not vary genetically, and of course xenophobia may not be a Darwinian adaptation, but we can't even discuss the possibility of its being a Darwinian adaptation unless we postulate a genetic basis for it. Lewontin himself has expressed the point as well as anybody: "In order for a trait to evolve by natural selection it is necessary that there be genetic variation in the population for such a trait" (Lewontin 1979). And "genetic variation in the population for" a trait X is exactly what we mean when we talk, for brevity, of "a gene for" X.

Xenophobia is controversial, so consider a behavior pattern that nobody would fear to regard as a Darwinian adaptation. Pit-digging in antlions is obviously an adaptation to catch prey. Antlions are insects, neuropteran larvae with the general appearance and demeanor of monsters from outer space. They are "sit and wait" predators who dig pits in soft sand which trap ants and other small walking insects. The pit is a nearly perfect cone, whose sides slope so steeply that prey cannot climb out once they have fallen in. The antlion sits just under the sand at the bottom of the pit, where it lunges with its horror-film jaws at anything that falls in.

Pit-digging is a complex behavior pattern. It costs time and energy, and satisfies the most exacting criteria for recognition as an adaptation (Williams 1966; Curio 1973). It must, then, have evolved by natural selection. How might this have happened? The details don't matter for the moral I want to draw. Probably an ancestral antlion existed which did not dig a pit but simply lurked just beneath the sand surface waiting for prey to blunder over it. Indeed some species still do this. Later, behavior leading to the creation of a shallow depression in the sand probably was favored by selection because the depression marginally impeded escaping prey. By gradual degrees over many generations the behavior changed so that what was a shallow depression became deeper and wider. This not only hindered escaping prey but also increased the catchment area over which prey might stumble in the first place. Later still the digging behavior changed again so that the resulting pit became a steep-sided cone, lined with fine, sliding sand so that prey were unable to climb out.

Nothing in the previous paragraph is contentious or controversial. It will be regarded as legitimate speculation about historical events that we cannot see directly, and it will probably be thought plausible. One reason why it will be accepted as uncontroversial historical speculation is that it makes no mention of genes. But my point is that none of that history, nor any comparable history, could possibly have been true unless there was genetic variation in the behavior at every step of the evolutionary way. Pit-digging in antlions is only one of the thousands of examples that I could have chosen. Unless natural selection has genetic variation to act upon, it cannot give rise to evolutionary change. It follows that where you find Darwinian adaptation there must have been genetic variation in the character concerned.

Nobody has ever done a genetic study of pit-digging behavior in antlions (J. Lucas, Personal communication). There is no need to do one, if all we want to do is satisfy ourselves of the sometime existence of genetic variation in the behavior pattern. It is sufficient that we are convinced that it is a Darwinian adaptation (if you are not convinced that pit-digging is such an adaptation, simply substitute any example of which you are convinced).

I spoke of the *sometime* existence of genetic variation. This was because it is quite likely that, were a genetic study to be mounted of antlions today, no genetic variation would be found. It is in general to be expected that, where there is strong selection in favor of some trait, the original variation on which selection acted to guide the evolution of the trait will have become used up. This is the familiar "paradox" (it is not really very paradoxical when we think about it carefully) that traits under strong selection tend to have low heritability (Falconer 1960); "evolution by natural selection destroys the genetic variance on which it feeds" (Lewontin 1979). Functional hypotheses frequently concern phenotypic traits, like possession of eyes, which are all but universal in the population, and therefore without contemporary genetic variation. When we speculate about, or make models of, the evolutionary production of an adaptation, we are necessarily talking about a time when there was appropriate genetic variation. We are bound, in such discussions, to postulate, implicitly or explicitly, genes "for" proposed adaptations.

Some may balk at treating "a genetic contribution to variation in X" as equivalent to "a gene or genes for X." But this is a routine genetic practice, and one which close examination shows to be almost inevitable. Other than at the molecular level, where one gene is seen directly to produce one protein chain, geneticists never deal with units of phenotype as such. Rather, they always deal with *differences*. When a geneticist speaks of a gene "for" red eyes in *Drosophila*, he is not speaking of the cistron which acts as template for the synthesis of the red pigment molecule. He is implicitly saying: there is variation in eye color in the population; other things being equal, a fly with this gene is more likely to have red eyes than a fly without the gene. That is all that we ever mean by a gene "for" red eyes. This happens to be a morphological rather than a behavioral example, but exactly the same applies to behavior. A gene "for" behavior X is a gene "for" whatever morphological and physiological states tend to produce that behavior.

A related point is that the use of single-locus models is just a conceptual convenience, and this is true of adaptive hypotheses in exactly the same way as it is true of ordinary population genetic models. When we use single-gene language in our adaptive hypotheses, we do not intend to make a point about single-gene models as against multigene models. We are usually making a point about *gene* models as against nongene models, for example as against "good of the species" models. Since it is difficult enough convincing people that they ought to think in genetic terms *at all* rather than in terms of, say, the good of the species, there is no sense in making things even more difficult by trying to handle the complexities of many loci at the outset. What Lloyd (1979) calls the OGAM (one-gene analysis model) is, of course, not the last word in genetic accuracy. Of *course* we shall eventually have to face up to multilocus complexity. But the OGAM is vastly preferable to modes of adaptive reasoning that forget about genes altogether, and this is the only point I am trying to make at present.

Similarly we may find ourselves aggressively challenged to substantiate our "claims" of the existence of "genes for" some adaptation in which we are interested. But this challenge, if it is a real challenge at all, should be directed at the whole of the neo-Darwinian "modern synthesis" and the whole of population genetics. To phrase a functional hypothesis in terms of genes is to make no strong claims about genes at all: it is simply to make explicit an assumption which is inseparably built into the modern synthesis, albeit it is sometimes implicit rather than explicit.

A few workers have, indeed, flung just such a challenge at the whole neo-Darwinian modern synthesis, and have claimed not to be neo-Darwinians. Goodwin (1979) in a published debate with Deborah Charlesworth and others, said, "neo-Darwinism has an incoherence in it ... we are not given any way of generating phenotypes from genotypes in neo-Darwinism. Therefore the theory is in this respect defective." Goodwin is, of course, quite right that development is terribly complicated, and we don't yet understand much about how phenotypes are generated. But *that* they are generated, and *that* genes contribute significantly to their variation are incontrovertible facts, and those facts are all we need in order to make neo-Darwinism coherent. Goodwin might just as well say that, before Hodgkin and Huxley worked out how the nerve impulse fired, we were not entitled to believe that nerve impulses controlled behavior. Of *course* it would be nice to know how phenotypes are made but, while embryologists are busy finding out, the rest of us are entitled by the known facts of genetics to carry on being neo-Darwinians, treating embryonic development as a black box. There is no competing theory that has even a remote claim to be called coherent.

It follows from the fact that geneticists are always concerned with phenotypic *differences* that we need not be afraid of postulating genes with indefinitely complex phenotypic effects, and with phenotypic effects that show themselves only in highly complex developmental conditions. Together with Professor John Maynard Smith, I recently took part in a public debate with two radical critics of "sociobiology," before an audience of students. At one time in the discussion we were trying to establish that to talk of a gene "for X" is to make no outlandish claim, even where X is a complex, learned behavior pattern. Maynard Smith reached for a hypothetical example and came up with a "gene for skill in trying shoelaces." Pandemonium broke loose at this rampant genetic determinism! The air was thick with the unmistakable sound of worst suspicions being gleefully confirmed. Delightedly skeptical cries drowned the quiet and patient explanation of just what a *modest* claim is being made whenever one postulates a gene for, say, skill in tying shoelaces. Let me explain the point with the aid of an even more radical-sounding yet truly innocuous thought experiment (Dawkins 1981).

Reading is a learned skill of prodigious complexity, but this provides no reason in itself for skepticism about the possible existence of a gene for reading. All we would need in order to establish the existence of a gene for reading is to discover a gene for not reading, say a gene which induced a brain lesion causing specific dyslexia. Such a dyslexic person might be normal and intelligent in all respects except that he could not read. No geneticist would be particularly surprised if this type of dyslexia turned out to breed true in some Mendelian fashion. Obviously, in this event, the gene would only exhibit its effect in an environment which included normal education. In a prehistoric environment it might have had no detectable effect, or it might have had some different effect and have been known to cave-dwelling geneticists as, say, a gene for inability to read animal footprints. In our educated environment it would properly be called a gene "for" dyslexia, since dyslexia would be its most salient consequence. Similarly, a gene which caused total blindness would also prevent reading, but it would not usefully be regarded as a gene for not reading. This is simply because preventing reading would not be its most obvious or debilitating phenotypic effect.

Returning to our gene for specific dyslexia, it follows from the ordinary conventions of genetic terminology that the wild-type gene at the same locus, the gene that the rest of the population has in double dose, would properly be called a gene "for reading." If you object to that, you must also object to our speaking of a gene for tallness in Mendel's peas, because the logic of the terminology is identical in the two cases. In both cases the character of interest is a *difference*, and in both cases the difference only shows itself in some specified environment. The reason why something so simple as a one gene difference can have such a complex effect as to determine whether or not a person can learn to read, or how good he is at tying shoelaces, is basically as follows. However complex a given state of the world may be, the *difference* between that state of the world and some alternative state of the world may be caused by something extremely simple.

The point I made using antlions is a general one. I could have used any real or purported Darwinian adaptation whatsoever. For further emphasis I shall use one more example. Tinbergen et al. (1962) investigated the adaptive significance of a particular behavior pattern in black-headed gulls (*Larus ridibundus*), eggshell removal. Shortly after a chick hatches, the parent bird grasps the empty eggshell in the bill and removes it from the vicinity of the nest. Tinbergen and his colleagues considered a number of possible hypotheses about the survival value of this behavior pattern. For instance they suggested that the empty eggshells might serve as breeding grounds for harmful bacteria, or the sharp edges might cut the chicks. But the hypothesis for which they ended up finding evidence was that the empty eggshell serves as a conspicuous visual beacon summoning crows and other predators of chicks or eggs to the nest. They did ingenious experiments, laying out artificial nests with and without empty eggshells, and showed that eggs accompanied by empty eggshells were, indeed, more likely to be attacked by crows than eggs without empty eggshells by their side. They concluded that natural selection had favored eggshell removal behavior of adult gulls, because past adults who did not do it reared fewer children.

As in the case of antlion digging, nobody has ever done a genetic study of eggshell removal behavior in black-headed gulls. There is no direct evidence that variation in tendency to remove empty eggshells breeds true. Yet clearly the assumption that it does, or once did, is essential for the Tinbergen hypothesis. The Tinbergen hypothesis, as normally phrased in gene-free language, is not particularly controversial. Yet it, like all the rival functional hypotheses that Tinbergen rejected, rests fundamentally upon the assumption that once upon a time there must have been gulls with a genetic tendency to remove eggshells, and other gulls with a genetic tendency not to remove them, or to be less likely to remove them. There must have been genes for removing eggshells.

Here I must enter a note of caution. Suppose we actually did a study of the genetics of eggshell removal behavior in modern gulls. It would be a behavior-geneticist's dream to find a simple Mendelian mutation which radically altered the behavior pattern, perhaps abolished the behavior altogether. By the argument given above, this mutant would truly be a gene "for" not removing eggshells, and, by definition, its wild-type allele would have to be called a gene for eggshell removal. But now comes the note of caution. It most definitely does not follow that this particular locus "for" eggshell removal was one of the ones upon which natural selection worked during the evolution of the adaptation. On the contrary, it seems much more probable that a complex behavior pattern like eggshell removal must have been built up by selection on a large number of loci, each having a small effect in interaction with the others. Once the behavior complex had been built up, it is easy to imagine a single major mutation arising, whose effect is to destroy it. Geneticists perforce must exploit the genetic variation available for them to study. They also believe that natural selection must have worked on similar genetic variation in wreaking evolutionary change. But there is no reason for them to believe that the loci controlling modern variation in an adaptation were the very same loci at which selection acted in building up the adaptation in the first place.

This consideration seems to me to be a reason for caution, not a reason for rejecting the whole genetic theory of natural selection! Never mind if living geneticists are debarred from studying the particular loci at which selection in the past gave rise to the original evolution of interesting adaptations. It is too bad if geneticists usually are forced to concentrate on loci that are convenient rather than evolutionarily important. It is *still* true that the evolutionary putting together of complex and interesting adaptation consisted in the replacement of genes by their alleles.

This argument can contribute tangentially to the resolution of a fashionable contemporary dispute, by helping to put the issue in perspective. It is now highly, indeed passionately, controversial whether there is significant genetic variation in human mental abilities. Are some of us genetically brainier than others? What I mean by "brainy" is also highly contentious, and rightly so. But I suggest that, by any meaning of the term, the following propositions cannot be denied. (1) There was a time when our ancestors were less brainy than we are. (2) Therefore there has been an increase in braininess in our ancestral lineage. (3) That increase came about through evolution, probably propelled by natural selection. (4) Whether propelled by selection or not, at least part of the evolutionary change in phenotype reflected an underlying genetic change: allele replacement took place and consequently mean mental ability increased over generations. (5) By definition therefore, at least in the past, there must have been significant genetic variation in braininess within the human population. Some people were genetically clever in comparison with their contemporaries, others were genetically relatively stupid.

The last sentence may engender a *frisson* of ideological disquiet, yet none of my five propositions could be seriously doubted, nor could their logical sequence. The argument works for brain size, but it equally works for any behavioral measure of cleverness we care to dream up. It does not depend on simplistic views of human intelligence as being a one-dimensional scalar quantity. The fact that intelligence is not a simple scalar quantity, important as the fact that is, is simply irrelevant. So is the difficulty of measuring intelligence in practice. The conclusion of the previous paragraph is inevitable, provided only that we are evolutionists who agree to the proposition that once upon a time our ancestors were less clever (by whatever criterion) than we are. Yet in spite of all that, it still does not follow that there is any genetic variation in mental abilities left in the human population today: the genetic variance might have been used up by selection. On the other hand it might not, and my thought experiment shows at least the inadvisability of dogmatic and hysterical opposition to the very possibility of genetic variation in human mental abilities. My own opinion, for what it is worth, is that even if there is such genetic variation in modern human populations, to base any policy on it would be politically undesirable.

The existence of a Darwinian adaptation, then, implies the sometime existence of genes for producing the adaptation. This is not always made explicit. It is always possible to talk about the natural selection of a behavior pattern in two ways. We can either talk about individuals with a tendency to perform the behavior pattern being "fitter" than individuals with a less strongly developed tendency. This is the now fashionable phraseology, within the paradigm of the "selfish organism" and the "central theorem of sociobiology." Alternatively, and equivalently, we can talk directly of genes for performing the behavior pattern surviving better than their alleles. It is always legitimate to postulate genes in any discussion of Darwinian adaptation, and it is one of my central points in *The Extended Phenotype* that it is often positively beneficial to do so. Objections, such as I have heard made, to the "unnecessary geneticizing" of the language of functional ethology, betray a fundamental failure to face up to the reality of what Darwinian selection is all about.

Let me illustrate this failure by another anecdote. I recently attended a research seminar given by an anthropologist. He was trying to interpret the incidence among various human tribes of a particular mating system (it happened to be polyandry) in terms of a theory of kin selection. A kin selection theorist can make models to predict the conditions under which we would expect to find polyandry. Thus, on one model applied to Tasmanian native hens (Maynard Smith and Ridpath 1972), the population sex ratio would need to be male-biased, and partners would need to be close kin, before a biologist would predict polyandry. The anthropologist sought to show that his polyandrous human tribes lived under such conditions, and, by implication, that other tribes showing the more normal patterns of monogamy or polygyny lived under different conditions.

Though fascinated by the information he presented, I tried to warn him of some difficulties in his hypothesis. I pointed out that the theory of kin selection is fundamentally a genetic theory, and that kin-selected adaptations to local conditions had to come about through the replacement of alleles by other alleles, over generations. Had his polyandrous tribes been living, I asked, under their current peculiar conditions for long enough – enough generations – for the necessary genetic replacement to have taken place? Was there, indeed, any reason to believe that variations in human mating systems are under genetic control at all?

The speaker, supported by many of his anthropological colleagues in the seminar, objected to my dragging genes into the discussion. He was not talking about genes, he said, but about a social behavior pattern. Some of his colleagues seemed uncomfortable with the very mention of the four-letter word "gene." I tried to persuade him that it was *he* who had "dragged genes in" to the discussion although, to be sure, he had not mentioned the word gene in his talk. That is exactly the point I am trying to make. You cannot talk about kin selection, or any other form of Darwinian selection, *without* dragging genes in, whether you do so explicitly or not. By even speculating about kin selection as an explanation of differences in tribal mating systems, my anthropologist friend was implicitly dragging genes into the discussion. It is a pity he did not make it *explicit*, because he would then have realized what formidable difficulties lay in the path of his kin selection hypothesis: either his polyandrous tribes had to have been living, in partial genetic isolation, under their peculiar conditions for a large number of centuries, or natural selection had to have favored the universal occurrence of genes programming some complex "conditional strategy." The irony is that, of all the participants in that seminar on polyandry, it was I who was advancing the least "genetically deterministic" view of the behavior under discussion. Yet because I insisted on making the genetic nature of the kin selection hypothesis explicit, I expect I appeared to be characteristically obsessed with genes, a "typical genetic determinist." The story illustrates well the main message of this chapter, that frankly facing up to the fundamental genetic nature of Darwinian *selection* is all too easily mistaken for an unhealthy preoccupation with hereditarian interpretations of ontogenetic *development*.

The same prejudice against explicit mention of genes where one can get away with an individual-level circumlocution is common among biologists. The statement, "genes for performing behavior X are favored over genes for not performing X" has a vaguely naive and unprofessional ring to it. What evidence is there for such genes? How dare you conjure up *ad hoc* genes simply to satisfy your hypothetical convenience! To say "individuals that perform X are fitter than individuals that do not perform X" sounds much more respectable. Even if it is not known to be true, it will probably be accepted as a permissible speculation. But the two sentences are exactly equivalent in meaning. The second one says nothing that the first does not say more clearly. Yet if we recognize this equivalence and talk explicitly about genes "for" adaptations, we run the risk of being accused of "genetic determinism." I hope I have succeeded in showing that this risk results from nothing more than misunderstanding. A sensible and unexceptionable way of thinking about natural selection – "gene selectionism" – is mistaken for a strong belief about development – "genetic determinism." Anyone who thinks clearly about the details of how adaptations come into being is almost bound to think, implicitly if not explicitly, about genes, albeit they may be hypothetical genes. As I shall show in this book, there is much to be said for making the genetic basis of Darwinian functional speculations explicit rather than implicit. It is a good way of avoiding certain tempting errors of reasoning (Lloyd 1979). In doing this we may give the impression, entirely for the wrong reason, of being obsessed with genes and all the mythic baggage that genes carry in the contemporary journalistic consciousness. But determinism, in the sense of an inflexible, tramline-following ontogeny, is, or should be, a thousand miles from our thoughts. Of course, individual sociobiologists may or may not be genetic determinists. They may be Rastafarians, Shakers, or Marxists. But their private opinions on genetic determinism, like their private opinions on religion, have nothing to do with the fact that they use the language of "genes for behavior" when talking about natural selection.

A large part of this chapter has been based on the assumption that a biologist might wish to speculate on the Darwinian "function" of behavior patterns. This is not to say that all behavior patterns necessarily have a Darwinian function. It may be that there is a large class of behavior patterns which are selectively neutral or deleterious to their performers, and cannot usefully be regarded as the products of natural selection. If so, the arguments of this chapter do not apply to them. But it is legitimate to say "I am interested in adaptation. I don't necessarily think all behavior patterns are adaptations, but I want to study those behavior patterns that are adaptations." Similarly, to express a preference for studying vertebrates rather than invertebrates does not commit us to the belief that all animals are vertebrates. Given that our field of interest is adaptive behavior, we cannot talk about the Darwinian evolution of the objects of interest without postulating a genetic basis for them. And to use "a gene for X" as a convenient way of talking about "the genetic basis of X," has been standard practice in population genetics for over half a century.

Note

This chapter draws directly from the second chapter of my *The Extended Phenotype* (Oxford: Oxford University Press, 1982), pp. 9–29.

References

Boden, M.: *Artificial Intelligence and Natural Man* (Brighton: Harvester Press, 1977).

Curio, E.: "Towards a methodology of teleonomy." *Experientia* 29 (1973), pp. 1045–58.

Dawkins, R.: *The Selfish Gene* (Oxford: Oxford University Press, 1976a).

Dawkins, R.: "Twelve misunderstandings of kin selection." *Zeitschrift fur Tierpsychologie* 47 (1979a), pp. 184–200.

Dawkins, R.: "Defining sociobiology." *Nature* 280 (1979b), pp. 427–8.

Dawkins, R.: "In defence of selfish genes." *Philosophy* (Oct., 1981).

Evans, C.: *The Mighty Micro* (London: Gollancz, 1979).

Falconer, D. S.: *Introduction to Quantitative Genetics* (London: Longman, 1960).

Goodwin, B. C.: "Spoken remark." In *Theoria to Theory* 13 (1979), pp. 87–107.

Gould, S. J.: *Ever Since Darwin* (London: Burnett, 1978).

Gould, S. J. and Lewontin, R. C.: "The spandrels of San Marco and the Panglossian paradigm: a critique of the adaptationist programme." *Proceedings of the Royal Society of London* B 205 (1979), pp. 581–98.

Gregory, R. L.: "The brain as an engineering problem." In Thorpe, W. H. and Zangwill, O. L., eds.: *Current Problems in Animal Behavior* (Cambridge: Cambridge University Press, 1961), pp. 307–30.

Hamilton, W. D.: "Altruism and related phenomena, mainly in social insects." *Annual Review Of Ecology and Systematics* 3 (1972), pp. 193–232.

Hofstadter, D. R.: *Godel, Esher, Bach: An Eternal Golden Braid* (Brighton: Harvester Press, 1979).

Hoyle, F.: *Man in the Universe* (New York: Columbia University Press, 1964).

Kempthorne, O.: "Logical, epistemological and statistical aspects of nature-nurture data interpretation." *Biometrics* 34 (1978), pp. 1–23.

Levy, D.: "Computers are now chess masters." *New Scientist* 79 (1978), p. 79.

Lewontin, R. C.: "Sociobiology as an adaptationist program." *Behavioral Science* 24 (1979), pp. 5–14.

Lloyd, J. E.: "Mating behavior and natural selection." *Florida Entomologist* 62 (1979), pp. 17–23.

Maynard Smith, J.: "The theory of games and the evolution of animal conflicts." *Journal of Theoretical Biology* 47 (1974), pp. 209–21.

Maynard Smith, J. and Ridpath, M. G.: "Wife sharing in the Tasmanian native hen, *Tribonyx mortierii*: a case of kin selection." *American Naturalist* 106 (1972), pp. 447–52.

"Nabi," I.: "Ethics of genes." *Nature* 290 (1981), p. 183.

Ridley, M.: "Konrad Lorenz and Humpty Dumpty: some ethology for Donald Symons." *Behavioral and Brain Sciences* 3 (1980), p. 196.

Rose, S.: "Pre-Copernican sociobiology?" *New Scientist* 80 (1978), pp. 45–6.

Rothenbulher, W. C.: "Behavior genetics of nest cleaning in honey bees. IV. Responses of F1 and backcross generations to disease-killed brood." *American Zoologist* 4 (1964), pp. 111–23.

Shuster, P. and Sigmund, K. "Coyness, philandering and stable strategies." *Animal Behavior* 29 (1981), pp. 186–92.

Symons, D.: *The Evolution of Human Sexuality* (New York: Oxford University Press, 1979).

Taylor, A. J. P.: *The First World War* (London: Hamish Hamilton, 1963).

Tinbergen, N. et al.: "Egg shell removal by the black-headed gull, *Larus ridibundus*, L.; a behavior component of camouflage." *Behaviour* 19 (1962), pp. 74–117.

Trevor-Roper, H. R.: *The Last Days of Hitler* (London: Pan, 1972).

Turing, A.: "Computing machinery and intelligence." *Mind* 59 (1950), pp. 433–60.

Weizenbaum, J.: *Computer Power and Human Reason* (San Francisco: W. H. Freeman, 1976).

Williams, G. C.: *Adaptation and Natural Selection* (Princeton, NJ: Princeton University Press, 1966).

Wilson, E. O.: *On Human Nature* (Cambridge, MA: Harvard University Press, 1978).

Winograd, T.: *Understanding Natural Language* (Edinburgh: Edinburgh University Press, 1972).

Young, R. M.: "Darwin's metaphor: does nature select?" *The Monist* 55 (1971), pp. 442–503.

Further reading

Dawkins, R.: *The Selfish Gene*, 2nd ed. (Oxford: Oxford University Press, 1989).

Dawkins, R.: *The Extended Phenotype* (Oxford: Oxford University Press, 1982).

Dawkins, R.: *The Blind Watchmaker* (Oxford: Oxford University Press, 1986).

Dawkins, R.: *River Out of Eden* (Oxford: Oxford University Press, 1995).

Dawkins, R.: *Climbing Mount Improbable* (Oxford: Oxford University Press, 1996).

Dawkins, R.: *Unweaving the Rainbow* (Oxford: Oxford University Press, 1998).

20

The Darwin Wars and the Human Self-image

JANET RADCLIFFE RICHARDS

I Introduction

One of the main achievements of the genetic revolution has been its placing beyond all serious scientific doubt the Darwinian theory of organic evolution by natural selection.

Darwin's theory seemed plausible to many people even at the time of its publication, and quickly gained widespread acceptance among scientists and naturalists. In its original form, however, it ran into various problems; and these genuine difficulties – along with other purely fanciful ones – were thankfully seized on by alarmed traditionalists as a justification for rejecting the theory outright. The resistance, of course, continues; anti-evolutionary creationism is still a powerful political force in the United States. But strength of feeling, no matter how widespread or influential, cannot show any belief to be rationally justified. Neo-Darwinism, the version of Darwinian theory that has emerged from the discovery of genes and the mechanisms of reproduction, has removed all the fundamental problems encountered by the classical theory. Now, as the philosopher Daniel Dennett (1995: 20) says:

> Like Gulliver tied down in Lilliput, it is unbudgeable, not because of some one or two huge chains of argument that might – hope against hope – have weak links in them, but because it is securely tied by hundreds of thousands of threads of evidence anchoring it to virtually every other area of human knowledge.

To worry about cloned human beings, or genetically modified tomatoes, or the access of employers to genetic information, while doubting the essential truth of Darwinism, would be like planning the details of space exploration while believing that the planets circled a stationary earth on crystalline spheres propelled by angels.

But even if the rearguard creationist defense of long-lost territory is discounted, the genetic revolution has not ended disputes about matters Darwinian. In many ways it has extended and intensified them. There are serious disagreements among people who have crossed the Darwinian threshold and accepted the idea of organic evolution, and this internecine strife is characterized by as much rancor and anxiety as the original disputes about evolution.

Since, as Dennett claims, the theory touches almost every aspect of knowledge, the scope for controversy is endless, and any concise account of what is going on is bound to cut corners. However, on the Baconian principle that truth emerges more readily from error than from confusion, even a simplified map is better than none.

The battle lines

The main focus of interest in these debates is (not surprisingly) ourselves, and the broadest disagreement is about the extent to which Darwinian explanation can cast light on our nature and our place in the scheme of things. That broad question of scope encompasses two narrower ones. The first concerns the relevance of Darwinism to questions about what we and other things ultimately consist of, and how we came to be as we are. The second concerns how much about the details of our deepest emotions and capabilities can be revealed by Darwinian enquiry.

Although these two questions are in many ways distinct, only people who give a strongly Darwinian answer to the first are likely even to raise the second. For practical purposes, therefore, it is useful to think of a single scale of deepening Darwinism, ranging from anti-Darwinians at the conservative end, to ultra-Darwinians (a term of abuse invented by their opponents) at the radical end.

Since the questions are about scope the potential answers are matters of degree, and a continuum does not, as such, offer any clear lines of dispute. But rather as gradually falling temperatures quite suddenly cause freezing, there seem to be points at which gradually deepening Darwinism abruptly produces a qualitative flip, and a significantly changed view of the world. These points are the boundaries over which the Darwin wars are being fought.

This is what figure 20.1 is intended to suggest. The explanation follows.

Cranes, skyhooks, and materialism

The essence of the first controversy, about the extent to which explanation of a Darwinian kind can account for the nature and origin of the world and what it contains, is strikingly caught by Dennett's metaphorical contrast of explanations that

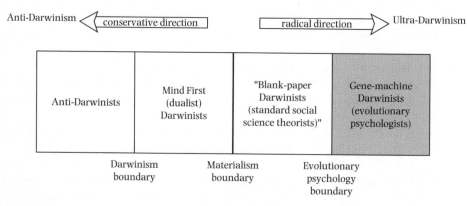

Figure 20.1 The scope of Darwinian explanation.

depend on *cranes* (devices that lift other things while themselves remaining rooted to the ground) with others that invoke *skyhooks* (things that descend from above to raise what cannot rise by itself) (Dennett 1995: 73ff).

Traditional explanations of order and complexity have always been of skyhook form, invoking the higher to explain what goes on among the lower. Since matter itself is inert, and can do no more than transmit motion imparted to it by other things, the capacity of some material things for growth, or movement, or thought, must be explained in terms of infusions of more powerful elements such as life and souls. This kind of thinking ultimately supports what Dennett (26ff) calls the Mind First view of things. A higher mind still – God – must be invoked to account for the existence of the world, and for all the complexity and design within it.

It was this top-down direction of explanation that Darwin's ideas began to upset. He showed in principle how natural selection and the ordinary forces of nature could bring complex organisms from simple ones, without any higher force or any design. In Dennett's terms, he gave an explanation in terms of cranes in a context where skyhooks had previously seemed essential.

Darwin himself – at least in public – performed this inversion only for organic matter: for what can be regarded as a section in the middle of the traditional Great Chain of Being, which ranged from inanimate matter at the bottom to God at the top. But, as Dennett points out, explanations of this cranes-only kind have no need to stop there. They might extend further down the chain, to account for the emergence of life from inanimate matter, or even – as some physicists speculate – the origins of universes. Or they might extend upwards, explaining human activity and thought without reference to immaterial souls, and in doing so eliminate the need for higher minds still to account for the existence of consciousness and purpose.

It is in this way that the question arises of how far a Darwinian, cranes-only explanation of origins can stretch; and people who have crossed the Darwinian threshold, and accepted evolution from micro-organisms to human bodies, disagree about how much further it can go. But although these disagreements are in theory matters of degree, there is a significant flip at the point when Darwinian explanations seem to stretch far enough to eliminate the need for skyhooks altogether, and justify a belief in *materialism*. Materialism – in this sense of the word, which is not the only one – is the monist view according to which matter is the only independently existing substance, with mind dependent on it in the sense that if all matter disappeared, so would all mind. It is opposed here to the Mind First view, which takes mind to be fundamental. This view is typically, though not necessarily, dualist, in the sense of regarding mind and matter as separate substances.

So the first significant controversy among Darwinians is whether explanation of a Darwinian, cranes-only type can stretch far enough to justify abandoning the Mind First view of things, or whether – as the Church has tended to claim since it got its breath back – evolution by natural selection may be understood as the means by which God produced animals and even the human body, but Mind must still be regarded as essential for getting things going in the first place, bringing life out of matter, and giving human beings immaterial souls. The two sides of this controversy coincide to a large extent with religious and secular views of the kind of thing we ultimately are.

Genes, cultures, and evolutionary psychology

The second controversy is also about the scope of Darwinian explanation, but in a different way. The main combatants here agree that our origins and constitution are entirely Darwinian and material, but they disagree about the extent to which an understanding of our evolutionary background and genetic constitution can provide insight into our fundamental psychology.

Darwin himself realized that the emotions and abilities of animals were as much a factor in their reproductive success, and therefore as open to evolutionary explanation, as any other aspect of them. This, however, was one of the contexts in which classical Darwinism ran into difficulties – in particular about the possibility of altruism – and the Darwinian study of psychology could make only limited progress until the advent of the gene theory and neo-Darwinism. But once the approximate resemblances between related organisms had been understood as resulting from overlapping combinations of precisely replicated genes, the way was open for a quite different approach. Some biologists began to think of organisms as – to use Dawkins' phrase – survival machines for the genes that constructed them, and to translate questions about why organisms behaved as they did into questions about how that behavior would have led to the success, not necessarily of individuals or even groups, but of genes.

The breakthrough to this way of thinking was made with William Hamilton's triumphant explanation, in 1964, of the baffling altruism of the sterile social insects. But the real controversy began when the idea was popularized and generalized, in 1975 by E. O. Wilson's *Sociobiology*. Nobody had been particularly bothered by Darwinian explanations of ants and bees, but what began with insects was extended by Wilson to speculation about human beings.

The dispute here is essentially about the extent to which we should regard ourselves as still characterized by our evolutionary origins, and to what extent as having transcended them to become creatures of our culture. The question of the relative input of genes and environment into an organism at any stage of development is obviously one of degree: nobody doubts either that the environment has an enormous influence on the way any complex organism develops, or that what that environment influences is something with a particular genetic constitution. But again there is on the continuum a sudden change of perspective and emphasis.

On one side of the divide are people who think that although human origins are entirely Darwinian, we have now evolved to a state of complexity that makes those origins irrelevant to the understanding of what we are. These are practitioners of the prevailing *standard social science* model of explanation, who work on the basis of what might be called a methodological blank-paper view of human nature, and look to the social environment for explanations of why we are as we are. Sociobiologists – or *evolutionary psychologists*, as sociobiologists concerned with human psychology are generally known – think our origins are still very much with us, that we can be understood only if we think of ourselves primarily as survival machines for our genes.

The nature of this methodological difference can be illustrated by one of the best-known disputes between the two sides: that of psychological differences between the sexes. Since the sexes have always been in systematically different environments it is impossible to tell directly the extent to which observed tendencies to difference between them are genetic in origin. We can try to make the environments more similar, as has now been done in many societies, but there are still many differences between the sexes on average. How should we pursue the enquiry into the origins of these differences?

Advocates of the standard social science approach, with their methodological blank-paper assumption, continue to look for the source in different social pressures, and if such pressures are not apparent they look for more subtle ones. Evolutionary psychologists approach the problem from the other end, from the point of view of genes trying (as it were) to get as many copies of themselves as possible into future generations; and from this direction there immediately appears a highly significant difference between the sexes, in their reproductive systems. A human female, reproducing flat out, can produce only about a child a year, while a sufficiently energetic male can produce hundreds – if he can get enough females to cooperate, and keep rival males out of the way. That difference alone suggests that successful genes are likely to adjust the emotional dispositions of their survival machines according to sex, and in particular suggests that males should tend to be eager for sex with large numbers of females and ready to dispute the matter with other males, while females – since nothing can increase the number of children they have – should tend to be more concerned with the quality of their mates.

Such ideas are only the beginning of an enquiry, to be tested against evidence from history and the social sciences as well as through continuing work in evolutionary biology. But they offer a new direction from which to approach the study of human nature; and evolutionary psychologists are pushing ahead with what they see as a new and exciting branch of science. Their opponents, in the meantime, regard the ideas as speculative or even fanciful and much of the work as unscientific, and continue to look for explanations of human characteristics in the social environment.

How to postpone, or even avoid, the conflict

Even if the fundamental Darwinian case has been settled beyond reasonable controversy, the same cannot be said of the more radical Darwinian ideas. This is not to say that the issues are finely balanced, but it does mean that anyone who wants to know what to think about the deeper levels of Darwinism needs to examine the arguments and assess them.

This, however, is not at all easy. For one thing, it is quite difficult to make out, through the smoke of what have aptly been called the Darwin Wars, even what the issues are. Much of what goes on amounts to direct or implied abuse of the other side's academic and moral credentials rather than direct discussion of the issues; and if you can get past that to the issues themselves, you have to know the terrain pretty well to know whether each side is arguing against what the other is really saying. As usual when academic problems become entangled with personal passions, the combatants tend to interpret their opponents' claims in the least plausible ways, treating the weakest arguments as representative of the whole position, quoting out of context, attacking

275

straw men, and generally seeming considerably more concerned with winning the public debate than reaching the truth. And even when the real questions are eventually identified, most of them turn out to involve not only detailed scientific and mathematical argument, but also large issues in epistemology, philosophy of science, and philosophy of mind. Most people are simply not in a position to reach a considered conclusion about these matters.

That very fact, however, raises one of the most significant aspects the Darwin wars: the engagement of people who have little real understanding of the issues at all, and who would not dream of involving themselves in controversies about quarks, or plate tectonics, or even philosophical theories of consciousness. Matters Darwinian seem, as they have always done, alarmingly close to home; and even now that many people are used to the idea that we are literally related to other animals, they are still concerned about the implications of Darwinism for ideas about the kind of thing we are, and are anxious that unless Darwinian thinking can be kept in check, much of what we have traditionally believed about our nature and potential will have to be abandoned.

The simple reply, of course, is that this is just too bad. Resistance of this kind no longer has the power to stop the course of science, and if science can establish the more radical Darwinian conclusions, they will just have to be taken on board, implications and all.

But the concern about implications raises a quite different, and rather neglected, part of the Darwin controversies. To the extent that these concerns about our self-image are what give the Darwin wars their ferocity, it is being taken for granted that the different positions actually have the implications attributed to them. But that is a substantial question in its own right, about which it is as possible to make mistakes as about the facts themselves; and unless the more radical forms of Darwinism really do have the alarming implications supposed, there is no need for anxiety about the scientific debate.

The subject is enormous, but it needs at least to be raised and illustrated. The rest of this chapter is about not which degree of Darwinism is right, but about what *turns* on the answer to that question.

II The Implications

Freedom and responsibility

The problem of human freedom and responsibility offers an ideal illustration of the fear that deepening Darwinism presents an increasing threat to our self-image. Blank-paperers often claim that gene-machinists cannot allow for human freedom – a capacity for genuine responsibility – and holders of the Mind First view typically think the same about materialists. This in turn illustrates the fact that the matter of implications cannot be as straightforward as it may seem, because these claims, simply understood, cannot both be right. If the capacity for responsibility is lost at the materialism boundary, it cannot be lost again to evolutionary psychology.

Freedom and responsibility: blank paper vs. gene machines
An illustration of the idea that freedom and responsibility are precluded by the gene-machine view comes in an ironic aside about the implications of sociobiology in a review by Steven Rose (1978) of Wilson's *On Human Nature* (quoted Dawkins 1982: 10):

> ...(don't blame your mates for sleeping around, ladies, it's not their fault they are genetically programmed).

The idea that some people are not capable of responsible action, and therefore cannot be blamed for what they do, is itself perfectly familiar. In spite of the inevitable gray areas, we routinely distinguish between people who are capable of understanding the consequences and implications of their actions and of controlling them (most of us), and others who are not (young children and sufferers from various mental abnormalities or illnesses). So the first question is whether the truth of sociobiological theories would show men's sexual urges to be a kind of mental illess that left them in a permanent state of diminished responsibility.

The reference to programming seems to imply this, but any such idea would depend on a serious misunderstanding of what evolutionary psychology was about. Evolutionary psychologists are not making any new claims about *how* inclined men are to philander. The issue between the two sides in this part of the Darwin wars is not what the phenomena *are*, but how they can best be *explained*. Gene machinists differ from blank paperers in claiming that the reason why men on average – in any society – seem so much more inclined than women to be tempted by a variety of sexual partners lies deep in their evolutionary origins. In this ordinary sense of capacity for responsibility, therefore – the one we use when deciding whether errant individuals should be punished for choosing to do wrong, or kept under control because they are incapable of responsible action – evolutionary psychology has no implications at all for the nonresponsibility of men for philandering, or of anyone for anything.

The quotation from Rose, however, also contains the hint of another idea: that if your genes cause your philandering, and you did not choose your genes, then you did not really choose to philander and cannot be blamed for doing so. This is quite different. The implication here is that even people who are capable of responsibility in the ordinary sense just considered may still not be really, or *ultimately*, responsible for what they do.

It is worth stressing here that no evolutionary psychologist believes in what is called genetic determinism: the idea that everything about you is fixed by your genes. On the contrary, it is taken for granted that a sophisticated genotype will be able to adapt its survival machine to different environments, and that a gene's-eye enquiry offers the best way of finding out how this adaptation works. But the claim can stand in a looser form. If you would not have philandered *but for* your genes, which you cannot help, you cannot, ultimately, be blamed for philandering.

This may seem self-evidently true. If so, however, it must be remembered that the question now at issue is whether the matter of responsibility *turns on* the outcome of this dispute, and that depends not only on the gene-machine view's *preventing* ultimate responsibility, but on the rival blank-paper view's *allowing for* it. But it clearly does not. Since we are no more responsible for our formative environment than for our genes, the kind of ultimate responsibility said to be ruled out by the gene-machine view is just as thoroughly ruled out by the blank-paper view.

This means that if the debate is about the *ordinary* capacity for responsibility, both positions allow for it. If it is about *ultimate* responsibility, understood in the way needed to support the accusation that the gene machine view precludes it, neither allows for it. Their implications, so far, are exactly the same.

Freedom and responsibility: cranes vs. skyhooks

This conclusion will not surprise the combatants on the conservative side of the other battle line, between materialists and the Mind First Darwinists. Of course – the Mind First advocate is likely to say – both the blank-paper and gene-machine positions preclude a capacity for ultimate responsibility – genuine free will – because both positions are materialist, and therefore *determinist*. It is determinism as such – not just genetic determinism – that conflicts with a genuine capacity for responsibility.

This response presupposes that the materialism/Mind First divide coincides with the determinism/nondeterminism divide, and this widely held assumption is disputable in both directions. However, that issue need not be pursued here, because it is forestalled by a more fundamental problem.

According to this line of argument, determinism rules out genuine responsibility for philandering because men are not responsible for the causes that make them act in the way they do. But how does this compare with the alternative possibility? Suppose the world is not deterministic, so that at least some events are wholly or partially uncaused. Uncaused events are, by definition, ones for which *nobody and nothing* can be responsible. Therefore wherever you imagine their occurring in any sequence of events, they cannot help to produce the kind of ultimate responsibility that determinism is said to rule out. Even if a nonmaterial world would indeed be nondeterministic, ultimate responsibility, understood in this way, would still be impossible.

The fact that this kind of ultimate responsibility is ruled out by both determinism and nondeterminism, however, shows where the real problem lies. Since the world must, as a matter of logic, be either deterministic or not (everything caused or at least some things not caused), the kind of responsibility at issue cannot exist *in any possible world*. Its elusiveness has nothing to do with Darwinism or determinism: the problem lies in the incoherence of this concept of responsibility itself. If determinism makes us not responsible for our choices because we did not choose to be the kind of person who is making the choices, the only thing that could make us responsible would be our choosing what we were from the beginning. But that would require our existing before we existed.

This illustrates the fact that questions commonly regarded as empirical may be at root philosophical. The first problem in this debate is to find a satisfactory answer to the question of what would count as a genuine capacity for responsibility, and only after that has been done can it be asked whether some Darwinian positions would allow for it while others did not. The problem now lies with anyone who thinks there is such a difference between these positions, first to produce an account of what would count as a capacity for genuine responsibility, and then show that some positions allow for it while others do not.

Altruism

Another familiar idea is that even if Darwinism leaves us capable of genuine choice, it still leaves us incapable of altruism, and therefore of genuinely moral behavior. It is not as clear in this case whether the dispute arises separately on the materialism and evolutionary psychology boundaries, but there is certainly a widespread view – among evolutionary psychologists themselves, as well as their opponents – that the gene-machine view implies that we must be fundamentally selfish.

As already mentioned, altruism – other than parent-to-child altruism – always presented problems for classical Darwinism. Because evolutionary change was supposed to work by the accumulation of tiny advantages, it seemed that even the slightest tendency to attend to the interests of others when they conflicted with your own should be rooted out by natural selection. But neo-Darwinism has found solutions, at least in principle, to these problems, by way of applying at the genetic level the familiar idea that individuals who cooperate may all be more successful than if they pursued their own interests directly. Such deliberately cooperative arrangements are typically mutually self-interested, rather than altruistic; but if creatures arise with genuinely altruistic attitudes that produce similar effects, natural selection may allow the genes that produce them – even if not always the individuals themselves – to prosper.

The first such possibility was the one demonstrated by Hamilton's solution to the problem of the social insects. Since relatives share copies of the same genes, more or less in proportion to their relatedness, any gene that helped to induce in its phenotypes a disposition to be altruistic to its relatives – also in proportion to their relatedness – could be highly successful. The genes could prosper even while many individuals, and even their individual reproduction, suffered.

Another possibility, first identified by Robert Trivers (1971), is known as *reciprocal altruism*. This is the idea that altruistic behavior even to unrelated others can benefit genes, as long as the altruistic impulses are shared by others and restricted in various ways. This possibility has been shown most famously in Robert Axelrod's computer tournaments between programs designed to respond in different ways to encounters with other programs (Axelrod 1984). The most successful at survival was a surprisingly simple program called Tit-for-Tat, with a rule of being nice at first, and then selectively nice or nasty according to what the other person (or programme) did to you. This suggests how natural selection might produce creatures of generous natures, as long as it tempered the generosity with a disposition to react fiercely to cheats. The experiment was purely formal, but Tit-for-Tat obviously has strong resemblances to apparently deep and universal human characteristics, such as feelings of gratitude and resentment.

It is, incidentally, ironic that the idea that evolution can produce only selfish organisms has been further entrenched by Richard Dawkins' well-known expression "the selfish gene" (1976). The selfishness of genes is anyway purely metaphorical, since genes obviously have no interests of any kind, even in making copies of themselves; and even this metaphorical selfishness is only retrospective, in that the genes that happened to survive are inevitably ones that have survived at the expense of others. Genes are not forward looking, and cannot plan their success. But even if genes were literally selfish, the transfer of selfishness to the genetic level is precisely what makes altruism possible at the phenotypic level, in organisms themselves.

But do these neo-Darwinian accounts really solve the problem of evolutionary altruism? They are often said not to be real solutions at all (e.g. Barash 1979: 133ff). Altruism involves the sacrifice of your interests to those of others; but on this account, it is argued, what appears as altruism is really in your own interests, because your apparently altruistic acts are in the interests of your genes.

This objection, however, depends on two mistaken assumptions. The first is that apparently altruistic acts are always in the interests of your genes, and this is not true. Characteristics of existing animals are ones that have been successful in evolution; but that does not mean they will go on being successful when environments (including other organisms) change. The eventual failure of what was once successful is the essence of evolutionary change, and, for instance, characteristics that developed when humans lived in small groups may turn out to be disastrous for the genes when they find themselves in large, technologically sophisticated, postfeminist societies. And even what is on the whole good for genes need not be so in any individual case. The dispositions that lead parents to sacrifice themselves for children may, for instance, result in their putting all their efforts into the care of a severely disabled child who will never reproduce, or helping their daughters to follow careers instead of producing grandchildren. Such altruism is not at all good for their genes.

The other mistaken assumption is that your genes' interests are identical with your own. One aspect of the metaphorical selfishness of the genes is their total unconcern about the interests of their survival machines, and to whatever extent your genes' as-it-were interests also happen to be your own real interests, you are *extremely* lucky. It was presumably in our genes' interests to make us bipedal and give us babies with enormous heads, for instance, but the result is emphatically not in the interests of individual childbearers. And if evolutionary psychologists are even close to being right about the nature of the sexes, it is, as Robert Wright says, "almost as though they were designed to make each other miserable" (Wright 1994: 58).

Conversely, what is in the best interests of your genes is most unlikely to be in yours. If some dictator, who liked you, took you over and turned you into a breeding machine – using surrogacy, cloning, artificial insemination, and anything else that would maximize your reproductive success – that would be wonderful for your genes, but probably not at all for you.

So far, then, there appears to be no reason to think that the gene-machine view of human nature rules out the possibility of altruism. The kind of altruism it allows is necessarily both selective and limited – indiscriminate and unconditional altruism are evolutionary impossibilities – but that is the case with all ideas of human altruism.

For anyone who disagrees, however, the challenge is the same as in the case of responsibility: the first problem is to produce an account of what would count as real altruism. Only after that can it be seen whether the radical Darwinian views make that impossible, and whether rival views have anything better to offer.

Hopes and ideals

Probably the strongest resistance of all to the deeper levels of Darwinism comes from a fear that they will undermine our hopes and ideals, and so remove everything that seems to give life any real purpose.

Once again, the anxiety seems to occur at both the materialism and evolutionary-psychology boundaries on the Darwinian spectrum. The anxiety about materialism is essentially religious; the anxiety about evolutionary psychology is social and political.

Hopes and ideals: blank paper vs. gene machines

There is a widespread belief that radical Darwinism is at odds with radical politics, and that to justify any kind of egalitarianism or social justice it is necessary to resist the gene-machine view out of hand.

A good deal of this impression comes from the notoriety of the early influences of Darwinism on political and social thinking. Evolution by natural selection depends on the existence of variations between individuals, and this gave rise to the ideas, first of Social Darwinism (roughly speaking, that you should not impede the Onward and Upward process of evolution by supporting nature's failures and encouraging them to breed), and then of eugenics (that you should actively assist the improvement of the species by encouraging the best to reproduce and discouraging the others). The resistance to sociobiology when it first appeared was fueled mainly by the conviction of its opponents that any claim about genetically ingrained characteristics must be the first premise of an argument for concentration camps, forced sterilization, and the abolition of the welfare state.

But – quite apart from any other problems – ideas of this kind completely mistakes the nature of sociobiology, which connects with Darwinian theory in a quite different way from the ideas of Social Darwinism. Its interest is not in the fact that evolutionary change depends on variation, but in the fact that certain variations *have been selected for*. All evolutionists take it for granted that there will be considerable variations within species; but the only intraspecific variations that interest sociobiologists are the ones that seem to have arisen *as a result of* selection – such as sex, and the divisions of function in the social insects – and are therefore part of the genes' (as-it-were) survival strategy. Variations of this kind have no possible use as the basis of sinister breeding programs: you can't – at least yet – breed with only one human sex, or keep a hive going with only worker bees.

However, people who defend rightish political views of other kinds do often support them with claims about characteristics said to be deep in human nature. Defenses of many kinds of tradition – hierarchies, economic inequalities, the subjection of women to men – typically appeal to premises of this kind, and in consequence people of leftward leanings have been inclined to resist evolutionary psychology out of hand, as a suborning of science by the political forces of conservatism and authoritarianism.

This reaction, however, in itself shows why questions about the implications of scientific claims must be considered independently of the claims themselves. In this context as in many others, the idea that if you are to resist an opponent's conclusion

281

you must deny the factual claims made in its support, may depend on giving too much credit to the rest of the argument.

This is well illustrated, for instance, by familiar traditional justifications of women's legal subjection to men, and their formal exclusion from male territory. One common argument was that women were weaker than men and the weak needed protection; but if you want to protect the weak, the last thing you do is make them weaker still by putting them into the legal power of the strong. Another was that women themselves liked their situation and were naturally suited to it; but in that case you should conclude that laws and institutions to keep them in their place were superfluous. Yet another was that women must be excluded from men's work because they were not capable of it; but if that were true they would be kept out by the selection processes already in place to exclude unsuitable men, and a special rule against women would be unnecessary. Many familiar lines of traditionalist argument fall into logical absurdities of this sort, so that even if the premises were true they would not support the conclusions.

The ultimate cause of such corkscrew reasoning is the fact that claims about human nature cannot on their own support *any* conclusion about what we should and should not do. As most philosophers have accepted since Hume, you cannot infer an "ought" from an "is" (Hume 1978). This means that an argument supporting a conclusion about what ought to be done needs premises asserting values as well as making claims of fact; and of course when people defend conclusions they feel strongly about, they want to appeal to attractive-sounding values. But you can use a claim about female weakness to support the conclusion that women should be legally subordinate to men only if you conjoin it with some such value premise as "the weak should be the slaves of the strong," or "the interests of the strong matter more than those of the weak." Conversely, if you want to use a benevolent premise about protecting the weak, your conclusion will have to be about restraining and limiting the power of the strong, not increasing it. Since political ideals lie in the value premises, rather than the claims of fact, nobody need feel that new claims about human nature can justify traditional laws and institutions.

Still, it may be objected, even if the claims of evolutionary psychology do not justify political conservatism, they still set limits to what can be achieved. We can change our laws and institutions; but if evolutionary psychology is right, the fundamental problems will remain. If women have genetically ingrained emotions that make them vulnerable to men and strongly inclined to care for their offspring, or men have natural inclinations to dominate or philander, the old problems will persist. Only if these traditionally male and female habits of mind are culturally induced, therefore, is there any hope of radical change.

But this line of argument depends on another assumption: that genetically ingrained characteristics cannot be changed, whereas culturally induced ones can. This is not necessarily or obviously true, in either direction. To make radical changes in culturally induced characteristics you would need to know in detail how these characteristics had been induced or could be reversed, and also have the power to manipulate the relevant parts of the environment. Given our lack of success so far in making radical changes to human nature, even convinced blank-paperers should agree that making radical changes was not an easy matter.

Conversely, the fact that some characteristic was rooted in our genes would not show that it, or its manifestations, could not be changed or controlled. Any characteristics open to identification by evolutionary psychology must indeed be resistant to change within ordinary environments, but that does not mean they cannot be altered by non-ordinary means. Scientists are making genetic and pharmacological strides every day; and as Dawkins says (1982: 13), things that are normally difficult to change may be easy if the right agent is applied. So there is no reason to think, in general, that social change must be easier on the blank-paper than the gene-machine view. Whichever is right, questions about ease of change arise case by case.

That, however, raises one final objection, which may well be the deepest root of the hope that the gene-machine view is not true. This is the idea that tampering with the fundamentals of human nature is wrong and dangerous, and that therefore that change can be *justified* only if the desired improvements can be brought about by social means alone.

Such a view makes sense on a Mind First account of the world. A deliberately designed world may have been planned as a harmonious whole, in which all would go smoothly were it not for creatures whose disruptive sinfulness sent the natural course awry. But the present question is about the implications of the skyhookless, gene-machine view of the world, and whether there is any reason on *that* assumption to regard intervention in human biochemistry as radically different from intervention in the environment.

It has often been assumed that in the world of materialist Darwinism, natural selection does the kind of work traditionally done by God: that trial and error have been making things progressively better, and that when we interfere we spoil the good work. That was the idea that underlay Social Darwinism. But this mistakes the nature of evolutionary change, because the *only* way in which later organisms are necessarily superior to the ones they replace is that they survived and the others did not. Even from the point of view of efficient survival, nonhuman nature is most unlikely to produce the design with the best possible prospects: natural selection can work only on what arises by chance from previous designs. But, more fundamentally, capacity for survival has no necessary connection whatever with anything else of value. If we want to achieve happiness, or harmony, or cooperation, or the absence of suffering, or artistic and scientific accomplishment, or an increase in human intelligence, or anything else we care about, refraining from intervention is likely to be the *least* reliable way of achieving it.

Of course we may make mistakes, and do harm. But that is true of everything we do – to our natural and social environment, as well as to our genes and biochemistry; and holders of the blank-paper view, according to which the most powerful influences on people are their formative environments, should presumably think that interfering with those environments carries the greatest danger of far-reaching unforeseen consequences.

If all this is right, there is once again no relevant difference between the blank-paper and gene-machine views. The differences lie in implications for ideas about *how* to bring about the improvements we want and therefore for the details of political programs, but not for the fundamental ideals themselves, or the possibility or justifiability of our implementing them. Any appearance of difference comes from slipping into Mind First habits of thought, and traditional ways of thinking about interference with nature that are incompatible with the materialist forms of Darwinism. Evolution by natural selection is not something that *can* be interfered with: it is just whatever happens.

Hopes and ideals: cranes vs. skyhooks
Finally there comes the controversy between these Mind First views and Darwinian materialism; and in this case it is impossible to avoid the conclusion that the difference of implications is considerable. Even so, however, there may be less at stake than first appears, and the issues need to be taken one at a time.

It is often thought, for instance, that Darwinian materialism precludes the possibility of objective values, because moral truth depends on the existence of God, and that if our moral ideas originate in the survival strategies of selfish genes they can have no objective value. But neither of these claims is at all obviously true. Few theists turn out to believe, when it comes to the point, that moral values depend on God. If they think it is wrong to torture for fun they are unlikely to think that this means only that God disapproves, and that if God approved there would be nothing wrong with it: they think God disapproves because torture is bad and God is good. If so, they do not think that the wrongness depends on the existence of God. Conversely, materialists who think that our origins are entirely evolutionary do not see this as a reason for doubting the existence of mathematical or scientific truths, or our ability to discover them, so there seems no good reason to regard the evolutionary origins of our moral ideas as a reason for doubting the existence of moral truth. The question of whether there could possibly be such things as moral truths is itself contentious, with some philosophers denying that there could be such things under any circumstances. But that is irrelevant to this particular question, which is specifically about whether the existence of moral truth *turns* on the question of materialism; and there seems no reason to think it does. Once again, the fundamental questions are philosophical.

In general, materialism in the metaphysical sense has no necessary connection at all with materialism in the familiar judgmental sense. Believing that you have arisen without design from purely material origins, and have no immaterial soul, does not commit you to valuing only the things that are usually called material. It does not even imply that so-called spiritual or religious experiences must be regarded as unreal, or less intrinsically (as opposed to instrumentally) valuable; only that they have to be given a different explanation and interpretation.

Still, even if such questions about fundamental values do not turn on the controversy about materialism, others obviously do. For anyone whose life is directed towards the service of a creator, or whose hopes lie in the immortality of an immaterial soul, or who believes that the world is underpinned by a moral order that will eventually manifest itself through the power of God, accepting a skyhookless form of Darwinism makes an enormous difference to ideas about what can be worked towards or hoped for.

This may even be one of the few contexts in which the difference between two positions on the Darwinian scale is greater than is generally realized, because, as already suggested, much supposedly materialist thinking still trails presuppositions and habits of mind that really belong only with the Mind First view. On the Darwinian materialist view there is no correlation at all between the natural and the moral order: no reason at all to think that if human beings keep to some appointed path, all will eventually go well. If things are to go the way we would like them to go, the only chance lies in our trying to find out how the world works and to influence it where necessary, but whether that means minimal or maximal interference in what would go on without us is an open question. Darwinian nature provides the raw materials, but gives no instructions about what to do with them.

So even though the transition from Mind First views to Darwinian materialism need not have a radical effect on values, it does limit reasonable hopes of the extent to which they can be fulfilled. It takes human beings from their secure position – a little lower than the angels – in an ordered universe and turns them into what may be the highest point yet reached through the accidental reconfiguring of inanimate matter. This is decidedly less comfortable, and it is no wonder that many people hope it is not true.

Conclusion

If these arguments are on the right lines, the disagreements between the factions within Darwinism have few or no implications for many ideas traditionally seen as essential aspects of humanity: our capacity for responsibility, the possibility of altruism, the objectivity of moral values, or beliefs about what kinds of thing are intrinsically – as opposed to instrumentally – worth trying to achieve. These questions are all fundamentally philosophical, and if the scientific questions disputed by the Darwin combatants are relevant to them at all, they cannot be asked until the problems themselves have been clarified. When that has been done, it seems that nothing turns on which variety of Darwinism is right. The impression that it does typically depends on mistaking logical impossibilities for empirical ones, or slipping between different ideas in different parts of the argument, or both.

With questions about what you can reasonably hope for and work towards, the matter is different. Here the answers must turn on the details of what the world is like and how it works, and this is just what the Darwin wars are officially about.

Even here it is possible to mistake the implications of the differences. In particular, questions about what is intrinsically – as opposed to instrumentally – valuable seem to be unaffected. And although the controversy between the blank-paper and gene-machine approaches to human nature has implications for the details of political ideologies, it has none for the fundamental criteria for determining what counts as a good society, or our chances of achieving one. But a great deal does seem to turn on the difference between the Mind First view and materialism, since this potentially affects everything about what we think we should be trying to achieve, and whether we think there is any external guidance about how to achieve it or have nothing more than ourselves to rely on. Dennett seems right to see this as the real Darwinian issue.

Still, the main purpose of these sketched discussions has not been to reach definitive conclusions about the implications of Darwinism in its different degrees. Their main point is to illustrate the more general claim that the implications of the different positions are nothing like as obvious as they are frequently taken to be, and need investigation independently of questions about which version is closest to the truth. Unless we are clear about the implications, we shall not know how much it matters who wins the Darwin wars.

Note

This chapter summarizes the central arguments of Janet Radcliffe Richards, *Human Nature after Darwin: A Philosophical Introduction* (New York and London: Routledge, 2000).

References

Axelrod, R.: *The Evolution of Co-operation*. Penguin Books, 1984.

Barash, D.: *Sociobiology: The Whisperings Within*. Fontana/Collins, 1979.

Darwin, C.: *On the Origin of Species by Means of Natural Selection*. Murray, 1859.

Darwin, C.: *The Descent of Man, and Selection in Relation to Sex*, 2nd ed. Murray, 1871.

Dawkins, R.: *The Selfish Gene*. Oxford University Press, 1976.

Dawkins, R.: *The Extended Phenotype*. Oxford University Press, 1982.

Dawkins, R.: *The Blind Watchmaker: Why the Evidence of Evolution Reveals a Universe Without Design*. Norton, 1986.

Dennett, D. C.: *Darwin's Dangerous Idea: Evolution and the Meanings of Life*. Penguin Books, 1995.

Hamilton, W. D.: "The genetical evolution of social behaviour." *Journal of Theoretical Biology* 7 (1964), 1–16, 17–52.

Hume, D.: *A Treatise of Human Nature*. Oxford University Press, 1978 ed.

Rose, S.: "Pre-Copernican sociobiology?" *New Scientist* 80 (1978): 45–6.

Rose, S.: *Lifelines: Biology beyond Determinism*. Oxford University Press, 1997.

Trivers, R. L.: "Parental investment and sexual selection." In Campbell, B., ed.: *Sexual Selection and the Descent of Man 1871–1971*. Heinemann, 1971.

Wilson, E. O.: *Sociobiology: The New Synthesis*. Harvard University Press, 1975.

Wilson, E. O.: *On Human Nature*. Harvard University Press, 1978.

Wright, R.: *The Moral Animal*. Abacus, 1994.

21

Religion and Gene Therapy: The End of One Debate, the Beginning of Another

GERALD P. MCKENNY

Religion and genetics are inextricably interwined. This is so not only in the sense that attributes of the divine or the sacred are ascribed to the gene in popular culture (Nelkin and Lindee 1995), among opponents of genetic engineering (Rifkin 1983), and even (wittingly or unwittingly) by distinguished scientists (Dawkins 1989; Avise 1998). It is also because of the tension (real or perceived) genetic knowledge and technology introduce in religious traditions that are strongly committed, on religious principles, to healing, feeding, and relieving the suffering of a fallen or broken world, but that are also committed to moral and other values that some uses of genetic knowledge and technology might challenge. I will explore this latter tension in the case of human gene therapy. My question is whether there are any reasons for religious traditions to object *in principle* to gene therapy as its development is currently envisioned, or any reasons why religiously based objections to the *means* by which it might be carried out need count decisively against gene therapy. My answer to both questions, derived from a careful analysis of arguments regarding human germline gene therapy, genetic enhancements, and the normative status of human nature, will be negative, and I will argue, in conclusion, that this phase of the "religion and gene therapy debate" is over and should make room for a new phase.

To focus on the question at hand will require doing considerable violence to the authors and ecclesial statements that have addressed gene therapy. In particular, it will require neglecting issues on which most religious perpectives either agree with their secular counterparts or display the same range of disagreements as do the latter: issues regarding levels of risk and benefit, informed consent, distributive justice, allocation priorities, etc. Among many religious perspectives, these are the most important issues at stake; by bracketing them here, I run the risk of perpetuating ill-informed stereotypes of religious traditions on the part of outsiders and misconceptions among some insiders that only what is uniquely religious is genuinely religious. Moreover, this approach will require a principle of selection that favors strong and clearly developed positions over expressions of points of view. It thus discriminates against those religious statements whose rhetorical purpose is catechetical rather than polemical, and presents a distorted impression of the range of religious perspectives to go along with the distortion of their content just mentioned. Fortunately, there are comprehensive surveys of religious perspectives on genetics and gene therapy that mitigate some of these wrongs (Chapman 1998; Shannon 1998; Shinn 1998; McKenny 2000). For the rest, I take responsibility.

Germline Gene Therapy

Public debates on human germline gene therapy (hereafter GLT) often take it for granted that religious hostility to GLT is widespread.[1] In the following paragraphs, I evaluate four kinds of arguments against GLT made on religious grounds and conclude that many of these objections are unsound while others could (as those who propound them often recognize) in principle be met by future developments in GLT.

The first kind of argument against GLT objects to the latter in principle. The strongest opposition to GLT follows from an identification of the human germline as the locus of the image of God in human beings (as more biblically-oriented theologies put it) or as the essence of human nature (in the terminology of humanistic theologies). The argument in both cases is that humanity-as-it-is, is normative, and since the germline is the locus of this "as-it-is," germline interventions are unjustifiable in principle. This argument is found with some frequency among theologians in Germany and Scandinavia (see von Kooten Niekerk 1992: 324–7), but almost never in the United Kingdom and North America.[2] The context in which the German and Scandinavian arguments have appeared is important in understanding their appeal in much of Europe (especially Germany) and their lack of appeal elsewhere – a context Kurt Bayertz refers to as a "moral culture" distinct from that of the English-speaking world and enshrined in the prohibition of GLT by the Council of Europe in 1982 and in its 1997 Bioethics Convention, and in similar prohibitions in German and Swiss law (Bayertz 1997). This moral culture has two aspects relevant to our topic. The first (discussed by Bayertz) is an understanding of human dignity and human rights shaped in part by the horrific Nazi abuses of genetic science. The second (which Bayertz does not address) is an element in the debate over humanism in the twentieth century: Is humanity yet to be realized in an act of self-overcoming, as some enthusiasts of Nietzsche once argued on the right, or in an "ontology of the not yet," as Ernst Bloch argued from a Marxist perspective? Or is humanity-as-it-is an objective good that demands our respect, as Hans Jonas argued in his powerful counterthesis to Bloch? (Jonas 1984).

Even within this context, however, it is doubtful whether the identification of the germline as the locus of the *imago Dei* or the essence of the human is theologically sound. The identification is almost always asserted rather than argued, and for good reasons. First, unless somatic cell gene therapy (hereafter SCT) is to be ruled out in principle, which few of these theologians are prepared to do, the essence of the human or the *imago Dei* must lie in germ cells but not in somatic cells. Unless germline interventions are wrong because they violate the consent of those who are not yet born or able to consent, this seems to locate the normatively human not in the genome itself but in the biological transmission of life. There are precedents in the Christian tradition on which such a view could draw, but these precedents court significant theological risks. Second, if the gene pool as a whole is the locus of the essence of the human or the *imago Dei*, then such theologians would have to show either why GLT is unacceptable while other activities that alter the gene pool – ranging from abortion and prenatal selection (which many such theologians would reject), to premarital carrier screening (which at least some would accept) – are acceptable, or why these latter activities are also unacceptable. One should not conclude that the concerns raised by these theologians (and many secular Europeans) are unfounded. The possibility that genetic knowledge and technology will facilitate or result in the devaluation of many human beings is a real one. However, GLT is not a necessary condition of this devaluation, and other practices, ranging from many uses of SCT to selective abortion and implantation, could be sufficient conditions for such devaluation. The problem is not any one technique, but the attitudes, commitments and social and cultural practices that govern our use of them.

Gilbert Meilaender offers a second objection in principle to GLT. While GLT could be therapeutic in intent and could spare future generations serious problems, the very feature that makes possible this beneficial effect, namely the exercise of control over future generations, renders GLT morally problematic. "Such interventions would aim . . . at shaping the nature of others still to come. Not only a human being but humankind is then the object of our intervention" (Meilaender 1990: 874). Meilaender's objection emerges from a consistent principle of respect for the person implicit in his account: medicine should focus on treating the person with the disease; it should not be used either to eliminate the person with the disease, as in the case of selective abortion, or to eliminate the disease from humanity, as in the case of GLT.[3] However, it is unclear that there is anything wrong *per se* with aiming to eliminate diseases from humanity as a whole. Surely Meilaender would not find either the smallpox vaccination or the Tay-Sachs screening programs objectionable, yet in both cases humankind or a significant subset thereof was the object of an intervention aimed at eliminating a disease from humanity.

If, as it appears, there are no theological arguments against GLT in principle, might GLT be ruled out because of the means it employs? This brings us to the second kind of argument against GLT. Respect for zygotes and embryos as potential persons led the World Council of Churches to call for a prohibition of research on zygotes and embryos in two reports during the 1980s (World Council of Churches 1982; 1989). Other religious groups and thinkers, including the Orthodox churches, the official teachings of the Roman Catholic Church, and most evangelical Protestant groups, make the stronger claim that zygotes and embryos are persons in the full sense of the term. In addition, the Roman Catholic magisterium (official teaching authority) holds *in vitro* fertilization (IVF) to be impermissible because, among other things, it violates the unity of conjugal love and openness to procreation that must never be separated (Congregation for the Doctrine of the Faith 1988). The most thorough attempt to address GLT with these concerns in mind is found in a report generated by the (UK) Catholic Bishops' Joint Committee on Bioethical Issues (Catholic Bishops' Joint Committee on Bioethical Issues 1995). The report, authored by a group consisting mostly of physicians and fellows of the Linacre Centre, concludes that the use of IVF and the destruction of embryos rules out most GLT research currently envisioned, but points out that these objections would not apply to the following interventions, none of which involve IVF or the destruction of embryos: (1) GLT performed on ova or spermatagonia followed by normal marital intercourse – a method also favored by the (US) Catholic Health Association (Catholic Health Association of the United States 1990: 21–2); (2) treatment *in situ* of the pre- or post-implantation embryo; (3) the removal and treatment of the preimplantation embryo followed by implanation. Of course, it is uncertain that GLT research will, at least in the early stages, proceed along the lines the report recommends: assuming that GLT eventually becomes safe and effective, this may well be due to what the report argues is immoral treatment of embryos. For this reason the report notes that even if, under ideal future circumstances, parents or prospective parents could make use of GLT without resort to IVF or the destruction of embryos, appearing to condone the means by which GLT was in fact developed and the witness to the sanctity of life entailed in refusing it would still be factors to consider in arriving at a decision. Moreover, as we will see, the report identifies other potential problems with GLT. Nevertheless, it is notable that the most thorough consideration of the morality of the means of GLT, undertaken from the perspective that makes the strongest and widest claims about the immorality of certain means, recognizes the possibility that morally licit means will contribute to making GLT permissible in the future. Arguments from the immorality of the destruction of embryos and/or IVF are the least tractable of all the arguments against GLT in the religion arsenal but, as we now see, even these arguments need not rule out GLT altogether.

A third set of arguments focuses on the moral impropriety of putting existing and future persons at risk and imposing costs on them. Risks to embryos are mentioned by many authors and statements. The report of the Bishops' Joint Committee also mentions the risks IVF and/or treatment of ova pose to the mother; they could have (but did not in this context) included also the risks to the mother posed by treatment of the embryo *in situ* and by its removal and replacement, should research on these methods proceed. The same report notes two additional problems that would remain even if technological advance reduces the foregoing risks to acceptable levels: (1) risks to descendants (assuming they would have existed at all) who will not be affected by the condition for which GLT was undertaken, and who therefore would be exposed to the risks of GLT without being subject to whatever disease or disorder prompted the resort to GLT; and (2) the fact that the costs of GLT would go toward individuals who (at least in many cases) will exist only because GLT will have become available, at the expense of the needs of those who will have existed whether or not GLT will have been available. Both arguments make controversial assumptions about the moral status of future persons. Assuming these assumptions can be defended, the first argument poses no obstacle as long as the risks are minimal. After all, we currently immunize all children against various diseases, exposing all of them to a small degree of risk even though some of them would have avoided contact with or warded off the disease without the immunization. If we tolerate minimal risks to all for the sake of an nonidentifiable subset in the case of presently existing persons, it seems permissible to tolerate such risks (and perhaps slightly greater ones) in the case of future persons. The second argument would place under suspicion not only GLT but the whole array of public health initiatives that have enabled millions of persons to live who otherwise would have died in infancy – at the expense, certainly, of the needs of those who would have survived infancy without such initiatives. In short, these risks and costs GLT poses to future persons need not worry us unless we have reason to worry about other means of eradicating diseases – means which we currently accept without hesitation.

A final set of arguments points to the unknown consequences of GLT on the germline and the gene pool. Given how little we know about the ways in which genes interact with each other and with other cellular mechanisms, could GLT irreversibly impair one kind of functioning even as it works to irreversibly eliminate another? And given how little we know about the various functions of genes, could we eliminate a deleterious gene from the gene pool only to destroy the only resistance against a new lethal virus or one that has been dormant for many millennia? The possibility of the first scenario in the case of individuals is an argument for postponing GLT research on human beings until such risks are known to be minimal. The second scenario is now recognized to be highly improbable: for better or worse, the likelihood of altogether removing a gene from the human gene pool is virtually nonexistent.

In conclusion, no authors or statements from a religious perspective have made a successful case for the rejection of GLT in principle. Immoral means and risks to embryos and mothers may be reasons to reject certain methods of research, now or permanently, while costs, potential harms, and unfairness in the allocation of research or therapy may be reasons not to pursue GLT in the present. But ideally any of these factors one deems problematic may be resolved in a satisfactory way. Finally, if (as some molecular geneticists now believe) GLT may in the future not require transmission of altered traits to progeny due to the use of artificial chromosomes, most of the foregoing objections to GLT other than those that address means and risks to present persons would simply disappear.

Genetic Enhancements

The term "enhancement" refers somwhat imprecisely to various phenomena ranging from increase or optimization of the performance or functioning of human capabilities to cosmetic alterations. Like their secular counterparts, religious responses to the use of gene transfer techniques for the enhancement or alteration of human characteristics often turn on the normative significance of a distinction between therapy and enhancement or, more accurately, between therapeutic and nontherapeutic uses of such techniques.[4] The most stringent religiously based criticisms of genetic enhancements are those that reject all nontherapeutic uses of such techniques in principle. Such blanket rejections, however, are rare, and of course, their degree of stringency depends on how narrowly the therapeutic is defined. In some cases neither the definition of "therapeutic" nor the grounds for rejecting the nontherapeutic are made clear (Church in Wales 1992). In other cases, the distinction between nontherapeutic and therapeutic interventions is equated, though without sufficient elaboration, with the distinction between interventions into essential human characteristics and interventions into secondary characteristics that give organic support to the essential characteristics (Torres 1997: 50–1; Taboada 1999). The intention in all of these cases seems to be to restrict genetic interventions to the treatment of serious diseases – an intention that is clearly stated by some German theologians (see Heselhaus und Schmidt 1994: 18).

There are two problems with these approaches. One is the familiar difficulty of distinguishing therapeutic and nontherapeutic. Some authors sympathetic to certain motives behind the distinction have sought to evade the problems with the latter by proposing alternative schemes. For example, John Feinberg proposes a line between gene therapy "to fight something in human beings that is clearly a result of the consequences of sin and living in a fallen world" and gene therapy to alter what is simply part of the diversity of creation (Feinberg 1997: 187). However, this scheme simply restates the therapeutic/nontherapeutic distinction. Feinberg classifies cystic fibrosis, Huntington's chorea, Parkinson's disease and other physical and psychological conditions as consequences of sin, while hair color, skin color, and left-handedness fall under the diversity of creation. Genetic interventions designed to alleviate the former are in principle permissible. As for the latter – whether is it permissible to change one's hair color, for example, even though this is a matter of human diversity rather than sin – everything depends on one's motive. Belief that certain of these traits are inferior to others, that changing them will increase one's own value as a human being, that those who possess other such traits are less valuable, or that everyone should possess a certain trait, are all immoral motives according to Feinberg. Feinberg thus does not rule out nontherapeutic enhancements altogether.

Nevertheless, there are problems with this approach. First, as Feinberg concedes, it is difficult to determine whether some traits, such as aggressive behavior or low intelligence, are consequences of sin or manifestations of diversity. Second, while certain characteristics – skin color or body shape, for example – are from Feinberg's standpoint due to genetic diversity and not sin, the discrimination some people face due to these traits is the effect of sin. Would Feinberg permit one to fight this consequence of sin by changing the trait? Third, one may question on theological grounds whether it is always justifiable in principle to fight the effects of sin. If, as Feinberg himself believes, death is a consequence of human sin, should Christians support the use of genetic technology to attain immortality?

A second problem with arguments that turn on the normativity of the therapeutic/nontherapeutic distinction or its equivalents (and not simply on the principle that only very serious conditions justify the costs, risks and uncertain benefit of genetic interventions at present) is that they seem to rule out not only genetic but also nongenetic means of nontherapeutic enhancement. But it is absurd to rule out all forms of enhancement or alteration that go beyond the treatment of disease or organic malfunction, however broadly the latter are defined. Rather than the therapeutic/nontherapeutic distinction, there are three issues regarding genetic enhancement that deserve attention: First, is there some feature of genetic interventions (perhaps shared by other medical interventions) that renders them problematic or less desirable than other interventions? Second, are there features of social and/or cultural contexts which make the pursuit of genetic (and perhaps other) enhancements problematic? Third, do particular kinds of genetic enhancements threaten human nature or dignity? Finally, does the genome itself possess normative status in a way that renders genetic but not other enhancements suspect? The first two questions will be addressed in this section; the final two questions will be addressed in the following section.

The Catholic Bishops' Joint Committee report recognizes the distinction between therapeutic and nontherapeutic but places greater normative weight on another distinction between "environmental" and "mechanical" interventions. The former involve "a mere *response* to *selected existing potential* of the child" and are "open-ended" in that they do not specify the exact characteristics or the degree to which the intervention will prove favorable. The latter, which include genetic interventions, involve "an *amendment* of existing potential" and "are something that *happens* to the child rather than something the child *does* in a certain environment" (Catholic Bishops' Joint Committee 1995: 39–40). The report offers two arguments in favor of environmental over mechanical interventions. First, the pursuit of health in general is subject to a *prima facie* principle that whenever possible, health should be promoted "through the normal channels of human *activity*, whether conscious or non-conscious" (ibid., p. 22). In other words, medicine should intervene only when a functional defect renders the normal means to fulfillment unavailable or unsatisfactory. This principle applies equally to "therapeutic" and "nontherapeutic" (or "perfective") interventions, and thus reduces the significance of the latter distinction, at least in principle (in practice, of course, factors such as risks and costs will keep distinctions between more and less severe conditions at the forefront). In the case of "perfective" interventions, this amounts to a presumption in favor of environmental over mechanical means. This presumption shifts the weight of ethical concern to two questions the report does not adequately address, namely what conditions and circumstances, if any, justify overriding this presumption, and whether mechanical interventions are *prima facie* justifiable for conditions that do not admit of environmental interventions. The second argument is that while both types of intervention run the risk that parents who make use of them will consider their child as a product or something they control, this risk is greater in the case of mechanical interventions.

Both of these arguments are open to challenge. First, the report focuses on enhancement of traits, such as intelligence, that will require a combination of mechanical and environmental interventions since (as the report notes) such traits involve both genetic and environmental factors. If so, it seems simplistic, relying on too narrow a description of the act, to argue that these enhancements bypass human activity – even if one succeeds in showing that gene addition or replacement (or whatever technique may be used) bypass the "normal" human activity of the recipient's own genes. Second, the argument that mechanical interventions more readily facilitate parental control and manipulation confuses two concerns, both serious. One is that parents who seek to enhance certain capabilities of their children will abdicate the parental role of interpersonal cooperation with children in favor of a technological fix. However, we have seen that many capacities parents seek to enhance will still require this parental role. The second concern is parental control and manipulation itself. However, the control parents are able to exercise over their children's environment is at least as severe as any control genetics is likely to facilitate, precisely because the former type of control acts directly and (if desired) continuously on the child's behavior, volition and personality. In short, genetic interventions will not necessarily exacerbate the first problem, while their absence will not necessarily diminish the second problem. Surely Meilaender is right here: cultivation of "a renewed sense of the mystery of the person and the limits to our own

293

efforts at shaping and transforming character" will be more effective in addressing these legitimate worries than will the disfavoring of any one technique at the expense of another (Meilaender 1990: 874).[5]

These criticisms do not imply that the concern with means is misplaced. What we know through genetic science and what we can do (or think we can do) through genetic technology determine to a large extent which aspects of ourselves we attend to, problematize, and seek to change, and what we take to be our responsibilities to and expectations of others – even (indeed especially) when the genetic interventions require environmental interventions to produce an effect. These matters raise the question of the role genetic knowledge and technology play in forming us as subjects in relation to ourselves and to others, and whether this kind of formation is or is not compatible with the kind of formation a given religious tradition seeks to accomplish in one. Regrettably, few religious ethicists have taken up this issue.[6]

There are a wide range of arguments to the effect that aspects of contemporary culture or society render genetic enhancement problematic. In this category belong criticisms of what may be called the "bad infinity" of modern societies: progress for its own sake, denial of finitude, flight from contingency, elimination of suffering – suspect attitudes or projects for which even the prospect of genetic enhancements provides further fuel (Hanson 1999; Shuman 1999). Also in this category are worries that the traits people choose for alteration or enhancement will strengthen the hold of certain stereotypes and forms of discrimination (World Council of Churches 1989; Zoloth-Dorfman 1998). Finally, many authors and statements point, with greater or lesser acuity, to the complex apparatuses through which modern societies optimize the capabilities of our bodies by measuring significant traits according to certain norms, stimulating our desires for traits that fall within those norms, and persuading us to seek and secure for ourselves and those for whom we are responsible the optimal traits. However, very few of these authors and statements rule out genetic (or other) enhancements on these grounds, and for good reason: these problems all point not to any intrinsic evil in genetic enhancements but to the need for constant vigilance and for the skills to determine how to resist and appropriate developing genetic interventions in accordance with a view of how such interventions and the goods and harms they may make possible fit into what a given religious tradition considers to be a worthy way of life (see Keenan 1999; McKenny 1997).

The Genome and the Normative Status of Human Nature

Are any (or all) gene therapy interventions problematic (wrong or at least suspect) on the grounds that they alter human nature in a way that is, from the perspective of a religious tradition, inconsistent with the normative status of human nature? This question is a subset of the much broader question, addressed elsewhere, of biotechnology and the normative status of nature more generally.[7] Both individual authors and ecclesial statements express concerns about the reductionist potential of gene therapy and the threats they believe it potentially poses to human dignity. Both of these concerns invoke claims about the normative status of human nature. That status, however, is conceived in two very different ways, and this difference leads to different conclusions regarding the alteration of the human genome.

Roman Catholics and Orthodox Jews tend to extend to the genome itself little or no privilege in defining human nature. On the Jewish side, arguments that genetic engineering falls under a class of illicit alterations of nature are not unknown, but the counterargument that genetic engineering falls within the physician's divine license to heal is nearly universally accepted (Rosner 1991). On the Catholic side, official or quasi-official statements, including two influential declarations by Pope John Paul II, consistently define the essence of human nature not in genetic terms but in language made familiar by the Vatican II document *Gaudium et Spes*, for which union of body and soul (*corpore et anima unus*) is what is essentially human. The Catholic Bishops' Joint Committee report explicitly rejects the view that our genes have a privileged role in constituting human nature or personal identity, arguing, in opposition to those who oppose human germline gene therapy in principle on grounds of the centrality of the genome to human identity or development, that the genome is neither central to the identity of a person nor is it morally untouchable due to its role in human development. Rather, "the genome is simply one highly influential part of our bodies"; like other parts, it "may *in principle* be altered, to cure some defect of the body" (Catholic Bishops' Joint Committee 1995: 32). The unity of the person as body and soul, and not the givenness of one's genome, is the essentially human.

Both the aforementioned papal declarations and the Bishops' report recognize senses in which genetic interventions are potentially reductionistic and threatening to human dignity. But these senses follow directly from this understanding of the essentially or characteristically human. Human dignity in this tradition includes three components: respect for life, union of body and soul, and liberty. These components are most clearly stated in the two papal declarations (Pope John Paul II 1982; 1983). The first component rules out most research on zygotes and embryos. More to the point of our present concern, it also rules out "manipulations tending to modify the genetic store and to create groups of different people, at the risk of provoking fresh marginalizations in society" (ibid., p. 388). It is unclear whether the marginalization the pope has in mind is that which would result from the creation of inferior beings or superior beings or both; in any case, any such violations are far off at best. The second component rules out the use of IVF and artificial insemination, which separate the procreative act from the biological and spiritual union of husband and wife. It also rules out interventions that would somehow distort or destroy the integral unity of body and soul – interventions, again, which are far off at best. The third component rules out any intervention that "reduces life to an object, when it forgets that it has to do with a human subject, capable of intelligence and liberty . . ." (ibid.). Once again, it is not clear what kinds of interventions or procedures would violate liberty in this sense, but it is notable that the problem of reduction and objectification refers to a human capacity that is threatened by being overridden or eliminated by potential (though again perhaps highly unlikely) uses of genetic technology. There is no indication whatsoever in these papal declarations that genetic interventions threaten human dignity or risk reductionism simply by virtue of carrying out alterations of the genome.

Of course, not all Catholics ground their theological anthropology on the integral unity of body and soul as the pope articulates it here. However, less conservative Catholic theologians reject genetic essentialism on similar grounds and draw similar conclusions regarding gene therapy. Considering whether genetic engineering alters human nature, Jean Porter argues that the characteristically human mode of life involves the subordination of biological processes to "the ongoing process of the rational formation and execution of purposes that is characteristic of human action" (Porter 1990: 422). No genetic intervention, then, can alter human nature unless it destroys the capacity for purposive action, and it is unclear how genetic engineering could accomplish such a result. From this perspective, even GLT is unlikely to affect human life as much as technological and cultural change do; the latter, presumably, more directly engage our purposive capacities.

For these Catholic commentators, then, humanity is defined in terms of a natural order, whether as a union of body and soul or a subordination of biological to purposive functions. While these definitions are fully compatible with a recognition of the genetic basis of human traits (indeed, the far-off scenarios the pope mentions depend on such a recognition) they deny DNA a privileged role in characterizing human nature and personal identity; the genome is neither the essence of the human nor the locus of the dignity of the latter. Rather, that essence and that dignity are constituted by the ordering of body and soul or by the subordination of biological to purposive capacities. It follows that genetic interventions are problematic only insofar as they threaten to distort or obliterate this natural ordering that defines human nature.

If Barry Freundel is correct, rabbinic Judaism arrives at a similar position. This tradition recognizes certain characteristics (Freundel lists speech, intellect, love, and creativity) as "manifestations of the presence of the soul, but not the same as the soul." It is permissible to discover the genetic sites of these characteristics. "Great concern, however, would exist about tampering with such sites either in terms of damaging something fundamentally human or in terms of potentially diminishing free will and individuality" (Freundel 1994: 123–4). Freundel stops short, however, of a permanent prohibition, arguing that a final judgment on such interventions would have to assess their nature and impact.

A very different understanding of the potential of gene therapy for reductionism and violation of human dignity emerges from some Protestant and ecumenical ecclesial statements on gene therapy. In many of these statements, the Christian doctrine of creation is consistently explicated not in terms of a natural order, but in terms of a very general concept of life: "God is Creator of all life. Life is precious; therefore we must speak in faith to the manipulation of life forms" (Harron, ed., 1984: 21). Christology also is understood in terms of life: "The theological task ahead is to make sense of the claim that Christ is the unity of all life in the light of the new knowledge" (World Council of Churches 1982: 2). The new knowledge, of course, is genetic knowledge; and since DNA plays a fundamental role in our concept of life, "[g]enetic science ... explores the essence of life" and "develops means to alter the nature of life itself" (United Methodist Church 1992). Genetic science and technology raise for these Protestants and ecumenists the now familiar concerns regarding human dignity and reductionism. However, these concerns are only superficially the same as those raised by Catholic authors and declarations. In the Protestant and ecumenical statements, the problems regarding dignity and reductionism follow not from the possible eradication, distortion or overriding of essentially human characteristics, but rather from certain implications of DNA as the essence of human life.

If DNA is the essence of human life, then the very act of intervening into it is problematic on two grounds: (1) such interventions threaten a reduction of human life to mechanistic terms, and (2) they threaten the very humanness of the human. We will examine these two problems in succession. First, because DNA is both the essence of living things and capable of being treated in thoroughly mechanistic terms, genetic interventions involve a reductionism that threatens human dignity. "[I]f practiced directly and deliberately on human beings, genetic engineering converts the human subject into a composite object of interchangeable elements" (World Council of Churches 1982: 8). Remarks such as this should not mislead us: no major Protestant or ecumenical body argues from this reductionism to a prohibition of, or even a presumption against, genetic interventions. The potential the latter offer for the treatment of diseases overrules the threat posed to human dignity by reductionism. However, reductionism is still a wrong or a harm done to the sacredness or dignity of human life. As such it would seem inevitably to leave a moral trace in every genetic intervention, however secure the ultimate justifiability of the latter.

Second, the essential role of DNA in defining the human ensures that genetic interventions inevitably alter human nature itself. Again, these ecclesial statements stop far short of prohibiting such interventions on these grounds, but at some point the threat to the humanness of the human becomes morally decisive. Often, this point is reached somewhere along the spectrum of germline interventions: "Many ethical and religious traditions endorse some human freedom to modify or transcend nature. But for us to change *substantially* the germline DNA is to directly alter the genetic foundations of the human. In what ways do we, by manipulating our genes in other than simple ways, change ourselves to something less than human?" (ibid.) Clearly, we are a long way from the Catholic Bishops' Joint Committee's description of the genome as "simply one highly influential part of our bodies." Because DNA, and not an order of functions or capacities, most essentially characterizes the human, any alteration of DNA changes human nature. Unable to specify the capacities whose loss or distortion would destroy human nature, and unwilling to prohibit GLT altogether, the *degree* of intervention becomes the morally decisive, if vague, criterion of what is morally acceptable and unacceptable.

In short, for these Protestant and ecumenical bodies, genetic intervention itself – not the potential threat to the order of nature that might follow from a genetic intervention – is charged with moral significance. The significance follows from the fact that DNA is both constitutive of the essence of the human and susceptible to manipulation. Of course, the significance accorded to genetic interventions does not amount to a prohibition of, or even a presumption against, those interventions. However, we have seen that the wrong or harm done to the human subject or to human nature as such by genetic interventions is always a factor, and at some unspecified point becomes a decisive factor, in the ethical evaluation of the latter.

What should we make of this argument? Does it justify a conclusion that there is a legitimate though indeterminate religious case against a currently envisioned use of

297

gene therapy? Probably not, for several reasons. First, what this argument most likely means in practice is that major innovations in gene therapy will generate ethical anxiety among those who share the outlook of these statements, but will probably not, on these grounds at least, elicit condemnation as long as their potential for the treatment of diseases and other disorders is significant and they do not pose disproportionate risks or violate other moral norms. Second, the concept of life on which the argument relies is riddled with problems of its own and generates further problems when given a normative status. Among the former are (1) the paradoxical dialectic of mechanism and vitalism it involves, in which a genetic understanding secures the triumph of physical and biochemical explanations which, by reducing life to the nonliving, imperil the status of these explanations as explanations of *life*, and thus elicit new outbreaks of vitalism; and (2) the question of whether "life" as the natural over against the artificial or the living over against the nonliving is even intelligible if DNA as the essence of life is best understood in terms of information science. Among the latter is the question of why human manipulation of the genome is suspect if, as molecular biology assures us, DNA is by its very nature infinitely manipulable and interchangeable. If DNA is the essence of human nature, and the nature of DNA includes the properties of infinite interchangeability of parts and infinite alterability, then the nature of human nature is infinite manipulability, and it is difficult to understand how human beings could reduce human nature to something less or other than itself or alter human nature simply by intervening into the genome, however extensively. Fortunately, the Christian doctrine of creation does not require these claims, which few Christians outside liberal Protestant and ecumenical circles are inclined to support.[8]

Both of the views of the normative status of human nature described above rely too heavily on the notion of the integrity of nature, disagreeing only on the content of this notion. A more appropriate approach to the normativity of the natural is to determine where nature falls in the metanarrative (for Christians) of creation, fall, and redemption, or (for Jews) of brokenness and restoration.[9] For Christians, the incarnation and resurrection of Christ and the eschatological character of the general resurrection, with its "already but not yet" status, would seem to provide grounds for a stance that affirms genetic advances as proleptic realizations of the resurrection, but warns against promises and expectations of a complete union of our bodies with our aims, ideals, and desires. For Jews, as Freundel points out, there are grounds for a strong affirmation of gene therapy as part of the divinely ordained task of *tikkun olam*, namely healing, repairing, and perfecting the world (Freundel 1994: 133, 136).

Conclusion

I have argued that up to now no arguments from a religious perspective have succeeded in showing why, from the relevant religious perspective, gene therapy as currently envisioned should be rejected in principle or because it inevitably employs immoral or otherwise suspect means, or that, other things equal, gene therapy should yield priority to more conventional methods of achieving its aims. It is time to move beyond the tired debate over whether religious traditions should support gene therapy or not, and to focus instead on other pressing issues. Among the latter are the issues involving appropriate levels of risk and benefit, the relativity of the benefits of gene therapy to its costs and to other biomedical (and nonbiomedical) priorities, fairness in allocating gene therapy research and ensuring access to its benefits, and mechanisms to ensure that all uses of genetic technologies are informed and consensual – matters on which the ranges of religious and secular viewpoints overlap significantly; the development of methods that minimize or eliminate the risk to embryos and future persons; and finally, determination of what place, if any, practices, and strategies of genetic self-formation should play in religious practices and strategies of self-formation by which ethical subjects are rightly related to themselves and to others.

Notes

1   See, for example, the comments by John Fletcher and James Watson at the 1998 Engineering the Human Germline Symposium at the University of California at Los Angeles, found in the summary report (Engineering the Human Germline Symposium, Summary Report, 1998).

2   Among ecclesial statements, the sole exception of which I am aware occurs in a 1995 statement adopted by the Seventh Day Adventist Church which simply rejects GLT, without argument or elaboration, on the grounds that the latter "could affect the image of God in future generations" (Seventh Day Adventist Church 1995: 95).

3   James Keenan argues similarly that GLT is morally problematic inasmuch as it collapses the distinction between the person and the disease, but unlike Meilaender he does not argue that this problem is sufficient to rule out GLT (Keenan 1990).

4   The latter distinction accounts for the use of enhancements in a therapeutic regimen, for example, an increase of the resistance of stem cells to anticancer drugs (Torres 1997).

5   There are, to my knowledge, no other arguments that find a presumption in favor of nongenetic over genetic means to enhancement. In at least one case, such a presumption is explicitly denied: according to Azriel Rosenfeld, rabbinic Judaism allows any procedure that is permissibly performed by standard forms of surgery to be performed by gene surgery. Hence, if (as many authorities agree) cosmetic surgery to relieve psychological distress is permitted, then gene surgery to achieve cosmetic effects would also be permissible (Rosenfeld 1979: 402).

6   Religious ethicists who assume this task could begin with sociologist Margaret Stacey's unpublished critique of the Clothier Report (Storer and Torrance 1995: 28), and from anthropologist Paul Rabinow's description of some of the ways in which genetic knowledges and practices produce ethical (self- forming) and pastoral (meaning-creating) forms (Rabinow 1992).

7   See McKenny 2000. The analysis that follows relies heavily on the second and third sections of this essay.

8   Nor do all liberal Protestants and ecumenists support them. Lutheran Ted Peters argues that neither nature generally nor DNA in particular has normative status or represents, in its present form, God's final plan for humanity. Because nature is created *ex nihilo*, it has no ultimacy in itself; because God continues to create (*creatio continua*), nature as it has evolved so far has no normative status (Peters 1998: 28). However, by describing creation entirely in terms of futurity and novelty and by describing human "co-creating" with God entirely in terms of technology, Peters risks simply baptizing a certain strand of modern utopianism.

9 Both Protestants and Roman Catholics explicitly refer to Christology in stating their respective views on the normativity of human nature. However, in both cases the Christology largely reaffirms the more fundamental importance of notions of life (Protestants) or order (Catholics).

References

Avise, R. S., *The Genetic Gods* (Cambridge, MA: Harvard University Press, 1998).

Bayertz, K., "The normative status of the human genome: a European perspective." In Hoshino, K., ed., *Japanese and Western Bioethics: Studies in Moral Diversity* (Dordrecht: Kluwer Academic Publishers, 1997), pp. 167–80.

Bloch, E., *The Principle of Hope* (Cambridge, MA: MIT Press), 3 vols.

Catholic Bishops' Joint Committee on Bioethical Issues, *Genetic Intervention on Human Subjects: The Report of a Working Party* (London: Linacre Centre, 1995).

Catholic Health Association of the United States, *Human Genetics: Ethical Issues in Genetic Testing, Counseling, and Therapy* (St. Louis: Catholic Health Association of the United States, 1990).

Chapman, A. R., "Christian perspectives on human genetics." *Annual of the Society of Christian Ethics* 18 (1998).

Church in Wales, Board of Mission, Division for Social Responsibility, *Human Genetic Screening and Therapy: Some Moral and Pastoral Issues* (Penarth: Church in Wales Publications, 1992).

Congregation for the Doctrine of the Faith, "Instruction on respect for human life in its origin and on the dignity of human reproduction." In Shannon, T. A. and Cahill, L. S., eds., *Religion and Artificial Reproduction* (New York: Crossroads, 1988), pp. 140–77.

Dawkins, R. *The Selfish Gene* (New York: Oxford University Press, 1989), 2nd ed.

Engineering the Human Germline Symposium, Summary Report, www.ess.ucla.edu/huge/ (June 1998).

Feinberg, J. S., "A theological basis for genetic intervention." In Kilner, J. F., Pentz, R. D., and Young, F. E., eds., *Genetic Ethics: Do the Ends Justify the Genes?* (Grand Rapids, MI: Eerdmans, 1997), pp. 183–92.

Freundel, B., "Personal religious perspectives: Judaism." In Nelson, J. R., ed., *On the New Frontiers of Genetics and Religion* (Grand Rapids, MI: Eerdmans, 1994).

Hanson, M. J., "Indulging anxiety: human enhancement from a Protestant perspective." *Christian Bioethics* 5 (1999): 121–38.

Harron, F., ed., *Genetic Engineering: Social and Ethical Consequences* (Cleveland: Pilgrim Press, 1984).

Heselhaus, D., und Schmidt, K. W., "Somatische Gentherapie – Aspekte aus der theologischen Diskussion." *Wiener Medicinische Wochenschrift* 5/6 (1994): 17–20.

Jonas, H., *The Imperative of Responsibility* (Chicago: University of Chicago Press, 1984).

Keenan, J., SJ., "What is morally new in genetic engineering?" *Human Gene Therapy* 1 (1990): 289–98.

Keenan, J., SJ, "Whose perfection is it, anyway? A virtuous consideration of enhancement." *Christian Bioethics* 5 (1999): 104–20.

von Kooten Niekerk, K., in Huebner, J. and von Schubert, H., Hg., *Biotechnologie und Evangelische Ethik* (Frankfurt: Campus Verlag, 1992).

McKenny, G. P., *To Relieve the Human Condition: Bioethics, Technology and the Body* (Albany, NY: SUNY Press, 1997).

McKenny, G. P., "Gene therapy, ethics, religious perspectives." In Murray, T. H. and Mehlman, M. J., eds., *Encyclopedia of Ethical, Legal and Policy Issues in Biotechnology* (New York: Wiley & Sons, 2000), pp. 300–11.

McKenny, G. P., "Religion, biotechnology and the integrity of nature: a critical examination." In Hanson, M. J., *Religion and Biotechnology: Critical Perspectives* (Washington, DC: Georgetown University Press, 2000).

Meilaender, G., "Mastering our gen(i)es: when do we say no?" *Christian Century* 107 (1990): 872–5.

Nelkin, D. and Lindee, S., *The DNA Mystique: The Gene as Cultural Icon* (New York: W. H. Freeman, 1995).

Peters, T., "Genes, theology and social ethics: are we playing God?" In Peters, T., ed., *Genetics: Issues of Social Justice* (Cleveland: Pilgrim Press, 1998), pp. 1–45.

Pope John Paul II, "Biological research and human dignity." *Origins* 12 (1982), pp. 342–3.

Pope John Paul II, "The ethics of genetic manipulation." *Origins* 13 (1983), pp. 385–9.

Porter, J., "What is morally distinctive about genetic engineering?" *Human Gene Therapy* 1 (1990): 419–24.

Rabinow, P., "Artificiality and enlightenment: from sociobiology to biosociality." In Crary, J. and Kwinter, S., eds., *Incorporations* (New York: Zone, 1992), pp. 234–52.

Rifkin, J. *Algeny* (New York: Penguin, 1983).

Rosenfeld, A., "Genetic engineering." In Rosner, F., and Bleich, J. D., eds., *Jewish Bioethics* (Brooklyn: Hebrew Publishing Co., 1979), pp. 402–8.

Rosner, F., *Modern Medicine and Jewish Ethics* (New York: Yeshiva University Press, 1991), 2nd ed.

Seventh-Day Adventist Church, *Statements, Guidelines and Other Documents* (Silver Spring, MD: Seventh Day Adventist Church, 1995).

Shannon, T. A., "Genetics, ethics and theology: the Roman Catholic discussion." In Peters, T., ed., *Genetics: Issues of Social Justice* (Cleveland: Pilgrim Press, 1998), pp. 144–79.

Shinn, R. L., "Genetics, ethics and theology: the ecumenical discussion." In Peters, T., ed., *Genetics: Issues of Social Justice* (Cleveland: Pilgrim Press, 1998), pp. 122–43.

Shuman, J. S., "Desperately seeking perfection: Christian discipleship and medical genetics." *Christian Bioethics* 5 (1999): 139–53.

Storer, W. and Torrance, I., eds., *Human Genetics: A Christian Perspective* (Edinburgh: The Church of Scotland Board of Social Responsibility, 1995).

Taboada, P., "Human enhancement: is it really a matter of perfection?" *Christian Bioethics* 5 (1999): 183–96.

Torres, J. M., "On the limits of enhancement in gene transfer: drawing the line." *Journal of Medicine and Philosophy* 22 (1997): 43–57.

United Methodist Church, *New Developments in Genetic Science* (Nashville, TN: United Methodist Publishing House, 1992).

World Council of Churches, *Manipulating Life* (Geneva: World Council of Churches, 1982).

World Council of Churches, *Biotechnology: Its Challenges to the Churches and the World* (Geneva: World Council of Churches, 1989).

Zoloth-Dorfman, L., "Mapping the normal human self: the Jew and the mark of otherness." In Peters, T., ed., *Genetics: Issues in Social Justice* (Cleveland: Pilgrim Press, 1998), pp. 180–202.

22

"Race," Genetics, and Human Difference

HUSSEIN KASSIM

The geneticist has a definite answer if questioned about the content of the word "race." It is that in the case of the human species the term does not correspond to any objectively definable entity.

Albert Jacquard (1984)

I Introduction

Discoveries in the field of genetics have had a profound impact on the conceptions of "race" and the conceptualizations of human difference that dominated elite and popular thinking in the Western world from the middle of the nineteenth century until after the Second World War. Belief in the inferiority of the nonwhite peoples with whom exploration, trade, and conquest had brought Europeans into contact during the "age of discovery" turned with the development of the natural sciences into the conviction that the differences between human groups were not cultural or social, but innate, permanent, and biological. "Race," it was believed, "explained individual character and temperament, the structure of social communities, and the fate of human societies" (Stepan 1982: 170). Considered "the prime determiner of all the important traits of body and soul, of character and personality, of human beings and nations . . . this thing called 'race' [was regarded as] a fixed and unchangeable part of the germ plasm, which transmitted from generation to generation, unfolds in each people as a characteristic expression of personality and culture" (Montagu 1997: 55). Behavior, both individual and collective, was held to be explicable in racial terms.

The development of genetics has substantially undermined this system of belief. It has refuted the idea that mankind is divided into different "types" or "races" which occupy preordained positions in a hierarchy of intellectual ability and moral worth. Genetic science has demonstrated that there is no biological entity that corresponds to the concept of "race" advanced by racial theorists or used in everyday language. The physical characteristics, once regarded as unchangeable, and on which racial categorization was founded, have been shown to be superficial and variable. The fact of overwhelming similarity rather than immutable difference between human beings has been established, and the mechanisms of heredity and the level at which human variability occurs – individual, not group – have been uncovered. Racial theorizing has been revealed as an instance of biological determinism, where differences between, and the positions of, individuals or socially-defined groups are explained as though they arise from inherited or inborn distinctions. The development of genetics has, moreover, coincided with the decline of "scientific racism," that is, the use of the "language, concepts and authority of science...to support the belief that certain human groups were inherently inferior to others as measured by some socially-defined criteria such as intelligence or civilized behavior" (Stepan 1982: ix).

Though revolutionary in its implications, the impact of genetics on thinking about human difference should not be exaggerated. First, the legacy of the nineteenth century has shown remarkable tenacity. The conviction that "races" are real still persists, even if the scientific underpinnings for such a belief have been removed. As an explanatory factor or meaningful category, "race" continues to figure in popular usage, as well as in some branches of science (Malik 1996; Kohn 1995). Second, to the extent that the typological conception has receded, factors other than gene theory have also played a part in forcing its retreat. Developments within anthropology and the emergence of the social sciences, as well as political factors, such as the opposition to Nazism and fascism in Europe between the wars and the enshrining of antiracism as part of the Cold War order, have been very important (Stepan 1982; Kohn 1995). Third, while the understanding of heredity and human variability brought by genetics may have answered important questions, it has also raised new fears and perhaps created new racist possibilities (Kohn 1995). Finally, ignorance and misunderstanding about genetics, as well as straightforward white supremacism, have ensured the survival of some of the myths associated with the typological conception.

The extent to which genetics has transformed the way in which human variation and racial difference are conceived can best be assessed by considering how "race" came to be conceptualized from the end of the eighteenth century, and the role of science which was instrumental in establishing and validating this new notion. The development of this conception and scientific arguments about "race" are examined in section ii. In section iii, the processes whereby the typological conception gradually gave way to a new understanding and the role in genetics in undermining the idea of "race" as type, are examined. Section iv, finally, explores the survival of "race" as an analytic category.

II Race as Type

Until the late eighteenth and early nineteenth century, it was believed that all human beings were descended from a single ancestral pair. This doctrine, *monogenism*, was rooted in a Christian cosmology that constituted the basis of understanding the natural world. In the words of St. Augustine:

> Whoever is anywhere born a man, that is, a rational, mortal animal, no matter what unusual appearance he presents in color, movement, sound, nor how peculiar he is in

some part, or quality of his nature, no Christian can doubt he springs from that one protoplast . . . if they are human, they are descended from Adam. (Cited in Stepan 1982: 1)

Unity, however, did not preclude difference. The striking variations in human physique, color, and temperament were explained, for example, by the naturalist, the Comte de Buffon (1707–88), in terms of a process of "degeneration" that began after the expulsion from the Garden of Eden. The impact of the environment was also invoked. The Swedish naturalist, Carl Linneaus (1707–78), in the first formal definition of human "races" in modern taxonomic terms, constructed a four-fold classification of man that associated differences in color, temperament, and stature with the climatic conditions prevailing in the four known regions of the world (1758). Other writers, such as Immanuel Kant (1724–1804), speculated on the existence of "internal powers," which caused the differences in human form. Common ancestry, moreover, did not imply equality. Blumenbach (1752–1840), a committed monogenist and cultural relativist, proposed a hierarchy which put "Caucasians" – a new term which he introduced to describe Europeans – at the top, since he considered them the most beautiful amongst humankind. For some, the appearance, habits, and practices of nonwhite peoples, in particular, their heathenism, nakedness, and blackness, signaled their inferiority.

Although contrasts in physique and habit between human groups were the subject of interest and speculation, understandings of the nature of human difference were very different from what they later became. The differences between peoples were regarded as social, moral, and cultural. They were regarded as the outcome of differing political arrangements or as the (reversible) effects of environment, climate, geography or landscape (Banton 1998; Hannaford 1996). The inferiority of non-European peoples was not generally construed as permanent or innate. Such an understanding only emerged with the development of new systems of thought and particularly of the natural sciences. Moreover, the notion of race, which came into use in the sixteenth century, had quite different connotations from its nineteenth-century usage. In earlier times, it was used to assert lineage, kinship, or descent (Banton 1998; Hannaford 1996). Employed in a genealogical sense, it was not used to signify differences in color or other physical attributes, nor did it carry implications of permanent, natural difference. It was not considered to hold any analytical value (Banton 1998).

From the end of the eighteenth century, however, a new perspective on human differences began to emerge. The retreat or defeat of nonwhite peoples in the face of European conquest and expansionism reinforced a sense of European superiority. Closer, increased, and more prolonged contact between European and non-European peoples raised questions about the adequacy of existing monogenist explanations of human difference. Environmental explanations were susceptible when the physical characters of human beings failed to change when they moved to different climes. Moreover, the variety of human cultures and the range of physiques encountered by "white" Europeans suggested considerable diversity. Within this context arose the conviction that the differences between human groups were not superficial or temporary, but deeply rooted and unamenable to change. *Polygenism*, the once heretical doctrine that humanity is divided into "races" that are aboriginally distinct, permanently different, and fundamentally unequal, challenged the monogenist ortho-doxy and became a respectable, widely held position.

The conflict between monogenism and polygenism was fought out on an increas-ingly scientific domain as the natural sciences developed in the late eighteenth and early nineteenth centuries.[1] Rationalist methods that eschewed metaphysical and theological approaches in favor of logical classification based on empirical inquiry came to be applied to natural history in general and to humankind in particular. Man, whom classical and Christian thought had kept apart from nature and thus "saved" from naturalism, came to be seen as part of the natural order and became the object of scientific inquiry. Crucially, the sciences supplied polygenism with the concepts and authority that enabled it to triumph by mid-century. A central concept was the notion of "type" – a term introduced by Georges Cuvier (1769–1832), the French scientist regarded as founder of geology, paleontology, and modern comparative anatomy – to convey the sense of permanent and essential difference between the races. (The notion of "type" had the advantage that it avoided the difficulties sur-rounding the definition of "species" which beset natural scientists.)

Polygenists contended that humankind was divided into different "types", distin-guishable by an assemblage of particular physical characteristics: skin color, hair texture, head size, or shape. These traits, they deemed, were innate and hereditary. Each "type" occupied a position in the natural hierarchy, commensurate with its endowments and abilities, as well as its level of cultural attainment. By identifying the particular "type" to which an individual belonged, they held that it was possible to determine his or her behavior, mental capacity and moral worth. For polygenists, therefore, "race" held the key to understanding all human action. Representative of this view was the declaration of the anatomist, Robert Knox (1791–1862): "with me, 'race' or hereditary descent is everything. It stamps the man."

The task of establishing the various human "types," as well the criteria by means of which the "races" of mankind might be defined and ranked, was taken up by anthropologists, using a range of anthropometric methods. Particular attention was directed toward the skull. Cuvier, like many others, employed the cephalic index – the ratio between the breadth of the skull and its length expressed as a percentage – which had been developed by the Dutch anatomist, Peter Camper, in the late eight-eenth century, to establish the differences between human groups. He argued that the three human races, Caucasian, Mongolian, and Ethiopian, were ranked in that order according to their respective level of intelligence. Similarly, in the USA, Samuel Morton (1799–1851) sought to establish that the "races" were separate and unequal by comparing the skull capacities of the five "races" of Blumenbach's classification. The results, published in *Crania Americana* and *Crania Aegyptica* in 1839 and 1844 respectively, led Morton to propose a ranking of "races" with Caucasians at the apex, followed in order by Mongolians, Malays, American Indians, and Ethiopians. Cauca-sians were further subdivided and ranked as follows: Teutons and Anglo-Saxons, Jews and Hindoos.

Morton's work was representative of the paradigm that became dominant in anthropology. The belief that humanity was separated into different types was taken as given. Evidence for the differences between the "races" and the inferiority of non-Europeans was, after all, it was claimed, plain to see. It was the task of anthropologists to see beyond the mixture of traits in any individual, to identify the underlying essence – the pure type – and to establish the various physical types by means of anthropomorphic measurement. Morton holds a special place as a practitioner in this enterprise due to his systematic empirical research.[2] His findings reached a wide and receptive audience due to their reproduction by other authors, including Arthur de Gobineau (1816–1882), who popularized them in his influential *Essai sur l'inégalité des races humaines* (Banton 1998).

Arguments in support of polygenism were grounded also in zoology. Louis Agassiz (1807–73), a Swiss naturalist, who became professor of Zoology at Harvard and the leading spokesman for polygeny in the US, argued that human "races" were created as separate species in "centers of creation" and that each race flourished within its home geographical range (Gould 1996: 74–82). This view was echoed by Josiah Nott (1804–73) and George Gliddon (1809–57), who emphasized the vital connection between aboriginal types and zoological "provinces" (Banton 1998: 54–62). Agassiz cited the depiction of ancient Egyptians in tomb paintings and the skin color of mummies, which he held demonstrated that racial differences had remained unchanged over thousands of years, as evidence of the antiquity of the races. Similar arguments were put forward in Britain by Charles Hamilton Smith (1776–1859), "the pioneer of racial typology in Britain" (Banton 1998: 68), and a follower and friend of Cuvier.

By the mid-nineteenth century, polygenism had supplanted monogenism as the new orthodoxy. It offered a more convincing account of human differences than its rival, was supported by scientific expertise and agreed with the sense that Europeans had of themselves in the world. Its dominance, indeed, lasted until well into the twentieth century. It not only survived, but was absorbed and reproduced in, Darwin's theory of evolution. The Darwinist revolution swept away many long-standing beliefs about the natural world, but it did not bring about a radical revision in thinking about race.[3] Although a monogenist and an abolitionist, Darwin (1809–92) subscribed to prevailing views of racial difference and inequality, and in *The Descent of Man*, used the theory of natural selection to account for differences between the "races" in their degree of civilization. With respect to physical differences between the "races," Darwin could see no evidence that characteristics such as skin color or hair texture conferred any biological advantage and concluded that their emergence could not, therefore, be explained by natural selection. To account for these traits, Darwin appealed to sexual selection, arguing that these non-adaptive racial characteristics persisted "not because of the advantage they conferred to an individual in the struggle for life, but because of the advantage they conferred in the struggle to find a mate" (cited in Stepan 1982: 59). "Early in the history of the human species, before man was civilized", Darwin argued, "all human individuals were racially alike. As the human population divided into small groups, and spread into new areas of the globe, different physical traits would appear by spontaneous variation, such as dark skin or woolly hair. By sexual selection, different traits in different groups of mankind would come to be favored and would be spread in the tribe" (cited in Stepan 1982: 64). The distinction drawn by Darwin between traits that were changeable, adaptive and evolutionary useful, and traits that were fixed, prehistoric and non-adaptive was of particular importance, since the latter – skull size, head-shape, skin color, and hair texture – were the very same that were regarded by polygenists as racial markers and served as the basis of racial typology.

Not only was Darwin's thinking consistent with many of the precepts of polygenism, but his theory of evolution provided "a new language to express old prejudice" (Stepan 1982: ch. 4). "Evolution" was interpreted as a linear progression towards higher levels of civilization. The inferiority of the "lower races" was explained in terms of a failure to advance along the evolutionary scale. Appeal was frequently made to the theory of recapitulation – "ontogeny recapitulates phylogeny" – according to which "an individual in its own growth passes through a series of stages representing adult ancestral forms in their correct order" (Gould 1996: 142–51). Recapitulation provided a criterion for the ranking of human groups by evolution (Gould 1996: 57). According to the theory, black people progressed no further than a stage equivalent to childhood among whites (Gould 1996: 132–5).

In addition, terms, such as "struggle," "fight," "conflict," and "survival," that were used by Darwin, offered a new vocabulary in which human action and interaction could be expressed. The language and concepts introduced – or that were believed to have been introduced – by Darwin were applied and misapplied by Social Darwinists, who used them in relation to human groups, including "race" (Banton 1998; Malik 1996). Gumplowicz (1838–1909), for example, wrote of the "perpetual struggle between the races for dominance" (cited in Banton 1998: 93). In an age of imperialist rivalry, where nations were conceptualized as racial entities, Darwinism was applied to relations between states and the imperial mission. Joseph Chamberlain, for example, declared that "the British race is the greatest of governing races the world has ever seen," while Lord Rosebery asked rhetorically, "What *is* Empire but the predominance of race?" (both cited by Malik 1996: 115). In Germany, Darwinism gave a new form of expression to a radicalized *völkish* nationalism that was associated with the Romantic tradition. Perhaps the best known exponent was the zoologist, Ernst Haekel (1834–1919), who wrote about "race" imperialism and the need for Lebensraum, and was later an important Social Darwinist source for Nazi ideologues.

Darwin was also drawn upon by advocates of eugenics, "the study of agencies which under social control may improve or impair the racial qualities of future generations either physically or mentally" (Stepan 1982), which emerged as a powerful intellectual movement in the late nineteenth century. Eugenicists called for the improvement of the racial stock by selective breeding. In the UK, their energies were directed towards the class system. Conservatives, such as Francis Galton, Darwin's cousin, and widely regarded as the founder of eugenics, proposed that steps be taken to encourage greater fecundity among the elite, while progressives called for eugenic measures to combat the established social order regarded by them as dysgenic (Malik 1996: 116). In the US, by contrast, "race" was the major concern. Eugenicists campaigned successfully for a halt to the immigration of inferior races.[4]

The assumptions about the nature of heredity that underlay these versions of Social Darwinism – that human attributes are "discrete measurable entities, fixed by heredity and found in different quantities in individuals and groups" (Stepan 1982: ch. 5) and that traits are "innate or acquired, but not both" (ibid.) – were widespread. They also highlighted a principal weakness of Darwin's theory of evolution, which lacked a satisfactory account of inheritance. Darwin himself subscribed to a "mixing" theory, according to which the characters an offspring inherits from its parents are averaged out. There was nothing in this view that contradicted the polygenist belief that the differences between the "races" were both ancient and fixed. It was only the rediscovery of Mendel's work on heredity that provided the microfoundations for Darwin's theory and the basis for work in genetics that ultimately demonstrated the falsity of the polygenist credo.

III A New Paradigm

The decline of the typological view was not sudden, but took place over a number of decades. The development of genetics undoubtedly played a major role in undermining the polygenist orthodoxy and replacing it with a new understanding of heredity. It was not, though, the only important factor. Racial science had been tarnished by the use to which it was put under, and the horrors perpetrated by, the Third Reich, such that the repudiation of its precepts formed an elemental part of the reaction to Nazism (Kohn 1995).[5] As Kohn has argued, scientific antiracism formed a central plank of the post-1945 order, as illustrated by the UNESCO Statements of 1950 and 1951. Also, the social sciences reached an important stage in their development in the 1930s and 1940s. Explanations for social action came to be sought in the social rather than the biological domain. Sociologists, such as Patrick Geddes, J. A. Hobson, and Leonard Hobhouse were no longer in the thrall of the natural sciences, ascribing poverty, not to the natural attributes of individuals, but to the operation of the social system.

Developments in anthropology – a third factor – put old certainties into question and downgraded the discipline's traditional preoccupation with human anatomy. First, the long-standing difficulty of identifying the relevant differences between the human types, which produced different estimates of the overall number of races, as well as competing racial taxonomies, was a problem that had always beleaguered the discipline, and which grew more difficult to justify. Second, Franz Boas (1858–1942) raised a more fundamental challenge. In his study of immigrants to the US, which involved the measurement of the skulls of more than 17,000 adults and their children, Boas showed that this key physical feature did not remain unchanged from generation to generation, but was susceptible to environmental influence. The impact of his demonstration of the plasticity of the skull, though not immediately felt, was utterly at odds with the traditional belief in the permanence of racial types. Third, anthropology had diversified. Culture emerged as a new field of inquiry, where anthropologists were no longer concerned with investigating the human anatomy. Malinowski and Radcliffe-Brown pioneered a different kind of anthropological enterprise, oriented towards ethnology. In these new areas, notions of inferiority and superiority were not as relevant, and indeed many rejected the notion of a scale of human worth and instead embraced forms of relativism.[6]

The emergence of modern genetics was critical. Heredity had been a concern of biologists since Darwin, but advances were made only after the rediscovery of the work of Gregor Mendel (1822–44) in 1900. Mendel had shown that heredity was not miscible, as Darwin had thought, but particulate and variable. Still, it was only when the dispute between Mendelians, whose approach to heredity involved examining Mendel's laws of the independent assortment and recombination of unit characters, and biometricians led by Karl Pearson, who approached heredity from a statistical perspective in the search for a mathematical expression of the correlation between traits and the intensity of resemblance between individuals, was resolved in the 1930s that the two methods merged in what became modern genetics. In the period between the wars, a new generation of geneticists, including Lancelot Hogben and R. A. Fischer, questioned the beliefs that undergirded polygenism and eugenics. Subsequent advances established a new understanding of human differences.

Genetics has identified the mechanism of heredity in human beings and the source of variation in humans, demonstrating that the idea of "race" in the typological sense has no basis in biology. It has shown that variability occurs at the level of individuals, not at the level of any mystical collective entity entitled "race." Variability results from the action of genes, independent units that are combined or recombined in human reproduction. Humans inherit two sets of genes, called "alleles," one from each parent. Individuals differ, because each offspring has a 50 percent chance of getting one or other allele from each parent or a 25 percent chance of receiving any particular gene. The fact of individual variability in hereditary characteristics undermines means that pure "races" do not exist in the sense of group of individuals corresponding to the same racial type.

Moreover, the physical traits regarded by the old anthropology as permanent racial markers, fixed and heritable, have been revealed by genetics to be in fact superficial and variable. The morphological characters used by anthropologists as the basis of their taxonomies for categorizing the various human types are categorized by geneticists as phenotypic; that is, they are observable traits, associated with certain genes, but environmentally sensitive and, therefore, changeable. For the geneticist, the genotype is the principal focus of attention. The significance of the distinction between genotype and phenotype for the typological conception of "race" is brought out well by Montagu:

> Taxonomic exercises in classification of assemblages of phenotypical...traits...will never succeed in elucidating relationships of different groups of humankind to one another, for the simple reason that it is not assemblages of traits that undergo change in the formation of the individual and the group, but rather the single complex units, the genes, which are physiologically associated with those traits...[It] is not possible to classify the various groups of humankind by means of the traits the older anthropologist have used, because those traits do not behave as complexes; they behave as the expression of many independent units, linked and unlinked, in interaction with the environment that have entered into their formation. (1997: 104)

In other words, the mistake of the old science lay in treating "as units the complexes of characteristics of individuals, races, and species, and [the attempt] to find rules governing the inheritance of such complexes. Mendel was first to understand that it was the inheritance of separate traits, and not complexes of traits, which had to be studied" (Dobzhansky 1937: 62). In addition, the physical characters relied on

309

for racial classifications involve "a minute fraction of the great number of genes that would be necessary to consider in attempting to make any real – that is to say, genetically analytic – classification of humankind" (Montagu 1997: 107).

Genetics has replaced the static typological conception with a dynamic view of human difference. The relevant differences between human groups or "populations," defined as a class of interacting individuals whose members have inherited common characteristics in different combinations subject to continual modifications are from a geneticist's perspective identifiable and measurable, but lie in gene frequency and the composition of the gene pool rather than the possession of race-specific physical traits. Importantly, populations differ in relative rather than absolute ways, tending to grade into each other. The unity of the human "race" is underlined by the fact that the various human populations share an overwhelming percentage of genes and that there is a small, but significant, gap between all human beings and even the closest nonhuman relative. As the geneticist Stephen Jones has remarked, "all families and all nations are connected by an invisible web of kinship" (1997: p. xiii).

Against the background of fundamental similarity, geneticists explain the differences between populations by migration from an original ancestral group, followed by geographical isolation. Two sets of mechanisms came into play with respect to those isolated groups, thus accounting for the differentiation of "a single collective genotype into several separate genotypes, and the subsequent development of a variety of phenotypes within these genotypes" (Montagu 1997: 114). The first are primary. They include genetic drift, where in a genetically heterogeneous group, "spontaneous random fluctuations in gene frequencies will . . . in the course of time, occur, so that originally relatively homogeneous groups will come to exhibit certain differences from other isolated groups which started with a similar genetic equipment" (Montagu 1997: 112), and genetic mutation, where a particular gene undergoes a physical change, "so that its physiological expression differs from that of the older form of the gene, and its action may express itself in the appearance of a new trait or new form of an old one" (ibid.). Both factors are constantly at work, indicating that the variation of human groups is a natural and continuous process. The second set of mechanisms involve the "action of factors such as environment, natural, social and sexual selection, inbreeding [and], outbreeding" (ibid.). Environmental conditions may, for example, favor some features above others, while social *mores* may prohibit marriage across ethnic groups, so perpetuating and consolidating differences, say, between blacks and whites in American society.

Genetics therefore offers a very different understanding of the differences between populations. Differences are explained in terms of the "frequency distributions of one or more genes within a population that differ from those of other populations . . . [representing] the effects of the action of different isolating agents on a common stock of genetic materials . . . ["Racial"] differences simply represent more or less temporary or episodic expressions of variation in the relative frequencies of genes in different parts of the species population" (Montagu 1997: 117). It rejects absolutely the idea that humankind is divided permanently into separate "races" with characteristic physical traits. According to Kohn:

What biology has done with "race" bears a certain resemblance to what physics has done with particles. It has extracted the contradictions and ambiguities hidden within the solid discrete certainties of traditional "race" theory and founded the populational concept upon them. Examined at the quantum level, races are revealed as fluid, elusive and paradoxical, if not illusory. (1995: 88)

IV The Survival of "Race"

Genetics may have demonstrated that "race" has no meaning as a biological concept, but it has not succeeded in eliminating use of the term in the old sense from either popular or scientific usage, nor has it rendered "race" redundant as an analytical term. In popular language, "race" is used as though synonymous with color. Differences in skin color and other physical attributes are interpreted as evidence that "races" possess an objective reality, and the basis for the idea that there is a difference in kind between human groups, so defined. Such beliefs in turn provide the foundation for the view that an individual's behavior or dispositions are explicable in terms of "race" conceived as a primordial entity, and that these visible differences are correlated with negative moral or intellectual attributes. One example of an appeal to "race" that demonstrates the survival of such views is that which appeared in an article in *Wisden Cricketers' Almanack* in 1995, entitled "Is it in the blood?," which claimed that the desire to play for England was a "matter of biology" and "that Asians and Negroes [*sic*] do not feel the same pride and identification with England as the white man" (quoted in Jones 1997: ix). The persistence of such beliefs can perhaps be attributed to a combination of what might be described as common-sense naturalism, the legacy of imperialism, and ignorance about genetics.

The conviction that "race" and racial difference are primordial can also take forms which make no appeal to biology. The essentialism that characterized the typological conception can be expressed in the language of culture and cultural difference. This is the basis of the "new racism," where racial or national identity is defined in terms of a cultural essence, which an individual either has or does not have, and which cannot be learned (Barker 1981).

"Race" is also perpetuated by government and law. The most common usage relates to the notion of "race relations," originally used in the United States at the beginning of the twentieth century to denote relations between blacks and whites. This phrase is problematic, misleading, and perhaps dangerous, in that it gives legitimacy to the idea that pure "races" exist, as well as implying "that the relations between persons thought . . . to belong in different 'races' differ in some important respect from relations between persons thought to belong in the same race" (Banton 1988: 2). A similar concern has been expressed by the same author regarding the inclusion of the category "Mixed-race" (1988: 1) in the UK population census of 2001.

In the social sciences, the use of "race" as an analytic concept continues, but has been vehemently contested. From one perspective, it is argued that, even though it has no biological meaning, use of the term is justified because "race" forms part of social reality, is created, constructed, and deployed by social actors, who attribute significance to skin color and differentiate groups accordingly, and contributes to the shaping of social interaction, the patterning of social order, and political outcomes. Investigating the processes that bring about conceptions of "race" and racial difference in different social environments is fundamental, according to proponents of this view, for understanding how a particular society functions, and "race," as socially defined, is indispensable as an analytic category. The competing perspective, closely associated with Robert Miles, argues that "race" has no place as a sociological concept. "Race" may indeed be a category that is socially constructed, produced and reproduced, but it cannot be used analytically without implying an acceptance of the "existence of biological differences between human beings, differences which express the existence of distinct, self-reproducing groups" (Miles 1993). Contending in addition that it has been turned by ethnic minorities into an ideological weapon, Miles argues that the term "race" keeps alive the assumption of biological difference and obscures the fact that racism is the real problem – a charge which may have some validity when more extreme versions of Afrocentrism are taken into account (Kohn 1995: 76–87).

Nor has "race" totally disappeared from science. Although the typological conception has largely vanished from mainstream anthropology, it survives in undiluted form in some extreme right-wing journals, many of which have connections with the racial science practiced under the Third Reich. It also exercises more than a residual influence in central and eastern Europe, where, for example, until the mid-1990s visitors to the Natural History Museum in Vienna were able to inspect human types in the "Races of Man" Hall (Kohn 1995: 9–27), and the Balkans, where political leaders use racial science in support of ethnic causes (Kohn 1995: 228–52).

In physiology too, "race" has been invoked in various attempts to explain why some human groups perform better in certain sports, sociobiologists have claimed that "interracial conflict" is the expression of a natural hostility to strangers, and in evolutionary biology arguments have been put forward that contend that the details of evolution have left human groups with significantly different capacities (Kohn 1995). However, it is in psychology that the typological conception remains most deeply embedded (cf. Kohn 1995: 7). Intelligence has always been a preoccupation for racial scientists seeking to establish differences between the "races" and to rank human groups. In the early nineteenth century, the search for the key to intelligence shifted from investigating bodies, and particularly skulls by craniometry, to measuring minds (Gould 1996). The belief that cranial capacity held the answer gradually fell into disrepute, though as late as 1962, Carleton Coon used differences in skull size – famously, using pictures of an Australian aborigine and a "Chinese sage" to contrast "the Alpha and the Omega of Homo sapiens" – to argue that the human "races" had evolved separately. The new approach gave up efforts to correlate the level of intelligence with anatomical characteristics in favor of an attempt to measure mental capacity directly.

The development of the IQ test was fundamental to this endeavor. Although its originator, the French psychologist, Albert Binet (1857–1911), devised the measure in order to identify educationally backward students for extra learning assistance, and counseled against its misapplication, his invention has been used for altogether different purposes. Against those – including Binet – who believed that intelligence consisted in a number of different qualities that were nonreducible, the British statistician and psychologist Charles Spearman found that there was a correlation between the score of individuals taking a range of tests designed to assess a range of mental abilities, and argued that this demonstrated the existence of a general intelligence or core cognitive ability, which he termed "*g*." Spearman contended, moreover, that *g* was hereditary, innate, and resistant to the effects of the environment, and that, quantifiable, it could be measured by intelligence testing. These elements constitute the basis of the hereditarian theory of IQ, adopted by a school of psychologists and social scientists, particularly in the US, to support arguments about racial difference.

The Binet scale was imported to the US from France by Henry Goddard, who argued that the test scores measured innate intelligence and that the results of testing revealed a fundamental inequality between the "races." It was refined by Lewis Terman, who developed the Stanford Binet scale. A major coup for the advocates of the hereditarian school was the success of Robert Yerkes in persuading the army to test 1.75 million men during the First World War. Yerkes used the data as evidence of innate racial difference, and his findings – and the used made of them by Carl Brigham, Professor of Psychology at Harvard – were influential in bringing about the Immigration Act of 1924, which strictly limited the entry of migrants from countries with "poor genes."[7]

In the more recent past, the best known advocates of the hereditarian position have been Arthur Jensen, and Richard J. Herrnstein and Charles Murray. Based on the differences scored in IQ tests, Jensen argued in 1969 in "How much can we boost IQ scores and scholastic achievement?" that "genetic factors are strongly implicated in the average Negro–white intelligence difference." He contends that the difference can be explained with reference to selective pressures operating on the brain, and that attempts to improve educational achievement among American blacks are futile, because intelligence is fixed at a certain level by heredity. Ten years later, he repeated his contention that there is an innate deficiency of intelligence among blacks, mounted a staunch defence of Spearman's *g* and IQ testing, and argued that all God's creatures can be ranked according to their quotient of *g*. In their book, *The Bell Curve*, Herrnstein and Murray rehearse similar arguments to those made by Jensen in 1969. Their central finding is that the normal distribution of IQ scores recorded by blacks and whites in the US show the black mean to be 15 points lower than the mean for whites, and their main argument is that this difference is due to heredity.

As a number of writers have observed, these arguments are founded on the old typological conception – the belief that there is such a thing as "race," that physical differences demarcate one "race" from another, and that "race" set limits to individual capacity and group achievement. Moreover, critics have leveled various objections against the *Bell Curve*, concerning methodology, statistics, sources, weaknesses of argument, and the failure to engage with alternative views. Stephen Jay Gould (1996: 176–350, 367–90) has challenged the hereditarian perspective by an attack on the four premises on which it rests – that intelligence must be a single thing ("abstractable"), that intelligence is capable of ranking people in a linear order

313

("rankable"), that intelligence is genetically based ("hereditable"), and that an individual's intelligence is stable ("immutable") – arguing that if any single one fails, the position collapses.

Against the first ("abstractable"), Gould argues that the alternative view – that intelligence is multifarious and multidimensional – is more compelling, that the hereditarians have brought forward no evidence to support their belief in a single overarching factor of general capacity and that the notion of g is no more than a statistical artefact that commits the fallacy of reification by turning an abstract concept into an entity – in the case of intelligence, a theoretical ability into a "thing in the head." Concerning the second ("rankable"), IQ tests do, of course, produce rankings, but the supporters of intelligence testing have not demon-strated either that what is being tested is in fact intelligence rather than school performance or social background, or that IQ tests are not culturally biased (Montagu 1997: 165–9). Until they have done so, the suspicion will remain that the attempt to rank by IQ is a strategy of biological determinism – an attempt to demonstrate that oppressed and disadvantaged groups are naturally inferior and deserve their status – particularly given that the most vociferous supporters are advocates of halting social programs. As Montagu notes (ibid.), testing has played a crucial role is sustaining black stereotypes. Regarding the third ("hereditable"), Gould contends that "heritable" is falsely equated by hereditarians with "permanent" and "unchangeable," and notes, to reveal this fallacy, that an inborn, fully heritable defect in vision can be corrected by glasses. Moreover, as Montagu (1997: 164) argues, "our knowledge of the genetics of intelligence is virtually non-existent," though it is "clearly a function of many genes in interaction not only with the environment but... with the verdicts of [i.e. interpretation and evaluation by] the organism itself." In view of the centrality of this view to their position, it is incumbent on hereditarians to provide more convincing evidence for the genetic determination of intelligence. Finally, with respect to the fourth premise, neither Jensen nor Herrnstein and Murray have produced convincing arguments or reliable data to support their claim that intelligence is immutable. Given the extremeness of their position – that a person's IQ is stable and permanent, and relatively resistant to the impact of social or educational intervention – this a serious weakness. The view that intelligence is amenable to environmental factors has greater theoretical and empirical support. Even data collected on the results of IQ testing tends to show that IQ scores are correlated with socioeconomic factors and that the scores have increased within a short period by a magnitude that cannot be explained by genetic transmutation (Kohn 1995: 104–5).

Although advocates of the hereditarian view of intelligence have not been able to answer its critics convincingly, it is unlikely that the position will be abandoned. Like "race," g and IQ testing have an intuitive, commonsense attraction that seems to be confirmed by everyday experience. Moreover, to some psycholo-gists, g is something of a "philosopher's stone." Finally, recognizing its potential use in defense of the social order, right-wing agencies have made generous funds available to support intelligence-focused, racially-centered research. For these reasons, the hereditarian view is unlikely to disappear, whatever its scientific credentials.

V Conclusion

In spite of the survival of the typological conception, the continued usage of "race" as an analytic concept and attempts to use the science in the service of national or ethnic conflict,[8] genetics has had a profound impact on the conceptualization of "race" and human difference. The way in which thinking about "race" has changed since the end of the eighteenth century illustrates, moreover, that scientific inquiry does not take place in an isolated scientific republic, but is a socially embedded activity whose practitioners are influenced by wider cultural beliefs and whose findings have far-reaching implications for the life chances of all human beings. The relationship between scientific inquiry and society is complex, and the insistence either that science is independent from other human activities or that science is subordinate to the interests of a particular group is too simple. What the history of "race" demonstrates is the importance of both ensuring scientific rigor and investigating social context.

Notes

1   Though biblical sources continued to be an authority and consistency with them sought. See, for example, the debate between the British physician, James Cowles Pritchard (1786–1848), a leading monogenist, and the polygenist Robert Knox (1791–1862) and James Hunt (1833–69). It is worth nothing that the biblical story of the "curse of Ham" was sometimes quoted in support of polygenism (Genesis 10). Ham, the son of Noah, was condemned to become a "servant of servants" by his angry father. The argument was put that blacks are the descendants of Ham, which explains their inferiority. However, there is nothing in the story to suggest that Ham was black.

2   In the more recent past, Morton's methods have occasioned intense debate about scientific objectivity (Gould 1996: 82–101; Banton 1988: 51–2).

3   At the same time, in chapter 7 of *The Descent of Man*, Darwin observed: "Although the existing races of man differ in many respects, as in colour, hair, shape of skull, proportions of the body, &c, yet if their whole structure be taken into consideration they are found to resemble each other closely in a multitude of points. Many of these are of so unimportant or of so singular a nature, that it is extremely improbably that they should have been independently acquired by aboriginally distinct species or races. The same remark holds good with equal or greater force with respect to the numerous points of mental similarity between the most distinct races of man."

4   Though concern about future generations led some US states to adopt a policy of compulsory sterilization of the mentally unfit.

5   In 1936, Julian Huxley and A. C. Haddon wrote *We Europeans*, an extremely important and influential book which condemned the use of racial science by the German dictatorship.

6   Lest it be thought that proponents of the older view gently laid down, the declaration in 1940 of Earnest A. Hooton, Professor of Anthropology at Harvard, should be noted: "We must rid ourselves of the false prophets of cultural salvation and the witless preachers of human equality. The future of our species does not hang upon forms of government, economic adjustment, religious or social creeds, and purely environmental education. The future of man is dependent upon biology" (quoted in Montagu 1997: 105).

7   It is instructive that Goddard, Terman, and Brigham all later recanted, retreating from many of the key hereditarian positions that they previously held (see Gould 1996). It is also noteworthy that data from the Army Tests, showing northern blacks to have a higher IQ than southern whites, was withheld (Montagu 1997: 168).

8   Research on the genetic background of the Roma, which appears to indicate that they originally hail from India, has been used by politicians in central and eastern Europe to argue that they (the Roma) do not belong in Europe and should return to their homeland. This example offers an illustration of how modern genetics may be used for xenophobic purposes (see Kohn 1995: 212–27).

References

Banton, M.: *Racial Theories* (Cambridge: Cambridge University Press, 1998).

Barkan, E.: *The Retreat from Scientific Racism: Changing Concepts of Race in Britain and the United States Between the World Wars* (Cambridge: Cambridge University Press, 1991).

Barker, M.: *The New Racism: Conservatism and the Ideology of the Tribe* (London: Junction Books, 1981).

Dobzhansky, T.: *Genetics and the Origin of Species* (New York: Columbia University Press, 1937).

Dunn, L. C.: "Race and biology." In Kuper, L., ed.: *Race, Science and Society* (Paris: UNESCO, 1975).

Gould, S. J.: *The Mismeasure of Man*, 2nd ed. (New York: W. W. Norton and Co., 1996).

Hannaford, I.: *Race. The History of an Idea in the West* (Baltimore: The John Hopkins University Press, 1996).

Hernnstein, R. J. and Murray, C.: *The Bell Curve: The Reshaping of American Life by Difference in Intelligence* (New York: Free Press, 1994).

Jacquard, A.: *In Praise of Difference: Genetics and Human Affairs*, trans. M. Moriarty (New York: Guildford, 1984).

Jensen, A.: "How much can we boost IQ and scholastic achievement?" *Harvard Educational Review* 33 (1969), pp. 1–23.

Jensen, A.: *Bias in Mental Testing* (New York: Academic Press, 1979).

Jones, S.: *In the Blood. God, Genes and Destiny* (London: Flamingo, 1997).

Kohn, M.: *The Race Gallery: The Return of Racial Science* (London: Jonathan Cape, 1995).

Malik, K.: *The Meaning of Race: Race, History and Culture in Western Society* (London: Macmillan, 1996).

Miles, R.: *Race after "Race Relations"* (London: Routledge, 1993).

Montagu, A.: *Man's Most Dangerous Myth: The Fallacy of Race*, 6th ed. (Walnut Creek: Alma Mira, 1997).

Stepan, N.: *The Idea of Race in Science: Great Britain 1800–1960* (London: Macmillan, 1982).

23

Self-ownership, Begetting, and Germline Information

HILLEL STEINER

Introduction

It is probably fair to say that although – and with one notable exception – philosophers talking explicitly about property rights in the human body has been a relatively
recent development, this idea is implicitly present in a good deal of philosophical
discussion going back quite a long time, as well as in ordinary moral reflection. The
concept of "self- ownership", currently made famous by Robert Nozick (1974), is now
widely deployed in much philosophical debate over issues ranging from taxation and
exploitation to suicide, organ transplants, abortion, and surrogacy. And it is slowly
beginning to make its way into analyses of the numerous complex ethical issues
thrown up by modern developments in biotechnology.

Why is this concept so useful? I guess it helps to begin with a definition of it. One of
the clearest I've come across is supplied by G. A. Cohen, who construes self-ownership
as implying that

> Each person is the morally rightful owner of himself. He possesses over himself, as a
> matter of moral right, all those rights that a slaveholder has over a complete chattel slave
> as a matter of legal right, and he is entitled, morally speaking, to dispose over himself in
> the way such a slaveholder is entitled, legally speaking, to dispose over his slave. (Cohen
> 1995: 68)

The idea here is quite simple. Slavery is the paradigm form of rightlessness. A slave is
a thing: a piece of domestic livestock, an energy resource, even a body tissue bank. So
self-ownership, as the right or bundle of rights that opposes slavery, implies that each
person's body is, as we might say, *owner-occupied*. Immanuel Kant's rendering of
essentially the same idea is that it is each person's innate right to be *"his own master"*
(Kant 1965: 63).

Now the concept of self-ownership is a useful analytical tool for philosophers
because one of the main jobs they're meant to do is to identify the smaller set of
often unfamiliar foundational premises that underlie a lot of our standard factual and
ethical beliefs. It is certainly true in this regard that, among the moral rights we have
or commonly think we have, the right of self-ownership is *not* one that comes readily

to mind. But what's also true is that many of the more familiar claims we *do* tend to make – about what's just and unjust or what is and isn't a violation of moral rights – are claims which would be arbitrary, inconsistent or simply unintelligible if we refused to endorse the right of self-ownership. Something like this right seems to be the ultimate basis on which we derive – and, equally importantly, *demarcate the scope of* – such diverse and more familiar moral rights as those against murder, assault, rape, arbitrary arrest and detention, interference with free speech, free contract, free association, and so forth.

Why does my right of free speech not protect my liberty to shout in your ear? Why isn't interference with an act of rape a violation of the rapist's right of free association? Why is consensual medical surgery not a form of assault? Questions like these all have their own particular answers, of course. But as soon as we press on those answers and ask why the rights they invoke count as reasons for forbidding or allowing the actions involved, we're invariably led to something like each person's self-ownership as the common underlying right that both sustains and circumscribes them. For it is this right that's needed to reconcile and render mutually consistent the various liberties and protections afforded by those more familiar moral rights.

To say this is not, of course, to deny that there can sometimes be other justifiable limits imposed upon at least some of those familiar moral rights: limits other than those implicit in duties to respect self-ownership. What it *does* imply, however, is that such limits are thereby to be understood as limitations on the right of self-ownership itself. And it perhaps goes without saying that such justifications usually need to be fairly complex ones, if they're not to serve as "slippery slopes" for limiting self-ownership in other less desirable ways.

Now one principal use to which the concept of self-ownership has been put in recent philosophical discussion is in the analysis of moral arguments about economic redistribution. Thus Nozick famously advanced the claim that taxing persons' earnings is tantamount to expropriating portions of their labor. And since their labor is the product of their bodies, such taxation is morally equivalent to seizing parts of those bodies. Nozick says that it is morally equivalent to partial enslavement. His argument here builds on one first offered in the seventeenth century by John Locke – generally acclaimed as the founder of modern liberal thought – who said

> every Man has a *Property* in his own *Person*. This no Body has any Right to but himself. The *Labor* of his body, and the *Work* of his Hands, we may say, are properly his. (Locke 1960: 305–6)

Locke, like Nozick, uses this self-ownership right to explain two things: why slavery is *un*just and why, contrary to many authoritarian political theories including the seventeenth-century doctrines of the Divine Right of Kings, private property *is* just.

It is not hard to see, I think, how this right can have very far-reaching economic and political implications. Since everything that's not a raw natural resource is *ex hypothesi* a thing embodying human labor, it would seem to follow that very little by way of government intervention – in either the provision of services or the regulation of the economy – can be justified or, at least, justified consistent with respect for self-ownership. For such intervention can be shown to require the enforceable diversion of persons' labor or its products from the uses to which they, or those to whom they've freely transferred those things, wish to put them. So any such intervention can, in that sense, be construed as a partial expropriation of that labor and, hence, as a partial enslavement or exploitation of the persons whose labor that is. And that's why the association of self-ownership with the doctrines of classical *laisser faire* liberalism is, I suppose, reasonably transparent and widely so perceived. Private ownership of labor-embodying things must be left pretty much unencumbered by any liabilities, except ones incurred by way of contractual or compensatory duties.

The Self-ownership Paradox

While it is both foundational for our moral rights and far-reaching in its distributive implications, the right of self-ownership is strikingly beset by a paradox. For *we ourselves* are the fruits of persons' labor, and we don't need to have undergone pregnancy or raised a child to appreciate this fact. Virtually everything that goes into the production of us up to adulthood is supplied by the labor of our parents and of persons they elect or employ for that purpose. Even in cases where eggs are harvested from some persons, fertilized, and then implanted in other persons (or for that matter, in test-tubes) – or in societies where noncontractual child-rearing duties are also vested in persons other than biological parents – how can the resultant offspring claim not to have been produced by parental labor? Their parents may be more numerous than the conventional duo, but these offspring are just as much those persons' products. How can something which is so evidently the result of others' labor expenditures *not* be the fruit of their labor? And if it is their labor's product, doesn't their self-ownership give them the right to that product? By extension, moreover, aren't they in turn owned by whoever previously produced them? Why, indeed, doesn't the ownership of persons operate like the ownership of livestock, with the offspring of each successive generation being owned by whoever owns their oldest living ancestors? (On the breeding of slaves for commercial purposes, see: Stampp (1964: 237–42); Escott (1979: 45); Fogel & Engermann (1974: 78–86); David et al. (1976: 154–61); Fogel (1989: 151–3).) In short, if self-ownership gives us the right to the fruits of our labor, how can we possibly all be self-owners? How can there be a *universal* human or moral right of self-ownership?

The short answer given to this question by Locke's great seventeenth-century opponent, Sir Robert Filmer, is that there can't (Filmer 1991). Allowing that self-owners are indeed entitled to the fruits of their labor, Filmer deployed the scriptural account of creation to break the above-indicated regress and resolve the paradox it generates. His argument is straightforward enough and runs as follows. God created the Earth and all that dwelt therein, including Adam to whom God then gave sole dominion over this creation. God similarly created Eve from a part of Adam's body, and she too was placed under Adam's dominion. Being the owner of Eve, Adam becomes the owner of their offspring and their offspring's offspring – their labor belongs to him – and, upon his demise, his ownership passes to his eldest son. And so it goes on from there, with this rather comprehensive sovereign title descending primogenitally through the ages to only one person at a time who is, therefore, the sole existing person who can be a self-owner. Everyone else is owned by that current successor. Hence, Filmer concluded, kings rule by divine right and absolute monarchy is the only justified form of government.

Now evidently there are a lot of problems with this kind of story, and Locke picked up many of them in the course of the ponderous counterargument he mounted in his *First Treatise*. We can ask why Adam should have had only one designated successor. Or why subsequent designated successors should have had only one designated successor. Or why singular succession need be primogenital. Or we can wonder about Noah and the Great Flood and ask how this might have interrupted the line of descent from Adam's successor. Or we can worry about why the Old Testament reports God as apparently countenancing a plurality of kings and nations at various subsequent times. And so on. All of these, as well as his own numerous inconsistencies, can fatally embarrass some of the particular political conclusions Filmer drew from his argument. But I don't think they come anywhere near to damaging its core structure insofar as that rules out universal self-ownership.

Nor do we get much closer to damaging it by simply shedding any commitment to the sexism and the creationism of the Old Testament and embracing evolutionism. For although the evidence supporting species' evolutionary origins is overwhelming and although it is possible that our own primordial human ancestors might have been more numerous than just the two persons of the Book of Genesis, such considerations offer no hope of expanding the class of self-owning persons to the extent of universal incidence.

This, because even if some of these primordial ancestors or their designated successors might have chosen to relinquish their ownership of some or all of their offspring – and might have emancipatorily conferred self-ownership upon them – there's no reason to suppose that all of them (to say nothing of all their self-owning descendants) would have chosen likewise. Whether any of us and if so, who, would be self-owners would thus depend upon the preferences of whoever owns our parents. Maybe they own themselves. Maybe not. If they or whoever else may own them were suddenly seized by a liberal impulse, then we and our siblings would stand a pretty good chance of being self-owners. Otherwise we are, as the core of Filmer's argument suggests, simply slaves.

One apparent way out of this conundrum might be simply to declare by moral fiat, so to speak, that everyone just *is* a self-owner. But this sort of exit looks to be a singularly unsatisfactory one, because it compels us to treat as open a question that most of us – and most conceptions of justice – treat as closed: namely, "Who is morally entitled to his or her own labor and to the products of that labor?" For if the labor of conception, gestation and postnatal nurturing *doesn't* in some way entitle the laborer, it is entirely unclear why any other types of labor do. If slavery and exploitation are paradigmatically unjust, how can the moral fiat solution to the paradox of self-ownership *be* a solution?

Hence what is needed, I think, is a solution that is endogenous to the paradox – that accepts all its moral premises – and, moreover, one that doesn't merely evade it by substituting for Filmer's preposterous historical claims an equally preposterous one: that all our begetters have invariably been good liberals. What we obviously want is an argument that vests us all with the ownership of ourselves and the fruits of our labor, and that doesn't rely on a fortuitously wide incidence of liberal impulses amongst our ancestors. We want to be able to sustain our offspring's self-ownership as well as our own, regardless of whether we or our parents are liberals.

Happily, the very same theories that explicitly deploy the concept of self-ownership also supply a key premise for fashioning just such a solution. For these theories, in insisting that private ownership of labor-embodying things must be unencumbered by any liabilities other than contracted or compensatory ones, typically acknowledge that self-ownership obviously does not, and cannot, extend such protection to the ownership of raw natural resources since these *ex hypothesi* contain no labor. So we find that philosophers who use the concept of self-ownership as an analytical tool – including Locke and Nozick – standardly infer that some egalitarian or public encumbarance on *natural resource ownership* is not only justified but even logically required (Locke 1960: 306–10; Nozick 1974: 174–82; cf. Steiner 1994: 234–6; more obscurely, see Kant 1991: 71–4). Such encumbrances constitute what amounts to the compensation owed by a resource owner to all others for their exclusion from the use of that resource.

Now the things that count as natural resources – as items not imputable to human labor – are evidently many and varied and can, for the most part, be compendiously construed as the nonartefactual components of geographical sites. For the most part, because some nonartefactual elements of the biosphere, being mobile, are less easily associated with particular locations. Nevertheless, their ownership too is subject to those encumbrances. How does this fact help us to resolve the aforesaid paradox?

Solving the Paradox

Here we first need to be clear about what solutions to paradoxes amount to. What's involved in many paradoxes is that the conjunction of several well-affirmed (factual or moral) propositions leads to a contradiction. The paradox of universal self-owner-ship amply displays this property, as the following statement of it indicates:

1   It is logically possible that all persons are self-owners.
2   All self-owners own the products of their labor.
3   All persons *are* the products of other persons' labor.
4   Therefore it is logically impossible that all persons are self-owners.

Historically, as we know, some paradoxes have proved simply insoluble. Others have lent themselves to solutions reached through operations of clarifying or modifying their constituent propositions. Obviously, the plausibility of any such strategy entirely depends upon whether the reasons for those operations are themselves independently plausible. What would count as a solution here is getting rid of (4), while still sustaining both (1) and (2). That is, we need to find a way in which – unlike the moral fiat solution – affirmation of (1) doesn't imply the denial of (2). (Thus Filmer, in rejecting (1), thereby implicitly denies the paradox's solubility. Becker (1977: 37–9) construes the paradox as a reason for rejecting (2); a similar view is presented by Okin

321

(1989: ch. 4)). And I propose to do this by clarifying (2) through a modification of (3) in a way which, I hope, possesses the requisite degree of independent plausibility. Consider the following sequence of examples, each of which involves the creation of labor-embodying objects.

Suppose I steal some lumber from you, sand it down, carve it carefully and fashion it into a table. Does the fact that I've poured so much of my labor and resources into this production process give me a clear unencumbered title to the table? Presumably few would disagree that the answer must be "no."

Suppose that instead of stealing your lumber, I steal a drawing you've made of Boadicea revolting against the Romans and, before returning it, I replicate it with my photocopier. Would we say that the fact that the photocopier, copy-paper, and labor used are all mine gives me an unencumbered title to that photocopy? Again, I think the answer must be "no."

Our third example invokes the previous discussion of the ownership of natural resources. Suppose I appropriate an unowned acre of land by cultivating it and transforming it into a fertile field. So I'm not guilty of stealing in the sense that I was in the previous two cases. Does my cultivation of that acre therefore give me an unencumbered title to that field? Again "no."

In the fourth example, we return to the previous case of the photocopied drawing. Here I am with the photocopy of the Boadicea drawing which I stole from you and copied with the use of my labor and materials. Suppose that Mrs. Thatcher comes along, takes that photocopy and, before returning it, she photocopies it with her photocopier onto a sketched self-portrait, thereby superimposing the one image on the other. Does she have an unencumbered title to this new photocopy? Once again, "no."

The fifth example is the one which finally brings us back to the problem of universal self-ownership. Consider a representative pair of primordial persons whom we'll uninventively call Adam and Eve. One thing we know from Darwin about Adam and Eve is that their parents were not persons. Nor, *ex hypothesi*, were they the products of persons' labor. So these parents (and their predecessors) were, in the requisite sense, natural resources.

Now consider how Adam and Eve were produced. According to molecular biology, the critical initial step in that production process consisted in the replication and recombination of DNA strands within and between the gametes of their respective parents. The DNA strands within their parents' germ cells were, so to speak, separately photocopied, and two of these copies were then superimposed on two others to yield two zygotes, each of which then got very busy generating an extended sequence of DNA-strand replications and recombinations which, with the concomitant cell divisions and differentiations, resulted in two sizeable clusters of somatic and germ cells whom we call Adam and Eve. And that same photocopying process was again at work in *their* germ cells, preparatory to the conception of their offspring, Cain.

So is Cain the product of Adam's and Eve's labor? Is Mrs. Thatcher's photocopy the product of her labor? We can hardly deny that Adam and Eve poured a great deal of their labor and other belongings into Cain's production, just as we cannot deny that Mrs. Thatcher made a significant corresponding contribution to the production of her photocopy. But what we can deny is that *all* the factors entering into either of these two processes were the products of those producers, or of other persons who voluntarily supplied them. In the case of the photocopy, one of these factors was involuntarily supplied by you. In the case of Cain, some of these factors were supplied by nature.

The conjunction of these examples furnishes us with the desired independently plausible reason for altering the terms of our paradox in a way that generates its solution. Universal self-ownership is nonparadoxically possible if Cain's self-ownership is permissible. What the example sequence shows is that, contrary to proposition (3), Cain is *not* fully the product of his parents' labor. His production required them to combine their labor with natural resources in the form of *germline genetic information transmitted from his grandparents*. Hence denying his parents unencumbered ownership of him doesn't amount to a denial of proposition (2). That is, encumbering that ownership is permissible. And this allows us to mobilize that permissibility to sustain proposition (1). For we are now logically at liberty to stipulate that this encumbrance can consist in the various constraints standardly imposed on parents' rights over their offspring. In particular, those rights can be liable to expiry on the occasion of Cain's attaining his majority and, in the interim, can be restricted in ways consistent with his interests as a minor. And this gives us the desired solution. For since Cain's self-ownership is thus compatible with proposition (2), so is ours (Steiner 1994: 237–48, 273–80).

That said, I would be remiss to conclude without acknowledging the fact – familiar enough to readers of this volume – that the above construal of germline information as a natural resource is subject to the caveat that the content of such information can now also be manipulated to an increasing extent. So it is not entirely clear, and I'm certainly not competent to say, which part of that information can in principle be regarded as what we might call the "natural residuum": that is, which part of it is *essentially* not a human labor product and must remain the legacy of our nonhuman ancestors. Presumably any general solution to the problems of classifying species will contain an answer to this question.

Acknowledgments

I am grateful to Kristina Stern and Pat Walsh for permission to reproduce several passages from my essay "Property in the Body: A Philosophical Perspective," published in their 1997 collection.

References

Becker, L.: *Property Rights* (London: Routledge & Kegan Paul, 1977).

Cohen, G. A.: *Self-Ownership, Freedom and Equality* (Cambridge: Cambridge University Press, 1995).

David, P. et al.: *Reckoning with Slavery* (New York: Oxford University Press, 1976).

Escott, P.: *Slavery Remembered* (Chapel Hill: University of North Carolina Press, 1979).

Filmer, R.: *Patriarcha and Other Writings* (1679), ed. J. Sommerville (Cambridge: Cambridge University Press, 1991).

Fogel, R.: *Without Consent or Contract* (New York: W. W. Norton, 1989).

Fogel, R. and Engermann, S.: *Time on the Cross* (Boston: Little, Brown & Co., 1974).

Kant, I.: *The Metaphysical Elements of Justice* (1797), ed. J. Ladd (Indianapolis: Bobbs-Merrill, 1965).

Kant, I.: *The Metaphysics of Morals* (1797), ed. M. Gregor (Cambridge: Cambridge University Press, 1991).

Locke, J.: *Two Treatises of Government* (1690), ed. P. Laslett (Cambridge: Cambridge University Press, 1960).

Nozick, R.: *Anarchy, State and Utopia* (Oxford: Blackwell, 1974).

Okin, S.: *Justice, Gender and the Family* (New York: Basic Books, 1989).

Stampp, K.: *The Peculiar Institution* (London: Eyre & Spottiswoode, 1964).

Steiner, H.: *An Essay on Rights* (Oxford: Blackwell, 1994).

Steiner, H.: "Persons of lesser value: moral argument and the 'Final Solution.'" *Journal of Applied Philosophy* 12 (1995), pp. 129–41.

Stern, K. and Walsh, P., eds.: *Property Rights in the Human Body*, Occasional Papers 2 (London: King's College London, Centre of Medical Law & Ethics, 1997).

Further reading

Ackerman, B.: *Social Justice in the Liberal State* (New Haven: Yale University Press, 1980).

Arneson, R.: "Property rights in persons." *Social Philosophy & Policy* 9 (1992), pp. 425–48.

Burley, J.: "Love's labours lost?: self-ownership, left-libertarianism and cloning." *International Journal of Human Rights* (forthcoming).

Gibbard, A.: "Natural property rights." *Nous* 10 (1976), pp. 77–86.

Gold, R.: *Body Parts* (Washington, DC: Georgetown University Press, 1996).

Gorr, M.: "Justice, self-ownership and natural assets." *Social Philosophy and Policy* 12 (1995), pp. 267–91.

Harris, J.: *The Value of Life* (London: Routledge & Kegan Paul, 1985).

Mack, E.: "Self-ownership and the right of property." *The Monist* 73 (1990), pp. 519–43.

Meyers, D.: *The Human Body and the Law* (Edinburgh: Edinburgh University Press, 1970).

Munzer, S.: "An uneasy case against property rights in body parts." *Social Philosophy and Policy* 11 (1994), pp. 259–86.

Roemer, J.: *Theories of Distributive Justice* (Cambridge, MA: Harvard University Press, 1996).

Scott, R.: *The Body as Property* (London: Allen Lane, 1981).

Van Parijs, P.: *Real Freedom for All* (Oxford: Oxford University Press, 1995).

Waldron, J.: *The Right of Private Property* (Oxford: Oxford University Press, 1988).

24

Justice, Genetics, and Lifestyles

INEZ DE BEAUFORT

"Life is a gamble, at terrible odds – if it was a bet, you wouldn't take it."
(Tom Stoppard, *Rosencrantz and Guildenstern Are Dead*)

Introduction

Mrs. D, aged 47, has been diagnosed with incurable lung cancer. Her life wasn't easy. She came from a broken family, raised her daughter alone after the father of her child left her when she was pregnant. She lived on social security, earning a little extra by cleaning. And yes, she smoked. Heavily. Many of her friends felt sorry but couldn't stop themselves from saying "If only you hadn't smoked so much. You brought it upon yourself." To which Mrs D answered "Smoking got me through the hard times. As I have many alcoholics in my family I was scared to death of becoming an alcoholic. I gambled I would survive smoking. Wrong. I should have realized that for those family members who didn't die from cirrhosis of the liver, it was not because they didn't drink but because they died from cancer at a young age. It's all in the family."

Mrs. D's story raises questions about the moral judgment of unhealthy lifestyles in general. Ought people to be free to take risks with, even ruin, their health? Can we blame and punish them for unhealthy habits or are they victims of their fate? It also raises questions about the relation between lifestyle, health and the genome. We all have genetic susceptibilities to diseases we can take precautions against contracting. We may at least lessen our chances of contracting them by living a certain lifestyle. Do we have a duty to find out about our susceptibilities and our individual risk? In this chapter I will very briefly, first, discuss the freedom to live an unhealthy lifestyle, for the remainder of the paper I will tackle some problems regarding genetic susceptibilities and responsibility for health.

Chance, Choice, and Circumstances

If factors (genetic or other) we cannot control fully determine our lifestyle, there would be no sense in arguing about moral responsibility. One cannot blame a mosquito for being drawn to the light. But we do advise people to stay out of the sun, to watch their diet, and to stop smoking. Some even take our advice. Persons can – generally speaking – change (part of) their lifestyles.

On the other hand, responsibility is matter of degree. We do not create ourselves *ex nihilo*: we are influenced by our genetic make-up, our family and social circumstances. The way we live our lives consists of a complex web of genetic predispositions, social circumstances, and personal character and choice. It is this mixture of chance, choice, and circumstances that makes personal responsibility with regard to lifestyle so complex. It is unfair and simplistic to attribute too much responsibility ("stupid and irresponsible of Mrs. D: she shouldn't have smoked") and it is wrong to attribute too little ("poor powerless Mrs. D: she couldn't help smoking").

Lifestyle

For the purpose of this chapter I will speak quite loosely of "lifestyle" as a more or less consistent composite of values, goals, habits, traditions, tastes, and choices concerning the way a person leads his life. One cannot, of course, go to a supermarket to choose the most appropriate or attractive lifestyle but equally, one is not born with a lifestyle. A lifestyle develops as the person grows. Moreover, lifestyles are important to persons. As one might say: "It is not just any lifestyle, it is *my* lifestyle." The amount of freedom an individual has to choose her lifestyle differs with social circumstances wealth or poverty for example, or with psychological factors such as being a creative person or being the sort of person who follows the crowds. Luck of course may play its part. Some persons are less free than others to make choices regarding their lifestyle. A 10-year-old homeless child sniffing glue because that is the only way to escape from his daily misery obviously has not freely chosen this lifestyle. There is often social pressure to live a certain lifestyle that holds for both healthy ("We didn't see you at the health club today!") and unhealthy lifestyles ("Don't spoil the party: have another drink"). It is surely astonishing that so much attention is played to the autonomy issues concerning unhealthy lifestyles, whereas the question as to what extent persons could or should be pressured into healthy lifestyles, is seldomly raised. Apparently the fact, or the presumed fact, that a certain lifestyle is healthy is a reason not to worry about the freedom of the persons living such a lifestyle.

One may change one's lifestyle wholly or partly, gradually or abruptly, for example a bohemien turning bourgeois or an *enfant terrible* growing up. Lifestyles can be evaluated from all kinds of perspectives: moral, aesthetic, economic, psychological, and many more. One can think of them as interesting, boring, healthy or unhealthy, fitting a person or not fitting a person. The healthy or unhealthy perspective is just one way to look at it, although it now seems to be quite a dominant perspective.

The right to be reckless

Elsewhere[1] I have argued that punishing people for an unhealthy lifestyle and introducing different forms of taxing unhealthy lifestyles raise many complex ethical issues. One of these is the problem, already mentioned, of the *degree of responsibility* which may differ in individual cases making it unfair to judge all who smoke in the same way, for example. Mrs. D may have more excuses for smoking, taking into consideration the difficulties in her life, than the affluent happily married lady whose house she cleans. An important question arises as to how much responsibility can be attributed to addicts? Clearly there is no straightforward answer to such a question, but it is important to bear the issue of addiction in mind when considering issues of autonomy and responsibility.

The scapegoat problem

Then there is what might be called *"the scapegoat problem."* We should be aware that the discussion of responsibility for lifestyle tends to focus on some unhealthy habits, such as smoking, but not on other lifestyle affected factors that may also be unhealthy, like being a "workaholic." It is not clear what could justify this selectivity if the issue is one of responsibility for adversely affected health.

The Popeye problem

We also have to be aware of what I term "the Popeye problem." Spinach used to be good for you and was promoted. But nowadays the advice is not to eat it more than once a fortnight. Although the body of knowledge on what is healthy and what is not grows and in some cases only the diehards stick to their own beliefs, there are also instances of doubt and changing insights. It is almost impossible to keep up, and what may be healthy today may not be healthy tomorrow. Popeye would surely carry tins of olive oil now.

Punishment and responsibility

Before punishment for the consequences of a lifestyle were to be considered in any form one would need to know very much about that persons' life. Addiction would have to be ruled out unless responsibility for aquiring an addiction could plausibly be attributed. Indeed, so much information would be required that it would impossible to acquire sufficient knowledge of the relevant circumstances without raising important and difficult issues about infringement of his *privacy*.[2]

"Paying your own way"

An argument in favour of "paying your own way" that often is brought forward is the following: it is suggested that unhealthy lifestyles impose costs on others and that that is unfair. Why, in conditions of scarcity should a dedicated nonsmoker pay for Mrs. D's healthcare? But not all unhealthy lifestyles are costly to others[3] (it may be cheaper to treat Mrs. D for her terminal cancer than to take care of her for 10 years when she suffers from Alzheimer's disease). And it doesn't seem to be fair to tax the alcoholics and the smokers but not, say, the mountain climbers. We would also have to agree which lifestyles are not to be taxed because the risks they imply are run for a higher, societally important goal. We would probably agree about the importance of policemen to society, but what should we say of stuntmen? There is also the risk of all too simple "philosophies" on the wrongness of the pursuit of pleasure versus the virtue of moderation or abstinence.

327

Lifestyle and personal identity

Finally, a lifestyle is not an arbitrary thing, one identifies with one's lifestyle: it has to do with who one is and how one lives. Lifestyles and the freedom to pursue them raise very fundamental issues of personal freedom. Just try to imagine circumstances in which a lifestyle would be imposed on you, so that you would have no choice in the matter. Suppose, for example, you receive a letter on your eighteenth birthday telling you that from now on you are going to be monk or a fitness junky. You would surely feel like a chained bear who has to dance.

One could argue that it is too grand for a habit like smoking to be called part of a lifestyle, and that calling it a lifestyle is an attempt to evoke sympathy and respect for what are only "bad habits." Smoking, so the argument would go, has nothing to do with something as honourable and worthy of protection as a lifestyle. That, however, is simplifying the issue. Mrs. D's smoking habit itself is not her whole lifestyle but it is part of a whole that is her lifestyle. She is in a sense a risk-taking person, but she didn't want to use alcohol because she felt very much responsible for her child, and thought that smoking was the most relaxing habit for her. One cannot separate a person's character and lifestyle from his habits.

Think of a poet who drinks too much. The fact may be that his best poems have been written under the influence of alcohol. Imagine an overweight philosopher who simply loves to eat and hates to exercise and whose intense reading and prolific writing unfortunately cannot compensate for his caloric intake. One may not be able to separate his dietary habits from his lifestyle as a whole.

If certain habits or dangerous activities were *not* part of a lifestyle it would probably be a lot easier to give them up. We wouldn't mind so much.

Genes and Lifestyle

Scientific developments in genetics confront us with data on the way in which our genetic make-up may make us susceptible to certain diseases: some cancers such as breast cancer would be clear examples. Some of those susceptibilities can be "diagnosed" because the particular gene location is known. In other cases there is a presumption for a familial/genetic factor, but the whereabouts of the particular genes causing the susceptibility have not yet been found. There is by no means always scientific evidence on how much of which factor contributes to the development of a certain disease in a certain case and how environment, genes, and bad luck intertwine.

Why is the genetic perspective important?[4] Why not simply say that one ought to live a healthy lifestyle. Not smoking diminishes the risks for many diseases. Had Mrs. D not smoked then her chances of dying from lung cancer would have been very much smaller. While this is true, the genetic angle is important because of the possibility that one's individual risk may differ significantly from a general risk, which may provide a different perspective on one's lifestyle. A person allergic to bees takes great care to prevent a sting because the stakes are much higher than for those who are not allergic. Red-haired persons usually have to be more careful about sunburn than people with dark skins.

Then there is the possibility that what is more healthy for you may depend on your genetic constitution. (Jogging may not be the preferred exercise for those whose backs are not too strong.) So although some things like smoking are unhealthy for everyone, some other habits and activities may be healthy for some but not for others (jogging), and some activities may be very dangerous for some but not for others (bee allergy). Genetic information can tell us more about our own risks.

Informed choices about lifestyles

Is there a moral obligation to find out about one's genetic susceptibilities and therefore one's individual risks, and to change one's lifestyle accordingly? There is a *prima facie* argument in favour of finding out about (some of) one's genetic susceptibilities because it will lead to *better informed choices* about one's lifestyle. It is rational to want to know material facts which might affect choices and, moreover, it is morally appropriate in so far as one thinks of well considered autonomous choices about lifestyles to be of moral value. To hold people responsible for their behaviour implies that one has an obligation to weigh risks and benefits of actions based on knowledge.[5] (This is not to say that taking risks itself is irresponsible or stupid, but that not taking the trouble of being informed can be stupid or immoral.) If you want to climb the Eiger you have to take into account weather conditions and prepare for it. It would be, for example, stupid to start climbing without knowing the weather forecast. Does that mean one is almost "automatically" morally obliged to *change* one's lifestyle if one knows one has a higher risk? The point of the weather forecast is preparing, not just shrugging your shoulders: "Yes, heavy snow storms are expected, up I go." With regard to changing one's lifestyle this question cannot be answered in general. It depends *inter alia* on one's view on lifestyles with unhealthy consequences in general and one's view on duties to self and to others. It also depends on how big the risk is, the circumstances of one's life, and the sacrifices one would have to make.

We are not, of course, morally obliged to be "health saints." Health is very important but some goals in life justify taking risks. And we are, after all, only humans with the cravings and weaknesses or irrationalities that are characteristic of our species. On the other hand: if a great risk can be diminished or removed without great sacrifices, we surely have powerful reasons so to do. If we can prevent a life-threatening situation developing we usually will want to do that. If an apple a day really helps it would be silly not to eat it. Some activities to be avoided, might not after all, in the light of the new knowledge, be worth the risks. (For a professional beekeeper it may be more difficult to change than for an amateur. Those who could die from a bee sting are in a different position than those who would just have the risk of a two-day fever.) These issues require individual weighing in individual circumstances and cannot, surely, be answered in general.

Two examples

Suppose that our overweight philosopher finds out that he suffers from a condition called hypercholesterolaemia, which implies that his cholesterol levels are very high. This can be treated by a diet and medication. The risks of very high cholesterol levels are

329

that he may have a heart attack or a stroke. Whether he will in fact change his diet depends on how much he cared about which kinds of foods and all kind of other things in his life. Is he the father of children, has he just only finished part 1 of a planned 10-volume *magnum opus* on how to make vegetables palatable etc. Since the stakes are very high I suppose that most persons ought to and in fact would change their lifestyle.

There is some indication that there is a relation between stress and a genetic predisposition to develop schizophrenia.[6] However, to decide to live a stressless life (if that is at all possible; think of the stress of trying to prevent stress) probably demands many sacrifices. Regarding both the uncertainty of the evidence as well as the almost impossible task of leading a stressless life, it is difficult to defend the proposition that there is an obligation to change one's lifestyle.

Third Parties' Susceptibilities

Lifestyles have consequences for others. The freedom to live a certain lifestyle is obviously limited by the rights and interests of others.[7] Suppose Mrs. D's daughter had the alpha antitrypsine deficiency which would make her more likely to suffer from the adverse effects of passive smoking. In that case the moral arguments against her smoking are even stronger, although they already existed when it was not known the child had the AAT deficiency. Passive smoking has long been recognized as harmful.

This duty not to harm others specifically holds for children, who often cannot escape suffering the consequences from other persons' activities. Suppose the philosopher we have been discussing has children; they may also suffer from hypercholesterolaemia. Early treatment and diet may be more effective. The philosopher, even if he decided for himself not to change his diet, ought to provide the diet for his children. In their case, keeping as many options open to allow them to choose their own lifestyle is an important consideration.

A general caveat

I have argued that it is *prima facie* morally right to be well informed about the risks before embarking on an activity that may entail risks. One should, however, be aware of possible general side-effects in the context of genetic developments. There is a possibility of a widespread panic and medicalization. We have to bear in mind that there is much scientific uncertainty on the importance of genetic factors in relation to multifactorial diseases. There is a danger of focusing too much on the genetic side. "Genetization" may be as risky as medicalization.

It might undermine a right not to know. Many have stressed the importance of a right not to know with regard to genetic information, in particular with regard to those conditions that one cannot change or influence ("the inescapable genetic predestination" cases like Huntington's chorea).[8] Along the same lines it could be argued that those who may have, for example, the BRCA gene, which is linked to a higher chance of developing breast and ovarian cancer, also have a right not to know, and could very well decide not to be told because they consider the treatment options to be unacceptable.

Those with predispostions enhancing their risk who do not change their lifestyle may become double scapegoats ("not only did you have an unhealthy diet, you knew it was specifically unhealthy for you") or may be discriminated against ("with your hyper-cholesterolaemia forget about the job"). Employers might insist on having full PPPPs (Personal Pedigree and Proper behavior Profiles) before hiring someone, which raises questions with regard to privacy and justice (after all: a genetic susceptibility is not a thing one chooses to have, and if there is no relation between the susceptibility and the qualifications needed for the job, it could be compared with discrimination on the ground of a disability). There is no guarantee that more knowledge about individual genetic risk will on the whole bring people to lead more healthy lifestyles. (If only they really knew they would change their wicked ways.) Those who find out they have a lower risk may consider this an "invitation" to take up an unhealthy habit, even though unfortunately in the case of multifactorial diseases having a lower risk does not provide a sort of genetic immunity to such diseases.

Genetic defeatism

Then there is the possibility of "genetic defeatism": knowing that he has a suscepti-bility to get a certain disease a person might think "I will get it anyway" and therefore not change his lifestyle (or even change it to a more unhealthy one). "Since I'm genetically doomed I had better start eating lots of nice fatty foods now, as much as I can before I have my stroke." Although also this shows a misunderstanding of the idea of multifactorial disease, I would not exclude the possibility that people will in fact suffer from such defeatism. They will look at it as a sort of genetic predestination instead of "proneness." It might also be used as an escape from the burden of moral responsibility. "I cannot help myself. I have very strong weakness of the will genes. All my male family members have been suffering from weakness of the will for centuries."[9]

Born to be wild?

An even more speculative area is the relation between character and lifestyle. It is possible that certain character traits and predispositions (a predisposition to become an addict) are genetically influenced. A very important argument for respecting (or accepting or tolerating) unhealthy lifestyles is that they are the personal and autono-mous choice of an individual. A kickboxer might not be someone who autonomously chose the career of kickboxing, but might be a person "handicapped" by an aggres-sion gene.

Would the argument "lifestyles ought to be respected because they are for an important part chosen" still hold? I think so. There are too many persons with an addiction who stop using what they were using to say that nobody can stop. After all, Mrs. D successfully fought her inclination to become an alcoholic. A person with an "aggression gene" might not have the choice to be without the gene, but he might direct his aggression in a number of ways: he might, for example, choose the career of a criminal, a kickboxer, an attorney, or even go into politics.[10]

331

I may be born with a novelty-seeking gene (rather born to be wild than born to be bored), but that still leaves me with many novelties to choose from, such as bungee jumping or philosophy. I'm not responsible for being born with the gene, but I am to a certain extent responsible for what I do with it. Genetic developments will continue to influence the debate on moral responsibility for one's health. More will be known about susceptibilities for disease in relation to lifestyle and the relation between genes and character.

Conclusion

Mrs. D will be dead by the time more is known about the relation between her genetic complement and her character. She told me, smoking: "I didn't have an easy life. I don't want to die, but I have few regrets. Such was my life." A psychological necessity to accept what is inevitable? A genetic tendency to endure fate? Or typical Mrs. D? The fact of the matter is that we just do not know the answer to these questions. Moreover, we may never have full answers to them. In debates about distributive justice and health-care (is the smoker eligible for a lung transplant?), our ignorance in these matters is often overlooked. It is convenient for the purposes of philosophical inquiry to simplify cases so that neat distinctions can be drawn and clear conclusions can be offered. Such inquiries serve a purpose, but they will not, for the foreseeable future (or possibly ever), provide clearcut guidance either to individuals or to policy-makers over what the appropriate response to many lifestyle choices should be. I have argued that third-party vital interests should command the attention of policy-makers when they may be harmed by the lifestyle choices of others. I have also argued that a *prima facie* case can be made for encouraging individuals both to learn as much as they can about their own levels of genetic risk and to modify certain of their existing lifestyles. But we should not lose sight of the complexity inherent in debates over lifestyle.

Notes

1   De Beaufort, I., "Whose lifestyle is it anyway?" In De Beaufort, I. & Hilhorst, M. T. (eds.), *Individual Responsibility for Health; Moral Issues Regarding Lifestyles.* European Commission, Brussels/Luxemburg, 1996; "Personal responsibility." In: Erin, C. & Bennett, B. (eds.), *Whispered Everywhere.* Oxford University Press (in Press).
2   See Harris, J., "Could we hold people responsible for their own adverse health?" *J of Cont Health Law and Policy* 1 (1996), pp. 100–6.
3   See for an interesting example: Barendregt J. J., Bonneux, L., and P. J. van der Maas, "The healthcare costs of smoking." *N Engl J Med* 337 (1997), pp. 1052–7.
4   See my "Will knowledge of our genome improve the quality of our lives?" In Evered, D., Kroes, R., and Klasen, E. C. (eds.), *Innovative research and Appropriate Healthcare for the Citizens of Europe,* Proceedings of the invitational conference on the occasion of the Netherlands' EU Presidency, Luxembourg, Office for Official Publications of the European Communities, 1997: 108–15.
5   Here I face the problem of those lifestyles that are by "nature" spontaneous, *carpe diem.* Is it always irresponsible to have such a lifestyle?

6   Hoek, H. W. and Kahn, R. S. "Erfelijkheid en omgevingsfactoren in de etiologie van schizofrenie." *Ned T voor Geneeskunde* 139 (10) (1995), pp. 498–501.
7   Lifestyles can have different kinds of consequences for others. Their health may be at risk (passive smoking). They may lose a person dear to them (philosopher dying from a stroke). The consequences to their health may be influenced by their own genetic constitution because they in their turn may be very sensitive to certain substances.
8   For the debate, see for example Chadwick, R., Levitt, M., and Shickle, D. (eds.), *The Right to Know and the Right Not to Know*. Avebury: Aldershot, 1997.
9   Weakness of the will being a condition that rarely afflicts women.
10   This is a central problem in Ken Follett's novel *The Third Twin* (1996).

References

R. E. Goodin: *No Smoking: The Ethical Issues* (University of Chicago Press, Chicago and London, 1989).
R. Klein: *Cigarettes are Sublime* (Duke University Press, Durham and London, 1993).
D. Wikler: "Persuasion and coercion for health: ethical issues in government efforts to change lifestyles." In T. L. Beauchamp and LeRoy Walters (eds.), *Contemporary Issues in Bioethics*, 2nd ed. (Wadsworth, Belmont, CA, 1999).

25

Commercial Exploitation of the Human Genome

RUTH CHADWICK AND ADAM HEDGECOE

Introduction

The topic of commercialization of the human genome is complex in at least two ways. First, a number of different kinds of activity might be encompassed in the term "commercialization." The patenting of genes has received perhaps the most attention, but it is not the aim of the present discussion to cover the ethics of patenting specifically. Three other areas are worthy of attention: the debate over the private–public competition in gene sequencing; the commercial marketing of genetic tests to the public; and the involvement of commercial companies in gene banking and in setting up population databases.

The second source of complexity relates to the attempt to apply ethical principles in the area of commercialization. This arises, at least partly, from assumptions that are made about the world of commerce, leading for example to the portrayal of business ethics as an oxymoron – a feature of discussions of commercialization that is not confined to the introduction of commercial interests in human genetics. There is an argument to the effect that the world of commerce structures relationships in particular ways – different from the ways in which gifts, for example, do. As Tom Murray writes:

> relationships based on gifts can and do play positive roles in regulating family and social life, in promoting solidarity in the face of powerful forces of alienation, and in serving essential social values that are not well served by markets, commerce and contract. (Murray 1987: 30)

If we speak of commercial "exploitation," moreover, we find the word "exploitation" is frequently used in a negative sense: one meaning listed in the *Oxford English Dictionary* is given as "the action of turning to account for selfish purpose, using for one's own profit."

It will be important in the context of the present discussion to examine what are the issues and problems that are held to be specific to the context to the commercial exploitation of the human genome. A brief examination of the debates surrounding the involvement of commerce in human genomics can swiftly lead to the conclusion that there is a tendency to take a negative view of such involvement, although there are arguments for more neutral and even positive interpretations.

As Michael Burgess has pointed out in connection with private genetic services, opposition to commercialization might be based on an argument that it is inherently immoral or that it has bad consequences not justified by benefits (Burgess 1999). Burgess proceeds to state that it is difficult to imagine the basis for a claim that private genetic tests are inherently wrong and that it is more likely that prohibitions or regulations will be justified on the basis of avoiding harms. It is worth, however, trying to tease out ways in which an argument might be constructed to the effect that commercialization in the context of the human genome is inherently immoral, whether as applied to marketing of genetic tests or in other ways. Beyond the concerns about the world of commerce in general, arguments might be constructed that it is undesirable for commerce to enter into certain areas of life, or to be applied to certain kinds of thing. Specifically, there are arguments that purport to show tensions between the values of commerce and science, or between the values of commerce and health – or at least between commerce and equitable healthcare. The healthcare context is one over which there has long been dispute about the rival merits of private and public provision and the competing values involved.

The thinking behind this kind of view might be based on a conception of the "good" or "telos" of a certain kind of activity or on a conception of what makes a good practitioner in a certain kind of activity. The argument that there is a (possibly irresolvable) tension between commerce and certain areas of life, or practices, might be found in some of the professions, for example, depending on a view that there are certain values that are "internal" to the profession in question. Such a view might be held to underlie, for example, the prohibition on advertising in certain professions or occupational groups, such as nursing (cf. Chadwick 1996). It is important to note that the argument need not be construed in terms of a consequentialist analysis of actual harms and benefits that may ensue to particular individuals or groups. The point is wider than that, suggesting that advertising is incompatible with what nursing *is or ought to be*.

Alternatively there may be an argument to the effect that there is an incompatibility between the nature of some particular *thing* and the values of commerce. Indeed there do seem to be arguments to this effect in the literature – that certain things are "beyond price" or that to enter them into the realm of commerce is an affront to their dignity. Thus anticommercialization arguments sometimes appeal not to the fact that the context is science or healthcare but to claims about the special significance of the human body in general, or of the human genome in particular, as in the Convention on Human Rights and Biomedicine (Council of Europe 1996) and the UNESCO Declaration on the Human Genome and Human Rights (UNESCO 1997). Another issue, however, is the question as to whether it is commercialization itself or the issue of commercial *monopoly* that is held to be problematic.

Insofar as arguments of a consequentialist kind are applied to these contexts, it is perhaps fair to say that a focus on the harms of commercialization has tended to dominate the debate. The question of recognition of and distribution of benefits where they exist, however, has recently demanded more explicit attention in the literature (e.g. HUGO Ethics Committee 2000). These themes recur in discussion of the different examples of commercialization identified above.

Commerce, Ethics, and Science: Gene Sequencing

Nobody could quite believe the whole thing would be done without making it available.
(Chris Mundy, MRC Human Genome Mapping Resource Centre, Cambridge, quoted in Kleiner 1994)

In October 1994 Craig Venter, a former researcher at the US National Institutes of Health, declared that he would only allow access to his database of DNA sequences to researchers who signed over rights to the commercial exploitation of their work to his company, Human Genome Sciences. The subsequent outcry from the scientific community suggested that this was more than just a minor disagreement over the right of access to research results; it has become a benchmark in discussions concerning the role of commercial companies in the sequencing of the human genome.

The story began in the late 1980s when Venter discovered a revolutionary new way of sequencing a genome; by rebuilding genes "backwards" from the messenger that is sent out to tell the body to make a particular protein, Venter found that there are stretches of DNA, hundreds of thousand bases long, which are unique to particular genes. These "express sequence tags" or ESTs can then be used to identify any gene in the body, since an EST will only bind to the particular gene from which it is derived. This provides a very rapid means of determining the sequence of any length of DNA; instead of having to find out the order of actual bases, ESTs allow you to work out the order of genes instead, and is thus far quicker than traditional sequencing. In the early 1990s Venter tried to patent a number of ESTs associated with the brain. Objections were raised to this, since many of the ESTs were available in the public domain, and although they could be associated with particular genes, Venter could not say what proteins these genes coded for. In September 1992, Venter's application was rejected by the US Patent and Trademark Office, because of lack of application of these ESTs.

Venter left the NIH to work for HGS, a company partly funded by the pharmaceutical company SmithKline Beecham and its nonprofit arm The Institute for Genomic Research (TIGR). It was here that he expanded his database of ESTs. The research community knew that Venter was carrying out the sequencing of ESTs on a very large scale and very little work was carried out on this elsewhere in the world, the assumption being that the results of his research would be made available. HGS, however, proposed that the EST database should be made available to researchers on condition that they signed a contract stipulating that HGS had first refusal on the marketing of any product that arose from the research. If a researcher and HGS failed to agree exact terms for the marketing after 9 months, then the researcher was free to take his/her product elsewhere. The contract did not prevent academic publication of results of research. When the details of this arrangement were made public, there was an outcry from the scientific community, which regarded such restrictions as an infringement of academic freedom. At the end of June 1997, TIGR terminated its 10-year deal with HGS early, forfeiting US $38 million of funding. Both sides appeared happy; HGS had now developed its own sequencing labs, and TIGR was free to use its research results as it wanted, and gain funding from other sources.

In May 1998 Venter announced that he had founded Celera Genomics, with backing from Applied Biosystems, and the race began between private and public efforts to produce the first draft of the human genome. Venter's approach to and technique of sequencing was different from that taken by the publicly funded Human Genome Project (Aldridge 2000; Brown 2000). Venter's statement that he would patent large numbers of genes as a way of recouping the financial investment in his technology raised the stakes in the discussion of commercialization of genetics to new importance (Marshall 1998; 1999). The question to be asked is how the actions of Venter should be regarded.

The values that are at stake in the debate over commerce and science are freedom of scientific inquiry, freedom of communication, and access to data. Traditional values celebrated openness of information and publication of results. Such openness is still embedded in university culture, but the point is that the culture of secrecy and protectionism required by commercial interests is inimical to those values held to be integral to academic research.

> The real problem with industrial involvement in fundamental research, in my view, is not that skills and ideas are being obtained at too low a price *but that the possibility of alternatives is shut down* ... [there] is an argument for a measure of university independence, guaranteed by the state to maintain a plurality of ideas, critical thought and a vision of social, economic, industrial and scientific alternatives. (Yoxen 1983: 225)

In this debate arguments about values traditionally inherent in science and the tension between those and commerce, sometimes shade into consequentialist arguments about the influence of commercial interests. Thus fears are expressed that the introduction of commercialization has led or will lead to skewing the direction of university-based research and to increased secrecy among scientists, involving the signing of nondisclosure agreements (cf. Caulfield 1998). In the case of Venter it is the issue of access to data which has caused major concern: for example, Paul Berg has said "these arrangements indenture you in a way you never had to contend with. It used to be if you wanted a gene, from work that had been published, you got it" (quoted in Kleiner 1994: 15).

The case that the increased prominence of commercial interests in biological research has had a pernicious effect upon the nature of university research is made by Seldon Krimsky in his book *Biotechnics and Society: The Rise of Industrial Genetics* (1991). Krimsky documents the rise of the influence of commercial interests in university research in biology, and outlines the objections that stem from such a process. The argument is essentially that it has had a deleterious impact upon the openness and freedom of opinion which previously characterized biological research:

> Critics of university–industry research relationships (UIRRs) proclaimed that openness of university research would be compromised as a consequence of unfettered industry support...they estimate that 41 percent of all biotechnology firms involved in UIRRs have acquired at least one trade secret from their university-sponsored research... growth of trade secrets is a reasonable proxy measure for erosion of free and open communication. (Krimsky 1991: 72).

Other surveys cited by Krimsky suggest that biotechnology companies have had a large say in the direction of academic research leading to conflicts of interest, shifts in the research agenda, and potential obstacles in the way of intellectual exchange. The difficulty, as Krimsky sees it, is that such restrictions involve a real change in culture within academic research.

While this argument may be applied to academic research in general, it is part of Krimsky's case that biology is in a special position within the sciences. Some of the reasons he suggests for this include:

- Biologists have been held to a higher ethical standard and greater public account-ability by virtue of the significance of their work for the health professions.
- The entrepreneurial relationships in biology have been more aggressive, experi-mental, and excessive than those in other disciplines, setting new norms for the academic community.
- The ethical issues associated with the application of recombinant DNA technol-ogy have focused special attention on all aspects of the "new biology," including the role of scientists in discovery, development, and evaluation of the technolo-gies.

Arguably Krimsky is looking back at a mythical golden age of biological research full of open exchange of information and scientific camaraderie. But as Paul Rabinow has argued "[a]nyone who has read James Watson's account...of the race to discover the structure of the DNA molecule may well wonder how free and open the situation ever was. What has changed is the entry of money and patents" (Rabinow 1991: 136). And the introduction of money and patents has not introduced self-interest into science: that was there already.

Rabinow also points out that "[W]hile attention has been focused on the impact of industrial models on the academy, the reverse exchanges have been ignored. The biotechnology words has its own particularities. Many companies have incorporated 'libraries', 'conferences', 'publishing', 'seminars'...this sector of industry has mim-icked elements of scholarly life in the biosciences" (Rabinow 1991: 134–5). Many of these changes occurred over the 1980s, before genome sequencing became a subject of interest to commercial companies.

There are, then, two competing perspectives on the interactions of commerce and science in this field: (1) that commerce is incompatible with the values of free and open communication in science and (2) that this depends on an over-idealistic picture of the way science has been conducted in the past. The issue of scientific freedom and the funding of research is not one that is either new or specific to genetics.

It does not, of course, follow, from facts about how science has been conducted, whatever the truth of that matter, that it ought to continue to be conducted in the same way. As large genetic databases are used both to generate and to test hypotheses, it is arguable that there are changes in the scientific paradigm. The question is whether the paradigms appropriate to ethics in science also are and/or should be subject to change.

Commercial Marketing of Genetic Tests

When we turn to the issue of commercialization as applied to the marketing of genetic tests, we move from the world of academic science into the arena of healthcare provision. A number of companies have offered direct-to-consumer tests, including University Diagnostics (cystic fibrosis carrier testing) and Myriad Genetics (predisposition to breast cancer). Of those breast cancers that are ascribable to genetic causes, a large proportion is thought to be influence of a mutation in the BRCA1 and BRCA2 genes. The BRCA1 gene was isolated at the end of 1994; the BRCA2 gene isolated just over a year later.

Although estimates vary, if BRCA1 and BRCA2 together account for approximately 70 percent of the incidence of breast cancer in large families with a strong family history, predictive testing for BRCA1 and BRCA2 susceptibility would not pick up 30 percent of factors. Thus even setting aside the possibility of false negatives, a negative test for BRCA1 and BRCA2 will not guarantee freedom from the disease. From October 1996 Myriad Genetics, however, began to offer a joint BRCA1 and BRCA2 comprehensive test, costing $2,400 with $395 follow-ups. Since the announcement of the discovery of the BRCA1 gene there has been a wide-ranging debate about the advisability of genetic testing for breast cancer.

What are the concerns about commercialization in this context? As mentioned above there is a debate about commerce and healthcare, which has a long history. This ultimately turns on a view that health is a special kind of good inappropriate for commercialization. Tom Murray has pointed to the inconsistencies with which physician–patient relationships are portrayed:

> On the one hand, physicians earn their money by seeing patients, and in that sense it is clearly a commercial relationship, a trade of money for service. At the same time, the noncommercial aspects of the relationship are stressed. The very words used to describe what physicians do – they "take care of" patients – come from the language of personal, moral, nonmarket relationships. (Murray 1987: 37)

While there are clearly cultural differences in perspectives on this topic, they will not be explored here since this argument is hardly specific to genetic services: it applies to provision of private healthcare generally. Another concern arising out of commercialization is the fear that services will be introduced too early, before there is adequate evidence of benefit (Caulfield 1998), and leading to unrealistic expectations. As Silverman has pointed out:

339

Employees and academic researchers associated with the enterprise participate in the stock benefits and are highly motivated to enhance the value of the initial public offering. (Silverman 1995: S15)

This again, however, is a problem that applies to commercialization generally. There is also an argument that the commercial marketing of private genetic tests promotes an inequitable distribution of healthcare, since, in so far as it is beneficial to individuals to have access to such services, they will more readily be available to those who can afford to pay (cf. Holtzman 1998).

What are the concerns specific to the genetic context? The debate seems to turn, not on the special nature of the human genome, but on the particular harms that might be thought to ensue from commercial marketing of genetic tests.

One argument arises from the supposed special nature of genetic information, although the extent to which it is special is controversial. Genetic testing of individuals, like population genetic screening, is a controversial healthcare intervention even in the public sector. There are concerns about the potential harm that may occur as a result of the finding and disclosing of genetic information, given the scope for misinterpretation of results not only by those to whom it applies but also by healthcare professionals (e.g. Hubbard and Lewontin 1996) in addition to use and abuse by interested third parties. This is partly because of its predictive nature. In the case of multifactorial conditions such as breast cancer, where the result of a test is likely to be not diagnostic but to inform an individual of their risk status, there are clearly possibilities for misunderstanding even if worries about false positives and false negatives can be discounted.

Because of the purported special nature of genetic information, there are arguments for a certain amount of justified paternalism and gatekeeping surrounding access to genetic tests (Burgess 1999: 183–5), with appropriate counseling to be available accompanying testing and disclosure of results. There are fears that commercial companies may not provide counseling which is arguably an aspect of quality control. Against this, an autonomy argument might be advanced to the effect that marketing of tests direct to the public does in fact enhance the autonomy of individuals who wish to buy this particular service (with perhaps a greater guarantee of privacy than they would have in a publicly funded system).

Opponents of commercialization claim that respect for patient autonomy may be undermined by the approach taken by the companies in marketing their tests. Marketing of their products may tend towards misinformation in so far as marketing is likely to exaggerate the benefits of taking a test in terms of both the accuracy of the test results and the positive outcomes of either reassurance or subsequent options for action. The Stanford Program in Genomics, Ethics, and Society suggested that "It is easy to imagine an advertisement for BRCA1 and BRCA2 mutation testing that preys on women's fear of breast cancer and then offers testing as a solution to this heightened concern" (Koenig et al. 1998: 541). This is how advertising works.

The issue is more complicated than false or misleading claims on the part of advertisers, however, as regards both genetic information and autonomy. First, individuals have very different attitudes to and interpretations of risk, and understanding the different ways in which genetic factors may influence disease processes *is* complex. The model of autonomy as being facilitated by the provision of information which enables individuals to make decisions about having or not having tests has also been challenged by arguments that the information may actually not do that but may be experienced as burdensome and a violation of a "right not to know" (Chadwick et al. 1997).

A division between genetic and nongenetic information is not helpful here. There are at the very least large differences of degree of precision and predictive power between different genetic tests – from a diagnostic test for Huntington's to a clarification of risk status for breast cancer; and between the different conditions and what can be done in the event of a positive test result. For this reason an argument that some account has to be taken of different types of tests and/or different types of condition in assessing the desirability and possibility of regulation in this area has appeared more attractive to some, such as the UK Government's Advisory Committee on Genetics Testing, which stated that:

> the main role for genetic tests supplied direct to the public should be limited to determination of carrier status for inherited recessive disorders in which an abnormal result carries not significant direct health implications for the customer. (Advisory Committee on Genetic Testing 1997: 10)

This position is open to challenge from two directions: first, that it is too permissive with regard to commercialization and opens the way to two tiers of care, putting those unable to pay for private tests at higher risk of having children with recessive disorders (Holtzman 1998); second, that it is too restrictive, in light of the strong perceived need of those with a strong family history of, say, breast cancer, for access to information, which may not be available in the public sector. Individual patients may experience a considerable benefit gain from commercial genetic testing – the liberation that may ensue from having the information facilitating a decision to take preventive action in the form of a prophylactic mastectomy, for example.

Another concern about commercialization of genetic testing is that it may have a subtle eugenic effect:

> For there to be a demand for a service – be it carrier testing, prenatal diagnosis, or individual testing – there must be a perceived need...Theoretically, the "genetech" industry would benefit from a broad definition of disease and disability and a narrow view of normalcy. If commercial interests help to foster this type of definitional shift, could it be considered a "eugenic" force? (Caulfield 1998: 149)

The dangers of eugenic thinking, however, have also been associated with genetic services in the public sector. Indeed, most of the concerns discussed in this section are relevant to genetic testing *tout court*. The issues specific to commercialization appear to be whether private marketing makes more likely the infliction of possible harms, the extent to which quality control is possible, and the weighing of potential harms and benefits.

341

Gene Banking and Population Databases

Developments in human genome analysis are leading to the storage not only of large amounts of information about gene sequences, but also to collections of DNA samples. The setting up of genetic databases for population genetic research is becoming increasingly an issue, most notably demonstrated in the case of the Iceland controversy. In the case of Iceland the proposals for a database of the country's health records have caused controversy for a number of reasons, including: the possibility of linking the information in these records to genetic and genealogical information; and the involvement of a single company, deCode Genetics, in the construction of the database. One of the key issues here has been the purported impact on academic research, as discussed in relation to the tension between academic science and biology. There are also concerns about the impact on the provision of healthcare, including the opportunity costs of focusing on particular models of disease and health research (cf. Chadwick 1999). The third area of concern, however, relates to the idea of the human genome as a source of financial gain, with claims made about commodification of a nation and "cashing in" a people's legacy (e.g. *New Scientist* 1998).

This particular debate relates to the wider one about the commercialization of the human body. Tom Murray writes:

> Individuals in market societies, especially intellectuals, may delude themselves into believing that needs are indistinguishable from desires, that the body is merely a commodity like any other, and that we have no moral bonds with the members of our communities other than those we have freely chosen . . .

> How we choose to handle the transfers of human biological materials from patients and research subjects to teachers and researchers will declare how we regard the human body. If certain human parts are "dignified", then our social relations suggest they may be given, but not sold. (Murray 1987: 38)

The issue of whether the human body is a suitable object for commerce, however, is hotly contested, and as Murray himself notes, we may regard some parts of the body differently from others – for instance according to whether they are capable of regeneration, or according to the symbolism associated with different parts of the body. The human genome is arguably particularly sensitive because of the gene's status as cultural icon and the view that DNA could be regarded as the modern secular equivalent of the soul (Nelkin and Lindee 1995).

What is at stake in setting up population databases, however, is not financial gain from the genome directly, in its "natural state" but rather facilitating research which will give rise to financial gain. Here the issues merge with those discussed above in connection with science and commerce. The discussion of commercial interests in the Iceland database has taken a predominantly harm-centered approach, of which the potential harm to academic research (the likelihood of which is contested by supporters), is one. The other harms discussed focus on the implications for informed consent; the impact on the doctor–patient relationship; and the opportunity costs of focusing on particular models of health (Chadwick 1999).

The tendency to concentrate on a harm-centered approach is easy to understand in the light of the uncertainty of benefit to parties other than commercial companies involved. The prospects for development of new pharmaceutical products in the light of research which illuminates the genetic factors at work in common diseases have the potential to make substantial profits for pharmaceutical companies, as does research into the genetic basis of drug response. Although it is argued that such developments inevitably bring with them benefits in terms of improved healthcare and new products, there is a tendency for cynicism about these claims in the light of the history of orphan diseases, which are pointed to in order to show that commercial companies are not typically moved by impulses to improve health unless there is a clear promise of profit.

In an attempt to avoid the problems which have beset deCode, the proposals for a UK national gene database have suggested a private–public partnership. The potential commercial benefits from the "exploitation" of the results of the Human Genome Project are vast. On the other hand, individuals who participate by donating DNA samples cannot expect the same kind of potential benefits as have been available as a consequence of participating in conventional medical research, such as the possibility of some therapeutic benefit. Even if it were the case, the potential commercial benefits to the companies may seem to be out of all proportion with the benefits available to those who offer samples.

In the light of these developments, there has been a noticeable shift in the debate towards specific attention to the notion of benefit-sharing. The HUGO Ethics Committee has stated that "the issue of benefit-sharing merits further discussion because expenditures by private industry for genetic research now exceed the contributions of governments." They have also taken the view that companies involved in human health may have special moral obligations. This is partly because public funding has contributed to the very possibility of private enterprise making a profit in this area.

The HUGO Ethics Committee states that "in the interest of justice, the last decade has witnessed an emerging international consensus that groups participating in research should, at a minimum, receive some benefit." Questions arise as to the type of justice argument at stake. There are questions about the extent to which the argument depends on a view that people deserve compensation or reward for their contribution, e.g. by donating their samples to a population genetic database. The point mentioned above, viz. that groups participating in research should receive some benefit, seems to support this kind of interpretation. To a certain extent, however, the belief in the importance of benefit-sharing has arisen, as acknowledged by the HUGO Ethics Committee Statement on Benefit-Sharing, in the context of special concerns regarding research involving indigenous populations.

Specific recommendations of the HUGO Statement include the suggestion that "profit-making entities dedicate a percentage (e.g., 1%–3%) of their annual net profit to healthcare infrastructure and/or to humanitarian efforts" (HUGO 2000). One potential problem with the benefit-sharing proposals is how they are supposed to relate to the harm-centered approach to the issues. If it is interpreted as a trade-off, there is a danger that it will be construed as a cynical attempt to buy people(s), including indigenous peoples, off, while failing to address the perceived potential harms of participating in genetic research at population level.

343

Conclusion

What has emerged from this survey of concerns about commercialization is that there are arguments to the effect that the values of commerce are in tension with the values of certain areas of life, namely science, and healthcare; and that there are certain types of thing which should not give rise to financial gain, of which the human genome is a prime candidate. These arguments are countered by other arguments to the effect that the involvement of commerce in science and healthcare is nothing new – as far as those arguments go, it depends on whether there is something special about human genetics in particular that makes it unsuitable for commerce.

Arguments that rule out commercialization in relation to the human genome altogether are unlikely to succeed. Both scientific research and healthcare depend to an increasing extent on commercial investment. There is an important point, however, that we need to ensure relationships that do not undermine the very point of social institutions (as we have seen in the debate on human genetics and insurance). The question is how commerce can be regulated in such a way as to promote the best consequences which will include maximizing benefits to individuals and groups, minimizing harms, and enabling social institutions to function. Policy-making bodies are examining this with regard to both genetic testing and benefit-sharing, but consensus in policy is not yet established, reflecting underlying philosophical disagreements about the appropriate way of regarding the human genome and its commercial possibilities.

References

Advisory Committee on Genetic Testing (1997), *Code of Practice and Guidance on Human Genetic Testing Services Supplied Direct to the Public* London: Health Departments of the United Kingdom.

Aldridge, S. (2000), "Who'll own your body?" *Focus* August: 54.

Brown, K. (2000), "The human genome business today." *Scientific American* 283 (1): 40–5.

Burgess, M. (1999), "Marketing and fear mongering: time to try private genetic services?" In T. Caulfield and Williams-Jones (eds.), *The Commercialization of Genetic Research: Legal, Ethical and Policy Issues*. New York: Plenum, 181–94.

Caulfield, T. (1998), "The commercialization of human genetics: profits and problems." *Molecular Medicine Today* April: 148–50.

Chadwick, R. (1996), "Nursing, advertising and sponsorship: some ethical issues." In K. Soothill, C. Henry, and K. Kendrick (eds.), *Themes and Perspectives in Nursing*, 2nd ed. London: Chapman and Hall, 209–21.

Chadwick, R. (1999), "The Icelandic database: do modern times need modern sagas?" *British Medical Journal* 319: 441–4.

Chadwick, R. et al. (eds.) (1997), *The Right to Know and the Right not to Know*. Aldershot: Avebury.

Council of Europe (1996), *Convention for the Protection of Human Rights and Dignity of the Human Being with regard to the Application of Biology and Medicine*. Strasbourg: Directorate of Legal Affairs DIR/JUR 96 14.

Holtzman, N. A. (1998), "The UK's policy on genetic testing service supplied direct to the public – two spheres and two tiers." *Community Genetics* 1: 49–52.

Howard, K. (2000), "The bioinformatics gold rush." *Scientific American* 283 (1): 46–51.

Hubbard, R. and Lewontin, R. C. (1996), "Pitfalls of genetic testing." *New England Journal of Medicine* 334 (19).

Human Genome Organisation (HUGO) Ethics Committee (2000), *Statement on Benefit-Sharing* (Released in Vancouver, April 2000). London: Human Genome Organisation.

Kleiner, K. (1994), "Squabbling all the way to the genebank." *New Scientist* (26 Nov.): 14–15.

Koenig, B. A. et al. (1998), "Genetic testing for BRCA1 and BRCA2: Recommendations of the Stanford Program in Genomics, Ethics, and Society." *Journal of Women's Health* 7 (5): 531–45.

Krimsky, S. (1991), *Biotechnics and Society: the Rise of Industrial Genetics.* New York: Preager.

Marshall, E. (1998), "Hubris and the human genome." *Science* 280: 994–5.

Marshall, E. (1999), "A high stakes gamble on genome sequencing." *Science* 284: 196–9.

Murray, T. H. (1987), "Gifts of the body and the needs of strangers." *Hastings Center Report* 17 (2): 30–8.

Nelkin, D. and Lindee, M. S. (1995), *The DNA Mystique: The Gene as a Cultural Icon.* New York: W. H. Freeman.

New Scientist (1998), "Selling the family secrets." 5 Dec.: 20.

Rabinow, P. (1991), *Essays on the Anthropology of Reason.* Princeton: Princeton University Press.

Silverman, P. H. (1995), "Commerce and genetic diagnostics." *Hastings Center Report* 25 (3) (Special Supplement): S15–S18.

UNESCO (1997), Universal Declaration on the Human Genome and Human Rights.

Yoxen, E. (1983), *The Gene Business: Who Should Control Biotechnology?* New York: Pan Books.

Part V

ETHICS, LAW, AND POLICY

26

Forensic DNA Typing

DAVID WASSERMAN

Introduction

Forensic DNA typing is a technique for identifying people from their organic traces – blood, semen, saliva, or hair – and their genetic idiosyncracies. It involves the comparison of small portions of DNA (deoxyribonucleic acid), the molecule containing the human genetic code, taken from different sources, e.g., from a bloodstain and a suspect, or a child and an alleged father. Its value as an identification technique arises from the fact that DNA is found in virtually all bodily residues, is extremely resistant to decay and contamination, and has many regions that are highly "polymorphic," or variable among individuals. It is a versatile technology, that can help implicate or clear a criminal suspect, distinguish serial from copycat crimes with no suspect, resolve parentage disputes, and help parents find missing children (see generally, NRC 1996: chs. 1 and 2; Weedn 1996).

Since its introduction in the mid-1980s, DNA typing has been employed in thousands of cases of disputed identity, in criminal, domestic, immigration, and other proceedings. In some of these cases, it merely gilded the lily, yielding more powerful and persuasive evidence for an identification that could have been made by other means. In other cases, however, there would have been no identification, or a mistaken identification, without DNA typing. This chapter will focus on its use in American criminal cases, and address the principal issues that have been raised about its accuracy, its role as legal evidence, its impact on the criminal justice and legal systems, and its threat to privacy. As we move from technology to policy, it will become apparent that DNA typing, like other controversial applications of genetic research, has not raised new issues in law and public policy so much as intensified the debate over long-standing ones.

In its use of genetic material, DNA typing accomplishes the same task as the scientific comparison of other bodily residues. To assess its impact on criminal investigation and adjudication, we must examine it in the context of those other identification techniques, especially fingerprinting and nongenetic serology (blood-marker testing).

DNA typing was first introduced to the public by the trademarked name of "DNA fingerprinting" (Gill et al. 1985). While that term has since lost currency, and has

349

been criticized for suggesting a discriminatory potential that DNA typing does not (yet) have, the comparison is instructive. Both fingerprinting and DNA typing use highly variable characteristics of biological residues to aid in criminal identification. While a DNA match cannot identify a suspect with the certainty claimed for a fingerprint match, DNA can be obtained in a far wider variety of settings, and the presence or absence of the suspect's DNA will often be more clearly incriminating or exculpatory. DNA typing has a greater capacity to discriminate among individuals than any other serological test, and it can be used on a wider variety of residues.

But although DNA typing may be more useful or versatile than other identification techniques, its marginal value as a forensic tool can hardly explain its extraordinary popular and judicial reception. The publicity and controversy it has generated may reveal less about its potential as an identification technique than about the strength of public expectations and anxieties concerning genetic research and technology. For while fingerprint identification uses features of the human body that are readily accessible and widely assumed to be unrevealing (apart from their potential for identification), DNA typing uses features that are widely, if misleadingly, thought to be among the most private and revealing. And while fingerprinting, despite its slow judicial acceptance, generated little scientific controversy, DNA typing, as an application of cutting-edge genetic research, has encountered both rapid judicial acceptance and intense, protracted controversy.

How it Works

In theory, we could identify people with absolute certainty by examining their entire genetic sequence, or genome, since each person's genome is unique. That is not a practical possibility, however, since the genome is spread over 46 chromosomes, each containing millions of smaller molecules. DNA identification was suggested by the discovery of small regions (loci) of DNA throughout the genome, varying in length and other characteristics from person to person. The capacity to use these variable loci to identify people resulted from earlier advances in molecular biology, which made it possible to break up the DNA molecule into very small segments and detect small differences in their length and weight. In the classical typing method known as "restriction fragment length polymorphism" analysis (RFLP), these variations, or polymorphisms, are detected by differences in the length of the segments left when DNA is cut up by restriction enzymes. More recent techniques employ the polymerase chain reaction (PCR) to make multiple copies of DNA segments, an "amplification" process that permits the typing of minute amounts of DNA by fragment length or molecular sequence (see generally, NRC 1996: chs. 1 and 2).[1]

Forensic typing typically involves the comparison of several loci, since even the most polymorphic locus has a limited number of "alleles," or variants. Typing is done with either a multiple-locus probe, which permits the comparison of several loci at the same time, or several single-locus probes, each comparing the alleles at a single locus, from the maternal and paternal chromosomes. While early forensic typing used multiple-locus probes, single-locus probes now predominate, for reasons that include the simplified interpretation of population data.

350

Consider a case in which a semen stain is found on the clothing of a rape victim. DNA typing can test whether the stain came from a suspect by comparing the DNA from his blood with the DNA extracted from that stain. The failure to obtain a match "excludes" the suspect as a source of the semen; a match "includes" the suspect in a subpopulation of potential sources. The more loci at which matches are obtained (and the rarer the matching alleles), the smaller the probability that someone besides the suspect was the source of the semen.

DNA typing can rule out identity categorically: if alleles from two samples do not match, those samples cannot have the same source. A match, however, yields only a probability of identity between suspect and source. A simple product rule will give the probability that the DNA could have come from anyone besides the suspect, if (1) a match is *correctly* found for the maternal and paternal alleles at each locus; (2) the alleles at each locus can be assumed to be statistically independent of each other and of the alleles found at other tested loci (e.g., the probability of finding a given allele at one locus must not depend on the probability of finding a given allele at another), and (3) the frequencies of the alleles at each locus can be estimated *for the appropriate population*. To continue with our example, if the suspect's DNA matches the semen for each pair of alleles at three tested loci, the alleles can be regarded as independent, and the frequency of each allele at each locus is 1 in 20, then the probability that the source DNA came from someone else will be 1 in 64,000,000: $[20 \times 20] \times [20 \times 20] \times [20 \times 20]$. The legal controversies over the admission and presentation of DNA matches have focused on the validity of the assumptions needed to yield such staggering odds.

Sources of Error and Uncertainty

The soundness of the theory and technique underlying DNA typing has never been in serious dispute; the controversy over the admission of DNA typing results has focused on the criteria for declaring a match, and the statistical interpretation of a match. The first issue was prominent in the early debate over the admissibility of DNA evidence, with critics concerned that the comparison of DNA typing from different sources left too much room for error, interpretation, and bias, notably in adjustments for "band-shifting," a phenomenon associated with certain methods of RFLP analysis (e.g. Neufeld and Colman 1990; Lander 1992). That concern has receded as techniques for comparing DNA fragments have become more precise and the criteria for declaring a match have been standardized.

Since the early 1990s, the second issue has predominated: the statistical interpretation of DNA matches. The vanishingly low odds often given for a chance match, as in our example above, rest on disputed assumptions about the frequency of specific alleles across population subgroups and the independence of alleles at different loci. They also rest on the assumption that a match has been correctly made, i.e., that the laboratory claiming a match has not done so erroneously – an assumption that laboratory errors in blind tests call into question, and that the absence of a standardized testing programs renders highly problematic. I will begin with the first concern, although some critics consider the second the more important.

Because of inbreeding, a racial, ethnic or other subgroup may have a significantly higher frequency for a given allele than the population average. If it does, and if any potential contributor of the source DNA comes from that subgroup, then the odds of obtaining a chance match on that allele will be significantly higher than the frequency of the allele in the general population.

Two distinct questions present themselves: do subpopulations differ in allele frequency? If so, what is the appropriate subpopulation to consider in a given case? The first is a scientific question, which has generated sharp disagreement among population geneticists, particularly about the validity of various tests for subpopulation heterogeneity. Proponents of forensic typing argue that current databases, based on broad population estimates, yield adequate frequency estimates, while some critics call for more refined subgroup data (see NRC 1992). The second question is evidentiary, because it concerns the population of potential contributors: if not the suspect, then who? If the suspect in a Crown Heights rape of a Hasidic woman is a Hasidic Jew, should the statistical interpretation of a match reflect the frequency of the matched profile in New York City, among Jews, among Hasidic Jews, among Crown Heights residents, or among some other subgroup? The choice of the most appropriate subgroup will depend on what is known or assumed about the offense or the offender, e.g., on whether the race or general appearance of the offender is known, on whether the rape occurred in an alley or a mikvah.[2] Some commentators argue that these uncertainties make it appropriate to use the general population frequency in all cases, others that the suspect's own racial or ethnic subgroup should be used, if adequate population data is available. Others question why the suspect's subgroup is appropriate unless the evidence limits potential contributors of the source DNA to that group; they suggest that the choice of subgroup must be left to judges or juries, on a case-by-case basis. Finally, some regard the multiplicity of possible subgroups, and the uncertainties about which is most appropriate, as militating against the use of frequency data or any statistical interpretation of a DNA match.

In 1992, the Committee on DNA Technology in Forensic Inference of the National Research Council (NRC) issued a report that called for using the highest allele frequency for any population subgroup if there were any significant differences among groups.[3] Under this "ceiling" principle, the probability that someone besides the suspect contributed the bloodstain would be assessed using the frequencies for the subgroup in which the matched alleles were most common, even if there was no reason to think that someone from that subgroup was involved in the incident. This proposal, intended to resolve the controversy by its simplicity and conservatism, only sharpened it, with critics finding the ceiling to be either overly conservative or ad hoc (e.g. Devlin et al. 1993; Kaye 1994). A new NRC panel issued a revised report on statistical issues in 1996, which rejected the ceiling principle in favor of much more modest downward adjustments in frequency when there is evidence of subpopulation differences. That proposal provoked less criticism that the one it replaced, and the 1996 Report helped shift the focus to other controversies in statistical interpretation (Symposium 1997: Introduction).

Several commentators have pointed out that the preoccupation with subpopulation differences had obscured a more important threat to the reliability of DNA typing results and their value as legal evidence: the prospect of laboratory error (Lempert

1991; Symposium 1997: 405–54). Sample-switching, contamination, and other laboratory errors, found to occur with disconcerting frequency in one highly publicized test of California crime laboratories, may be a more significant source of error than mistaken frequency estimates. Some critics have argued that the probability presented to the fact finder that someone other than the defendant was the DNA source can be no lower than the false-positive rate of the laboratory doing the testing. The debate over this proposal leads to the next general topic, the issue of integrating DNA typing results with nonquantitative evidence into the framework of legal proof.

DNA Typing Results as Legal Evidence

Even if DNA typing is reliably performed and analyzed, the significance of its results may be misunderstood by juries and judges. The statistical interpretation of a DNA match introduces a conspicuously large (or small) numerical probability into a criminal trial characterized by informal, nonquantitative evidence. The integration of DNA evidence into legal proof presents several challenges that go beyond the usual doubts about lay comprehension of scientific and quantitative evidence.

The probability of a match vs. the probability that the suspect was the source of the DNA

The statistical interpretation of a DNA match is usually given in terms of the probability that someone picked at random from the relevant population would match the source DNA. In our example, we calculated that probability as 1 in 64,000,000. But that impressive statistic does not give the probability that the fact finder is interested in – the probability that the suspect contributed the source DNA. Establishing that probability is more complex.

On the prevailing Bayesian approach, the match is seen as a piece of evidence that modifies the prior probability, whatever it was, that the suspect contributed the source DNA. The modification is made by multiplying the prior probability by the "likelihood ratio," which compares the probability of a match if the suspect was the DNA source with the probability of a match if he was not. The former probability can be assumed to be 1 (with no false negatives); the latter is just the random match probability. So the likelihood ratio will just be the reciprocal of the match probability. That ratio indicates that a match was 64,000,000 times as likely if the suspect was the DNA source than if he was not, *not* that the suspect is 64,000,000 times more likely than anyone else to be the source. It is easy to confuse the two claims, and treat the match probability as indicating the latter. This error has been called the "prosecutor's fallacy," and it will yield a mistakenly large probability that the suspect was the source whenever the prior odds that he was the source are less than 50:50.

The complementary "defendant's fallacy" involves the assumption that anyone in the reference population with the same DNA profile as the suspect is as likely to be the source (both terms are from Thompson and Shumann 1987). This would mean that if the match probability in our example had been 1 in 640,000, and the reference population 6,400,000, the suspect would have had only a 1 in 10 chance of being the source, since we would expect there to be 9 other people in the population with the same profile. The assumption will be mistaken, and the odds substantially higher, in any case where the suspect was initially identified by evidence other than the DNA match. In cases where the suspect is identified only through the search of a DNA data bank containing his profile, there is no prior evidence linking him to the specific offense, and the match will therefore have far less probative value. The simplest way to deal with this problem would be to attempt to match the DNA of the data-bank suspect to the source DNA at several different, independent loci. If this is not feasible, the 1996 NRC report proposes a downward adjustment of the match probability that reflects the greater likelihood of a coincidental match in larger databases.

The laboratory false-positive rate and the probability that the suspect was the DNA source

Some commentators have proposed that the statistical interpretation of a match incorporate the false-positive rate of the crime laboratory performing the typing: the frequency with which it mistakenly declares a match (Symposium 1997: 405–64.) They argue that the probative value of a match reflects the probability that a match would have been declared if the suspect was not the source (this is the probability expressed by the denominator of the likelihood ratio). But there are two ways that could happen. First, the lab could accurately declare a match with the suspect's DNA when someone other than the suspect was in fact the source. Second, the lab could declare a match mistakenly. The probability of such an error, given by the laboratory's false-positive rate, may be vastly greater than the probability of a coincidental match, and it must be factored into any statistical presentation of the match.

Other commentators point out, however, that information on false-positive rates is not available in the absence of routine blind-proficiency testing of crime laboratories, and they argue that even if such testing were routine, the false-positive rates it yielded could not be generalized to the laboratory's ordinary case work. They propose that evidence of laboratory error be presented separately from the statistical interpretation of the match, with the fact finder invited to discount the latter by the former in some substantial but unspecified way, a recommendation adopted by the 1996 NRC Report (ch. 3). Critics, however, doubt that judges or juries will discount adequately; research on eyewitness testimony suggests that lay fact finders tend to take little account of the reliability of identification evidence (Symposium 1997: 405–54).

The integration of nonquantitative evidence and the neglect of "softer" variables

If DNA evidence is difficult for lay fact finders to interpret in isolation, it is also difficult to integrate with the standard kinds of evidence produced at a criminal trial – eyewitness testimony, evidence of motive, means, and opportunity, character evidence – where, for example, a DNA match confronts an airtight alibi, or where a DNA exclusion confronts strongly incriminating eyewitness and circumstantial evidence. It is possible that judges and juries will give too much weight to DNA evidence in cases

354

of conflict, but it is also possible that they will give it too little weight. There are several reports of juries having convicted defendants implicated by eyewitness or circumstantial evidence in the face of clear exclusions, a subject I will take up in discussing the exculpatory potential of DNA typing. There are few reports of DNA evidence prevailing in the face of a strong alibi or other strong exculpatory evidence; this may be because prosecutors are less likely to use DNA evidence to plug the gaps in weak cases than to reinforce strong ones.

A second concern is that the complexities and controversies surrounding the introduction of DNA evidence may divert attention from critical issues to which DNA is not material. Inclusion cannot establish guilt, only source identity; exclusion cannot establish innocence, only noncontribution. A match will have limited inculpatory value when there are other disputed issues besides identity, such as intent. Conversely, a failure to match will have limited exculpatory value where the offense was likely to have been committed by a number of people, or where there are likely to have been "innocent" sources for the tested residue, such as consensual sexual partners.

The Legal Reception of DNA Typing

The reception of DNA typing evidence by criminal courts in the United States has three striking features. The first is the short interval between the introduction of typing and the admission of its results in criminal trials. The second feature is the vigor and persistence of the challenges to its admissibility. The final feature is the extent to which those challenges have been resolved outside the usual confines of adversary litigation.

DNA typing was taken up by the criminal justice system far more quickly than either fingerprinting or conventional serology. It was almost 30 years from the first scientific use of friction ridge patterns on the fingertips for identification purposes to the routine admission of fingerprint evidence in criminal cases. There was a similar lag between the discovery of ABO blood-group typing around 1900 and the admission of blood-type evidence for identification purposes in the 1930s. In contrast, it was less than two years between the first published scientific discussion of the use of DNA typing for identification purposes, in 1985, and the introduction of typing results in an American criminal trial, in 1987.

Some of this difference may be due to the greatly increased pace of scientific testing and validation between the turn of the century and its final two decades. But that is only part of the story. The enormous cachet of genetic research and technology helps explain both the rapid acceptance of forensic DNA typing and the vigor of the challenges to it. A survey of court cases in 1992, when the admission of scientific evidence in federal and many state courts was still governed by the restrictive *Frye* standard (discussed below), suggested both the extent of judicial acceptance and the magnitude of the challenge. Forensic typing results had been admitted in well over 700 cases in 49 states, but they had been subject to full-dress evidentiary hearings in almost 10 percent of these (Wasserman and Weedn 1992).[4]

This tally, however, does not fully capture the intensity of the challenge to typing evidence. In several highly publicized cases in the late 1980s and early 1990s, the

355

courts conducted extensive evidentiary hearings, in which some of the nation's leading geneticists and forensic scientists offered sharply conflicting testimony on the reliability and interpretation of DNA matches. The duration, acrimony, and repetitiveness of these hearings convinced many observers that the controversies about DNA typing would be better resolved in an extrajudicial setting, where the admissibility of scientific evidence would not rest on the findings of individual judges and the vagaries of adversary combat.

There was precedent of a sort for this approach in the informal "consensus conference" held by prosecution and defense experts in the *Castro* (1989) case, the first criminal case in the US in which DNA typing was subjected to a sustained challenge, and one of the few in which it was excluded. Many observers hoped that a blue-ribbon commission could replicate on a larger scale the success of the *Castro* experts in resolving their differences outside the confines of adversary litigation. This hope now seems naive; the most prominent panel to address scientific issues in DNA typing remained sharply divided by the issues it was convened to resolve.

The first major extrajudicial examination of forensic DNA typing was conducted by the congressional Office of Technology Assessment. Its 1990 report found the technology to be generally reliable, and it dismissed some of the objections to its forensic use as "red herrings." Not surprisingly, the OTA report was dismissed by many critics of forensic typing as a whitewash. The National Research Council attempted to achieve a broader consensus by convening a panel that included leading critics as well as proponents of DNA typing. That panel, which met in 1991–2, vacillated between a highly qualified endorsement of forensic typing as then practiced and a call for a temporary moratorium on the presentation of match statistics. It finally opted for the former (so close to its reporting deadline that a *New York Times* headline story the previous day announced that it was going to opt for the latter). While the panel endorsed both the theory of forensic typing and many of the standard typing procedures, it also called for much stricter standards for certifying and testing laboratories, and it adopted the controversial ceiling principle discussed above.

In the seven years since the NRC report was released, its endorsement has had more impact than its qualifications. While crime laboratories have improved their performance and self-regulation, they remain a long way from the proficiency testing program the report called for. And, as discussed above, a second NRC panel (1996) rejected the ceiling principle, which had found only partial acceptance (and comprehension) in the courts (Kaye 1994).

DNA Typing and the Judicial Assessment of Scientific Evidence

The prominent role of extrajudicial panels in attempting to resolve controversies about DNA typing may have resulted in part from the premium that federal and much state law placed on expert consensus in the admission of scientific evidence. Under the *Frye* standard, which governed the admission of scientific evidence in federal and many state courts when DNA typing evidence was first introduced, judges were required to exclude scientific techniques and tests that did not have "general acceptance" in the relevant scientific community. The fact that DNA typing was rarely excluded in the face of scientific controversy suggests that the courts focused on the general acceptance of its theory and standard methods, not on the sharp disagreement about its controls, quality assurance, and statistical interpretation. But it also suggests that *Frye* (1923) may have lost its hold well before the United States Supreme Court adopted new standards for the review of scientific evidence in 1993. The controversy over the admissibility of DNA typing results highlighted some of the tensions in *Frye*, and may have hastened its demise.

Frye can be seen as a reasonable if unsuccessful effort to preserve the authority of lay judges in reviewing scientific evidence. Rather than requiring the judge to educate herself in the relevant science, or to delegate her authority to a court-appointed expert, *Frye* let the judge resolve controversy by counting heads. In effect, it substituted a social for a scientific criterion: the existence of a consensus in the relevant scientific community.

There are obvious problems in deciding what the relevant scientific community is: the boundaries may be drawn more widely or narrowly, and it sometimes takes an expert to know one. The early controversies over forensic typing dramatized the problem: initially, there was far greater consensus about the reliability of typing among forensic scientists than among population geneticists. To decide that the relevant scientific community included the latter as well as the former was to reduce the odds of finding general acceptance. But how was a lay judge to decide what the relevant community was, without grasping some of the underlying science and technology? Such critical boundary determinations undermined the division of intellectual labor established by *Frye*.

The DNA typing controversies also provoked resistance to *Frye* by appearing to confer a "dissenter's veto" on mavericks and zealots within the scientific community. Under *Frye*, judges are not supposed to evaluate disagreement among experts, but merely to regard it as bearing on the issue of consensus. *Frye* thus appeared to give disproportionate weight to dissenters, allowing a small but persistent minority to block a finding of general acceptance. The fact that the articulate, persistent critics of DNA typing so rarely succeeded in doing so suggests that this fear may have been exaggerated. But it certainly influenced the climate of judicial opinion in the early 1990s, when the federal courts were re-examining the *Frye* standard.

In late 1993, the United States Supreme Court finally overruled *Frye*. In *Daubert* (1993), it required federal judges to assess the scientific validity of a test rather than canvass its acceptance. Although *Daubert* may have the effect of relaxing the standards for admitting scientific evidence, its intent was rather to increase the responsibility of judges for evaluating that evidence.

Daubert defined two roles for the trial court: first, to assess the threshold reliability of scientific evidence, based on such factors as its conformity to accepted research methods, its peer-review, and its replication; second, to assess the "fit" of scientific evidence to the case at hand. The latter role requires the judge to understand what is properly a scientific question and what is not – an understanding that has often been lacking, as we have seen, in the debate over the appropriate reference population for a DNA match. While a judge lacks the expertise to assess the extent of subpopulation differences or the adequacy of a population database, she is well equipped to assess how or whether the evidence in the case restricts the range of potential contributors of the source DNA: whether the location, time, or other feature of the offense, or any other evidence in the case, limits potential contributors to certain subpopulations. *Daubert* affirms the competence and responsibility of trial judges to make such determinations of "fit."

Social Impact: Criminal Investigation and Adjudication

In contrast to the large body of scholarly writing on the reliability and interpretation of forensic DNA typing, little research has been done on its routine utilization and impact. Almost nothing is known about the vast majority of cases in which DNA typing is performed – cases where typing is employed in the investigatory or pretrial stage, but never introduced at trial. We know very little about how frequently DNA typing is being employed in cases where it is feasible and potentially useful; whether its utilization is limited by a lack of suitable material, budgetary constraints, or institutional inertia; or what role DNA evidence plays in the cases where it is employed.

This is a significant gap in our understanding. The 1992 National Research Council report on forensic DNA typing cautioned that "the introduction of a powerful new technology is likely to set up unwarranted or unrealistic expectations." DNA typing is particularly likely to give rise to unwarranted expectations because of the way it establishes identity: through a person's genetic code. Public perception of DNA typing may be distorted by the same "genetic essentialism" that exaggerates the significance of genetic links in custody disputes and genetic predispositions in risk assessment (Dreyfuss and Nelkin 1992).

DNA typing may give rise to exaggerated expectations in two areas. One, which has already been discussed, is in the level of confidence it can provide about source identity. The second is in its impact on the resolution of criminal cases and the operation of the criminal justice system. Forensic typing greatly increases the discriminatory potential of biological residues, and permits a far wider range of biological residues to be analyzed, in far smaller quantities. But it can only make a difference in cases where (1) identity or the occurrence of physical acts is at issue and (2) biological material whose source is relevant to that issue is available for typing, and (3) other evidence bearing on identity is unavailable or inconclusive.

The research of Peterson and his associates suggests that identity is not at issue in most criminal cases, and is less likely to be at issue in cases where forensic evidence is available. Peterson et al. (1987) found, for example, that in about 60 percent of rape cases, the complainant had a prior relationship with the accused, making identity less likely to be an issue. In addition, Peterson et al. (1984) found more biological evidence collected in cases with more extensive victim-perpetrator interaction, which suggests that biological material is more likely to be available in cases where it is less likely to be needed for identification. (At the same time, a recent FBI survey found that DNA was submitted to crime laboratories in less than 10 percent of all rape cases and tested in only 6 percent (Weedn and Hicks 1998: 5). These figures certainly suggest that the potential of DNA typing to resolve identification issues has not been fully realized.) While DNA typing is relevant to other issues besides identity, these and similar findings suggest that it may not be relevant to the disputed issues in a majority or large minority of criminal cases. Moreover, the impact of DNA typing on cases that do have relevant issues is uncertain. While anecdotal reports suggest that many cases rest heavily on DNA typing, an assessment of its marginal impact requires an appraisal of the other evidence that was available in the case, or could have been made available.[5]

The role of DNA typing on the investigation of criminal cases is virtually certain to increase with the advent of forensic data banking. By 1999, almost every state required DNA samples from convicted sexual or violent felony offenders for inclusion in a computerized database. As these databases become operational, law enforcement officials can check the residues in new or unsolved cases against the profiles of prior offenders. Prosecutions in several states have been initiated by such "cold hits" (Weedn and Hicks 1998: 5–6). The impact of forensic DNA data banking has been more immediate and dramatic in the United Kingdom, which allows profiles to be obtained from suspected as well as convicted offenders. In 1995, the year the British DNA database system went into operation, it had 360,000 profiles and was reported to have linked 28,000 people to crime scenes (though how many of those would have been linked by other evidence is not known). The system, eventually expected to include a third of all British males between the ages of 16 and 30, is already reported to have a 50 percent chance of yielding a "hit" on the first try (Wade 1998; Weedn and Hicks 1998).

The most striking effect of DNA typing, however, may be in exonerating suspects who would otherwise have been charged, arrested, or convicted. Of the more than 400 tests conducted by the FBI Crime Laboratory by early 1990, over a third excluded the suspect. These high rates of exclusion have persisted; a 1996 national telephone survey of crime laboratories conducted by the Justice Department, that included 13 state and local and 4 private laboratories, as well as the FBI and an armed forces laboratory, found an overall rate of exclusion of 23 percent, with 16 percent of tests inconclusive (Conners et al. 1996).

While some of these exclusions served to eliminate "usual suspects" and some may have limited exculpatory value, an unknown percentage vindicated suspects who would have been, or already were, charged or arrested. The most compelling evidence of the exculpatory potential of DNA typing comes from a 1996 Justice Department report. It identified 28 cases in which a convicted defendant was ultimately released as the result of a DNA test excluding him as the source of organic material found on the victim or at the crime scene. All 28 cases involved sexual assault; in 6, the victim was murdered (Connors et al. 1996).

Forensic DNA typing may have a significant effect not only in vindicating particular defendants, where its impact will be limited to cases with preserved residues, but in increasing skepticism about other forms of identification evidence. Even a handful of well-publicized cases where DNA typing unambiguously exonerates a suspect implicated by eyewitness or other standard evidence may sensitize law-enforcement officials to the risk of mistaken accusations. The attention paid to DNA typing may also promote the more frequent and careful utilization of other forensic evidence. The accuracy of criminal adjudication might be greatly enhanced by placing less reliance on conventional forms of identification and greater reliance on forensic evidence.

359

Social impact: privacy

The threat to privacy from DNA typing arises from two sources: the ease with which DNA can be obtained and the amount of data it can yield. Usable DNA can be extracted not just from blood and semen, which may only be taken with probable cause and a court order, but from trace amounts of tissue and saliva. The courts have not yet resolved what constraints govern the "search and seizure" of such material by oral swab or hair sample, or whether people have any constitutionally protected expectation of privacy in such material once it leaves their bodies (see generally, Office of Technology Assessment 1988). Federal courts have, however, upheld the taking of DNA samples from all convicted felony offenders for use in forensic databases (Wade 1998).

More broadly, civil libertarians are concerned about the potential for abuse arising from the inclusion of increasingly large segments of that population in DNA data-banks. Now limited to profiles from convicted defendants, those data-banks may be augmented by DNA from other groups, such as military personnel and employees in high-security positions. It may soon be technically possible to screen a large portion of the population for involvement in any crime where testable body residues are found. Perhaps more worrisome, these data banks may also be augmented by other types of information, such as fingerprints, criminal records, and behavioral profiles.

The DNA molecule itself is becoming an increasingly rich source of personal information. Thousands of medical conditions have already been mapped to specific regions of the genome, and genetic "markers" are likely to be found for many physical traits and behavioral and psychiatric conditions. While most of the loci used in typing do not appear to have functional significance, the mapping of the human genome may place some of these loci in close proximity to the genes associated with significant traits. Access to personal data could be limited by storing only DNA profiles, but there are reasons for preserving DNA, such as the opportunity for reanalysis by an independent laboratory or with a new technique. As typing becomes more reliable and more standardized, however, preserving samples for reanalysis may become less of a concern.

Conclusion

Forensic DNA typing is unlikely to either revolutionize criminal investigation or radically undermine privacy. In the area of criminal prosecution where it has had its most visible impact, sexual assault, it may well effect an enduring increase in the frequency and accuracy of convictions. And its role in vindicating wrongfully convicted defendants has a moral significance that is not reflected in the small number of cases.

The most encouraging long-term effects of the DNA typing may lie in its contribution to more professional law enforcement, to a healthy skepticism about the standard types of evidence by which most convictions are obtained, and to closer collaboration among scientists, policy-makers, and lawyers in the review of scientific evidence.

Notes

1   Mitochondrial DNA, which is inherited from the mother, has also been used in recent years for identification purposes, although rarely in criminal cases. It can be recovered from residues where nuclear DNA cannot be found, is available in insufficient quantities, or is too degraded to analyze. But because only a small region of mitochondrial DNA is highly polymorphic, it lacks the discriminatory potential of nuclear DNA (Weedn 1996).

2   There is also the problem of considering siblings and other relatives as alternative suspects. The probability that the DNA sample came from an (untested) relative of the suspect may be far greater than the possibility that it came from someone picked at random from some larger population, and some commentators have argued that any match statistic presented to the fact finder must be qualified by this possibility, unless all relatives can be tested, or ruled out as suspects (see Lempert 1991; Symposium 1997: 454–61).

3   Actually, it proposed both an interim ceiling principle, for use until adequate subpopulation databases were developed, and a permanent ceiling principle once they were. Both principles have complexities that I have ignored in the text.

4   The few cases to exclude match results altogether did so because of doubts about the laboratory's performance, not about the underlying theory or the population statistics; in a larger number of cases, still a small minority, the match was admitted, but its statistical interpretation was excluded or restricted.

5   The only published study on the impact of forensic DNA typing (Purcell et al. 1994), a survey of the prosecutors in about a quarter of the first 200 recorded cases in which DNA evidence was introduced at trial, found that testimony from a DNA expert significantly increased the odds of conviction and the length of sentence. The prosecutors surveyed regarded DNA typing as important in winning cases involving stranger-crimes and cases involving older, employed defendants. In an ongoing study of the utilization and impact of forensic DNA typing in four Maryland jurisdictions, conducted by the author and several colleagues, preliminary analyses indicate that typing is more likely to be employed in stranger crimes, crimes without confessions, and crimes involving weapons, and that matches are associated (in one or more jurisdictions) with higher conviction rates and longer sentences (Wasserman et al. 1999).

References

Connors, E. et al.: "Convicted by juries, exonerated by science: case studies in the use of DNA evidence to establish innocence after trial." *National Institute of Justice* (1996).

Devlin, B., Risch, N. N., and Roeder, K.: "Statistical evaluation of DNA fingerprinting: a critique of the NRC's report." *Science* 259 (1993), p. 5.

Dreyfuss C. R. and Nelkin, D.: "The jurisprudence of genetics." *Vanderbilt Law Review* 45 (1992), pp. 313–48.

Gill, P., Jeffreys, A. J., and Werrett, D. S.: "Forensic applications of DNA fingerprints." *Nature* 318 (1985), p. 577.

Kaye, D. H.: "The forensic debut of the National Research Council's DNA report: population structure, ceiling frequencies and the need for numbers." *Jurimetrics Journal* 34 (1994), pp. 369–82.

Lander, E.: "DNA fingerprinting: science, law, and the ultimate identifier." In Kinles, D., Hood, L., and Cambridge L., eds.: *The Code of Codes* (Cambridge, MA: Harvard University Press, 1992).

National Research Council (NRC), Committee on DNA Technology in Forensic Inference: *DNA Technology in Forensic Science* (Washington, DC: National Academy Press, 1992).

National Research Council (NRC): *The Evaluation of Forensic Evidence* (National Washington, DC: Academy Press, 1996).

Neufeld, P. J. and Colman, N.: "When science takes the witness stand." *Scientific American* 262 (1990), p. 46.

Office of Technology Assessment: *Criminal Justice: New Technologies and the Constitution.* OTA-CIT-366 (Washington, DC: US Government Printing Office, May 1988).

Office of Technology Assessment: *Genetic Witness: Forensic Uses of DNA Tests.* OTA-BA-438 (Washington, DC: US Government Printing Office, July 1990).

Peterson, J. L., Mihajlovic, S., and Gilliland, M.: *Forensic Evidence and the Police: The Effects of Scientific Evidence on Criminal Investigations* (Washington, DC: US Government Printing Office, 1984).

Peterson, J., Ryan, J., Houlden, P., and Mihajlovich, S.: "The uses and effect of forensic science in the adjudication of felony cases." *Journal of Forensic Sciences* 32 (6) (1987), pp. 1730–53.

Purcell, N., Thomas, L., Winfree, L. Jr. and Mays, G. L.: "DNA (deoxyribonucleic acid) evidence and criminal trials: an exploratory survey of factors associated with the use of 'genetic fingerprinting' in felony prosecutions." *Journal of Criminal Justice* 22 (1994), p. 145.

Symposium on the 1996 NRC Report on DNA Typing: *Jurimetrics Journal* 37 (1997), pp. 395–506.

Thompson, W. C. and Schumann, E. L., "Interpretation of statistical evidence at criminal trials: the prosecutor's fallacy and the defense attorney's fallacy." *Law and Human Behavior* 11 (1987), p. 167.

Wade, N.: "F.B.I. set to open its DNA database for fighting crime." *The New York Times*, Oct. 12, 1998, p. 1, c6, p. 16, c1–2.

Wasserman, D., Tully, L., and Prenger, V.: "The impact of DNA typing on criminal investigation and adjudication in four Maryland jurisdictions: a preliminary report." *College of American Pathologists Conference XXXIV*, Feb. 27, 1999, Bethesda, MD.

Wasserman, D. and Weedn, V.: "Forensic DNA typing: consensus and controversy." *Scientific Evidence Review* 1 (1992), pp. 32–6.

Weedn, V. W.: "Forensic DNA tests." *Clinics in Laboratory Medicine* 16 (1996), pp. 187–96.

Weedn, V. W. and Hicks, J. W.: "The unrealized potential of DNA testing." *Research in Action* (National Institute of Justice, June, 1998), pp. 1–8.

Cases

Daubert v. Merrell Dow Pharmaceuticals, 509 U.S. 579 (1993).
Frye v. United States 293 F. 1013 (1923).
People v. Castro, 545 N.Y.S. 2d 985 (1989).

Further reading

Ballantyne, J., Sensabaugh, G., and Witkowski, J., eds.: *"DNA Technology and Forensic Science"*: *Banbury Report 32* (Cold Spring Harbor, NY: Cold Spring Harbor Press, 1989).

Billings, P. R., ed.: *DNA on Trial: Genetic Identification and Criminal Justice* (Plainview, NY: Cold Spring Harbor Laboratory Press, 1992).

Kaye, D. H.: "The admissibility of DNA testing." *Cardozo Law Review* 13 (1991).

Lempert, R.: "Some caveats concerning DNA as criminal identification evidence: with thanks to the Reverend Bayes." *Cardozo Law Review* 13 (1991).

Mays, G. L., Purcell, N., and Winforce, L. T.: "DNA (deoxyribonucleic acid) evidence, criminal law and felony prosecutions: issues and prospects." *Justice System Journal* 16 (1992), pp. 111–22.

National Research Council (NRC), Committee on DNA Technology in Forensic Inference: *DNA Technology in Forensic Science* (Washington, DC: National Academy Press, 1992).

National Research Council (NRC): *The Evaluation of Forensic Evidence* (Washington, DC: National Academy Press, 1996).

Symposium on the 1996 NRC Report on DNA Typing: *Jurimetrics Journal* 37 (1997), pp. 395–506.

Wasserman, D. and Weedn, V.: "Forensic DNA typing: consensus and controversy." *Scientific Evidence Review* 1 (1992), pp. 32–6.

27

Privacy and Genetics

MADISON POWERS

Introduction: Promise and Perils

The growth of scientific knowledge about the contribution of genetics to disease and human behavior brings in its wake both promise and peril. The promise lies in the increased understanding of the pathways of disease and, eventually, new interventions that can cure existing medical conditions or, perhaps more importantly, interventions that prevent premature mortality and excess morbidity. The peril lies in the discovery of the genetic basis of disease for which no cures or preventive interventions are available, while the knowledge of increased genetic susceptibility to disease can result in harm when disclosed to others. The fear of the unintended, adverse consequences of such disclosures to patients and research subjects has led to considerable discussion of the moral importance of protecting genetic privacy (Andrews et al. 1994; Rothstein 1997; Nuffield Council 1993).

Recent interest in the threats to individual privacy posed by the genetic revolution comes at a time of renewed interest in medical privacy generally, especially in light of the increased commercial and governmental claims for a need for access to such information for the purposes of controlling the costs and monitoring the outcomes of healthcare interventions. Moreover, the expansion of genetic knowledge and the increased ability to learn more about an individual's current medical condition, as well as predictive information about his or her susceptibility to disease in the future, arises in a context in which the revolution in information technology has by itself heightened fears that highly sensitive personal information of all sorts is increasingly difficult to protect from access by a wide variety of persons and used for a wide variety of purposes. Many of these purposes are in conflict with the interests of the person about whom the information is obtained.

The combination of the genetic revolution, the informatics revolution, and the increased desire by government and commercial interests for expanded access to information has potent consequences. The genetic revolution holds out the promise of obtaining an unprecedented degree of personal information about individuals not otherwise obtainable through ordinary medical testing techniques. The informatics revolution produces the new capabilities for collecting, storing, transmitting, sorting, combining, and analyzing personal information. A consequence of these new capabilities is that a more fine-grained, highly detailed profile of an individual is possible, including data about medical condition, susceptibility to disease not yet clinically manifested, psychological predispositions, individual behaviour and consumer preferences, and legal and other public records. The mere possibility that more personal information can be obtained and analyzed in ways that reveal more about individuals than once was possible, in turn, further stimulates an interest among researchers, marketers, insurers, employers, law enforcement officials, educators, and social workers for information for which they can claim a plausible need to know in order to do their jobs more effectively.

Among the many pressing moral issues raised by the genetic revolution is the question of how the seemingly reasonable claims of a legitimate "need to know" should be balanced against the equally compelling demands of individuals to retain control over access to personal information. In short, the contest is between the claims about the moral importance of preserving an individual's genetic privacy versus the medical, scientific, social, and economic benefits that might accrue if privacy restrictions are relaxed.

The aim of this chapter is to examine: (i) the history of moral views about the value of individual privacy generally and of medical privacy in particular; (ii) how, if at all, genetic information differs from other types of highly sensitive, personal medical information; (iii) the range of morally significant interests that count in favor of privacy protection for such information and the major options for addressing the interests that give rise to claims of a need for enhanced genetic privacy; and (iv) the rise of genetic paternalism and the desire of some to override individual privacy concerns for the sake of third parties or society at large.

The History of Privacy as a Moral Concept

Philosophers, academic lawyers, and social theorists disagree over how the concept of privacy is best understood. Privacy, on one popular account, is an expansive notion, connoting a state in which public access to the thoughts, actions, decisions, and personal facts about persons is and should be limited or restricted. This expansive account treats privacy as a claim about those spheres of personal life that are inherently private, or not the proper subject for intervention by the state or persons other than those for whom access is explicitly consented to by an individual.

One problem with expansive privacy definitions is that it is exceedingly difficult to defend a conception of what kinds of matters are inherently private. Historical accounts of the history of the human desire for maintaining some sphere of privacy reveal considerable cultural and individual differences in views of what matters are justifiably restricted from public scrutiny and intervention (Ariès and Duby 1987–91). A second problem with expansive privacy definitions is that they often conflate accounts of what a state of privacy *is* with moral claims about what weight privacy interests *ought* to be assigned when they conflict with other morally significant interests (Parent 1983). It is one thing to describe what a condition of privacy is in terms of the limited access others have to aspects of an individual's life, but quite another to articulate what matters are so important – and why – that they merit some insulation from the public. A third problem is that expansive definitions tend to be too sweeping in their account of the nature of privacy rights. For example, a famous definition of privacy rights treats the right of privacy as derivative from a broader right to be left alone, and a widely criticized view of privacy that developed in United States constitutional doctrine views privacy as a right broad enough to encompass some restriction on interference with certain medical choices (e.g., abortion) (Warren and Brandeis 1984; Parent 1983).

For the purposes of this chapter, privacy is defined in a narrow, less controversial sense, focusing on informational access. Privacy on this narrow view is a condition or state in which cognitive access to personal information is restricted (Powers 1996). The narrow definition reflects three key assumptions. First, whatever the merits of a view of political morality that condemns some types of state interference with intimate actions and personal decisions, the moral case for restriction of access to information often varies from the moral justification for insulating an individual from the efforts of others to gain knowledge about that individual. Although some decisions may be much more difficult to make (e.g., whether or not to bear a child to term) without some measure of informational privacy, many justified claims for keeping certain kinds of information from public view (as we shall see below) do not rest on the assumption that autonomous decision-making is undermined without restriction of others' access to information.

Second, cognitive access can be obtained by any of the senses, as well as through verbal or written communication or any indirect means of obtaining information, such as through the use of medical tests. Accordingly, the kinds of threats to informational privacy are as various as the means to learning about an individual. With each new technological development, such as a genetic test for increased susceptibility to a disease, the risks to personal privacy expand.

Third, since no one can ensure complete restriction of the cognitive access to personal information by others, short of living in total isolation, concern for personal privacy is always a matter of degree and is typically confined to specific kinds of information. Individuals may have good reasons for medical professionals and family members having access to certain genetic information, but they may not want that information made available to employers, insurers, or the public at large. Similarly, they may have stronger reasons for guarding genetic information relating to behavioral predisposition than other forms of disease susceptibility on the grounds that the former is more likely to be misused or misconstrued. Moreover, any claim about the moral importance of privacy and its loss must be tied to some argument about why it is reasonable to want to deny others access to some specific kind of personal information. All losses of privacy therefore are not on par morally, and only those that are nontrivial and not outweighed by competing moral considerations give rise to a justifiable claim of a moral right to privacy.

Although concerns about privacy may, for many observers, seem like a distinctively modern worry, or indeed, a uniquely contemporary preoccupation, the history of privacy in medical contexts goes back at least 2,500 years in Western culture to the origin of the Hippocratic Oath. The ancient physician's Oath holds, "What I may see or hear in the course of treatment in regard to the life of men, which on no account one must spread abroad, I will keep to myself holding such things shameful to be spoken about." This Hippocratic tradition, which has remained a important influence even in contemporary medical education, reflects an absolute, unqualified commitment to maintaining the privacy of medical information obtained from the course of the confidential physician–patient relationship.

However, the Hippocratic tradition contrasts sharply with more recent formulations of the physician's duties of confidentiality. The statement of the American Medical Association adopted in 1980, for example, reflects a far more qualified commitment. It states that the physician "shall safeguard patient confidences within the constraints of the law." The clear implication is that other considerations given legal preeminence can override moral concerns about privacy, and that the law reflects morally justifiable exceptions to duties of confidentiality. Among the most widely discussed exceptions are duties to warn third parties of imminent threats to third parties, such as threats of physical violence disclosed by psychiatric patients in the course of a therapeutic relation or the existence of communicable diseases such as HIV infection and the physician has reason to believe that the patient is putting others at risk of infection. The upshot is that the long-term trend within the ethical codes of physicians has been toward a weaker view of the felt importance of patient privacy in relation to other social goals.

Other factors also tend to weaken the strength of the shared public commitment to keeping medical information private. Some commentators have noted that the traditional commitment to privacy is a "decrepit" concept, out of sync with the realities of clinical medicine and the institutional demands of practicing modern medicine (Seigler 1982). The old model of the physician–patient relationship is one in which no other parties are involved in the delivery of care. By contrast, the delivery of care now requires access to medical information by a large number of persons, including nurses, orderlies, medical testing personnel, hospital and primary care center administrators, auditors in charge of obtaining third party reimbursement for services, independent evaluators concerned with monitoring quality of care, and numerous other persons having a bona fide need to know a patient's medical information.

Medical information is widely disseminated in many other nonmedical contexts as well, such as military records, school and counseling records, records of court proceedings, local and regional local public health office records of neonatal screening tests administered at birth, employee personnel files containing information from employment physical examinations, applications for life and health insurance, and the data sets of researchers and epidemiologists who have access to medical records but no direct involvement in the delivery of clinical services. In many cases, some of the persons having ready access to personal medical information are not bound by quite the stringent legal duties of confidentiality that apply to physicians, and many are not constrained by the traditional codes of professional ethics that elevate the value of individual privacy above competing social values which can and often conflict with privacy concerns (Rothstein 1994–5).

In sum, clinical reality, as well as the prevailing institutional arrangements developed outside of the context of clinical medicine, render medical privacy an illusion. The perception of many privacy advocates – those Alan Westin aptly terms privacy fundamentalists – is that the pervasive lack of privacy protection is deeply troubling, and that legal and other institutional realignments are needed to restore a greater

367

degree of privacy protection for individual medical and other similarly sensitive personal information (Westin 1994). Numerous privacy protection laws have been passed or proposed over the last 30 or 40 years, especially in European countries. The aim of most of the proposals is to grant individuals greater control over access to such information and to establish data privacy protection boards to restrict and regulate the subsequent use of medical information over which individuals no longer exercise control once disclosed initially for limited purposes to physicians and others (Rothstein 1996; Schwartz 1997).

From a short-term perspective, the growing public concern about the loss of individual privacy may appear as a relatively recent phenomena, inspired by an increased awareness of the threats to personal privacy posed by advances in information technology and social and economic institutions that seem to have an unquenchable appetite for more and more information. However, from the longer term perspective, the relatively recent resurgence of those making the moral case for privacy fundamentalism is a response to what can only be seen as a wholesale retreat from privacy that has characterized the last 50 years, especially in the realm of medicine.

Genetic Exceptionalism

In addition to worries about privacy threats posed by technological advances and institutional arrangements are anxieties about the capacity for genetic testing research to reveal unprecedented knowledge about individuals heretofore unimaginable. The rapid pace of efforts to map and sequence the human genome, as well as the almost daily reporting of genetic associations with various diseases, has placed the special issue of genetic privacy, as opposed to medical privacy *per se*, prominently on the public policy agenda in many industrial nations. Many privacy advocates favor stronger privacy protections for genetic information than for other types of medical information based on the premise that genetic information and its unwanted dissemination have potentially greater adverse consequences than the loss of privacy with regard to other types of medical information (Annas 1993; Annas 1995). However, the moral case for privacy fundamentalism within the realm of genetics depends both on the plausibility of that assumption – that genetic information is fundamentally different in nature – and the further assumption that special or different levels of privacy protection for genetic and other medical information is feasible or wise. The claim that genetic information merits a higher standard of protection against privacy loss is sometimes referred to as genetic exceptionalism (Murray 1997).

The argument for genetic exceptionalism rests on a number of claims about the putatively unique nature of genetic information and its greater capacity to produce harmful consequences if disseminated. There are a number of closely related themes underlying this claim. One assertion is that genetic testing reveals information about conditions likely to manifest themselves in the future, even though the subject of testing has no clinical symptoms at the time of testing. Another claim is that, as more is learned about how genes can be responsible for a variety of seemingly unrelated conditions, testing for one condition also has the potential to reveal the existence of other medical conditions or genetic susceptibilities not contemplated at the time of consent to testing. Because of genetic testing's potential to reveal information relevant to one's medical future and its potential to convey information not contemplated at the time of testing, one concern is that genetic testing has greater potential for serious economic and social consequences than other types of medical information, and that individuals have less opportunity to protect their interests. Moreover, it is claimed that genetic testing, unlike other types of medical testing, reveals information about the current or future health status of other family members. A further worry is that the risk of misinterpretation, inaccuracies inherent in testing, and the public's willingness to attribute too much weight to predictive information obtained, together with the relevance of individual testing to the privacy interests of other family members, make the need for special precautions greater. Finally, some may also conclude that all of the above stated implications of genetic testing carries with it an added psychological and emotional burden caused by their awareness of the potential for an expanded range of adverse consequences.

All of these concerns are reasonable causes for caution. However, none of these features of genetic information makes it unique, either in the kinds of ancillary or subsequent information genetic testing yields or in its potential for social, psychological, or economic burdens. Many other sorts of medical tests, including cholesterol testing, provide the basis for prediction of future illnesses. Many routine blood tests simultaneously yield information about a multiplicity of current or future medical conditions. Moreover, nongenetic medical tests which yield information about especially sensitive medical conditions, such as mental illness, may, if revealed to others, pose a greater threat to an individual's social and economic interests than genetic information about relatively benign, less socially stigmatized medical conditions or predispositions. In addition, a great deal of medical information currently collected bears on the risk factors for disease for other family members, either because of the family history suggesting a common genetic basis or because of shared increased risk associated with a common environment.

A second set of objections raised against genetic exceptionalism rest on the lack of feasible or justifiable alternatives for treating genetic information differently from other kinds of medical information. One argument is that there is simply no conceptually bright line that can be drawn between genetic information and a host of other kinds of medical information already relied on in clinical contexts (Yesley 1997). Family histories offer clinicians clues to the possible genetic basis of illness, as well as providing some basis for prediction of future illness. Unless the suggestion is that such information be segregated from other medical information contained in patient files, then special treatment would require excision of data that clinicians already collect and retain as part of their patient's medical records. Moreover, the argument for special treatment of information obtained from genetic testing is further undermined by the need of clinicians to have ready access to and rely on all of the relevant information they can get in order to provide high quality medical care to their patients. The force of that argument is likely to be magnified as more conditions can be diagnosed and treated as a result of genetic tests.

Although criticisms of both the uniqueness claim and the reasonableness of genetic exceptionalism view go a long way in undermining the claim for a need of more stringent level of privacy protection for genetic information, these arguments, however, do not automatically favor the status quo. The case for raising the standards for privacy protection for genetic information and other kinds of medical data will fail or succeed on the strength of the arguments for the importance of the interests that underlie concerns for medical privacy in general.

The Moral Basis of Medical Privacy Rights

Unwanted access to personal information including medical information undermines a variety of morally significant individual interests. Perhaps no one interest accounts for all of the reasons personal privacy is highly valued, but a family of related values have been put forward by various privacy theorists (Reiman 1976; Fried 1984; Rachels 1975). One important consideration is that of autonomy, or the ability to make important life choices free from the scrutiny of others. Individuals may seek to keep genetic and other medical information inaccessible to others on the grounds that the judgments of others may unduly influence their reproductive decisions.

A second kind of interest underlying the case for privacy rights is the fact that disclosure of personal information such as the existence of some physical or mental disability may interfere with a person's social and economic prospects. Employers may be reluctant to hire or promote persons (correctly or incorrectly) thought to have significant limitations that might affect job performance or length of service in the job. Insurers and mortgage lenders might take such conditions into account when making underwriting decisions for fear that the individual poses a greater than average financial risk.

A third interest sometimes cited as a major reason for privacy protection is that a measure of insulation from public scrutiny is necessary for the formation of intimate relationships and that the essence of such relationships is the selective disclosure of highly personal matters to persons having a special bond of intimacy.

Two other interests center around the psychological consequences that loss of privacy might entail. The fourth interest lies in the direct impact of privacy loss for the individual. Individuals are said to have an interest in retaining privacy in virtue of the role privacy plays in the formation of one's own self-concept. The claim is that unwanted disclosures may result in emotional distress, loss of self esteem, and an inability to form a stable sense of self when details about one's frailties and vulnerabilities are widely known (Reiman 1976). The fifth concern focuses on the judgments of others. Disclosure of highly sensitive, personal information can lead to social stigma, embarrassment, and a loss of the respect of others (Rachels 1975).

The list of relevant interests arguments underlying the moral importance of privacy rights might include many other concerns as well, but three points are worth noting about the nature of the interests at stake. First, the kinds of interests individuals have tend to cleave into two broad categories. The first category involves losses of valuable social and economic opportunities. Privacy protection is not the only way such losses could be prevented. Instead of ensuring privacy, public policies can be fashioned such that unwanted disclosures do not have the undesirable consequences they have under some particular set of social arrangements. On this view, the moral focus shifts from restricting access to restricting use of information. For example, if the risk is to one's employability or insurability then that risk may be mitigated by antidiscrimination policies. Keeping information inaccessible to others is therefore not the only way to address the moral claims that lie at the heart of some privacy concerns. This observation suggests that in an important range of cases, the fundamental moral concern is not privacy per se but rather some claim about the requirements of distributive justice such that the use of personal information to determine what distributive share of valuable social opportunities and individual gets is unfair (Powers 1997). In short, not all arguments many put forward for more stringent privacy rights decisively show that inaccessibility of others to personal information is what is morally required to protect the interests individuals are most concerned to safeguard. The second category of interest, however, is not so easily guaranteed by policies designed to curb the undesirable uses of personal information. The threats to autonomy, the potential impact on self-esteem, the ability to form intimate relationships, and the potential for social stigma identify interests that only some restrictions on access to information – as contrasted with restrictions on its use – is likely to successfully combat. One could argue, of course, that change of public attitudes and efforts to educate and reduce prejudice might render the need for privacy protection less important. Although a not implausible suggestion, fundamental change of social attitudes is not as easily accomplished as the change of social and economic arrangements that make certain uses of information illegal or unprofitable.

The difference between interests that can be best satisfied through curbs on information use and curbs on information access points up the second observation about the moral basis for privacy rights. Privacy in itself is not intrinsically valuable. Privacy protection only takes on moral importance in light of the contingent threats to other valuable human interests, and the existence of those threats are a function of whatever social attitudes and social arrangements happen to be in place (Powers 1994). In a world of fewer prejudices, a smaller differential in economic and social power and opportunities, the need for privacy protection would diminish. Therefore, the issue of how weighty genetic privacy interests are in comparison to competing social interests is a question that can only be answered by an assessment of how much the proliferation of individual genetic information would shift the balance of power and distribution of opportunities within society. To the extent that dissemination of genetic information renders individuals more vulnerable to the vicissitudes of the marketplace, genetic privacy takes on greater importance. To the extent that access to individual genetic information reinforces ethnic, social, and other forms of prejudice, or fuels beliefs in a crude biological determinism or a movement for eugenics, then the case for genetic privacy is strengthened (Wolf 1995).

That the moral justification for moral rights to privacy is dependent upon human vulnerabilities that can vary depending on differing social contexts suggests a further conclusion. The need for either stronger or weaker forms of privacy protection will depend upon the extent of the risks to individual interests inherent in each context. Liberal access to genetic information in contexts where the interests of individuals are not inherently in opposition is better justified than in instances in which the interests are not in conflict. Employers and employees often have opposing interests, as do health insurers and persons seeking insurance. By contrast, it is less obvious that epidemiologists and other medical researchers have interests that are in direct opposition, and thus the case for greater access to genetic information for the sake of scientific advancement may be stronger.

In many instances, nonetheless, some of the strongest advocates for privacy protection have been found in the research context (Knoppers and Laberge 1995; Clayton 1995). Many researchers argue for the need for access to individual genetic information having personal identifiers in order to correlate genotypic and phenotypic information and thereby advance scientific knowledge more efficiently. However, researchers often defend the need for stringent privacy protections such that third parties including insurers and employers do not gain access to that information, and they argue for a high standard of informed consent, which includes disclosure of privacy related risks. They thus argue for acting an abundance of caution so that the bonds of trust will be strengthened and the public will be reassured that researchers are acting in the public interest without compromising the interests of individuals in the process. To the extent that third party risks to privacy losses are mitigated, while ensuring adequate access for research purposes, many of those who have addressed genetic privacy questions in research contexts argue along the lines Alan Westin describes as a privacy pragmatist position. Indeed, if the risks to individual interests are less in such contexts than in some other contexts in which interests are inherently antagonistie, then the case for a privacy pragmatist approach may be persuasive.

A third observation about the family of interests that underlie privacy rights claims is that, although the interests are conceptually distinct, they often travel together. Social prejudice, for example, often tracks risks to employment. In many instances, the threat to one's future employment opportunities may not be a result of an accurate assessment of an individual's capacity to be a productive employee, but rather an assessment of that individual's potential based on social prejudice. The upshot is that the best case for genetic privacy protection is often built out of a combination of rationales, each mutually supporting one another because of the fact that individuals need restriction of access to personal information in order to protect themselves against a battery of harms that tend to cluster. In some instances, the implication may be that more privacy protection, rather than curbs on use of information, may have the better moral argument.

If the arguments of this section are persuasive, then one conclusion emerges: privacy fundamentalism may be a more appropriate moral view in some contexts, while a privacy pragmatism may be better justified in others.

Genetic Paternalism

One arena in which the privacy pragmatist and privacy fundamentalist views appear in sharpest dispute is the clinical care context. The issue is one in which duties of confidentiality to the patient are pitted against the interests of third parties who may be benefitted or protected from harm by the disclosure of genetic information about the patient to third parties. Physicians and genetic counselors face an exceedingly difficult moral dilemma, for example, when an individual patient refuses to allow other family members to know the results of tests that reveal information relevant to their health. The dilemma is especially acute when knowledge of their genetic condition, predisposition, or status as carrier of a trait inheritable by their children could result in treatment, preventive steps to postpone or avert some future medical condition, or aid in making of reproductive decisions.

The standard model most widely discussed focuses on fatal, debilitating, unpreventable, and largely untreatable diseases such as Huntington's disease. Others highlight the relevance of such knowledge for the reproductive decisions of others who may be carriers of genes relating to cystic fibrosis, thalassaemia, or Tay-Sachs. Perhaps most difficult of all, however, are those which may be severe, ultimately fatal, but which may be preventable, ameliorated, or postponed if genetic information is shared. Familial breast cancer and colon cancer are examples.

Many take a somewhat wary view of the significance of individual privacy claims in such contexts. Some of this skeptical view about the weight of privacy considerations owes much of its appeal to analogous arguments made in some other medical contexts in which patient privacy is pitted against the interests of third parties. On some occasions, it has been seen as both legally and morally permissible – perhaps even obligatory – for providers of healthcare to disclose confidential information to others in order to protect them from harm. Both moral and legal concerns about this issue are traceable to a famous court case known as the *Tarasoff* case (Pelias 1991). In that case and in similar cases subsequently, courts have held that psychiatrists may have a duty to protect third parties from harm, even when it requires a breach of patient confidentiality.

Analogous duties have been argued for in the context of contagious diseases such as HIV. More recently, lawyers and ethicists have begun to consider the extension of these duties in cases involving genetic information (Suter 1993; Hannig 1993; Andrews 1997). Two questions have emerged as central concerns. First, what are a healthcare professional's moral duties to protect third parties potentially at risk of harm by disclosing to them confidential genetic information obtained from a patient? Second, to what extent ought these moral duties to be reflected in the law?

Several positions on these questions can be found in the literature. Some, including the members of a 1983 President's Commission on Biomedical Issues in the United States, the Nuffield Council on Bioethics in Britain, and the authors of the Institute of Medicine (IOM), report on genetic testing, favor a legal duty to disclose any medical information including genetic test results, when it might prevent harm to third parties. However, they support such a duty only in narrowly defined circumstances (Andrews et al. 1994; President's Commission 1983; Nuffield Council 1993).

The analytic framework of the President's Commission provides the starting point for the IOM recommendations and for most other discussions of duties to disclose genetic information. They recommended four necessary conditions which should be met before disclosure is justified. First, there must have be an unsuccessful attempt to persuade the patient to disclose the information to the relevant party. Second, there must be a high probability of harm without disclosure and a high probability that the disclosure itself will avert the anticipated harm. Third, the potential harm must be serious. Fourth, only the degree of informational detail necessary to avert harm should be disclosed.

Some other commentators favor disclosure in a broader array of cases. They appear more concerned, for example, about the role of health professionals in promoting the public health generally, especially when no one else appears to be in a position to avert harm to innocent third parties. One strand of this view favoring broader disclosure seeks to dissolve the conflict between patient and family members by reconceptualizing the identity of the patient. Dorthy Wertz and John Fletcher, for example, claim that "hereditary information is a family possession rather than simply a personal one" (Wertz and Fletcher 1991). Because the healthcare professional's duty is seen as one directed toward the whole family as patient, patient-oriented duties of confidentiality do not conflict with duties to outsiders, but rather the professional's duties are seen as obligations to do the best for the interests of their patients, understood as the family unit.

A more moderate view concludes that there may be a morally sufficient justification for giving healthcare professionals a qualified legal *privilege or prerogative* to disclose, even when there is not a morally sufficient justification for imposing a legal duty requiring disclosure. That is to say that, while it rejects the idea that the moral case for imposing a duty on healthcare professionals is strong enough to hold professionals legally liable for not doing so, it accepts that there is enough conflict of opinion that professionals should be able to follow their own conscience on the issue. Accordingly, healthcare providers would not be held legally liable either to a patient who might sue for breach of confidentiality, *or* to a third party who might sue on the grounds that the professional failed to take steps that might have prevented harm to him or her.

Some privacy fundamentalists, however, appear strongly opposed to any legal duty for healthcare professionals to disclose confidential information over the objections of patients, even if it can be argued that professionals have some *prima facie* moral duty to prevent harm to others. Their arguments, typically turn on the greater weight of the potentially harmful consequences of further weakening the relationship of trust between patients and providers (Orentlicher 1997).

There are three other more powerful reasons for taking the privacy fundamentalist position in the clinical context involving conflicting familial interests.

First, there are significant worries about the wisdom of putting the healthcare professional in the role of enforcer of otherwise commendable social goals and of presuming that a decision about what is in the best interest of the family unit is within the scope of their moral authority or in principle a matter about which medical professionals are competent to judge. If one is in the grip of a largely paternalist view of the role of healthcare professionals, one may be easily tempted to see this task as part of one's legitimate professional brief. This is especially likely if one argues that the *family*, rather than the individual, is the patient. In that case, one naturally sees the case as less of a conflict between patient interests and third party interests.

However, healthcare professionals may not be well suited to assume the role of enforcers of a particular view of family communication or of an ideal of familial loyalty and connectedness which everyone does not share. Family dynamics, as well as the understanding of what a family is, are not uniform or determined solely by biological connection. While medical professionals may have superior insight into the strictly medical aspects of the dilemma, even there we do not ordinarily presume that superior medical insight entitles them to override the purely medical aspects of their patients' decisions. Medical paternalism of this sort has been roundly rejected. That we should presume that healthcare professionals have superior moral insight into whether the expected medical benefits to the recipient of the information outweigh all of the other potential harms that might ensue grants to the medical professional a degree of moral authority that exceeds even that of the widely discredited versions of medical paternalism. Healthcare professionals do not train to be clairvoyants or family values police; nor should we want them to.

Moreover, this first line of criticism cuts against even the qualified privilege view. If one is skeptical of vesting in the healthcare professional the moral authority to decide whose interests predominate, one should be equally cautious in granting even a qualified legal privilege to health professionals to take on this role as ultimate decision-maker. For the main thrust of this argument is that they lack both the moral warrant and the epistemic credentials to be assigned the job of striking the proper balance.

A second general reason for a cautious attitude toward leaving it to healthcare professionals to decide when to breach a patient's confidentiality is that the patient, whose interest in confidentiality is sacrificed, is not normally the direct cause of potential harm to third parties. Recognition of a professional's duty to disclose genetic information to family members imposes burdens on persons who simply fail to assist others, not on persons who, for example, through their own violent or risky behaviors impose risks on innocent third parties. Thus, most cases of a patient's failure to disclose genetic information to a family member are not quite like the psychiatric or HIV cases, where we can claim that individuals, through their own behavior, may have forfeited their privacy rights.

A third ground for caution is that there are, other more appropriate ways for healthcare professionals to discharge their moral obligations. Some of these involve a fairly substantial shift away from the nondirective end of the counseling continue. Some have considered the shift away from the norm of nondirective counseling, only to reject that option as undermining the values of patient autonomy (Rhodes 1998). However, a merit of this alternative is that it allows the healthcare professional an avenue for moral integrity and allows him or her to do more than stand idly by when a patient makes a choice the healthcare professional finds morally objectionable. A more directive approach to *encouraging* the disclosure of information during the post test counseling phase arguably is less of an interference with patient's autonomy than the unilateral decision to take matters into one's own hands in order to prevent harm to others. If done with sensitivity, and presented as a form of dialogue among moral equals, the more explicit approach to the discussion of the values of the provider may actually *facilitate* rather than *frustrate* autonomous decision-making.

In sum, there are good grounds for skepticism toward many of the moral rationales put forward for a legal duty to warn of genetic risks, and these grounds are equally forceful against the more moderate claim for a qualified privilege for healthcare professionals to decide either way. As important as the needs to protect others is, it is perhaps more important not to succumb to the temptation to assign to ourselves the moral responsibility for correcting all of the ills that come within our reach. Although some measure of this noble impulse is necessary to keep us from the opposite vice of doing nothing in the face of evil, we should be modest about the scope of our individual moral authority to redesign the world according to our own moral visions. This lesson applies no less to healthcare professionals than to others who occupy positions of great responsibility, and as a consequence, naturally feel the tug of conscience in the face of the decisions of others with whom we morally disagree.

Conclusion

The genetic revolution has arrived just at a time in which the privacy fundamentalist view in medicine is in considerable decline, the threats to personal privacy are exacerbated by developments in information technology, and the concentration of power in market economies limits the life options of many individuals. In some instances, the case for privacy fundamentalism seems quite compelling; in other cases, the privacy pragmatist position seems better justified. Those cases in which genetic privacy fundamentalism seems most plausible are ones in which individuals are most vulnerable when they lack ability to control access to personal information, restrictions on use of information are less likely to protect the underlying interests at stake, and the moral authority of other individuals and institutions to decide the proper balance between privacy and the public good is most in doubt.

References

Andrews, L.: "Gen-etiquette: genetic information, family relationships, and adoption." In Mark Rothstein, ed.: *Genetic Secrets: Protecting Privacy and Confidentiality in the Genetic Era* (New Haven, CT: Yale University Press, 1997), pp. 255–80.

Andrews, L. et al.: *Assessing Genetic Risks: Implications for Health and Social Policy* (Washington, DC: National Academy Press, 1994).

Annas, G.: "Privacy rules for DNA databanks: protecting coded 'future diaries.'" *Journal of the American Medical Association* 270 (1993), pp. 2346–50.

Annas, G.: "Genetic prophecy and genetic privacy – can we prevent the dream from becoming a nightmare?" *The American Journal of Public Health* 85 (1995), pp. 1196–7.

Ariès, P. and Duby, G., gen. eds., *A History of Private Life*, vols. 1–5 (Cambridge, MA: Belknap Press, 1987–91).

Clayton, E. et al.: "Informed consent for genetic research on stored tissue samples." *Journal of the American Medical Association* 274 (1995), pp. 1786–92.

Fried, C.: "Privacy: a moral analysis." Reprinted in F. Schoeman, ed.: *Philosophical Dimensions of Privacy: An Anthology* (New York: Cambridge University Press, 1984), pp. 203–22.

Hannig, V. et al.: "Whose DNA is it anyway? Relationships between families and researchers." *American Journal of Medical Genetics* 47 (1993), pp. 257–60.

Knoppers, B. and Laberge, C.: "Research and stored tissues: persons as sources, samples as persons?" *Journal of the American Medical Association* 274 (1995), pp. 1806–7.

Murray, T.: "Genetic exceptionalism and 'Future Diaries': is genetic information different from other medical information?" In M. Rothstein, ed.: *Genetic Secrets: Protecting Privacy and Confidentiality in the Genetic Era* (New Haven, CT: Yale University Press, 1997), pp. 60–73.

Nuffield Council on Bioethics: *Genetics Screening: Ethical Issues* (London: The Council, 1993).

Orentlicher, D.: "Genetic privacy and the physician–patient relationship." In M. Rothstein, ed.: *Genetic Secrets: Protecting Privacy and Confidentiality in the Genetic Era* (New Haven, CT: Yale University Press, 1997), pp. 77–91.

Parent, W. A.: "Privacy, morality, and the law." *Philosophy and Public Affairs* 12 (1983), pp. 269–83.

Pelias, M.: "Duty to disclose in medical genetics: a legal perspective." *American Journal of Medical Genetics* 39 (1991), pp. 347–54.

Powers, M.: "Privacy and the control of genetic information." In M. Frankel and A. Teich, eds.: *The Genetic Frontier: Ethics, Law and Policy* (Washington, DC: American Assoc. for the Advancement of Science, 1994), pp. 77–100.

Powers, M.: "A cognitive access definition of privacy." *Law and Philosophy* 15 (1996).

Powers, M.: "Justice and genetics: privacy protection and the moral basis of public policy." In M. Rothstein, ed.: *Genetic Secrets: Protecting Privacy and Confidentiality in the Genetic Era* (New Haven, CT: Yale University Press, 1997), pp. 355–68.

President's Commission for the Study of Ethical Problems in Medicine and Biomedical and Behavioral Research: *Screening and Counseling for Genetic Conditions* (Washington, DC: The Commission, 1992).

Rachels, J.: "Why privacy is important." *Philosophy and Public Affairs* 4 (1975).

Reiman, J.: "Privacy, intimacy, and personhood." *Philosophy and Public Affairs* 6 (1976), pp. 27–44.

Rhodes, R.: "Genetic links, family ties, and social bonds: rights and responsibilities in the face of genetic knowledge." *Journal of Medicine and Philosophy* 23 (1998), pp. 10–30.

Rothstein, M.: "The use of genetic information for nonmedical purposes." *Journal of Law and Health* 9 (1994–5), pp. 109–20.

Rothstein, M., ed.: *Genetic Secrets: Protecting Privacy and Confidentiality in the Genetic Era* (New Haven, CT: Yale University Press, 1997).

Rothstein, M. and Knoppers, B.: "Legal aspects of genetics, work and insurance in North America and Europe." *European Journal of Health Law* 3 (1996), pp. 143–61.

Schwartz, P.: "European data protection law and medical privacy." In M. Rothstein, ed.: *Genetic Secrets: Protecting Privacy and Confidentiality in the Genetic Era* (New Haven, CT: Yale University Press, 1997), pp. 392–417.

Seigler, M.: "Confidentiality in medicine – a decrepit concept." *New England Journal of Medicine* 307 (1982), pp. 1518–21.

Suter, S.: "Whose genes are these anyway?: Familial conflicts over access to genetic information." *Michigan Law Review* 91 (1993), pp. 1869–87.

Warren, S. and Brandeis, L.: "The right to privacy." Reprinted in F. Schoeman, ed.: *Philosophical Dimensions of Privacy: An Anthology* (New York: Cambridge University Press, 1984).

Wertz, D. and Fletcher, J.: "Privacy and disclosure in medical genetics examined in an ethics of care." *Bioethics* 5 (1991), pp. 212–32.

Westin, A.: "Privacy and genetic information: a socio-political analysis." In M. Frankel and A. Teich, eds.: *The Genetic Frontier: Ethics, Law and Policy* (Washington, DC: American Assoc. for the Advancement of Science, 1994), pp. 53–76.

Wolf, S.: "Beyond 'genetic discrimination': toward the broader harm of geneticism." *Journal of Law, Medicine and Ethics* 23 (1995), pp. 345–53.

Yesley, M.: "Genetic privacy, discrimination and social policy: challenges and dilemmas." *Microbial and Comparative Genomics* 2 (1997), pp. 9–35.

Further reading

Andrews, L. et al.: *Assessing Genetic Risks: Implications for Health and Social Policy* (Washington, DC: National Academy Press, 1994).

Frankel, M. and Teich, A., eds, *The Genetic Frontier: Ethics, Law and Policy* (Washington, DC: American Assoc. for the Advancement of Science, 1994).

Nuffield Council on Bioethics: *Genetic Screening: Ethical Issues* (London: The Council, 1993).

President's Commission for the Study of Ethical Problems in Medicine and Biomedical and Behavioral Research: *Screening and Counseling for Genetic Conditions* (Washington: The Commission, 1992).

Rothstein, M., ed.: *Genetic Secrets: Protecting Privacy and Confidentiality in the Genetic Era* (New Haven, CT: Yale University Press, 1997).

Schoeman, F., ed.: *Philosophical Dimensions of Privacy: An Anthology* (New York: Cambridge University Press, 1984).

28

DNA Banking: A Retrospective-prospective

BARTHA MARIA KNOPPERS

Introduction

In August 1999, the National Bioethics Advisory Commission (NBAC) released its long-awaited report: *Research Involving Human Biological Materials: Ethical Issues and Policy Guidance.*[1] For the past decade there has been a good deal of confused debate over DNA sampling and banking, which, as I argue below, the Report goes only some way towards dispelling. Why has there been such heated controversy over human genetic materials? The short answer to this question is that DNA, found in all biological materials, can, without the consent of the source, be readily obtained and subjected to unwanted scrutiny or study.

Collectively, we humans constitute the human genome as opposed to the plant or animal genomes, with whom however we share most of our DNA. But individually, we are uniquely different. DNA is found in every human cell. DNA samples provide the scientific opportunity to prove difference and diversity. Yet genetic information is also necessarily "familial," to say nothing of its possible socioeconomic implications if released to third parties (e.g. employers and insurers). It also carries the baggage of historical (eugenics) and social (stigmatization) misuse. Thus, a single stray strand of hair *qua* DNA sample is not so simple in its connotations, and study of it may entail egregious consequences for the individual.

The NBAC Report makes 23 recommendations which fall into the following eight categories:

1 Adequacy and interpretation of existing federal policies for the protection of human subjects;
2 Federal and state legislation governing medical record privacy;
3 Informed consent;
4 Waiver of consent;
5 Reporting of research results to subjects;
6 Consideration of potential harms to others;
7 Publication and dissemination of study results; and
8 Professional education and responsibilities.

Leaving the first two USA-specific areas aside, below I concentrate on the remaining six, in turn, and analyze whether and how each advances the debate or, perhaps, settles certain issues. First, however, it will be helpful to indicate which definitions the Committee employed when framing its Report, since the way in which the terms are characterized is central to my ensuing discussion.

Definitions

The Commission adopted the following definitions:

Unidentified samples – sometimes termed "anonymous" – are those supplied by repositories to investigators from an unidentified collection of human biological specimens.

Unlinked samples – sometimes termed "anonymized" – are those that lack identifiers or codes that can link samples to identified specimens or particular individuals. Typically, repositories send unlinked samples from identified human biological specimens to investigators without identifiers or codes so that identifying particular individuals through the clinical or demographic information that is supplied with the sample or biological information derived from the research would be extremely difficult for the investigator, the repository, or a third party. Unlinked samples also include those that are already in an investigator's possession and whose identifiers have been removed by a disinterested party.

Coded samples – sometimes termed "linked" or "identifiable" – are those supplied from identified specimens by repositories to investigators. However, these samples do not include any identifying information, such as patients' names or Social Security numbers. Rather, they are accompanied by codes. In such cases, although the repository (or its agent) retains the ability to link the research findings derived from a sample with the individual source by using the code, the investigator (or one reading a description of the research findings) would not be able to do so.

Identified samples are those supplied by repositories from identified specimens with personal identifiers (such as names or patient numbers) that are sufficient to allow the researcher to link directly the biological information derived from the research with the individual from whom the material was obtained.

Several preliminary remarks about these definitions are in order. First, the Commission makes clear that the use or study of samples during clinical care or for other activities such as quality control procedures (e.g. calibration) or teaching does *not* reside within the ambit of *research*, defined as "a systematic investigation designed to develop or contribute to generalizable knowledge." This is not as obvious as it may, at a glance, appear. For a decade now certain guidelines or laws have tended to "sacralize" the sample[2] and have restricted the use of any products of the body in the absence of consent. Second, the Commission also deems that for such samples to be considered "human subjects" under federal regulations, these samples must be *identifiable*. Hence protection is stipulated only when research can be *linked to specific human subjects.* The Commission qualifies this, however, with the caveat that attention ought to be paid to the possibility of group harms, such as loss of health insurance coverage, should "group or family interests be revealed or placed at risk because of research that is conducted on a class of similar, albeit individually unidentifiable samples" (p. 61). NBAC also warned that unlinking samples (so as to avoid recontact and consent as well as ethics review) could seriously "reduce the scientific value of the research" (p. 61).

Informed Consent

Distinctions must be drawn between the informed consent for samples obtained during routine medical care and those obtained specifically for research. It goes without saying that samples obtained during clinical care cannot be used for research without an explicit informed consent and that refusal to consent should in no way affect clinical care. But what if at the time of medical care, there is no research project and it is only later that the researcher wants to use an archived sample for research?

To answer that question the Commission further distinguished between coded or identified samples and unlinked or unidentified samples. By their very nature, the use of unidentified samples irrespective of origin does not require consent. Moreover, if originally identified and obtained with consent during either routine care or for research and then unlinked, it is impossible to go back for consent. Thus, the Commission considered that it would be "appropriate for research on unlinked samples to be exempt from IRB [Institutional Review Boards] review in most circumstances" (p. 58). While then obtaining a new consent for research on unlinked samples is neither necessary nor possible, it should be emphasized again that NBAC warned that unlinking samples (so as to avoid recontact and a new consent as well as ethics review) could seriously "reduce the scientific value of the research" (p. 61). All future research would also be limited.

It goes without saying that consent to sampling for research purposes includes not only an informed agreement on the purposes and risks and benefits of the possible research uses but also of any future uses. What happens if new research purposes arise? Can one agree in advance to a general release of the sample for *any* future research?

To answer that question requires distinguishing between two classes of samples, those obtained prior to the adoption of a policy such as NBAC's and those since. The tendency had been for the use of samples to be limited to the purposes explicitly mentioned and general releases were generally frowned upon as not constituting a truly informed consent. Indeed, often there were four classes of samples, those limited to a single project studying a certain condition, those limited to research on a particular condition but not to one project, those permitting research on related conditions, and those permitting genetic research generally (the latter "blanket" clause often refused by ethics committees). In the situation of a sample taken prior to the NBAC report, where the sample is still coded or identified, NBAC recommends that the investigator and the IRB should review existing consent documents to determine whether the subjects anticipated and agreed to participate in the type of research proposed. If the existing documents are inadequate and consent cannot be waived, the investigator must obtain informed consent from the subjects for the current research, or, in appropriate circumstances have the identifiers stripped so that samples are unlinked.

Even though the report had the support of a majority of Commissioners, controversy arose within the Commission on the proper policy for sampling in the future. Among the options for informed consent suggested for potential participants were:

a)   refusing use of their biological materials in research,
b)   permitting only unidentified or unlinked use of their biological materials in research,
c)   permitting coded or identified use of their biological materials for one particular study only, with no further contact permitted to ask for permission to do further studies,
d)   permitting coded or identified use of their biological materials for one particular study only, with further contact permitted to ask for permission to do further studies,
e)   permitting coded or identified use of their biological materials for any study relating to the condition for which the sample was originally collected, with further contact allowed to seek permission for other types of studies, or
f)   permitting coded use of their biological materials for any kind of future study.

The last two options were considered by one commissioner as undermining the evaluation by the IRB of the risk–benefit ratio, to say nothing of the criterion of a fully informed consent. Yet, according to another commissioner: "Without a general consent option, I am concerned that consent forms in the clinical setting will become too complicated and patients will be overly concerned and opt not to sign. Even when the research will be minimal risk and not require informed consent, such biological materials will be forever lost to research, because they would have been excluded at the time of biopsy or excision from any future research use" (p. 65).

It has taken over a decade to move the debate past the "DNA is just biological stuff" to the "DNA is the person" position, and finally, in the NBAC report, to the position which we could qualify as "all human biological materials require respect." This constitutes a significant milestone in that the debate has contained allegations that research on such materials without a specific informed consent runs afoul of the Kantian imperative, in that it uses "a person" as a means to an end. Terms to describe this phenomenon range from "instrumentalization," to "commodification," to "reification."

The impact on research has not been negligible. Research ethics committees were often spending more time pondering the need to obtain consent from the "sources" of samples long deceased, or on whether the risk–benefit ratio could include an evaluation of an open-ended consent to any research, or, whether that latter should be proscribed altogether. As the number of options offered to participants grew, the number of contradictory positions of professional societies did as well. In spite of a certain conservatism or hesitancy on some issues, the NBAC Report constitutes an important innovative landmark.

NBAC innovates in its position that research can only be said to be "human subject research" when it involves an identifiable sample. While not denigrating the significance of human biological material, the Commission took a pragmatic and practical approach. One can only speculate that this is due in part to the worrisome trend of unlinking (anonymizing) samples to enable such research to be done. While ethically expedient and efficient, the long-term risks of this approach to circumvent the "DNA sample as person" conservatism were already noted by HUGO's (Human Genome Organization) Ethics Committee in its "Statement on DNA Sampling."[3]

Moreover, other than the position of professional organizations of pathologists, this is the first time in the DNA banking world that research subjects can (if the recommendations are followed) permit the use of coded or identified samples for any related study and also give permission for further contact to seek permission for other studies.

One might question the open-ended, unknown obligations that further contact would entail. If such permission were given, issues of a limit on the length of time of the obligation, the mobility of participants or of researchers, lack of response, and so on would have to be considered. Indeed, the even more revolutionary suggestion that permission could be given for the use of "coded materials" for *any kind* of *future study*, with no specific obligation to recontact, opens the door for a broader base of participation. This position finally recognizes the meaningful distinction that should be drawn between research involving living persons, embryos, gametes, nonregenerative tissues such as organs, and, finally, biological materials.

Waiver of Consent

One particular aspect of the American federal regulations (the "Common Rule") is the possibility of avoiding consent of the person altogether when a study is of minimal risk. Obviously, the actual physical risks of sampling are negligible, but the psychosocial harms are not, if future uses run contrary to personal cultural and spiritual values, for example. The Commission preferred an interpretation of the concept of minimal risk as meaning the "risks of everyday life." Accordingly, the risks of harm resulting from the improper use of medical records would not be a risk of daily life.

> Nonetheless, NBAC believes that most research using human biological materials is likely to be considered of minimal risk because much of it focuses on research that is not clinically relevant to the sample source, as compared to research with medical records, for example, which is likely to be filled with clinically relevant findings that could harm the individual is misused or used inappropriately by third parties. (p. 67)

Thus, if adequate confidentiality mechanisms are in place especially as concerns third parties, and also for communication to the physician if need be, then research protocols on coded samples of minimal risk would not require IRB review. This "liberal" interpretation of the regulations applies only to samples collected before the adoption of the Report since its recommendations foresee the possibility of offering an open prospective consent to the participant.

Reporting of Research Results to Subjects

Considering the current disagreement on whether findings should be communicated to subjects, the Commission left it to IRB's to develop guidelines. Should only confirmed, reliable and clinically significant and relevant information be provided? In general, "the disclosure of research results to subjects represents an exceptional circumstance" (p. 72). Obviously, this restriction as well as a plan for how to manage disclosure when necessary forms part of the consent procedure. According to the Commission, disclosure should occur only when the following apply:

a)   the findings are scientifically valid and confirmed,
b)   the findings have significant implications for the subject's health concerns, and
c)   a course of action to ameliorate or treat these concerns is readily available.

Most importantly, at the time when research results are disclosed, "appropriate medical advice or referral should be provided" (p. 72).

The reporting of results constitutes another thorny issue. While anonymization also avoids any duty to report back since a "person" cannot be found, there comes a point where findings become valid and clinically significant and anonymization is ethically questionable. Nevertheless, to avoid confusion and possibly needless psychological harm, NBAC rightly limits reporting back. New communication tools need to be developed however. Considering the current public and private discomfort with genetic information even if the conditions are met, we might wish to consider limiting reporting back to the person's family physician. Are we ready to permit refusal without any idea of the consequences when such information is received with no health professional intermediary?

Considerations of Potential Harms to Others

Both group risks already mentioned earlier and risks and benefits to relatives (e.g. the disease or condition being studied is genetic or involves infectious agents or toxins) are raised by the Commission. Currently, the regulations do not require that the concerns of first-degree relatives be considered. Such harms where foreseeable should be minimized and when appropriate, researchers should consult the representatives of the relevant groups. If the specific research protocol poses a risk to a specific group this should be disclosed. The Commission avows that living relatives of a "deceased sample source might have an interest in the research, particularly if the investigation has focused on hereditary traits" (p. 73). No position is taken an access by such relatives except to say that people are human subjects under the federal regulations only while they are living.

It is unfortunate that NBAC did not use this report to clarify the situation of the rights of relatives to access such materials or information during the life of a person or after his/her death, or of a possible duty to warn at risk relatives. On the latter issue, HUGO's Ethics Committee[4] and others[5] have maintained the existence of an ethical duty to warn the relative, if the person refuses and the condition is preventable or treatable. With respect to the former, there may be an implicit acquiescence to access to the DNA of the deceased relative by family members (limited to cases of medical need?) with NBAC's simple pronouncement that people are human subjects only when they are living. Similarly, NBAC shirks the larger issues of publication of research results (including negative results?) and of access to medical records and the (continued?) use of information therein). This latter issue is relevant to pharmacogenomic studies that combine classical, clinical drug trials with DNA banking. The issues may simply be too vast and important. The Report itself was already four years in the making.

Publication and Dissemination of Research Results

No inroads are made by NBAC concerning the publication of research results especially with regard to pedigrees. The Commission merely repeats that potential harms to the privacy of individuals or gorups should be minimized. Crucial statements do, however, address both the issue of the source of funding, i.e. public or private, and the ethical requirements of journals. On the former, NBAC does not find it to be "an important consideration in determining the ethical acceptability of the research" (p. 74). On the latter, NBAC specifically recommends that

> [j]ournals should adopt the policy that the published results of research studies involving human subjects must specify whether the research was conducted in compliance with the requirements of the Common Rule. This policy should extend to all human subjects research, including studies that are privately funded or are otherwise exempt from these requirements. (p. 74)

Professional Education and Responsibilities

Education refers not only to information but to "the ongoing effort to inform, challenge and engage" (p. 75). This may sound like standard exhortation, the need for public understanding of research and resources being a universal concern. But NBAC goes further and maintains (as distinct from recommends) that "because it is the research community that seeks access to these materials, for policy purposes the moral burden should fall upon researchers to elicit from prospective contributors, both individuals and groups, the values and meaning that they attach to the requested samples" (p. 75).

Use of Medical Records

Finally, the Commission skirts the issue of the conditions governing access to medical records, access necessary for any meaningful research on human biological materials. It notes however, that debates about confidentiality are relevant in two ways. Firstly,

385

access to medical records for research involves information about human beings and so constitutes human research and thus its recommendations could provide a model framework. Secondly, there may be a tendency to create a dual system – one for medical records and one for human biological materials. Harmonization is necessary, and any legislation should "ensure that appropriate access for legitimate purposes is maintained" (p. 75).

Conclusion

In short, one can only hope that NBAC's enlightened approach will find its way into banking politics. The actual and future societal benefits of research are often forgotten in the "atomistic" age of individual rights. While the proper and necessary barrier to collective abuse, the extension of such rights to unidentified or even coded samples thwarts such benefits, and ultimately belittles respect for "real" persons, that is, persons who are more than their DNA.

Notes

1 National Bioethics Advisory Commission. *Research Involving Human Biological Materials: Ethical Issues and Policy Guidance.* Vol. I (Rockville, Maryland, 1999).
2 B. M. Knoppers and C. M. Laberge, "Research and Stored Tissues: Persons as Sources, Samples as Person?" *JAMA* 274(22) (1995), 1806.
3 HUGO Ethics Committee, "Statement on DNA Sampling: Control and Access." *Eubios Journal of Asian and International Bioethics* 8 (1998), 56.
4 Ibid.
5 President's Commission for the Study of Ethical Problems in Medicine and Biomedical and Behavioral Research, *Screening and Counselling for Genetic Conditions* (Washington, DC, US Govt. Printing Office, 1983).

29

Genetic Difference in the Workplace

MICHAEL S. YESLEY

Introduction

In recent years, there has been a cascade of discoveries of genetic mutations associated with various health disorders. Identification of these mutations will enable the determination of who is at risk for the disorders and also the development of treatments. Until the treatments become available, however, genetic technology will permit diagnosis and prediction, but not prevention of disorders. The increasing ability to determine healthy individuals' genetic risks of future disorders, coupled with the inability to alter those risks through treatments or preventives, has raised concern about genetic discrimination. Many fear employers will use genetic testing to identify at-risk individuals and exclude them from employment in order to reduce absenteeism and the cost of health insurance in the future. Commentators have cautioned about the creation of a "biological underclass" of healthy persons barred from employment and other opportunities solely because of genetic abnormalities (Nelkin and Tancredi 1997).

The specter of genetic discrimination has prompted international organizations and governmental bodies to take action. In 1997, UNESCO adopted the Universal Declaration on the Human Genome and Human Rights, which proclaims, "No one shall be subjected to discrimination based on genetic characteristics that is intended to infringe or has the effect of infringing human rights, fundamental freedoms and human dignity" (UNESCO 1998: Article 6). Similarly, the Council of Europe's Convention on Human Rights and Biomedicine, also adopted in 1997, prohibits "any form of discrimination against a person on grounds of his or her genetic heritage" (COE 1997: Article 11). The Convention bars tests to predict genetic disease or detect genetic susceptibility to disease except for health purposes or scientific research (ibid., Article 12). Official bodies in several countries, including Canada, the United Kingdom, Germany, and the Netherlands, have recommended controls on the use of genetic information by employers (Rothstein and Knoppers 1996).

In the United States, President Clinton has stated, "We must prevent the misuse of genetic tests to discriminate against any American" (Clinton 1998). A recent report by several executive agencies recommended the adoption of a federal law to bar employers from requiring genetic tests or using genetic information to discriminate against employees (DOL; DHHS; EEOC; DJ 1998).[1] Several states have already adopted laws prohibiting genetic discrimination in employment, but the executive report argues a federal law is needed to assure nationwide protection.

The decade-old Americans with Disabilities Act (ADA),[2] generally bars employers from discriminating against job applicants or workers with disabilities. The ADA does not specifically mention genetics, but the Equal Employment Opportunity Commission has issued an interpretation that an employer who discriminates on the basis of a worker's unexpressed disease gene "regards" the worker as disabled and consequently may be violating the ADA.[3] This interpretation has not yet been judicially reviewed (EEOC).[4]

In the absence of a federal statute specifically barring genetic discrimination in employment, 18 states have adopted laws that prohibit employers from discriminating on the basis of any genetic characteristic.[5] Most of these laws include measures to protect genetic privacy, such as prohibitions of mandatory testing as a condition of employment. Several of the laws permit voluntary genetic testing to determine whether an employee is susceptible to a workplace exposure.[6] New York is the only state that specifically permits an employer to require genetic testing for susceptibility to disease from a workplace exposure.[7] Whether the testing is voluntary or mandatory, none of the laws permits exclusion if the test results show that an individual is genetically susceptible to a workplace exposure. The decision whether to work in the risky environment is left to the employee.

A few states provide exceptions to their prohibitions against genetic discrimination in employment when "based on a bona fide occupational qualification"[8] or "directly related to a person's ability to perform assigned job responsibilities."[9] These exceptions reflect a misconception of genetic anomaly. An unexpressed genetic characteristic, by definition, cannot affect job performance, and the exceptions are therefore meaningless.

New Hampshire's 1995 law is typical. It bars employers from (1) requiring genetic testing as a condition of employment, or (2) affecting the terms of anyone's employment on the basis of genetic testing.[10] The statute excludes from the definition of genetic testing any test to determine whether an individual meets "reasonable functional standards" for a specific job,[11] which, as noted above, is a meaningless clause since genetic testing cannot determine ability to function. With consent, an employee may be tested to determine susceptibility to toxic substances in the workplace, provided the employer does not take any adverse action as a result of the test.[12]

The international proclamations and legislation against genetic discrimination in employment do not reflect evidence that such discrimination is actually occurring. Legislators in the United States have often cited three surveys of genetic discrimination, but these reports provide only anecdotal evidence of discrimination or what survey respondents considered to be discrimination. The studies acknowledge their results are not based on representative sampling and therefore cannot support estimates of overall incidence. Moreover, one of the studies, published in *Science* (Lapham, Kozma, and Weiss 1996), failed to distinguish between having a genetic disease and merely being at risk for genetic disease. As a result, the extent to which asymptomatic persons experienced the discrimination reported in this study cannot be determined.

(Discrimination against individuals with existing disorders is not customarily considered genetic discrimination.)

A more recent survey of more than one thousand geneticists and their patients also provides scant evidence of genetic discrimination. The geneticists reported a total of 550 asymptomatic individuals who were refused employment or insurance because they were carriers or genetically predisposed to disease. Since the geneticists collected these reports in nearly 3 million patient sessions, the response rate of about one report of discrimination in 5,000 sessions indicates a very low level of discrimination. Further, the patient-respondents reported only 2 percent had been refused employment, and the surveyor concluded that "it is not clear from the data that genetics is a separate, or even a major, cause for such refusals."

Last year the American Management Association asked about genetic testing in its annual survey on workplace testing at major US firms. Although more than three-quarters of the respondents reported that they perform some medical testing, less than 1 percent conduct genetic testing (AMA 1998). These results represent mid-sized and large companies, which conduct more comprehensive testing of new hires than smaller firms. Thus, probably well under one percent of all employers conduct genetic testing of new hires. Since employers conduct so little genetic testing, there is little opportunity for them to practice genetic discrimination.

In the absence of actual experience of genetic discrimination in employment, the flurry of state laws and congressional proposals to prohibit such discrimination is being driven by concern for the future. Congressman Obey has stated, "It would be a tragedy...if those dollars [spent on the Human Genome Program], instead of winding up producing a net good for the American people, wind up simply producing a greater ability for different powerful parties in this economy to discriminate on the basis of genes which individuals could not order beforehand but were stuck with after they were born" (Obey 1996). That result would indeed be a tragedy, but there is little evidence it has yet occurred. It might be argued that the genetic antidiscrimination laws have succeeded in preventing this outcome, but the laws are recent and surveys going back a decade and longer have consistently reported little use of genetic testing, not to mention genetic discrimination, by employers (USCOTA 1983, 1990).

Thus, the genetic antidiscrimination laws are proactive, intended to prevent problems from occurring in the future, in contrast to more customary legislation that reacts to existing problems. The forward-looking genetic legislation presents a challenge to its drafters. Without actual experience of genetic discrimination, it is difficult to envision the many nuances of genetic discrimination and the likely impacts – positive and perverse – of attempts to prevent it. Consequently, the recent genetic anti-discrimination laws paint with a broad brush. Most statutory prohibitions of genetic discrimination in employment are absolute or near-absolute, like the civil rights measures barring race and sex discrimination. The laws assume genetic discrimination can never be justified, thereby ignoring the possibility that the exclusion of individuals with certain genotypes from certain jobs might sometimes be warranted in the interest of public safety or the health of the workers. The prohibitions lack flexibility to protect workers and the public when the employment of an individual with a certain genotype will create a substantial risk to health or safety.

389

The remainder of this chapter will explore the need for flexibility that is missing from the genetic antidiscrimination laws adopted to date.

The circumstances under which genetic discrimination might be justified on grounds of health or safety are limited and, at present, largely hypothetical. Many conditions must be satisfied to overcome moral and social objections to differential treatment of employees on the basis of their genetic characteristics. When genetic mutations for occupational susceptibilities are identified, employers should first be required to eliminate the exposures (rather than the susceptible workers), thereby making the workplace safe for all workers. Next, in most cases where an exposure cannot practicably be eliminated from a workplace, the employer should inform the workers or applicants of the genetic risk, make testing available, and permit those identified as susceptible to determine for themselves whether to take a job entailing the exposure. Only substantial risks to susceptible workers' health may warrant mandatory exclusion rather than self-determination by the workers.

Similarly, when genetic mutations are identified for predispositions to late-onset disorders that could threaten public safety, there may be alternatives to the exclusion of workers with those mutations. Such threats could occur when a genetic disorder results in mental deterioration or physical collapse of a worker whose actions could endanger many lives, such as an airline pilot. However, the onset of most disorders is detectable by physiological or functional tests before the disorders create a hazard. In those cases, it is unnecessary to exclude asymptomatic individuals from the work-place merely because they have the genetic mutations predictive of the disorders. Safety concerns justify exclusion only when the initial expression or effect of a genetic characteristic is so subtle or sudden that periodic medical or functional tests cannot detect the onset of the disorder before it endangers the public.

As a general matter, any proposal to exclude individuals from employment on the basis of genetic difference should be suspect. Genetic difference must not become an unchallenged rationale for excluding individuals who can be productive members of society. Any exclusion from employment on the basis of a genetic characteristic must not only be supported by conclusive scientific evidence of the effects of the mutation, but also a lack of feasible alternatives to avoid those effects and a likelihood of serious consequences if the effects are not avoided. On the other hand, the possibility that genetic risk may justify exclusion from employment under certain conditions should not be ignored. The challenge is to balance two goals: preventing misuse of genetic information and achieving the potential benefits from such information.

Under what circumstances might predictive genetic information be relevant and its use be appropriate in making hiring decisions? Some distinctions among job appli-cants are appropriate to hiring decisions, others not. Certainly employers may select applicants on the basis of their training, experience, and other aspects of professional qualification. However, characteristics such as race, sex and ethnicity are generally irrelevant and inappropriate (as well as unlawful) considerations for hiring, because they usually reflect prejudice rather than any rational basis for exclusion.

Disability is also considered an unfair basis for employment discrimination when an individual is "otherwise qualified" or, under the ADA, capable of performing a job with "reasonable accommodation." Unlike race, sex, and ethnicity, which are seldom relevant to job performance, disability may bear on an individual's ability to perform.

Accordingly, the ADA does not absolutely prohibit consideration of disability but requires that disability not play a disproportionate role in hiring decisions and that needless impediments to job performance be removed.

To accomplish this goal, the ADA prohibits discrimination based on disability against an individual who "with or without reasonable accommodation, can perform the essential functions of the employment position."[13] The jurisprudence applying the ADA to particular circumstances is complex and ongoing,[14] but the pertinent lesson of this law is that the principle of equality does not bar all consideration of disability in making a selection for employment. Disability may serve as the basis for exclusion when it unavoidably prevents the performance of a crucial aspect ("essential function") of employment.

We may ask, then, whether genetic abnormality should be treated like disability or like race, sex, and ethnicity. If race, sex, and ethnicity are the model, then an absolute or near-absolute prohibition on the use of genetic abnormality as a basis for employment discrimination is justified. But if disability is the model for protection against genetic discrimination, a prohibition against discrimination should be qualified, to permit consideration whether a genetic abnormality is relevant to the job at hand. There is also the possibility that certain kinds of genetic abnormality should be treated like race and sex, almost never justifying discrimination, and other kinds of genetic abnormality should be treated like disability, that is, a potential disqualification depending on the particular circumstances of the disorder and the employment position.

Genetic abnormality is not a uniform characteristic with an unvarying risk message. To the contrary, the predictive value and implications of genetic information vary substantially. A genetic abnormality in a healthy individual may indicate a probability or certainty (usually the former) that the carrier will be affected by a disorder, irrespective of environmental influences. Or the abnormality may indicate that the carrier is susceptible to a particular environmental influence, related or unrelated to the workplace, exposure to which is likely to result in a disorder. Although a genetic risk signifies an above-average relative risk, it may still be a very small absolute risk. If the abnormality is recessive, it may affect offspring but not the carrier of the trait. The disorder itself may vary unpredictably in severity and time of onset, and it may or may not be treatable. The test for the abnormality may have high or low false positive and false negative rates. Further, the early manifestation of the disorder may, or may not, be detectable and may have consequences primarily for the affected individual or may also endanger others. This substantial diversity of genetic risk requires a legislative treatment that "discriminates" according to the type of risk.

Most genetic risks are clearly not relevant to fitness for employment and should be prohibited as a basis for discrimination, following the model of race and sex. The most obvious type of genetic characteristic that should play no role in selection for employment is a recessive trait that presents no risk to the carrier. The only reason for not hiring an applicant on the basis of a recessive trait is to avoid the expense of providing healthcare to the applicant's affected offspring. This expense would ultimately be reflected in the employer's cost of providing healthcare benefits. Since employers play a substantial, quasi-public role by supplying health insurance to half the covered population in the United States, they have a broader obligation than their own profit in this regard. Until the United States institutes a more inclusive healthcare system, it is appropriate to require that employers disregard the possibility that certain applicants are more likely than others to have children with genetic disorders.

Another type of genetic characteristic that should play no role in selection for employment presents a risk to the carrier unrelated to any occupational exposure or to the safety of others. The employment will not endanger the employee with this characterstic, nor will the employee endanger anyone else by virtue of the characteristic. The carrier is now healthy but has an above-average likelihood (or certainty) of a late-onset disorder, a predisposition to cancer, or a susceptibility to a non-occupational exposure. None of these events will endanger others, because the job does not threaten safety under any circumstances (for example, a clerical position) or because the disorder for which the individual is at risk is detectable before it threatens safety.

Thus, the only person at risk in this situation is the worker, and this risk is not altered by susceptibility to an occupational exposure. The employer who discriminates in this situation wishes to avoid future costs of healthcare, as in the case of a recessive gene, and also the costs of absenteeism due to the employee's anticipated illness. The discriminating employer's position may seem stronger here than in the previous situation involving a recessive gene, since the worker's attendance – not merely the cost of healthcare benefits – is likely to be affected in the future. In both situations, however, the quasi-public role of employers in providing health insurance, as well as our social commitment to equal opportunity and the fundamental importance of earning a living, outweigh the employer's speculative economic benefit from discriminating.

If a disorder will threaten the safety of others before its symptoms can be detected, being genetically predisposed to the disorder might present an unacceptable risk that should outweigh both privacy and antidiscrimination rights of a worker. In such fields as transportation and construction, where the safety of the public or fellow workers is a major concern, the rights of the employee and the risk to others must be balanced. For the same reason that drug testing of transportation workers is permitted or required, test results ruling out the presence of certain genetic characteristics may be an appropriate condition for employment in these fields.

As noted in the foregoing discussion of alternatives, however, it will not always be necessary to exclude individuals from employment when their genetic characteristics raise safety concerns. Very few mutations are likely to be associated with disorders that will threaten safety before their symptoms can be detected. Consider the case of an asymptomatic 30-old pilot with a family history of Huntington's disease (HD) and therefore a 50 percent risk of getting the disease himself. At present, the pilot is quite competent to fly. If he inherited the mutation, HD will likely occur by age 50. The initial symptoms will be subtle but incompatible with flight safety. When the pilot applies for a flying position, should the airline (a) refuse to consider him for employment under any circumstances, or (b) require him to be tested for the HD mutation and then refuse to hire him if the test is positive?

In fact, neither action may be necessary to preserve safety. If the pilot agrees to be tested for the HD mutation, there is an even chance of discovering the mutation is absent. Even if the pilot inherited the HD mutation, the first symptoms of the disease can be detected, and the pilot removed from flying duties, before safety is threatened. Although a routine physical examination would be inadequate, a more rigorous neurological examination would detect the first symptoms. If the pilot does not wish to be tested for the HD mutation or tests positive, the neurological examination can be required annually and will assure safety.

Some disorders, however, may not be detectable before they threaten safety. For example, about half of all heart attacks cause sudden cardiac death, in which the heart abruptly stops working and death occurs within an hour. This can occur in a person who does not have detectable blockage of a heart artery. A recent study found that sudden cardiac death runs in families and therefore has a genetic cause. If researchers succeed in identifying a mutation that predicts sudden cardiac death with a high likelihood, it may be justified to require job applicants with a family history of sudden cardiac death to be genetically tested and, if they have the mutation, excluded from positions in which sudden incapacity could threaten public safety.

Many variables would have to be taken into consideration. Not only the greater risk relative to someone without the mutation, but also the absolute risk associated with the mutation would be relevant. For example, a mutation that increases a risk for sudden incapacity tenfold from one in 10,000 to one in 1,000 might be insignificant, whereas a mutation that increases risk tenfold from one in 1,000 to one in 100 might be significant. Also, a sudden incapacity might have substantial consequences in the case of an airline pilot but insignificant consequences in the case of a train engineer with a "dead-man's switch" that will automatically stop the train if the engineer is incapacitated.

Unfortunately, factors such as these cannot be taken into account under the laws of the 18 or so US states that have prohibited genetic discrimination in employment. These laws absolutely bar discrimination on the basis of genetic information about an applicant or employee. The laws provide, for example, that it is an unlawful employment practice to discriminate against any individual based on the results of a genetic test;[15] an employer shall not discriminate with respect to compensation, terms, or conditions of employment on the basis of genetic information, refusal to submit to, or make available results of, a genetic test;[16] an employer shall not use any genetic information or test results of an employee or prospective employee to distinguish between, discriminate against, or restrict any right or benefit;[17] an employer shall not solicit, require or administer genetic testing as a condition of employment, or affect the terms, conditions, or privileges of employment or terminate employment based on genetic testing;[18] an employer may not make any inquiry which expresses discrimination as to genetic predisposition;[19] it is an unlawful employment practice to limit, segregate, or classify an employee in such a way that would adversely affect the status of an employee on the basis of genetic information concerning the individual.[20] (As noted above, the exceptions to some of these prohibitions cover inability to perform the job, not risk of a future incapacity.)

Absolute prohibitions of genetic discrimination require employers, and permit employees, to disregard genetic warning signs of disorders that are undetectable before they threaten public safety. Although scientists have not yet identified such predictors, their discovery can be anticipated. Unfortunately, the statutory prohibitions require this potentially valuable genetic information to be ignored.

An employee or prospective employee may be genetically susceptible to a workplace exposure that threatens only the employee's own health. Several state genetic antidiscrimination laws recognize the potential usefulness of testing for genetic susceptibility, but none of the laws permits an employer to exclude an employee or applicant whose test results show susceptibility to a workplace exposure. An employer may offer or, in New York, require genetic testing, but may not base any adverse employment action on the test results. The decision to avoid the exposure, possibly by not accepting or resigning from employment, is left to the susceptible employee.

Thus, in balancing occupational safety against antidiscrimination concerns and respect for employees' privacy and autonomy, the states have placed greater value on the latter considerations. Some of the laws recognize the safety concern by permitting voluntary testing for genetic susceptibility, but safety is outweighed by the other considerations, since the employees themselves determine whether to be tested (except in New York) and what use to make of the test results.

This approach seems appropriate for the present. It maintains pressure on employers to eliminate hazardous exposures rather than exclude susceptible employees. Also, mutations for occupational susceptibilities probably have not yet been identified. Further advances in genetics may enable the identification of susceptible employees, however, and there may be circumstances under which exclusion of those individuals would be prudent. Although several steps should be taken before permitting exclusionary policies, for example, making the workplace safe for everyone, verifying scientific evidence of genetic susceptibility, and informing employees of the risks, situations justifying exclusion – albeit hypothetical at present – are conceivable.

Several factors would be relevant in determining the acceptability of mandatory exclusion. These factors include the relative and absolute risk of the disorder if an individual with the susceptibility mutation receives the occupational exposure, the accuracy of the genetic test in detecting the mutation, the seriousness of the disorder, the availability of treatments or preventives, and, of course, the practicability of eliminating the exposure from the workplace. Balancing these many considerations would require a complex calculus.

Under some circumstances, the answer will be clear. If a mutation is common and does not substantially increase the risk from an occupational exposure; if the disorder associated with the mutation is mild, slow to manifest, and treatable; and if the hazardous exposure could be practicably eliminated, an exclusionary policy would not be justified. Instead, we would expect the employer to eliminate the exposure from the workplace.

At the opposite extreme, if a rare mutation in combination with an occupational exposure will cause a disorder that is invariably fatal within a short time of exposure; if the disorder always occurs with, and never without, the presence of the mutation; and if elimination of the exposure from the workplace is not practicable, there would be a strong argument for mandatory testing of all employees and mandatory exclusion of employees found to be susceptible. Under these circumstances, the concern for occupational safety should dominate the antidiscrimination and privacy interests of the employees, but only one state law would permit mandatory testing, and none of the current state laws would permit mandatory exclusion.

394

In an intermediate, gray zone, a moderately prevalent mutation confers susceptibility to an occupational exposure resulting in a serious but nonfatal disorder that will
not manifest for several years and may be treatable. If the exposure to which the
mutation is susceptible can be eliminated from the workplace at reasonable cost, it
should be. But if it is impracticable to eliminate the exposure, the occupational safety
interest may or may not outweigh the employees' interests in privacy and equality.
Some would insist only that notice of the potential risk be given to employees and a
test for the susceptibility mutation be offered or required, but that the employees
determine for themselves whether to avoid the risk. Others, placing more weight on
the safety or efficiency interests, would favor mandatory genetic testing and exclusion
of susceptible persons. Unfortunately, the state laws provide no flexibility to make this
determination.

Conclusion

At present, there are few, if any, genetic characteristics that identify individuals who
would be a threat to public safety in certain jobs or susceptible to certain workplace
exposures, and exclusion from employment based on genetic characteristics is not
justified. However, scientists are likely to discover such genetic indicia in the future. If
there are no alternatives to avoid untoward consequences, it may be appropriate to
exclude those individuals from certain employment positions. Unfortunately, the
recent laws on genetic discrimination in employment prohibit any exclusion based
on genetic information, even in the limited circumstances where exclusion would be
justified.

Notes

1 Department of Labor, Department of Health and Human Services, Equal Employment
   Opportunity Commission, and Department of Justice, *Genetic Information and the Workplace*
   (Jan. 20, 1998). Several bills to bar genetic discrimination in employment have been
   introduced in Congress, but none has yet received a hearing.
2 The employment provisions of the Americans with Disabilities Act are set forth at 42 United
   States Code secs. 12201–13.
3 Equal Employment Opportunity Commission, Definition of "disability" in *EEOC Compliance
   Manual*, vol. 2, sec. 902 (1995). The EEOC administers the employment provisions of the ADA.
4 The validity of the EEOC's interpretation may be determined by a pending decision in which
   the Supreme Court will analyze the "regards" provision of the ADA for the first time.
   Albertson's, Inc. v. Kirkingburg, No. 98–591.
   There have been two federal court decisions involving constitutional challenges to
   genetic testing by employers. *Norman-Bloodsaw v. Lawrence Berkeley Laboratory*, 135 F.3d
   1260 (9th Cir. 1998), challenged a national laboratory's practice of selectively testing new
   hires' blood and urine for sickle-cell trait, syphilis, and pregnancy, unbeknownst to the
   employees. An appellate court found that unconsented testing could violate the constitutional right of privacy and statutory civil rights protection. By contrast, a federal district
   court in *Mayfield v. Dalton*, 901 F.Supp. 300 (D.C. Haw. 1995), found the mandatory

collection of DNA from members of the military in order to provide a means of identifying their remains is not an unreasonable seizure barred by the Constitution. The Ninth Circuit dismissed an appeal for mootness and vacated the district court's judgment, since the complaining soldiers had left the military. *Mayfield v. Dalton*, 37 Fed.R.Serv.3d 458 (1997). The applicability of these cases is probably limited by their unusual facts, but they indicate to employers that genetic testing should not be conducted secretly or without a job-related basis.

5 See Ariz. Rev. Stat. sec. 41-1463.B.4 (1997); Cal. Govt. Code sec. 12926 (1998); Conn. Gen. Stat. sec. 46a-60(a)(11) (1998); Del. Code Ann. tit. 19, sec. 711 (1998); Ill. Comp. Stat. Ann. 513/1–25 (1997) (adopts ADA standards); Iowa Code Ann. sec. 729.6 (1992); Me. Rev. Stat. Ann. tit. 5, sec. 19302 (1998); Mo. Rev. Stat. sec. 375.1306 (1998); N.C. Gen. Stat. sec. 9528.1A (1997); N.H. Rev. Stat. Ann. sec. 141-H:3 (1995); N.J. Stat. Ann. sec. 10:5–12 (1996); N.Y. Exec. Law sec. 296 (1996); Okla. Stat. tit. 36, sec. 3614.2 (1998); Or. Rev. Stat. secs. 659.036, 659.227 (1996); R.I. Gen. Laws sec. 286.7–1 (1992); Tex. Lab. Code Ann. sec. 21.402 (1997); Vt. Stat. Ann. tit. 18, sec. 9333 (1998); Wis. Stat. sec. 111.372 (1992).

6 See e.g. Wis. Stat. sec. 111.372(4)(b) (1992).

7 New York Exec. Law sec. 296, subd. 19(B) (1996).

8 Me. Rev. Stat. Ann. tit. 5, sec. 19302 (1998).

9 Mo. Rev. Stat. sec. 375.1306 (1998).

10 N.H. Rev. Stat. Ann. sec. 141-H:3.I (1995).

11 N.H. Rev. Stat. Ann. sec. 141-H:1.IV (1995).

12 N.H. Rev. Stat. Ann. sec. 141-H:3.IV (1995).

13 42 United States Code sec. 12111(8).

14 For example, the Equal Employment Opportunity Commission and reviewing courts must construe what constitutes a disability, what is "reasonable accommodation" of a disability, and what are the "essential functions" of an employment position.

15 Ariz. Rev. Stat. sec. 41-1463.B.4 (1997).

16 Me. Rev. Stat. Ann. tit. 5, sec. 19302 (1998).

17 Mo. Rev. Stat. sec. 375.1306.1 (1998).

18 N.H. Rev. Stat. Ann. sec. 141-H:3 (1995).

19 N.Y. Exec. Law. sec. 296, subd. 1(d) (1996).

20 Tex. Lab. Code Ann. sec. 21.402(d) (1997).

References

(AMA) American Management Association: *1998 AMA Survey: Workplace Testing and Monitoring* (1998).

Ashford, N. A. et al.: *Monitoring the Worker for Exposure and Disease: Scientific, Legal, and Ethical Considerations in the Use of Biomarkers* (Baltimore: Johns Hopkins University Press, 1990).

Billings, P. R., Kohn, M. A., de Cuevas, M., et al.: "Discrimination as a consequence of genetic testing." *American Journal of Human Genetics* 50 (1992), p. 476.

Clinton, W. J.: State of the Union Address (Jan. 27, 1998).

Council of Europe, *Convention on Human Rights and Biomedicine* (April 4, 1997).

Draper, E.: *Risky Business: Genetic Testing and Exclusionary Practices in the Hazardous Workplace* (Cambridge: Cambridge University Press, 1991).

Epstein, R. A.: "The legal regulation of genetic discrimination: old responses to new technology." *Boston University Law Review* 74 (1994).

Geller, L. N., Alper, J. S., Billings, P. R. et al.: "Individual, family, and societal dimensions of genetic discrimination: a case study analysis." *Science and Engineering Ethics* 71 (1996), p.2.

Jouven, X., Desnos, M., Geurot, C. et al.: "Predicting sudden death in the population: the Paris prospective study." *Circulation* 99 (1999), pp. 1978–83.

Lapham, E. V., Kozma, C., and Weiss, J. O.: "Genetic discrimination: perspectives of consumers." *Science* 621 (1996), p. 274.

Nelkin, D. and Tancredi, L.: *Dangerous Diagnostics*, 2nd ed. (Chicago: University of Chicago Press, 1997).

Obey, D.: Statement, 142 *Congressional Record* H7220-02 (1996).

Rothenberg, K., Fuller, B., Rothstein, M. et al.: "Genetic information and the workplace: legislative approaches and policy challenges." *Science* 275 (March 21, 1997), pp. 1755–7.

Rothstein, M., ed.: *Genetic Secrets: Protecting Privacy and Confidentiality in the Genetic Era.* (New Haven, CT: Yale University Press, 1997).

Rothstein, M. and Knoppers, B. M.: "Legal aspects of genetics, work and insurance in North America and Europe." *European Journal of Health Law* 3 (1996), pp. 143–61.

Smith, D. H., Quaid, K. A., Dworkin, R. B. et al.: *Early Warning: Cases and Ethical Guidance for Presymptomatic Testing in Genetic Diseases* (Bloomington: Indiana University Press, 1998), pp. 62–7.

UNESCO, *Universal Declaration on the Human Genome and Human Rights* (Nov. 11, 1997), Article 6. The General Assembly of the United Nations endorsed the UNESCO Declaration in Dec. 1998. United Nations Press Release GA/9532 (Dec. 9, 1998).

US Congress, Office of Technology Assessment: *The Role of Genetic Testing in the Prevention of Occupational Disease* (Washington, DC: US Government Printing Office, 1983).

US Congress, Office of Technology Assessment: *Genetic Monitoring and Screening in the Workplace* OTA-BA-455 (Washington, DC: US Government Printing Office, 1990).

Wertz, D. C.: "Society and the not-so-few genetics: what are we afraid of? Some future predictions from a social scientist." *Journal of Contemporary Health, Law and Policy* 13 (1997), p. 299.

Further reading

Ashford, N. A. et al.: *Monitoring the Worker for Exposure and Disease: Scientific, Legal, and Ethical Considerations in the Use of Biomarkers* (Baltimore: Johns Hopkins University Press, 1990).

Draper, E.: *Risky Business: Genetic Testing and Exclusionary Practices in the Hazardous Workplace* (Cambridge: Cambridge University Press, 1991).

Epstein, R. A.: "The legal regulation of genetic discrimination: old responses to new technology." *Boston University Law Review* 74 (1994).

Rothenberg, K., Fuller, B., Rothstein, M. et al.: "Genetic information and the workplace: legislative approaches and policy challenges." *Science* 275 (March 21, 1997), pp. 1755–7.

Rothstein, M., ed.: *Genetic Secrets: Protecting Privacy and Confidentiality in the Genetic Era* (New Haven, CT: Yale University Press, 1997).

Rothstein, M. and Knoppers, B. M.: "Legal aspects of genetics, work and insurance in North America and Europe." *European Journal of Health Law* 3 (1996), pp. 143–61.

US Congress, Office of Technology Assessment: *Genetic Monitoring and Screening in the Workplace*, OTA-BA-455 (Washington, DC: US Government Printing Office, 1990).

30

The Insurance Market and Discriminatory Practices

TOM SORELL

Introduction

Insurers try to guard against what they call *adverse selection*: the situation in which those at high risk of some sort of insured loss are covered by policies at prices suited to low or average risk. For individual companies, adverse selection can lead to a vicious spiral of high pay-outs for claims, leading to higher premiums for everyone in their insurance pool, leading to the migration of low risk policy-holders to competing companies. If adverse selection became quite widespread in companies with a large market share, it would lead to general disarray, at any rate in one branch of the insurance business. Income and reserves would simply not meet claims and normal running costs of individual firms. Markets may also break down where claims, income, and reserves are in rough equilibrium, but where the profits of the insurance business are much lower than the profits of other kinds of business, and where it is relatively easy for a commercial provider of insurance to leave the insurance market and enter another in which more money can be made. Both kinds of breakdown are preventable, if commercial risks are accurately assessed and minimized. But success in managing commercial risk can also be morally risky.

To begin with, managing risk can involve intrusive investigation. Because facts relevant to estimating risk are often highly personal, there is a danger that the investigation will be *too* intrusive, violating the right to privacy of people who apply for insurance. Relatedly, an investigation can test the limits of obligations to maintain confidentiality on the part of the doctors of insurance applicants. Managing risk may also lead to refusals of insurance, or offers of insurance at prohibitively high cost to applicants. The financial consequences of being denied insurance can be catastrophic for individuals, especially where commercial markets are the only protection against large potential losses, and the advantages of group insurance are not available. For the purposes of this chapter, only the risks of claims on life, health, and disability insurance are in question, and the main kind of information relevant to risk that will be considered is medical information in general, and genetic information in particular. What special moral risks, if any, are raised by the increasing availability, and increasing scientific understanding, of genetic information, including the results of gene sequencing and mapping?

Suppose that in the relatively near future genetic tests are available for a whole host of inherited diseases and predispositions to disease, some carrying very high costs of treatment or income support. Might not insurance companies require intending customers to take these tests and communicate the results – as a condition of being considered for insurance? And would not such a requirement carry heavy penalties for those already unfortunate enough to suffer from one of the diseases or predispositions? Wouldn't their bad luck be compounded by the prospect of either being refused insurance or paying prohibitively high prices for it? Or, if it is not normally individuals but the companies employing them that bear insurance charges, as in the USA, wouldn't the added costs of insurance to the companies make someone a less attractive prospect as an employee than someone whose good luck it was to have a less disease-prone constitution? Wouldn't some people suffer the triple misfortune of having a genetic predisposition to a certain disease, bad prospects of insurance cover, *and* bad prospects of employment? A similar question arises if life insurance is a condition of taking out a mortgage: in that case the prospects of house-owning may significantly be set back by one's genetic inheritance and the disadvantage it confers in the insurance market.

It is easy to exaggerate both the novelty of the risks posed by genetic information, as well the seriousness of the risks, if current insurance practice is a guide to the future. Tests that screen for sickle-cell anemia and Tay-Sachs disease have been available for a long time; and there are established techniques for establishing whether one will contract Huntington's disease or suffer from Fragile X syndrome. Some of the genetic tests already available detect diseases – Huntington's is a case in point – for which old-fashioned personal and family medical histories have anyway provided good evidence. In short, some of the moral risks of new genetic information are risks already presented by other, less up-to-date medical information, and by well-worn underwriting (risk-assessment) techniques.

Even where the science of genetics has made it possible to test very accurately for health risks, insurers have sometimes been reluctant to require that the relevant tests be taken. What has deterred them is the potential marketing disadvantage of requiring the tests, and the cost of the test procedures themselves, which must be borne whether or not the insurance applicant ever takes up a policy. Some of the diseases for which tests exist are extremely rare. An expensive test for a rare disease is unlikely to be a cost-effective means of minimizing future claims. A moderately cheap test for indications of more common sources of insured losses – cigarette smoking or alcohol consumption – may also not be cheap to conduct often. And even cost-effective tests are likely to discourage potential customers who would rather not know if they have a serious genetic disease or a chance of developing its symptoms, or who dislike undergoing medical tests. Insurers who insist on tests are likely to face competition from other companies who see the market opportunity of offering cover with relatively few questions asked. In life insurance markets as they are already known in the West, certain preferred risks – nonsmokers in their thirties – are sometimes offered life policies with cover over $200,000 on the basis of a telephone conversation – with no medical examination at all. Such practices underline the fact that, in North America and the UK at any rate, insurance companies tend to want to write new business

399

more than they want to avoid risk. In the UK, 95 percent of proposers of life insurance are offered policies on standard terms, and only 1 percent of applications are refused.

Is there more to this risk-taking than meets the eye? In Britain, where insurance contracts are subject to a convention of utmost good faith on the part of insurance applicants, insurers can avoid liability for health or life insurance claims if they can show that an applicant failed to reveal the results of genetic tests or other tests relevant to the insured risk. In practice, however, it is very difficult for insurers to find out whether relevant information about genetic tests is being suppressed unless they are party to a testing process that they set in motion. So not asking for tests may have adverse commercial consequences that the utmost good faith convention does not mitigate. Despite that, a policy statement issued in 1997 by the UK insurers' association specifically disavows plans to ask for tests (ABI 1997). The same policy statement leaves it to individual insurance companies to decide whether to take account of the results of genetic tests voluntarily taken by applicants and made known to the companies. It seems that in the commercial judgment of some members of the insurers' association it may be better for business to overlook evidence of risk than to appear to potential applicants to be reluctant to offer coverage.

Whether or not commercial insurance practice moves in the direction of compulsory testing, and of underwriting that sets premium levels in keeping with test results, it is possible to ask whether it would be morally permissible for it to do so. We can pursue this large question with the aid of three more specific ones. (1) Would compulsory testing and the associated underwriting unfairly overburden certain members of the commercial insurance pool, or unfairly exclude certain people from that pool? (2) Would the testing regime compromise professionals who are third parties to insurance agreements? (3) Would the testing and underwriting regime unreasonably insulate commercial insurers from risks they are in business to cater for, boosting profits with no real benefit to policy-holders or those who need insurance most? Don't those in the most need of insurance have a right to try to circumvent or manipulate the regime?

Unfair Burdens

Insurance companies do not treat all individual applications for insurance in the same way: does this make them guilty of discriminating against some applicants? If someone is refused insurance or offered it at a higher cost than someone else, is that necessarily a case of discriminatory, in the sense of unfair, treatment? Not if the two applicants belong to groups that, statistically, run different risks of loss, and if it is fair for insurance charges to vary with risks of loss. Cases of voluntary risk-taking seem to tell in favor of charging more to the higher risk. After all, why should someone who smokes heavily and overeats in the face of repeated health warnings, and who will probably have contributed by his actions to heart or lung disease if he develops either, be treated the same as someone who, for health reasons, has given up cigarettes and kept their weight down? Equal treatment might be in order if the medical effects of smoking were unknown or undemonstrated, or if the connection between obesity and conditions like diabetes was hidden, but the connections being known, the known risks are different, and if the risks are run willingly, then so much the worse for the overweight smoker who applies for insurance. No doubt things stand differently if someone has tried hard but failed to minimize health risks. But even this sort of case does not affect the conclusion that it is sometimes permissible for different insurance applicants to be offered different terms. The conclusion is perhaps all the more compelling in the case of people who pursue risk for its own sake through a sport or recreation that is particularly dangerous.

When it comes to disorders with a genetic basis, the risk does not result from what the one with the disorder has done, but from his physical make-up. If he is charged more than someone with a different make-up, is he treated unfairly by the insurance company? In dealing with this question it is important not to be seduced by a certain rhetoric. There is a certain naturalness in saying that the policy-holder who is charged more than a standard premium because of a genetically based risk is *penalized* for a condition he cannot help. If this rhetoric were strictly and literally acceptable, then being charged the higher rate *would* be unfair, because it is unfair to be penalized, and therefore held responsible, for a risk one is not responsible for. The fact is, however, that an insurance applicant need no more be penalized when he is charged more for a genetically-based risk than a holder of a certain currency is necessarily penalized when an exchange rate movement unexpectedly makes his foreign holiday more expensive. It is true that the insurance applicant is disadvantaged by his condition and that the tourist is disadvantaged by the exchange-rate movement. It is true that both conditions are normally beyond the control of individuals. But there is no unfairness, no avoidable injustice, necessarily, in being disadvantaged by circumstances beyond one's control. Our tourist is not singled out. *Anyone* holding the same currency is in the same boat. Similarly, the insurance applicant is not singled out if anyone running the same risk of costly illness is charged the same. There is no disrespect or disapproval standardly involved in the forces that underlie exchange rate movements, as there is in acts of penalization. Similarly for actuarial calculations, which give the chances of loss for different risks, based on all the evidence thought to be relevant about the client group that has been accumulated over time. If experience indicates that some people in the client group constitute a risk, it does not seem to follow that the relevant actuarial conclusions penalize people. One might as well say that, through weather forecasts, climatic history penalizes those who find themselves in Siberia in winter. To the extent that is true, it is not necessarily unfair.

If we are not carried away by the rhetoric of penalization, what other basis might there be for thinking that genetic testing and underwriting based upon it might be unjust? A natural line of thought in this area arises from thinking of highly debilitating genetic diseases, like Huntington's: "No one who suffers from this or a similarly debilitating genetically based disease can justly be left unsupported financially, and if a regime of genetic testing and underwriting prevents financial support reaching these people, then that regime, too, is unjust." Natural as it is, it is not altogether to the point. First, it does not bear on mildly debilitating genetically based diseases that would involve insured loss. For presumably we do not believe that all mildly debilitating conditions – a permanent limp brought on by jogging, for example – must be financially supported no matter what. Second, the line of thought may fall short of calling into question the risk-screening methods of private insurance. It may simply show that some risks that are screened out by private insurers have to be borne by some institution or other. Perhaps the institution of last resort is should be a public health service, or perhaps it should be a private insurer. It would not follow from the debilitatingness of the disease that the burden should fall on the private insurer.

As for a private insurer's selling policies on the basis of genetic tests and at prices that reflect actuarial evidence, it is in fact easier to mount a moral argument from justice *in favor* of this practice, than an argument against. For an important potential source of injustice in insurance practice is the failure to base premium levels on *evidence* of incidence of insured loss, and to operate instead on the basis of hunches, some adversely affected by prejudice. The supposition that British home-owners run a relatively manageable risk of illness and premature death led to adverse selection in the mortgage-related life insurance market in the UK in the late 1980s (Sorell and Draper 1999). The supposition that a single man in his twenties applying for very high life cover is at significant risk of death from AIDs probably led to the loading of life premiums for young single men in both the UK and the USA in the 1980s (Fenn and Diacon 1998). The untested supposition that someone who had taken an AIDs test probably had a high-risk sex life probably accounted for questions about AIDs tests and AIDs test results on insurance application forms in places where such questions are legal. The untested supposition that someone in even a monogamous homosexual relationship is at much higher risk of AIDs than a heterosexual probably continues to affect premium levels. Similar untested assumptions underlie differentially high premium levels for disabled people for life, health, and even automobile insurance. It is true that the switch from hunches to evidence can sometimes be expensive for insurance companies, since actuarial bases for premiums cannot be conjured out of thin air. It is true that if premiums reflect the costs associated with actuarial expenses, premiums for e.g. the disabled will still remain high, at any rate in the short term (Fenn and Diacon 1998). Still, this can be considered a reasonable (short-term) expense of dismantling a regime in which groups against which there is already considerable prejudice can avoid having to pay higher insurance premiums for no good reason. In the case of the disabled, the change is being required by legislation recently introduced in the USA and the UK.

Discussions of the ethics of insurance and genetics often focus, perfectly properly, on the disadvantages suffered by those whose genes put them at risk of disease and high premiums. But the other side of the coin is the advantages that might be enjoyed by those whose genes are revealed by testing to be correlated with low risk of disease and premature death. These people stand to benefit from genetic tests. Perhaps the tests will show that they can safely do without some forms of health or life insurance altogether. Or perhaps the results of tests will put them into the "preferred risks" category, entitling them to very low premiums. The protest that certain people are unfairly penalized for their bad genes does not seem to be echoed in a protest that people are or might be unfairly advantaged by their good genes. Yet some established insurance practice does turn biological advantage into insurance advantage. For example, women standardly live longer than men, and are therefore better life policy risks, which makes them eligible for lower premiums than men. The fact that this is one of the few areas in which women as a group are at an advantage over men might mean that the arbitrariness of the advantage is of little or no significance morally. And perhaps this conjecture generalizes: wherever economic advantages from genetic testing accrue differentially to an otherwise unfairly disadvantaged group, they are tolerable.

Things are not so clear where the higher insurance risks of a certain genetic make-up fall on already disadvantaged groups and where insurance advantages fall on certain already advantaged groups.

In such cases, it is tempting, from a moral point of view, to look for means of minimizing the further disadvantage *and* the further advantage. One way of doing this is by having universal compulsory insurance with contributions geared to ability to pay rather than risk of insured loss, as in certain public insurance schemes. Or one can have group insurance delivered privately with relatively relaxed underwriting if the insured pool is big enough. The trouble with the group insurance option is that it usually has conditions of entrance that the disadvantage of the already disadvantaged group might make it difficult to meet. The trouble with the public scheme is that its costs and compulsory nature are likely to make it vulnerable to political pressure requiring it to be scaled back.

Compromised Professionals?

An application for an insurance policy often involves parties other than the applicant and the insurer or insurance broker. Doctors, either working for insurers, or for applicants, can also be called upon to provide information. Applicants' doctors may be privy to information that would adversely affect their patients' insurance prospects – either by giving grounds for higher premiums or for being excluded from insurance coverage altogether. Should they only disclose this information to their patients with warnings about what insurers might do with it? Or should they be silent about the insurance consequences, because it is not their moral responsibility to comment on it? Should they disclose it, if asked, to insurers? As this information is normally confidential, there is good reason to think it should never come from the applicants' doctor. Instead, it should be gleaned by independent medical testing. But where it is customary for applicants' doctors to provide the information, and refusal to do so might itself be construed by insurers as evidence of increased risk, the reluctance of a scrupulous doctor to cooperate might have the same effect as full disclosure of all evidence of elevated risk. These issues arise for doctors in relations with insurers well outside the area of genetics, and in transactions with insurers beyond the application process – for example, in cases where a disability policy is already in force, an insured loss under that policy arises from a household accident, and it is convenient for the insured to try to get his doctor to overdraw the severity of the accident in order to maximize the pay-out. But related issues could also arise in areas where developments in genetics are highly relevant.

Suppose that a couple covered by private health insurance decide to have children, and intend to have the policy apply to the newborn child. Suppose that antenatal testing would reveal a high risk of cystic fibrosis, but that the couple decide not to have the test done when the doctor advises them to do it. If the baby is born with cystic fibrosis, is it permissible for the insurers to investigate if the testing was done and if not, why not? If the answer is "Yes," there may be some temptation on the parents' part to suggest that they were ignorant of the risk or improperly advised about the testing. If that happens, can the doctor fairly be expected to keep silent and not reveal that his advice about antenatal testing was ignored?

Suppose that the tests themselves carry some health risk or some measurable risk to the fetus. Should a doctor advise against its being done, if he runs the risk of having his advice questioned by the insurers, or if as a result of following his advice, his patients find themselves in difficulty over insuring the newborn? Similar issues arise outside the antenatal case, where what is in question is advising for or against taking a test that will remove all doubt about whether a patient will develop a disease like Huntington's. If there is a choice between saying nothing and advising against, where having this advice followed will lead to all insurance being refused to the patient, what should the doctor do? In the roughly analogous case of advising people to get AIDS tests, some doctors in sympathy with their patients often advised against testing, because of the insurance questions about the tests that their patients were likely to face if they were traveling or intended to buy a house.

To the reasonably familiar questions that arise for doctors of insurance applicants, we can add much less familiar ones relating to doctors working for insurance companies. Suppose that family history would make it clear to a patient that there was a high chance of developing a certain disease, and that a genetic test would establish for certain whether that would happen. Would it be right for a medical officer of an insurance company to advise his employers to require the test to be taken as a condition of getting insurance, if the medical officer knew the distress that certain knowledge might produce? Suppose that the medical officer's company is unwilling to pay for counseling for people who take genetic tests. Or suppose that the company does provide for genetic counseling in the form of a videotape, refusing on cost grounds to pay for counseling sessions. Is this a set-up that a doctor, even one employed by an insurance company, should live with? Again, and keeping to the case of the family medical history suggesting the risk of genetic disease, would it be right for the medical officer to agree to a policy of putting family names on a database alerting an association of insurance companies about the elevated risk? The fact that a medical officer provides advice for commercial purposes and probably does not treat patients may not free him from an obligation to think about the consequences for insurance applicants of his insurer's policies. Indeed, if the medical officer does not take these things into account, it might be thought that he prostitutes his medical knowledge, or frustrates its proper purposes.

Selective Disclosure and the Management of Risk

In considering the ethics of insurance it is natural to put the individual insurance applicant in the role of David opposite a Goliath of an insurance company. Especially if the insurer has a long record of high profits, why shouldn't it be deprived of some information about applicants that would enable it to minimize its already success-fully controlled risks still further? Why shouldn't it be deprived of this information, including the results of genetic tests, if gathering it and making it available is anyway intrusive, if it is information whose effects are likely to add to the disadvantage of people who are ill, and if the losses from risks can be borne without driving the company out of profit?

The idea that insurance losses fall only on institutions, and that the institutions are probably already too rich, is widespread. People who would not dream of keeping the extra change that the neighborhood shopkeeper gives them through oversight are often quite prepared to inflate their losses on insurance claims, because the company is thought to be impersonal, faceless, and large, with a size and shape so different from that of the local shopkeeper that it cannot feel personal financial pain. Businesses, even big businesses, are not like this, and some insurance companies are very far from being like this, having kept up some of the traditions of the cooperative association, or specializing in risks in the not-for-profit or public sector. In mutual insurance companies, where premium income is the sole or main source of claims, any pressure that increases claims puts upward pressure on premium levels and gives added reason for pervasive and accurate risk-assessment based on the burdens of individual policy-holders. People like the local shopkeeper feel the insurance company's pain. In insurance companies funded out of the proceeds of premiums and investment or other income, the effects of big losses arising from concealed risk or fraud are also higher premiums for policy-holders, and lower returns to shareholders. The shareholders need not be tycoons or large profit-making institutions. They can be local shopkeepers, or, differently, the pension funds of people who have no shares and small savings.

It is sometimes true that insurance fraud is perpetrated against rich companies, even ones that overcharge for policies or make questionable savings by contesting defensible insurance claims. This does not turn fraud into permissible activity, any more than robbery is made right by the fact that some people who are robbed came by their money or goods with unbecoming ruthlessness. Perhaps in the same way selective disclosure to insurers is bad, for reasons similar to those that might be brought up against lying. Politicians who self-servingly defend a policy of being economical with the truth are objects of contempt. Why should selective disclosure by private individuals not put them in the wrong as well? There is a difference, admittedly, between refusing to disclose information that would raise one's insurance premium and lying one's head off about one's insurance losses. For one thing, the refusal may have nothing to do with the higher insurance premiums: it may be based on the reasonable belief that the information requested is too personal to be asked for. Still, there is a background fact that connects nondisclosure and lying, and that insurers make much of, namely the huge asymmetry between what the insured knows about his losses and potential losses and what the insurer knows or can find out cost-effectively, if at all. When it comes to knowledge about losses or potential losses under a particular policy, the insurer is David and the insured is Goliath.

Might one asymmetry, the knowledge asymmetry, counterbalance the other asymmetry – in financial strength and sophistication – between insurer and insured? If the asymmetries do cancel one another out, and parties to insurance contracts accept the asymmetries as facts of life, then there is a presumption in favor of not disturbing the balance too much. The more that insurance companies try to make up for the knowledge deficit by intrusive questioning or by raising premiums across the board, the more the balance is disturbed, just as the balance is disturbed the more that policy-holders try to stay ahead of the costs of premiums through fraudulent claims or nondisclosure in insurance applications. If considerations about maintaining this balance were decisive in insurance ethics, then there would be a strong presumption in favor of not allowing health and life insurers suddenly to increase their powers of discovery through genetic tests, and a strong presumption in favor of life and health policy-holders not weakening the financial position of companies through fraudulent claims or misleading insurance applications. But of course, as things are, there are other destabilizing forces in the insurance market – notably the increasing costs of treatment resulting from innovation, and the increasing costs of treatment resulting from increased demand.

These forces give an incentive to companies, especially in the health insurance market, to raise premiums and screen out risks even if all policy-holders are honest and informative when asked to be. The same forces give policy-holders an incentive to evade the screening and to be selective in their disclosure of information relevant to risk. Those who are excluded by screening techniques and who are poor are likely to add to the already big burden on public health services. Such people are forced to cope with the problems of belonging to a healthcare underclass in addition to having to cope with membership in an economic underclass. Against this background, it is not just economically but morally important to control health costs. There is some evidence, however, that when the controls take the form of incentives to doctors to act as insurers' gatekeepers in the healthcare market, other moral risks are run. It may be that in the rich, industrialized countries the most cost-effective as well as least morally objectionable way of dealing with health insurance is by nonmarket means – by a universal, compulsory health insurance system, with contributions geared to ability to pay. Under these arrangements the insurance pool is large enough to make it likely that the rich and healthy will be able to pay for the ill and poor, and risk of mortality or ill health is not made the ground of a lighter or heavier financial burden. Under these arrangements the side costs of a genetic disorder or predisposition are minimized without concealment, and the enforced sharing of risk is in a cause everyone can agree is good. As the cases of the UK and Canada show (Marmor 1994), a public health insurance regime cannot only deliver high-quality modern treatment; it can co-exist with a profitable life insurance market, and, for the wealthy, a small but profitable private insurance market as well.

References

Association of British Insurers, Policy Statement on Life Insurance and Genetics, Feb. 18, 1997 (London: ABI).

Fenn, P. and Diacon, S.: "Disability and insurance." In Sorell, T., ed.: *Ethics, Healthcare and Insurance* (London: Routledge, 1998)

House of Commons Science and Technology Committee: Third Report, *Human Genetics: the Science and its Consequences* (London: HMSO, 1995), vol. iv (Minutes of Evidence), p. 25.

Marmor, T.: *Understanding Healthcare Reform* (New Haven, CT: Yale University Press, 1994).

Sorell, T. and Draper, H.: "AIDS and insurance." In Bennett, R. and Erin, C. A., eds.: *HIV and AIDS Testing, Screening, and Confidentiality – Ethics, Law, and Social Policy* (Oxford: Oxford University Press, 1999), ch. 14.

Further reading

Annas, G. J.: "Who's afraid of the human genome?" *National Forum*, Spring (1993), pp. 35–7.

Arnow, E.: "What is socially responsible insurance?" *Business and Society Review*, Winter (1991), pp. 34–5.

Kevles, D.: "Social and ethical issues in the Human Genome Project." *National Forum* Spring (1993), pp. 18–21.

Knoppers, B.: "Who has the right to know the genetic constitution of a person?" In Burley, J., ed.: *The Genetic Revolution and Human Rights* (Oxford: Oxford University Press, 1998), ch. 3.

Lander, E.: "The new genomics: global views of biology." *Science*, 242 (1996), pp. 536–9.

Mosely R., Crandall, E., Dewar, M., Nye, D., and Ostrer, H.: "Ethical implications of a complete human gene map for insurance." *Business & Professional Ethics* 10, no. 4 (1991), pp. 69–82.

Sorell, T., ed.: *Healthcare Ethics and Insurance* (London: Routledge, 1998).

Wright, R.: "The end of insurance." *New Republic*, July 9 and 16 (1990), p. 26.

31

Legal and Ethical Issues in Biotechnology Patenting

PILAR OSSORIO

Introduction

This chapter examines arguments concerning the ethics of patenting human DNA. I will give some background in the patent law and its underlying premises, and then examine two species of argument against patenting human DNA. The legal discussion in this essay refers to the US patent law; however, the major conceptual points are relevant to any jurisdiction.

Patent law is a system designed to promote the common good by maximizing the dissemination of new and useful information and products. Patents are not simply a reward for the hard work, high expenditures, or great insight of inventors. Rather, patents provide a limited monopoly to inventors as a *quid pro quo* for inventors' providing knowledge of how to make new and useful items to the public. Patents aid in the dissemination of knowledge because (1) patents are published and available to the public; and (2) they remove incentives for inventors to hoard information as trade secrets (at least in theory). The patent law can be described as serving a positivist, functionalist strategy: we choose the rules governing patentability to accomplish the goal of getting new and useful knowledge disseminated, and the rules are justified according to whether or not they accomplish this goal. In practice, this is an empirical determination which is difficult, if not impossible, to make with any confidence.

The patent system is designed to address purported economic inefficiencies associated with the use and exploitation of ideas. Ideas are a form of "public good" because people who do not pay for an idea may still "use" it once it has become publicly available, and because one person's use of an idea does not deplete what is left over for others. These are the characteristics, respectively, of non-excludability and nonrivalrous competition. Real property, such as a bicycle, generally is not a public good. If I am riding a bicycle then others cannot simultaneously ride that bicycle (at least not many others!), but if I am using my knowledge of how to design a bicycle, others could be doing the same thing simultaneously. Other examples of public goods include national defense (because everybody in the country will be protected whether or not they pay taxes or participate in the defense) and statues in public parks.

One commentator has noted that it is *prima facie* irrational for a society to grant monopoly rights over something that all could use at once (Hettinger 1995: 279), and thus intellectual property faces a special burden of justification. The justification stems from the concept of market failure. Non-excludability and nonrivalrous competition may lead to market failure because they prevent investors from recouping their investments or from profiting. To prevent this market failure, to encourage the investment of intellect and capital in invention and innovation, the patent system grants inventors a limited monopoly which allows them to control the use and manufacture of their inventions. As of 1995, the term of a patent begins when the patent is granted and runs until 20 years from the date when the patent application was filed. When the term expires, the public gains the right to use freely the information contained in the patent.

An underlying assumption of the patent system is that other, nonmarket incentives will not lead to as good or as much development of new and useful knowledge and products. One problem with this assumption is that the patent system is designed primarily to stimulate research and development through private investment, but biology research, including genetics research, has traditionally been supported through public funding. This raises the question of why anybody should get even a limited monopoly over knowledge generated by public funds. Would that knowledge have been generated anyway, without the trade-off of giving somebody some additional rights to control how it is used?

Moreover, is it unfair to charge monopoly prices if the public has already paid for the research – is this a kind of double dipping? In the US, biotechnology patent policy has been based on the perspective that although "basic science" research may be done with public support, product development traditionally has not been. The justification for encouraging patents on university research has been that it will enhance the pace of private sector product development. Overall, the public good will be promoted because the public will obtain more products, which are the concrete embodiments of the research for which it has paid. The assumption is that without patents the biotechnology industry could not compete for private capital against other industries, such as the computer industry.

Although patents were intended to enhance information sharing, under some circumstances they can instead create disincentives which lead to the opposite result. In publicly funded research laboratories, where a norm of information sharing exists (although this norm by no means controls all behavior), the opportunity to obtain patents may lead researchers to delay publication of scientific results until patent applications have been filed (Blumenthal et al. 1997). In addition, the opportunity for patents may lead to large, and some would say wasteful, expenditures for filing, prosecuting, and litigating patents. Finally, patents on the tools necessary for basic research may slow down research if investigators must negotiate royalty agreements each time they transfer technologies (Eisenberg 1996). Whether the opportunity to obtain patents does maximize the number of inventions or the information sharing in a particular field will depend on the cumulative effect of the incentive structures in that field. It is by no means a foregone conclusion that biotechnology patents lead to the greatest number of biotechnology inventions or products. Furthermore, it is not clear that the socially optimal rate of invention equals the maximum rate of invention.

Biotechnology patenting has raised a great degree of interest, anxiety and opposition throughout the world. Despite the controversy, as of the writing of this essay, the US has granted thousands of patents covering DNA sequences, cell lines, and transgenic animals. This essay focuses on legal and ethical issues in the patenting of human DNA. While similar arguments might be relevant to other aspects of biotechnology patenting, I believe that each particular area deserves independent analysis.

The arguments presented here are primarily directed toward the patenting of genomic DNA as opposed to complementary DNA ("cDNA"). Genomic DNA is the DNA found in chromosomes; it is the DNA we inherit, the DNA carried in the egg and sperm, and later replicated in the cells of our body. The term genome describes all of the DNA carried in any one cell of an organism. With minor exceptions, each cell in an organism contains the same DNA as every other cell. cDNA, on the other hand, is artificially constructed DNA, made in the laboratory by creating DNA copies of RNA. For the most part, cDNA is not ever found in our bodies, however, it *represents information* encoded in our bodies and is much more useful than genomic DNA for many biotechnology applications.

When an inventor patents DNA, she obtains rights over a DNA sequence. This sequence is represented by a series of the letters "A," "G," "C," and "T," each of which denotes one of the four chemical components ("nucleotides") of DNA. It is the particular sequential arrangement of nucleotides which encodes the information cells use to produce proteins. To obtain rights over a sequence it must be "claimed" by being included in a portion of the patent termed "the claims."

Background on Patent Law: Fighting the Myths and Misconceptions

Patents, property, and ownership

Patents are one form of "intellectual property." It is difficult if not impossible to devise a unitary definition of property; however, scholars do agree that the term property does not describe a thing (tangible or intangible) but rather a "bundle of rights" associated with a thing. All property is not equal – different properties and types of property are comprised of different bundles of rights. The rights granted by patents are different than the rights granted by real and personal property (rights to land and objects). Real and personal property rights typically, although not always, include rights of *possession* and *use*, and the right to *exclude others* from possession and use of the thing. These rights may be constrained in various ways; for instance, if a person owns land, zoning or environmental laws may limit her use of the land. The right to exclude others from one's land may be limited by easements. One's use of automobiles, a form of personal property, may be limited by the driving laws. Although the rights of possession, use and exclusion may be limited, and occasionally one of these will be absent altogether, they are nonetheless commonly presumed to be included, in some form, in the bundle of rights associated with owning real and personal property.

In addition, rights of real and personal property apply to particular instances of land or objects. If a person owns land, she possesses one or more particular pieces of land. If a person owns a shirt, there may be many other identical shirts but she only has rights in one particular shirt.

Patents do not confer all of the rights typically associated with real or personal property. A patentee has the right to *exclude others* from making, using, selling, offering for sale, or importing patented items for a specific term of years. A patentee also may exclude others from importing products made by a patented process. A patentee has no affirmative rights to do anything; patents do not grant rights of use or possession, only rights to exclude. A person could patent a new kind of gun and yet never possess a single gun. An inventor could patent a particular variety of drug, but not be able to market that drug because it had not passed FDA approval.

Patents do not confer ownership of the thing patented. No particular thing or class of things belongs to a patentee by virtue of her patent. If a person owns a bicycle then a particular bicycle belongs to her, but if a person has a patent on a bicycle, it is entirely possible that no bicycles belong to her. It is not the case that all bicycles covered by the patent belong to her. Although an investigator at Harvard holds a patent on transgenic mammals, it is not the case that "Harvard owns any mammal with any recombinant cancer-causing gene" (Hettinger 1995: 277). Unfortunately, literature discussing the ethics of patenting human-derived materials frequently incorporates the assumption that patents confer ownership of the item or process patented. The analysis then focuses on whether owning people, or parts of people, is ethically acceptable. While the question of owning people is an old and well traveled ethical debate, it is not particularly relevant to the ethics of patenting human DNA or cell lines. Analyses of the ethics of patenting should examine whether the right to exclude which is conferred by patents undermines other rights, conflicts with particular interests, conflicts with important values, or interferes with utility maximization.

Patentability

For an invention or discovery to be patentable, the threshold issue is whether it is *patentable subject matter*. Laws of nature (such as the law of gravity), principles, and abstract ideas are not patentable subject matter. Only practical, applied ideas are patentable; a patent must teach other people how to make or do something. Things found in nature, and which have not been altered by human manipulation, are not patentable – a person who discovers a novel variety of pine cone lying on the ground could not obtain a patent, regardless of how much money and time was spent searching for that cone.

Under US law, DNA, cells, and animals are all patentable subject matter, but *only if* they have been manipulated or altered by human beings in some way. The foundational case in biotechnology patenting is *Diamond v. Chakrabarty*, in which the US Supreme Court held that a scientist could patent a strain of bacteria into which he had introduced new segments of DNA. The introduced DNA purportedly altered the nature of the bacteria such that they attained the capacity to digest oil. In *Chakrabarty* the Court stated that "anything under the sun made by man" is patentable (447 US 303 (1980)).

411

The patentability of DNA thus turns on the question of whether it can be characterized has having been "made by man." This standard raises questions such as: what exactly must be altered, how much must it be altered, and what scope should the patent rights cover? With respect to these questions, it is instructive to know how sequence data are obtained and what DNA sequence patents teach. There are several methods of sequencing DNA, but all of them require at least some of the following steps: isolating DNA, purifying DNA, removing a small segment of the DNA from its place in the genome and connecting it to bacterial DNA (termed "cloning," but not to be confused with the kind of cloning which produces an animal that is genetically nearly identical to another animal), chemically unwinding DNA, and constructing radioactive or fluorescent copies of the genomic DNA fragment. When a patent claims a particular DNA sequence, it must teach how to "make" that sequence; the patent must give enough information that another investigator can synthesize the sequence de novo or clone the sequence herself.

The US courts, and the Patent and Trademark Office ("PTO"), have accepted the argument that the degree of manipulation required to obtain DNA sequence is generally great enough so that DNA sequences can be described as having been "made by man." The patented sequence is thus perceived as representing and teaching a DNA molecule which is different from the DNA inside of a person's cells, even if this "manufactured" sequence is identical to a DNA sequence in the person's cells, and even though the original genomic DNA was isolated from a person's cells. For this reason, patents on human DNA do not give the patentee any rights over DNA as it occurs naturally in a person's body. Patents on human DNA cannot be used to exclude a person from "using" her own DNA – they do not prevent a person from replicating new cells or having children.

The characterization of DNA sequences as things which are made by humans is open to criticism. The inventor of a machine determines the form of the object, the relations between each part of the object, and the qualities and properties of the object. None of these statements is true with respect to a naturally occurring DNA sequence. Some argue that, for a gene truly to be made by humans, a new and useful sequence would have to be constructed de novo, with little reference to genes in our bodies. Under this theory, a gene which encoded a novel, nonnaturally occurring protein would be patentable subject matter, but genomic DNA sequence would not. Determining the sequence of naturally occurring DNA molecules would be analogous to finding and describing a pine cone. A great deal of expenditure, ingenuity, time and determination may be required to find the pine cone, but none of these make it patentable. Likewise, all of the manipulation and experimentation necessary to determine the sequence would not make DNA patentable.

To be patentable an invention or discovery must be novel (35 USC §102), useful (35 USC §101), and nonobvious (35 USC §103); each of these terms is a "term of art," the meaning of which has been defined through extensive litigation. Under the General Agreements on Tariffs and Trade, patentability requirements for the EC countries are synonymous with the US requirements (General Agreements on Tariffs and Trade, 1994, Art. 27). Opponents of DNA patents argue that the novelty requirement for patentability should prevent DNA patents from issuing. They argue that the strand of DNA, with nucleotides ordered in a particular sequence, existed prior to our elucidation of the sequence and therefore nothing new was invented or discovered. DNA sequence data is merely descriptive of a preexisting molecule. Unfortunately, it is difficult to reconcile this argument with the legal definition of novelty. The novelty requirement, as articulated in the statute, prevents patents from issuing on inventions which were already known or used by others, or which have previously been described in a printed publication. Possibly, one could characterize the natural processes of a person's body as "use" of DNA; however, the uses which typically justify DNA patents are the "nonnatural" ones, such as cloning and expressing human proteins in bacteria, or creating a diagnostic test (Eisenberg 1990: 724–9).

The legal force of the arguments against DNA patenting is also undermined by long-standing precedent allowing patents to issue on natural substances which have been isolated, purified, or modified. In the influential 1911 case, *Parke-Davis & Co. v. H. K. Milford & Co.*, the court held that a naturally occurring bodily substance, adrenaline, could be patented because it had been purified and slightly modified. In *Parke-Davis*, Judge Lerned Hand stated that even if the adrenaline had not been altered in kind, the mere fact of purification meant that the adrenaline became "for every practical purpose a new thing commerically and therapeutically" (*Parke-Davis* at 102). Under this line of cases, proponents of DNA patenting have argued that isolated, purified, and cloned DNA is a "new thing."

The Ethics of Patenting Human Genes

Human dignity

Several arguments against the patenting of human DNA arise from the possibility that such patenting constitutes an affront to human dignity. I take these arguments to mean, roughly, that allocating human DNA to the realm of patentable subject matter implies a diminished conception of who we are. Furthermore, this diminished conception is less good than other conceptions because it leaves us vulnerable to one or more negative outcomes, such as exploitation of persons, commodification of persons or their parts, or inappropriate tinkering with human identities.

Although I have claimed that the rights granted by a patent do not constitute ownership of the thing patented, many who oppose the patenting of human genes on the affront-to-human-dignity grounds do so because they believe that patenting human DNA constitutes a form of ownership by one person of part of another person. Furthermore, they believe that it is wrong for one person to own or have proprietary interests in part of another person. The claim that it is wrong for one person to own part of another apparently derives from the claim that it is wrong for one person to own another person. For instance, the Commission of the European Communities has stated: "whereas, in the light of the general principle that the ownership of human beings is prohibited, the human body or parts of the body *per se* must be excluded from patentability" (Commission of the European Communities 1992).

Even if human gene patents did constitute ownership of another person's DNA, an extension of the traditional arguments is required to move from the impropriety of owning intact people to the impropriety of owning body parts or macromolecules.

Although this is not the place to review the large literature on self-ownership and why it is wrong for one person to own another, it will suffice to say that arguments against the ownership of persons appeal to the diminishment of autonomy and agency, and to the fact that a self-aware being would understand and revile what was being done to her. A self-aware being can create life plans which would be undermined by another's ownership and control of her body. These considerations do not apply to body parts or macromolecules. People have interests which can be thwarted, body parts and DNA do not have interests of their own. In addition, if we believe that a human body exists as a manifestation of the person, and that this has moral implications, it is still not clear that any particular part of the body, or macromolecule from the body, should be taken as a manifestation of the person. In fact, such an approach could reflect a demeaning and inappropriately reductionist conception of what it means to be human. Thus, even though we agree that it is wrong for one person to own another, it is not self-evident that it is wrong to own parts of others, or macromolecules derived from others.

Furthermore, a person who held a human gene patent, and obtained the further right to make, use, or sell DNA constructed according to that patent, would be trafficking in *copies* or *representations* of the DNA inside of another person's body. As discussed above, technically a patent cannot apply to DNA as found *in situ* in the human body, and the patentee would not have access to or control over the actual DNA inside of a person's body. Making, using or selling the patented DNA would not interfere with the bodily integrity or functioning of the person from whom the patented sequence was derived. The "ownership argument" against patenting would therefore rest on the claim that it diminishes us if one person can make, use, or sell copies of another's extracorporeal, nonparticularized body parts (Barody 1999). Some may want to defend this claim; for me, it does not carry much persuasive force.

Several of the human-dignity arguments against patenting human DNA refer to the notion that our DNA is unique and uniquely involved in our identities. However, it is difficult to formulate a credible argument based on this premise. While any person's total genome is unique to her, any particular part of it probably is not. And when we are discussing the possibility of patenting particular human genes or gene fragments, we are discussing only a tiny fraction of a genome. Each of our genomes is over 99 percent identical to those of other humans, and 98.5 percent identical to chimpanzee genomes. By sequencing genes from mice, rats, and other primates we can elucidate sequences that are remarkably similar to, and sometimes identical to, human gene sequences. If we excluded from patentability only that part of the human genome which is unique to human beings, then only a tiny fraction would be unpatentable. If we excluded from patentability only those gene sequences that were unique to a particular person, then any human gene or DNA sequence would probably be patentable. A valid argument might be constructed against producing a single patent on one person's entire genome, but this would be an argument of very limited utility, because it is highly unlikely that any such patent would be sought or issued.

One interesting argument relating dignity, human DNA and identity concludes that patenting of human DNA is wrong because it commodifies something which is part of our personal identities. By commodify I mean that it makes DNA into an object for exchange in the market ("market alienable"), placing it in the realm of supply and demand pricing, marketing, arbitrage, advertising, stockpiling, etc. (Radin 1987: 1851–9). The commodification argument may be formally stated as follows:

a) Each person's DNA is, in some manner, constitutive of her/his personal identity.
b) It is bad to commodify things which are constitutive of somebody's personal identity because it [interferes with her self-actualization, or undermines her as a moral agent or ... and thereby diminishes her.
c) Patenting is a form of commodification.
d) Therefore, it is bad to patent a person's DNA.

I have tried to formulate the first premise so that it is not a simple genetic determinist claim. A person need not believe that her DNA is determinative of her identity to believe that it is at least partially constitutive of her unique identity. Some have argued that even extracorporeal objects, such as a wedding ring or piece of art, can be constitutive of personal identity if they are invested with sufficient meaning and emotion that the person has partially identified herself with the object (Radin 1987: 1903–9). When a person identifies with an object in this manner it becomes a "personal attribute." Under this conception of identity, the boundary separating self and other is malleable and mobile. Under this conception, our DNA may be something which is invested with enough symbolism and personal meaning that it is a personal attribute much of the time. If this is the case, then commodifying it may do violence to our sense of having worth which cannot be expressed by market price. (Here I do not take any position as to whether or not people should identify with their DNA so as to make it a personal attribute; the claim is descriptive only.)

One obvious problem with this view is that objects which may become part of our personal identities, such as wedding rings, are frequently bought and sold and this does not strike us as problematic. We would have to argue that it is only wrong to commodify such objects, including DNA, if and when they became personal attributes.

A more fundamental problem arises from the conceptual difficulties of relating the patented DNA to the DNA purportedly associated with personal identity. To sustain the argument we must show that the identification which created a personal attribute was not with a person's particular, embodied DNA, but with any piece of DNA that had an identical sequence to hers. This is unlikely to be true, given that for any particular gene an individual is likely to share sequence identity with other people and often, with nonhuman animals. It is more likely that, if we have any sense of identification with DNA, it is the DNA inside of our cells, the DNA which is physically part of us. When a wedding ring becomes a personal attribute, it is the particular ring which was given as symbolic of a union, not any wedding ring of the same manufacture. Thus, we find a lack of clarity in the argument above, because the a DNA commodified by a patent probably is not a personal attribute.

An additional problem with the argument appears when we examine the question of whether a patent itself commodifies the thing patented (premise (c) of the argument). Patents only confer the right to exclude others from doing something. Although patents may be integral to the process of creating commodities, it is the affirmative rights and the actions of manufacturing and selling which actually constitute commodification. Thus, premise (c) of the argument is incorrect as stated. To formulate a valid argument we should describe some relation between patent rights and commodification. This should not be difficult given that patents are intended to encourage not just the pursuit of knowledge, but the practical application of that knowledge in marketable form.

If one takes a slightly more determinist view of the relationship between a person's genome and her identity, then commodifying human DNA may appear quite threatening to personal identity. If one believes that a particular person's DNA has some causal relationship to her personal identity, then there is a manner in which that DNA is essential to who she is. The DNA is solidly within the boundaries of the self. To take such an attribute and make it alienable, and therefore separable from the self, is to take what was essential and make it inessential. And commodification is not any kind of alienability, but market alienability, which incorporates a set of values about arm's-length transactions and impersonal interactions. To separate from what was formerly "self" in an arena governed by values of impersonalism may be particularly threatening or demeaning.

However, determinist views of personal identity encounter the same problems in the commodification argument as the personal attribute theory. Even if the genes in my body are somehow causally related to my personal identity, this does not mean that DNA of identical sequence but which is sequenced or produced outside of my body is causally related to my identity. It is difficult to imagine how copies of my DNA which were produced in bacteria or a goat could be causally related to my personal identity!

This realization raises the question of whether our concerns about personal identity, commodification, and DNA are directed towards DNA as a physical molecule, or DNA as an information carrier. It is certainly the case that bacterially-produced copies of a person's gene might yield information related to her identity, even if the gene sequence is not unique to that one individual. The information could be embarrassing or dangerous. If a researcher were to sequence some of my DNA, and discover that I carried a mutation associated with cystic fibrosis, this would be knowledge pertinent to my identity, and it could endanger my prospects for employment or insurance. It may be that we do not want this personal information commodified, both because of its symbolic significance, and for instrumental reasons such as the potential for discrimination. The philosophical implications of the distinction between DNA as a physical molecule and an information carrier bear further exploration. As we undertake this task, we should keep in mind that the patent system is primarily concerned with DNA as a physical molecule, whereas scientists are more interested in DNA as an information carrier.

Common heritage arguments

A second category of arguments against patenting human DNA relies on the claim that human DNA is part of the common heritage of humanity. These arguments conceive of human DNA as a form of commons, something which is either owned by all or owned by none. For those who think that patents confer ownership of the thing patented, there is a self evident incompatibility between genomic DNA as a form of commons and genomic DNA patents. However, even for those who recognize that patents do not confer ownership, the commons notion carries with it implications that all people should have the right to access beneficial uses of the human genome or of human-genome-derived knowledge, and that for one person to obtain special economic benefits through the exploitation of the human genome might be unjust enrichment.

Also encompassed in or related to the common heritage argument is the belief that information about the human genome has the same deep importance for further scientific progress as do laws of nature, and therefore anything that impedes access to or use of this knowledge should be avoided. Under this scenario, because patents may impede access and use, granting them is wrong.

Note the tension between conceiving of genomic DNA as something common to all people and conceiving of it as something unique, individual, and particular to each of us (the underlying concern of some dignity arguments). The two characterizations can both be correct, however, because an individual's complete genome may be unique and particular, and at the same time people are biologically connected to each other through our genomes, parts of which shared among us.

The two obvious questions are (1) whether human genomic DNA can be part of the common heritage of humanity; and (2) if it is part of our common heritage, then should it be unpatentable? With respect to the first question, it is not clear what attributes, if any, are necessary for something to qualify as belonging to the common heritage of humanity. I suspect that the designation is assigned instrumentally to things we wish to preserve or whose uses we seek to control; the designation signals that certain constraints or protections are appropriate. If this is true, then the statement that the human genome should not be patented because it is part of our common heritage would be a tautology. We must instead identify reasons which justify both particular protections and the "common heritage" designation.

By international agreement, certain natural phenomena and cultural artifacts, as well as the resources of the open sea, have been designated as part of the common heritage of humanity (The Convention for the Protection of the World Cultural and Natural Heritage, 27 United States Treaties and Other International Agreements 1997: 37; United Nations Convention on the Law of the Sea, United Nations Document A, 1982, Art. 136). Rights to the resources of the open seas are "vested in mankind as a whole," and activities in the open sea must be carried out "for the benefit of mankind as a whole." Proponents of the common heritage notion of human DNA may wish to see similar agreements concerning its uses and patenting. Note, however, that the common heritage designation has not prevented us from charging people to see cultural treasures, and it has not prevented companies from obtaining rights to mine the deep sea bed. What it means to use a resource for the benefit of all humanity is open to a wide variety of interpretations, and it is not clear that this stricture would rule out patenting.

Although there is no international agreement stating that genomic DNA belongs to the common heritage of humanity, it has attributes which would make this designation reasonable. Genomic DNA, in the form of chromosomes, is physically shared among people. The sharing of DNA unites us as members of families, and as members of the human species, both literally and symbolically. It connects us to past and future generations. The value of this interconnection may motivate us to designate genomic

417

DNA as part of our common heritage. If we did so, we would probably seek protections or constraints on the uses of information derived from genome research. These constraints might reflect some, but not all, of the concerns underlying the common heritage designation of natural resources and cultural treasures. Natural resources and cultural treasures are designated as our common heritage in part so that they cannot be depleted or destroyed, but genomic DNA cannot be depleted or destroyed through commercial exploitation. One person's use of genome sequence information in a product would not change or prevent the natural functioning of another person's genome, nor would it prevent reproduction and the passing of genomes from one generation to the next.

To determine whether genome patenting was ethical under a particular set of constraints, we would have to determine whether the patent right furthered or undermined the goals underlying those constraints. Many believe that, to the extent that knowledge about the human genome is used to generate new and beneficial products or processes, it should be as widely available as possible. One might then suspect that patenting is unethical precisely because it is an exclusionary right which allows the patentee to prevent others from using information. Some might describe this as unfair or unjust. At the very least, one might suspect that it would be wrong for a patentee to refuse either to license or develop a beneficial use of genome information, thereby preventing anybody from benefiting.

There is also a question of whether it is unjust enrichment for somebody to benefit from patenting our common heritage. If products are made using patented information from genome research, the patentee or her licensee can charge monopoly prices and/or royalties, which some might perceive as either unjust enrichment or an unjust barrier to access. The perception might be that the patentee is selling back to us, at unreasonably high prices, something which should already be ours. Also incorporated here would be distributive justice concerns about relations between wealthier countries (which have the capacity to conduct research and produce biotechnology products) and less wealthy countries. Citizens of less wealthy countries would partake of the genome as our common heritage, but they would be unlikely to share equally in medical benefits generated by human genome research under the current regime of international trade relations, which includes patenting as a trade-related concern.

For a valid argument to be constructed based on the common heritage notion, one issue which must be addressed is whether the common heritage incorporates both DNA and knowledge about DNA. Or alternatively, what is the relationship between genomic DNA as our common heritage, and any rights we have to knowledge about genomic DNA or products derived from it? We must engage the question of why people who actually generate the knowledge do not deserve some compensation for their efforts and contributions; having a common interest in the genome does not necessarily mean that we can appropriate the fruits of other people's labor. In addition, we should remember that an underlying assumption of the patent system is that beneficial products would be generated more slowly in the absence of patents, so an argument could be made that patents maximize the common good by providing incentives for research and product development. As stated previously, this is essentially an empirical question which should be addressed through economics research.

References

Barody, B.: "Protecting human dignity and the patenting of human genes." In Chapman, ed.: *Perspectives on Genetic Patenting: Religion, Science and Industry in Dialogue* (Washington, DC: American Association for the Advancement of Science, 1999).

Blumenthal, D., Campbell, E., and Anderson, M. et al.: "Withholding research results in academic life science." *Journal of the American Medical Association* 277 (1997), pp. 1224–8.

Commission of the European Communities: "Amended Proposal for a Council Directive on the Legal Protection of Biotechnology Inventions." *COM* (92) 589 final-SYN 159, Brussels, Dec. 16, 1992.

Diamond v. Chakrabarty, 447 U.S. 303, (1980), quoting S. Rep. No. 1979, 82d Cong., 2d Sess., 5 (1952).

Eisenberg, R.: "Patenting the human genome." *Emory Law Journal* 39 (1990), p. 721.

Eisenberg, R.: "Public research and private development: patents and technology transfer in government-sponsored research." *Virginia Law Review* 82 (1996), p. 1663.

General Agreements on Tariffs and Trade: "Agreement on the trade related aspects of intellectual property rights." *International Legal Materials* 81 (1994), Art. 27.

Hettinger, N.: "Patenting life: biotechnology, intellectual property, and environmental ethics." *Boston College Environmental Affairs Law Review* 22 (1995), p. 267.

Opinions of the Group of Advisers on the Ethical Implications of Biotechnology of the European Commission, Brussels, 1996.

Radin, M.: "Market-inalienability." *Harvard Law Review* 100 (1987).

Parke-Davis & Co. v. H. K. Mulford & Co., 189 F. 95 (S.D.N.Y. 1911), aff'd 196 F. 496 (2d Cir. 1912).

The Convention for the Protection of the World Cultural and Natural Heritage, 27 United States Treaties and Other International Agreements, 1997, p. 37.

United Nations Convention on the Law of the Sea, United Nations Document A, 1982, Art. 136, New York.

Further reading

Curien, H.: "The Human Genome Project and patents." *Science* 254 (1991).

Human Genome Organization: *Ethical Implications of the Human Genome Project: International Issues* 10 (1992).

Perspectives on Genetic Patenting: Religion, Science and Industry in Dialogue, ed. A. Chapman (Washington, DC: AAAS Press, 1999).

32

Are Genes Inventions? An Ethical Analysis of Gene Patents

MARK SAGOFF

Introduction

Patents serve the legitimate economic purpose of encouraging by protecting innovation and investment. Recent US Patent and Trademark Office (PTO) policy creating intellectual property rights in such things as cell lines, organisms, DNA fragments, and genetic codes, however, has occasioned a great deal of controversy. Critics argue, among other things, that to patent living things is to imply that they are designed by human beings, in other words, that they are artifacts rather than products of nature. These critics deny that genes, cell lines, and organisms should be classified as inventions, like photocopiers and lawn mowers, that people in a clear sense design rather than discover. Members of religious groups, in particular, oppose current policy because they believe that God rather than biotech firms is the designer of life and therefore has a prior claim on whatever intellectual property rights may issue on living things.

Proponents of current PTO policy reply that these critics fail to understand the purpose of patent law. According to the industry view, patents create temporary legal monopolies to encourage useful advances in knowledge; they have no moral or theological implications. As Biotechnology Industry Organization President Carl Feldbaum noted: "A patent on a gene does not confer ownership of that gene to the patent holder. It only provides temporary legal protections against attempts by other parties to commercialize the patent holder's discovery or invention."[1] Lisa Raines, Vice President of the Genzyme Corporation, summed up the industry position, which is that their opponents in the religious community just don't get it. "The religious leaders don't understand perhaps what our goals are. Our goals are not to play God; they are to play doctor."[2]

This essay will argue that industry leaders and their critics differ, indeed, on the way they conceive the nature of patent law. Religious and other critics of current patent policy believe that just as a person who bakes a loaf of bread owns it, so, too, an inventor has a natural property right to the idea, design, or invention of which he or she is the author. "Justice gives every man a title to the product of his honest industry," wrote Locke in the *First Treatise on Civil Government*.[3] If invention is an example of industry, this principle suggests that patents secure a pre-existing moral

420

property right of inventors to the products of their ingenuity and industry US Congress Office, 1989).[4] Religious leaders, who believe that God is the creator of nature (even those who allow that evolution may have been part of the divine plan) take umbrage, therefore, when mortals claim as their own what was produced by a superhuman intelligence.

Industry leaders, in contrast, regard patent policy as serving an entirely utilitarian or economic purpose that has nothing to do with natural property rights. To obtain the benefits that biotechnology offers humanity, these leaders argue, society must allow patent protection on genes, cell lines, organisms, and other genetic resources. This practical purpose says nothing about the true moral authorship of the natural world. Industry representatives suspect that religious and other critics oppose gene patenting primarily because they wish to impede the growth of genetic engineering and biotechnology generally. It is their Luddite attitude, so industry representatives may hold, that causes these critics to read into patent policy moral and theological implications that simply are not there.

If religious leaders and industry representatives disagree primarily over the nature of patent law – one side viewing it as recognizing natural rights and the other as serving a utilitarian or economic function – then it is easy to imagine how to fashion a statutory framework on which both sides can agree. Such a framework would do two things. First, it would grant biotechnology firms the legal protections associated with utility patents. That would satisfy industry. Second, such a framework would distance itself explicitly from the implication that human beings design or invent genes, cell lines, and organisms. By explicitly recognizing that these are products of nature not artifacts, it would concede the principal point of critics of current patent policy. In other words, a new statutory framework may gain a consensus by providing patent-like protections without the honorific moral implications that are usually associated with intellectual property rights.

Such a statutory solution would resolve a problem that derives from the logical ambivalence of the patent system itself. On the one hand, this system honors individual inventors by recognizing their ingenuity, skill, and inspiration. By "securing for limited Times to Authors and Inventors the exclusive Right to their respective Writings and Discoveries,"[5] the government, on this view, recognizes rights individuals themselves create by their own activity. In other words, these property rights are "bottom up" rights derived from individual acts of creativity, not "top down" rights derived from the policy goals of the government.[6]

Religious and other critics of gene patents contend that biotech firms do not design or in that sense create genes, cell lines, and other products of nature and therefore do not deserve to claim them as intellectual property. These firms merely manipulate genes using by now conventional means, or they simply copy genetic material, which they claim as their own. Even if it could be shown society benefits by allowing biotech firms to patent objects of nature, they have no moral right to claim them as intellectual property.

On the other hand, patent law serves society as a whole by encouraging investment to "promote the Progress of Science and the useful Arts."[7] In this context, patents are seen as "top down" artificial legal monopolies constructed by the state to serve broadly economic or utilitarian ends. One could argue, as the biotech industry does, that the temporary monopolies of the sort patents create are necessary not to recognize individual genius but to encourage investments beneficial to society as a whole. On these grounds, the biotech industry contends that the gene patenting, by serving strictly utilitarian goals, makes few if any claims about the provenance or authorship of life.

One might say that patents on genes and other forms of life present moral issues that are the mirror opposite of those involved in the patenting of medical procedures. In order to give the inventors of medical procedures the recognition they deserve, society acknowledges their intellectual property in them. The recent statute that allows doctors to patent medical procedures, however, does not allow them to charge a fee for their use, apparently because doctors are supposed to develop cures as a moral duty not simply for personal gain.[8] In contrast, society may believe that it must encourage the biotech industry by allowing firms to license for a fee the genetic materials they discover or manipulate. At the same time, nobody – not even these firms – may believe that they design genes and other life forms and thus have a moral or natural right (as doctors may to the procedures they invent) to claim them as intellectual property.

Patent Policy prior to the 1980s

Critics of current PTO policy often point out that legal practice traditionally excluded as nonpatentable such objects as scientific principles, laws of nature, physical phenomena, abstract ideas, and products of nature.[9] While denying the patentability of these products of nature, traditional practice recognized the property right of inventors to their own ideas. In that way, patent policy at least prior to the 1980s did not justify itself simply on economic or utilitarian grounds. Rather, by refusing to issue patents on objects of nature as distinct from those of human design, PTO policy remained broadly consistent with a Lockean conception of natural property rights.

Thomas Edison received a patent to the light bulb because he contributed the novel idea that constituted the design that made it work – in this instance, the idea of a glowing carbon filament. Edison was thus able to satisfy the "description requirement" of patent law, which demands that an inventor set forth the new knowledge or novel idea his invention represents in a written "description of the invention ... in such full, clear, concise, and exact terms as to enable any person skilled in the art ... to make and use the same."[10]

Similarly, King Gillette improved the lot of mankind by conceiving a design that solved the problem of keeping a thin and flexible blade rigid enough to shave whiskers. His patent specification describes his solution, namely, to "secure [the] blade to a holder" so that "it receives a degree of rigidity sufficient to make it practically operative."[11] What made the light bulb, the disposable razor, and – to mention another important invention, the golf tee – clear instances of intellectual property is that their inventors not only produced these objects, but also designed them. To put this distinction in Aristotelian language, the inventor can claim an intellectual property right if he or she provides not just the *efficient* but also the *formal* cause of the mechanisms he or she creates.

Unlike Edison and Gillette, plant and animal breeders, such as Luther Burbank, could not obtain patents on the many wonderful hybrids they created. Breeders did provide the efficient cause of these new varieties, that is, the tools or labor needed to bring them into being, but they did not provide the formal cause in the sense of designing these varieties. In the absence of this "inventive" step, the law could not provide protection because no intellectual property existed. Edison is reputed to have told Burbank, "The things you have created for the American people are worth far more than what I have created for them. The law protects my creations but gives no protection to yours."

The reason utility patents did not issue to plant and animal breeders was clear at the time. Edison could claim an intellectual property right in his inventions – and therefore a "utility" patent in them – because they arose from a design he devised and disclosed. Burbank, a superb breeder for whose work we cannot be too grateful, did not provide new ideas or knowledge that would enable others to build further varieties. He relied entirely on his skill in conventional techniques of breeding. Thus, the Shasta daisy for which Burbank is justly famous can be reproduced biologically but not intellectually. Burbank gave us many wonderful plants, but he left plant science essentially unchanged.

Confronted with the inapplicability of intellectual property law to new varieties of plants and animals, Congress enacted the Plant Patent Act of 1930 and the Plant Variety Protection Act of 1970, which protect new varieties respectively against unauthorized asexual and sexual reproduction. Congress recognized that plant breeders could not claim to design the new varieties they created; indeed, they could hardly claim that the methods they used were anything but obvious, nor could they describe the design of the plants they produced. Nevertheless, Congress wished to give an adequate economic incentive to breeders and reward their efforts, even if those efforts involved production not invention and thus did not result in the creation of intellectual property.[12] Perhaps for this reason, religious leaders and others did not complain that Congress, in giving breeders certain rights to capture the economic benefits of their work, confused their creativity with that of God. On the contrary, even if (contrary to fact) breeders' rights and utility patent rights offered exactly the same legal protections, they do not appear to carry the same moral or theological implications. The reason may be that the latter but not the former connote not simply a legal remedy but a natural right inherent in the creation of intellectual property.

Before the 1980s, there seemed to be a general consensus that those who manipulate the powers or mechanisms inherent in nature cannot claim those powers or mechanisms as intellectual property. This consensus covered all technology – not just plant and animal breeding. The electromagnetic spectrum and the principles that underlie it, for example, belong to nature not art. Accordingly, Samuel Morse could patent telegraphic instruments he invented but not – as he wanted – the use of electromagnetic waves to send and receive signals. Morse claimed as intellectual property "the use of the motive power of the electric or galvanic current, which I call electro-magnetism, however developed, for making or printing intelligible characters . . . at any distance." But the Supreme Court held that Morse invented only a particular instrument to take advantage of electromagnetism, and that he could not prohibit others from harnessing by other means the same natural materials or forces.[13]

The distinction between what one invents or designs and what one merely produces or discovers underlies the traditional refusal of the Patent Office and the courts to allow patents on objects that belong to nature. In a leading case, an appeals court in 1928 held that the General Electric Company could not patent pure tungsten, but only its method for purifying it, since tungsten is not an invention but a "product of nature."[14] In its pure form, tungsten possesses the ductility and tensile strength needed for constructing filaments for incandescent lamps and radio vacuum tubes. William Coolidge, working for General Electric, had developed a process for removing the impurities, chiefly oxygen, which are always combined with tungsten in nature. A lower court, under the impression that the metal Coolidge had produced was a new alloy, had upheld a patent on it. In invalidating the patent, the appeals court observed that Coolidge had not invented an alloy, but had purified an elemental mineral. Even though tungsten in a pure form is not found in nature but occurs only when human beings purify it, the appeals court concluded that Coolidge "cannot have a patent for it because a patent cannot be awarded for a discovery or for a product of nature or for a chemical element."[15]

In a more recent but similar case, a patent applicant had devised an efficient way to remove the head and sand vein from a shrimp. The applicant wished to patent not just the method of cleaning the creature, but also the resulting product, i.e., headless and veinless shrimp. To be sure, shrimp never occur in nature without heads or veins, yet the court determined that the resulting product was still a shrimp and therefore rejected the patent application under the products of nature doctrine.[16] The question arises, of course, what makes pure tungsten and headless and veinless shrimp "products of nature" and therefore unpatentable even though they are never found in nature. This question goes to our intuitions about what counts as natural and as artificial – a distinction worth preserving insofar as it underlies many or even most moral judgments and perceptions.

The Landmark *Chakrabarty* Decision

In the past, the Patent Office and the courts have generally observed Jeremy Bentham's principle that a patent must be confined "to the precise point in which the originality of the invention consists."[17] The "precise point of originality" may extend to the processes or instruments adequate to produce a result, but not necessarily to the result itself, if it is found in nature.[18] At any rate, the PTO once insisted that products of nature – especially those found in nature – are not patentable. In these matters, as one court said, "It is basic to the grant of a patent that the scope of a patent should not exceed the scope of invention."[19] This is no longer true. In recent years the PTO has awarded patents on naturally occurring proteins and gene sequences. Patents have been awarded, for example, for a DNA sequence for erythropoietin,[20] for plasminogen activator protein,[21] for a human T-cell antigen receptor,[22] and for various cell lines. There has been a sea change in patent policy.

The change occurred after the Supreme Court, by a 5–4 majority, decided in *Diamond v. Chakrabarty* (1980),[23] that Chakrabarty, a biologist, could patent hybridized bacteria because "his discovery is not nature's handiwork, but his own."[24] The majority opinion did not intend to reverse the long tradition of decisions that held products of nature not to be patentable. The majority opinion reiterated that "a new mineral discovered in the earth or a new plant discovered in the wild is not patentable subject matter."[25] The Court apparently believed that the microorganisms genetic engineers design are not found in nature but are "the result of human ingenuity and research."[26]

Although Dr. Chakrabarty's patent disclosure, in its first sentence, claims that the microorganisms were "developed by the application of genetic engineering techniques,"[27] this is not true, if genetic engineering techniques involve the use of restriction enzymes. (The bacteria in question were produced a year before restriction enzymes had come into use.) Chakrabarty had simply cultured different strains of bacteria together in the belief that they would exchange genetic material in a laboratory "soup" just as they do in nature.[28] Chakrabarty himself was amazed at the Court's decision, since he had used commonplace methods that also occur naturally to exchange genetic material between bacteria. "I simply shuffled genes, changing bacteria that already existed," Dr. Chakrabarty told *People* magazine. "It's like teaching your pet cat a few new tricks."[29]

The *Chakrabarty* decision had the immediate effects of reversing a series of court rulings that had rejected the idea that hybrids were inventions. In 1948, for example, the Supreme Court in *Funk Brothers Seed Company v. Kalo Inoculant* had held invalid a patent on a mixture of bacteria that did not occur together in nature. The *Funk Brothers* Court stated that the mere combination of bacterial strains found separately in nature did not constitute "an invention or discovery within the meaning of the patent statutes."[30] According to the Court, "a product must be more than new and useful to be patented; it must also satisfy the requirements of invention or discovery." In *Funk Brothers*, the Court regarded the repackaging of genetic information taken from nature as a commercial not a scientific advance.[31] "Even though it may have been the product of skill, it certainly was not the product of invention."[32]

In April 1987, in response to *Chakrabarty*, the US Patent Office said that it "now considers nonnaturally occurring non-human multicellular living organisms, including animals, to be patentable subject matter."[33] The PTO did not discuss what "nonnaturally occurring" meant – e.g., whether the concept would include pure tungsten and headless shrimp. It certainly would seem to include the products of conventional plant and animal breeding. The trade paper *Genetic Engineering News* immediately inferred that the PTO ruling "will lead to protection of animals developed not only through genetic alteration but also through animal husbandry and breeding."[34] At first, the PTO was unwilling to draw this inference.[35] But a 1985 decision established a precedent whereby, as a law journal noted, "a plant breeder may obtain a utility patent on a newly developed plant variety."[36]

Organisms produced by conventional breeding techniques now routinely receive utility patents on the same terms as products of genetic engineering.[37] This adds support to the view that the distinction between a product of skill and an invention, once sufficient to keep breeders from obtaining utility patents, no longer matters in PTO policy. Even though plant varieties developed today by conventional methods of artificial selection may exhibit no more inventive conception or design than those Burbank bred, they will receive utility patents as intellectual property.[38] Invention is no longer necessary; utility is all.

Public Debate over *Chakrabarty*

Public debate concerning the patenting of genetic resources began in the 1980s, when the US Patent and Trademark Office (PTO), following the *Chakrabarty* decision, first issued utility patents on organisms. The debate greatly intensified after 1991, when the National Institutes of Health (NIH) proposed to patent thousands of fragments of human DNA identified by government researchers.[39] In congressional hearings on the Biotechnology Competitiveness Act (which passed in the Senate in 1988), witnesses testified that America was locked in a "global race against time to assure our eminence in biotechnology" – a race in which the Patent Office had an important role to play.[40]

If Americans could not get patents on genetic resources, many observers warned, other nations would profit from research undertaken in the United States. One commentator describes the mood of the late 1980s: "Everything patentable should be patented as quickly as possible, including the maximum number of private claims resulting from government-funded research. [As] 'the first order of business'... human genome sequences themselves should be considered patentable."[41]

On the other side, critics of gene patenting, at least at first, appeared to oppose the progress of genetic engineering in general. According to an Office of Technology Assessment report issued in 1989, these critics had little to say about the appropriateness of patents per se, "focusing instead on the consequences of the commercial use of patented organisms or the underlying merits of biotechnology itself."[42] Critics at the time pointed to the possibility that a genetically engineered organism would run amok, causing environmental damage. This argument was directed less against the patentability of organisms, however, than against their environmental release, whether or not they were patented.

During the 1980s, those who opposed gene patenting lost their cause in part because they directed their objections primarily to the risks of biotechnology – even though those risks did not bear directly on the question of patentability. In *Chakrabarty*, for example, lawyers told the court "that genetic research and related technological developments may spread pollution and disease" and lead to other untoward consequences. But the court found, predictably, that it should not "weigh these potential hazards in considering whether respondent's invention is patentable subject matter" under patent law.[43] The Supreme Court, briefed by the opponents of gene patenting largely on the risks of biotechnology, held for the proponents. Risks or hazards, after all, hardly bear on the question of patentability, since even dangerous inventions, such as automatic weapons, if they have any use at all, may be as patentable as those that are perfectly safe.

Today, the locus of the debate has greatly changed. While there continues to be discussion about the risks and benefits of biotechnology, these no longer stand at the center of ethical, cultural, and religious reservations about gene patenting. Rather, critics of gene patenting, while deeply unhappy with the outcome of *Chakrabarty*, take some comfort in its holding that products of nature are not patentable – "a new mineral discovered in the earth or a new plant discovered in the wild is not patentable subject matter."[44] Religious and other opponents of current PTO policy point out that biologists who discover a useful organism in the wild should not able to patent that creature as their own invention. On the same principle, these critics deny that biotech firms should be able to patent naturally-occurring organisms they take into the laboratory even if they slightly alter them.

These critics point out that PTO policy, in opposition to the explicit doctrine of every relevant Supreme Court decision including *Chakrabarty*, now routinely awards patents on what are plainly objects of nature, such as genes, gene fragments and gene sequences. Harvard University in 1988 acquired a patent on glycoprotein 120 antigen (GP120), a naturally occurring protein on the coat of the human immuno-deficiency virus (HIV).[45] Very broad patents have issued on plant genomes. By using a well-known process to put a foreign gene in cotton, the firm Agracetus received in 1992 US Patent 5,159,135, covering "all cotton seeds and plants which contain a recombinant gene construction (i.e., are genetically engineered)." Agracetus gained the right (which has since been challenged) to control the cotton genome as its invention. "All transgenic cotton products... will have to be commercially licensed through us before they can enter the marketplace," a vice president of Agracetus said.

If the genomes of other plants besides cotton are claimed as intellectual property and patented as subjects of genetic manipulation, one may wonder whether conventional distinctions which once carried important moral or cultural significance – for example, distinctions between "nature" and "artifice," between "living being" and "inanimate thing," between "discovery" and "invention," and between "basic" and "applied" science – have any meaning in the wake of the current PTO policy. If these distinctions and concepts no longer matter, what sorts of concepts and distinctions are to take their place?

In the face of increasing intellectual reservations about gene patenting, in February 1994, Dr. Harold Varmus, the new Director of NIH, withdrew the NIH patent applications, thereby resolving a deep dispute within the Institutes.[46] In contrast to current NIH policy, several private companies continue to pursue intellectual property rights to human gene fragments and sequences.[47] The PTO has denied some of these applications on the grounds that the applicants, not knowing the function of the gene sequences they hoped to patent, could not specify a "utility" or use for them.[48] By 1995, in spite of these hurdles, the PTO had issued approximately 450 patents on gene sequences.[49]

A lively debate has ensued on whether these patents serve the interests of the pharmaceutical and biotechnology industries or, on the contrary, may inhibit investment, research, and product development.[50] Industry observers note that at any time half the members of the Biotechnology Industry Organization, the leading trade association, are suing the other half over patent claims and infringements. Patents, in effect, function as little more than licenses to sue for infringement, and given the fast-changing and unfamiliar technological terrain of genetic engineering, it is difficult to predict how cases will turn out. The availability of gene patents has certainly increased litigation and therefore transaction costs, but it is unclear whether these patents have improved predictability, efficiency, or creativity in the biotechnology industry.

The major firms appear divided on this question. Almost half of the patents on gene sequences and fragments that have been issued are owned by a consortium of SmithKline Beecham and Human Genome Sciences, which is trying to map, sequence, and patent as much as possible of the human genome.[51] On the other hand, Merck & Co., another pharmaceutical giant, is supporting geneticists at Washington University in St. Louis in their effort to sequence the human genome and place the information as quickly as possible in the public domain – on a website, in fact. The Merck database now contains nearly 400,000 sequences, and more are being added at the rate of about 4,000 a week. Art Caplan and Jon Merz comment: "This has created a remarkable situation in which two corporate giants are engaged in a competition in which one seeks to give away what the other wishes to sell."[52]

The principal objection to gene patenting no longer centers on the risks of biotechnology but on the appropriateness of claiming objects of nature as intellectual property. The information represented in genes, gene fragments, or sequences appear to common sense to be a public good – like the laws of science or mathematical formulas – that should not be acquired from the intellectual commons and converted to private property. What is more, by "fencing" this commons, as it were, patent policy may serve to desacralize life by making its most mysterious secrets fungible commodities like any others. Ethicists who do not represent religious faiths voice concern not necessarily about the economic but the moral implications that may follow when industries own living nature as intellectual property. As John Fletcher, an ethicist at the University of Virginia, has said, "You don't have to be religious to realize there ought to be a debate about patenting."[53]

The Joint Appeal

As the PTO, NIH, and industry groups have grappled with legal issues concerning the patenting of gene sequences, critics, many of them from the religious community, have raised moral objections to the patenting of genes, cell lines, organisms, and forms of life generally. These objections do not simply reiterate earlier qualms about the risks of biotechnology. Nor do they rest on technicalities of patent law – whether, for example, the requirements of "nonobviousness" and "specific utility" rule out most applications to patent gene sequences. Rather, the emerging debate engages ethical beliefs, commitments, and attitudes concerning the authorship of the genetic design of living things.[54]

On May 18, 1995, about 200 religious leaders representing 80 faiths gathered in Washington to call for a moratorium on the patenting of genes and genetically engineered animals. In their "Joint Appeal Against Human and Animal Patenting," this group stated:

> We, the undersigned religious leaders, oppose the patenting of human and animal life forms. We are disturbed by the U.S. Patent Office's recent decision to patent body parts and several genetically engineered animals. We believe that humans and animals are creations of God, not humans, and as such should not be patented as human inventions.[55]

The Joint Appeal attracted a great deal of criticism, both within and without the religious community, in part because of its association with the activist Jeremy Rifkin, who had organized the event.[56] The Center for Theology and the Natural Sciences (CTNS), for example, argued that Rifkin had "hoodwinked" representatives of various faiths into making a "vague and inflammatory" statement.[57] On the other hand, even these critics of the Joint Appeal agree "that the dignity and integrity of life be safeguarded."[58] Ted Peters, one of the directors of CTNS, adds that patent policy should maintain the distinction

> between discovery and invention, between what already exists in nature and what human ingenuity creates. The intricacies of nature, no matter how fascinating to the one who uncovers them, ought not to be patentable. This applies to knowledge of the existing human genome.[59]

The religious leaders who wish to maintain "the distinction between discovery and invention, between what already exists in nature and what human ingenuity creates" are not necessarily opposed to the progress of genetic discovery, genetic engineering, or biotechnology, but generally acknowledge its "enormous potential for enhancing creation and human life."[60] In a speech to the Pontifical Academy of Sciences in 1994, Pope John Paul II hailed human genome sequencing "which will open new paths of research for therapeutic purposes." While supporting progress in genetic science and technology, however, the Pope said: "we rejoice that numerous researchers have refused to allow discoveries made about the genome to be patented."[61]

Broadly speaking, religious leaders have joined with academic commentators who recognize that a "subtext in all this is the distinction, if any, between discovery and invention"[62] – a distinction nearly ignored in earlier discussions, which centered on risks. Those who wish to maintain this distinction generally believe that intellectual property rights should not issue for discoveries – or, more broadly, for products of nature – but only for inventions, such as transistors or light bulbs, which common sense would say human beings design and create.

Inventions or Objects of Nature?

Many conceptual and normative perplexities surround distinctions between "nature" and "artifice," "Creation" and "contrivance," or "discovery" and "invention" within the patenting debate. Those who object to patents on genetic materials and transgenic animals offer as one of their most frequent arguments the view that these are products of nature and, accordingly, part of the common heritage of mankind. For example, French science minister Hubert Curien argued in 1991 that "It would be prejudicial for scientists to adopt a generalized system of patenting knowledge about the human genome . . . [S]uch a development would be ethically unacceptable. A patent should not be granted for something that is part of our universal heritage."[63]

Are lifeforms that have received utility patents better described as objects of nature or as products of human design and invention? The academic literature expresses

429

perplexity over this question. For example, Daniel Kevles and Leroy Hood wonder whether copy DNA (cDNA) sequences[64] may best be described as objects of human design and invention, and therefore as patentable, or as objects of nature and therefore as belonging to the common heritage of mankind. They argue, on the one hand, that cDNA could be considered an object of human design or devising "since it can be physically realized... using the enzyme reverse transcriptase" in the labora- tory. On the other hand, Kevles and Hood write, "If anything is literally a common birthright of human beings, it is the human genome. It would thus seem that if anything should be avoided in the genomic political economy, it is a war of patents and commerce over the operational elements of that birthright."[65]

Industry representatives and others who support gene patenting may respond to this kind of objection in either of two ways. First, they may reply that cDNA sequences, transgenic plants and animals, and related products of biotechnology would not exist without human intervention into nature. Hence they are novel inventions, not products of nature. Second, they may claim that the distinction between "invention" and "discovery" or between products of nature and of design is no longer relevant to patent policy, if it ever was. They may concede, then, that genetic resources are products of nature, but argue that these discoveries are patent- able compositions of matter nevertheless.[66]

Consider, first, the assertion that genes, gene sequences, and living things, if they are at all altered by human agency, are novel organisms and therefore not products of nature. This defense of gene patenting would encounter several difficulties. First, patents have issued on completely unaltered biological materials, for example, the patent mentioned earlier on glycoprotein 120 antigen (GP120) to Harvard in 1988. Second, the techniques by which biological material is altered quickly become routine and obvious, for example, cDNA replication, the immortalization of cell lines, and so on. These techniques could be analogized to that of grafting plants or breeding animals. The exercise of microinjecting genetic material into a mouse embryo after a while may seem to involve no more an inventive step than the exercise of grafting a plant. Where the techniques of producing a hybrid plant, animal, or bacterium are well known and have become routine, it might seem that they are obvious. The result of employing such a technique, therefore, might be the result of skill, but one cannot easily say that it is the product of invention.

On the other hand, proponents of gene patenting might deny that patenting makes any claim to invention, design, or authorship but only creates a legal monopoly to serve certain utilitarian purposes. In that event, defenders of gene patents might agree with their critics that God or evolution or nature is the true designer or inventor of the human genome, cells, and animals. Advocates of gene and animal patenting would deny, in other words, that anything of moral, theological, or cultural significance follows from a determination, basically for economic or utilitarian reasons, to allow patents on knowledge gained as a result of genomic research. They may then seek to find common ground with religious leaders and others by denying, rejecting, or abjuring any ethical, metaphysical, or theological implications associated with patents. This would require a revised statutory framework – one that provides the equivalent of utility patents but in the form (or under the concept) of breeders' rights rather than rights of intellectual property.

Conclusion

Interestingly, those who decry current PTO policy in granting intellectual property rights to organisms and other biological and genetic resources do not necessarily oppose the development of biotechnology *per se*. Rabbi David Saperstein, director of the Religious Action Center of Reform Judaism in Washington, DC, a prominent member of the coalition that issued the Joint Appeal, for example, acknowledged the "benefit of the drugs or the benefit of the techniques, the benefit of the genetic engineering process" associated with the Human Genome Project. Saperstein said, "[T]here are ways through contract laws and licensing procedures to protect the economic investment that people make without going to the step of giving these corporations or these groups of scientists the right to own new forms of life."[67] Even the activist Jeremy Rifkin may be open to monopoly protections that do not engage moral issues involved with intellectual property. Characterizing the position of the 80 religious leaders he led to Washington in 1995, he emphasized that they had "no problem" with process patents nor even with protecting biotech products with the sort of marketing exclusivity conferred on "orphan" drugs.[68]

On the industry side, spokespersons have been anxious to assure their clerical critics that they do not want to "play God" by claiming to be the authors of life. What industry wants, they argue, is not to upstage the Creator but to enjoy a legal regime that protects and encourages investment. In a widely published letter written in response to a recent controversy involving the patenting of a gene associated with breast cancer, Carl Feldbaum wrote, "Biotechnology researchers do not own genes. Rather, they borrow genes from nature and pay back humanity with treatments and cures."[69]

It is not only utility – the practical result of patent policy – that counts. We must also consider the expressive function of the law. Karen Lebacqz, a theologian, makes this point: "the question is not so much what we *do* but how we *think* about it."[70] Industry is concerned with utility and practical results; religious and other critics are understandably upset with the expressive or symbolic implications of current PTO policy. A new policy approach or statutory framework could accommodate all these concerns if it provided the kinds of monopoly commercial rights industry seeks without creating the implication or connotation that industry "invents" or "owns" genes as intellectual property. In other words, some middle ground modeled on the earlier plant protection acts might achieve a broad agreement among the parties now locked in dispute.

Notes

1   See Reginald Rhein, "Gene Patent Crusade Moving from Church to Court," *Biotechnology Newswatch*, June 5, 1995, p. 21.
2   ABC World News Tonight, 6:30 p.m. ET, May 18, 1995, transcript no. 5099.
3   John Locke, *Two Treatises of Government*, ed. Peter Laslett (Cambridge: Cambridge University Press, 1967), First Treatise, I, Sec. 32, p. 205. Locke's principal treatment of property rights is found in the Second Treatise, chapter 5. For an excellent analysis of the Lockean

argument, see Lawrence Becker, *Property Rights* (London: Routledge & Kegan Paul, 1977), esp. ch. 4.

Alan Goldman understands the underlying premise to state "a person's right to the fruits of his or her labor, perhaps considered as an extension of his or her activity and therefore of him or herself." Goldman, "Ethical issues in proprietary restrictions on research results," *Science, Technology, and Human Values* 12 (1987), p. 23. For further discussion, see Robert Nozick, *Anarchy, State, and Utopia* (New York: Basic Books, 1974), p. 175.

4 Commentators generally agree that the basis of patent law consists, first, in the natural entitlement of inventors to the fruits of their labor and, second, the enhancement of social welfare or utility that follows from the patent protection. See, for example, US Congress, Office of Technology Assessment, "New Developments in Biotechnology: Patenting Life – Special Report," OTA-BA-370 (Washington, DC: USGPO, April 1989), p. 130.

5 Constitution of the United States, Article 1, section 8.

6 See, for comparison, Richard A. Epstein, "Takings: of private property and common," AEI paper, March 7, 1996, p. 4.

7 Constitution of the United States, Article 1, section 8.

8 While US physicians may patent medical procedures, this right is honorific only, since a statute enacted in 1996 prevents them from suing for patent infringement. For a detailed study of this statute and its history, see W. E. Havins, "Immunizing the medical practitioner 'process' infringer: greasing the squeaky wheel, good public policy, or what?" *University of Detroit Mercy Law Review* 77 (Fall 1999), pp. 51–71.

9 For an example of this argument, see Elizabeth Joy Hetch, "Note: beyond Animal Legal Defense Fund v. Quigg: the controversy over transgenic animal patents continues," *American University Law Review* 41 (1992): 1023, 1030.

10 U.S.C. Section 112, first para.

11 US Patent 775,134, issued Nov. 15, 1904. For litigation, see *Gillette Safety Razor Co. v. Clark Blade & Razor Co.*, 187 F. 149 (C.C.D.N.J. 1911), aff'd 195 F. 421 (3rd Cir. 1912).

12 These laws greatly weaken the nonobviousness and enablement tests; in fact, the 1970 statute does away with them entirely, mandating only that seeds be deposited in a public repository. This may represent good social policy, insofar as it encourages plant breeders to continue their useful endeavors. It may also be fair, since Congress, by giving breeders rights over the use of their plants for reproduction, may recognize the rights of creators to control their personal property, including the seeds and tubers of the plants they produced. The genetic information contained in these seeds and tubers, which might be considered intellectual property, however, is the work not of the breeder, who could hardly specify what it is, but that of nature. For this reason, the Plant Protection Act does not give a breeder intellectual property rights to this information. Rather, the statute provides that anyone who develops the same variety independently does not infringe the patent.

13 *O'Reilly v. Morse*, 15 How. 62, 112–29 (1853).

14 *General Electric Company v. De Forest Radio Co.*, 28 F.2d 641 (3rd Cir. 1928, cert. denied 278 U.S. 656 1929).

15 *De Forest*, 28 F.2d at 642.

16 *Ex parte Grayson*, 51 U.S.P.Q. (BNA) 413 (PTO Bd. App. 1941).

17 Jeremy Bentham, *The Rationale of Reward* (London: R. Heward, 1830).

18 See Edmund J. Sease, "From microbes, to corn seeds, to oysters, to mice: patentability of new life forms," *Drake Law Review* 38 (1989): 551, 566.

19 *Monsanto Co. v. Rohm & Hass Co.*, 312 F. Supp. 778, 790 (E.D. Pa. 1970), aff'd 456 F.2nd 592 (3rd Cir.), cert. denied 407 U.S. 934 (1972).

20 US Patent No. 4,703,008, Lin, inventor, 1083 Off. Gaz. Pat. Off. 2038 (Oct. 27, 1987).

21 US Patent No. 4,370,417, Hung, et al., inventors, 1026 Off. Gaz. Pat. Off. 1315 (Jan. 25, 1983).

22 US Patent No. 4,713,332, Mak, inventor, 1085 Off. Gaz. Pat. Off. 1386 (Dec. 15, 1987).

23 *Diamond v. Chakrabarty*, 447 U.S. 303 (1980).

24 *Diamand v. Chakrabarty*, 447 U.S. 303, 310 (1980). This was not the first patent to be placed on an organism. In 1873, the United States granted Patent No. 141,072 to Louis Pasteur, for a "yeast, free from organic germs of disease, as an article of manufacture." For discussion, see Fredrico, "Louis Pasteur's patents," *Science* 86 (1937), p. 327.

25 *Diamond v. Chakrabarty* at 309.

26 *Diamond v. Chakrabarty* at 310.

27 US Patent 3,813,316, May 28, 1974.

28 For a description of the process Dr. Chakrabarty used, see Robert H. Sprinkle, *Profession of Conscience: The Making and Meaning of Life-Sciences Liberalism* (Princeton: Princeton University Press, 1994), pp. 177–8.

29 Quoted by Philip L. Bereano, "Patent nonsense – patent pending: the race to own DNA," *Seattle Times*, 27 Aug. 1995, p. B5.

30 *Funk Bros. Seed Co. v. Kalo Inoculant Co.*, 333 U.S. 127, 132

31 The Supreme Court in *Chakrabarty* emphasized that the bacteria in question there were different from those in *Funk Brothers* because they had been genetically manipulated and were not naturally-occuring strains. Yet the manipulation in this instance was no more than commonplace hybridization that differed little from previous practice. The bacterial inoculant at issue in *Funk Brothers* comprised bacteria that also did not and could not coexist naturally. The novel combination of bacteria that was unpatentable in *Funk Brothers* would seem to be patentable after *Chakrabarty*. There appears to be no "inventive step" in the latter instance that is absent in the former.

On the strength of the *Chakrabarty* decision, the Patent Office began routinely to award patents on hybridized and recombinant organisms – and very broad patents at that. The current high-water mark in this flood of patents came with the application of Agracetus of Middletown, Wisconsin, which received in 1992 US Patent 5,159,135, covering "all cotton seeds and plants which contain a recombinant gene construction (i.e., are genetically engineered)." By using a well-known process to introduce foreign genes into a cotton plant, Agracetus gained the right to exclude other companies from introducing any other genes into that plant without its consent. "All transgenic cotton products ... will have to be commercially licensed through us before they can enter the marketplace," a vice president of Agracetus said.

The Patent Office apparently reasoned that anything that is not a product of nature must therefore result from invention or design. This is perhaps not an unwarranted inference from *Chakrabarty*, but it does confuse *invention* with the *production* of anything novel and useful. The Patent Office went further to establish as intellectual property the genome of any organism – Agracetus also received a patent for soy – that a company managed to alter using novel technical means. In several instances when a company seeking to patent an organism had used fairly well-known, if laborious, methods for manipulating its genome, the Patent Office still allowed a patent on that genome as the material for further genetic manipulation. The Patent Office, in other words, failed to distinguish manipulating or changing a genome from designing or inventing it.

Competitors were slow to challenge the Agracetus patent, perhaps believing that their time and interest would be better served by acquiring similar intellectual property rights to broccoli, bananas, and a host of other organisms whose genomes they could alter using the same technique Agracetus applied. Eventually challenges mounted up, including a major and successful suit by the US Department of Agriculture. The Patent Office is reviewing the Agracetus patent and it is unlikely to be sustained.

32 *Funk Brothers*, at 131–2.

33 *Official Gazette of the U.S. Patent and Trademark Office* 8 (1987), p. 1077. A year later the Office issued a patent to the Harvard mouse.

34 Sterling, "Patent Office Decides," p. 1.

35 Commenting on the 1987 ruling, a PTO official said: "This won't affect our policy that products found in nature, such as farm animals produced by natural breeding, are not considered patentable...For an animal to be covered under patent statutes, they [sic] have to be somehow created by man." See "New animals will be patented," *The New York Times*, April 17, 1987, p. 9.

36 Neil D. Hamilton, "Why own the farm if you can own the farmer (and the crop)?" *Nebraska Law Review* 73 (1994), p. 91.

37 For example, several patented herbicide-tolerant crops, such as DuPont's sulfonylurea-tolerant soybeans, were developed through conventional breeding.

38 The intellectual contribution of breeders, after all, may be as great as or greater than that of genetic engineers with respect to the organisms they create. Breeders have to keep dozens of traits in mind and navigate among them, while engineers make a far more surgical strike on the genome of the organism. Plant breeding and artificial selection generally, moreover, typically change the genome of target animals far more broadly than the more surgical technique employed by genetic engineers, which is usually to micro-inject many fewer foreign genes into fertilized eggs. Experts have testified, indeed, that "centuries of selective breeding have altered domestic animals far more than the next several decades of transgenic modifications are likely to alter them." Reid G. Adler, "Controlling the applications of biotechnology: a critical analysis of the proposed moratorium on animal patenting," *Harvard Journal of Law and Technology* 1 (1988): 1–61; quotation at p. 20, n. 126, citing various sources. Reid cites expert testimony to the effect that the new biotechnologies do not depart radically from historical practices. See p. 18, n. 99.

39 In June 1991, Dr. J. Craig Ventner, a researcher at the National Institute of Neurological Disorders and Strokes of the National Institutes of Health (NIH), filed for patent rights on 337 gene fragments and, eight months later, on 2, 375 additional partial gene sequences. Ventner had conceived of a way to identify that small portion (about three percent) in cells that function as genes. Since only the genes create messenger RNA (mRNA) coding for proteins, Ventner saw that if he could clone the mRNA (which is too fragile itself to work with), he could derive usable complementary copies (he called these cDNA) or the original genes. Ventner could then sequence the nucleotides in the original genes by working with the cDNA copies of clones taken from mRNA – thus making gene sequencing far cheaper, faster, and easier to do. Ventner used this method to sequence short streches from cDNA clones – a few hundred bases – to identify what he called "expressed sequence tags" or ESTs. Building on Ventner's work, he and many other researchers have developed auto-matic sequencing machines to identify ESTs quite rapidly.

Ventner's work in relation to patent policy has been widely covered in the literature. See, for example, Rebecca S. Eisenberg, "Genes, patents, and product development," *Science* 257 (Aug. 14, 1992), p. 905 (pointing out that a lack of known utility presents an obstacle to patenting ESTs); see also Christopher Anderson, "Genome project goes commerical," *Science* 259 (993): pp. 300–2.

40 H.R. 4501 and S. 1966, The Biotechnology Competiveness Act, Hearings, quoted and cited in Robert H. Sprinkle, *Profession of Conscience*, p. 187. As one industry representative testified:

America's competitiveness is the centerpiece for international trade discussions today... America's competitiveness can be strengthened by providing more effective legal protection for American technology. Congress would be going in the wrong direction to consider limiting protection for biotech inventions...

W. H. Duffey, testimony before US Congress, Committee on the Judiciary, Subcommittee on Courts, Civil Liberties, and the Administration of Justice, *Patents and the Constitution: Transgenic Animals*, hearings June 11, July 22, Aug. 21, and Nov. 5, 1987 (Washington, DC: USGPO, 1988).

41 Sprinkle, *Profession of Conscience*, pp. 187–8.

42 U.S. Congress, Office of Technology Assessment, "New developments in biotechnology: patenting life – special report," OTA-BA-370 (Washington, DC: USGPO, April, 1989), p. 30.

43 *Diamond v. Chakrabarty* at 303.

44 *Diamond v. Chakrabarty* at 309.

45 Marjorie Sun, "Part of AIDS virus is patented," *Science* 239 (Feb. 26, 1988), p. 970. For discussion, see Sprinkle, *Profession of Conscience*, pp. 180–1.

46 See Christopher Anderson, "NIH drops bid for gene patents," *Science* 263 (Feb. 18, 1994), p. 909. See also: Diane Gershon, "US and British researchers agree not to seek gene fragment patents," 367 *Nature* 583 (1994); and Natalie Angier, "US dropping its effort to patent thousands of genetic fragments," *New York Times*, Feb. 11, 1994, p. A16. Dr. James Watson, who headed the National Center for Human Genome Research at the time when Dr. Bernadine Healy, as NIH director, pressed for patenting, resigned in part over the matter. See James D. Watson, "A personal view of the project," in Daniel J. Kevles and Leroy Hood, eds., *The Code of Codes: Scientific and Social Issues in the Human Genome Project* (Cambridge, MA: Harvard University press, 1992), pp. 164–73. On April 9, 1996, the National Center for Human Genome Research (NCHGR) declared that human genomic DNA sequence data "should be released as rapidly as possible and placed in the public domain where it will be freely available." In order to stimulate research by making "DNA sequence information available as rapidly and freely as possible," NCHGR discouraged investigators and researchers from patenting genetic sequences identified in the context of projects to which it contributes funds. "Policy on Availability and Patenting of Human Genomic DNA Sequence Produced by NVHGR Pilot Projects," April 9, 1996, distributed in photocopy by the NIH.

47 See John Carey, "The gene kings," cover story, *Business Week* 3423 (May 8, 1995), pp. 72–8.

48 NCHGR, in its policy statement, observes that when a "raw human genomic DNA sequence... lacks demonstrated specific utility," it is therefore "an inappropriate material for patent filing." "Policy on Availability and Patenting," p. 3. The Patent and Trademark Office, moreover, has recently released Utility Examination Guidelines to strengthen the requirement that the applicant assert a credible and specific utility for the claimed genetic invention. Department of Commerce, Patent and Trademark Office, Docket Number 950706172–5172–01, Utility Examination Guideliness, 60 FR 36263, July 14, 1995. Sequences may have a known utility if they are derived from genes of known function. This prior knowledge, however, if it is already published, belongs to the public domain, and may therefore prevent a patent application that passes the tests of specific and credible utility from meeting the conditions of novelty and nonobviousness. The requirement that patent applications for genes, sequences, or fragments specify a clear and credible application or utility has limited the number of successful patent applications. Even by 1992, a consensus among experts had begun to form that the sequencing a genetic material could be accomplished routinely and that the important step that required creative knowledge – whether patentable or not – had to do with interpreting the data to learn what the

435

function of the gene is. Absent this knowledge, there could be no knowledge new, useful, and nonobvious enough to be patentable. This was the general view reached by the Gene Patent Working Group, an interagency task force convened by the White House Office of Science and Technology Policy. For discussion, see P. Zurerm "Critics take aim at NIH's gene patenting strategy," *Chemical and Engineering News* 70 (1992), pp. 21–2.

49   Because of the inherent differences in and variety of patent applications, this number must be treated as a rough estimate. It results from a careful LEXIS search and subsequent culling undertaken by Diana Sheiness. For details, see Diana Sheiness, "Patenting gene sequences," *Journal of the Patent and Trademark Office Society* 78(2) (Feb. 1996): 121–37. Arthur Caplan and Jon Merz, in their interesting editorial, "Patenting gene sequences: not in the best interests of science or society," also use the 450 figure (in the *British Medical Journal* 312, April 13, 1996, p. 926).

50   The desirability of patent protection for genes, gene sequences, and methods of genetic recombination and engineering remains controversial even within the biotechnology industry. Thomas J. White points out that a great many unpatented genetic compositions and processes have been commercialized successfully, for example, the commercially successful restriction enzymes that serve as the basis for recombinant DNA techniques. Processes for making monoclonal antibodies and for sequencing genes were invented and commercialized without benefit of patents. As far as patenting policy is concerned, White writes, "there is no industrywide consensus on many of these issues, and there are specific disagreements among the various trade associations, large phramaceutical corporations, and entrepreneurial firms." Thomas J. White, "Intellectual property and genetic testing: a commentary," in Mark S. Frankel and Albert H. Teich, eds., *The Genetic Frontier: Ethics, Law, and Policy (Washington*, DC: AAAS, 1994): 199–208; quotation at p. 202.

51   For discussion, see G. Poste, "The case for genomic patenting," *Nature* 378 (1995): 534–6.

52   Arthur Caplan and Jon Merz, "Patenting gene sequences: not in the best interests of science or society," *British Medical Journal* 312, April 13, 1996, p. 926.

53   Reported by Richard D. Land and C. Ben Mitchell, "Brave new biopatents," forthcoming in *First Things: A Monthly Journal of Religion and Public Life*.

54   For discussion, see E. Richard Gold, *Body Parts: Property Rights and the Ownership of Human Biological Materials* (Washington, DC: Georgetown University Press, 1996), esp. chs. 4 and 7.

55   Press release, May 18, 1995, Joint Appeal Against Human and Animal Patenting, Washington, DC. See Richard Stone, "Religious leaders oppose patenting genes and animals," *Science* 268 (May 26, 1995), p. 1126. See also, "Religious leaders prepare to fight patents on genes," *New York Times*, May 13, 1995, p. 1.

56   See, for example, Ronald Cole-Turner, "Religion and gene patenting," *Science* 270 (Oct. 6, 1995), p. 52.

57   Press Release, The Center for Theology and the Natural Sciences, May 18, 1995. The organization address is 2400 Ridge Road, Berkeley, CA 94709. A longer and well-argued version of this press release has recently appeared in the journal *Dialog*, vol. 35, Spring 1996, pp. 117–32, written by Ted Peters, who teaches ar the Pacific Lutheran Theological Seminary and is one of the directors of the Center for Theology and the Natural Sciences.

58   Ted Peters, "Should we patent God's creation?" p. 132.

59   Ted Peters, "Should we patent God's creation?" p. 132.

60   Statement of the United Methodist Church meeting in 1992, reported by Ronald Cole-Turner, "Religion and gene patenting," *Science* 270 (Oct. 6, 1995), p. 52.

61   Pope John Paul II, speech before the Pontifical Academy of Sciences, Oct. 28, 1994; reported with text in *L'Osservatore Romano*, Weekly Edition (in English), number 45, Nov. 9, 1994, p. 3.

62   Kate H. Murashige, "Intellectual property and genetic testing," in Mark S. Frankel and Albert H. Teich, eds., *The Genetic Frontier: Ethics, Law, and Policy* (Washington, DC: AAAS, 1994), pp. 181–98; quotation at p. 187.

63   Hubert Curien, "The Human Genome Project and patents," *Science* 254 (1991): 1710, 1710.

64   For an explanation of this term, see note 2.

65   Daniel J. Kevles and Leroy Hood, eds., *The Code of Codes* (Cambridge, MA: Harvard University, 1992), pp. 313–14. See also Kate H. Murashige, "Intellectual property and genetic testing," in Mark S. Frankel and Albert Teich, eds., *The Genetic Frontier: Ethics, Law, and Policy* (Washington, DC: AAAS, 1994), pp. 181–98.

66   At a recent meeting of the AAAS committee, the author of this essay engaged in a detailed conversation on this point with Lawrence Goffney, Jr., Acting Commissioner of Patents and Trademarks. Goffney stated that products of nature are now patentable if they meet the other conditions of patentability, e.g., specific utility, nonobviousness, and novelty in the sense that the relevant knowledge had not already been published. Goffney argued that if current PTO policy were in place in the 1920s, the PTO would have had to grant a patent on pure tungsten. After all, there seems to be no principled difference in relation to the "product of nature" doctrine between DNA codes for particular proteins and pure tungsten. Accordingly, Goffney apeared willing to accept the central contention of religious leaders that genetic materials were "products of nature" or of Creation. He did not believe, however, that this fact was relevant any longer to PTO policy.

67   For these remarks and discussion, see Reginald Rhein, "Gene patent crusade moving from church to court," *Biotechnology Newswatch*, June 5, 1995, p. 1.

68   Ibid.

69   Feldbaum's letter appeared in many newspapers, including, for example, *Indianapolis News*, June 21, 1995, p. A7.

70   Karen Lebacqz, "The ghosts are on the wall: a parable for manipulating life," pp. 22–41 in *The Manipulation of Life*, ed. Robert Esbjornson, Nobel Conference XIX (San Francisco: Harper & Row, 1983), p. 35.

33

Property, Patents, and Genetic Material

STEPHEN R. MUNZER

I Introduction

Should there be property rights in genetic material? This is an intriguing question for those who see property rights in land and automobiles and livestock as unproblematic. They might view the molecular building blocks of life as *sui generis*, and doubt that any of the standard justifications of property could apply.

This essay surveys various property rights that arguably can exist in genetic material. To make progress on this topic it is useful to introduce the term "genetic material" rather than use only the word "gene." Very roughly, a gene is a sequence of deoxyribonucleic acid (DNA) or, rarely, ribonucleic acid (RNA), that encodes a protein. The DNA sequence of a gene in a chromosome includes regions preceding and following (the "leader" and "trailer") the coding region as well as intervening sequences ("introns") between individual coding sequences ("exons"). For simplicity, "overlapping" and "alternative" genes are ignored. The term "genetic material" includes chromosomal genes but also embraces larger and smaller sequences of DNA (and, rarely, RNA). Above the level of chromosomal genes, it covers gene families, chromosomes, and the genome of one or more individuals. Below the level of chromosomal genes, "genetic material" includes viruses, viroids, plasmids, and certain sequences of complementary DNA (cDNA) known as expressed sequence tags. Anyone who asks "Are there property rights in genetic material?" must reckon not only with chromosomal genes but also with these supragenetic and infragenetic stretches of DNA.

Moreover, the questioner must distinguish among different sorts of property rights. As a practical matter, it is the law of patents that governs the most important aspects of currently recognized property rights in genetic material. Yet it would be a mistake to overlook other varieties of such rights – for example, trade secrets, or copyrights to books or articles that describe genes or identify their place on a chromosome. The components of property rights include a liberty-right to use; a (normative) power to sell, give, bequeath, license, or exclude; a claim-right to profits; and an immunity against governmental expropriation of the right without compensation. These various "rights" are normative modalities that exist among persons with respect to things (Munzer 1990: 15–27). Philosophically, the issue is what property rights, if any, can

438

be justified in genetic material. Legally, the issue is what protection, if any, is afforded by the legal system of a particular nation such as the United States, by agreement among various nations such as the European Union, or by international law.

Because even a philosophical inquiry finds different sorts of intellectual property to be central, a brief discussion of them is in order. A copyright is a property right, not in ideas themselves, but in the original expression, fixed in a tangible medium, of ideas broadly understood. In the United States, a federal statute protects such expression against unauthorized reproduction. An author can register a work with the Copyright Office. But neither registration nor public dissemination is a condition of copyright protection. Since protection does not extend to any idea, process, principle, or discovery embodied in the work, copyright is of subordinate importance to legal property rights in genetic material.

A trade secret is information that can be used in a commercial enterprise and that is sufficiently confidential and valuable to provide an economic advantage over others. The protection of secret business information goes back to Roman law. In the United Kingdom and the United States, the protection of trade secrets dates from the nineteenth-century legal response to the technical knowledge and employee mobility characteristic of the Industrial Revolution. Trade secret law, in its origins, stems from judicial decisions in the areas of contract, tort, and unfair competition; now it is often codified in statutes. In the United States, no governmental agency issues or registers trade secrets, and their protection is a matter of state rather than federal law. The holder of a trade secret must make reasonable efforts to keep it confidential. Protection continues until the information becomes public knowledge – through, for example, independent discovery by others. Violations of trade secret law consist of unauthorized disclosure by employees or others and improper acquisition by outsiders, for instance, by theft or biotechnological espionage. Someone whose trade secret is misappropriated may sue for conversion, breach of contract, unjust enrichment, or various statutory violations. If successful, the holder of a trade secret may obtain damages – sometimes treble damages – for past injury and injunctive relief against future misappropriation. Theft of a trade secret is also a crime.

A patent is a specially protected form of intellectual property granted by a governmental authority, such as the Patent and Trademark Office (PTO) in the United States or the European Patent Office (EPO) in the European Union. It is usually a more robust set of property rights than a trade secret, for the patentee can exclude others from making or selling the patented invention or discovery, even if these others arrived at the invention or discovery independently. Patents are available for certain inventions and discoveries and have a time limit – currently in the United States a term of up to 20 years from the date of application. Patents, if granted, make information concerning the invention or discovery open to public inspection. However, patent applications that are pending, abandoned, or denied are usually not available for public inspection, and applicants can still try to protect the information as trade secrets.

To give the ensuing analysis some practical verisimilitude, it will be supposed that patents exhibit the following legal features. First, the subject matter of a patent must be some process, machine, manufacture, or composition of matter. Second, necessary conditions for granting a patent are that the putative invention or discovery be new, useful, non-obvious in light of previous knowledge ("prior art"), and described in enough detail to enable others who are skilled in the art to make or use it. Third, exceptions to patentability include inventions whose use is immoral, such as a letter bomb, or whose processes are essentially biological, such as cross-breeding. The first two features derive from the United States Patent Act (2000). The last comes from Article 53(a) of the European Patent Convention (1973). United States courts treat genetic material as a "composition of matter" and typically use the rules that have developed for the patentability of smaller, less complicated chemical compounds (Eisenberg 1997). The EPO wrestles with, among other issues, what "morality" forbids and whether technical intervention renders a process no longer "essentially biological."

Insofar as property rights are rights among persons with respect to things, it is vital to ask what the "things" in question are. Are the rights in one or more gene tokens, or in the type of those tokens, or both? (Tokens are particulars; types are universals or some other sort of abstract object (Hale 1987: 54–7, 191–3).) Are the rights in a variety of a plant or animal – say, the onco-mouse? Are the rights in a product of genetic manipulation – say, genetically engineered bacteria that do not occur in nature? Are they in a process or machine – for instance, a patent on an automated DNA sequencing machine? Does it make a difference how sophisticated the life form is – on a scale, say, from bacteria to plants to animals to chimeras to humans?

It is time to get down to business.

II The Range of Genetic Material

Different issues arise depending on the stretch of genetic material under consideration. This section addresses in turn genes, supragenetic sequences, and infragenetic sequences of DNA.

Genes

There are two main arguments for property rights of at least some sort in genes. First, it is useful to recognize property rights in genes. If one did not, much important research would never be undertaken or at least would proceed at a slower pace. It requires substantial energy and capital investment to carry out genetic research, and unless the researchers receive some legal protection for their discoveries, they would avoid such work and direct their energy and capital elsewhere. Granted, governments could fund genetic research and place the results in the public domain. But this point suggests only that governments might act wisely by supporting genetic research. It does not show that private researchers or firms should be barred from such research or that property rights in the results should be withheld from them. It does intimate, however, that some reasons for government-funded genetic research could be to reduce market incentives for private research, to limit the extent of private property rights in genes, and to support research that entrepreneurs might find unprofitable. All the same, anyone who believes that a principle of utility or efficiency justifies some property rights (Munzer 1990: 191–226) has a ground for recognizing some property rights in genes.

Second, it is a fitting response to the labor put into genetic research to recognize property rights in genes. By pursuing such investigations the researchers deserve some appropriate recompense for their work, and sometimes the fitting response is the acknowledgment of property rights. The rights are, however, qualified in various ways. For example, the research activities should not interfere with the ability of other molecular biologists to vie for similar discoveries. And any property rights that are *prima facie* justifiable under this argument should be commensurate so far as possible with the desert of the researchers. Hence, anyone who holds that a principle of desert based on labor justifies some property rights (Munzer 1990: 254–91) has a ground for recognizing some property rights in genes. This principle should not be identified with Locke's views on property (ibid.: 256 n. 1).

But which rights might it be useful or fitting, or both, to acknowledge? Some candidates are easy choices. Researchers who publish an article describing for the first time a gene that regulates pollen production in plants should have a copyright in the article. A private firm that employs molecular biologists to do genetic research should have a trade secret in their discoveries. The firm should be allowed to protect the discoveries from biotechnological espionage and to license others to use them. Although the protection of trade secrets is a vital spur to innovation, there is legitimate concern that advances in molecular genetics might occur largely in secret, for such a pattern would depart from a paradigm of science in which researchers make their work publicly available after peer review.

A patent is a trickier candidate. It is at least a start to require the applicant for a patent to meet the conditions laid down in the United States Patent Act and not to fall within the exceptions listed in Article 53(a) of the European Patent Convention (1973). Beyond that, the applicant should normally receive a patent, say, in a *process* for sequencing the gene or in *information* regarding the DNA sequence of the gene. To say that a biotechnology firm holds a patent on, for example, a gene that causes breast cancer is to say that the firm has a patent on the gene *type* and can get legal protection for, say, a diagnostic test that can identify who has the gene. It is not to say that the firm has a property right in all *tokens* of that type, such that individuals who have the gene are somehow committing patent infringement.

If these arguments are sound, then one must decide, on a case-by-case basis, whether a patent on a gene is justifiable. Applicants must show that the process, machine, or information regarding the DNA sequence is in fact new, useful, and nonobvious. They must describe it in sufficient detail; under Section 112, para. 1 of the Patent Act and *Regents of the University of California v. Eli Lilly & Co.* (1997), they must give the complete and exact sequence of nucleotides that make up the cDNA of the gene. Applicants must also show that a patent would not violate morality, and establish that the genetic material involves enough technical intervention so as not to be essentially biological.

Opponents of property rights in genes might attack their justifiability in a number of ways without having to descend to case-by-case wrangling. To begin, they could contest the principle of utility and efficiency and the principle of desert based on labor. Quite enough disagreement exists in the theory of property to make a cavalier confidence in general principles unconvincing as moral argument. Furthermore, opponents could appeal to egalitarian considerations. To do so effectively, however, requires justifying these considerations, such as in the form of a principle of justice and equality (Munzer 1990: 227–53). It also requires showing precisely how property rights in genes offend defensible egalitarian considerations.

A rather different argument against property rights in genes is that genes are inherently unownable. One might elaborate this argument in various ways; some versions are more interesting than others. One version is that genes are the stuff of life, and that it demeans the sanctity of life to allow ownership of them. Whatever the theological merits of this argument, it is a weak piece of secular moral philosophy. Genes are not alive; they are only parts of things that are alive. Even if genes were living things, it hardly follows that they cannot be owned; few believe that crops growing in a field are unownable. And even were one to concede that genes cannot be owned, it would scarcely follow that information about genes, such as their DNA sequences, is unownable, or that one cannot own machines or processes relating to genes.

A more interesting version is that knowledge about genes belongs to the common dominion of humankind, and information about them cannot be wrested from this intellectual commons and reduced to private ownership. Here it is wise to avoid Platonism about genes. It is going out on a limb to talk as if all propositions about DNA sequences already exist in a transcendental strongbox. So it is more cautious and plausible to talk about all potential (as well as actual) propositions about genes as belonging to an intellectual commons.

Yet the argument remains incomplete. It is not clear that researchers "discover" such propositions rather than entertain or formulate them. Even if they discover them, it is not plain why the propositions should remain closed to private ownership. It is usually said that one cannot patent laws of nature, such as $F = ma$ or $E = mc^2$. One should not recite this patent dogma uncritically, because a principle of utility and efficiency or a principle of desert based on labor, or both, arguably could support the patentability of laws of nature. Still, the DNA sequence of a gene is not a law of nature – at least not in the same sense that $F = ma$ or $E = mc^2$ is a law of nature. The DNA sequence is, rather, a partial description of the structure of a complicated molecule, and in that respect is like the structural formulae for glyburide and paclitaxel in pharmaceutical chemistry.

If one concludes that the arguments favor the patentability of some genes, there should be a public-interest exception to patent suppression. In the United States, the holder of a patent on, for instance, a machine can generally "suppress" the patent by not making the machine, assigning the patent, or licensing anyone else to make the machine. But suppose that a pharmaceutical company has 10 years left on its patent on a highly profitable drug for alleviating the symptoms of Huntington's chorea. Now suppose that the company's researchers modify the relevant gene so that, through gene therapy, it is possible to cure the disease. The company receives a patent on the modified gene but suppresses the patent because it can make far greater profit by selling its existing drug than it could by using gene therapy to cure the disease. Because the consequences of Huntington's chorea are so grave, even when the symptoms are alleviated by the existing drug, it seems morally wrong, and legally unjustifiable, for the company to suppress its new patent.

442

This argument for a public-interest exception to patent suppression requires some qualification. First, its conclusion is not the current state of the law in the United States. Under Section 271(d)(4) of the United States Patent Act (2000), the suppression of a patent is at present not illegal. Also, scholars of intellectual property wrangle over whether patent suppression has actually occurred – as distinct from rumors of its occurrence. The foregoing argument is, then, merely the beginnings of a case for making a public-interest exception, should it be appropriate and needed, to the general permissibility of patent suppression in the United States. The exception, as briefly advocated here, does not dictate which limitations on the patent would be appropriate. For example, it leaves such options as exclusive use vulnerable to challenge through evidence of suppression, exclusive but mandatory use, and a right to profits in a mandatory licensing scheme.

Second, even as a moral consideration the argument makes relevant the issue of whether and, if so, how patent suppression could make economic sense from the perspective of the patent holder. In the example of Huntington's chorea, it might appear that the patentee could make more money from its patent on the pertinent gene than from its patent on the drug. Given a free market and an incentive to make as much money as possible, the pharmaceutical company would charge an even higher price for its superior product – namely, the gene therapy. If that is correct, clear-eyed economic thinking would seem to eliminate patent suppression as a genuine problem.

This line of reasoning, it is submitted, proceeds too swiftly to be convincing. For one thing, it ignores the availability of revenue over time. Sufferers from Huntington's chorea and their medical insurers may have more money for treatment over a long period of drug therapy than over a short period of gene therapy. Thus, the company may be able to maximize its profits by running out its drug patent before exploiting its genetic patent. Furthermore, this line of reasoning ignores some of the factors that can affect decisions on pricing. If the company were to charge an enormously high price for gene therapy, public outcry and political pressure could move the company to lower its price. The company might even be able to predict such outcry and pressure, and avoid high pricing for that reason. Hence, patent suppression could make sense from an economic point of view, and in that case the moral argument against some forms of patent suppression would have a point.

The foregoing are general arguments for and against property rights in genes. The balance of this essay takes up specialized arguments concerning other stretches of genetic material and the difference between human and nonhuman genetic material.

Supragenetic sequences of DNA

Assume *arguendo* that one can justify at least some property rights in some genes. It remains to consider DNA sequences that are greater than genes, such as gene families, chromosomes, and the genome. For brevity's sake consider just the human genome. Readers can fill in the gaps for the intermediate cases.

It is extraordinarily hard to justify the assignment of all property rights in the human genome to any single individual, firm, or government. No principle of utility and efficiency is likely to justify doing so. A monopoly on, say, the sequence of the human genome would give enormous economic and social power to its owner, and such broad monopolies typically lead to abuse, anticompetitive practices, and other inefficient results. Nor can a principle of desert based on labor rescue the case. In fact, a great many researchers are involved in the Human Genome Project. Other researchers are employed by private firms such as Celera Genomics Group. Besides, to obtain a patent on a gene a researcher must under current law not only give the exact sequence of the gene but also describe a use for the gene and its protein product. So no one entity deserves all of the property rights that are severally justifiable. Neither should all of the various owners be allowed to transfer their rights to a single entity. Not only would this create an objectionable monopoly, it would also run afoul of moral restrictions on transfer that qualify a plausible labor-desert principle (Munzer 1990: 276–9).

Infragenetic sequences of DNA

It is tempting to suppose that if it is more difficult to justify property rights in the genome than in a chromosomal gene, it must be easier to justify them in a shorter sequence such as a virus, plasmid, or expressed sequence tag (EST). The supposition beguiles but, like the serpent's calling attention to the fruit of the tree, should be resisted. Here it is possible to discuss only ESTs, which have been the subject of intense intellectual and practical debate.

An EST is a length of cDNA that is almost always only a partial sequence of a gene being expressed at the time a specific tissue is sampled. Most ESTs are about 400 to 500 nucleotides in length, whereas genes are usually between 2,000 and 25,000 nucleotides long. ESTs can be useful in isolating genes, locating coding regions on genomic DNA, and identifying patterns of gene expression in tissues other than the tissue of origin or in the same tissue under different conditions. Yet these uses are typically intermediate. They do not themselves result in a product but rather allow one to continue down the path to a useful end result. In the United States, patent applications are pending on millions of ESTs. As of June 2000 the PTO had issued three patents on ESTs, although the ESTs were highly atypical in that they came from known protein families (e.g., kinases) with known functions (e.g., signaling).

What intellectual property rights, if any, should be allowed in typical ESTs about which little is known at the time of sequencing? On the one hand, it would be quite unwise to allow patents on them. For utility is hard to establish. And severe economic consequences would ensue for biotechnology firms and consumers, because an EST patentee could "hold up" other research and product development. On the other hand, ESTs are worth more than trade-secret protection, for they do have some value even if they lack what some patent lawyers call end-use utility. A sound intermediate answer is to give ESTs specialized protection that is both shorter and less robust than a standard patent. A carefully tailored registration system can provide justifiable limited intellectual property rights in ESTs without the adverse economic consequences of allowing patents on them (Holman and Munzer 2000).

444

III Nonhuman Genetic Material and Life Forms

Consider a scale and a distinction. The scale is from bacteria to plants to animals to chimeras. The distinction is between property rights in genetic information and property rights in the life forms themselves.

One may begin with bacteria and use as an example the genetically engineered bacteria that figured in the case of *Diamond v. Chakrabarty* (1980). Chakrabarty, a microbiologist, devised a process whereby two to four different plasmids could be transferred to and maintained in *Pseudomonas* bacteria. A plasmid is a self-replicating extrachromosomal circular molecule of DNA that can function stably in a host cell. The unaltered bacteria have no capacity to break down hydrocarbons, but the altered bacteria do. By breaking down various components of oil, such as camphor and octane, the altered bacteria have potential for cleaning up oil spills.

The following property rights seem unproblematic. Chakrabarty should have a trade secret in the information, and the process, for inserting the plasmids into unaltered bacteria. Moreover, the altered bacteria are not found in nature. The information and process are new, useful, nonobvious in light of prior art, and described in ample detail. Thus under usual legal criteria in the United States, they are patentable. Hence Chakrabarty has a more robust package of property rights than a trade secret.

The most interesting question is what property rights, if any, Chakrabarty has in the genetically engineered bacteria themselves. The United States Supreme Court settled the question as a legal matter when it decided, by a 5–4 vote, that he could patent the living micro-organisms themselves. But is this the right answer as a moral matter? It seems easy to justify an affirmative answer using a principle of utility and efficiency or a labor-desert principle. But, it will be protested, bacteria are *living things*. Granted, in this respect they differ from viruses, plasmids, and other bits of genetic material. Yet bacteria have no will. The altered bacteria do not occur in nature; their genetic material as a whole, including that supplied by the plasmids, is peculiar to bacteria. So it is hard to see why Chakrabarty should not have full property rights over the altered bacteria.

What about plants? Consider the genetically engineered plants at issue in the *Plant Genetic Systems* case (1995). Some herbicides inhibit glutamine synthetase. Plants that resist glutamine synthetase inhibitors are selectively protected against certain weeds and fungi. Plant Genetic Systems NV developed a process in which a foreign nucleotide sequence is stably integrated into the genomes of the plants in question. The sequence encodes a protein that neutralizes or inactivates a glutamine synthetase inhibitor. The company applied for and received a patent from the EPO. Later, Greenpeace Ltd requested revocation of the patent. The Opposition Division of the EPO rejected the position of Greenpeace, and the Technical Board of Appeal upheld the decision.

The present issue is not whether this ruling is a legally sound application of Article 53(a) of the European Patent Convention (1973), but whether it is morally justifiable that anyone should have property rights in genetically engineered plants. It seems unproblematic that one can have a trade secret or a patent in the process of genetic

445

manipulation. But it is debatable whether one should have a patent on, or even a trade secret regarding, the plants themselves.

To pursue this matter it will help to consider two objections made by Greenpeace. One is that the costs outweigh the benefits. The benefits presumably include the engineering of sturdier plants without the time, uncertainty, and instability of cross-breeding. The costs, according to Greenpeace, are the risks that herbicide-resistance could spread to other plants, particularly weeds, in which that characteristic is undesirable; that the treated plants could become weeds; and that ecosystems could be damaged (*Plant Genetic Systems* 1995: 552). The chief difficulty with this argument is that the risks that Greenpeace identified are all, to judge from the then available evidence, unlikely to materialize. The documentary evidence adduced by Greenpeace speaks in terms of "possibility," "may," and "potential" (ibid.: 566–7). If one holds that plants have no will and cannot feel, then the cost–benefit argument is unsuccessful.

Although Greenpeace's first argument fails in the case of these herbicide-resistant plants, this sort of argument might succeed in other cases. To the extent that patentability rests on consequentialist considerations, one must think through the effects of granting a patent. Therefore, if a patent on a genetically engineered plant would impose substantial external diseconomies on persons other than the patent holder, that would be a reason for refusing to issue the patent.

A second objection rests essentially on this assertion: "As plant genetic resources [are] the heritage of mankind, they [have] to remain available to all without restriction and to be preserved intact for future generations" (*Plant Genetic Systems* 1995: 551). This assertion suggests one form of the commons argument considered in section II: that no one may raid the intellectual commons that belongs to all.

This objection is more of a gesture than an argument. Under the strongest language in the assertion ("preserved intact"), one seemingly meets a claim that would rule out all interference with nature – even by cross-breeding. This claim is atavistic and silly, because it is unwise public policy to prevent, for instance, the cross-breeding of food plants that will produce better crops. Now consider the weaker language ("heritage of mankind . . . remain available to all"). Even if plants, micro-organisms, and foreign nucleotides are part of the patrimony of humanity, this language does not confront a standard Lockean argument that labor on these resources can take them out of the commons to some extent. So if one buys plants and materials for genetic engineering, and then develops plants that have a special property not found in nature (say, resistance to herbicides), under a labor-desert principle one should have some property rights in the results of one's labors, viz. the herbicide-resistant plants. It does not follow that these rights last forever. In fact, all patent systems put a time limit on the exploitation of inventions and discoveries.

As to animals, nowhere is the "morality" exception to patentability more salient than in the *Onco-mouse/Harvard* case (1992). Scientists at Harvard University engineered transgenic mice that are highly likely to develop malignant tumors early in life. The mice are useful in research on cancer. Harvard obtained a US patent in 1988, and sought European patents on both the process of genetic manipulation and the transgenic mice themselves. The EPO Examining Division refused a patent on the animals in 1989, but the Technical Board of Appeal remitted the case in 1990. After further consideration, the Examining Division issued a patent on the onco-mice in 1992, but stressed that the patent gave Harvard only the right to exclude others rather than a "positive right to use the invention" (1992: 591).

The most interesting point in the opinion is that deciding the "morality" of the patent requires the "balancing" of "three different interests": humans' interest in being free from dangerous diseases, the interest of various parts of the environment in avoiding the risk of the dissemination of unwanted genes, and the interest of onco-mice in not feeling pain ("cruelty to animals") (p. 591). The first interest favors patentability; the last two interests argue against patentability. "In the overall balance the Examining Division concludes that the present invention cannot be considered immoral" (p. 593).

The EPO opinion wrestles with a difficult problem, but its resolution, albeit politically adroit, does not touch the deeper issues. First, it affords no guidance on what counts as, or how one identifies, "morality" in such a case. Ill-thought-out moral judgments should not qualify. Some suggest a critical morality – specifically, an emerging European critical morality (Beyleveld and Brownsword 1993). Others retort that patent examiners are not trained to identify or apply such a morality (Armitage and Davis 1994). Second, even the critical morality of a nation or group of nations is not decisive of what morality requires or forbids. The critical morality of Aristotle's Greece is not decisive of the morality of slavery. The moral philosopher must press the inquiry further. Third, the EPO opinion supposes that various effects, risks, and interests can be "weighed and balanced" (*Onco-mouse/Harvard* 1992: 591), but many philosophers would doubt that a scale of commensurable values exists on which these items can be compared, or even that these terms are the only appropriate terms for referring to such values. In particular, perhaps animals that can feel pain have rights not to be treated in certain ways – even if that treatment greatly benefits human interests. A complication remains: different populations of mice are in question. If onco-mice are used, they are specially engineered for the purpose. If other mice are injected with malignant cells, they will be the animals to suffer. So one must reckon not only with pain to mice but with which group of mice will suffer pain. From a moral point of view it may be particularly objectionable to create a strain of mice whose genetic makeup virtually guarantees that they will suffer pain.

Last come chimeras. In Greek mythology, the Chimera was a fire-breathing monster usually depicted as having a lion's head, a goat's body, and a serpent's tail. In contemporary biology, a chimera is a transgenic creature that is part animal and part human. No chimeras exist at present (Iwasaka 2000: 1532). But the possibility of creating them raises knotty questions of morality and patent law.

As to morality, nonconsequentialist arguments of the sort advanced below in section IV would cut against property rights in chimeras and even against the creation of chimeras. Institutionalized moral principles, such as Article 53(a) of the European Patent Convention, which disallows patents contrary to "morality" or *ordre public*, and the Thirteenth Amendment to the US Constitution, which outlaws slavery, probably also undermine creating and owning chimeras. These principles have some distinctive nonconsequentialist content. Doubtless European "morality" needs clarifying. And perhaps not all uses of chimeras would involve enslavement. Yet it may be harder to rule out chimeras on purely consequentialist grounds, for

447

half-human, half-animal creatures might be useful for doing work or serving as research subjects. The consequentialist who wishes to rule out chimeras morally thus might have to invoke slippery-slope problems or long-range adverse consequences of using chimeras.

So far as the patenting of chimeras is concerned, special difficulties arise. From a European perspective, Grubb (1999) aims to get beyond visceral objections and the broad language of Article 53(a). He asks, tartly: "Given that the genome of a human is 98 per cent identical with that of a chimpanzee, how many genes does it take to really make a difference?" (260). From a US vantage point, Iwasaka is chary of moralizing and tries to advance the discussion beyond the Thirteenth Amendment and misapplications of the utility requirement. Drawing on evolutionary biology, Iwasaka suggests intriguingly that a chimera should be patentable if the applicant can show that it meets two conditions: first, that the organism would have little chance of developing naturally, and second, that natural selection would work against the organism's survival but for the intervention of human interest and technology (2000: 1519–20, 1532–4).

IV Nonconsequentialist Arguments against Property Rights in Human Genetic Material

Although some argue that to allow property rights in human genes would on balance have bad consequences, the core of many arguments is nonconsequentialist. These arguments maintain that, even were the consequences on balance good, it would nevertheless offend some principle of morality to have patents, trade secrets, or other property rights in human genetic material. The most prominent nonconsequentialist arguments draw inspiration from Immanuel Kant and Alan Gewirth. The discussion to follow distinguishes as necessary between genetic material that is peculiar to humans and that which is shared with at least one other species. Those who desire a more complete account of *consequentialist* arguments than that afforded by sections II and III above can easily adapt the ensuing discussion to their desires. They can reckon such effects as reductions in human freedom, offenses against human dignity, violations of self-respect, "commodification," and "generic inconsistency" to be "bad consequences."

Kantian arguments

Because Kant died well before the development of Mendelian genetics and contemporary molecular biology, he could not have discussed genes in any remotely modern sense. Yet he does discuss the human body and its parts from the perspective of his moral philosophy. One can identify in his works at least three arguments against property rights in bodily parts: arguments based on human freedom, human dignity, and self-respect (Munzer 1993).

The first two arguments, if transposed into a genetic key, proceed as follows. The argument based on human freedom runs: Human beings have free will. If they had property rights in their own genes and exercised those rights by sale or licensing, they would lose that freedom and move to the level of things. But things have no free will. Hence the move ends in contradiction (Kant 1963: 124–5, 165). The argument based on human dignity, in one version, goes: Human beings exhibit humanity (*Menschheit*) and dignity (*Würde*); they are priceless. If they had property rights in their own genes and exercised those rights by sale or licensing, they would treat their genetic material in ways that conflict with humanity and dignity. They would decline to the level of things with a price (Kant 1948: 96–7; cf. Kant 1963: 124, 165).

Both arguments might seem to have an obvious flaw. People have some rights with respect to their bodies, including their genes, and it is plausible, the objection runs, to regard these rights as property rights. For example, one has a claim-right with a correlative duty on others not to take one's genes. Again, one has a power to exclude others from controlling one's genes. These rights are consistent with human freedom and human dignity. The exercise of these rights, in the face of threats or efforts to take or control one's genes, is essential to the preservation of one's freedom and dignity. If one did not exercise them, one would be vulnerable to freedom-depriving or dignity-offending genetic manipulation by others. Consequently, the possession and exercise of such property rights in genes is, *pace* Kant, compatible with and sometimes even required by human freedom and human dignity.

Kant might be able to avoid this objection by responding that the genetic rights in question are not *property* rights. Specifically, he can invoke a distinction between personal rights and property rights in regard to human bodies (Munzer 1990: 37–56). One can subdivide property rights in the body into weak and strong varieties. A "weak property right" involves only a choice to transfer gratuitously. A "strong property right" involves a choice to transfer for value. All other interests and choices regarding one's body involve at most "personal rights," such as the claim-right against theft and the power to exclude. Hence the examples adduced do not require Kant to recognize any property rights, in the sense explained, in one's body. This way of avoiding the objection tallies with Kant's concern with transferring – and above all selling – parts of one's body.

There is, however, a more serious objection to the first two arguments. As presented, both commit, or at least seem to commit, the fallacy of division. A gene, or a chromosome, or even the genome of an individual is not identical with the human being or person. It is fallacious to argue that what is true of the whole is true of these various genetic parts. Therefore, even if human beings have freedom, humanity, or dignity, it does not follow that these genetic parts do.

To rescue a version of the argument based on human dignity from the fallacy of division, one can pursue a pair of strategies (Munzer 1994: 275–7). The "integration strategy" insists on the unified organization of various bodily parts, and can stress that each individual's genetic material plays a fundamental molecular biological role in that organization. The "derived-status strategy" points out that various bodily parts have more or less personal connections with the entire human being, and can underscore that each individual's genetic material plays a vital role in the status of the whole person. Neither strategy provides a knockdown argument against property rights in human genetic material.

Yet both strategies together suggest that it could offend human dignity to sell or license for cloning genes that relate to, say, the shape of one's face, key features of

449

one's temperament, or salient aspects of one's intelligence. The reasons for offense differ somewhat in these examples. Cloning the many genes that influence the shape of one's face is, perhaps, offensive because that is an intimate feature of one's body. To duplicate a key feature of one's temperament – for example, perseverance – is problematic because a character trait such as perseverance typically requires development by overcoming obstacles. It may offend dignity to replicate the trait without the history of its acquisition. As for intelligence, one might have a knack for unusually penetrating comments or articulating complicated philosophical arguments. To clone this salient aspect of one's intelligence, rather than to teach someone else how to develop this capacity, is perhaps offensive to both the seller and the buyer. There may, then, be a range of related grounds for suggesting that it could offend human dignity to make one's genes available for cloning in return for money. This suggestion is one way to make sense of worries about the "commodification" of human genetic material and human beings, even in cases in which other species share some of that material.

Lastly, there is Kant's argument based on self-respect, which is here transposed into a genetic key: Human beings should respect themselves. If they had property rights in their own genes and exercised those rights, they would treat their genetic material in ways that interfere with self-respect (*Selbstschätzung*). They would descend to the level of things, and violate the prescription to treat themselves with respect (cf. Kant 1991: 402–3, 417–18; Kant 1963: 169–71). Violations of a duty of self-respect, in Kant's view, sometimes make people like animals, and moral worth consists partly in what distinguishes human beings from animals (Kant 1963: 159; Kant 1991: 427).

The argument based on self-respect provides no decisive case against property rights in human genetic material. One has to assemble the argument from scattered passages in Kant's corpus on self-respect, duties toward the body, and sexual morality. One also has to develop a rather tricky casuistry of self-respect (Munzer 1993: 328–41). A man who sells or licenses his genetic material for purposes of gambling or pornography would, for Kant, usually be violating a duty of self-respect. Yet he could, without violating his self-respect, sell his genetic material to researchers to establish a cell line that would produce proteins useful in treating cancer. Judged from this perspective, it was morally unfounded for the Supreme Court of California to hold that John Moore lacked a property right in his cells and genetic material (*Moore v. Regents of the University of California*, 1990). Besides, as is often pointed out, it is bizarre that Moore should lack such a right, and yet his physician, a pharmaceutical company, and others with whom his physician dealt should have property rights in Moore's blood, tissues, cells, and genetic material.

Gewirthian arguments

The centerpiece of Gewirth's moral philosophy is the principle of generic consistency: "Act in accord with the generic rights of your recipients as well as of yourself" (Gewirth 1978: 135, italics omitted). "Generic rights" are rights to the necessary conditions of agency, freedom, and well-being (p. 64). Gewirth argues that the principle of generic consistency is not only a necessary but also the supreme principle of morality. It prescribes, moreover, equality of generic rights.

This dizzyingly abstract principle receives down-to-earth unpacking in Gewirth (1996). He argues that among the included generic rights are rights to education, to limited private property, to employment, and to work in firms over which workers have substantial control. The later book does not depend entirely on the earlier; Gewirth's objections to libertarianism and especially communitarianism stand largely independently. The key development in his thought is the use of the principle of generic consistency to defend a wide array of economic rights.

Plainly, one needs further development to bring this principle to bear on property rights in human genetic material, and Deryck Beyleveld and Roger Brownsword (1997) try to fill in the gap. The *Relaxin* case (1994) is an intriguing illustration because it concerns a specifically human cDNA sequence. The Howard Florey Institute used donated tissue from a pregnant woman to isolate human H2-relaxin mRNA. Relaxin is a polypeptide hormone secreted from the corpus luteum of the ovary. Because the genomic DNA encoding this protein contains an intron that interrupts the coding region, it was necessary to isolate the cDNA that encodes the protein by splicing out the intron. The Institute did so and received a patent from the EPO. Thereafter the Fraktion der Grünen im Europäischen Parlament (the Green Party) opposed, unsuccessfully, the patent on various grounds relating to immorality under Article 53(a) of the European Patent Convention (1973). The sole ground discussed here is that what the Institute did "infringes the human right to self-determination" (*Relaxin* 1994: 397).

One possible Gewirthian argument is wholly philosophical in character. A human right to self-determination relates to the necessary conditions of agency, freedom, and well-being. It is therefore a generic right. To infringe that right is to violate the principle of generic consistency.

Another possible Gewirthian argument melds moral philosophy, European critical morality, and Article 53(a) of the European Patent Convention (1973). Beyleveld and Brownsword (1997) agree with the Opposition Division that the Fraktion der Grünen got their facts wrong in key respects. The pregnant woman did not have the tissues taken from her – she consented to donate them; the patent did not give the Institute rights to any particular human being; the patent did not enslave, dismember, or sell piecemeal any woman; it is not necessary to get additional human tissue, because the Institute can use the cDNA to synthesize the protein. Still, the Opposition Division failed to get to the root of the Fraktion's case. It did not weigh the moral arguments on each side under "the critical cultural morality of the Contracting States" (Beyleveld and Brownsword 1997: 22).

The central difficulty with both arguments is that they do not show why granting this patent violates anyone's human rights. Beyleveld and Brownsword say as much (1997: 22). Indeed, it is not clear that Gewirth himself would hold that the patent would violate the principle of generic consistency. One could allow the law to carry the load by, say, invoking UNESCO's preliminary draft of a *Universal Declaration on the Human Genome and Human Rights* (Dec. 1996). But then one must acknowledge that law, not moral philosophy, is doing the heavy lifting. And some will protest what they view as the promiscuous coining of new human rights.

451

V Conclusion

The philosophical picture is complex. At a general level, two main arguments exist for property rights of at least some sort in genes. One argument is that it is useful to recognize such rights, because the prospect of gaining these rights has incentive effects that are, on balance, desirable. The other argument is that sometimes the fitting response to the labor put into genetic research is to recognize property rights in genes.

These two arguments play themselves out in a complicated fashion along several dimensions. First, one must look carefully to see what sorts of property rights – patents, copyrights, trade secrets – they might justify. Second, the arguments lend themselves best to property rights in genes. Less clearly do they support property rights in supragenetic stretches of genetic material, especially the genome of an individual, and infragenetic stretches of genetic material, such as expressed sequence tags. Third, other things being equal, the arguments tend to justify genetically related property rights in bacteria more readily than in plants, in plants more readily than in animals, in animals more readily than in chimeras, and in chimeras more readily than in humans.

Of profound importance, here as elsewhere in moral and political philosophy, is the distinction between consequentialist and nonconsequentialist arguments against property rights in human genetic material. The chief nonconsequentialist arguments stem from the work of Gewirth and Kant. Gewirthian arguments, as currently developed, appear too abstract to pose much of a constraint. His principle of generic consistency does not lead obviously to the conclusion that, say, granting a patent on a human gene must violate anyone's human rights. Kantian arguments – particularly those based on human dignity and self-respect – seem more powerful. For instance, it could offend human dignity to sell or license for cloning genes that relate to salient aspects of one's intelligence.

The law of intellectual property receives subordinate attention here, but the discussion brings out some points of legal interest. Scientists who publish an article describing a gene that regulates the production of pollen should have a copyright in the article. Molecular biologists should have a trade secret in their discoveries. Patents present the most difficult legal issues. Though patents on processes, machines, and information relating to genetic material are in principle justifiable, many complications remain. There should be a limited public-interest exception to patent suppression. Very few expressed sequence tags should be patentable; for most ESTs a weaker form of intellectual property rights is in order. Some genetically engineered bacteria and plants should be patentable – as held in *Diamond v. Chakrabarty* (1980) and *Plant Genetic Systems* (1995). The suffering of genetically engineered mice should cast doubt on their patentability under the European Patent Convention – at least insofar as a patent confers a right to engage in cancer research that causes them pain. The *Onco-mouse/Harvard* (1992) case, which upheld the patentability of onco-mice, is a dubious decision under the European Patent Convention.

References

Armitage, E. and Davis, I.: *Patents and Morality in Perspective* (London: Common Law Institute of Intellectual Property, 1994).

Beyleveld, D. and Brownsword, R.: *Mice, Morality and Patents: The Onco-mouse Application and Article 53(a) of the European Patent Convention* (London: Common Law Institute of Intellectual Property, 1993).

——: "Patenting human genes: legality, morality, and human rights," in Harris, J. W., ed., *Property Problems: From Genes to Pension Funds* (London: Kluwer Law International, 1997), 9–24.

Diamond v. Chakrabarty: *United States Reports* 447 (1980), 303–22.

Eisenberg, R. S.: "Structure and function in gene patenting," *Nature Genetics* 15 (1997), 125–30.

European Patent Convention (5 Oct. 1973). Reprinted in Empel, M. van, *The Granting of European Patents* (Leiden: A. W. Sijthoff, 1975), 339–77.

Gewirth, A.: *Reason and Morality* (Chicago and London: University of Chicago Press, 1978).

——: *The Community of Rights* (Chicago and London: University of Chicago Press, 1996).

Grubb, P. W.: *Patents for Chemicals, Pharmaceuticals and Biotechnology: Fundamentals of Global Law, Practice and Strategy* (Oxford: Oxford University Press, 1999).

Hale, B.: *Abstract Objects* (Oxford and New York: Blackwell, 1987).

Holman, M. A. and Munzer, S. R.: "Intellectual property rights in genes and gene fragments: a registration solution for expressed sequence tags," *Iowa Law Review* 85 (2000), 735–848.

Iwasaka, R. M. T.: "From *Chakrabarty* to chimeras: the growing need for evolutionary biology in patent law," *Yale Law Journal* 109 (2000), 1505–34.

Kant, I.: *Groundwork of the Metaphysic of Morals*, trans. by H. J. Paton as *The Moral Law* (London: Hutchinson University Library, 1948).

——: *Lectures on Ethics*, trans. L. Infield (Indianapolis and Cambridge: Hackett, 1963).

——: *The Metaphysics of Morals*, trans. M. Gregor (Cambridge: Cambridge University Press, 1991) (page references are to the Academy pagination given in the margin).

Lewin, B.: *Genes VI* (Oxford: Oxford University Press, 1997).

Moore v. Regents of the University of California: *Pacific Reporter* (Second Series) 793 (Cal. 1990), 479–523.

Munzer, S. R.: *A Theory of Property* (Cambridge: Cambridge University Press, 1990).

——: "Kant and property rights in body parts," *Canadian Journal of Law and Jurisprudence* 6 (1993), 319–41.

——: "An uneasy case against property rights in body parts," *Social Philosophy & Policy* 11, no. 2 (Summer 1994), 259–86.

Onco-mouse/Harvard: European Patent Office, Decision of the Examining Division (April 3, 1992), Grant of European Patent No. 0 169 672, *Official Journal* (Oct. 1992), 588–93.

Plant Genetic Systems: European Patent Office, Decision of the Technical Board of Appeal (Feb. 21, 1995), T 356/93–3.3.4, *Official Journal* (Aug. 1995), 545–85.

Regents of the University of California v. Eli Lilly & Co.: *Federal Reporter* (Third Series) 119 (Fed. Cir. 1997), 1559–75.

Relaxin: European Patent Office, Decision of the Opposition Division (Dec. 8, 1994), *Official Journal* (June 1995), 388–407.

UNESCO Draft Bioethics Convention: *Preliminary Draft of a Universal Declaration on the Human Genome and Human Rights* (Dec. 1996) <http://www.ruhr-uni-bochum.de/zme/unesco-1296.html>.

United States Patent Act: *United States Code* (2000 edn.), Title 35, esp. sections 101, 102, 103, 112, 154, 271. Washington, DC: United States Government Printing Office, 2001.

Further Reading

Beyleveld, D.: *The Dialectical Necessity of Morality: An Analysis and Defense of Alan Gewirth's Argument to the Principle of Generic Consistency* (Chicago and London: University of Chicago Press, 1991).

Beyleveld, D. and Brownsword, R.: "Patentability of genetically engineered animals: the emerging European view," *Asia Business Law Review* 8 (April 1995), 19–26.

Czmus, A. F.: "Biotechnology protection in Japan, the European Community, and the United States" *Temple International & Comparative Law Journal* 8 (1994), 435–63.

Eisenberg, R. S.: "Intellectual property at the public–private divide: the case of large-scale cDNA sequencing," *University of Chicago Law School Roundtable* 3 (1996), 557–73.

Epstein, R. A.: "Property rights in cDNA sequences: a new resident for the public domain," *University of Chicago Law School Roundtable* 3 (1996), 575–9.

Gold, E. R.: *Body Parts: Property Rights and the Ownership of Human Biological Materials* (Washington, DC: Georgetown University Press, 1996).

Nuffield Council on Bioethics: *Human Tissue: Ethical and Legal Issues* (London: Nuffield Council on Bioethics, 1995).

Resnik, D. B.: "The morality of human gene patents," *Kennedy Institute of Ethics Journal* 7 (1997), 43–61.

Thomas, S. M., Davies, A. R. W., Birtwhistle, N. J., Crowther, S. M., and Burke, J. F.: "Ownership of the human genome," *Nature* 380 (April 4, 1996), 387–8.

34

Genetic Screening from a Public Health Perspective: Three "Ethical" Principles

SCOTT BURRIS AND LAWRENCE O. GOSTIN

Introduction

The disciplines of medicine and public health are different in their goals and practices (Mann 1997: 6), and this difference is centrally important in the context of human genetics. Medical genetics concerns the clinical decision made by a doctor to use genetic technology for the benefit of his or her patient. Public health genetics, on the other hand, may be defined as the systematic application of human genetic technologies to identify, prevent, or ameliorate genetic conditions in whole populations. Genetic testing, then, involves the decision to test an individual patient, while genetic screening involves a decision to systematically test a discrete population (CDCP 1997).

The ethical and policy implications are quite different depending on whether genetics is applied in the medical or the public health context. From a public health perspective, the benefits of testing are assessed against different criteria, and the line between providing care to the individual patient and providing it to the population represents a dramatic investment of scarce resources, both political and economic. Medical ethics, which can guide the clinical decisions of healthcare providers, do not adequately address the distributional issues and health–health trade-offs (Sunstein 1996) that arise in public health decision-making. In this chapter, we discuss the emerging idea of *public health ethics*, and set out three principles, rooted in public health, for deciding whether a genetic test should be deployed in a program of population screening (Burris and Gostin 1997).

Public Health Ethics

The language of medical ethics "has been developed in a context of individual relationships, and is well adapted to the nature, practice, settings, and expectations of medical care" (Mann 1997: 8). It does not provide a vocabulary and analytical framework for addressing the fundamental social causes of disease that must be addressed to provide "the conditions in which people can be healthy" (IMNAS 1988), nor the deep social divisions that a recognition of the social roots of disease reveals (Burris 1997). An ethics for public health remains to be written, and such a task is beyond our reach in this chapter. We can, however, make a small contribution in the form of a definition of public health that captures the essential moral choices that public health requires.

We define "public health" as *the process of maximizing, within the bounds of possibility set by the resources allocated, the level and distribution of satisfactory health in a population*. This definition stresses several foundational points. First, public health is devoted to the health of populations, not individuals. Geoffrey Rose has brilliantly described the practical implications of this difference for disease prevention, including the "prevention paradox" that the measures that will most improve the health of a population may also have negligible benefits for particular individuals, and vice versa (Rose 1985). Second, public health operates in a world of choices in the allocation of limited resources. The great sanitarian Herman Biggs famously remarked that "public health is purchasable," but because there will always be limits on how much we are willing to buy, public health will always turn on allocational decisions. Thus public health is as inherently political – i.e., concerned with the allocation of resources in society – as it is technological – concerned with the deployment of professional knowledge of illness. Finally, while the principle of maximization suggests that measures should be compared for their costs and benefits, imposing a strong utilitarian element to the analysis, it is not necessary to see an ethics of public health as a purely utilitarian exercise. It has its consequentialist side to be sure, but our definition offers the possibility of a deontological claim based on the intrinsic value of a fair distribution of reasonable health and equitable access to the conditions in which it is possible to achieve it (Soskolne 1991–2).

The Public Health Interest in Genetic Screening

In the absence of a developed ethics of public health, we offer three principles (Brandt et al. 1990) that follow from a definition emphasizing the population, the struggle for resources, and the importance of an equitable distribution of health.

Principle 1: Screening should enhance the health of the population

Much of the impetus for using genetic testing has and will continue to come from the healthcare sector, so it is well to keep in mind that public health and healthcare aspire to complementary but meaningfully different ends. Public health aims to improve the health of the group, as measured by aggregate outcomes. Medicine aims to improve the health of the individual, as measured largely by improvements in quality of life and the individual's satisfaction with her own outcome. Any number of differences follow from this basic distinction, among which are: population health depends more on the causes of incidence of disease in populations than the causes of illness in individuals, and, from the population standpoint, it is the distribution of cases, rather than the accidental fate of any particular person, that matters. Individual risk factors, which seem to explain why certain people get sick, do not tend to explain why certain ills are prevalent in certain populations. Thus genetic differences may help explain why people exposed to the same environmental co-factors differ in their health, but the environmental factors provide the chief explanation of health differences between populations living in different environments. Because health risks that are constituted in a population are different than those expressed in individuals, even a very powerful individual risk factor may not constitute a public health priority if the prevalence of the marker is low, or if there exists no cost- effective intervention from a population-based perspective (Rose 1985: 8; Mann 1997; Lo 1992; Northridge 1995; Keeney 1994) The discovery of the relationship between the BRCA1 trait and breast cancer provides an illustration of a genetic technology that may have beneficial application for an individual, but perhaps not for whole populations. As Lerman and Croyle observe, "much of breast cancer is not caused by inherited susceptibility at all, but results from somatic events that produce genetic changes in a woman's breast cells during her lifetime. Moreover, the majority of women who develop breast cancer have no known major risk factors" (Lerman and Croyle 1994).

Even if we can fully prevent breast cancer among women with the BRCA1 trait, breast cancer will continue to be a significant burden on the health of the population.

To find a genetic screening measure "ethical" in the public health sense, then, we need to determine that it has a reasonable probability of leading to information that can be used to reduce the incidence of genetic illness or mortality in the society as a whole or in a significant population facing a special threat. If it does not, the measure, however useful to individuals, ought not be an important public health priority, and may not be worthy of significant public sector resources.

A genetic intervention that benefits individual patients may actually be harmful from a population perspective. Health and disease being to a considerable extent socially constructed (Brandt 1987), a new technology providing new forms of information about health and disease can have dramatic effects on how these concepts are understood in society. A widespread belief that health is "in the genes" could further attenuate popular understanding of behavioral and environmental factors influencing health, making it harder to win support for and compliance with public health interventions. Nor can we blithely ignore the risks that the genetic information so desirable to individuals may support the revival of eugenic ideas and policies in new guises (Stone and Stewart 1996; 1992). Susan Wolf has warned of the rise of what she calls "geneticism," which, "like racism and sexism, ... is a long-standing and deeply entrenched system for disadvantaging some and advantaging others based on their genetic traits" (Wolf 1995).

Principle 2: The measure should be an efficient and just use of resources

While it is ethically problematic for many doctors, rationing in public health is a "moral imperative ... in the face of scarce resources" (Morrow and Bryant 1995). Ideally, each public health dollar will be spent to achieve the greatest marginal increase in the level and distribution of well-being in the population. Although the problems of comparing incommensurate values quickly bursts any illusions about the objectivity or mechanical quality of this analysis, this principle is nevertheless a useful reminder to build water pipes and sewers before cholera wards, and to bear in mind the relative costs and benefits of oral rehydration kits and heart transplants. The high cost of healthcare accentuates the resource problem. Often doctors can do things for individual patients that are clearly miraculous, yet which not only do not add measurably to the level and distribution of good health in the population, and whose cost may drive out nonmedical forms of prevention (Kliegman 1995).

Screening programs often illustrate the significance of marginal cost in public health planning. There is an impulse in medicine to routinize the use of a test or treatment that seems to work for the individual, an impulse that is often quicker off the mark than the validation of the measure's efficacy on a large scale (MacDonald 1996; Nelson et al. 1996). Making a useful test routine sometimes carries with it in turn the impulse to make it "mandatory." Yet, apart from the difficulties of enforcing compliance, which we will discuss next, the move to routine or mandatory testing makes a more fundamentally faulty assumption: that the cost–benefit ratio of reaching hard-to-find or resistant targets is comparable to that of reaching the compliant and eager. Indeed, where a test offers useful relative risk information or even therapeutic options to the patient, one might most logically start with the assumption that the majority of people at risk will accept the test without any intervention from public health authorities at all.

Both the efficiency and fairness of a public health intervention should be evaluated in more than just monetary terms. It must be recognized that genetic conditions will be experienced by individuals within a web of social relations. We frequently discuss the social implications of having a disfavored trait in terms of stigma, but there is far more to the social risk of a genetic illness or predisposition to genetic illness than the psychosocial experience of a "spoiled identity" (Goffman 1963). Social risk in health may be defined as "the danger that an individual will be socially or economically penalized should she become identified with an expensive, disfavored or feared medical condition" (Burris 1998). So defined, social risk has two distinct components, each of which imposes its own costs on a health measure: (1) "the threat," i.e. attitudes and behavior that cause or threaten social harm; and (2) "the perception of risk," i.e. the attitudes and beliefs about the threat among those who are in some way tied to the trait or disease. Social risk in these terms is a complex phenomenon, or, better, a constellation of phenomena, that will vary with the type of condition, other traits of the person who has it (such as socioeconomic status, race, gender) and the culture of the relationships in which the trait arises.

Again the experience of HIV is instructive: people at risk of HIV have resisted testing for social reasons, it seems, not because of some clear-cut fears about privacy and discrimination as such, but rather a complicated mix of anxieties tied to racism, homophobia, and alienation from authority. The same may be said for genetic carrier traits, genetic markers (predispositions to disease), and genetic illness. A person's genetic composition has an intimate character that says a great deal about her individuality, her family, and her ethnic community. This deep personal meaning suggests that individual behavior may change when faced with decisions to acquire and use genetic information. Social risk, then, includes fears about societal perception of *self*: what discrete or complex illness do I have or might I acquire in the future? What personality characteristics may be revealed, ranging from shyness or risk-taking to aggression or criminal propensities? Social risk may also involve concerns about family: what does this genetic characteristic mean for my parent, sibling, or child? Finally, social risk may involve concerns about my community: what does the incidence of this genetic characteristic (e.g., Tay-Sachs or sickle cell) mean for my religious or ethnic group?

The notion that legal protection can palliate perceptions of social risk is especially problematic, given that for many people social risk comes from the law, or that their experiences with the legal system have not been positive (Burris 1997). True justice requires that the perspective of the test subject, in all its complexity, be included in the analyses of the costs and benefits of the measure.

The morality of public health's utilitarianism is rooted in the imperative to improve the distribution as well as the level of health. Were there truly a mechanical formula for achieving the greatest good for the greatest number, ethics would be largely self-executing, for the marginal gains of measures helping a large number of needy would almost always be greater than the benefits of helping the fortunate few (Morrow and Bryant 1995: 16). In fact, however, nothing could be more complicated and controversial than deciding who is needy and should get what help. In a politicized world of scarcity, there is a constant danger that health expenditures will reflect existing distributions of wealth and influence. Ill-health follows and reflects social disadvantage; social differences create different health problems (Sorlies et al. 1995; Blane 1995; LaVeist 1993). Spending money to address the leading killers of the population as a whole may exclude expenditures on the leading killers of subgroups in the population. Though cancer is the leading cause of death in the population as a whole, spending to find its genetic causes must be seen in light of such facts as the proportion of cancers affected by genetics, the harm of accidents, and the toll of violence on young black men (McGinnis and Foege 1993). We believe that a just health policy requires recognition of the pernicious synergies of socio-economic disadvantage, and of the problematic nature of exiting social entitlements. To the extent that disease is a social product, public health ought to act as a conscience (Susser 1993).

Principle 3: The measure should be as acceptable as possible to its targets

This principle has roots in both practicality and morality. Public health depends largely on voluntary compliance with its guidelines. This is equally true of "voluntary" advice, like wearing a bicycle helmet, and of "mandatory" rules, like wearing seat-belts. Resistance can raise costs enormously, the more as prevalence of the condition rises. It has proven possible, with a fair amount of money and talent, to impose directly observed therapy on a few hundred recalcitrant TB patients in a few major cities (Frieden et al. 1995); it is unlikely ever to have been feasible to isolate and monitor the sex lives of tens of thousands of people with HIV. Even most "mandatory" measures are either largely voluntary in effect (e.g., premarital screening) or are so broadly acceptable that they are not resisted (like PKU screening of newborns). The success of a public health intervention, and its cost, therefore depend significantly on the degree to which its targets perceive it to be more beneficial than costly.

Resistance to health measures is rarely as irrational as it might seem to the paternalistic professional observer. A measure that leads to immediate and short-term health benefits for targeted individuals is obviously more desirable than one that does not; there is the difference between screening for ALS and screening for PKU. Monetary or other incentives may increase the benefits of compliance, as is sometimes done with DOT. The costs of compliance are often in something like inverse proportion to the treatability of the condition: the less we can do for a trait, the more social costs screening is likely to entail. Being marked as having a dangerous, untreatable condition may be costly in psychological terms, and may expose the subject to social risk. These sorts of costs may be addressed to some extent through counseling and the legal protection of social status, but this is difficult and problematic in its own way (Burris 1997). In moral terms, this principle emphasizes the fairness of allocating both the benefits and burdens of a disease that threatens public health on the public generally, rather than primarily on the shoulders of those who have the illness.

In the HIV epidemic, resistance to public health rules has taken on a perhaps unprecedented but now widely followed political dimension. Legal and advocacy organizations, capable of generating grassroots action and of effectively lobbying and litigating, have demonstrated their capacity to influence the development of public health policy (Bayer 1991; Wachter 1991). In many respects this has proven a boon to public health, facilitating the social negotiation necessary to design broadly acceptable measures. It has also, however, added even more complexity to the rich symbolic politics of health and disease. Thus a final caution under the heading of the principle of acceptability is that measures may not always be judged for their intrinsic merits, or even their objective likelihood of causing harm to the target population. HIV reporting in the United States typifies a measure that has in many places been strongly opposed by advocates, despite the excellent record of health departments in protecting the confidentiality of their records (Gostin et al. 1997: 1162–7). In this instance, the fear of what government might someday do with an "AIDS list" outweighs health departments' excellent track record (Siegel et al. 1989). The same, of course, can be said about genetics, where the public has strong beliefs, and some irrational fears, about the application of genetic technologies to human populations. The principle of acceptability thus becomes a good heuristic for analyzing and responding to a health measure's social meaning.

Discussion

Putting aside the assumption that widespread collection of genetic data is both desirable and inevitable sets a very different genetic agenda for public health law. As a preliminary matter, we are required to ask, what are the criteria that need to be satisfied to justify a particular genetic intervention in public health terms, and to what extent have they been satisfied? It is well beyond the purpose of this chapter to apply the principles we offer to any particular genetic screening initiative. Nevertheless, a general overview of genetic screening shows the need for caution in designing large-scale screening programs in the name of improving the public's health. Genetic illness is an important threat to public health. Historically, genetic disease has been seen as both a major source of ill-health and premature mortality, and as largely intractable (McKeown 1980). With its significant impact on both the population as a whole and on distinct subpopulations, genetic illness is obviously an important challenge to public health (CDCP 1993, 1995).

Some level of pure research would surely be a wise and just use of resources for population health, provided always that information about the impact of genetic factors on health is integrated into a broader examination of the determinants of health (Clarke 1995). There is good historical evidence that the facts of the germ theory had a greater impact on the decline in mortality in the United States in the past century than did the medical interventions derived from them (Preston and Haines 1991). Research may help identify important co-factors for illness in the environment, or help provide behavioral guidance. Likewise, epidemiological research, including formal surveillance, is justified precisely because of the difficulty of assessing the potential of genetic knowledge on public health (Hanson 1995). Public health data collection is a prerequisite for according genetic illness greater public health priority.

The value of screening individuals in medical care depends from a public health point of view on factors like the extent and severity of the condition in the population, the cost of detecting it, and the availability of some intervention to cure or prevent the expression of the condition. In those relatively few instances in which the identification of a genetic trait leads to effective, life sustaining therapy at a reasonable cost – PKU for instance – screening evidently has real public health value. And, of course, as more is known about human genetics, science is likely to offer more effective means to prevent and treat genetic illness. More controversial but comparably effective at the population level is prenatal screening to which the preventive response is contraception or abortion, raising the specter of eugenics. CVS and amniocentesis, for instance, have led to a substantial reduction in the prevalence of Down's Syndrome at birth, but possibly at the cost of further stigmatizing those children who are born with the condition. To the extent one regards preventing the birth of children with Down's syndrome to be desirable, there are now racial and ethnic differences in prevalence that may reflect unequal access to prenatal diagnostic services (CDCP 1983–90: MMWR 1994). As the complexity and cost of the response increases – as might happen in the area of prenatal surgery – the eugenic issues, the public health cost–benefit ratio, and the problem of access, all increase.

The most problematic use of genetic screening, from both the medical and the public health standpoint, is where there is little or nothing to be done to prevent an illness or intergenerational transmission of illness. Genetic screening is also problematic where the genetic factor is but one contributor to a higher relative risk of an illness that depends also on unknown individual or environmental co-factors. The psychological value of knowing about something one cannot alter may be positive or negative for the individual (Wiggins et al. 1992; Lerman and Croyle 1993), and likewise may make for a net increase or decrease in the sum total of public well-being. Stigma and stress add to the social costs of screening for risk factors, as does an increase in the prevalence of that most modern of ills, being "at risk." In the case of illnesses that have behavioral co-factors, there has been some support for the proposition that personalized relative risk information can enhance the chances of behavior change, but the impact may be slight and short term, and in any event must be placed in the context of the difficulties of behavior change overall (Rose 1985). In a larger sense, genetic screening threatens to be a readily commodifiable, culturally powerful

461

approach to dealing with disease that will further complicate the discovery and alteration of the pathogenic elements of the ecology. One could argue that "the focus on genetic factors may distract attention from 'the real challenge of the future which appears to be the behavioral and social issues of risk reduction'" (Clarke 1988).

Although the potential costs of genetic screening are high, they are not uniformly distributed across all uses of the technology. Genetic databases collected by the government, or under its auspices, for research purposes can be reliably protected, even in a largely electronic records environment, because there is no need to allow access for medical care or payment purposes. Such programs could move as much as possible to blinded collection or storage, and can maintain rigid barriers to access without significantly burdening bona fide research.

The acceptability of genetic screening is also likely to be very diverse, reflecting the variety of social and medical impact genetic information can have, and the varying degrees to which various populations have access to those benefits and confidence in legal protection of social status. There is likely to be a fair amount of resistance on the general ground of state intrusion into privacy, including spillover from efforts to gather and use genetic information for identification and law-enforcement purposes (Gostin 1995). Markers of serious future or inheritable diseases are likely to be socially risky to some degree, particularly to the extent they are used by insurers and employers to avoid healthcare costs. As genetic factors have more and more influence on individual social status, we can expect more principled resistance to screening. The popularity of prenatal screening, for example, is giving rise to concerns about the perceived value of disabled lives (Shepherd 1995). More broadly, much will depend upon the degree to which the benefits of genetic knowledge are distributed in the population: if genetic technology leads to improvements in healthcare, its practical value will depend upon the population's actual access to the care; if it identifies environmental pathologies, its value will depend on the degree to which society is prepared to alter how it produces, distributes, and consumes (Link and Phelan 1995).

Conclusion

The use of genetic screening for public health purposes will tend to be most effective when it serves a clear population goal, has a healthy ratio of overall economic and social benefits to costs, entails a just use of resources, and is acceptable to the populations it targets. We recognize that the public health agenda is never written by fully autonomous, fully informed rational actors on a clean slate (Vickers 1965). Yet precisely because public health policy is so heavily influenced by social and political factors, it is important to seize the opportunity for reflection before the time for action arrives, and to at least aspire to rationality in the heat of action.

References

Bayer, R.: *Private Acts, Social Consequences: AIDS and the Politics of Public Health* (New Brunswick, NJ: Rutgers University Press).

Blane, D.: "Social determinants of health – socioeconomic status, social class, and ethnicity." (editorial) *American Journal of Public Health* 903 (1995), p. 85.

Brandt, A.: No Magic Bullet: A Social History of Venereal Disease in the United States Since 1880 (1987).

Brandt, A. et al.: "Routine hospital testing for HIV: health policy considerations." In *AIDS and the Healthcare System*, Lawrence O. Gostin ed. (New Haven: Yale University Press, 1990).

Burris, Scott.: "The invisibility of public health: population-level measures in a politics of Market Individualism." *American Journal of Public Health* 1607 (1997), p. 87.

Burris, Scott: "Law and the Social Risk of Healthcare: Lessons from HIV Testing." *Albany Law Review* 831 (1998), p. 61.

Burris, S. and Gostin, L. O.: "Genetic screening from a public health perspective: some lessons from the HIV experience." In Rothstein, M., ed.: *Genetic Secrets: Protecting Privacy and Confidentiality in the Genetic Era* (1997), pp. 137, 139.

Burris, Scott.: "Driving the epidemic underground? A new look at law and the social risk of HIV testing." *Aids and Public Policy Journal* 66 (1997), p. 12.

(CDCP) *Surveillance for and Comparison of Birth Defect Prevalences in Two Geographic Areas – United States, 1983–88*, 42 MMWR SS-1 (1993).

(CDCP) *Surveillance for Anencephaly and Spina Bifida and the Impact of Prenatal Diagnosis – United States, 1985–1994*, 44 MMWR SS-4 (1995).

(CDCP) Centers for Disease Control and Prevention: *Translating Advances in Human Genetics into Public Health Action: A Strategic Plan* (1997).

Clarke, Angus.: "Population screening for genetic susceptibility to disease." *Brit. Med. J.* 35, 311 (1995).

Clarke: quoting Williams, R. R.: "Nature, nurture and family predisposition." *New England Journal of Medicine* 318 (1988), p. 769.

Frieden, R. Thomas et al.: "Tuberculosis in New York – turning the tide." *New England Journal of Medicine* 229 (1995), p. 333.

Goffman, I.: *Stigma: Notes on the Management of Spoiled Identity* (Harmondsworth: Penguin, 1963).

Gostin, O. L., Ward, W. J., and Baker, Cornelius, A.: "National HIV case reporting for the United States: a defining moment in the history of the epidemic." *New England Journal of Medicine* 337 (1997), pp. 1162–7.

Gostin, O. Lawrence: "Genetic privacy." *Journal of Law and Medical Ethics* 23 (1995), pp. 320–30.

Hanson, W. J.: "Birth defects surveillance and the future of public health." *Public Health Reports* 110 (1995), p. 698.

Harper, P.: "Genetics and public health." *British Medical Journal* 304 (1992), p. 721.

Institute of Medicine, National Academy of Sciences: *The Future of Public Health* (Washington, DC: National Academy Press, 1988), pp. 38–40.

Kliegman, R. M.: "Neonatal technology, perinatal survival, social consequences, and the perinatal paradox." *Am. J. Pub. Health* 909 (1995), p. 85.

Keeney, L. Ralph.: "Decisions about life-threatening risks." 331 *New England J. Med.* 193 (1994).

Kliegman, M. R.: "Neonatal technology, perinatal survival, social consequences, and the perinatal paradox." *Am. J. Pub. Health* 909 (1995), p. 85.

LaVeist, A. T.: "Segregation, poverty, and empowerment: health consequences for African Americans." *Milbank Q.* 41 (1993).

Lerman, C. and Croyle, R.: "Psychological issues in genetic testing for breast cancer suscepti-bility." 154 *Arch. Int. Med.* 609 (1994).

Link, G. B. and Phelan, J.: "Social conditions as fundamental causes of disease" (extra issue). *Journal of Health and Social Behavior* 80 (1995).

Lo, B.: "Ethical dilemmas in HIV infection: what have we learned?" *Med. & Healthcare* 92 (1992), 20.

MacDonald, D.: "Cerebral palsy and intrapartum fetal monitoring." *New England Journal of Medicine* 659 (1996), p. 334.

Mann, J. M.: "Medicine and public health, ethics and human rights." *Hastings Center Report* (May–June, 1997), p. 6.

Marantz, R. P.: "Blaming the victim: the negative consequence of preventive medicine." *American Journal of Public Health* 80 (1993), p. 1186.

McGinnis, J. M. and Foege, W.: "Actual causes of death in the United States." *Journal of the American Medical Association* 2207 (1993), p. 270.

McKeown, T.: *The Role of Medicine: Dream, Mirage, or Nemesis* (London: Nuffield Provincial Hospitals Trust, 1980).

Morrow, H. R. and Bryant, H. J.: "Health policy approaches to measuring and valuing human life: conceptual and ethical issues." *American Journal of Public Health* 1356 (1995), p. 85.

Nelson, B. Karin et al.: "Uncertain value of electronic fetal monitoring in predicting cerebral palsy." *New England Journal of Medicine* 613 (1996), p. 334.

Northridge, M.: "Public health methods: attributable risk as a link between causality and public health action." *American Journal of Public Health* 85 (1995), p. 1202.

Preston, H. S. and Haines, R. M.: *Fatal Years: Child Mortality in Late Nineteenth-Century America* (Princeton: Princeton University Press, 1991).

Rose, G.: "Sick individuals and sick populations." *Journal of Epidemiology* 32 (1985), p. 14.

Shepherd, Lois: "Protecting parents' freedom to have children with genetic differences." *Univer. Il. L. Rev.* 761 (1995).

Siegel, K. et al.: "The motives of gay men for taking or not taking the HIV antibody test." *Social Problems* 36 (1989), p. 368.

Sorlies, P., Backlund, E., and Keller, J.: "US mortality by economic, demographic, and social characteristics: the National Longitudinal Mortality Study." *American Journal of Public Health* 85 (1995), p. 949.

Soskolne, C. L.: "Rationalizing professional conduct: ethics in disease control." *Public Health Review* 19 (1991–2), pp. 311–12.

Stone, H. D. and Stewart, S.: "Screening and the new genetics; a public health perspective on the ethical debate." *Journal of Public Health and Medicine* 18 (1996), p. 3.

Sunstein, R. C.: "Health–health tradeoffs." *University of Chicago Law Review* 63 (1996), p. 1533.

Susser, M.: "Health as a human right: an epidemiologist's perspective on public health." *American Journal of Public Health* 83 (1993), p. 416.

Vickers, G.: "Who sets the goals of public health?" In Katz, A. H. and Felton, J. S., eds.: *Health and the Community: Readings in the Philosophy and Sciences of Public Health* (New York: Free Press, 1965).

Wachter, R. M.: *The Fragile Coalition: Scientists, Activists and AIDS* (New York: St. Martin's Press, 1991).

Wiggins, S. et al.: "The psychological consequences of predictive testing for Huntingdon's disease." *New England Journal of Medicine* 327 (1992), p. 1401.

Wolf, S.: "Beyond 'genetic discrimination': toward the broader harm of geneticism." *Journal of Medicine and Ethics* 23 (1995), pp. 345, 349.

Afterword

SIR DAVID WEATHERALL

It is impossible to do justice to a work of this size and diversity of views in but a few pages. Given that, I settle here for a short commentary from the viewpoint of somebody who, though their research and clinical practice is closely related to the new genetics, has no expertise in the fields of ethics or philosophy, or, indeed, in any of the disciplines that are grappling with the ethical framework needed for doctors and the community at large to live with this complex and rapidly moving field.

There is no doubt that the developments in biology of the post-DNA era have had an extraordinary impact both on those who work in fields related to genetics and on the public. By British standards, the subject has received an enormous amount of coverage by television and radio, has generated numerous books and articles in both the scientific and popular press, and its ethical issues have even spawned a neologism all of their own, an unwelcome newcomer to our language which, I see, has been perpetuated by the editors of this book! And, even more remarkably, the level of public interest in this topic shows no sign of decline.

Why has modern genetics raised so much excitement and concern? Undoubtedly a major factor is the speed of development and discovery in modern biology. When this book was first planned the notion of mammalian cloning still seemed like an Orwellian pipedream. Yet Dolly now seems to be one of the family, and more recently cloned mice peered at us from the pages of *Nature*. Who will be next? Although historians of science use the term jealously, I suspect that few of them would disagree that the years following Watson and Crick's discovery of the self-replicating properties of DNA reflect a revolution in biology equal to that which occurred in physics in the early part of this century. Within less than 20 years after recombinant DNA technology was born, methods had become available for finding almost any gene of interest, they could readily be transferred from one species to another, and the Human Genome Project became a reality. Overnight, DNA was widely perceived as the very essence of life itself, and, perhaps for the first time, it appeared that we might have control over our destinies.

Not surprisingly it was not long before the alarm bells started to ring. Although few outside the field of genetics knew very much about the eugenics movement of the period between the two world wars, it was not long before they became better informed. As molecular genetics started to be applied in clinical practice several

465

writers rather emotively coined the term "the new eugenics." Where might it all end? Although we had been prepared to think about these things by fictional accounts of what might be achieved by genetic manipulation, kindled by J. B. S. Haldane's *Daedalus*, Aldous Huxley's *Brave New World*, and by George Orwell's *1984*, and expanded with relish by later science fiction writers, what we were reading every time we opened our newspapers seemed very much stranger than fiction, and much more frightening.

The other important contributors to this uneasy scene were the scientists themselves. Although many molecular biologists have behaved themselves, others have not. Exaggerated claims for the speed of the applications of molecular genetics were made: "gene therapy just round the corner"; "in a few years a simple DNA test will provide an accurate profile of the pattern of one's health from birth to grave"; "the gene for homosexuality discovered"; and many more. The hunger of the media for the words of these false, or at best premature, prophets seemed unassuageable, and even if the language of many scientists was more guarded, the journalists themselves felt it fair game to add the appropriate embellishments. Even those who were cautious often found their articles published under torrid headlines dreamt up by their commercially minded colleagues.

And there is another factor which has discouraged rational debate in this field, particularly regarding its medical applications. Because its science is so new and complex, many doctors and specialists in the ethics of medicine and science have had little more understanding of what is going on than the general public. Although a few molecular geneticists attempted to interpret the field for their clinical colleagues and the community at large, the potential medical applications of the new genetics were often publicized by basic scientists who, though they knew a great deal of molecular biology, had only the flimsiest idea about the problems of sick people. In short, because research has moved so rapidly there has been a rapidly widening communication gap between the basic biological sciences, the clinical world, ethicists, and the public. At the same time doctors have had many more immediate ethical issues to worry them, including an increasingly aging population, rare resources, assisted reproduction, and so on. For many the ethical concerns of the new genetics seemed to be of very little immediate relevance to their day-to-day practice.

In a scene of such complexity, and with such diverse input, it has been extremely difficult to put the problems of modern genetics into perspective and to distinguish between the important questions and those that are futuristically frivolous. But it would be foolish to ignore them or to try to play down the concerns of society about the effects of meddling with our genes.

Some of the issues that have been raised have been around for a long time and have simply been highlighted by the effectiveness of our new technology. The prenatal detection and termination of pregnancies for babies with Down syndrome, or other easily identifiable chromosomal abnormalities, has been practiced for many years. The DNA era has greatly expanded the number of conditions that can be identified prenatally, and hence has greatly broadened the spectrum of parental choice about what kind of children they wish to have. The ability to identify individuals who will develop the effects of monogenic diseases later in life, and the necessity of testing their relatives as part of the counseling process, has undoubtedly posed new dilemmas. Similarly, when they relate to easily definable monogenic diseases, there are well-defined questions arising from the possibilities of unfair distribution of healthcare, life insurance, employment, patenting of human DNA, and similar issues. All these problems seem to be well understood, and there is no reason, given time and sensible debate, why there should not be a rational outcome.

Similarly, a broad-based debate over the issues of somatic gene therapy has led to the recognition that this (still potential) form of treatment is no different in principle to any other type of organ transplantation; the major questions are not ethical but about safety and the development of more effective technology. Germline gene therapy has been recognized for what it is, a completely new step into the unknown, and has been at least temporarily banned in most countries. I suspect that this is based more on the grounds of lack of scientific knowledge rather than major ethical issues. In the field of gene transfer across species the transgenic approach to studying gene expression and other basic biological mechanisms seems to cause little difficulty, while the use of the same principles for producing human therapeutic products in animals has been accepted much less easily. I find it difficult to understand the attitudes of some of my colleagues who, while tucking into a large steak, regale me with the evils that will result from the pharmaceutical industry transferring human genes into cattle, whether to produce therapeutic agents in their milk or to modify their immune systems to allow their organs to be used in place of diseased human parts. Many of these arguments seem to be based more on the "ugh" factor than on any easily definable ethical grounds, or (and despite the fact that we have been doing it for centuries by artificial breeding) a feeling that it is wrong to alter the genetic make-up of living things.

While some of these concerns may be illogical and not easily defined as crossing ethical boundaries, nevertheless they are real and cannot be ignored. Mary Warnock was well aware of them in her wise handling of the problems of embryo research. There may well be a case for holding back on some research of this kind until there has been a chance for both professional and public debate and reflection. So much of it is now closely tied up with industrial exploitation that this may not be easy, particularly since we have still not reached a stage of genuine clarity about the questions of patenting inventions relating to genetic material.

Some of the most nonproductive debates on the ethics of the new genetics have revolved round the consequences of our increasing ability to identify one or more of the genes that are involved in complex multigenic disorders such as coronary artery disease, stroke, diabetes, the major psychoses, and some forms of cancer. There is no doubt, at least as judged from twin studies and related approaches, that all these conditions reflect the complex interplay of many environmental factors and variable genetic susceptibility based on the action of several, and in some cases many, different genes. The degree of heritability of these diseases varies widely and in many cases the environment seems to be a much more important factor. The belief that we will be able to identify individuals early in life who will succumb to these diseases in middle or even old age has raised concerns about life insurance, discrimination at work, and, in particular, stigmatization and difficulties in providing medical treatment in the increasingly commercial world of healthcare delivery.

467

There are two reasons why research into a better understanding of the genetic component of polygenic disease is important. First, by defining the genes involved, and understanding why variation in their function and products renders some individuals more or less susceptible to environmental agents, it is possible that we may come to understand the pathogenesis of these conditions. This should lead to better approaches to their prevention and treatment and, in particular, may offer the pharmaceutical industry the possibility of moving into the "designer drug" era. Second, it might be possible, by defining groups of individuals who are at high genetic risk of developing these diseases due to environmental exposure, to concentrate efforts in public health and preventative medicine on subgroups of the population.

It is easy to understand why there have been concerns about misuse of genetic information of this type. However, as in other areas of this field, the possibilities for precision of diagnosis may have been prematurely oversold. From what little is known so far we are moving into a research field of extreme complexity that will require the development of completely new bioinformatic systems before its place in predictive genetics can be defined. For example, "total genome" searches for the susceptibility genes for type 1 diabetes have shown up to 15 different potential loci. Although it is likely that, of these, only a handful may be of genuine importance, even if this is the case, predictive genetics may be quite difficult and depend very much on the number of environmental triggers that are defined. I suspect that the prediction of coronary artery disease or hypertension, for which the degree of heritability is approximately the same as type 1 diabetes, may be equally or even more complex. Thus we are a very long way away from the time when we will be able to say with confidence whether a baby will develop these diseases in middle life, and when this information will be of any actuarial use. Those who have oversold the likely speed of progress in this field, and hence who have raised serious ethical concerns about its application, have simply disregarded the enormously complex interactions between nature, nurture, and the pathology of aging on which most of our common polygenic diseases are based. Until this field is much further advanced, and adequate pilot studies have been done to find out how effective it is in practice, it will be difficult to develop an adequate ethical framework for its wide-scale application.

Similar problems and misunderstandings have formed the basis for much of the overheated debate on the role of genes in psychiatric disease, homosexuality, criminality, intelligence, and different personality traits. The debate has become so heated in the USA that there has been a major movement to ban genetic research in some of these fields. Again, it appears that many of these concerns have arisen from an overstated and biologically deterministic view of just how much our genetic make-up as compared with our environment combines to make us what we are. There seems to be no reason whatever not to pursue research in these very difficult fields. After all, if there is a major biochemical component to the major psychoses, the most likely way of discovering its nature is through the genes which make us more or less susceptible to developing these conditions. And, equally, it is of enormous biological interest to know to what extent such traits as homosexuality or behavioral disturbances are genetically determined. But it is abundantly clear that the environment plays an extremely important role in shaping human behavior. As Peter Medawar has pointed out, there are, in effect, two patterns of inheritance, endosomatic through our

DNA, and exosomatic, by which he implies the transfer of information from generation to generation by nongenetic routes; we are what we are as the result of our physical inheritance and the environment in which we are raised, with its attitudes and traditions that have been passed down from our forebears by word and deed.

At the far end of the spectrum of debate on the new genetics we reenter the world of Aldous Huxley and the later science fiction writers. Here the fears are about the serious misuse of genetics for changing the behavioral patterns of individuals for political ends, the augmentation of various physical traits for nefarious purposes, and the rest. These more extreme examples of the "slippery-slope" argument make for exciting reading, though because as yet they are based on virtually no scientific data whatever, discussions of their ethical aspects are not yet very productive. However, provided that they are set in a background that recognizes the current state of scientific progress, or lack of progress, they may serve a purpose. We simply don't know what will be possible while we are in the throes of a major biological revolution. It was widely believed until a short time ago that it would simply not be possible to clone human beings. And yet this view had to be revised almost overnight with the appearance in all our newspapers of pictures of Dolly, a sheep that had been generated by some remarkably sophisticated cloning technology. If nothing else, this reminded us that we must keep a completely open mind about the future possibilities of human biology.

Index

470